Economics of Maritime Business

This book provides a comprehensive introduction to the economics of the business of maritime transport. It provides an economic explanation of four aspects of maritime transport, namely, the demand, the supply, the market and the strategy.

The book first explains why seaborne trade happens and what its development trends are; it then analyses the main features of shipping supply and how various shipping markets function; the book finally addresses the critical strategic issues of the shipping business. The full range of different types of shipping are covered throughout the chapters and cases. The book combines the basic principles of maritime transport with the modern shipping business and the latest technological developments, particularly in the area of digital disruption. The ideas and explanations are supported and evidenced by practical examples and more than 160 tables and figures. The questions posed by the book are similar to those that would be asked by students in their learning process or professionals in the business environment, with the answers concentrating on the reasons for what has happened and will happen in the future rather than merely fact-telling or any specific forecast.

The book is most suited for students of shipping-related disciplines, and is also a valuable reference for maritime professionals.

Shuo Ma is Professor of Maritime Economics and Policy at the World Maritime University, Sweden. Since 2001, he has been Vice-President of the university. He is responsible for the university's outreach programmes, which include Asia-based MSc. programmes, post-graduate diploma courses by distance learning and executive professional development courses.

Routledge Maritime Masters

1. Port Economics
Wayne K. Talley

2. Port Economics
Second edition
Wayne K. Talley

3. Management of Shipping Companies
Ioannis Theotokas

4. Managing Human Resources in the Shipping Industry
Edited by Jiangang Fei

5. Shipping Business Unwrapped
Illusion, Bias and Fallacy in the Shipping Business
Okan Duru

6. Maritime Business and Economics
Asian Perspectives
Edited by Okan Duru

7. Economics of Maritime Business
Shuo Ma

For more information about this series, please visit: www.routledge.com/Routledge-Maritime-Masters/book-series/RMM

Economics of Maritime Business

Shuo Ma

Routledge
Taylor & Francis Group
LONDON AND NEW YORK

First published 2021
by Routledge
2 Park Square, Milton Park, Abingdon, Oxon OX14 4RN

and by Routledge
52 Vanderbilt Avenue, New York, NY 10017

Routledge is an imprint of the Taylor & Francis Group, an informa business

British Library Cataloguing-in-Publication Data
A catalogue record for this book is available from the British Library

Library of Congress Cataloging-in-Publication Data
Names: Ma, Shuo, 1955- author.
Title: Economics of Maritime Business / Shuo Ma.
Description: First Edition. | New York : Routledge, 2020. | Series: Routledge maritime masters ; 7 | Includes bibliographical references and index.
Subjects: LCSH: Shipping. | Merchant marine--Management. | Management—Technological innovations.
Classification: LCC HE571 .M293 2020 (print) | LCC HE571 (ebook) | DDC 387.5/1—dc23
LC record available at https://lccn.loc.gov/2020007729
LC ebook record available at https://lccn.loc.gov/2020007730

ISBN: 978-1-138-99964-0 (hbk)
ISBN: 978-1-138-99965-7 (pbk)
ISBN: 978-1-315-65812-4 (ebk)

Typeset in Bembo
by Swales & Willis, Exeter, Devon, UK

Contents

Figures

Tables

Abbreviations

3PL	third party logistics.
AI	artificial intelligence.
AIS	automatic identification system.
ALARP	as low as reasonably practicable.
BAF	bunker adjustment factor.
BDI	Baltic Dry Index.
BIMCO	Baltic and International Maritime Council.
CBA	cost benefit analysis.
CIF	cost, insurance, freight.
CNY	Chinese yuan (currency).
CO_2	carbon dioxide.
COA	contract of affreightment.
COLREG	Convention on the International Regulations for Preventing Collisions at Sea.
CRM	customer relationship management.
dwt	deadweight tonnage.
EBITDA	earnings before interest, taxes, depreciation and amortisation
ECA	emission control areas.
ECDIS	electronic chart display and information systems.
EEDI	Energy Efficiency Design Index.
EMSA	European Maritime Safety Agency.
ERP	enterprise resource planning.
EU	European Union.
EXW	ex-works.
FAK	freight all kinds.
FDI	foreign direct investment.
feu	forty-foot equivalent unit.
FFA	forward freight agreement.
FIATA	Federation of International Freight Forwarders Association.
FMC	Federal Maritime Commission.
FOB	free on board.
FSA	formal safety assessment.
GATT	General Agreement on Tariffs and Trade.
GDP	gross domestic product.
GHG	greenhouse gases.
grt	gross registered tonnage.
GSC	global supply chain.

gt	gross tonnage.
GVC	global value chain.
Handysize	bulk carriers or oil tanker of up to 50,000 dwt.
IACS	International Association of Classification Societies.
ICC	International Chamber of Commerce.
ICD	inland clearance depot.
ICS	International Chamber of Shipping.
IFO	intermediate fuel oils.
ILO	International Labour Organization.
IMARSAT	International Maritime Satellite Organization.
IMSAS	IMO member state audit scheme.
Incoterm	International commercial terms.
INTERTANKO	International Association of Independent Tanker Owners.
IoT	internet of things.
IRR	internal rate of return.
ISF	International Shipping Federation.
ISM	International Safety Management.
ISMA	International Ship Managers Association.
ISO	International Organization for Standardization
ITF	International Transport Workers Federation.
ITOPF	International Tanker Owners Pollution Federation.
JIT	just-in-time.
Knot (kn)	nautical mile per hour.
LIBOR	The London inter-bank offered rate.
LNG	liquefied natural gas.
lo-lo	lift-on lift-off.
LPG	liquefied petroleum gas.
MARPOL	International Convention for the Prevention of Pollution from Ships.
MASS	maritime autonomous surface ships.
MDF	maritime dependence factor.
MEPC	marine environment protection committee.
MFO	marine fuel oil.
MLC	Maritime Labour Convention.
MOU	memorandum of understanding.
MPA	Maritime and Port Authority.
MSC	maritime safety committee.
NAFTA	The North America Free Trade Agreement.
NGO	non-governmental organisation.
NOx	nitrogen oxides.
NVOCC	non-vessel-operating common carriers.
OBO	ore bulk oil.
OECD	Organisation for Economic Co-operation and Development.
OPEC	Organization of Petroleum Exporting Countries.
OPRC	International Convention on Oil Pollution Preparedness, Response and Co-operation.
OSRA	Ocean Shipping Reform Act.
P&I	protection and indemnity.
Panamax	mid-sized cargo ships capable of passing through the original Panama Canal.
PSC	port state control.

R&D	research and development.
ROI	return on investment.
ro-ro	roll on, roll off.
SCFI	Shanghai Containerized Freight Index.
SCM	supply chain management.
SEEMP	ship energy efficiency management plan.
SOLAS	International Convention for the Safety of Life at Sea.
SOx	sulphur oxides.
SSE	Shanghai Shipping Exchange.
STCW	International Convention on Standards of Training, Certification and Watch-keeping for Seafarers.
STV	seaborne trade in value.
teu	twenty-foot equivalent unit.
TFP	total factor productivity.
THC	terminal handling charge.
UNCLOS	United Nations Convention on the Law of the Sea.
UNCTAD	United Nations Conference on Trade and Development.
USMCA	United States–Mexico–Canada Agreement.
VLCC	very large crude carrier.
VLOC	very large ore carrier.
WTO	World Trade Organization.
WS	Worldscale.
WTA	willingness to accept.
WTP	willingness to pay.

Preface

International maritime transport deserves more attention from and the interest of many people in the world. For more than half a century the shipping sector should have been given credit for many global social and economic achievements, be it the continuous economic stability and prosperity in most countries or the hundreds of millions of people lifted out of poverty. Presently, like most other economic activities, maritime transport will be disrupted and reshaped by digital technologies and the related new business models. The sector is at the crossroads, facing rapid economic, environmental and technological changes and the associated uncertainties. There is a need for a thorough, broader and new review of maritime businesses, about not only the economic principles that have guided the functioning and operation of the sector but also the root causes of changes and the development directions for the future. Having spent many years on research and teaching in the subject at the Master's level, I decided to write this book as a contribution to the fulfilment of the need.

The book aims to give economic explanations of the shipping business and what can happen in the future. An effective way of doing this is to ask relevant questions. Therefore, the book consists of more than 280 specific questions and answers. The ideas and explanations are evidenced by practical examples and supported by more than 160 tables and figures. The book explains why seaborne trade happens and what its development trends are; it analyses the main features of shipping supply and how various shipping markets function and it addresses the critical strategic issues of the shipping business. The book has 16 chapters divided into 4 parts, dealing with the issues concerning maritime transport demand, supply, market and strategy.

Part I has four chapters discussing maritime demand or seaborne trade. *Chapter 1* explains why maritime transport has a derived demand from trade. In this chapter we go through different trade theories to explain why trade happens and the impact of tariffs and transport on trade. *Chapter 2* concentrates on the seaborne trade of natural resources and primary materials. We demonstrate the close correlation between a country's GDP per capita and its seaborne trade per capita over a long period. *Chapter 3* examines the international trade of manufactured products from three aspects: the impact of the global supply chain, the growth of the middle class and the changes in consumption and trade patterns. *Chapter 4* evaluates the future of seaborne trade from a macro and long-term perspective. We also look into the impact of the continuous shrinking shipping cost on trade and the role of seaborne trade in the economy of countries.

Part II has four chapters covering the supply of maritime transport. *Chapter 5* begins with an examination of ship productivity and the structural changes in the shipping sector. We then explain the reasons for and the impact of the specialisation of ships and the containerisation of the liner shipping sector as well as the future development trends. *Chapter 6* looks at the economic and operational characters of ships. Some key factors which define a ship's cargo-carrying capacity, such as size, speed, time in port, etc., are analysed. *Chapter 7* discusses the economic and operational characteristics of the two forms of commercial shipping services: tramp shipping and liner shipping. *Chapter 8* explains why shipping is a capital-intensive sector and why asset management plays an important role. In this chapter, the issues of ship finance and financial risks are discussed.

Part III has four chapters examining the market of maritime transport. *Chapter 9* analyses the operational, regulatory and technological systems of maritime transport and the enormous challenges involved. *Chapter 10* talks about ports. In this chapter, we explain the relationship between port and state, port and shipping and why port plays a decisive role in shipping development. Port evolution and port competition are also discussed. *Chapter 11* focusses on maritime services, particularly those related to seafarers, ship registration, marine insurance, shipbrokers and marine fuel supply. *Chapter 12* concentrates on the freight market. The economic features of tramp and liner shipping freight markets, the competition and evolution of the freight market and the associated risks are analysed.

Part IV has four chapters dealing with the strategic issues of the shipping sector. *Chapter 13* is an economic review of the maritime competition between countries and between companies in different shipping sectors and with specific focusses. *Chapter 14* evaluates shipping in the context of logistics. The chapter also assesses the logistic activities of the shipping companies and the possibilities of integration between shipping and logistics. *Chapter 15* is devoted to maritime safety and environmental economics. We explain what externality is and why it is better to internalise it by using market-based measures. *Chapter 16* examines the impact of digitalisation on maritime transport. We demonstrate why shipping activities can be expressed and treated digitally and how the recent breakthroughs of digital technologies have triggered a disruptive transformation of the shipping sector. We discuss the likelihood of digitalisation and automation of most shipping sectors, the driving forces for the disruption and the principles for a successful company strategy.

The book is most suited for the students pursuing shipping-related programmes. It is also a valuable reference for maritime professionals. The "questions-and-answers" format is particularly useful because the over 280 questions reflect those likely to be asked by the students in their learning of the subject or by the professionals in the business environment. In the book, the answers to the questions concentrate on an analysis of the causes and reasons for current and possible future maritime businesses. Most readers would benefit most by reading the chapters in sequential order. But those who have already the basic knowledge of shipping can begin anywhere and read the chapters selectively. It may even be a good idea to start the book with *Chapter 16* because this last chapter focusses on the issues of digitalisation and disruptive changes which can lead to a complete transformation of the maritime transport sector within the next couple of decades.

Part I

The demand

Chapter 1

International trade explained

Demand is the desire of a consumer to pay a specific price for having a product or service. Supply is, therefore, the response to the desire through the provision, at the price agreed, of the product or service. Without need, a maritime transport service will not be provided. So we will, first of all, discuss maritime transport demand, before trying to find answers to the fundamental questions on supply such as what, how and to whom the shipping services shall be provided. But the demand for maritime transport is a derived demand from trade. Shipping exists because of trade or, in other words, trade is the *raison d'être* for shipping. That is the reason why the first chapter is devoted to international trade. In this chapter, we will begin with an explanation of what a derived demand is. We will then look at the main characters of trade, the trade theories and their critiques. This will be followed by discussion of the changes in the environment for trade. We will also have a brief review of new economic theories and explanations of trade. We will finally analyse the differences between the trade of primary commodities and that of manufactured products.

1.1 Maritime demand derived from trade

Why does maritime transport have a derived demand from trade?

A ferry ship provides services to the passengers, a cruise ship offers packages to the tourists and a cargo ship provides transport to trade for the transportation of goods. In such cases, the demand for the service is a downward slope curve representing the relationship between the price charged by the shipping companies and the quantity of services desired by the users. The lower the price is, the more the demand will be. However, there is a difference between the demands for passenger ships or cruise ships and the demand for cargo ships. The services provided by the passenger or cruise ships are final consumption goods (services), but the service provided by the cargo ship is a part of the trade. What a final consumer wants are the goods, not the transport. But trade will not be completed without transport. The customer satisfaction from cargo transport is only indirectly obtained from the completion of the trade. The more successful the trade is, the bigger the demand for shipping. As people do not want maritime transport services per se, rather they want the products that have been transported by ships, the demand for shipping depends on the demand for the delivered goods.

Such a demand is called *derived demand*. Shipping is an intermediate service with a derived demand from trade. As a good illustration of such a demand, we can refer to one of the most commonly used terms; an ICC (International Chamber of Commerce) term for international trade, "CIF", which means the cost of the cargo, the insurance cost and the transport freight. In this case, the transport service is purchased together with the cargo. If trade terms other than CIF are used, maritime transport is always considered as a part of the trade, though the payment may or may not be included in the cargo's price.

What are the implications of a derived demand?

Because shipping has a derived demand, for a better understanding of shipping we need to have a detailed discussion about international trade. Among many characteristics of the trade-derived maritime demand, the following four aspects deserve more attention.

1 ***Alternative transport modes***. While an increase in the demand for shipping in terms of cargo transported must come from the corresponding rise in trade in volume, the opposite may not be true. This means that more trade does not always lead to more demand for shipping, even in volume terms. Shipping is not an exclusive mode of transport for trade. This is particularly true between the countries sharing common borders, where rail or road transport may be more suitable options. Pipelines and aeroplanes are other modes of transport carrying importation portions of international trade. The exact mode of transport to use depends on many elements of the characteristics of each transport mode. But one can also not estimate future maritime transport demand by merely relying on future trade development and without considering other modes of transport.
2 ***Variable impact on the demand***. Unlike passenger or cruise shipping, for which price changes directly affect the demand level, in cargo transport, price changes may or may not have a noticeable impact on the demand. This is about price elasticity of demand, a topic which will be discussed in more detail later in the book. What is important to note now is that, for maritime transport of cargo, the same degree of change in price will have very different effects on the final prices of the goods delivered, thus leading to very different degrees of changes in the demand of trade. For example, the freight cost could be at the same level as or even higher than the price of some cargoes, such as raw materials to be transported over a long distance. In this case, a small change of the freight cost, say by 10%, would have a significant effect on the price of the cargo and subsequently on the level of demand. However, the maritime transport cost could be less than 1% of the price of some high-value cargo, such as electronics or clothes. In this case, even a 50% rise or fall in the freight level would only have a limited effect on the price of the final product and thus the level of demand.
3 ***Indirect competition***. With a derived demand, maritime transport contributes to the final value of trade and it is, therefore, an element of the trade's competitiveness. So even in a case where there is no direct competition in shipping services, maritime transport may still be a decisive factor in the trade competition between nations. In other words, the success of the shipping depends on the success of the trade it serves. It is also true that maritime transport strengthens or weakens the competitiveness of trade. For example, from 2011 the Brazilian mining company Vale S.A. took delivery of a series of very large ore carriers (VLOC) capable of carrying about 400,000 tons (deadweight) of iron ore from Brazil to China and other destinations. As China has become the world's top producer of iron and steel, Australia enjoyed a competitive edge over Brazil in exporting iron ore to the Chinese market due to its proximity. So maritime transport was a determining factor in the competition. By using such large ships, the intention was to cut transport cost through scale economies to improve the competitiveness of iron ore.

4 ***Weak public awareness.*** Operating in support of international trade shipping is invisible to the public. For instance, ordinary people generally do not appreciate the importance of shipping because they cannot see it when they pick up at the supermarket a product imported from a country on the other side of the globe or fill up their cars with gasoline that has been transported all the way by a tanker ship. Most people normally only care about what they see and feel and have little interest in knowing how the product has been brought to them. It is difficult for people to appreciate the role of international shipping and the tremendous contributions made by truck drivers, warehouse keepers and crane drivers at the port. So knowing that maritime transport has a demand derived from trade allows us to better understand why improving public awareness of the maritime sector is so hard a task.

1.2 The need for trade

Why is trade at the centre of a modern economy?

Trade can simply be described as the transfer of the ownership of goods or services from one individual or firm to another in exchange for monetary payment or other products or services. This definition applies to demand and supply, though usually the topic of demand/supply and that of trade are discussed under separate headings. Trade is an exchange or a transaction of goods or services between a buyer or the demand and a seller or the supply, that may or may not take place in a market.

Gross domestic product (GDP) is commonly used to measure a country's economy or its output for a period of time, normally a year. Gross domestic product is measured by the calculation of the total prices or market value of the final goods and services produced within a year. Such prices or market value are equivalent to the final transactions, or trade. For example, the food in a restaurant is traded between the restaurant owner and the customer, it thus has a price and enters into the country's GDP. But a self-prepared dinner at home is not traded with an attached price and is not included in the GDP. So the GDP can be calculated either based on the total consumer prices, which is on the demand side, or based on the total value-added or all producers, which is on the supply side. For a firm, the value-added is the difference between its sales and its purchases of input from other firms. Once again, trade is at the centre of both sales and purchases. So we may say that a country's GDP is realised in the form of the outcomes of trade.

Why are national trade and international trade often discussed separately?

A trade is a trade. There are no fundamental differences whether it is within a country or between countries. In an extreme case, if the entire world were just one country, all trade would be national or, at the other extreme, if countries were divided into small enough pieces to separate every producer and consumer, then all trade would be international. So, if trade is almost a synonym of demand and supply and it also has a central position in the creation of GDP and the development of national economy, why are national and international trade usually treated as separate topics? There are some reasons and we would like to discuss the following three of them.

- ***Sovereign nations.*** Although trade is the same no matter where trade partners are from, in most textbooks on economics trade is usually discussed in the international context. The role of domestic trade for a national economy is only elaborated on briefly if at all. Concerning the reasons for this, Samuelsson[1] explained that international trade differs from domestic trade in three aspects: it has a larger scope of trade, it involves national sovereignty with possible trade barriers and it is subject to currency issues. The last two differences are the sources of most trade disputes and the main areas for which government policies are established. It also means that if trade-related national borders are removed and a common currency is used, the differences between domestic and international trade should disappear. This is what has happened in the Eurozone countries in Europe and the reason for the WTO to treat the within-EU trade as one single entry.

- ***Specific focusses.*** Another reason why trade needs to be looked at separately from demand and supply is related to the difference in the focus. While the discussions of trade place emphasis mostly on everything related to the transaction process of goods and services, the analysis of demand/supply concentrates on the need and the production aspects of products and services. It is for this reason that, for example, in a typical demand/supply equilibrium model, the basic elements of trade, such as transaction cost, are not considered; likewise, in the classical trade theory, which will be further discussed later, the focus is not on the changes in the production pattern, such as effects of scale economies or cluster networks.
- ***Methods of measurement.*** Trade is measured in the price of transactions, while GDP is measured in value-added of productions. For a firm, trade refers to all revenues received for the outputs plus all costs incurred for the external inputs. This is also equivalent to all its sales and procurements. But what enters into the GDP is only the difference between the two or the value-added created by the firm. So, a fundamental difference between trade and GDP is that the former is based on the prices of all transactions, while the latter is based on the prices of final transactions only. Consequently, there is, indeed, a lot of double-counting in trade statistics. In the US dollar, for example, a country's trade, such as Singapore's, may even be bigger than its GDP.[2] The more intermediate transactions in the production process, the higher the amount of trade, while the market value or the price of the product to the final consumer remains just the same. This has become the origin for some serious divergence in interpreting the balance of trade issues between nations. So, the WTO and OECD took the initiative to calculate and publish trade statistics based on the value-added of countries with an indication of foreign content of gross exports of some selected countries. The calculation is very complicated, so the value-added-based statistics of international trade are not published on an annual basis. For this book, the traditional trade data on actual import and export, not the data on value-added, are far more relevant.

Why do people trade?

Economics is about using limited resources efficiently for the maximum benefit of society. Just as Adam Smith described in *The Wealth of Nations*, people are much more productive if they specialise and trade. This is because specialisation leads to skilfulness and scale economies, which in turn improve the quality of and reduce the cost of production. This is also called a division of labour. Consequently, people's time, which is a limited resource, is used more efficiently than without specialisation and trade. So people specialise for the sake of economic efficiency and people trade as a result of specialisation. Consequently, the more efficiently the resources are used, the more developed the economy, the more prosperous and wealthier the society will be.

In the pre-Industrial Revolution era, the level of trade was low, because it was mostly a village economy in which farmers produced most of what they needed by themselves. Very little was left for trade with other people. With almost no specialisation, the productivity was very low and resources such as land and labour were used inefficiently. As a consequence, people were very poor. This is still the case in, unfortunately, too many places even today. Starting in Europe, the Industrial Revolution changed such a situation completely. The symbol of modern society is specialisation and trade. Since GDP is the price for the trade to the final consumers, the richer the country, the higher the trade level; the higher the GDP per capita and the higher the trade per capita (domestic and foreign). In the end, the more sophisticated and advanced an economy is, with a larger service sector and more intermediate transactions, the higher the trade level will be. The aspects of trading countries will be discussed later in this chapter. Trade is a synonym for wealth.

What are the main implications?

In this section we have discussed the relationship between the economy and trade. There are two important implications that we should emphasise more.

- A poor country trades less than a rich country and when the country becomes richer, its trade level shall increase. This is indeed what happens in many countries such as India, whose domestic trade boomed, or China, which has become an international trade champion. It is, therefore, logical that future trade should be generated by those countries that are likely to have faster economic growth. How much of the new trade would be international? The answer may depend on many factors, which we shall discuss in more detail in the following sections of this chapter. But with a faster than average growth rate, it looks almost certain that the potential trade growth should come from Asia, Africa and Latin America.
- Although it is often taken for granted that trade refers to international trade, there are no fundamental differences between domestic and foreign trade with regard to why people trade. In practice, however, sovereignty and currency issues make international trade a special and more complicated case. It is uncertain in which direction the issue of international versus national trade will develop: more open and integrated or more protection and division? Various trade talks currently going on between major trading countries and regions as well as on the global level seem to give reasons for optimism that the economic globalisation will continue. So far, only a small portion of the world population has benefitted from the economic globalisation. That should be a hopeful perspective for the maritime transport sector.

1.3 Classical trade theories and their limitations

It is still worth having a brief review of the basics of the trade theory because it is far from being evident, even today, that everyone has understood and accepted the fundamental principles. There are two different attitudes toward trade. The first is the unilateral benefit attitude, which is based on the belief that one gains what the other loses or that the size of the "cake" remains fixed. Hence, the less one buys from the others, the better it is for himself. The corresponding national policy under such an attitude is usually in the form of "import substitution" which focusses on enhancing the degree of self-sufficiency to ensure maximum economic independence from foreign countries.

The second is called the mutual benefit attitude, which is founded on the belief that trade can improve productivity for all trade partners through specialisation according to the absolute or comparative advantages of each country. This kind of trade benefits both importers and exporters because the bigger the market of trade is, the broader the specialisation will be, the higher the productivity will become, and the larger the benefit for all will be. And in the end, the size of the cake – the production of all participating countries – will increase.

What is the "absolute advantage" trade theory?

As we conclude that trade is the result of the division of labour and of specialisation, a question may be asked about how the division should be made or in which sector a person or a country should specialise. Well, if people specialise in gaining economic efficiency, then such efficiency is naturally the guide to specialisation. If efficiency is defined as the output to input ratio, the bigger the ratio, the higher the efficiency. In the economic system both output and input are measured in terms of cost. So a person should choose the product which he can produce at less cost than other people can. In such a case the producer is said to have an absolute advantage in this production over the others. Adam Smith[3] described the situation in the following words "Every individual is continually exerting himself to find out the most advantageous employment for whatever capital he can command". Regarding the meaning of the expression "advantageous", he also said that "every prudent master of a family, never to attempt to make at home what it will cost him more to make than to buy". And in respect of whether such an idea would also apply between nations, Smith said: "What is prudence in the conduct of every private family, can scarce be folly in that of a great kingdom". International trade allows a broader division of labour, thus opening up a bigger room for economic benefit and more efficient use of resources.

What is the "comparative advantage" trade theory?

The idea of choosing what you are better at or, with a cost advantage, what to specialise in, is rather straightforward. But how about a situation in which one has no such choice, which means that there is nothing the person can produce cheaper than his peers? There are plenty of such cases in our life. For example, in an office with two persons there are two tasks to be completed during office hours – answering customer requests and compiling cost data – and both tasks need to be done in an equal amount of time. It is not uncommon that one person is capable of doing both tasks more efficiently than the other person. In this case, according to the "absolute advantage" principle, there should not be any specialisation or trade, since one of the two persons lacks absolute advantage.

The English economist David Ricardo proved at the beginning of the 19th century that even if one person could do both tasks more efficiently than the other person, specialisation and trade are still beneficial as long as the efficiency gap between the two persons is different in doing one job than in doing the other job. The principle applied here is called "comparative advantage". The main reason for trade being mutually beneficial is because the resource, e.g., people's time, is limited. A division of labour based on comparative advantage would allow a more efficient use of the limited resources by letting each party concentrate on the task in which he has either the biggest absolute advantage or, in the absence of absolute advantage, the smallest absolute disadvantage. By specialising and trading, both parties will be better off. The biggest absolute advantage and the smallest absolute disadvantage are called comparative advantage. So in the above case of two office workers, the one who has the absolute advantage should choose the task with the biggest efficiency difference between them and leave to his co-worker the other task with which his absolute advantage must be smallest.

Of course, the same principle applies to trade between countries. Let's take a classic example of international trade of cotton and wheat between two countries A and B. Figure 1.1 shows that, with the same amount of land, country A can produce 8 units of cotton and 4 units of wheat, while country B can produce 6 units of cotton and 2 units of wheat. Country A has an absolute advantage in the production of both products compared with country B. However, country A has a comparative advantage in wheat because the efficiency ratio compared with that of country B is 4 to 2, bigger than 8 to 6 for cotton. Country B has a comparative advantage in cotton because its efficiency ratio compared with country A is 6 to 8 for cotton, bigger than 2 to 4 for wheat. In other words, wheat is relatively cheaper in country A while cotton is relatively cheaper in country B, assuming that in each country the price of the products is determined by land productivity. So, in country A, the price ratio of wheat and cotton is 2 to 1, and in country B it is 3 to 1.

With free trade and under the assumption of zero transaction costs, a trader would see the opportunity to import wheat from country A, which is 100% more productive than country B, and sell it in country B where the price is relatively higher. With this, he would import cotton in country

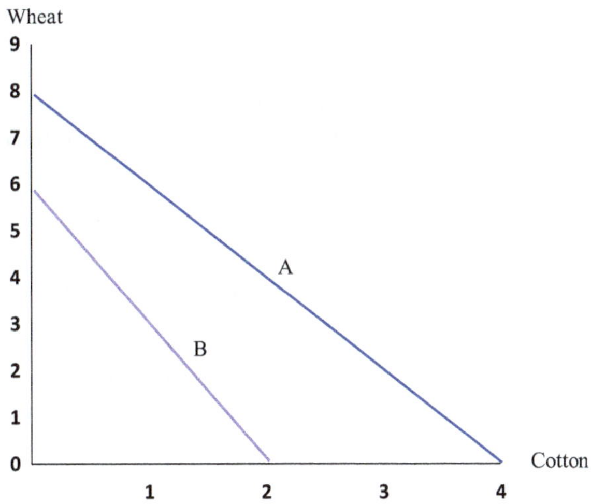

Figure 1.1 Trade based on comparative advantage.

Note: country A has a comparative advantage in cotton, because it is 100% more efficient, bigger than that in wheat; country B has a comparative advantage in wheat because it is 25% less efficient than country A, smaller than that in cotton.

B, which is 25% less productive than country A, and sell it in country A where the price is relatively higher. Overall, the trader is better off and has the motivation to trade more. Subsequently, as more wheat enters into country B, the price will fall, forcing wheat farmers to reduce their production and eventually to leave the sector. At the same time, as more cotton is exported from country B, the price will rise, attracting farmers to move in. Likewise, the same thing will happen in country A, where the production of wheat will increase at the expense of cotton. With the effect of free trade, the prices of the two commodities in both countries will equalise. Each country will naturally specialise in the areas of its comparative advantage and both countries will be better off. The economic benefits of trade based on comparative advantage are in the form of price reductions of wheat in country A and of cotton in country B, originating from more efficient use of land.

What is the "factor endowment" trade theory?

As we can see, the comparative advantage trade theory focusses on the differentiation of production efficiency between trading parties, but it did not give an explanation on what are the causes for such efficiency differences. Two Swedish economists, Hechscher and Ohlin,[4] argued that the comparative advantage came from different factor endowment between the countries. For example, the US has more capital, Russia has more land, India has more labour, etc., and such endowments can be considered as fixed factors for a given period. So, comparatively, trading nations have different factor endowments which form the origins of comparative advantage for trade because the more abundant the factor endowment is, the cheaper the factor price will be.

They also argued that for producing different goods the different proportions of production factors must be used. For any production, where the factor proportion remains unchanged, there will be a constant return to scale. Therefore, different productions and products can be divided into categories depending on their factor proportions. For example, textile products are labour-intensive, soya beans are land-intensive and machinery is capital-intensive, etc. Matching the production of right factor proportion with the country factor endowment is the central idea of the Hechscher-Ohlin trade theory. So, according to this theory, China, with 1.4 billion people, should concentrate on labour-intensive production and Australia should be focussing on the agriculture sector, while Japan or South Korea should not, etc.

What are the main limitations of classical trade theories?

The comparative-advantage-based trade theory has been the intellectual foundation for the free trade economic thinking for a very long time. Yet, it also has a number of shortcomings, particularly with regard to the severe omissions and over-simplistic assumptions which were necessary and important for the construction of the theory and building of the model. For example, the theory assumes that the use of a factor, labour or land, is perfectly interchangeable and substitutable across sectors and between individuals. It also assumes that there are no un-used factors, therefore producing more of one product would systematically mean producing less of the other products. It assumes that prices equal costs, that there are no transport costs and customs and it assumes that there are no effects of scale economies or diminishing return when the size of production changes. It assumes that the market is free of government intervention or large corporations' influence; and more. To a different extent, all these assumptions may be problematic, unrealistic or even untrue. This is the main reason for the theory having limited value for real-world applications.

In 1953 the American economist Leontief[5] challenged the "factor endowment" theory by calculating the capital and labour requirements for the production of US exports and US production in import-competing industries. He found that US export industries required a higher proportion of labour than the industries in which the US had substantial imports. Compared with its trading partners, the US is labour scarce but capital abundant. But a capital-rich country was exporting labour-intensive products. Why? This is called the "Leontief paradox" because it proved contrary to the well-accepted Hechscher-Ohlin factor proportion proposition.

What are the main implications?

The above discussions reveal a number of implications, not only for this section but also for the whole book. There are mainly three of them. First is that the central ideas of economics are also applicable to maritime transport. For example, we can use the trade theory to explain the specialisation of maritime activities. Different shipping activities require different factor proportions and different maritime nations have different factor endowment. The modern shipping industry is a perfect demonstration of international specialisation. From shipbuilding and ship operation, to seafaring and maritime services, the activities are concentrated in a small number of countries. The knowledge of economics enables people to see the rules behind what is happening and to understand why, which will help them make better decisions.

The second implication is about economic assumptions and the importance of empirical analysis. One of the most striking features of economics is that it relies on assumptions. A fundamental assumption in economics is that people take a decision "rationally". For example, when the price goes down, one buys more. But, for example, a decision of an exporter on which shipping company to use is more complex and is influenced by many more factors. It is rarely just a matter of price even if the quality of service between suppliers is identical. We see more people making emotional rather than rational decisions, including in the maritime sector, such as the behaviour of ship sales and purchases. So assumptions are often sources of invalidity of the theories. But assumptions are needed for economic analysis. For example, when the effect of a factor can only be observed if other factors are assumed to be constant. Such a situation is not always possible in real life. So to make sure that the assumptions are correct and the results are valid and stable, empirical testing and analysis should be made. This is to verify the theory in real-world situations. If the empirical analysis fails to support the conclusion, more verification is needed.

The third implication from the above discussions is about the need for the economic theories to adapt to the changing environment with adjustments, modifications and new ideas. This is actually the topic of the following sections in this chapter and later chapters. We will see that enormous changes have happened since the classical trade theories were first introduced, particularly for the last half a century, and that disruptive changes will occur to maritime transport in the future. Such changes will happen in both the demand and supply aspects of shipping. But most of the changes are mere reflections of broader evolutions and new development in the world economy, trade, production, consumption and technologies.

1.4 New economic explanations of trade

With the recognition of the limitations of the classical trade theories, let's take a look at some new thoughts in the area of international trade. Since the Second World War, international trade has entered a new era with a large volume of trade and broader geographical coverage. It is necessary for us to briefly discuss some most important ideas, in particular the following three which have a direct influence on maritime demand: the demand-driven trade theory, scale-economies trade theory and the business-cluster trade theory.

What is demand-based trade theory?

Most of the trade theories, traditional or new, can be called supply-based because the drivers of trade in these theories are producer, production and products related. In 1961 the Swedish economist Staffan Linder[6] proposed an "overlapping demand theory" to explain international trade. According to him, international trade is simply the extension of national trade, therefore the country needs to have a domestic demand for a product which then can also be exported overseas. The amount of foreign trade a country has depends on the consumer preference of the country. And such consumer preference is affected by the income level of the country. Consequently, the proportion of foreign trade in total trade is bigger in small countries than in big countries; the higher the country's income per capita, the more it takes part in foreign trade; countries with similar consumer preference would trade more between themselves, and this is called overlapping demand.

According to this trade theory, the higher the income of a country, the more it takes part in foreign trade; and the more similar the income level of two countries, the bigger the need for trade between them. This is an interesting observation because such similarity between the trading countries implies similar technology and an insignificant difference in factor endowment such as labour or capital that are the origins of comparative advantage. In reality, the biggest bilateral trade flows are not those between countries with different factor endowments or comparative advantages, but those with similar conditions, such as between the US and Canada, and those between France and Germany. These are countries with similar levels of income and consumer preference. As usual, this theory has received criticism, for example on how to explain the fast growth of trade in semi-finished products and the intra-firm trade, which are not closely related to the local demand or the level of income of the exporting countries. Nonetheless, the theory does provide a fresh angle of analysis: looking for the motivations of the trade from the demand side is an excellent idea. This explains why container shipping mostly concentrates between rich and industrialised countries.

What is the new trade theory based on scale-economies?

As the world economy grew and international trade expanded, people found that the traditional trade theory was insufficient to explain the situations that arose. For example, trade in differentiated products, mostly manufactured, is far more important than that in homogenous goods, mostly primary commodities. But the factor endowment proposition seemed to have ignored this by assuming that products, as well as production factors between countries, are identical and perfectly substitutable. Although the factor proportion theory explained the effects of diminishing return, it did not take into account the effect of the gains in unit cost reduction thanks to economies of scale, known as increasing returns to scale. The ever-increasing cross-border trade within the same firm cannot be explained by traditional trade theories. In order to address these unexplainable issues, theorists began to look for other reasons for trade and in the late 1980s the "new trade theory" emerged, mainly to explain trade of similar goods between similar countries. One of the leading theorists is American economist Paul Krugman.[7] The new trade theory is based on three reasons for trade: increasing returns to scale, imperfect competition and differentiated goods.

Increasing returns to scale is also called economies of scale, which means that as the size of production increases, cost per unit of output decreases. The main reasons behind this are (a) a larger scale of production allows fixed costs to be spread out over more units of output; and (b) as the size of production increases, generally, operational efficiency is also higher, such as improved skills and speed of operation or reduction in idle time. So if, for some reason, a country has economies of scale in a product due to, e.g., a quick growth or a big local demand, it will be able to export. This theory explains the reasons for trade independently from the traditional theories based on comparative advantage. In the case of a competitive market, trade can be explained by comparative advantage theory, while in the case of imperfect competition and monopoly, the new trade theory provides more suitable explanations.

The idea of customer preference is also at the centre of the new trade theory. People do not always choose the least costly products. Their satisfaction is often based on a diverse choice of marks and brands. Such customer preference is also an important reason for trade. However, there may be a conflict between pursuing low production cost through economies of scale on the one hand and satisfying customer preference for more diversity on the other. This is because the former implies a consolidation of production, thus with fewer choices, and the latter means small scales of production. International trade, according to the new trade theory, offers a perfect solution to the problem: by having a more concentrated production at home for both domestic and foreign demand to benefit from economies of scale, while importing more foreign-made products to give consumers more diverse choices. When it comes to maritime transport services, the balance between the loyalty to a supplier for the sake of stability and the diversity of service providers for the sake of risk management is always a challenge.

What is the national competitive advantage theory?

In 1990 Michael Porter proposed a new framework of international trade in his book entitled *The Competitive Advantage of Nations*.[8] He argued that a country's competitiveness in participating in international trade is determined by 4 key attributes, which are factor endowments, demand conditions, cluster effects and firm strategies.

1 **Factor endowments**. Here Porter extended the traditional concept of factors endowment to include infrastructure and quality of education and research. Just having a good reserve of factors, such as natural resources or labour, is not enough. The key is how to use them effectively. The natural blessings such as land, natural resources, climate, etc., are called basic factors, which

are essential. But equally or more important are the so-called advance factors, which include skilled labour force, technology, infrastructure, communication, etc. A country may lack favourable basic factors, like the Netherlands, Singapore or South Korea, but it may excel in advanced factors to acquire a competitive advantage to be strong exporters of high-tech products or services.

2 **Demand conditions**. For competing abroad, strong local demand is essential, not only in quantity but also in sophistication. Many examples show that demanding customers in the domestic market would drive the suppliers to actively engage in research and innovations to improve the quality of products. This will, in turn, provide the industries with a strong competitive margin in the international market. The IT products in the US and electronic products in Japan are examples in this respect. Large domestic demand will also help the exporters to benefit from the effect of scale economies. The huge domestic market in China has allowed many Chinese manufacturers to enjoy a big advantage from economies of scale in their exports, which has offset the disadvantages of fast-rising labour costs.

3 **Related and supporting industries or clusters**. If the above two attributes are not new, the third factor is a new perspective in Porter's analysis. It is what we know today as cluster effects. No product for export can be made in isolation. So one cannot just derive the direct contributing factors in a product to estimate the comparative advantage. The competitiveness of a product in the foreign market depends on the existence and the efficiency of the product cluster, which includes home-based suppliers and related supporting industries in terms of cost-effective and quality inputs. For example, the Japanese and Korean success in many electronic products, including memory chips and cameras, is greatly attributable to a large number of local suppliers, most of which are small- and medium-sized companies. Logistics services, including shipping and port, are another important determining factor for the international competitiveness of a country's export sector.

4 **Firm strategy, structure and rivalry**. One of the omissions in the classical trade theories is about the role of companies. Porter emphasised that it is the firms, not the nations, that are competing and trading in the international market. So company strategies are of significant importance and the conditions concerning how companies are created, organised and managed are decisive. The role of entrepreneurs is paramount in the effective use of production factors. So even if an enterprise had all necessary factors at comparatively low costs, success in the international market is still not a guarantee if the factors are not used effectively with good strategies and management. Usually, company innovation, product improvement, cost reduction, etc., are most effectively driven by competition. So the existence of a strong domestic competitive environment is also one of the key elements.

What are the main implications?

We have so far discussed some new leading ideas answering the question about the reasons for international trade. These ideas emerged because the old theories could not fully explain international trade as the world economy, production and consumption evolved. The world economy has kept changing and re-shaping the international trade environment. The biggest change is most probably economic globalisation. As we will later see, for about 60 years cross-border trade has grown almost twice as fast as the world economy. As a result, countries are more closely connected with each other by trade. The barriers to trade like customs duties have on the whole been declining. The growing and accelerated international mobility of factors such as capital and labour has made national comparative-advantage-based theories less relevant. The establishment of export processing zones (EPZs) means that a country can become an exporter of a product without a local demand. Among the important implications we can draw from the above discussions, we will elaborate on the following three.

- ***From country to company***. Traditional trade theories are based on cost advantages between countries, as if the country is the trading entity with the power to choose which sectors to focus on and which others to forego. However, in reality, never has a state or a market economy been in such a place or had such a power. The real trading entity is an individual firm. So many new economic thoughts on trade place more emphasis at the company level to see how the factors are utilised. For example, they look at advantages obtained from increasing returns to scale of a firm, or from industry clusters, or a good company strategy. The state has certainly a role to play to influence the country's foreign trade, via, for example, tariffs or currency-related trade policies, but the real competitiveness of a country's trade comes from the performance of individual companies.
- ***From international trade to trade***. We explained above that as far as the reasons for development are concerned, there was not any fundamental difference between domestic and international trade. Seventy country borders and different currencies are the unique features of international trade as compared with domestic trade. For a company, the most important concern is to sell the product, no matter where it is sold. It should make no difference for the company whether the product is sold domestically or internationally. People trade every day and as long as they are happy with the quality and price of the product or service, it does not matter where it is made. In this sense, Linder's demand-based trade theory reveals a lot of truth. Trade grows together with people's income. Driven by economic globalisation, multinational companies and cross-border capital flows, the world economy is more integrated and provides more favourable conditions for the further growth of international trade.
- ***From trade to the connections of trade***. While the traditional trade theories concentrate more on the production and outputs, ignoring how the goods are transferred from the producer to the consumer, new trade theories also look at the transaction process and the way in which trade is conducted. Krugman[9] developed a model on trade geography and Porter analysed the role of infrastructure and supporting industries. The success of IKEA, the world's largest furniture maker, is greatly attributable to the way the products are stored and transported. The competitiveness of Walmart and Dell computers has a lot to do with their superior logistics systems. Today, for an increasing number of companies, logistics is one of the most important sources of competitiveness. The performance of shipping and port services often play a decisive role in the success or failure of a country's trade on the international market.

Communication is another dimension of trade connections. Trading locally or between large and well-known companies is less difficult than trading between remote companies, especially between the small ones. The complexity does not only come from a long physical distance but is also related to the difficulties in communication between the sellers and buyers. Thanks to the internet, the situation is changing. Alibaba, a B2B trading platform, allows many small buyers and sellers, normally remote from each other, to trade in goods which were previously untradeable due to the lack of communication. There are online shipping service networks which start to create platform service by providing communication between the supply and demand which were close by but did not know each other.

1.5 The administrative cost of international trade

What is the transaction cost of trade?

If you trade your own home-grown vegetables with a next-door neighbour for his fruit, the cost of trading is probably next to zero. But if you buy fruit from a shop in town, it would incur transport and time cost. If you buy from abroad, more costs will need to be added in terms of tax and procedures. The further away you buy things from or sell them to, the higher the cost. Such cost associated with trade is called transaction cost. Since the cost of trade has to be absorbed by the traders, it must not be bigger than the benefit from trade. So, the higher the transaction costs, the less the benefit of trade. In other words, if the transaction cost is more than the benefit from trading, trade will not happen. From this perspective, the transaction cost is considered as a trade barrier.

There are two types of transaction costs for international trade: one is related to policy, the other is related to transport and logistics. Trade policy refers to government attitude and regulations at the national level with respect to trade. With an attitude to discourage trade in order to protect domestic production, the protective measures can be in various forms such as customs duties, trade quotas, special standards, conditions, requirements, currency control, etc. Under an attitude to encourage trade, promotional measures can be in the form of subsidies, tax reliefs, foreign exchange rate control, etc. The transport and logistics-related trade barriers refer to all activities involved in transferring the goods from the seller to the buyer. It includes transport, packaging, cargo handling, warehousing, storage, etc. Time and cost spent on these activities are logistics barriers to trade.

A country's GDP is driven by consumption, investment and export. All three involve the trade of individuals, corporations and governments. Such trade can either be completed domestically or internationally. Transaction cost is higher for international trade than for domestic trade. For a large country, transport and logistics costs for domestic trade can be higher than similar costs for international trade. But, generally speaking, international trade incurs a higher transport cost than domestic trade. With regard to policy-related trade cost, which is, in most cases, not applicable for domestic trade, it is entirely a phenomenon of international trade. On the one hand, policy-related trade cost may change at any time, going up or down, or disappear as in the situation in Euro-zone countries in Europe, in which case there is little difference between domestic and international trade. On the other hand, transport-related trade costs will always remain, although there is a difference between countries and the general tendency is for such costs to decrease. If the size of a country's total trade is defined by its GDP, the relationship between national and international trade is a function of several factors as illustrated in Figure 1.2. We can see how the relationship is affected by the national competitiveness of products and services on the global markets as well as by customs tariffs and transport costs as the barriers to trade. We will discuss the administrative cost first. On the one hand, when the international price and quality differences in goods and services between countries are bigger, international trade

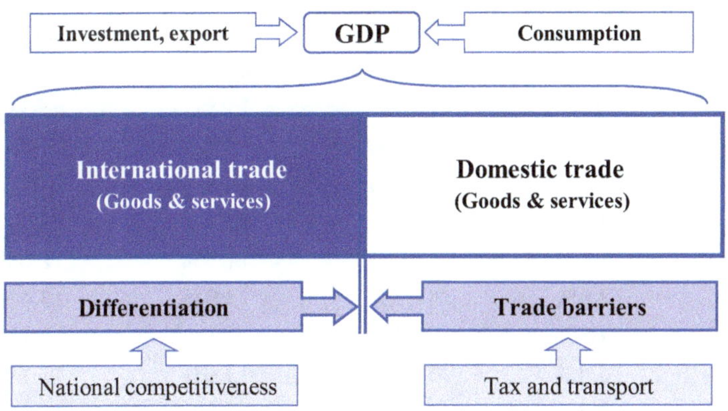

Figure 1.2 Trade model and the influential factors.

Source: Shuo Ma.

Note: international trade is affected by the level of GDP, the competitiveness of products/services on the international market and the trade transaction cost.

will increase. On the other hand, when the transaction cost changes, e.g., due to a change in tax level or shipping freight, the balance between national and international trade will also shift.

What are the impacts of "administrative costs" on trade?

Generally speaking, policy-related trade barriers include tariff and non-tariff measures on trade. They are mostly applicable to a country's imports. Import taxes levied on goods and services are the most popular form of such government intervention in free trade. The aims are to protect the domestic producers and to generate an income. The economic impact of such policy-related extra cost to trade is straightforward: it makes trade more expensive and less beneficial. So the higher the tariffs are, the less the trade will be. For example, if international trade can bring the price of cloth in the domestic market down from US$20 per unit to US$10, the benefit of trade is US$10/unit, which will boost the demand to a higher level. In the case that a tariff of US$2/unit is imposed on the import, the benefit of trade is reduced and the price will be at US$12/unit instead of US$10, depriving the chances of those customers who can only afford to buy the cloth with a price reduction of more than US$8/unit.

The level of customs duties in the world varies from country to country and from one product to another. Table 1.1 shows the average tariff rates of selected economies in 2006 and 2018. At the World Trade Organization, which consists of 164 member states as of 2018, negotiations between countries are going on continuously to reduce trade barriers further. Compared with the situation in the 1980s, the average tariff rates applied in most countries, particularly in the less-developed

Table 1.1 Average trade tariffs of selected economies, 2006 and 2018.

Economies	*2006*		*2018*	
	Non-agri.	*All*	*Non-agri.*	*All*
Singapore	0.0%	0.0%	0.0%	0.0%
USA	3.3%	3.5%	3.1%	3.4%
Japan	2.8%	5.6%	2.5%	4.4%
European Union	3.9%	5.4%	4.2%	5.2%
Switzerland	2.1%	7.6%	1.8%	6.6%
Russia	11.1%	11.4%	6.1%	6.8%
Mexico	13.3%	14.0%	5.8%	7.0%
China	9.0%	9.9%	8.8%	9.8%
Nigeria	11.4%	12.0%	11.5%	12.0%
Brazil	12.6%	12.3%	13.9%	13.4%
South Korea	6.6%	12.1%	6.7%	13.7%
India	16.4%	19.2%	13.6%	17.1%
Egypt	12.2%	19.3%	11.8%	19.1%
Sudan	18.5%	20.1%	20.1%	21.5%
Bahamas	31.2%	30.2%	35.0%	32.5%

Source: WTO World Tariff Profiles (2006, 2019).

Note: the table is the simple average tariffs (MFN applied) in 2006 and 2018 for non-agricultural products and all products.

economies, have been decreasing. According to the WTO, the average import tariff of the developed countries fell from between 20% and 30% in 1947 to 14% in 1952 and 3.9% in 2005.[10] A similar evolution has also been true in the less-developed world. India, for example, made a great effort to bring the average tariff rate down from 33% in 2003 to 17.1% in 2018 and China's 9.8% average tariff rate in 2018 was the result of a massive reduction from about 40% in 1985.[11] A similar development has also happened in many other countries. Tariff rates of more than 20%, which were common amongst poorer countries in the 1990s, are now exceptions. On the whole, global trade is freer now than it was in the past, with a progressive reduction of not only tariff-related barriers but also of non-tariff-based barriers. An increasing number of countries have adopted more trade-friendly economic policies. Consequently, the membership of the WTO had grown by about 30%, from 123 countries and territories in 1995 when the organisation was established, to 164 in 2018, covering around 97% of global trade.

Will the administrative cost to trade increase or decrease in the future?

A very crucial question which remains to be answered is whether the above development reflects the general trend of global trade or not. In other words, to what extent would the barriers to free trade stop falling or even rise in the future? As the demand for the shipping industry is derived from trade, this question is particularly important. What could be the factors that might derail the course of trade-driven economic globalisation? If history can serve as a guide, significant reverse development would possibly happen at the time of economic crisis. A typical example is the Great Depression of the 1930s when the World GDP fell by 15% from 1929 to 1932.[12]At that time, the market demand dropped massively and the unemployment rate was high in all industrialised countries. Protectionist policies started to be implemented by individual countries, which triggered retaliatory tariffs by other countries. International trade became a victim of economic crisis. Between 1929 and 1932 for example, foreign trade declined by 70% in the USA, 61% in Germany, 60% in the UK and 54% in France. The trade level of 1929 was not recovered until 1950.

According to the World Bank, during the recent recession the world's average GDP growth rate dropped from more than 3% per annum to 0% in 2009 with negative growth rates in most industrialised countries. World trade suffered a big decline of 12% in 2009.[13] People called it the "Great Recession", based on the resemblance to the magnitude of the economic crisis in the 1930s. Yet to the surprise of many people, the last big recession did not trigger widespread protectionism similar to that experienced in the 1930s. Figure 1.3 shows that after a considerable decline of 12% in 2009, world trade grew by 14.5% in 2010.[14] The down-turn of trade was quickly reversed and the global economy rebounded from the following year, though the recovery was rather timid and uneven between economies. Why did history not repeat itself? And why did the world trade continue to grow despite the severe economic recession? It is believed that the economic and trade resilience in the wake of the economic crisis of 2008 is attributable to the following 4 reasons.

- One of the main reasons causing the Great Depression of the 1930s was the macroeconomic policy misjudgement and unilateral intervention.[15] Thanks to the inter-governmental bodies like the WTO and the creation of high-level international institutions such as G-20, a group of the world's 20 biggest economies, the leading economies managed, through dialogues, negotiation and discussions, to reach some agreements and coordinated policy principles in order for the governments to safeguard the global trade against protectionism and actively help with the economic recovery.[16]
- Compared with the situation in the 1930s, the world economy is much more diversified. Many less-developed countries enjoy fast economic growth. Most of these emerging economies have a common characteristic of high dependence on foreign trade. So the pro-free-trade force comes

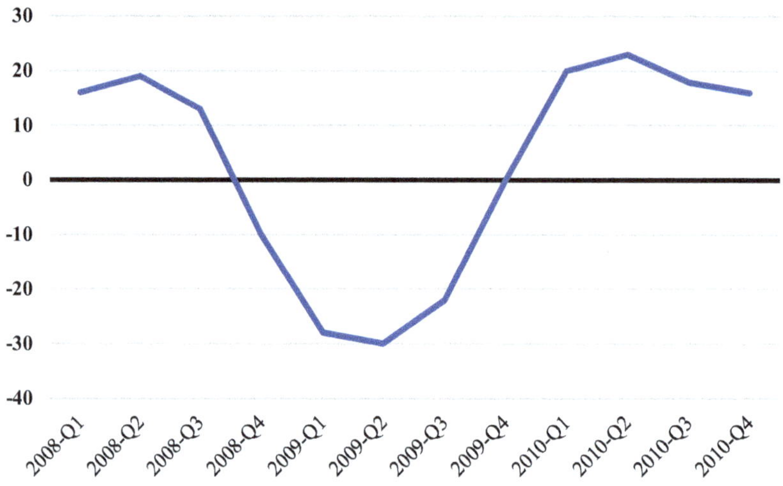

Figure 1.3 World export of manufactured goods, 2008-Q1 to 2010-Q4.

Source: WTO (2014b)

Note: in the wake of serious financial crises, world trade dropped massively. But it recovered to the same pre-crisis level within a year. The situation of the Great Depression of the 1930s was avoided.

no longer from the traditional industrialised countries only. These countries trade not only with rich economies but also between themselves. So any kind of reduction in trade would hurt them more than most advanced economies. During the economic crisis of 2008 the major emerging economies were all committed to free trade.

- With 164 members, most countries are today members of the WTO. As such, they have committed themselves to the trade agreement and WTO rules. Thanks to the trade monitoring mechanism of WTO in keeping traditional instruments of protectionism at bay, member states are restrained in the use of trade-restrictive measures at the time of economic crisis. For the WTO, there is certainly a lot of room for improvement for better efficiency and effectiveness.
- Empirical evidence has shown that the rise in intra-industrial trade and the global supply chain played a vital role in curbing the motivation for protectionism.[17] Firms rely increasingly on not only imported raw materials but also on parts, semi-finished and intermediate goods. Consequently, countries are more and more inter-dependent and more integrated into the global value chain, all linked by international trade.

What are the main implications?

In essence, the real reason to divide trade into domestic and international is due to the existence of borders, which may prevent international trade from moving across these borders freely. Such barriers may take various forms. Tariffs, quotas, inconsistent or opaque regulations and exchange rate manipulation are the most common measures taken by governments to interfere with free trade flows. From the above discussions, the following implications can be drawn.

- ***Widespread protectionism is unlikely to happen due to deeper economic integration***. Thanks to the global value chain, which includes virtually all major economies in the world, a country would find that it is in its best interest to safeguard free trade, unless it is for political reasons, because a protectionist action would hurt its own interest as much as that of its trade partners. So economic interdependence and integration are a very powerful and effective guarantee of free trade.

- ***Protectionism proved to be ineffective for long-term economic growth.*** The argument for protectionism is always to protect the long-term economic benefit of the country. But international trade has been fully recognised as a driving force for growth. Protectionist policies may help domestic producers in the short term, but it often hurts the country's long-term interest since the protected local producers lose the motivation to improve efficiency and the quality of their products or services.
- ***The development of institutions and agreements for free trade.*** As the benefit and importance of international trade are recognised by an increasing number of countries, rich and poor alike, different sorts of free trade agreements and institutions at international, regional and global levels have been made. This creates a multi-layer international coordination network or constraints with an effect to prevent major unilateral protectionist actions to be taken against all trade partners.

1.6 The transport cost of international trade

Trade transaction costs include both administrative and transport-related costs. It has been argued that the reduction of trade cost contributed to the trade expansion from 1870 to 1913 by 55% and to the trade boom since World War Two by 33%.[18] It is estimated that trade costs expressed in tax-equivalent terms would be 170% for industrialised countries and much higher for the developing world. Out of these costs, the biggest are retail and distribution costs (55%) and border-related trade barriers (44%). Transportation cost makes up the bulk of the distribution cost.[19] Based on the US data, logistics costs consist of transport freight and costs related to the time value of goods transported.

Transport cost is the cost of distance. This cost should be understood in a broader sense to include both time and money involved in moving the goods from the seller to the buyer. An assumption in the economic analysis that transport cost is zero would lead to wrong conclusions. The existence of transport cost explains why international trade has not been at the level that most trade theories suggest that it should be. In the 1940s and 1950s, when tariffs applied by the major trading countries were typically as high as 20% to 30% of the value of goods, customs tariffs were the biggest cost of a trade. Over recent decades, with the average import tariffs dropping to 3–4%, transport cost has become the major cost of trade. In this section we will look at the transport cost with an emphasis on international maritime transport.

How much does transport cost in a national economy?

As shown in Figure 1.4, in 2018 the total freight transport costs in the US were US$1,040 billion, which was equivalent to about 5.1% of the US GDP in 2018.[20] The overall logistics cost for US businesses was 8% of the US GDP in 2018. This percentage during the last couple of decades has been stabilised at between 7.5% and 8.5% in the US. However, the ratio of transport cost to inventory cost increased from about 1 to more than two between the 1980s and the 2010s, and it is still rising. Similar proportions of logistics cost to GDP and of transport cost to inventory cost are also present in other industrialised economies in Europe and Japan. One of the reasons is the stagnation or even decline in inventory cost due to better inventory control and lower capital cost. Such a development trend has an important impact on the competition between different transport modes, in favour of maritime transport, which is slow but cheaper. Not all cargo moved is trade between companies;

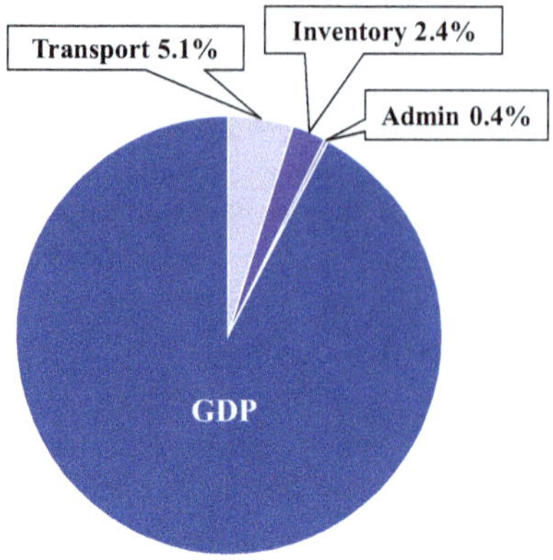

Figure 1.4 Percentage of transport cost in GDP in the US (2018).

Source: CSCMP (2019).

Note: in 2018, 1.6 trillion US dollars was spent on logistics. This is 8% of GDP, of which 5.1% was transport cost and 2.4% was inventory cost.

the transportation of goods in the production process within the same firm is also included. This percentage is, by and large, representative for other wealthy countries with similar advanced and high-performance transportation sectors. So, for countries with a less efficient transportation system, inadequate facilities and backward institutions, the proportion of transport cost in GDP could be as high as 15% or more. With such a high price, transport weighs very much in trade. Or, in other words, transport can be a "killer" of business, as it can, in many cases, cost more than the benefit of trade. Measuring the costs of transport in GDP allows us to have an idea about the size of the transport market, but not necessarily about the impact of transportation on trade. This latter could be observed from the proportion of the transport cost in the value of the trade. Similar to the effect of the administrative costs, which are also an add-on to trade, the transport costs can be seen as a burden or a reduction of the benefit of trade.

How much of the world's international trade is moved by maritime transport?

There are six modes of transport which can be used to move international trade. Transport by sea is one of them and the other modes are by road, rail, air, inland waterways and by pipelines. Not all modes of transport are available to a particular country or trade. For example, generally, road and rail transport is not an option for the international trade of an island country, unless by putting the trucks or railway wagons on ships. Similarly, a land-locked country does not have direct access to international sea transport. Sometimes a mode of transport is unavailable only due to the lack of adequate infrastructure such as port, rail, etc., or services. So long as different modes of transport are available, the choice of the modes to use is by and large an economic one, as illustrated in Figure 1.5. If all relevant factors, such as transport cost, cargo handling cost, storage and in-transit inventory cost, safety, etc., are measured in terms of cost, the mode of transport with the lowest cost per unit is usually used.

As far as the international transport of cargo is concerned, transport and inventory costs are the two essential elements to consider. Compared with other modes, maritime transport provides cheap

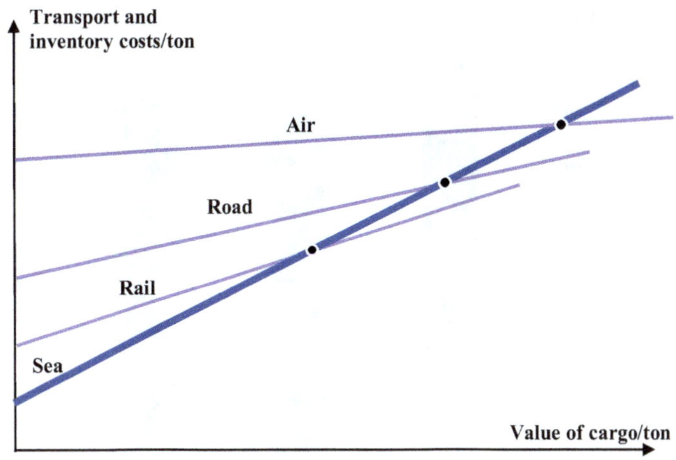

Figure 1.5 Value of cargo and transport cost by mode.

Source: Shuo Ma.

Note: faster modes of transport are more suitable for high-value cargo. Also note that both transport cost and time costs may change even in the short term due to factors such as scale economies, fuel cost or interest rate fluctuations.

but slow transportation. It is, therefore, the most suitable for low-value cargoes. High-value cargoes are more time-sensitive and long transit time will typically lead to an inventory cost that is too high. So, as shown in Figure 1.5, if the value of freight is taken as an independent variable, the most suitable mode of transport depends on the unit value of cargo to be transported.

International trade can be measured in two different ways: by value and by weight or volume. Natural resources, such as minerals, cereals, forest products and energy goods such as oil, coal and gas, are generally of low value. These goods are also traded in large quantities, which provides a possibility to reduce the transport cost through economies of scale. Compared with other modes of transport, ships are capable of carrying as much as half a million tons of cargo each time. So, apart from some energy products such as oil and gas which are transported by pipelines, most natural resources are transported by ships. It is estimated that,[21, 22] if intra-European Union trade is excluded, about 90% of international trade measured in tons is transported by ships. However, when measured in value terms, the share of maritime transport is believed to be at about 60% of world trade. Because Europe is the world's largest region for international trade and most trades between European countries are moved by land-based transport, if intra-EU trade is included, the share in volume terms of maritime transport is lower than 90%, as shown in Figure 1.6.

In 2015 between 20% and 25% of world trade in US dollar terms was between neighbouring countries sharing a common border, such as that between the US and Canada or between France and Germany. This percentage varies from one region to another, but is relatively stable over time.[23] For example, cross-border trade is at a low level, usually less than 5%, between the countries exporting mostly natural resources in Africa and the Middle-East. On the other hand, it is about 30% in Europe and North America where most of the exports are manufactured goods. Obviously, it is most likely that land-based modes of transport, such as road, rail and inland waterways, are used for trade between countries sharing the same borders.

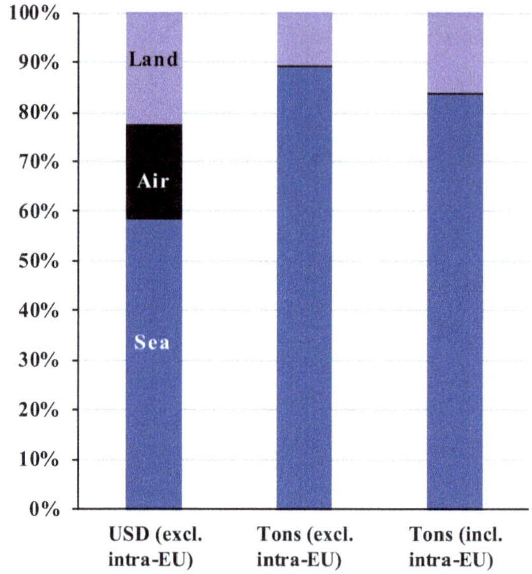

Figure 1.6 Transport modal split of world trade (2018).

Source: IATA (2019), UNCTAD (2018), Clarksons (2019).

Note: air transport's share is very low in volume (metric tons) terms, but much bigger if measured by value. Most intra-EU trade is moved by land, so the land-based portion is high when intra-EU trade is counted.

How much does maritime transport cost to international trade?

To transport a 40-foot container (forty-foot equivalent unit or FEU) from the Far East to a main US west coast port would cost approximately US$2,000.This cost has not changed much since the beginning of containerisation. Such a container has a cargo loading capacity of about 25 metric tons and 72 cubic metres. If 40-inch TV sets are packed in such containers, each can load about 500 of them. Supposing the retail value of the TVs is US$700 apiece, the total value of the cargo is US$350,000. With US$2,000 as the maritime freight cost, the trans-Pacific international maritime freight for TVs is 0.6% *ad valorem* or US$4 per TV set.

Today the price for transporting containers by sea is usually charged in FAK (freight all-kind) terms. It is a flat rate per container applicable to all containers regardless of types of cargo loaded. In this case, the sea transport cost will constitute a more significant proportion of the total value of cheap products and a smaller percentage when it comes to expensive goods. In 2011, for example, the largest item exported from China to the US was furniture, which had an average FOB value of about US$21,000/FEU.[24] If the same maritime freight should apply, the maritime transport cost for Chinese-made furniture is 9.5% *ad valorem*. Even calculating the retail value, the proportion of transport cost would still be high. The high *ad valorem* shipping costs are more remarkable for low-value natural resources transported by ships in bulk. Take, for example, one of the commodities which had the most dynamic growth from the year 2000, iron ore from Brazil to China. In 2003 the *ad valorem* maritime transport cost of iron ore from Brazil to China was as high as 60%.[25]

The different dynamics of the price evolution of the goods and of the transport lead to changes in *ad valorem* shipping cost. Even without considering price fluctuations, maritime transport costs still

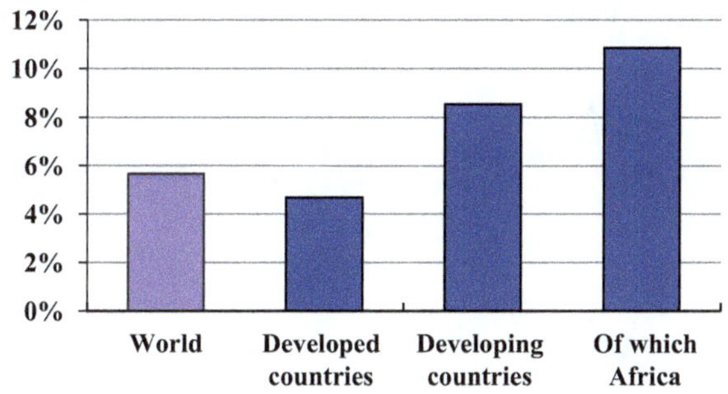

Figure 1.7 Freight as % of import value, 1980–2005 average.

Source: Shuo Ma, based on data of UNCTAD (1980–2005).

Note: such a percentage was in decline until the year 2000, when freight levels surged. Currently the world proportion is about 5%, though countries not on the main shipping routes are still paying more on transport for their imports.

vary greatly for trade between different countries and regions, as demonstrated in Figure 1.7. Africa has been paying the most on maritime transport for its imports on an *ad valorem* basis. From the 1980s to the 2000s the average maritime freight as a percentage of import value was 5.8% globally. But the proportion was much lower for industrialised countries at about 4.2%. The developing countries were paying almost twice as much as the developed countries paid and Africa paid the highest, almost 11% of the import value, on maritime transport. The variations of the *ad valorem* freight cost compiled by UNCTAD are based on the IMF's FOB/CIF ratios of trade data.[26] Although such a method has to be used with caution,[27] it does reveal an idea of the different impacts of transport cost on trade. Why should countries or regions pay transportation bills for their foreign trade with such big differences? There are multiple reasons for this to happen, such as the average value of import, the size of the market, the average distance with the main trading partners, the facilities and efficiency of ports, the import/export balance, the situation of competition of maritime services, etc.

Has the maritime transport cost increased or decreased?

It is evident that, compared with the early days of maritime transport, today the cost either measured in constant currency or *ad valorem* terms is much lower. During more recent times, some researchers found that the maritime transport cost to trade over the last half century or so has not fallen as much as that for other modes of transport, particularly aviation.[28] But in constant dollar terms the price of shipping still follows a downward trend. On 4 January 1985 a dry bulk freight index was created by the Baltic Exchange based on the representative freight rates in US dollars of the day. The index was set as 1,000 points on its first day. More than 30 years later, on 16 July 2015, the same index was still trading at 1,000 points.[29] Of course, there had been ups and downs during this period. However, given the cumulative inflation of the US dollar by as much as 76% between 1985 and 2015, the same level of the Baltic Dry Index of 1,000 points over 30 years means that the cost of maritime transport has significantly decreased.

Another example of the transport cost of maritime containers shows a similar trend. In the 1960s maritime transport of cargo by containers started to expand rapidly from North America to Europe and Asia. The typical freight for electrical/electronic products was US$2,000 for transporting a forty-foot container (FEU) from the basic ports in the Far East, e.g., Hong Kong, Pusan or Kobe, to the

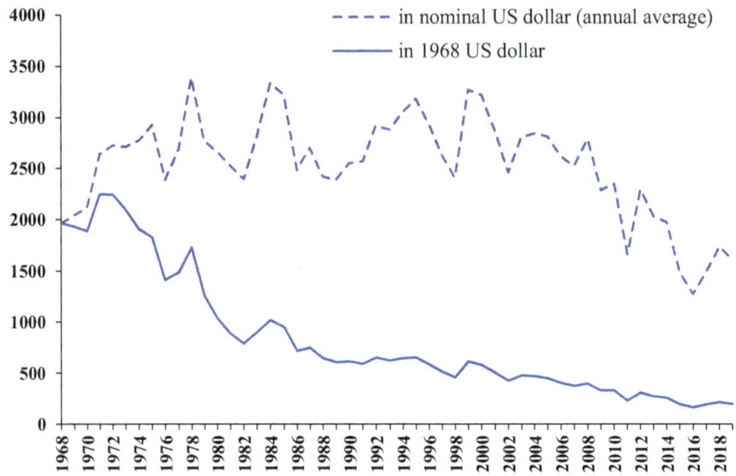

Figure 1.8 Trans-Pacific container freight rates, US$ per FEU, 1968–2019.

Source: Shuo Ma, based on data of Informa, Clarksons, SSE and USDL.

Note: this is about a FAK flat rate per FEU from basic ports in the Far East to basic ports on the West Coast of the USA. While the rate in nominal dollars has been up and down and in 2019 is 82% of 1968 level, the inflation-adjusted rate in 2019 is merely 9.8% of that in 1968.

West Coast of the US, e.g., Seattle or Long Beach. Since then the freight was fluctuating between US$1,500 and $3,500. In July 2018 the annual average freight rate for the same route was about US$1,750 per FEU.[30] During this period the US dollar has lost a lot of its value due to inflation. Measured in 1968 dollars, the Trans-Pacific freight rate of 2018 was only US$225 per FEU or 9.8% of the 1968 level. This development of price is shown in Figure 1.8. It should be noted that if the improvements in the quality of container shipping services, e.g., a shorter transit time, during this period are taken into account, the real benefits for trade from a better and cheaper maritime transport are much more significant.

What are the main implications?

Although overall international trade transaction cost has been decreasing, for most countries today the transport-related costs remain the biggest cost to international trade, particularly for low-value cargoes. For the future of maritime transport and the impact of shipping cost on trade, the following summary can be made.

- Low cost remains the most distinguishable and attractive feature of maritime transport as compared with other modes of transport. The primary cause of the low cost comes from the high productivity achieved through specialisation and continuous exploitation of scale economies and the innovations in marine technology and operations. The cost advantage of maritime transport is large and significant, particularly for the transport of natural resources of huge volume but low value. So, as world trade continues to grow, the importance of maritime transport will not diminish. These points will be further discussed in more detail in other chapters of the book.

- Despite a general downward trend of maritime transport cost of trade, transportation and distribution have remained the biggest cost element for international trade. So further reducing maritime transport-related costs is of great importance for trade development. Because poorer countries are paying a higher transportation bill for their trade than rich ones, the improvement of the transport system, especially of maritime transport, is a prerequisite of economic development and should be a top priority for those countries.
- While some clear evidence can be given to demonstrate a sensible reduction of maritime transport costs, other studies have shown that the air and land-based transport costs have decreased as well. International shipping is a highly competitive sector. Competition drives the industry to innovate and adopt new technologies and new production methods to improve the quality and reduce the cost of services. It was the main reason which triggered the productivity improvement of maritime transport in the past and it remains the most powerful driving force for further cost reduction in the future. We will take a closer look at these aspects in the following chapters.

1.7 Summary

Maritime transport exists because trade needs it. Maritime transport has a derived demand from trade in goods. So knowing about the need or the demand is the first step in learning maritime economics.

Trade is the result of the division of labour through specialisation. Although based on the same logic, international trade is usually treated separately from domestic trade due to its global scope, the special barriers related to national sovereignty and national currencies. International trade is generally measured in value terms when the cargo passes national borders.

The classical trade theories include the concepts of absolute advantage and comparative advantage. The theory of absolute advantage suggests that buying is better than making so long as buying costs less than making. The theory of comparative advantage indicates that each trading partner ought to produce the goods for which it has a comparative advantage or the biggest absolute advantage by leaving the other party to deliver the products on which it has a comparative advantage or the smallest absolute disadvantage. By doing so, both parties will benefit, even if one party has an absolute advantage in producing all goods.

New trade theories have been developed to emphasise, for example, factors such as intra-industry trade between countries with similar factor endowments, or consumer preference that cost need not be the sole element to consider. People trade to satisfy a demand for diversity or effect of scale economies, and the large domestic market can also affect cost. The roles of supporting industries, including maritime infrastructure and services, and of firms have also been considered to explain the development of trade.

Trading between countries is not free. Administrative costs of international trade include all costs borne by trade in the forms of either tariffs like customs duties or non-tariff administration like quotas or particular standards, formalities or procedures. Thanks to continuous efforts at various international levels, administrative costs of trade have been on the decline. There are reasons for being optimistic about a continuous course of free trade in the future.

The level of economic development and the demand for seaborne trade have a high level of correlation. Such a close relation has been proven both at the country and global levels, though variations exist between nations based on a country's size and disposition of resources. As economies continue to grow, the average seaborne trade per capita can only be expected to increase in the future.

Transport-related costs have become bigger than the administrative costs of trade in most countries. It is estimated that about 90% of international trade in tonnage is moved by sea, although in value the percentage of maritime transport is lower. The *ad valorem* maritime transport costs vary greatly from a tiny fraction of the value of some manufactured goods to an amount higher than the value of the bulk cargo. Some countries are paying twice as much *ad valorem* costs than other countries. Globally, maritime transport freight cost is about 5% of the import value. Maritime transport freight cost has decreased over time, thanks to productivity improvement and market competition.

Notes

1 Samuelsson P. and Nordhaus W. (2010).
2 WTO (2014a).
3 Smith A. (2003).
4 Ohlin B. (1967).
5 Leontief W. (1953).
6 Linder B. S. (1961) Linder argued that there is no difference between national and international trade as "If we divide the World into a sufficiently large number of countries, all trade would be foreign trade. If there were only one big country, all trade would be domestic trade" (p. 112).
7 Krugman P. (1980).
8 Porter M. (1990).
9 Krugman P. (1991).
10 WTO (2009).
11 WTO (2014b).
12 Eichengreen B. (2015).
13 WTO (2011).
14 WTO (2012).
15 See reference Eichengreen (2015).
16 In the middle of the crisis, the G-20 leaders made a collective commitment to "refrain from raising new barriers to investment or to trade in goods and service, imposing new export restrictions, or implementing WTO inconsistent measures to stimulate exports". See Declaration of the Summit on Financial Markets and the World Economy, Washington D.C., 15 November 2008.
17 Gawande K., Hoekman B., and Cui Y. (2011). Gawande found that many firms were not motivated to lobby for import protection due to the fact that both their production and market relied heavily on international trade.
18 Jacks D., Meissner C., and Novy D. (2008). Not only were the booms explained to a high degree by trade costs, the decline of trade during the Great Depression can also, to a large extent, be attributed to the surge of trade costs.
19 Anderson J., and Wincoop E. (2004). According to Anderson, trade costs are defined to include: "all costs incurred in getting a good to a final user other than the marginal cost of producing the good itself: transportation costs (both freight and time costs), policy barriers (tariffs and nontariff barriers), information costs, contract enforcement costs, costs associated with the use of different currencies, legal and regulatory costs, and local distribution costs (wholesale and retail)."
20 CSCMP (2016, 2019). The US business logistics cost was US$1.45 trillion in 2014 or 8.3% of US GDP. Of this, about 67% was transportation costs and most of the rest was inventory carrying costs. The ratio of expenses on transportation to that on inventory change ranged from about 1 in the 1980s to more than 2 in the 2010s. This is mainly due to a stagnation of inventory cost thanks to better cost control and low capital cost.
21 UNCTAD (1980–2006).
22 ICS (2015). It is stated by the International Chamber of Shipping as one of the key facts of shipping and world trade (www.ics-shipping.org/shipping-facts/key-facts) that "The international shipping industry is responsible for the carriage of around 90% of world trade". Based on the data of Global Insight, it was calculated that, globally, about 90% of world trade in volume and about 70% in value was moved by ships (see UNCTAD, 2008).

23 Intra-regional trade, of which cross-border trade is a part, is at a low level in Africa, the Middle-East and Latin America, but is much higher in Europe, North America and Asia. For more details see WTO, *International Trade Statistics*, multiple years.
24 Dong Z. (2011). FOB (free on board) prices vary greatly from one product to the next. Fashion clothes can be worth a million US dollars.
25 OECD (2010). The *ad valorem* costs are affected by both the changes in the price of the product as well in the price of the transport.
26 IMF (2014).
27 Hummels D. (2001). Hummels draws attention to the quality problems of the IMF data on freight cost, because a high proportion of the observations are rough estimates and there are compositional shifts in trade flows. The IMF data based on freight as a percentage of import value should only be used as an indication of general trend rather than a precise measure of cost.
28 Hummels D. (2007). Hummels argued that the cost of ocean transport has risen in current dollar terms, although the price with a GDP deflator did show a reduction.
29 Baltic Exchange (2015).
30 Clarksons (2015–2019).

References

Anderson J. and Wincoop E. (2004) "*Trade Costs*", Journal of Economic Literature, Vol. XLII, September 2004, pp. 691–751.

Baltic Exchange (2015) Retrieved from www.balticexchange.com.

Clarksons (2015–2019) "*Seaborne Trade Monitor*", July 2015, Volume 2, No. 7, Clarksons Research, London.

Clarksons (2019) *"Seaborne Trade Monitor"*, Volume 6 No. 9, Sept. 2019, Clarksons Research, London.

CSCMP (2019) "*Annual State of Logistics Report*", (Executive Summary) The Council of Supply Chain Management Professionals, USA. Retrieved from https://info.tranzact.com/cscmp-state-of-logistics-report-2019-executive-summary

CSCMP (2016, 2019) "*The 26th Annual State of Logistics Report*", *Council of Supply Chain Management Professionals (USA)*, 2015, 2018.

Dong Z. (2011) "*Economic Analysis on the Sustainability of Slow Steaming in Liner Shipping*", MSc. research paper, ITL2011, World Maritime University.

Eichengreen B. (2015) "*Hall of Mirrors: The Great Depression, the Great Recession and the Uses-and-misuses of History*", Oxford University Press, Oxford.

Gawande K., Hoekman B., and Cui Y. (2011) "*Determinants of Trade Policy Responses to the 2008 Financial Crisis*", World Bank Policy Research Working Paper 5862, World Bank, October 2011.

Hummels D. (2001) "*Toward a Geography of Trade Costs*", Working Paper, Purdue University, September 2001.

Hummels D. (2007) "*Transportation Costs and International Trade in the Second Era of Globalization*", Journal of Economic Perspectives, Vol. 21, No. 3, pp. 131–154.

IATA (2019) "*World Air Transport Statistics 2019*", International Air Transport Association.

ICS (2015) "*Shipping Facts*", International Chamber of Shipping, Retrieved from www.ics-shipping.org/shipping-facts/key-facts.

IMF (2014) "*International Financial Statistics 2014*", International Monetary Fund, Vol. LXVII, Washington, DC, pp. 69–74.

Jacks D., Meissner C., and Novy D. (2008) "*Trade Costs, 1870–2000*", American Economic Review, Vol. 98/2, pp. 529–534.

Krugman P. (1980) "*Scale Economies, Product Differentiation, and the Pattern of Trade*", The American Economic Review, Vol. 70, No. 5 (December 1980), pp. 950–959.

Krugman P. (1991) "*Increasing Returns and Economic Geography*", The Journal of Political Economy, Vol. 99, No. 3 (June 1980), pp. 483–499.

Leontief W. (1953) "*Domestic Production and Foreign Trade: The American Capital Position Re-examined*", Proceedings of the American Philosophical Society, Vol. 97, No. 4 (September 28), pp. 332–349.

Linder B. S. (1961) "*An Essay on International Trade and Transformation*", Almqvist & Wiksells Boktryckeri AB, Uppsala.

OECD (2010) "*Clarifying Trade Costs in Maritime Transport*", STD/TBS/WPTGS(2010)21, OECD, September 2010.

Ohlin B. (1967) "*Interregional and International Trade: Revised Edition*", Harvard University Press, Cambridge MA.

Porter M. (1990) "*The Competitive Advantage of Nations*", Free Press, New York.

Samuelsson P. and Nordhaus W. (2010) "*Economics*", 19th Edition, McGraw-Hill Irwin, New York.

Smith A. (2003) "*The Wealth of Nations*", Reprint Edition, Bantam Classics, New York (March 4, 2003).

UNCTAD (1980–2006) "*Review of Maritime Transport*", United Nations Conference on Trade and Development, Geneva. UNCTAD/RMT/1980 to UNCTAD/RMT/2006.

UNCTAD (2018) "*Review of Maritime Transport*", United Nations Conference on Trade and Development, UNCTAD/RMT/2018, Geneva, Switzerland.

WTO (2009) "*World Trade Report – 2008*", World Trade Organization, Geneva.

WTO (2011) "*International Trade Statistics*", 2010, World Trade Organization, Geneva.

WTO (2012) "*International Trade Statistics*", 2011, World Trade Organization, Geneva.

WTO (2014b) "*World Trade Report 2014*", World Trade Organization, Geneva.

Chapter 2

Seaborne trade in natural resources and primary materials

International trade consists of all kinds of goods. Among these, there are two most prominent groups: natural-resource-based goods and manufactured products. According to the World Trade Organization, natural resources are "stocks of materials that exist in the natural environment that are both scarce and economically useful in production or consumption either in their raw state or after a minimal amount of processing".[1] So all mining goods, energy goods and forest products are included. Agricultural products do not fall within this definition as they are cultivated by people, using natural resources such as water and land, rather than extracted from the natural environment. We include agricultural products in this chapter under the definition of primary materials. More than two-thirds of seaborne trade in volume terms is raw materials. The second group is manufactured products. These are industrial goods, such as machines, and consumer goods, such as clothes, furniture, etc. The manufactured goods make up the biggest share of international trade in value terms. In this chapter we will concentrate on the first group of seaborne trade: the natural resources and primary materials. We will examine the influential factors concerning the supply and demand of this maritime trade, its evolution and the relationship between a country's demand for seaborne trade and its economic development.

2.1 Maritime demand for natural resources and primary materials

If we have a map showing the natural resources, such as minerals, energy products and grain, needed for industrial use or people's consumption and at the same time showing the locations of industrial activities and population, we can see that the two are often separated by oceans. For example, the Middle East has a lot of oil/gas reserves but few industries. In 2018 China produced over half of the world's steel, but only about 15% of iron ore. Japan is the third biggest industrial power in the world but has virtually no natural resources. About 70% of global seaborne trade is in raw materials. Maritime transport is vital for the world economy.

What are natural-resource-based goods?

During the pre-Industrial Revolution era natural resources were not main items of trade because, on the one hand, a massive demand for mining and energy products did not exist in non-industrial societies and, on the other hand, people usually lived where sufficient food could be produced, with therefore no need to move grain over a long distance. In this sense, trade and maritime transport of natural resources and primary materials are directly related to industrialisation, population growth and urbanisation. Such developments have led to a spatial separation of production and consumption and, as a consequence, created the need for transport.

For maritime transport, natural resources and primary materials are divided into two categories: liquid and dry cargos (see Figure 2.1). Within liquid cargo, crude oil is by far the biggest cargo. It is followed by oil products, liquefied gas and other liquids such as water, juice, eatable oil, wine, etc. Although the amount of processing varies from one product to another, all the goods listed above are considered as natural resources and primary materials. With regard to dry cargo, the three biggest commodities are iron ore, coal and grain. Under grain, there are different agriculture products, such as wheat, corn, rice, etc., and within coal we have also coking coal or steam coal. Apart from the three main dry cargoes, there are some other commodities in smaller quantities, such as alumina, phosphate, other minerals, etc.

What are the main differences between natural resources and manufactured products?

We want to discuss natural resources and manufactured products separately for the following reasons: the nature of competitive advantages is different; the trade flows evolve differently; the situation of exhaustibility and substitutability, the mobility and price dynamics are different. We now look at these reasons one by one.

Trade, according to most trade theories, is mutually beneficial thanks to productivity improvement through specialisation. Such specialisation is different in the case of trade in natural resources. Porter divides the factors affecting trade into two levels: the basic factors and the advanced factors. The conditions in natural resources, or primary materials, are typically determined by basic factors. The disposal of natural resources is uneven in the world. So those countries which need such resources but do not have them will have to import them from other countries. Or in some countries, as compared with other countries, natural resources like oil, coal or minerals are more easily accessible, or cheaper to exploit, or are of the quality required. As long as the reserves of the natural resources have not run

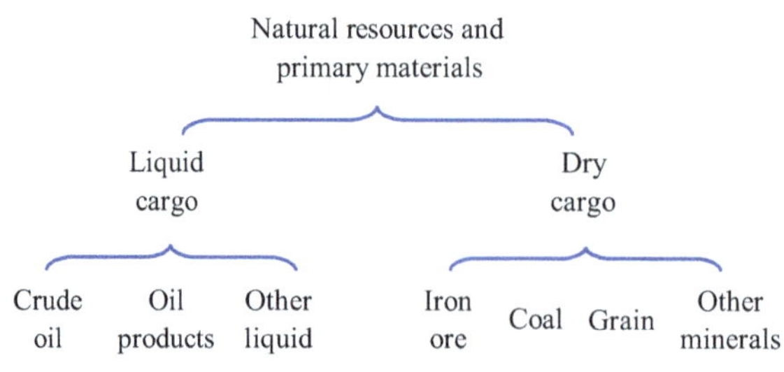

Figure 2.1 Natural resources and primary materials.

Note: oil, coal and liquefied gases fall under "energy" goods, while most of the rest, bar agricultural products, are under mining products.

out, these countries can continue to enjoy the advantages. Since the natural resource is a factor, the trade of natural resources can be seen as direct factor trading. The production of manufactured goods is more human-based and determined by advanced factors. This is because manufacturing depends on the level of education, research, technology, labour skills and know-how in the countries concerned. Often it also requires the existence of industry clusters. So the competitive advantages of natural resources are based on the conditions of natural resources; those of manufactured products are mostly based on the capabilities of human resources.

Competitive advantages of a country are not static, which means that it may move from one product to another depending on the changes in conditions of production factors. The typical example is about labour cost and skills. As the economy develops, the labour cost may become higher and, as a result, this makes the labour cost advantages disappear. For natural resources as compared with manufactured products the factors evolve differently. First, while the bases of natural resources are discovered, the foundations of manufacturing production are built. So, with the necessary capital investment, a newly found oil field can relatively quickly be turned into an export source and remain so for a long time. In the case of manufactured products, it usually takes many years or generations to build the capacity and to sustain the growth. Second, natural reserves are limited resources, so the advantages are constrained by the rate of exploitation. However, manufacturing depends mainly on human resources, which are only constrained by the demographic conditions of a country. So the advantage may be more sustainable. This is mainly for two reasons. First, such advantages depend on the relative position of a country compared with other countries; second, the advanced factors, particularly technology, are dynamic and sometimes can change rapidly. It is essential to understand such differences and to know the future sources of competitiveness of a country and thus the trend of trade flows.

Most natural resources extracted from the environment are non-renewable, or need to take a long time to renew, such as forests. For example, with the current known reserves and production level, the Middle-East, with the largest reserve and production of oil in the world, will only have enough oil to exploit for about 80 years and Brazil, with one of the biggest reserves and production of iron ore, can only continue to produce for about 100 years.[2] This contrasts with manufactured goods which can always be produced by man, as long as there is a need. Another striking feature of natural resources and primary materials is that they do not have ready substitutions, although interchangeability may exist between some energy products in the middle-term. The situation is quite different in the case of manufactured goods, for which it would be much easier and more common to find substitutes.

Natural resources are unevenly distributed in the world and have to be extracted from where they are found. But manufactured products can be produced in different places. Today, capital as a production factor is internationally mobile. Technology can also be transferred from one place to another. The typical example of the mobility of manufacturing activities is what has happened during the last couple of decades in Europe, North America and East Asia where the export of manufactured products migrated from one region to another. This is mainly because manufacturing activities move to places where cheap production factors such as labour and land are available. Such migration of manufacturing has happened many times in Asia, e.g., from Japan to Korea/Taiwan then to China. The driving force is the combination of productivity rise, improvement in technology and skill and increases in the cost of labour. During such production movement, processes of product upgrading are completed as results. Countries are moving up the ladder by taking in productions with more technological content while letting out those with lower technology-intensity. The "upgrading" effect in manufacturing activities does not exist in the production of primary materials. In the case of natural resources, the production takes place where the resources are and it continues until the resources have been exhausted or the demand disappears. The value or unit prices of major natural resources are relatively low compared with those of manufactured products. In terms of the total amount of weight in tons, natural resources are in a much higher number than manufactured goods.

What are the special characteristics of natural resources for maritime transport?

The characteristics of trade in natural resources described above have a noticeable impact on the maritime transport of them. The following four aspects are of particular importance.

- ***Cargo in big volume and of a homogeneous nature.*** In terms of weight, natural resources occupy the largest portion of global trade. According to the United Nations,[3] more than 11 billion metric tons of cargo were transported by ships in 2018. Out of this amount, about 7 billion tons or about 65% were natural resources. The big volume requires enormous transportation capacity to complete trade. It also allows very large ships to be constructed and operated for the transport. Given the homogeneous nature of most natural resources, the cargo is usually transported in loose form without packing, in bulk. Such cargo is generally loaded and discharged on and off ships quickly by using specialised cargo handling equipment.
- ***Cargo with low unit value.*** Apart from precious stones and minerals, most natural resources are of low market value. This is mainly because the materials are in abundant supply and there are only the costs, or value-added, from exploitation and transport. Consequently, transport cost constitutes usually a big proportion of the total value of the cargo. Sometimes, when the distance between traders is long and the freight cost is high, the cost of maritime transport is higher than the value of the cargo. In view of the fluctuation of the maritime transport freight market, the high proportion of transport cost increases the volatility of the prices in natural resources. The low unit value of raw materials and a high proportion of transport cost also mean that slow transport speed is justified to reduce transport costs even at the expense of longer transit time, which, as inventory cost, is less costly for low-value cargo.
- ***Concentrated and relatively stable sources of export.*** As explained above, the disposition of natural resources does not directly relate to those factors, such as labour and capital, which are dependent on the level of economic development of a country. As a result, the natural distribution of raw materials and the natural conditions of exploitation are fixed factors. When a country with rich natural resource reserves does not have as big a need for the resources it produces as other countries, it becomes an exporter. So, for each of the main commodities, the number and location of the exporters are relatively few and stable. For example, Brazil and Australia have been, for many years, the leading exporters of iron ore and Saudi Arabia and Venezuela have been, and will continue to be for a long time, the leading exporters of oil. Some countries are no longer exporters due to an increase of local consumption, e.g., the oil exports of Indonesia or the iron exports of India. However, natural resources are less stable and more diversified commodities for the importers. This is mainly because import depends not only on the size of local production but also the development level, the structure and the growth of the economy.
- ***Volatile volume and prices of trade.*** The need for natural resources depends on the economies of the importing nations as well as of the world as a whole. As the economic situation varies over time, the trade in natural resources can fluctuate. When the Chinese economy slowed down in 2015, for example, its import of iron ore also decreased, which led to a reduction of the freight rate.[4] Sometimes weather conditions can also affect the level of trade: e.g., the import of grain changes due to weather conditions of the importing as well as exporting countries, and the need for imported coal for heating varies according to the average temperature of the winter.

What are the main implications?

A closer and specific review of the transport demand of natural resources allows us to understand one of the most important features of modern shipping: specialisation. It is the result of two major forces: the enormous size of demand and the continued pursuit for higher productivity driven by competition. The maritime transport of raw materials is now divided into tanker ships for liquid bulk transport, large bulk carriers for iron and medium-sized bulk carriers for coal/grain and other natural resources. Subsequently, ports are also specialised. In general, specialisation improves productivity and quality of services and at the same time reduces the cost. The specialisation of shipping services is the subject of more detailed discussions in the following chapters.

The maritime transport of raw materials is relatively simple and straightforward. A company can offer such services with one single ship or multiple ships. As a result, the entry barrier is low and the degree of competition is high. As most of the port-to-port operations are undertaken on international waters, it is largely a free market open to all. So the freight level is solely determined by the market based on the balance of demand and supply.

2.2 Relationship between sea trade and economic development

Why should per capita volume rather than total volume be used?

The measurement of seaborne trade and economic development level is country-based. Yet there is an issue of the unequal sizes of countries. Usually the total volume of trade or economy of a country is used. The obvious reason for this is that the total volume of trade is the actual demand and supply to or from a country, and therefore the exact amount of cargo for maritime transport. We have discussed in the last section the changing geography of seaborne trade in terms of total trade volume between major importers and exporters. From such discussions we observe that the trade in natural resources has been much driven by the economic development of the importing countries. Natural resources and raw materials are usually imported by those countries with a high level of economic growth, such as those in Western Europe, the Far East and North America. However, there is a problem if only the total amount is counted because it does not reveal the causes of trade directions as well as their changes and it fails to reflect the development potential of a country and the future dynamics of trade.

The economic development level of a country is more accurately measured in terms of GDP per capita rather than total GDP. A large economy in terms of total GDP, such as India's, may have a lower level of economic development than that of a much smaller economy such as Singapore or Malaysia. A country's economic development is also more closely linked to the growth of GDP per capita and to the increase in people's purchasing power. Since economic development is now measured on the basis of GDP per capita, seaborne trade should also be measured in the same way in order to examine the relationship between the two.

What are the driving forces for seaborne trade in natural resources?

As discussed in the previous chapter, trade means buying and selling. So the richer the country is or the higher purchasing power the country has, the more it trades. But when it comes to natural resources such as described above, the buyers are not final consumers, but producers. These materials are primary inputs needed by the industries. It is, therefore, the industry which is the driving force behind trade in natural resources. So, there are, between final consumers and natural resources, industries which may be located in a different country.

Natural resources and raw materials are only used by specific industries. Crude oil is for the petrochemical industry; iron ore is for the steel industry; coal is for the power generation and steel industries; logs are for the paper and furniture industries and rubber is for the car industry, etc. At a certain development stage, a country's need for raw materials can be extremely high for construction projects to build the stock of basic infrastructure. This happened in the 1960s in Europe and Japan and in the 2000s in China.

The output of industrial production can, therefore, be for both local and international markets. Many countries with strong industrial and manufacturing capabilities import raw materials for local consumption and also export some finished or semi-finished products. On the other hand, a rich country may not be a big importer of raw materials if it does not have a large industry base. For example, Japan produced 6.9% of world total steel production in 2013 but only used 4.4% of the world's total.[5] The difference was for export. It is mainly for this reason that Japan has one of the highest levels of per capita steel production in the world at more than 1 ton per person.

Why do countries with available domestic resources still rely on imports?

One important condition is the situation of domestic supply of the raw materials. International imports are only necessary if the local supply is either insufficient, in quality and/or quantity, or uneconomical for the production. A good illustration of this point is the difference between Japan and the US. Both countries have highly developed industry bases. While Japan has virtually no local supply of natural resources for its industries, the US is a resource-rich nation. Consequently, Japan is more dependent on foreign supplies than the US.

However, the concept that countries import raw materials because they do not have such resources available in their countries is not correct. Actually the basic trade theory of cost advantage does apply to the trade in natural resources as well, which suggests that a country would use imported rather than locally produced materials as long as the imports are cheaper. While some large industrial countries in East Asia, such as Japan or South Korea, rely on international supplies of almost every kind of raw materials due to unavailability of such materials domestically, many other countries prefer using imported instead of locally produced materials.

For example, China has large reserves of iron ore and coal. Yet, due to quality and cost reasons, China is still a major importer of a huge amount of both materials. It is reported that the price of coal from domestic production at the power stations located in coastal cities in China is higher than that of coal imported from the international market. In 2012, for example, the price of thermal coal was CNY410/t at the coal mine of northern China, CNY582/t at the loading port and CNY613/t at the discharging port in southern China. During the same period, the price of coal of the same quality at the same discharging port was CNY580/t, including 17% import tax. This is CNY33/t cheaper than the locally produced coal. The price difference was as high as CNY90/t for thermal coal and CNY320/t for coking coal in 2009. This is because the prices of both coal and sea transport fluctuate more in the international market than in the domestic market.[6]

When it comes to another important raw material, iron ore, the situation in China is very similar. Most of the local mines are of small size, for example, in a 2015 report,[7] about 80% of them were as small as an annual production of 200 thousand tons or less. The quality of locally produced ore is also not good enough, so an additional cost has to be spent to increase the iron content. The break-even price is typically 50% higher for the local producers compared with that of big international producers in Australia or Brazil.

Is a positive relationship between seaborne trade and economic development level a coincidence or rule?

As seaborne trade in this chapter refers to natural resources and raw materials, we will examine the relationship between such trade and the level of economic development of importing regions and countries. Two special remarks should be made before the discussion. The first is that we separate import from export and concentrate on the former. This is mainly because export or supply of raw materials is based on natural distribution and location of resources, rather than economic development level. It is the consumption, or import, of the country that is under discussion. We only compare large countries, regions or economies. This is mainly because natural resources are consumed by heavy industries, as we discussed above, which small economies with a high level of economic development may or may not have.

With a close look at the major importers of natural resources, it is not difficult to observe that they are mostly countries or regions with high income per capita or a high level of economic development. Such a trade pattern has been consistent since the end of World War Two. Figure 2.2 shows the seaborne trade imports in terms of tons of cargo per capita of selected countries and regions in 2017. Even though China is the biggest importer of natural resources in the world, in per capita terms Japan is almost three times bigger than China with more than 6 tons of seaborne imports per person. It is also interesting to note that North America, i.e., Canada and the US, is a rich continent in terms of natural resources and has traditionally been an exporter of some major raw materials. But, even so, the seaborne trade import in tons of cargo per capita is still very high, despite a bigger gap between the level of GDP per capita and seaborne trade imports per capita. For North America, oil had been the biggest import cargo, though the situation has changed during recent years. The volume of containerised cargo imports to the North American market is also very substantial. There is a close relationship between the level of economic development in terms of GDP per capita and the level of seaborne trade in terms of tons of imported cargo per capita. The coefficient of correlation (R^2) between these two variables, even including North America, is 74%.

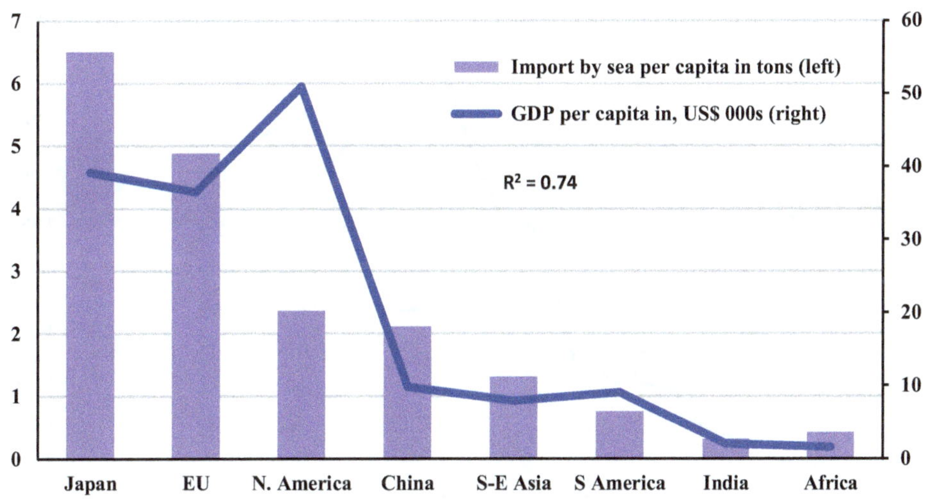

Figure 2.2 Seaborne imports per capita (tons) and GDP per capita (USD), 2017.

Source: Shuo Ma, based on the UN publications (2019).

Note: most seaborne trade has been transported to rich economies where industries are located and the level of development is high. While the resource-rich US imports less per capita and resource-scarce Japan imports more per person, China's import per capita increased with its economic growth. The two variables are correlated.

The above analysis is about the relationship between the level of economic development of some large countries or economic regions and their level of seaborne trade. It is found that a high coefficient of correlation, R^2 at 74%, exists between the two variables. However, since not all countries are included, it is only for one single year and there is one case of inconsistency, i.e., North America, we should investigate further. We choose two countries: Japan and China. This is because, on the one hand, both countries are large economies with rapid economic growth, since the 1950s for Japan and the 1980s for China, and, on the other hand, there is one big difference between them. For most natural resources, Japan does not have local supplies while China does.

In 1965 Japan's GDP per capita was US$920 and its total seaborne trade was 221 million tons.[8] This was a period when the Japanese economy was continuing to grow very rapidly. As the world's second-largest economy, Japan had an enormous need for raw materials for its industry, construction and expanding consumer market. The country does not have any significant reserves of minerals or energy resources, but with more than 100 million inhabitants it has one of the highest population densities in the world. So Japan has been heavily dependent on foreign trade for cargoes such as oil, coal, minerals and grain. Being a highly industrialised country, it exports manufactured goods for the international market as well. Japan is an island country so, apart from some high-value goods which are transported by air, all Japan's foreign trade is moved by ships. Figure 2.3 shows the relationship between two developments in Japan between 1964 and 2018: the GDP per capita and the total seaborne import trade per capita. In the 1960s the growth of GDP per capita and that of seaborne import trade per capita were both very rapid. Then by the middle of the 1970s, while GDP per capita continued to

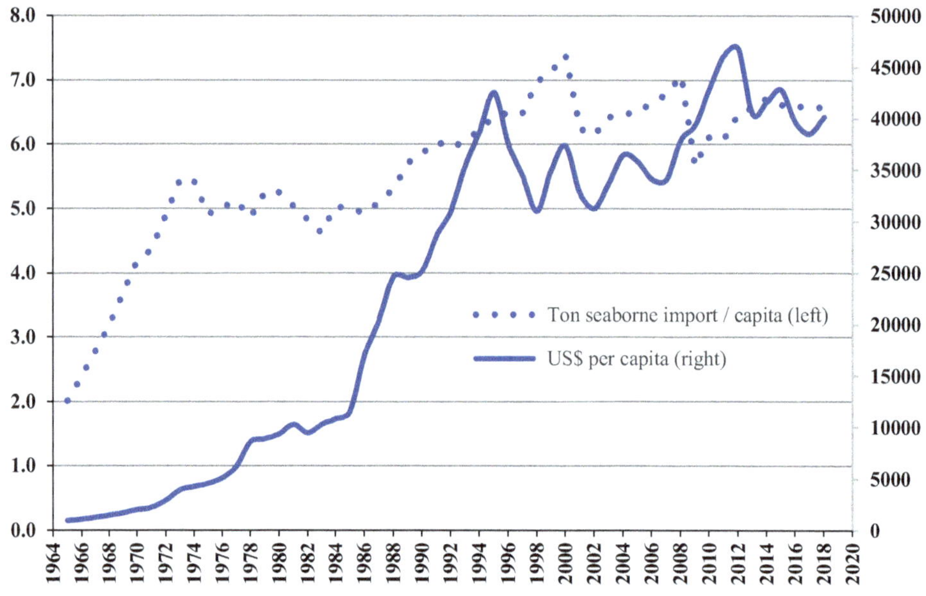

Figure 2.3 Japanese international seaborne import per capita and GDP per capita 1965–2018.

Source: Shuo Ma, based on World Bank and UN statistics.

Note: without natural resources, Japan started to import large amounts of raw materials when its economy took off. However, as the GDP per capita reaches a higher level, the seaborne trade per capita growth rate slows down.

increase at high speed beyond US$5,000, seaborne trade of import per capita started to experience only modest growth. This reflects the stage of cumulative stocks of infrastructure and the change of the economic structure from heavy-industry-centred to electronics, high tech sectors and services. On the whole, Japan's seaborne trade per capita is closely correlated to its GDP per capita level. The growth rate of seaborne trade per capita reaches the peak earlier than that of GDP per capita.

The Chinese example differs from that of Japan in many respects. China is a large economy with more than 1.3 billion people. Since the end of the 1970s, China has experienced rapid economic development, changing itself from a country with GDP per capita as low as barely US$200 in 1978 to about US$97,000 in 2018. Unlike Japan, China has reserves of many natural resources it needs. Yet such local supplies, e.g., oil, were quickly proving inadequate as the demand soared or were becoming uncompetitive against imports. We have taken the data on China's seaborne import trade per capita and GDP per capita during the period of 41 years from 1978 to 2018 to test the relationship between them, which is illustrated in Figure 2.4. So in 1978, when the GDP per capita was about US$200, the seaborne import was about 0.1 ton per person, while in 2018, with the GDP per capita at US$97,000, the imported seaborne trade for every Chinese person was 3 tons. There is high positive coefficient of correlation between these two variables, which means that the change of seaborne import trade level can be explained by the change of economic development. The Chinese economic development model shares some common characteristics with that of other developing countries. For example, it uses enormous raw materials, from both local production and imports, to build infrastructure and to provide energy. Such a pattern was followed not only by Japan and Western Europe after World War Two but also, more recently, by smaller economies such as Korea, Malaysia and Taiwan, etc.

As discussed above, the existence of local supplies of natural resources may reduce the need for importing them from abroad, provided the local productions are cost-competitive. Low reliance on

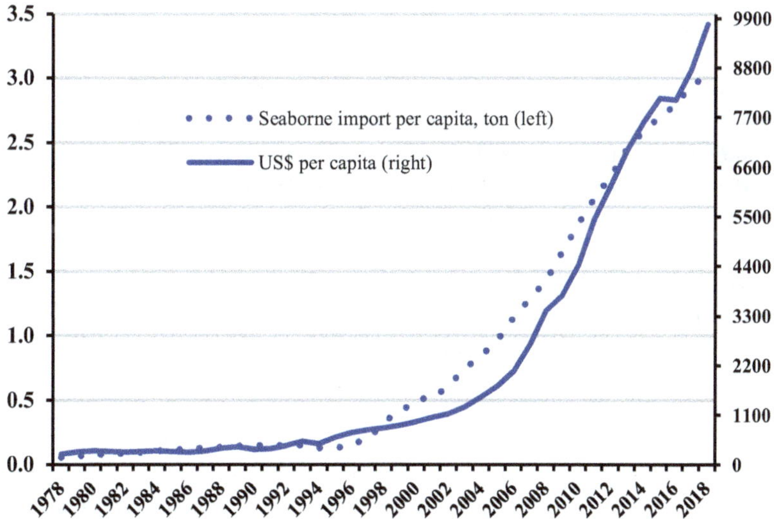

Figure 2.4 Chinese seaborne import per capita and GDP per capita, 1978–2018.

Source: Shuo Ma, based on Chinese official statistics.

Note: in China, the changes of seaborne import per capita are highly correlated with the change of (nominal) GDP per capita during the period of fast economic expansion.

import materials often happens at the early stage of economic development in countries where local supplies are available. There are two main reasons. The first is related to the quantity of the materials needed. At the early stage of economic development, the local supplies would be sufficient for the demand. But in the process of continued economic growth, demand increases and the local resources may have been exhausted or are not enough for the need. In such cases, the supplies will mostly come from imports. The second reason is related to cost. At the early stage of development, local resources may enjoy a cost advantage due to low production and transport costs. For example, the factor costs in relation to land and labour would be low when a country is relatively under-developed. But such costs will rise as the country becomes more affluent. Imported raw materials will also be more competitive when the size of demand is large thanks to the scale economies of purchase and maritime transport.

For a country, the amount of seaborne trade is closely related to the stage of the country's economic development. But, as a general rule, when a country's stocks of infrastructure and durable products are close to the level of maturity, there will be less need for raw materials. So, if the Chinese experience is a guide, it is probable that a country's demand for raw materials will be at the highest level when its GDP per capita is between US$1,000 and US$8,000. Or, if GDP in PPP is used, the range will be from US$1,500 to US$12,000 per head. After this level, a country usually enters into a stage of economic maturity, with, on the one hand, a stock of basic infrastructure and durable goods that is sufficiently large and, on the other hand, a service sector that is becoming a dominant contributor to the country's GDP. Massive construction would generally pass its peak period and, consequently, the growth of seaborne trade will be much slower.

What are the main implications?

The above discussion leads to the conclusion that seaborne trade, mainly imports, depends on the economic development level. For a country or region, it means that the amount of seaborne trade in terms of tons of cargo per habitant is positively correlated to the level of its economic development in terms of GDP per capita. Therefore, a perspective on world economic development would provide us with an indication of the global seaborne trade in the future. In the wake of the economic recession in 2008, the world economy was at risk of a general decline. To avoid the worst situation from happening, a more coordinated action plan needed to be discussed and agreed on among the world's leading economies. Many countries shared such an idea. It was clear that the existing mechanism of the so-called "G-7" was not enough to represent the world economy. Subsequently, a new group, "G-20", was created, which embraced many "emerging" economies whose GDP per capita was low, but those economies were large and had grown fast. The creation of G-20 is a clear sign that the potential economic growth comes from the countries with low income per capita but a fast growth rate. With more than half of the global population and almost 2 billion people turning into middle-class consumers, the emerging economies and the developing world, in general, are where the new maritime demand will come from in the future.

In volume terms, seaborne trade consists mostly of raw materials and energy goods. The demand for such products is closely related to the level of economic development of a country. This phenomenon is particularly apparent at the early stage of a country's economic development when basic infrastructure and the stock of durable products are to be built. As the country's economy matures, the growth of such imports will slow down. There is a difference between countries with or without the reserves of such natural resources. While those countries without local supplies would see the import of raw materials increase at a fast pace early on, those countries with available local supplies will eventually start to import, depending on some other factors such as specific natural conditions of local raw materials, population density, economic structure and speed of development. The two examples of Japan and China show such differences. In the case of Japan, a country with virtually no natural resources, the fast increase of seaborne trade started early when the GDP per capita was still relatively low at about US$400. In the case of China, where local supplies of natural resources could satisfy the need of the initial stage of development, the country started to experience fast growth of seaborne trade at a GDP per capita of US$1,000. The growth of seaborne trade generally starts to slow down when the per capita GDP is about US$5,000–10,000. Given that there are many countries whose economic development is within such a range, we can have a general idea about the future of maritime transport demand.

2.3 The evolution of seaborne trade in natural resources

Since the 1950s the world seaborne trade in natural resources has experienced very rapid and continuous growth. In 1950 total seaborne trade was about 500 million metric tons of cargo but in 2018 it was more than 11 billion tons.[9] Most of the seaborne trade consists of natural resources and raw materials. Although the proportion of manufactured products, or general cargo, has steadily increased over the last decades to reach a level of about 20% of the total seaborne trade, crude oil and oil products remain the largest cargo item for international shipping. In 2018 about 26% of seaborne trade was oil and oil products; 14% was iron ore; 12% was coal and 4% was grain. Together, these four main types of cargo made up about 56% of the total seaborne trade. It is for this reason that we will now examine the evolution of the major seaborne trade of natural resources, namely, oil, iron ore, coal and grain. Over time, there has been an integration process of various commodity markets in the form of price convergence.[10] We have found evidence of such price convergence for oil, coal and iron ore, with only grain as an exception. Figure 2.5 shows the evolution of world seaborne trade from 1990 to 2018.

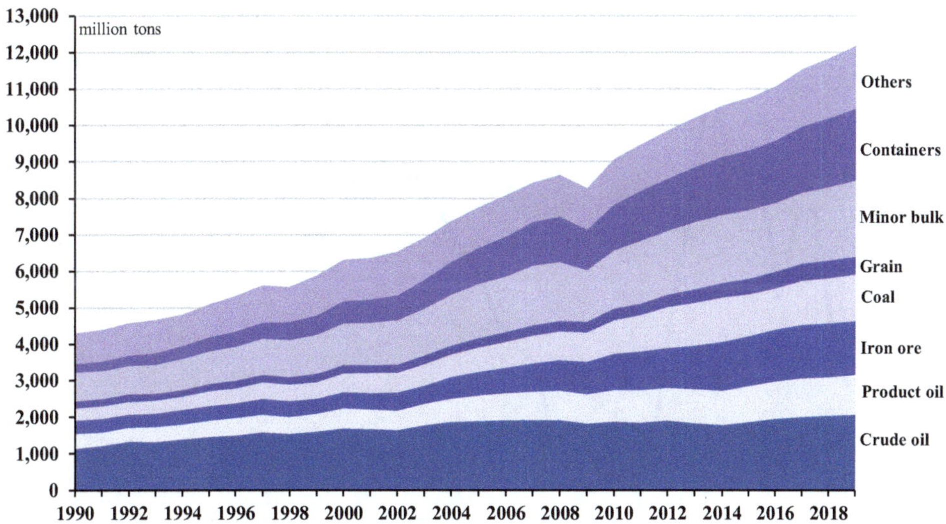

Figure 2.5 World seaborne trade by main types of cargo, 1990–2018 (in metric tons).

Source: Shuo Ma, based on data from Clarksons Shipping Intelligence.

Note: the share of crude oil and oil products dropped from 55% in 1970 to 36% in 1990 and 26% in 2018. At the same time, the share of dry bulk cargo increased from 40% to 45% and the share of containerised cargo increased from 5% to 16%.

The total size of the seaborne trade increased from 4,286 million tons in 1990 to 12,168 million tons in 2018. The increase is equivalent to an average annual growth rate of 3.7%. The economic crisis of 2009 did have an impact, but it did not change the course of the development. The leading position of seaborne trade has shifted from liquid bulk cargoes to dry bulk cargoes. Very rapid growth has also been registered for containerised trade.

What is the market of the seaborne trade in oil?

Crude oil is still the single largest item of seaborne trade. The amount traded varies between one and two billion tons. Figure 2.6 shows the world seaborne trade in crude oil between 1970 and 2018. The influential factors on the levels of demand include the price of oil, the economic situation of the major oil-importing countries and the competitiveness of alternative modes of transport, such as pipelines. Take the oil price as an example. In 1973/4, as a result of the "first oil shock", the price of oil went from around US$3 per barrel to more than US$10 per barrel. The economies of oil-importing countries were badly affected. But the demand did not decrease immediately, mainly because shifting to alternative energy sources would not be possible in the short term. That was what happened again in the wake of the so-called "second oil shock" which took place in 1979 when the oil price increased

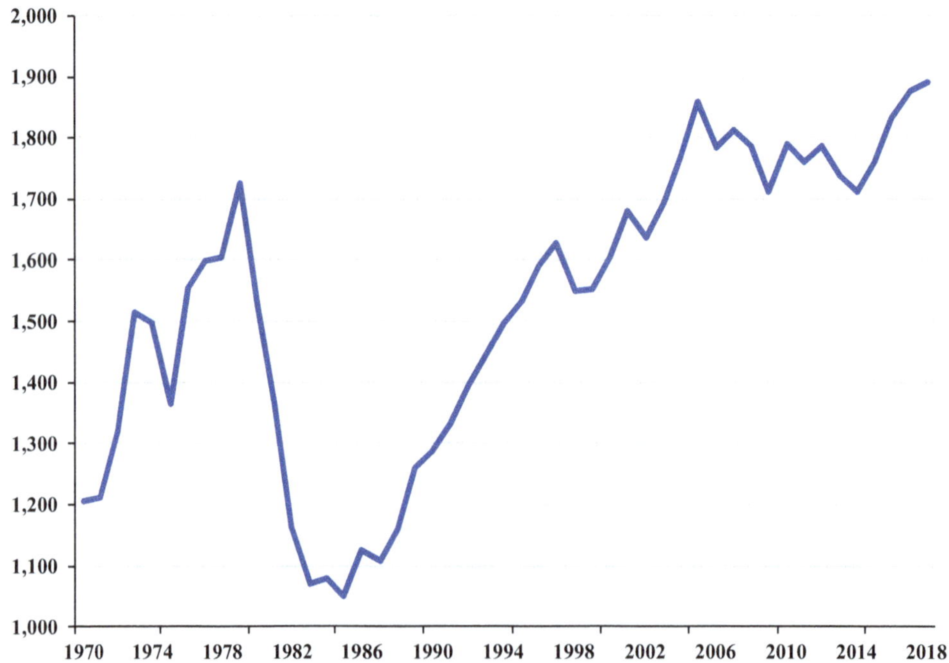

Figure 2.6 World crude oil seaborne trade, in million tons, 1970–2018.

Source: Shuo Ma, based on data from ISL, Clarksons, Fearnleys, UNCTAD.

Note: seaborne trade in oil dropped greatly after the second oil shock by the end of the 1970s. Strong demand from the emerging economies is the main driving force for the more recent increase.

further from around US$13/barrel to about US$35/barrel. As a consequence, the seaborne trade in oil decreased from more than 1,700 million tons in 1979 to just over 1,000 million tons in 1983, a 41% drop. This is a typical example showing that the demand for oil is price inelastic in the short run, but elastic in the long term.

Concerning the main exporters of oil transported by sea, as shown in Figure 2.7, the situation has been relatively stable, with three regions, namely the Middle-East, Africa and Latin America, being the major sources of export. Combined, they provide about 80% of the world's total seaborne trade in oil. While the Middle-East continues to be the largest exporter, since the 1970s the share of Latin America has steadily increased, thanks particularly to the exports of Venezuela. Russia is also a big exporter, but its oil is mostly moved using pipelines to Europe as well as to the Asian countries. New discoveries in West Africa have led to an increase in market share of this region, while the share of North Africa has reduced. Other regions, such as South-East Asia, Europe and North America, are also exporting oil, but in relatively small quantities.

As far as the import of oil is concerned, the picture of the main importers is quite different. It evolves chiefly according to the situation of economic development in the world. Over the last half a century, the most noticeable economic change is probably the increasing role of the emerging economies, particularly those in Asia, and such a development affected global seaborne trade. Figure 2.8 shows the percentage changes over the period from 1970 to 2018 between the major oil-importing countries and regions. Europe's market share decreased from about 50% to less than 25%. During the same period, the Asian share increased to over 50% of the world's total. China, for example, had been by and large self-sufficient and even had some surplus for export until the late 1990s, but since then the country quickly became a major importer worldwide. By 2015 China overtook the US to be the largest oil importer in the world. A similar situation of "exporter-turning-to-importer" can be seen in Indonesia as well. India is another new oil importer and potentially one of the largest in the world. Oil pipelines have been constructed linking Russia, Central and West Asia to European and Asian markets. But the bulk of oil demand is still transported by ships.

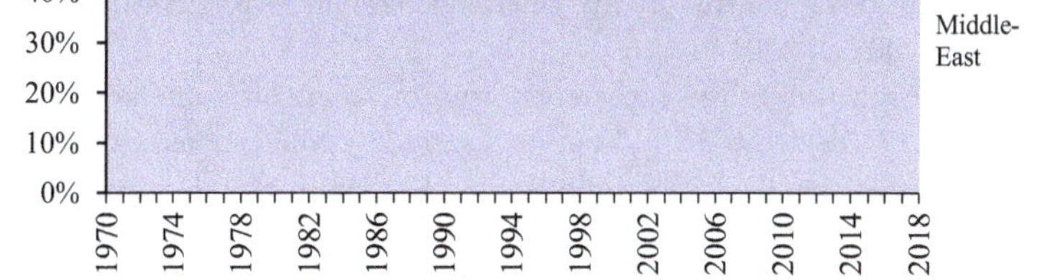

Figure 2.7 Market share in % of exporters of crude oil by sea, 1970–2018.

Source: based on data from ISL, Clarksons, Fearnleys, UNCTAD.

Note: the Middle-East remains the main exporting region in the world of seaborne trade in oil. Russia is a big oil exporter, but mainly by pipelines.

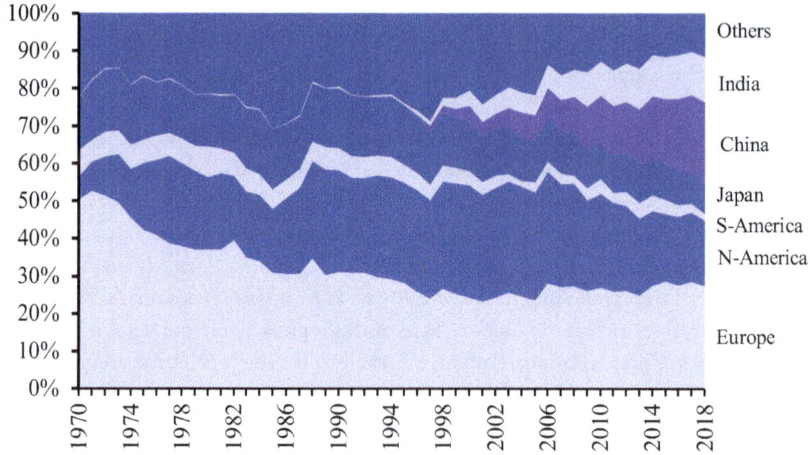

Figure 2.8 Market share in % of importers of crude oil by sea, 1970–2018.

Source: based on data from ISL, Clarksons, Fearnleys, UNCTAD.

Note: the European share reduced due to rapid growth of demand from the emerging economies, the oil production in Europe and the increase in oil transported to Europe by pipelines.

What is the market of seaborne trade in iron ore?

International trade in iron ore is the second-largest single seaborne trade commodity after crude oil. Since 2000 there has been a tremendous increase in the volume of iron ore trade. The demand for iron ore is directly dependent on the industry of iron and steel. So, depending on the availability of economically viable local sources in a steel-producing country, the amount of iron ore import is determined by the size of the steel industry of a country or region. Figure 2.9 shows seaborne trade in iron ore from 1970 to 2018. Over almost half a century, the volume grew about six-fold from around 200 million tons to about 1,200 million tons with an average growth rate of 3.6% per year. The development of the iron ore trade can be broadly divided into two periods: before and after 2002. The first period was characterised by a relatively stable growth at an annual rate of 2.3%. After 2002 the commodity was in strong demand by the emerging economies, particularly China. The average growth rate between 2002 and 2014 was 6.1%.

If we look at the situation of the exporters of iron ore, there are some noticeable changes that have happened since 1975 (Figure 2.10). Exporters were less concentrated in the 1970s but, since then, Brazil and especially Australia have steadily reinforced their market dominance with a combined market share of 80% in 2015. This is because, on the one hand, the iron ore production cost is much lower in Brazil and Australia compared with that of other countries and, on the other hand, the steel production has moved from North America and Europe to Asia over the last couple of decades. Consequently, Australia has benefitted from its proximity to the market and thus has become the leading exporter of iron ore. India was the third-largest iron ore exporter until around 2010, by which time the local demand started to absorb an ever-larger portion of the mineral so that, eventually, the country is no longer an exporter.

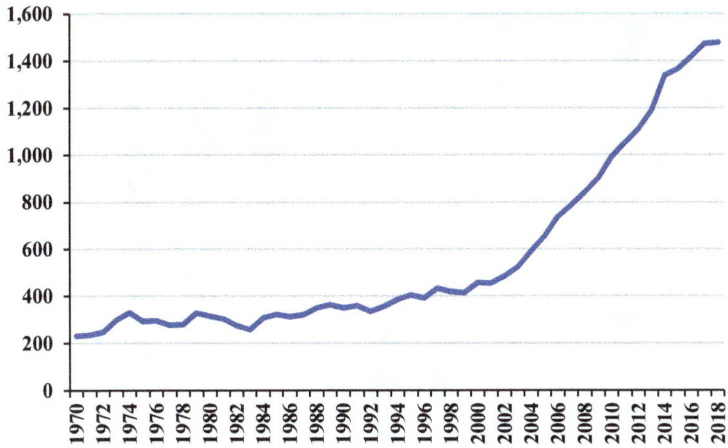

Figure 2.9 Seaborne trade in iron ore, in million tons, 1970–2018.

Source: based on data from ISL, Clarksons, Fearnleys, UNCTAD.

Note: the international seaborne trade in iron ore had been stable until about 2000, when China started to import in a big way.

When it comes to the situation of import, the biggest change since the 1970s is the shifting of traffic from traditional industrial countries toward the emerging economies in Asia (Figure 2.11). Virtually all the increase in this trade has been from Asia, particularly China. The European import of iron ore by sea has not changed much over the last decades with an amount between 120 and 150

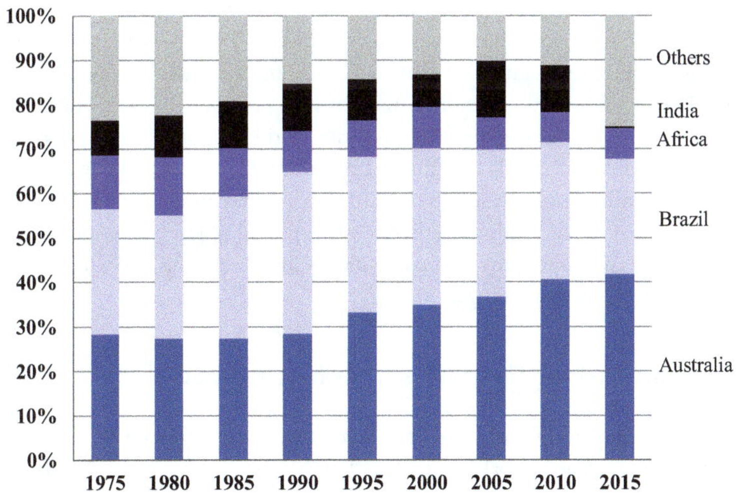

Figure 2.10 Market share in % of exporters of iron ore by sea, 1975–2015.

Source: based on data from ISL, Clarksons, Fearnleys, UNCTAD.

Note: two exporters have dominated the export of iron ore: Australia and Brazil, for the reasons of low production cost and the continued reduction of transport cost.

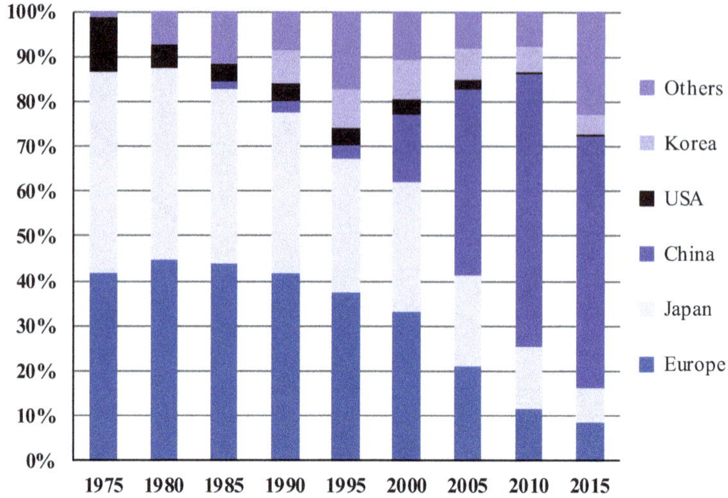

Figure 2.11 Market share in % of importers of iron ore by sea, 1975–2015.

Source: Based on data from ISL, Clarksons, Fearnleys, UNCTAD.

Note: with the US being mostly self-sufficient, Europe and Japan were the main importers of iron ore until the 1990s, when other East Asian countries and especially China became big importers.

million tons per annum. It has been the same situation regarding Japanese import, which is at around 130 million tons per annum. The import of the USA has been in decline. The imports of Korea and Taiwan and other Asian economies increased steadily during this period. However, the biggest surge of the seaborne trade of iron ore happened from the year 2000 and was because of the Chinese imports. The demand from China is so significant that in 2014 about 68% of the global export of iron ore went to China. The changes in the seaborne trade of iron ore over the last couple of decades are a perfect reflection of the new development trend of the world economy. The rapid economic growth in the less-developed countries in Asia transformed them into new industrial powerhouses. Korea is an excellent example in point. From the 1970s onward, this country underwent a process of industrialisation and urbanisation. The steel industry entered into a period of fast expansion. The import of iron ore surged. When much the same process took place in China from the 1990s, a similar development happened, but only about 20 times bigger.

What is the market of the seaborne trade in coal?

In 1970 about 80 million tons of coal were traded internationally by means of maritime transport. In 2018 the global seaborne trade in coal rose to 1,240 million tons, an increase of more than 15 fold in 48 years (Figure 2.12). This represents an average growth rate of more than 6% per year.[11] This is a very high growth rate in view of the total global seaborne trade, which increased at a much slower rate of 3.2% per year during the same period. Today, coal is mostly consumed in the steel and electricity sectors. Such areas have experienced fast growth from the 1970s, partly because of the economic growth in both industrialised and emerging economies and partly because of the substitution effects following the two oil shocks that happened in the 1970s.

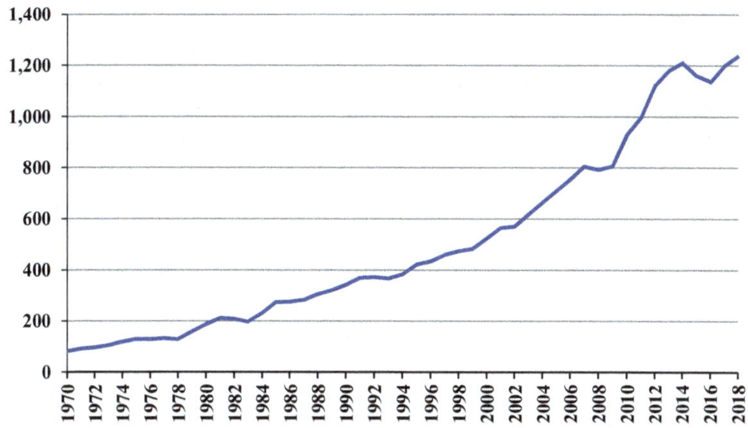

Figure 2.12 Seaborne trade in coal, in million tons, 1970–2018.

Source: based on data from ISL, Clarksons, Fearnleys, UNCTAD.

Note: the international trade in coal increased steadily, mainly due to the demand from the emerging economies.

As a basic natural resource with a large quantity of reserves, the availability of coal is well spread out in the world. So it is more often the case that coal is provided by local sources. For example, the US produces more coal than it needs. China also has most of its need satisfied by domestic productions. The picture of major exporters has, however, undergone some big changes since the 1970s, and particularly from the 1990s, as demonstrated in the graph (Figure 2.13). In 1975, for example, North America, Eastern Europe and Australia dominated the global export of coal. While East European export kept growing slowly, the American coal export declined from 113 million tons in 1990 to

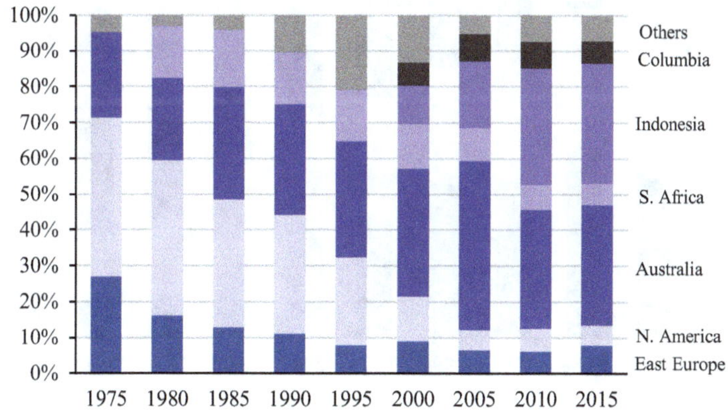

Figure 2.13 Market share by exporters of coal by sea, 1975–2015.

Source: based on data from ISL, Clarksons, Fearnleys, UNCTAD.

Note: the share of North America reduced due to rapid growth of Indonesian export and the strengthening of Australia's leading position as coal exporter.

about 40 million tons in 2005. In the meantime, new supplies of coal emerged. South Africa has exported more than before and Columbia has become one of the major exporters. But it is Indonesia which has experienced the most spectacular growth of coal export to be, with Australia, one of the two leading coal exporters in the world: it exported, for example, over 400 million tons of coal in 2018, which is almost a third of the global total seaborne trade in coal. The evolution of coal exporters is shown in Figure 2.13.

When it comes to the market of import of coal, the situation is more diversified today than it was in the 1970s, as shown in Figure 2.14. In 1975, for example, about 90% of the seaborne trade in coal was for Japan and Europe. Then some natural-resource-poor but fast-industrialising economies in Asia, such as Korea, started to import more and more raw materials including coal in the 1990s, when their domestic resources were exhausted or became increasingly less competitive compared with imported supplies. Such a situation happened later in China and India, the two big countries with relatively large reserves of coal, as shown in Figure 2.14. As we have explained previously, due to the low-cost production in Australia or Indonesia and declining maritime transport cost, countries like India and China found that it is more cost-effective to feed their steel plants and power stations, particularly those located along the coast, with imported coal rather than the domestic products.

What is the market of the seaborne trade in grain?

Compared with iron ore and coal, the seaborne trade in grain has increased modestly since 1970, as illustrated in Figure 2.15. During the 48 years between 1970 and 2018, the seaborne trade in grain increased 4.7 times from about 100 million tons to about 470 million tons (see Figure 2.15). This represents an average annual growth rate of more than 3%. Seaborne trade in grain depends, in the long term, on factors such as demographical changes and the rising living standards, etc., and, in the short term, on factors such as weather conditions, harvest situation, etc. With an improved living

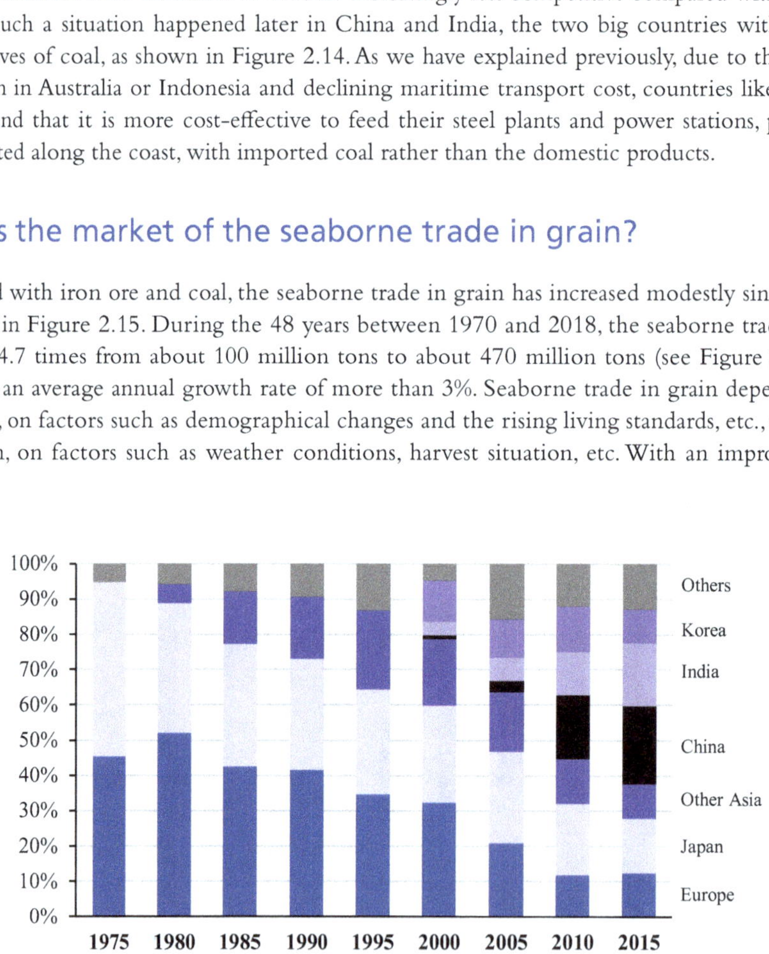

Figure 2.14 Market share by importers of coal transported by sea, 1975–2015.

Source: based on data from ISL, Clarksons, Fearnleys, UNCTAD.

Note: the European share reduced due to rapid growth of demand from the emerging economies, the oil production in Europe and the increase in oil transported to Europe by pipelines.

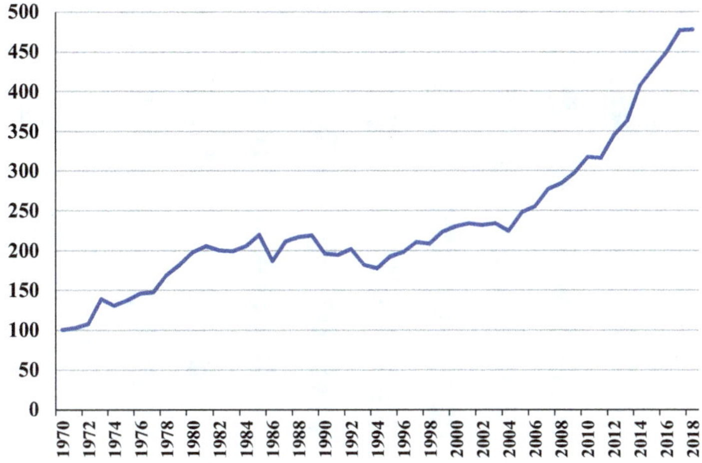

Figure 2.15 Seaborne trade in grain (in million tons), 1970–2018.

Source: based on data from ISL, Clarksons, Fearnleys, UNCTAD.

Note: between 1970 and 1980, and since 2005, the seaborne trade of grain expanded rapidly thanks to an increasing demand from Asia driven mainly by enhanced living standard and reduction of arable land.

standard, the consumption of meat usually increases and so does the grain for animal feed, which in turn would lead to more import of grain. The import of grain can also be affected by a reduction of arable land, which is often experienced in some countries due to economic structural changes and development.

There are different kinds of grain that are traded on the international markets, for example wheat, corn, rice, soya and barley, etc., are the main kinds of grain moved by ships. North America and Australia export wheat. Russia used to be an importer of wheat but is now an exporter. Corn is mainly exported by the US, Ukraine, Brazil, Argentina, etc. Rice is mainly exported by Thailand, India, Vietnam, etc. China used to be a big exporter of rice but it now imports much more than it exports due to the expanded domestic demand. As shown in Figure 2.16, the USA has been the biggest exporter of grain in the world, despite the fact that their market share decreased from about 60% in the 1970s to about 40% more recently. Europe has traditionally been an important grain-exporting region. In 2015, for example, the European Union exported more than 30 million tons of grain. Some European countries, like France, are big exporters of grain. East European countries such as Russia or Ukraine are also exporting grain by tens of millions of tons each year. A very large proportion of the European grain exports are for the demand of the neighbouring countries and is therefore not transported by ships.

With regard to importers of grain, as shown in Figure 2.17, Asia is in a dominating position. Asia is not only the most populous continent in the world, but it also has a high population density and the fastest economic growth. The living standard of many newly industrialised Asian countries has risen rapidly, which has, in turn, led to an increased demand for grain consumption. This happened not only in Japan in the past, but has also been repeated in other Asian countries such as South Korea and, more recently, China. Countries in the Middle-East are naturally depending to a large extent on imports for their consumption of grain. Today, Africa is also a net importer of grain. Countries like Nigeria, with more than 100 million people, import millions of tons of wheat and rice each year.

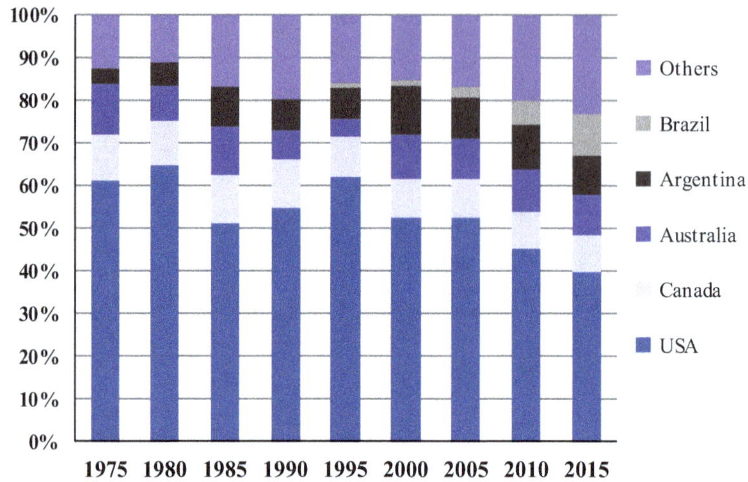

Figure 2.16 Market share in % of exporters of grain by sea, 1975–2015.

Source: based on data from ISL, Clarksons, Fearnleys, UNCTAD.

Note: the US remains the biggest exporter of grain. Europe is also an important exporter of grain, though most intra-European trade is not seaborne.

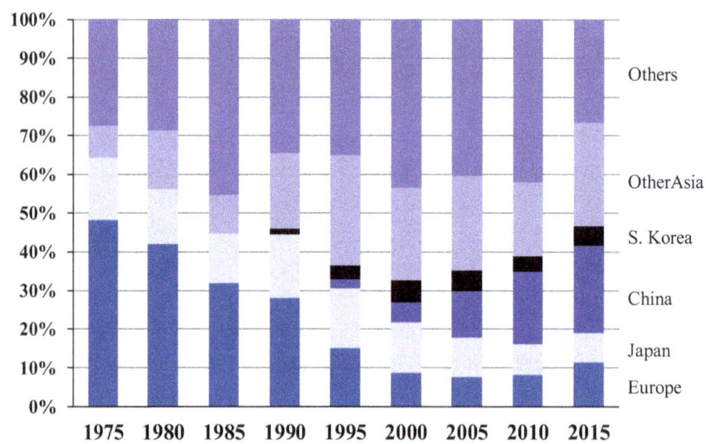

Figure 2.17 Market share in % of importers of grain by sea, 1975–2015.

Source: based on data from ISL, Clarksons, Fearnleys, UNCTAD.

Note: Asia has been the biggest importing region for grain. While China has become a major importer, India is still self-sufficient.

The local production of grain has improved in Africa, yet such an increase of local supply has not kept pace with the growth of population.

2.4 Price changes of resource-based demand and price elasticity

The international trade in natural resources is by and large a competitive market. The supply of most materials is available in more than one country or place. There is no administrative barrier to prevent new suppliers from entering the market. In 1960 some major oil-exporting countries established the Organization of the Petroleum Exporting Countries (OPEC), which produces about 40% of the global oil production or about 60% of the world oil exports. With such a dominant market share, this organisation is in a position to influence the oil price on the international market.[12] For most other commodities, the prices are determined mostly by the market forces of demand and supply.

Why does the price level of demand for commodities fluctuate?

International trade of natural resources is known for fluctuating prices. A good example is what has happened since 2000. There are many reasons for this. The first is the nature of demand and supply of the commodities. The demand for most raw materials changes due to many influential factors, most of which are unpredictable. In the short term, for example, temperature and climate changes can affect the demand for energy or grain. For example, good weather or natural disasters can influence the import or export of grain and a mild or severe winter may also lead to a decrease or an increase in trade of energy products for heating. Such weather-related and seasonal elements usually only have a relatively limited impact on the demand for raw materials. The need for commodities is more affected by cyclical changes in the market, such as the economic boom and bust.

In the longer term, the changes in demand are more related to the economic development of a country or group of countries when large-scale construction of infrastructure takes place. Such development, as we discussed previously, could lead to a strong and continuous new demand for natural resources. Such a "resource thirsty" type of growth may typically last for 15 to 20 years or even longer. This happened after World War Two in Japan and Europe, and also in the 2000s in China and other emerging economies. Such developments have created the two largest maritime trade expansions in modern times.

Yet, on the other hand, supply would generally not be able to cope with the changes in demand both in the short and long term. In the short term, the supply of raw materials, such as energy or agriculture products, can hardly adjust the production scale to align with the changes in demand. In the long run, when demand increases, new reserves are more difficult and costly to exploit. For example, the possibilities of developing new arable land would not only be limited in many cases but it would also be time-consuming. Often insufficient transport infrastructure can also prevent new sources from being added. Consequently, the supply of natural resource-based commodities also has low price elasticity.

As we can see in Figure 2.18, until the 1970s the prices of most raw materials were relatively stable due to the fact that the demand fluctuation was within supply's adjustable range of the production. Take crude oil as an example. Although the demand increased in the 1960s, the discovery of new reserves of oil that could be produced cheaply accommodated the new demand and prevented the price from rising. The production cost of crude oil in many Middle-East countries was as low as less than US$5 per ton.[13] The two oil crises in the 1970s and early in the 1980s pushed the price almost seven times higher. However, thanks to cheaper production, the increased production of

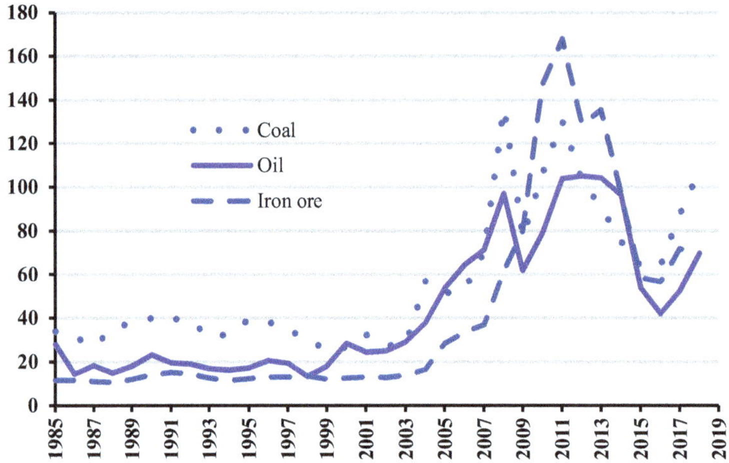

Figure 2.18 Price of coal, oil and iron ore, in US$ per ton, 1985–2019.

Source: World Bank and IMF (terminal coal, Australia; Spot oil; Iron ore, CFR Tianjin).

Note: the price of three main commodities increased extensively from 2003 due to the extremely strong demand increase from the emerging economies, particularly China. The demand persisted at a very high level for about 10 years before dropping.

non-OPEC oil-producing countries and the use of other energy sources as a substitute for oil led to a continuous decline of oil price. Then from the year 2000, a new and strong demand emerged in some newly industrialised countries, in particular in China. Unlike the previous industrialisation processes, the one that happened recently in the so-called "emerging" economies has a completely different level of impact because these countries represent, combined, more than half of the global population. Consequently, the price of all raw materials, including oil, was pushed up to a new and historical height.

What are the price changes in the major commodities during recent years?

Since the beginning of the 20th century, the prices of primary commodities such as oil, iron, coal and grain have followed a tendency of gradual decline, along with the improvement of technology and reduction of production cost, until around 2010 when the price of virtually all natural resources experienced substantial increases.[14] Figure 2.18 shows the prices between 1985 and 2019 of the three major commodities of coal, oil and iron ore, which are mostly moved by ships. We can make some observations particularly in the following areas: stable prices in the 1980s and 1990s; a sudden increase around the year 2000; rapid decline from the year 2012; and, lastly, the close correlation between the major commodities.

The sharp price increase from 2003 was mainly driven by new demand in the market. China joined the WTO in 2001 and, since then, the Chinese economic growth has maintained at a very high speed. Although the construction of basic infrastructure such as road, rail, ports, houses and others had led to a demand for raw materials before 2003, the need was mostly met by the local supplies.

The situation started to change around 2000, mainly due to a very rapid expansion of demand which could hardly be fulfilled in its totality by the local supplies for reasons of quantity, quality and price. Consequently, international supplies became the main sources. Given the size of the market, the Chinese import of natural resources had a big impact on prices and pushed them to a very high level for more than ten years. The prices of coal, oil and iron ore increased to four to five times higher, which erased virtually all the price declines of the 20th century. What is interesting to note is that there is clear evidence of price convergence for these commodities.

According to some research,[15] the benefits from price increases went mostly to the mining stage rather than to the production stage or processing of the materials. Taking steel production of the hot-rolled coil as an example, the profit split between steel production and raw materials changed from about 81% that went to steel production and 19% for raw materials in 1995 to merely 28% for steel production and 72% for raw materials in 2009. This is a clear indication that the natural resources were the scarcest input along the production chain. It is also the situation for other commodities such as coal and oil. There are two main reasons for this to happen. The first is the extraordinary increase in demand for raw materials from the emerging economies, particularly China; the second is the long time needed for the supply to adjust to the changes of demand. To a large extent the maritime transport supply has a similar character. So, at the time of a sudden increase in demand for shipping, the supply of ship capacity can only adjust with extensive delays, which usually leads to the high price of transport.

Compared with pure natural resources such as oil, coal or iron ore, grain is an agricultural product, with a different level of input in human and, in the case of modern agriculture, capital resources. Another difference is that both demand and supply of grain are much affected by natural conditions such as drought, flooding or temperature in the short term, as well as by the demographic changes and urbanisation process of countries. Consequently, over the period between 1985 and 2019, the price of grain followed a different development path, as shown in Figure 2.19. The degree of fluctuation is more modest in the price of grain than in that of the materials driven mainly by industrial needs.

The high price volatility of commodities is not just a phenomenon of recent decades, it has been so ever since such trade existed. Recent research[16] reveals that from 1700 until the end of the

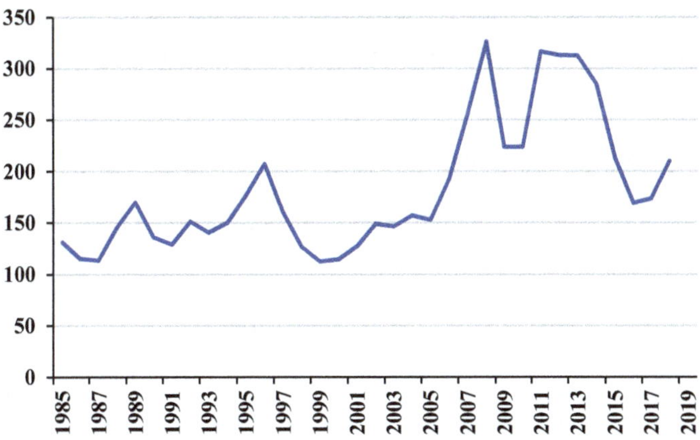

Figure 2.19 Price of grain in US$ per ton, 1985–2019.

Source: based on the World Bank, Databank (wheat, FOB Gulf of Mexico).

Note: the price of grain changes in a different way than that of energy and mining products. The price also increased, to a lesser extent, to over US$300 per ton before decreasing.

20th century, the price volatility of commodities was higher than the average price volatility of all goods. In contrast to commodities, the prices of manufactures have been less volatile. Between 1700 and 1896, commodity prices were 40% more volatile than the prices of manufactures. It is also found that the price volatility of commodities in modern times has not been higher than that of 300 years ago.

Why is the demand and supply of natural resources price inelastic?

The response of demand level to the changes in the price of a product is called the price elasticity of demand, usually expressed as the percentage change of demand to the percentage change in the price. The elasticity is high if the level of demand changes swiftly and robustly in response to the price changes. Otherwise, the demand is not price-elastic. Given the law of demand and supply, an increase in price would generally lead to a reduction of demand. So the reaction is in the opposite direction or a negative relationship. Generally speaking, there are three situations of price elasticity of demand. If, for example, there is a 1% increase in price and the demand reduces by 1%, it is said that the demand has a unit price elasticity. If a 1% increase in price leads to less than a 1% reduction of demand or an increase in demand by whatever percentage, the demand is price inelastic. If a 1% increase in price leads to more than a 1% decrease in demand, such a demand is price elastic.

Price is only one of many factors affecting the level of demand. Some of those factors are specific for a particular environment or condition and others are valid for a specific period of time or use; some are internal factors and others are external factors. For this reason it is difficult to calculate the exact price elasticity of a commodity. However, an examination of the influential factors would be beneficial to have an idea about the price elasticity of demand for natural resources and primary raw materials in general. The following five factors are the most important ones, namely: economic value and usages, the situation of substitute, shifting cost and time, consumption postponement possibility and share in total expenditure. The demand for natural resources and commodities is not price-elastic due to these five factors. Let's take a more detailed look at them.

- ***Economic value and usages***. This is about the usefulness or the economic utility of a commodity for consumers. Such utility can be broadly divided into three levels: necessity, comforts and luxuries. The demand for necessities, such as food or water, is so essential that it is price inelastic. On the other hand, the demand for comforts or luxuries is usually price elastic. The main raw materials carried by ships as discussed in this chapter, namely oil, iron ore, coal and grain, are those commodities that are essential for the importing countries[17] and therefore are price inelastic. There is another situation of associated demand elasticity which can be observed in the demand for iron ore. Such a demand is associated with the demand for steel which is price inelastic. Consequently, the demand for iron ore is also price inelastic.
- ***The situation of substitutes***. Producers are always looking for ways to reduce cost. When the price of a commodity rises, the producer would be interested to know the possibility of substituting a cheaper input for the more expensive one. Sometimes, substitutions are possible between different kinds of energy goods. For example, an electricity power station could replace coal with oil or gas. In such a case, the demand is price elastic. When substitutes are unavailable, for example in the case of iron ore, or are very limited, as in the case of grain, demand will be inelastic.
- ***Shifting cost and time***. When substitutes exist, the elasticity of demand depends on two other important factors. The first is the cost of substitution. This is the cost involved in the shifting from one material to another. Although many energy products are substitutable, high cost may prevent a substitution from happening should the price change be not big enough and/or not sustainable. In this case, demand is inelastic. The second factor is the time needed for completing the substitution. During the first oil shock of 1973, the market did not decrease a lot because time was needed

for a power plant to change from burning oil to gas. So demand is inelastic in the short term but elastic in the long term.

- ***Consumption postponement***. In the case where a demand can be postponed, it will be price elastic. In reality, however, the demand for the raw materials discussed in this chapter is almost always not deferrable since they are often essential inputs for production. Consequently, the demand for natural resources and raw materials is generally price inelastic. Because the demand cannot be deferred, reserves in stock are often made, particularly when the price of the commodity is low.
- ***Share in total expenditure***. In most cases the cost of a commodity is only a small proportion of the cost of the final product. For example, the cost of iron ore constitutes only a very small proportion of the cost of a car or a house. So the smaller the share of the material in the total cost of the final product, the less elastic the demand will be. If the demand for the final product, for example a house, is price inelastic, the demand for iron ore, which is an associated demand with the need for the house, will also be price inelastic.

Energy products, grain and many minerals are usually considered as strategic commodities due to the essential roles such products have for people's subsistence. When the commodities are needed, no delay or interruption would be tolerated. So such a demand is not very sensitive to price changes. The second reason is the lack of substitutes. For most natural-resource-based commodities there is a lack of substitutes, particularly in the short and medium term. Consequently, due to the above two reasons, the demand for natural-resource-based commodities has low price elasticity.

2.5 Summary

In this chapter we have discussed the characteristics of seaborne trade in natural resources and primary materials. Such trade can be divided into liquid cargo, such as oil and oil products, and dry cargo, such as iron ore and coal. Although many commodities are included in the category of dry cargo, three of them, iron ore, coal and grain, are analysed in more detail because they together constitute the bulk of the dry cargo carried by ships. Commodities are different from manufactured goods in many ways: the producers' comparative advantages are different. While the natural conditions are the determining factors for the comparative advantages of primary commodities, for manufactures the comparative advantages are mainly based on human resources. While the producers of raw materials remain relatively stable, those of manufactures change from one group of countries to another according to the changes in production factors. While natural resources are exhaustible, manufactured products are not. We have also examined the transport characteristics of raw materials and concluded that such cargo is in large quantity, of a homogeneous nature and low value with relatively stable exporting locations.

We then discussed the relationship between seaborne trade of commodities and economic development processes. Because most raw materials are needed by the industrial sector, the stage of industrialisation and the economic development of a country would be the primary determining factor for seaborne trade. Such a hypothesis was verified first by the examination of the economic development level, in terms of GDP per capita, and the seaborne trade level of the world's leading economies. We found that the two variables are positively correlated. For example, the growth of the GDP and seaborne trade in Japan between 1964 and 2015 has a high correlation. Another test was made for China by analysing the evolution of the two variables during the period between 1978 and 2018 when the Chinese economy maintained a very high annual growth rate. Once more, a tight correlation is found. Such findings are of high importance because the expected industrialisation and economic development in the future will provide us with an idea of where and how big the future seaborne trade will be.

We then discussed the evolution of seaborne trade in natural resources. The volume of trade has increased enormously since World War Two. During the last couple of decades another big change is the shifting of the importing countries from the traditional industrialised countries in Europe and

North America to the emerging economies, particularly those in Asia. Such a shift is related to the development of infrastructures in those countries. As the more developing countries are building their infrastructure, they will be the motors for the growth of seaborne dry bulk trade in the future.

Finally we examined the price changes of trade in natural resources. Historical statistics show that prices of commodities are more volatile than prices of manufactures. This is because of, on the one hand, the fluctuating nature of the demand for commodity products and, on the other hand, that the supply can hardly cope with the demand changes. For the supplies to adjust there are resource constraints and time constraints. So the supply of raw materials is generally not price-elastic. The demand for commodities also lacks price elasticity because the products have high economic utility, there is a lack of suitable substitutes and a low proportion of the cost of raw materials in the total expenditure for the importer.

Notes

1 WTO (2010). Since "natural resources" are defined as objects of trade, they have to be scarce in supply and they have to have an economic value.
2 BP (2015). Although natural resources exist in many countries, their production has been relatively concentrated, due to the production and transport costs as well as the quality of the resources.
3 UNCTAD (2019, 2015).
4 Lloyd's List (28 August 2015). China was a major importer of iron ore in the 2000s and 2010s. Yet the demand is much affected by the economic development and policy of the country. A very big reduction of shipping freight rates happened in 2015 caused by a decrease in demand from China.
5 World Steel Association (2014). In 2013 the net export of steel by Japan was 42.5 million tons.
6 Gao L. (2013). About 75% of coal consumed in China is for electricity generation. The cost of coal consists of production, logistics and tax. The Chinese imported 330mt of coal in 2013.
7 Zhang J. (2015). Out of a total of 2,147 iron ore mines investigated, only 19 had an annual production level of 5m ton and 30% of them had an annual production as small as 10,000 tons.
8 UNCTAD (from 1972) *Review of Maritime Transport* and data on seaborne trade from UNCTAD and data on GDP per capita from IMF and the World Bank.
9 Clarkson Shipping Intelligence Network (website, 2019). In 2014 a total of 9,842 million metric tons of international merchandise trade was transported by ocean-going ships.
10 Findlay R. and O'Rouke K. H. (2003).
11 Fearnleys (from 1980). The statistics on international seaborne trade of coal are published by various organisations. The data for the early years are collected from UNCTAD (from 1972) and Fearnleys (from 1980). The data for different regions and countries are collected from *ISL Shipping Statistics Yearbook*, Bremen, Germany, from 1982. The data for more recent years are taken from Clarksons Shipping Intelligence Network, Clarkson Research Service Limited.
12 The OPEC-led oil embargo triggered the oil crisis in the 1970s. For OPEC's share in world oil production and export, see OPEC (2015) "*Annual Statistical Bulletin 2015*", p. 65.
13 IMF (2015).
14 McKinsey & Company (2013).
15 McKinsey (2012).
16 Jacks D., O'Rourke K., and Williamson J. G. (2011).
17 Dahl (1993). Research using econometric models on the US energy demand, including oil, coal and gas, found that the price elasticity of demand for coal is, for example, at about –0.3.

References

BP. (2015) "*Statistical Review of World Energy*", 64th Edition. June 2015, p. 7. Retrieved from Statista.com (2015) and other sources.

Clarkson (2019) "*Seaborne Trade Monitor*", Volume 6, No. 9, Clarkson Shipping Intelligence.

Dahl C. A. (1993) "*A Survey of Energy Demand Elasticities in Support of the Development of the NEMS*", MPRA Paper 13962. Retrieved from http://mpra.ub.uni-muenchen.de/13962/, 1993-12 d.

Fearnleys. (from 1980) "*Fearnleys Review*", Oslo, Norway.

Findlay R. and O'Rouke K. H. (2003) "*Commodity Market Integration 1500–2000*", in "*Globalization in Historical Perspective*", edited by M. Bordo, A. Taylor, and J. Williamson, pp. 1–56. Chicago Scholarship Online (February).

Gao L. (2013) "*Domestic Freight Higher than International Freight*", (Chinese) First Financial Daily, 11 July 2013.

IMF. (2015) "*Commodity Special Feature – From World Economic Outlook*", IMF, Washington, DC, April 2015, p. 35.

Jacks D., O'Rourke K., and Williamson J. G. (2011) "*Commodity Price Volatility and World Market Integration since 1700*", The Review of Economics and Statistics, Vol. 93, No. 3 (August 2011), pp. 800–813.

Lloyd's List. (2015) "*Rates Weaken amid Slack China Demand, by Tom Leander*", Lloyd's List, Dry Cargo, 28 August 2015.

McKinsey. (2012) "*Manufacturing the Future*", *McKinsey Global Institute Report*, p. 79.

McKinsey & Company. (2013) "*Resource Revolution: Tracking Global Commodity Markets*", p. 6

OPEC (2015) "*OPEC Annual Statistical Bulletin 2015*", p. 65.

UNCTAD. (from 1972) "*Review of Maritime Transport*", UNCTAD, Geneva, Switzerland.

UNCTAD. (2015) "*Review of Maritime Transport*", UNCTAD/RMT/2015, Geneva, Switzerland.

UNCTAD. (2019) "*Review of Maritime Transport*", UNCTAD/RMT/2018, Geneva.

World Steel Association. (2014) "*World Steel in Figures*", WSA, Belgium.

WTO. (2010) "*World Trade Report 2010*", World Trade Organization, Geneva.

Zhang J. (2015) "*Cost of Iron Ore*", *(Chinese) International Finance News*, 27 April 2015.

Chapter 3

Seaborne trade in manufactured products

The rapid growth of general cargo trade from the 1970s and 1980s is attributable to the new pattern of globalised production and consumer society which have been gradually expanding from Europe, North America and Japan to some other parts of the world. Such developments will define the demand for maritime transport of general cargo in containers. During more recent years, the manufacturing sector has registered a steady growth of 2.8% per annum from US$5.7 trillion in 2000 to US$7.5 trillion in 2010. The even faster increase of the service sector means that the manufacturing industry employed more than 476 million people and represented 16.6% of global GDP in 2010, down from a much higher level of 27% in 1970.[1] Although the proportion of manufactures in the global GDP has been on the decline at the benefit of the service sector, the international trade of manufactures has been growing very fast, at about 7% per annum on average since 1950. In 2018, in value terms, about two-thirds of trade of merchandise, or nearly half of total global trade if trade in services is included, was manufactures. In this chapter we will analyse such developments. As far as maritime transport is concerned, the manufacturing sector is extremely important and liner shipping contributes about half of the total freight income of the shipping industry.

3.1 Maritime demand for manufactured products

If world trade is measured in value terms, it consists mostly of manufactured products. Manufacture uses raw materials and transforms them by man or machines or chemical processing, especially on a large scale, into various finished products. So manufactures are also often referred to as industrial goods to distinguish them from agriculture and services. These products include two groups of goods. The first group is consumer goods or home products such as electronic products, clothes, furniture and everything else people buy from shops and use in their daily life; the second group is capital goods, which are for the purpose of production rather than final consumption, such as machinery, office equipment, aeroplanes, ships, etc. In maritime transport, manufactured products are referred to as *general cargo*. Recently, some small bulk commodities are increasingly transported in containers. These include agricultural products such as grain, coffee, soya beans and other goods like forest products, steel products, cotton and even minor ores. Such relatively heavy and low-value cargo, sometimes in large quantities, is often loaded in containers as backhaul cargo on the routes with container trade imbalance.

What are the main characteristics of trade in manufactured goods?

The first characteristic of manufactures is their high value, both in total amount and unit value of trade. Today manufactured goods make up the largest portion of international trade in value. For example, in 2018 about 68% of world merchandise exports were manufactured goods. For most countries, manufactured products are also the single largest sector of foreign trade. Figure 3.1 shows the share of manufactured goods in the total merchandise exports and imports of selected economies in 2017. Japan is a highly industrialised country with very limited natural resources. Its exports are therefore predominantly manufactured products, but its imports consist of more basic materials. On the other hand, resource-exporting countries like Brazil and South Africa import mostly manufactured products. Measured in value terms, one item of manufactured product, for example, office and telecommunication equipment, can almost be twice as valuable as an entire cargo of iron ore.[2] It is difficult to tell the proportion of manufactured goods moved by maritime transport in value terms, as seaborne trade has always been measured in volume.

During the last couple of decades, not only is trade in manufactured goods much bigger than that in natural resources and raw materials, but manufactured goods have also registered a much faster growth rate than fuel, mining products or agricultural goods. Figure 3.2 shows that between 1950 and 2018 the volume of trade in terms of the current value in US dollars has registered an extraordinary growth of 80-fold for manufactured goods. This represents an average annual growth rate of 7%. While, during the same period, trade in fuel and mining products grew only about 11-fold, at an average annual growth rate of 3.8%. Similarly, trade in agricultural products grew even more slowly, by less than 10-fold, at an average annual growth rate of 3.5%. There are several reasons to explain why manufactured goods have grown so much faster than other trade in commodities. We will discuss these reasons

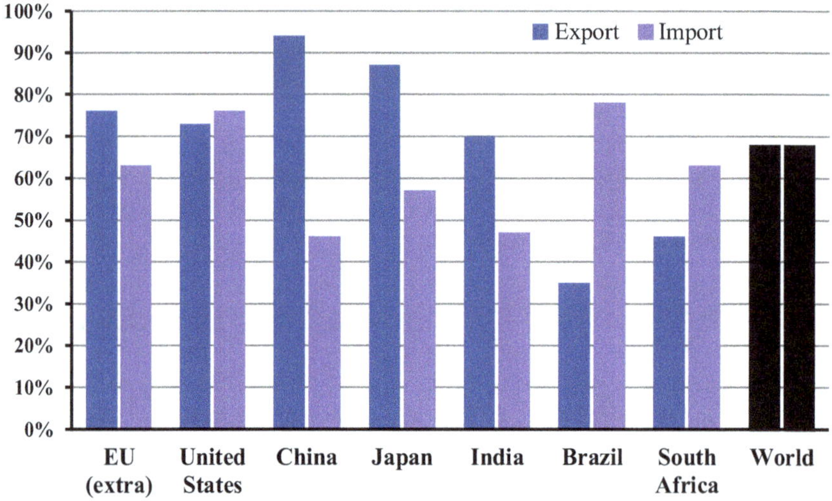

Figure 3.1 Manufactures in total merchandise trade of selected economies, 2017.

Source: Shuo Ma, based on data from WTO.

Note: resource-rich countries, like Brazil or South Africa, export less manufactures than raw materials. Industrialised but resource-insufficient countries, like China or Japan, export more manufactured goods than commodities.

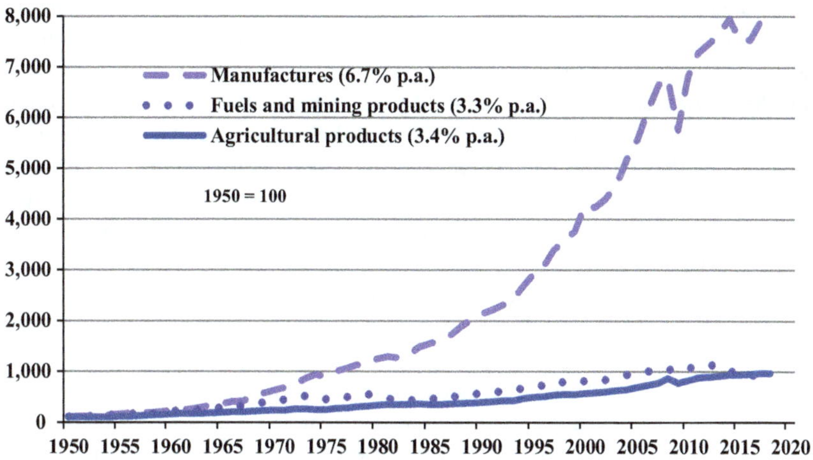

Figure 3.2 World trade growth in value index by type of cargo, 1950–2018 (1950=100).

Source: Shuo Ma, based on data from WTO.

Note: from 1950, the average annual growth rate of trade in manufactured goods is twice as fast as that of trade in primary materials. This is the result of both a faster expansion of trade in absolute terms and a steady increase in unit value of manufactured goods.

in more detail in the following sections. It is worth mentioning that not all international trade of manufactured goods uses maritime transport. Given the high unit value of this cargo, and therefore its sensitivity to transit time on the one hand and the geographical conditions between trading nations on the other hand, a significant proportion of manufactured goods are transported by aeroplane, train or trucks.

The high value of manufactured goods as compared with primary materials contrasts with the picture of trade in terms of volume that we discussed in the previous chapter. Measured in metric tons, manufactured goods, which are also referred to as general cargo, represent about 30% of total seaborne trade in 2018, while measured in value it is about 65%, down from about 75% in the year 2000. It decreased mainly because of the rise of commodity prices in the 2000s. Even in terms of tons, the market share of general cargo in total seaborne trade has increased steadily from, for example, about 25% in 1990 to 30% in 2018. Among the manufactured goods, more than half are transported in containers, for instance, out of a total of over 11 billion tons of global seaborne trade in 2018, about 2 billion tons were manufactured goods or about 16%.[3] The increase of market share in value terms has been more spectacular, as shown in the above figure.

The main reason why manufactured goods are always of high value comes from the fact that a large quantity of production factors are invested in production, particularly in the form of labour and capital. Apart from some specific minerals, most natural resources and raw materials are in relatively abundant supply. Therefore, depending on each case, a substantial part of the value accumulated in the production of these materials is mainly related to exploitation and transport. However, the production of manufactured goods requires much more of production factor inputs. The higher the technology and the more sophisticated the product is, the more production factors and the higher the value of the product will be. Consequently, the unit value of the manufactured product is often high. For example, electronic products can have a unit value as high as US$30–50,000 per ton, which contrasts with raw materials such as coal, ore or oil usually of low unit value at, e.g., US$10–100 per ton.

For the same reason as described above, production factors such as labour and capital play a more decisive role in determining which countries will be competitive to export manufactured products. The situation is very different for trade in raw materials, in which case the disposition of natural resources is the decisive factor. Because the conditions of production factors, scale economies, local consumptions and competitive advantages are different between the countries or between regions, and at the same time these conditions change over time, a country's position as importer or exporter evolves. This can clearly be observed in Asia since the 1960s, where the leading export hubs of manufactured products moved from high-cost countries such as Japan and Korea to relatively low-cost countries such as Malaysia, Thailand and China.

Consequently, the value of manufactured products is not determined by their size, weight or dimension, but by the contents of production factors. That is why a mechanical watch or a laptop computer would have a higher value than 10 tons of coal extracted out of a mine. Generally speaking, manufactured goods are of high total value but not necessarily in big volume. High value means high capital cost tied up in the products. Such a cost is determined in relation to the time during which the capital is deployed by the holder. This is the reason why maritime transport is more attractive for low-value products that are sensitive to cost rather than time. Subsequently, a lot of high-value manufactured products are moved by faster modes of transport, such as road or air transport, even at a higher cost.

In terms of volume in metric tons, seaborne trade of general cargo has also registered robust growth. For example, as shown in Figure 2.5 of Chapter 2, during the period between 1990 and 2018, the total seaborne trade grew from 4.3 billion tons to about 11 billion tons at an average annual growth rate of 3.7%. In 2018, as compared with the situation in 1990, the share of liquid bulk cargo dropped from 36% to 26%, while that of dry bulk cargo increased from 39% to 45% and that of general cargo increased from 25% to 29%. The total amount of general cargo increased from about a bit over 1 billion tons in 1990 to more than 3 billion tons of cargo in 2018, which represents an average annual growth rate at about 4.5%. Figure 3.3 shows the growth of seaborne container trade from 1990

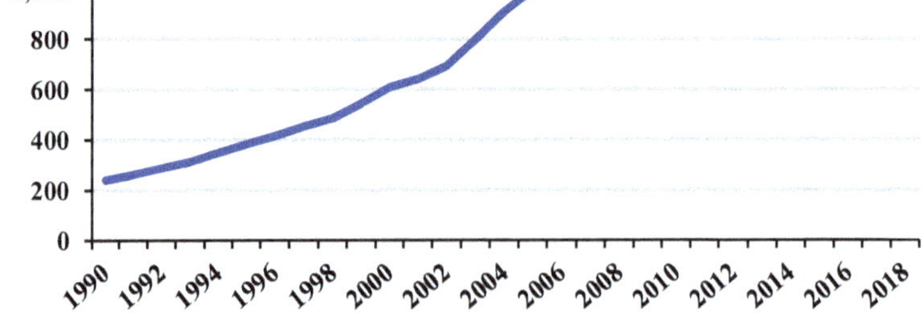

Figure 3.3 World seaborne container trade in million tons, 1990–2018.

Source: Shuo Ma, based on data from Clarksons.

Note: between 1990 and 2018, general cargo increased by 4.5% per year on average, of which containerised cargo increased by 7.7% per year on average.

to 2018. The average annual growth rate during this period is 7.7%, which is much higher than that for the dry bulk and tanker trades.

Manufactured goods are called "general cargo" for the reason of their diversification. Unlike raw materials, which are usually of a homogeneous nature, manufactured products are different in form, dimension, weight, etc. Such diversity poses problems for transport. So unitisation is necessary for more efficient transport. The most important unitisation is containerisation, which was first introduced in maritime transport in the 1950s. This is about loading general cargo into steel containers of standard sizes, usually of the dimension 8 x 8 x 20 feet or 8 x 8 x 40 feet. Containers have enormously improved transport efficiency, so gradually they have become the mainstream of transporting general cargo by ships. Today, most of the seaborne trade in manufactured goods is moved in standard sea transport containers. The so-called multi-purpose general cargo ships have been replaced by ships specifically designed to transport containers. For example, the world's general cargo fleet by the beginning of 2015 was only about 13 million deadweights (dwt), which is about half of the size of this fleet in 1996. According to Clarksons Shipping Intelligence, the general cargo ships trading in regular liner services, which is the main shipping pattern for manufactured goods, are fewer than 50 ships. While the seaborne trade of general cargo continues to grow at a fast speed, the general cargo ship fleet has kept shrinking. Today virtually all manufactured goods that can be loaded into containers have been moved by container ships. Consequently, the global container trade increased from 237 million tons in 1990 to 1,870 million tons in 2018, with an annual growth rate of over 8%. The global container fleet in 2015 had increased 6.3 times since 1996.[4] Depending on different shipping markets and ports, the rate of containerisation is about 70% for the general cargo market and on some main East–West shipping routes the penetration rate is as high as 90% or more. It is generally believed that most "containerisable" cargo has by and large been transported by containers.

What are the main categories of manufactured goods?

Manufactured products traded between countries can be divided in two different ways. First of all, the division is based on the nature of use; that is, either for consumption use or industry use. The former includes all products that are ready for final consumption, such as finished furniture, footwear, clothes, electronics, etc. These goods are traded and transported for people to consume. The latter is the manufactured products for industrial use which include either capital goods or intermediate goods. Capital goods are those needed to carry out production processes. They are generally durable goods such as machinery, tools, or goods for making other goods or services. These goods include equipment, parts, tools, etc. Intermediate goods, on the other hand, are semi-finished products or processed materials to be used by industry in the production of goods or services, or they are the intermediate goods in production processes.

There is another way of dividing manufactured products which is based on the stage of production of either finished or unfinished products. Finished products are goods for industries such as capital goods described above or for final consumption such as consumer goods like clothes or TVs. Unfinished, sometimes also referred to as semi-finished, products are those intermediate materials traded and transported in the production processes before a product is finished. Finished products can be for both industry and consumers. However, unfinished products are for industry's needs only. The differences between a finished product and an unfinished product are large and vary in many ways. The most important difference is that unfinished products are traded in the middle of the production process, while finished products are traded at the end of the production process. During recent decades, unfinished products have grown at a very rapid pace as compared with finished products. Figure 3.4 is the structure of the global manufactured trade by type of products in value in 2018. Most of the goods, except for intra-European and intra-North American trade, are transported by ships.

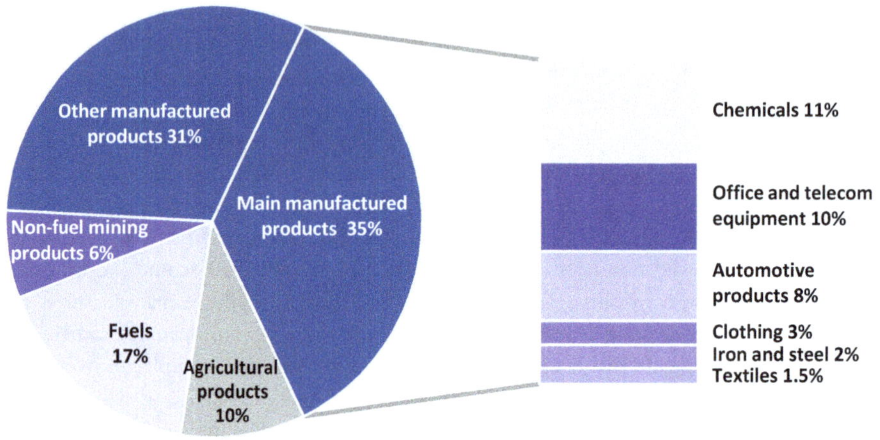

Figure 3.4 Structure of world merchandise trade by type of products, in US$, 2018.

Source: Shuo Ma, based on WTO International Trade Statistics, 2019 and World Bank and UNCTAD trade statistics.

Note: in value terms, about two thirds of world trade is in manufactured products. The percentage changes mainly due to price fluctuation of commodities.

The main reason why unfinished manufactured products are traded internationally with a fast growth rate is economic globalisation. A globalised production system has become the main form of industrial production for an increasing portion of products, at the expense of a system in which the manufactured goods are produced within a single nation. It is called the *global supply chain* or GSC. We, therefore, will take a more detailed look at such a trend in the seaborne trade of manufactured goods later in this chapter.

Which countries are the leading traders of manufactured goods?

We will discuss this question from two aspects: the exporters and importers of manufactured goods and the seaborne trade of general cargo, particularly container traffic. The main reason for doing so is that although our central interest is seaborne trade, we have to understand the situation and changes in the trade of manufactured goods in general. There is only a portion of manufactured products that are transported by ships, yet the trade evolution of the manufactured goods as a whole determines the future of seaborne trade of general cargo.

First, we should look at the exports. Industrialised countries and economies are producing manufactured products. So Europe, North America and Japan have been the leading exporters. The newly industrialised countries and territories, particularly those in Asia, have caught up very quickly. According to the World Trade Organization[5] (see Table 3.1) the world trade of manufactured products increased from 2,390 billion US dollars in 1990 to 4,690 billion dollars in 2010 and 12,616 billion dollars in 2017. If the European Union is considered as a single economic entity, then in 2017 close to 90% of the world's total manufactured products were exported by the top ten economies. Table 3.1 also shows that over 75% of manufactured goods were exported in 2017 by five economies, namely the EU, China, the USA, Japan and South Korea. This is a high level of concentration. The EU is the biggest exporter, but about two-thirds of the EU trade is carried out within the EU. Given the fact

Table 3.1 Leading exporters of manufactured products, 1990, 2000, 2017.

	(Billion dollars and percent)	*1990*	*2000*	*2017*
	World total exports (bn$)	*2,390*	*4,690*	*12,161*
1	EU (EU 28)	50%	43%	38%
2	China	2%	5%	17%
3	United States	12%	14%	9%
4	Japan	12%	10%	5%
5	South Korea	3%	3%	4%
6	Hong Kong	3%	4%	4%
7	Mexico	1%	3%	3%
8	Taiwan	3%	3%	2%
9	Singapore	2%	3%	2%
10	Switzerland	2%	1%	2%
11	India	1%	1%	2%
12	Canada	3%	4%	2%
13	Thailand	1%	1%	1%
14	Malaysia	1%	2%	1%
15	Turkey	0%	0%	1%
	Of the world total	**91%**	**93%**	**91%**

Source: WTO, International Trade Statistics.

Note: about two thirds of the EU's trade is between EU countries. A big portion of Hong Kong's and Singapore's export is re-export.

that the EU has been a free trade region since 1994 and the adoption of the Euro by most EU countries as a common currency, trade between EU member countries is increasingly seen as "domestic" trade. In 2017, 38% of the EU's export of manufactured products was for the market outside the EU, which represents about 15% of the global export of manufactured products measured in value.

A noticeable development between 2000 and 2017 is the rise of Asia, particularly the extraordinary increase in the Chinese export of manufactured products. China joined the WTO in 2001, which symbolises the integration of the country into the world trade system. As a consequence and given the size of China, its impact on world trade is huge. The rise of China is a reflection of a more general development trend of international trade and economic globalisation. International trade has been growing very fast, mainly driven by the participation of many newly industrialised or emerging economies. We will discuss in more detail the impact of economic globalisation on maritime transport demand later in the chapter.

With regard to the situation of major importers of manufactured products, the picture is on the whole similar to that of exporters. Once again, Europe takes the lead, given the fact that the intra-European trade is included, and is followed by the USA and China. Again, Hong Kong and Singapore are among the 15 leading importers of manufactures thanks to their role as re-exporters. Table 3.2 shows the largest 15 importers of manufactured products in 2017 and, for comparison, their positions in 1990 and 2000. Similar to the situation of exports of manufactures, China has registered the most robust growth since 1990. At the same time, the market shares of other economies in Europe, North America and Asia declined. This is mainly the effect of industrial migration, which happened as a result

Table 3.2 Leading importers of manufactured products, 1990, 2000, 2017.

(Billion dollars and percent)		*1990*	*2000*	*2017*
World total imports (bn$)		*2,376*	*4,630*	*12,161*
1	EU (EU 28)	47%	39%	35%
2	United States	16%	21%	15%
3	China	2%	4%	7%
4	Hong Kong	3%	4%	4%
5	Japan	4%	5%	3%
6	Canada	4%	4%	3%
7	Mexico	1%	3%	3%
8	South Korea	2%	2%	2%
9	Singapore	2%	2%	2%
10	India	1%	0%	2%
11	Switzerland	2%	1%	2%
12	Chinese Taipei	2%	2%	2%
13	Russia	0%	0%	1%
14	Australia	1%	1%	1%
15	Brazil	1%	1%	1%
	Of the world total	**82%**	**87%**	**78%**

Source: WTO, international trade statistics data.

Note: the USA has been the largest importer of manufactured products, while China is catching up fast. Data on Russia starts from 2000.

of economic globalisation and turned China into the "world factory". Out of the imports of China, a large portion is "intermediate" products needed in the production of goods for export. The combined share of the top 15 importers is smaller than that of exporters, which is evidence of a lower degree of concentration. Countries like Brazil and Australia are exporting raw materials rather than manufactured goods but, in 2017, more than 70% of the imports of these two countries were manufactured goods.[6]

Who are the leading traders of manufactured goods transported by sea?

One question remains to be addressed: if manufactured goods constitute about two-thirds of the world's total merchandise trade, how much of this manufactured product is carried by ships? The situation varies greatly between the regions and there is no straight answer. As far as the largest trader, Europe, is concerned, it is important to separate the European trade between the intra- and extra-EU trades for our discussion of the maritime demand. This is because most European countries share common borders and the land-based transport system is well developed in Europe. Consequently, about two-thirds of the intra-EU trade uses land-based transport, such as rail, road and inland-waterways.[7] Some of the intra-EU trade by sea is also protected as domestic transport. As far as the extra-EU trade is concerned, which is about a third of the total EU foreign trade, most cargo is transported by ships.

Table 3.3 Modal split in percentage of the transport of extra-EU export and import freight, by value and volume, 1998, 2008 and 2018.

	1998 (EU-15)		*2008 (EU-25)*		*2018 (EU-28)*	
	Value	*Weight*	*Value*	*Weight*	*Value*	*Weight*
Sea	41.4%	70.8%	50.7%	72.4%	50.3%	75.7%
Road	22.6%	7.9%	16.3%	6.1%	16.2%	3.0%
Rail	2.2%	4.2%	1.6%	4.2%	1.4%	3.8%
Waterways	0.8%	2.9%	0.3%	0.9%	0.2%	0.8%
Pipelines	1.4%	10.9%	4.4%	12.0%	2.3%	11.6%
Air	24.1%	0.3%	20.1%	0.6%	25.5%	0.8%
Other/unknown	7.6%	3.0%	6.5%	3.6%	4.1%	4.3%

Source: Based on European Commission, EU transport in figures.

Note: for extra-EU trade, maritime transport is the dominating mode of transport, particularly in volume terms.

Table 3.3 shows the modal split for the EU's external trade in value as well as in volume. Air transport takes a lot of high-value cargo, while, in volume terms, about 75% of cargo was moved by sea transport in 2018. Between 1998 and 2018 the share of maritime transport increased, due to the fact that more countries joined the EU and that trade with Asia, which is very much maritime-transport-dependent, grew at a much faster speed than that with other non-EU markets. To conclude, if, in 2018, 38% of the EU trade by value of manufactured goods is extra-EU trade, of which about 50% is moved by maritime transport, then the high market share of the EU in international trade of manufactured products is less significant for maritime transport than the percentage suggests.

The situation is similar for North America. For a long time the world's largest bilateral trade was the one between the USA and Canada. About 50% of NAFTA, the free trade area covering the USA, Canada and Mexico, is within USMCA or formerly NAFTA.[8] In 2014 the three North-American countries had a combined market share of 15% for export and 20% for import of the world's total trade in manufactured products. About half of such trade is mainly carried by land-based transport.

When it comes to Asia, particularly Far East Asia, the situation is quite different. Although the intra-Asian trade is massive and growing, most of this trade is relying on maritime transport. This is because of the pattern of intra-Asian trade and particular geographical conditions. China's main trade partners are not its neighbouring countries with which land-based transport can be used. Japan, Indonesia and the Philippines are island countries. South Korea is not trading much with North Korea. Other Asian economies are also trading with the countries separated by oceans. ASEAN, the ten-member South-East Asian association, only trades up to about 25% of their total trade between themselves. So a vast majority of Asian countries' foreign trade is dependent on maritime transport.

To summarise the above discussions, both Europe and North America rely to a considerable extent on land-based transport for their export and import of manufactured products. Asia, on the contrary, is highly dependent on shipping for its trade of manufactures. Such a situation is best demonstrated by the global market of container trade (see Figure 3.5). In 2018, for example, Europe's share of the global manufactured exports in value was 39%, but its share of seaborne containerised exports in volume was only 17% of the world's total. This is because a large portion of the European exports of manufactures was transported by land. Similarly, about 15% of the world's manufactured exports in 2018 was from the three North-American countries, yet only about 8% of the global containerised

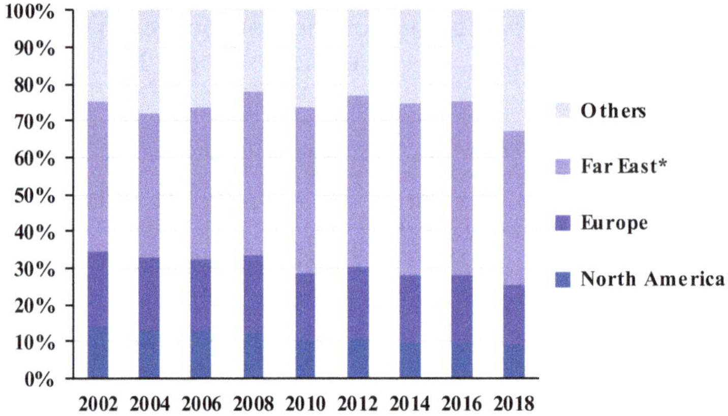

Figure 3.5 Regional shares of global container trade, 2002–2018.

Source: Shuo Ma, Based on data from Clarksons.

Note: this is about import and export of container trade by main regions.
*Far East – does not include West Asia and South Asia.

exports were from North America. With only about 33% of the global export by value, the Far East, which includes the economies of East and South-East Asia, counted for more than half of the global containerised exports. This is mainly because the intra-Asian trade, which is very large, is mostly seaborne. When it comes to import of manufactures by containers, the shares of Europe and particularly North America in the world's total are higher than exports. But with export and import combined, the Far East, as shown in Figure 3.4, is still by far the largest seaborne trade market for manufactures.

3.2 Globalised production and trade in manufactured goods

If we look at Table 3.1 above, we see that China's share of manufactured export increased from 5% in 2000 to 17% in 2017 and, at the same time, Europe's share decreased from 43% to 38%, the US's share dropped from 14% to 9%, Japan's from 10% to 5% and Taiwan's from 3% to 2%. This phenomenon cannot simply be explained by a sudden increase in the international competitiveness of the home-grown manufacturing capability of China. Rather, a large part of this development is attributable to a new and fast-expanding globalised production pattern, or the global supply chain, GSC. This is about the migration of a lot of manufacture productions from traditional industrialised countries to newly industrialised regions. It is the globalisation of industrial and service processes, rather than the migration of the whole production. It started before 2000 and China was certainly not the first place to receive migrated production processes. But, with much rapid growth and China as a giant participant, this process has gone to such a high level with a far-reaching impact on many sectors, including the demand for maritime transport.

Why have manufacturing activities been globalised?

In the discussions of the previous chapters we attributed the faster growth of international trade compared with the growth of the world's production to the following two main developments. The first is the expansion of traders, especially those capable of offering more significant production-cost differentiation; the second development is the reduction of trade cost or the transaction cost, which includes administrative costs and transport costs. As such costs decrease, the benefits of trading grow, which in turn stimulates more products, that were previously not traded due to price differences too small to cover the transaction costs, to be included in international trade. So, the further the transaction costs reduce, the more products will be included in international trade and the further the trade will reach. For example, it is now common that goods such as flowers, vegetables, stone, plaster, tiles and other low-value goods are traded between distant markets such as the Far East and Europe. The continuous reduction of transaction costs and the widening of the cost of production between traders have expanded international trade from about 6% of global GDP in 1900 to 12% in 1950 and more than 26% in 2014.[9] The effect is illustrated in Figure 3.6.

We can use Figure 3.6 to explain two driving forces of the trade growth: the effect of production cost and of trade cost. The figure shows the trade of two products A and B with changes in trade cost. In other words, we would like to see how the amount of trade is influenced by the interplay of the changes in the cost of product between trade partners on the one hand and of the changes in trade cost on the other hand.

- ***Impact of product cost changes.*** The rapid trade expansion should not be attributed solely to the reduction of trade cost. Larger participation in trade by more countries has played an important role as well. Assume trade cost is T-1 and there are two traders, A and B, in the market. There is no trade of product A because the benefit of trade, which is the difference between A-1 and A-2, is not enough to offset the trade cost T-1. There is, of course, no trade of product B either for the same reason. However, when a third country 3 joins with the capability of producing product A at a lower cost, trade will happen between countries 1 and 3 thanks to the bigger difference in

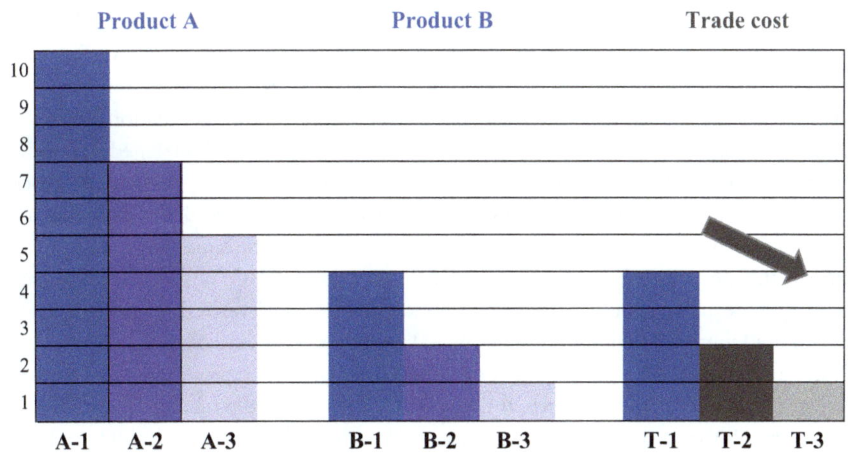

Figure 3.6 The effects of production and transport cost on trade of different products.

Source: Shuo Ma.

Note: product A is of high value and is made by countries at different costs. Assuming the trade cost is the same between the countries, trade happens if the trade cost is smaller than the difference of production cost. For low-value product B, trade cost is often too high for trade to happen.

product cost, which is more than the trade cost T-1. This simulates the trade expansion caused by newly industrialised countries, such as China, capable of producing at low cost thanks, e.g., to scale economies or know-how acquisition. There is always less of a chance for a low-value product, such as product B, to be traded internationally, even with the participation of low-cost countries like B-3. This is because trade cost is proportionally large for the low-value product and thus more difficult to be offset by cost differences. Urbanisation stimulates the situation of products like building materials, fresh food, etc.

- ***Impact of trade cost changes.*** As discussed previously, the trade cost includes both administrative and transport costs. When this cost reduces from T-1 to T-2, usually as a result of productivity improvement, products with smaller cost differences may become tradable and, as a result, trade increases. For example, with trade cost at T-2, product A, which could not be traded between countries 1 and 2 due to too small a cost difference, would now be traded. Similarly, product B will be traded between countries 1 and 3. So, thanks to a reduced trade cost, low-value products will be traded internationally. This is exactly what has happened over the last decades as low transaction cost helped expand international trade in a vast variety of products. The lower the trade cost is, the more traded products will be and, at the same time, more remote trade partners can be included.

But the impact of lower transaction cost is not just to allow more products and producers to participate in international trade. The product-based exchanges discussed above are only a part of the story. The reduction of trade costs also leads to some profound changes in the patterns of how a product is made, particularly in the manufacturing sector. The product-based international trade assumes that the production is completed in one country and the cost comparison is made either on the raw materials or on the final product. Such an assumption was justified for two main reasons. First, the technical know-how needed for the manufacturing process was usually only available within a country. So it was typical in the past that a product was labelled with the expression of "made in" a specific country. The second reason was the relatively high trade cost. As discussed in the first chapter, that, compared with 2018, the container freight rate in 1968, measured in constant dollars, was approximately 9 times higher. Administrative cost to trade was also much higher in the 1960s, 1970s and even 1980s. So efforts were made to minimise transaction cost by concentrating production processes as closely as possible.

With a continuing decline of the transaction cost, a new type of international trade started to emerge, which meant that, instead of finished products, semi-finished and intermediate products were traded between countries. So international trade was introduced into the production process. With the fast growth of multinational companies and the expansion of foreign direct investment, this kind of trade has taken an ever-increasing share of total trade. Various expressions are used to describe this development, the most commonly used being global value chain (GVC) or global supply chain (GSC), intra-industry trade, trade of tasks, process-based trade, international vertical specialisation, etc.

We can use Figure 3.7 to illustrate such trade. Take product A as an example. Its production consists of three production stages or processes or tasks. The total cost of production A-1 and A-2 is the same between countries 1 and 2, so there is no benefit from trade in the final products, even if transaction cost is zero. However, it is possible that the cost of each production stage is different between the two countries, even if the costs of the final products do not reflect all these differences. For product A, process 3 is less costly in country 1 than in country 2, but processes 1 and 2 are cheaper in country 2. If the transaction cost is at T-2, a trade of production process, by combining the best processes of the two countries, would result in a more competitive product, such as A2+3 plus T2, which is cheaper than A-1 or A-2. So the product is made in two countries instead of one. It can certainly be made in more countries, which is the reality today for many products. The trade of intermediate products also helps offset high transaction cost and subsequently increases trade, which would not take place due to too small a cost difference, as shown in Figure 3.7, regarding product B. If transaction cost is at T-2, product B would not be traded between countries 1 and 2 because of the insufficient cost difference.

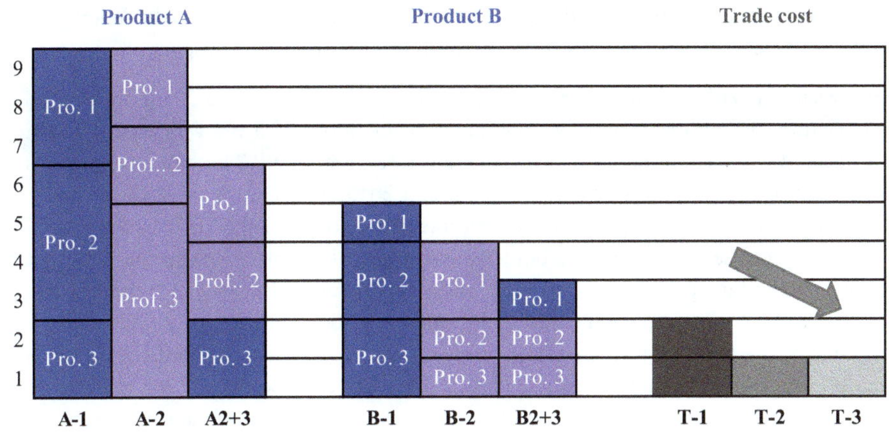

Figure 3.7 From trade in product to trade in process, the impact of trade cost.

Source: Shuo Ma.

Note: when "tasks" instead of "products" are traded, additional benefits can be made when transaction cost is low. So, by combining the most attractive production processes of the trade partners, additional benefits, 3 units for Product A and 1 unit for Product B, are made. So even countries with the same costs can benefit from trade.

But when the product is made in both countries, by combining the most attractive production stages of each, the outcome is a cheaper product. When trade cost further reduces, from T-2 to T-3, such intra-industry trade would expand more broadly.

A product is usually made through a multiple-stage value chain, each stage often requiring different types, quality and quantity of factor inputs. Some need more labour skills, others less, some require more land, others less, some are more technology-intensive, others less, etc. Such differences are the source of the benefit of a trade if a division of labour between countries could be done according to the comparative advantage of individual stages rather than that of the completed product. When the individual production process is consolidated through the trade of intermediates, an effect of increasing the return to scale could further reduce the cost of the final product. Such intra-industry trade can take the form of outsourcing or sub-contracting by trading in intermediate goods such as parts or components; it can also be an intra-firm trade through foreign direct investment (FDI). It means that a company invests in production capacities in a foreign country under its control or that of a joint venture. With regard to the recipient country, such outsourcing and foreign direct investment are usually welcome and encouraged with incentives because of their contribution to the local GDP and employment market. Given such attractiveness, trade of intermediate products has entered, during the last couple of decades, a high-speed expansion phase, particularly since the 1990s. About 30% of merchandise trade is now in intermediate goods or components.[10]

What is the impact of GVC or GSC on international trade?

As the globalised production expanded and has become a fixed feature of modern manufacturing, international trade of manufactures is no longer the same as before. There have been many discussions and analyses on the developments of the *global value chain* or *global supply chain*. The following changes are among the ones that have the most important impacts on maritime transport.

- ***Fast growth of trade of intermediate goods.*** As discussed earlier, in the 2010s about 50% of the manufactures traded internationally were intermediate goods. This is a very high proportion and it is rising. They include more than just manufactured products.[11] The best example of a global value chain is probably in Asia: between 1995 and 2013, for example, while Asia's trade of final goods grew about four times, its trade of intermediate goods increased by a factor of six.[12] Today, it is common to see multiple cross-border transactions taking place during the production process before the final product is made. Each time a semi-finished product is exported, its value is counted as international trade. Therefore the value of trade concerning a product is higher than the value of the final product itself. The international trade statistics are inflated due to multiple calculations of the semi-finished products each time they cross borders. This is also the main reason that the international trade of manufactures has increased so much during the last couple of decades. For example, in 2008, 65% of the global trade in merchandise was manufactured products. But if such multiple calculations of the value of intermediates are eliminated by counting only the value-added to the product, the share of manufactures shrinks down to merely 37% of the world total.[13] The increasing part of intermediates in trade has a very profound impact on maritime transport. We will discuss this impact in more detail in the following section.
- ***From market penetration to value-added acquisition.*** When trade mostly consisted of finished goods, products, market share and profits were the primary aim of the exporters. For example, the number of TV sets exported to a market was usually taken as a target or as an indicator of performance. Today, as intermediate products have become a mainstream of trade, production tasks are shared between countries. Not only are finished products imported and exported but also components and parts. This is a fundamental change. Producing a part of a product is quite different from exporting a final product. It is the *value-added* that traders are looking for. When value-added is the objective, the unit of trade is not bound by a finished product any longer. Consequently, *specialisation moves from product-based to process-based*. The international division of labour is not product-based but task-based. Depending on the transaction cost, outsourcing and division of labour can be more extensive and the scope of the scale economies can be explored to a higher level. As a result, trade expands.
- ***Emerging economies as the main players.*** Foreign direct investment has been one of the major driving forces for the growth of intra-industry trade. A country with some attractive resource factors, such as land or labour, but missing the capability of product development, manufacturing, marketing or other know-how, may hardly be able to be a competitive producer in a traditional product-based trading system. However, thanks to the global value chain, such a country, with the help of foreign direct investment, can participate in the production process by trading in intermediate goods. Consequently, many poorer economies are among those with the fastest trade growth. The global distribution of value-added from manufacturing has gradually shifted from traditional industrialised countries in North America, Europe and Japan to the developing and emerging industrial economies. Between 1990 and 2014 the global share of the former decreased from 82% to 64%, while the global share of the latter increased from 18% to 36%.[14] This happened in Latin America, East Europe and particularly in Asia. China is the best example in point. The Chinese trade in 1980 was merely 1% of the world's total, but in 2011 its share became 11%[15] and the contribution of trade of intermediates to this extraordinary growth is tremendous. According to the WTO, developing economies' share of merchandise imports increased from 26% in 1995 to 39% in 2014.[16] Between 1963 and 2014, the European share of the USA's export dropped from about 30% to 20%, the Japanese share dropped from 7.5% to 4%, but the share of newly industrialised East Asian economies, including China, increased from 3% to 18%.[17] Since then, the trend has continued.

- ***The rising similarity of two-way trade***. Product-based trade suggests that countries specialise in producing those products in which comparative advantage is found. As a result, different products should be exchanged between trade partners. But when international trade is changed to task-based or process-based, countries may import and export similar kinds of intermediate goods. With the effect of foreign direct investment and globalised production, even the newly industrialised countries or emerging economies have also seen the structure of their export becoming increasingly similar to that of the more advanced economies. For example, measured in overall export similarity index,[18] between 1995 and 2008 the similarity index of the Japanese and Chinese exports increased from 24% to 36%, that of the US and Chinese exports increased from 25% to 33% and that of German and Chinese exports increased from 24% to 35%.[19] The same type of changes happened in other emerging economies as well.
- ***The important role of the global supply chain***. If transaction cost is the main influential factor of international trade of intermediates, the change of this cost can also cause the trade to rise or decline. The two elements of the transaction costs, administration-based and transportation-based, have to be low for intra-industry trade to prosper. During the last couple of decades, only those countries capable of offering excellent administrative and transport services benefitted from the globalised production of manufactures. Efficient transport is a prerequisite for a country to be integrated into the world production system and global supply chain. It is one of the key ingredients for the Asian countries to have experienced the fastest growth of trade in intermediates.

3.3 Globalised consumption and trade in manufactured goods

We have discussed so far the production side but the consumption of manufactured goods has changed too. The consumption of manufactured products was traditionally concentrated in industrialised countries in North America, Europe and East Asia. But this situation has changed over the last few decades. Increasingly, the newly industrialised economies have become not only main players in the globalised production of manufactured goods but also consumers of raw materials as well as manufactured goods. For example, in 2015, a total of about 25 million commercial vehicles, of which about 21 million were private passenger cars, were sold in China, or more than 25% of the total global production.[20] How did it happen? Will the trend continue? We are going to discuss in this section some of the key issues in this regard, particularly the issues of urbanisation and the rise of the middle class in the main emerging economies.

What have been the changes to the global middle class?

One of the most important changes which has a profound impact on trade of manufactures is population growth. According to the UN, the world population will increase from 7.3 billion in 2015 to around 9.7 billion in 2050.[21] Another closely related aspect which is equally important is urbanisation. In 1900 only about 15% of the world population lived in cities and the ratio went up to approximately 30% in 1950. By about 2005, for the first time, more people lived in cities than in the rural areas and in 2018 the ratio was 55%.[22] It is expected that by 2050 66% of the world population will be urban. The emerging economies and newly industrialised countries are not only homes of global manufacturing productions, but they also become increasingly homes of consumption too.

The world urbanisation since 1900 seems to be rising hand in hand with economic growth and global trade. Generally speaking, urbanisation will lead to productivity gains, cost savings and output improvements by transferring people from agriculture in rural areas to industry and services in cities.

Although urbanisation is often associated with social-economic challenges and may not necessarily lead to improvement of quality of life, by living and working in cities people are more specialised and meet a much bigger part of their need through trade, which can either be domestic or international. It was observed in the 1970s that a country could hardly reach income levels of US$10 thousand per capita before about 60% of its people were urban.[23] Using the United Nations data on urbanisation rates and IMF data on GDP per capita for 170 countries, we found that the two variables are positively correlated up to almost 70% as shown in Figure 3.8.[24] Some samples fall outside the norm, sometimes by large margins, because there are countries with a relatively high urbanisation rate but still not reaching a high level of income.

Recent experiences in Asia, Africa and Latin America have demonstrated that successful industrialisation and development of the manufacturing sector are among the key factors and conditions to make sure that urbanisation and economic growth happen together. Such a phenomenon is best illustrated with the evolution of the Chinese urbanisation process since its economic reforms from the end of the 1970s and the income level growth during this period. As shown in Figure 3.9, as the level of urbanisation increased, say from 20% to 40%, the income per capita grew at a more or less similar pace, which might reflect the effect of people moving from lower productivity rural activities to higher productivity activities of the industrial and service sectors in cities. Then, in later phases, the productivity improvement accelerates, which resulted in a more rapid increase in income levels. Other fast-growing emerging economies have followed a similar path, though some countries may see the take-off in their income level happening at a different, usually higher, urbanisation rate.

In spite of disparities between countries, a general positive correlation exists between the level of urbanisation and economic growth and the subsequent development of international trade, especially when people come to cities in search of better-paid jobs and a higher living standard. As shown in Figure 3.10, two regions, Asia and Africa, were below the world average urbanisation rate in 2015.[25] Europe's urbanisation rate varies between countries. In 2015 the average urbanisation rate was 69% in Eastern Europe and 70% in Southern Europe, but 79% in Western Europe and 81% in Northern Europe. The differences in urbanisation reflect the differences in the economic development levels

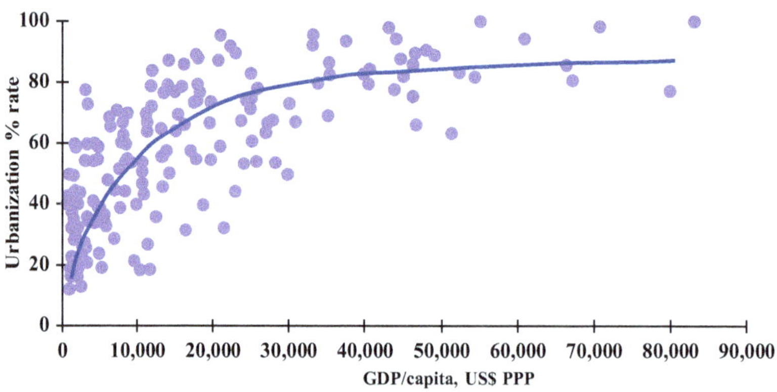

Figure 3.8 Relationship between urbanisation rate and GDP per capita in PPP$, 2015.

Source: Shuo Ma, based on data of UN and IMF 2015.

Note: a total of 170 countries are included in the data set. The GDP per capita numbers are based on US dollars in purchasing power parity. The R^2 is 0.693.

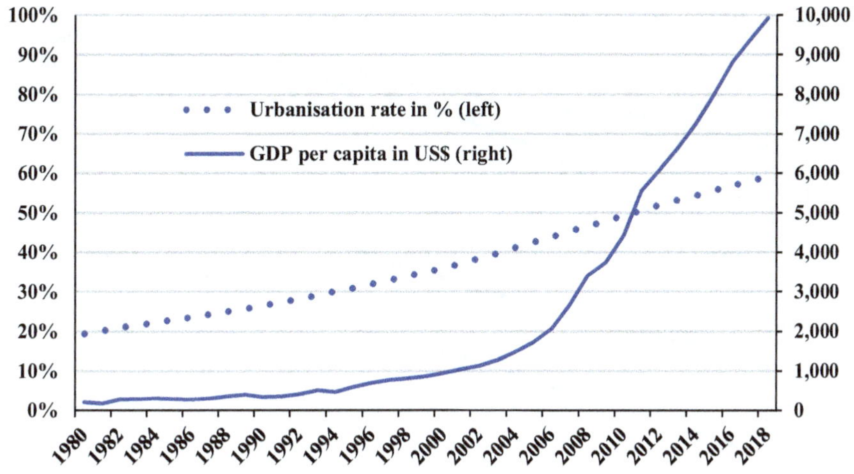

Figure 3.9 Relationship between urbanisation and GDP per capita in China, 1980–2018.

Source: The World Bank, United Nations.

Note: the Chinese urbanisation rate is affected by a large number of migrants who keep their homes in the countryside but live and work in coastal cities.

within Europe. It is Asia that has caught up very quickly since 1995. All industrialised Asian economies have high rates of urbanisation. For instance, in 2015, the urbanisation rate was 94% for Japan, 83% for South Korea and 75% for Malaysia. It is interesting to note that, as in Europe, the urbanisation rates of these Asian countries also correspond closely to their individual levels of income growth. If what happened in these countries is a guide to predict future income growth, Asia and Africa will be the sources for more potential development. In 2015 the urbanisation rate was only 33% in Vietnam and India, with GDP per capita in both countries also at a similar level of about US$2,000. There are, therefore, strong reasons to expect the income level to rise in these and other similar countries. As purchasing power grows, trade will increase.

What are the impacts of globalised consumption on maritime demand?

We have discussed above the issues of urbanisation and concluded that the current fast process of urbanisation in the developing world will lead to an increase in income level in these countries, which in turn will drive international trade to a higher level. Of course, simply moving from the countryside to a city may not necessarily mean more international trade, particularly at the early stage of migration. However, when the "new blood" of the city population has been absorbed by the industry and service sectors, productivity will rise and income will increase. With time, people's purchase power will increase to the extent that they become more affluent as middle-class consumers. Their consumption needs will change, according to *Engel's Law*, and people will spend more on goods and services beyond their non-basic needs. Many of such goods and services (e.g., music, film, education, tourism) are more internationally tradable and more easily satisfied by non-domestic firms. It is the size of such a middle class that is important for maritime transport demand.

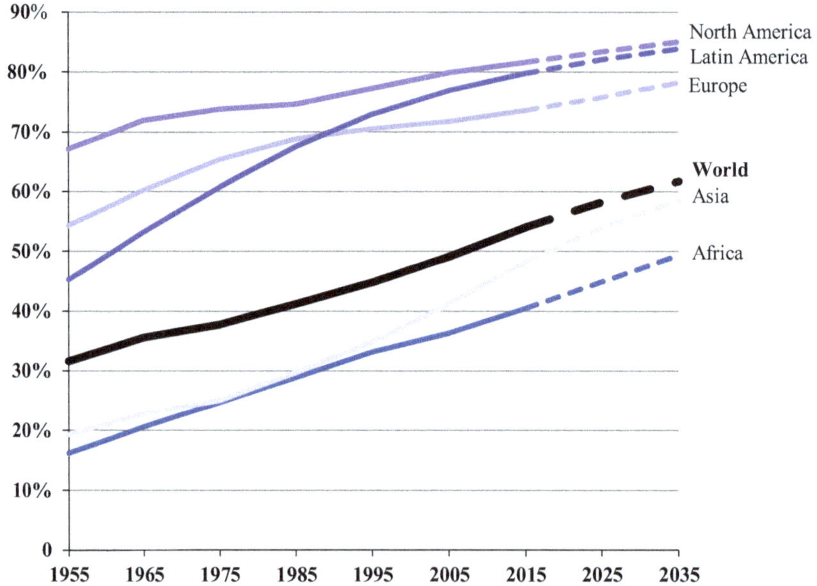

Figure 3.10 Urbanisation rate (%) by region, 1955–2015, projection to 2035.
Source: based on data from the *UN World Urbanisation Perspective* (2018).
Note: within each region, big differences exist between countries. In Asia, for example, in 2015 Japan has 94% while Sri Lanka has 18%; Northern Europe has 81%, while Southern Europe has 70%.

There is no straightforward way of defining the term "middle class" that can be more or less accepted and used universally. The term is so broad and sometimes expands to cover political and social dimensions. Even when focussing on the economic aspect to measure the impact of the middle class on consumption, different methods and benchmarks are used. When defining the middle class, the international institutions such as the World Bank, Asian Development Bank and African Development Bank use a range of personal income between US$2–US$20 per day, or with a further breakdown into categories, such as "lower middle" (US$2–4/day), "mid middle" (US$4–10/day), "upper middle" (US$10–20/day) and "affluent" (>US$20/day).[26] Concentrating on more effective purchasing power, an OECD study put the bar higher to define the middle class as those households with an income of US$10–100 per person per day.[27] Figure 3.11 shows the size of the global middle-class population based on such an income range and the distribution of the middle-class population by region. Accordingly, the size of the middle class was 1.8 billion people in 2009. The majority of them, or 64%, lived in Europe, North America and Japan. The number is expected to increase to 3.2 billion in 2020, which will be about 40% of the global population, and most of the additional middle class will be from the emerging economies of Asia, particularly China. By 2030, the global middle class will be 4.9 billion people. India's middle class will overtake China's to be the biggest in the world. About two-thirds of the global middle class will be living in Asia.

The projections shown in Figure 3.11 are based on an optimistic view and the understanding that what has happened in China and India during the recent decades in terms of poverty alleviation, economic growth and living standard improvement will continue in the future. However, it is evident that although the share of the global middle class for North America will drop to 7% and that for

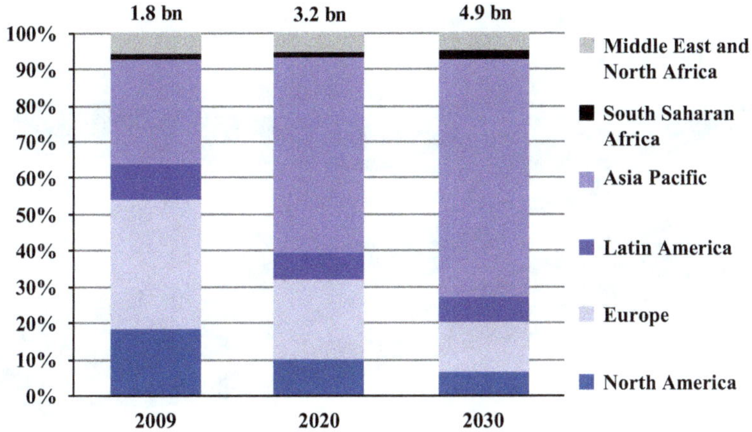

Figure 3.11 Size and distribution of middle class (billion people, percentage).

Source: based on data from OECD (2010).

Note: the absolute number of the middle class in North America remains constant, but the numbers for Europe will decline due to population decrease in Eastern Europe.

Europe to 14% by 2030, the purchasing power will still be much more than these percentages suggest. There is a considerable difference between the high middle class, mostly in OECD countries, and the low middle class in emerging economies. Already in the definition of the middle class used in the figures there is a difference as big as ten times between US$10 and US$100 per person per day. The fact is that the majority of the middle class in the emerging economies are those with a daily income just above the threshold of US$10, while a much bigger proportion of people in the OECD countries are in a higher range of income than those in the emerging economies, and many of them will earn, in effect, more than US$100 per day.

So, in addition to the size and distribution of the middle class in the future, we have to know about the spending patterns and levels of the middle-class population. It is expected that the spending of the middle class of a country reflects to a large extent its level of GDP per capita. And the increase in spending comes together with an increase in the level of GDP per capita. Since GDP per capita increases at a much faster pace in many emerging economies than in the OECD countries, the future trade demand will come more from the developing world. Given the huge size of the population and very fast economic growth in terms of GDP per capita, India and China will be the main contributors to the future global middle-class consumption. Other emerging economies in Asia as well as in other parts of the world will also see the middle class continue to grow. For example, it is estimated that by 2020 the number of households with disposable incomes of over US$50,000 per year will reach 7.1 million in Mexico and 9.4 million in Brazil, doubling the number in 2013 in both cases.[28] When it comes to the future spending of the middle class, India and China will dominate. Figure 3.12 shows the distribution by major countries and regions of the world's middle-class consumption measured in 2005 US dollars based on purchasing power parity between the year 2000 to the current day and with a long-term projection to the year 2050.[29] The OECD countries will no longer be the biggest consumption markets as they still are today. By 2020, Asian consumption will count for about 40% of the global total, by 2030 the percentage will be 56% and by 2050 Asia's share will be 69%. Such a situation, should it indeed happen, will alter the general layout of maritime transport demand completely. When

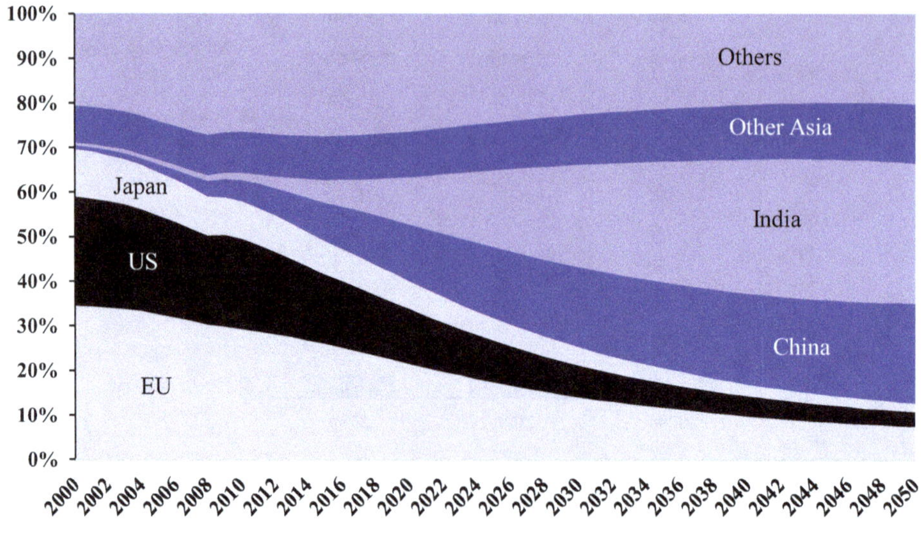

Figure 3.12 Share of global middle class consumption, 2000–2050 (2005 PPP$).

Source: Shuo Ma, based on OECD (2010), Brookings (2011).

Note: this is based on the assumption that both China and India continue to grow and India overtakes China to be the world's most populous nation.

considering the impact of the long-term changes in middle-class consumption, many factors are to be considered. The structure of trade will also be different and most of the consumption, particularly in large countries such as India and China, will be locally supplied rather than imported.

As the new middle class grows and upgrades in income level, their consumption behaviour will change in two aspects, which will have some impact on maritime transport demand. First, there is what some economists have called a "growth sweet spot", which means a threshold of rapid consumer growth and a wakening up of certain purchasing habits that are of interest to international trade and business in general. It was argued that the time when a country hits its sweet-spot is when the per capita income reaches US$6,000. Although the sweet-spot is different for different countries, it was revealed that the sweet-spot for the automobile market is between US$5,000 and US$12,000 per capita, with a peak at about US$8,500.[30] China's GDP per capita was about US$5,000 in 2009 when about 13 million cars were sold, overtaking the USA to become the world's biggest market for private vehicles. In 2018 some 25 million cars were sold in China and this may signify the closeness to the peak because the per-capita income of that year was close to US$10,000.

The second aspect is what we discussed in the first chapter, which is the consumer preference for diversification. As more and more people enter into the group of the middle class, their consumption structure changes. Their desire for manufactured goods will increase and, as the income level rises, they will also develop a preference for diversification. All this will mean more international trade. There will be more future increase coming from the countries of a similar development stage, including what is referred to as "South–South" trade. The share of "South–South" trade out of the total world trade rose from 8% in 1990 to about 27% in 2013, matching the trade between developed countries. The so-called "North–North" trade saw its share slide from 56% in 1990 to some 30% in 2018.[31] Figure 3.13 shows the structural changes in China's export by destination. Between 2004 and 2018, the biggest market for

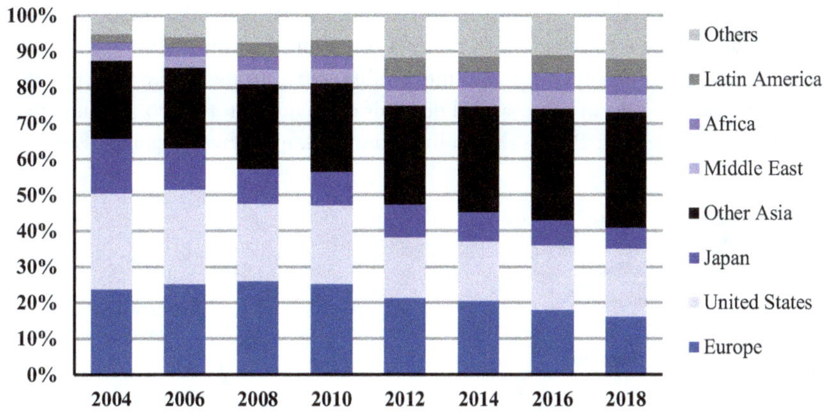

Figure 3.13 China's export by destination, 2004–2018 (in US$ percentage).

Source: Shuo Ma, based on data of WTO (2015) and other sources.

Note: most of China's merchandise exports are manufactured goods, which include both final consumer goods and intermediate products.

the Chinese export shifted from the North, i.e., Europe, Japan and North America, to the South, i.e., the rest of the world. If the economic growth in the South continues, pushing more people to the higher middle-class income ranges, the balance of trade market will tip more to the emerging economies.

3.4 Changes in maritime transport demand for manufactured goods

Not only has the international trade of manufactured goods grown faster than energy, mining and agriculture products, the types of goods and therefore the way they are moved between countries have also undergone many changes. The development of a global supply (value) chain of production and the start of the income convergence process between countries with the rise of the emerging economies has made maritime transport – the link between the countries – more important and critical than ever. So it is necessary that the changes and the responses are understood.

What are the new features of maritime demand for manufactured goods?

In view of the global supply chain or globalised manufacturing process, the single biggest change is the move from "product"-based to "process"-based international division of labour. In other words, this is the transformation from the trade of product to the trade of tasks. International trade happens when a country specialises by not producing everything it needs. In the era of the global supply chain, a country specialises by not producing one entire thing alone. Such new maritime transport demand has a number of distinct features.

One of the most significant new features of the global supply chain is the high level of concentration of production. Different stages of production which used to be integrated, such as design, development, manufacturing, sales and distribution, etc., are now separate from the manufacturing.

The activities can be carried out in different places and, increasingly, across national borders based on comparative advantage for each stage of production. From the point of view of a product value chain, each stage contributes a different amount of value-added to the final product in the hands of consumers. The exact amount of value-added depends on many factors, such as competition, standardisation, scale economies, etc. But, as shown in Figure 3.14, manufacturing and assembling usually

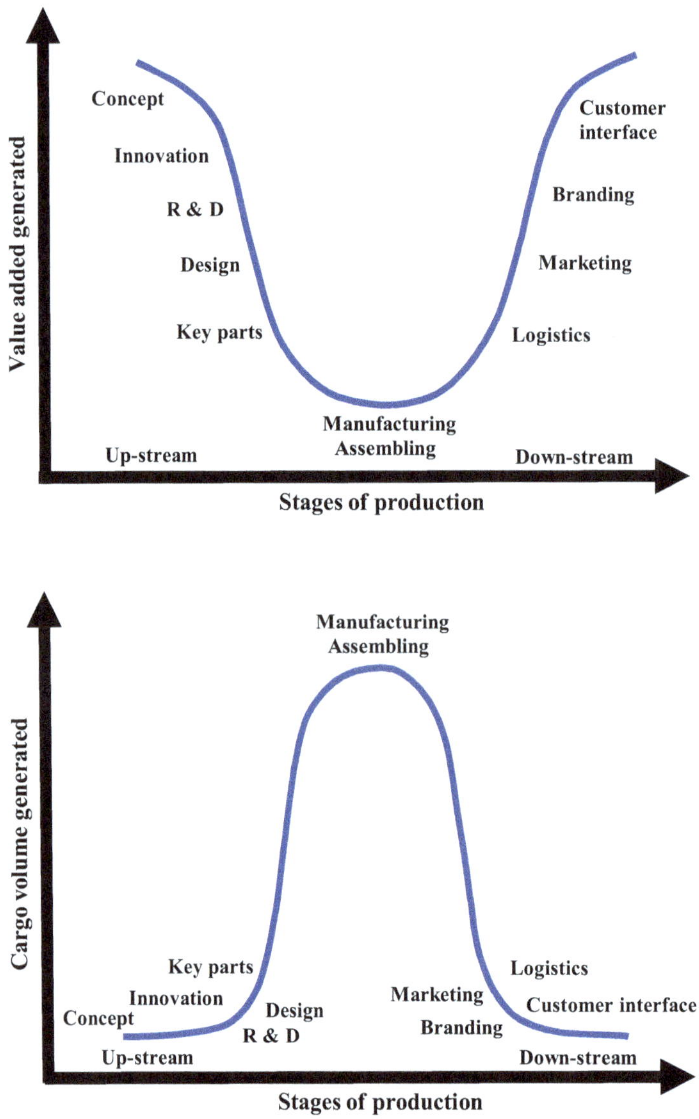

Figure 3.14 Value added and cargo volume generated by production stages along the supply chain.

Source: Shuo Ma (2015).

Note: affected by many factors, manufacturing stage generates a small portion of value added but has the biggest concentration of cargo volume.

have the lowest level of value-added. It was revealed that by assembling earlier generation iPhones, China contributes merely about US$7 to the total value.[32] However, such insignificant value-added does not reflect the real value of the process of maritime transport. It is quite to the contrary. Manufacturing and assembling are more important to shipping than other production stages. What is more is that one of the consequences of the task-based division of labour between countries is the bigger concentration of production and, therefore, of cargo. This is because the comparative advantages of the production factors, such as labour or land, are explored to a greater extent. For example, shoes as a whole are not necessarily labour-intensive, but the manufacturing of them is, while the design or marketing of them is not. When design and manufacturing are tied together, the same products are made in different countries, often due to the customer's preference for diversification. This will lead to a lower level of production concentration. But when manufacturing can be separated, such activity will go to the most attractive location. Such a concentration will further reduce production cost thanks to the effects of sectorial cluster and economies of scale, as the lower chart of Figure 3.14 shows.

The second important feature regarding location is about the relocation of the manufacturing activities from one country to another or the moves of production centres. Relocation of production usually happens when the comparative advantages between countries evolve, resulting in changes in the most attractive location. When manufacturing is globalised, it becomes more "footloose" than before. This is best observed in Asia, where manufacturing centres moved from more advanced countries, such as Japan, to less advanced ones, such as Korea, and then to Malaysia and Thailand, then to China, and then to Vietnam and Indonesia. Land and labour costs are certainly very important, but they are not the only factors leading to the final relocation. China is labelled as the "factory of the world", simply because the size of the country is so big that it absorbed a very large portion of the global manufacturing sector, not only for the international markets but also for the domestic consumers. A similar pattern existed before in Korea or Taiwan. The only difference is that China is about 20 times bigger. China will by no means remain as the "factory of the world" forever. It will pass on that role to other countries when its labour force becomes scarce and pricy. Such a process has already begun.

Another essential feature of maritime demand in the era of global manufacturing is the growing risks and sensitivity to the supply chain performance. When manufacturing was a purely national business, cross-border transactions would only happen either before production, for example to import raw materials, or after it, to export finished products. But when intermediate products need to be traded and transported between countries, the reliability of the supply chain becomes very critical and the system is more vulnerable. Risks rise with the stronger possibilities of trade flow disruptions caused by political, social, technical and natural uncertainties.

Manufacturing and services are becoming increasingly integrated and the share of service inputs in manufacturing output varies between stages of production. But the general trend is that the service content in the manufacturing value chain is increasing.[33] A thriving global value chain relies more and more on the effective and efficient coordination, communication, logistics and transport services. Production-related factors, such as labour and land, alone are no longer enough to determine where the production will take place.

How does the new manufacturing model affect maritime transport?

When ships are transporting intermediates, instead of finished products or raw materials, there will be some new characteristics of the transport demand. The main and real change comes from the fact that maritime transport is no longer either before or after the production process, *it is now in it*. As part of the production, maritime transport contributes directly to the outcome in terms of quality and price of the production.

- ***Importance of service reliability.*** With manufacturing activities more fragmented, the linkage is not just between neighbouring factories, but between faraway countries separated by oceans. Yet the dependence of production on reliable transport is the same whether the distance is short or long. On the one hand, because maritime transport is not only cost-effective but also more reliable than before, it has been an enabler for manufacturing processes to be globalised. On the other hand, long transport distances and the more complex operational environment of maritime transport increases risks of different kinds. As the globalised production is exposed to more uncertainties associated with maritime transport than before, when only local transport was necessary, customers will favour those shipping companies that can provide more reliable service, e.g., with more ships, more flexibility to cope with demand changes and better capability of solving problems in case of emergency, etc.
- ***Cargo imbalance.*** As illustrated by Figure 3.14, globalised production leads to a bigger concentration of goods. Although in value terms a two-way trade may well be in balance, in volume terms it is often not. The situation of imbalance is particularly serious when it comes to container transport between the Far East and other regions outside Asia. For example, China needs to export tens of millions of shirts loaded in thousands of maritime containers in exchange for a Boeing aircraft which can not be transported by a ship. In addition to the value/volume differences of trade and the various modes of transport to use, there is also the effect of what we just discussed above, which is the different stages of production that each country specialises in. The American company Apple generates most export dollars from each iPhone sold abroad by concentrating just on the most upstream and downstream stages such as R&D, design or branding and customer interface. Consequently, globalised production creates a huge imbalance of cargo flows in the system. Take the main East–West container cargo flows as an example, as shown in Figure 3.15, where typically

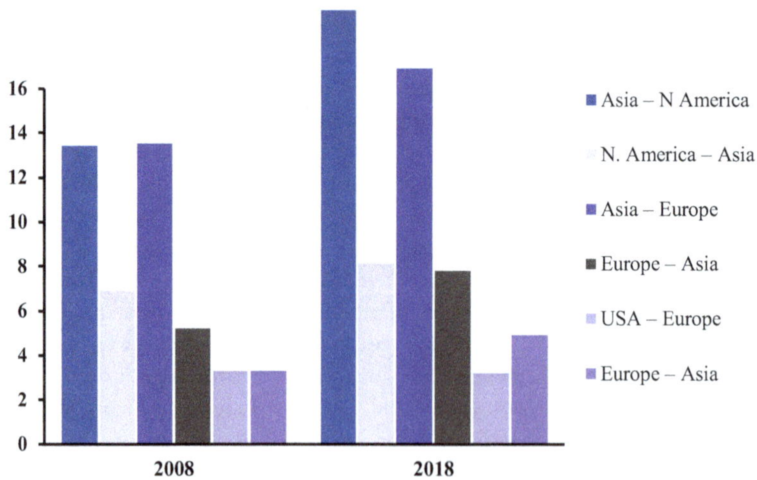

Figure 3.15 Container cargo volumes on East–West trade routes (million teus, 2008 and 2018).

Source: Shuo Ma, based on data from UNCTAD.

Note: the situation of cargo flow imbalance exists on other trade routes as well, with, in virtually all cases, Asia being an exporter rather than an importer.

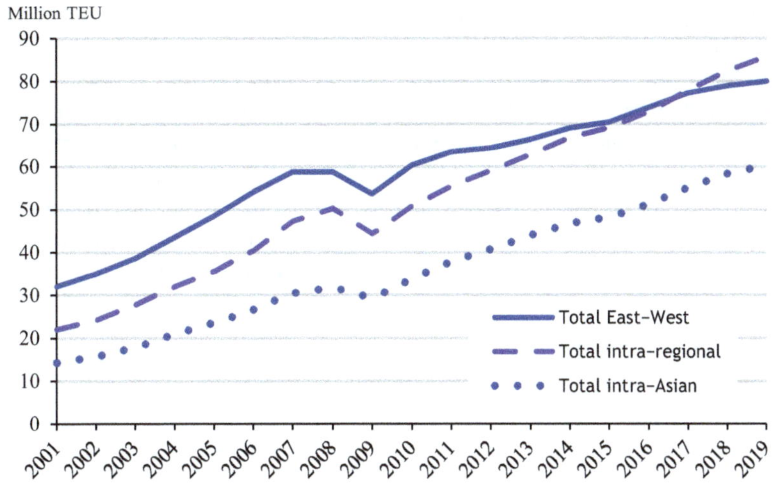

Figure 3.16 Container trade: East–West vs. intra-regional markets 2001–2019, million teu.

Source: Shuo Ma, based on data from Clarksons.

Note: the East–West container trade (transpacific, transatlantic and Asia–Europe) was overtaken by intra-regional trade in 2017. In 2001 the intra-Asian trade was 44% of the East–West trade and in 2018 it was 75%.

Asia exports twice as many containerised goods to Europe and North America as it imports from them. Such a serious traffic imbalance has been persistent and, as long as the pattern of globalised production continues, the situation will not change. One of the major consequences is the high volume of empty containers on the shipping routes, where there is a cargo deficit. It is a big challenge to the shipping industry that increases the operational costs.

- ***Rise of intra-regional trade***. We explained that most manufactured goods are traded between rich countries with similar per capita income levels, driven primarily by customer preference for diversification and also by globalised production. The high-income countries with similar income levels in Europe or North America are close to each other. So, as we discussed earlier, a big portion of the trade of manufactured goods is intra-regional trade, such as intra-European and intra-North-American trade. By the same logic, when low-income countries are more developed and the per-capita income becomes high enough, the demand for manufactured goods and imports will grow. So, driven by both the global supply chain and the growing middle-class consumption in the newly industrialised countries, regional trade has been flourishing, particularly in Asia. As shown in Figure 3.16, in 2017 the total intra-regional trade was bigger than the Transpacific, Transatlantic and Asia–European markets combined or the East–West container trade. In 2014 more than 54% of Asia's trade was within the region. Given the special geographical conditions, most of the intra-Asian trade is carried by ships. Consequently, intra-Asian trade is the largest market of containerised freight in the world. In 2018 the ten biggest container ports in the world were all in Asia.[34]
- ***Logistics and supply chain***. The higher the level of globalised production and integration, the more dependent the system is on the connection, transport, logistics and supply chain. At the same time, the international supply chain has become increasingly longer and more complex. Such

dependence implies two issues: on the one hand, there is an increase of transport and logistics out of the total time and cost of the production. On the other hand, there is a higher risk due to various uncertainties associated with the prolonged supply chain. The sources of uncertainties may be administrative, political, social, technical or operational. The performance and reliability of supply chain and logistics services are becoming more and more decisive factors for the success of the globalised production system and, therefore, for the successful participation of a country to join the system. Numerous examples have shown that comparative advantages in traditional production factors such as land and labour are often not sufficient for a country to be internationally competitive if excellent logistics and supply chain infrastructure are not in place.[35]

What is the role of shipping in the expansion of trade in manufactures?

Globalised production has only been possible thanks to the efficiency of the "connections" between the different stages of production often separated by oceans and seas. High transport costs can severely undermine the competitiveness of the manufacturing industry, especially for the products that have relatively low unit value. Similarly, better logistics and supply chain services will help bring the cost of manufactures down in the international markets. There is proof of a strong correlation between transport connectivity and economic outcomes in terms, for example, of participation in the global value chain measured by trade in manufactured components.[36]

The *ad valorem* maritime freight cost for international trade, as described earlier, is about 5%. Given the competitive nature of the international market for manufactures, the shipping cost plays an important role in the competitiveness of a country's trade. The freight elasticity of trade demand in manufactured products measures the magnitude of this role. It is the impact of maritime transport cost on trade. Assuming that the quality aspects of maritime transport, such as transit time, customer service, safety, reliability, frequency of services, etc., are all expressed in terms of cost, there is a negative freight elasticity of demand in trade, which means the lower the freight cost, the more the trade. There has been a lot of research work carried out in this area. The OECD concluded that an increase in maritime transport costs of 10% will be associated with a 6–8% decrease in trade.[37] A similar conclusion was given by Behar that every percentage reduction of transport distance would lead to 0.9% increase in trade and freight costs account for two-thirds of the effect of distance, while the remaining third was related to time delays.[38] In a World Bank study of more than 140 countries throughout the world, it revealed that every percentage reduction of shipping cost would boost 1.4% of additional trade in value terms.[39]

In the process of becoming the "factory of the world", China turned itself from an insignificant export in the 1990s to the world's largest exporter with 12.4% of the global export of merchandise.[40] Much of this achievement is attributable to the development of its maritime transport sector. In the World Bank's Global Logistics Performance Indicators of 160 countries, China ranked number 28 for general logistics performance, number 23 for logistics infrastructure, such as ports, and number 22 for international shipments.[41] It is estimated that had Chinese port and maritime transport services remained at the same level as 1978, the country's foreign trade would be about 25% less than the actual amount of 2007. Subsequently, the national GDP in 2007 would have been about 0.68% lower than the actual level,[42] which is a very significant impact coming from one sector on a large economy.

3.5 Summary

This chapter deals with maritime demand for manufactured goods. This market segment is not as big as that of raw materials and natural resources in terms of volume, but it represents more than half of global seaborne trade in value terms. Over the last many decades, international trade in manufactures has grown at a faster speed than that in natural resources. China is the biggest exporter of manufactured goods, although the EU as a whole exports more, despite the fact the about two thirds of the trade is intra-EU, thus primarily transported by land-based modes of transport. Different from Europe and North America, Asia is the most important market of seaborne trade in manufactures, given its fast-growing manufacturing capability and consumption power, as well as the specific geographical conditions.

One of the main reasons for the rapid growth of trade in manufactures is the development of the "global value chain", which means that the production of manufactures is divided into stages and carried out separately in different countries. Better and cheaper transportation and communication are the enablers of this new pattern of production, transnational companies helped by foreign direct investment are the executors and cost-cutting through exploring advantages of specific factors and the effect of scale economies is the main driving force. As a consequence, the trade of intermediate goods is bigger than that of finished consumer goods or capital goods. For maritime transport, the globalised production system brings more business, but also more challenges, such as trade imbalance.

Another reason for more trade of manufactured goods is the emergence of new consumption centres in emerging economies due to the urbanisation process and the growing middle-class population. This development happened in Latin America and Eastern Europe and Asia. The newly industrialised Asian countries have become not only a global base of the production and consumption of manufactured goods. It is expected that in the future, the role of Asia will increase further, as the region will be the home of the world's largest middle-class population. As a result of both the global value chain and the rise of new consumption centres, trade between the newly industrialised countries has increased fast.

Most of the manufactured goods are transported by containers. Containerisation, which will be further discussed in more detail in later chapters, leads to very large ships being deployed. This has been the situation in the shipping industry when the volume of trade grows at a fast pace thanks to the development of the global value chain and the expansion of the middle class in many emerging economies. Consequently, loading centres shift as the global value chain extends to new countries and intra-regional trade, in Europe, America and particularly Asia, has registered a more dynamic growth than inter-regional trade. Other remarkable results are the concentration of cargo and persistent imbalance of trade. With the production process extending over several countries, the reliability of maritime transport becomes a critical factor. While the globalised production has an important impact on the shipping industry, it is equally true the other way round that maritime transport has become a decisive element for the effective participation of a country in the global value chain.

Notes

1 UNIDO (2014).
2 WTO (2015).
3 UNCTAD (2018).
4 Clarksons (Shipping Intelligence Network, 2018).
5 WTO (2018).
6 WTO (2018).
7 In 2018 the market share of maritime transport, or short sea shipping, in intra-EU freight transport was 33%. Source: European Commission, Eurostat (http://ec.europa.eu/eurostat/statistics-explained/index.php/Freight_transport_statistics_-_modal_split).
8 According to WTO, in 2014 50.2% of the trade of NAFTA members (the USA, Canada and Mexico) is within NAFTA. In the same year, about 63% of the EU's trade is intra-EU and 25% of ASEAN's trade is within ASEAN. For details see "WTO, International Trade Statistics, 2015", table A3.

9 In 1820 world trade was only about 1% of the world GDP. Today, some countries have a trade to GDP ratio as high as 60% or even higher. See: *World Bank Development Report*, 2009.
10 In 2014 about 65% of merchandise trade was manufactures. Most intermediate goods are manufactures, so the 30% of all merchandise trade represents a higher percentage in manufactured goods. See WTO (2014) *World Trade Report*, WTO, Geneva, p. 43.
11 According to the UN trade statistics, intermediate goods include many categories such as food, industrial supplies and parts and accessories (see http://unstats.un.org/unsd/tradekb/Knowledgebase/Intermediate-Goods-in-Trade-Statistics).
12 IMF (2015).
13 WTO (2014), p. 82.
14 UNIDO (2015), p. 176.
15 WTO (2014), p. 58.
16 WTO (2015), p. 24.
17 The share of South America and Africa in the USA's export did not change much during this period, which shows the effect of the global supply chain. Source: WTO International Trade Statistical Review, 2015, WTO.
18 Export similarity is measured as *S(a,b)=sum[min(Xia, Xib]* where *S* is the export similarity index of countries *a* and *b*, *Xia* is the share of product *i* in the export of country *a* and *Xib* is the share of product *i* in the export of country *b*. *S* is zero when there is an absence of similarity and 1 for identical export composition. For more details see: Finger J. and Kreinin M. (1979) *The Economic Journal*, Vol. 89 No. 356 pp. 905–912.
19 Similar increases of export similarity between other emerging economies and advanced economies have also been observed during the last couple of decades. For details see: IMF (2012) *Changing Patterns of Global Trade*, January 2012, p. 27.
20 According to the China Association of Automobile Manufacturers (www.caam.org.cn), in 2015 a total of 24,503,300 vehicles were produced and 24,597,600 vehicles were sold in China. Out of this total, 21,079,400 and 21,146,300 passenger cars were produced and sold. The rest are commercial vehicles. In 2014 a total of 90,717,246 vehicles, of which 72,068,994 were passenger cars, were produced in the world.
21 According to the UN, by 2050 the world's most populous country will be India with about 1.75 billion people, Nigeria will be the third most populous nation with 413 million people and the biggest increase of the world population, from 7.3 billion in 2015 to 9.3 billion in 2050, will be in Africa. Source: United Nations, Department of Economic and Social Affairs, Population Division (2015). *World Population Prospects: The 2015 Revision*, ESA/P/WP.241.
22 UN (2018).
23 Lewis A. (1977).
24 Clarke Annez P. and Buckley R. (2009).
25 UN (2014).
26 Asian Development Bank (2010).
27 OECD (2010).
28 Ernst and Young/Oxford Economics (2014).
29 Brookings (2011).
30 Ernst and Young (2013), p. 6.
31 In the South-South trade, the share of consumer goods has been growing, although the lion's share is in intermediates and primary products. Countries from East Asia take the largest part in the South-South trade. Source: WTO (2019) "International trade statistics, 2019" and UNCTAD (2019) "Key statistics and trends in international trade, 2018". UNCTAD/DITC/TAB/2014/2, pp. 12–15.
32 Asian Development Bank (2011).
33 McKinsey (2012), pp. 38–45.
34 Lloyd's List (2018).

35 World Bank (2016).
36 World Bank (2015a), p. 6.
37 OECD (2009).
38 Behar A. and Venables A. (2010).
39 World Bank (2005).
40 WTO (2015).
41 World Bank (2015b), p. 34.
42 Ma S. (2009), pp. 82–86.

References

Asian Development Bank. (2010) "*Key Indicators for Asia and the Pacific, 2010*", Special Report on the Rise of Asia's Middle Class. ADB, 2010, Manila, the Philippines.

Asian Development Bank. (2011) "*How the IPhone Widens the United States Trade Deficit with the People's Republic of China*". ADBI Working Paper No. 257, 2011.

Behar, A. and Venables A. (2010) "*Transport Costs and International Trade*", University of Oxford Department of Economics Discussion Paper Series No. 488, June 2010. P.

Brookings. (2011) "*The Emerging Middle Class in Developing Countries*", by Kharas Homi, Brookings Institute.

Clarke Annez, P. and Buckley R. (2009) "*Urbanization and Growth: Setting the Context*", in "Urbanization and Growth" edited by Michael Spence, Patricia Clarke Annez, and Robert M. Buckley, The World Bank, Washington, DC.

Clarksons. (2018) "*Shipping Intelligence Network*".

Ernst and Yong/Oxford Economics. (2014) "Rapid-Growth Markets Forecast", July 2014.

Ernst and Young. (2013) "*Hitting the Sweep Spot, The Growth of the Middle Class in Emerging Markets*", p. 6.

Finger, J. and Kreinin M. (1979) "A Measure of "Export Similarity' and Its Possible Uses", *The Economic Journal*, Vol. 89, No. 356, pp. 905–912.

IMF. (2012) "*Changing Patterns of Global Trade*", January 2012, p. 27.

IMF. (2015) "*Reaping the Benefits from Global Value Chains*", Working paper WP/15/204.

Lewis, A., (1977) "*The Evolution of the International Economic Order*", Princeton University Working Paper 74, Research Program in Development Studies. March 1977, Princeton University, Princeton, NJ.

Lloyd's List. (2018) "*Top 100 Ports 2018*", Retrieved 10 July 2019 from https://lloydslist.maritimeintelligence.informa.com/one-hundred-container-ports-2018.

Ma, S. (2009) "*The Impact of Shipping and Ports on China's 30-year Rapid Economic Expansion*", (in Chinese), published on China Navigation, March 2009, Shanghai, China, pp. 82–86.

McKinsey. (2012) "*Manufacturing the Future: The Next Era of Global Growth and Innovation*", McKinsey Global Institute, Washington, DC, November 2012, pp. 38–45.

OECD. (2009) "*Maritime Transport Costs and Their Impact on Trade*", OECD Working paper TAD/TC/WP (2009), p. 7.

OECD. (2010) "*The Emerging Middle Class in Developing Countries*", OECD Development Centre, by Kharas H. (2010) Working Paper 285, DEV/DOC(2010)2, January 2010. OECD, Paris.

UN. (2014) "*World Urbanization Prospects*", UN, ST/ESA/SER.A/352.

UN. (2015) "*World Population Prospects: The 2015 Revision*", United Nations, Department of Economic and Social Affairs, Population Division (2015). ESA/P/WP.241.

UN. (2018) "*2018 Revision of World Urbanization Prospects*", UN, ST/ESA/SER.A/352.

UNCTAD. (2018) "*Review of Maritime Transport*", UNCTAD/RMT/2014, United Nations, New York, pp. 4–20.

UNCTAD. (2019) "*Key Statistics and Trends in International Trade, 2018*". UNCTAD/DITC/TAB/2014/2. pp. 12–15.

UNIDO. (2014) "*The Future of Manufacturing: Driving Capabilities, Enabling Investment*", UNIDO, Vienna, Austria.

UNIDO. (2015) "*Industrial Development Report, 2016*", UNIDO/ID/447, UNIDO, p. 176

World Bank. (2005) "*Global Logistics Indicators, Supply Chain Metrics and Bilateral Trade Patterns*". World Bank Policy Research Working Paper No.3773, Washington, DC: 2005-11.

World Bank. (2009) "*World Development Report*", World Bank.

World Bank. (2015a) "*Connecting to Compete: World Bank Logistics Performance Indicators*", 2014, The World Bank, Washington, DC, p. 34.

World Bank. (2015b) "*Connecting to Compete: World Bank Logistics Performance Indicators*", 2014, The World Bank, Washington, DC, p. 6.

World Bank. (2016) "*Connecting to Compete: World Bank Logistics Performance Indicators*", 2015, The World Bank.

WTO. (2014) "*World Trade Report, 2013 Factors Shaping the Future of World Trade*", pp. 43, 58, 82.

WTO. (2015) "*International Trade Statistical Review, 2015*", World Trade Organization, table A3.

WTO. (2018) "*International Trade Statistics, 2018*", World Trade Organization, Geneva, Switzerland.

WTO. (2019) "*International Trade Statistics, 2019*", World Trade Organization 2019.

Chapter 4

The future of seaborne trade and its economic importance

In the last two chapters we have discussed the maritime transport demand for natural resources and manufactured goods, the two broad segments of seaborne trade. We have examined the evolution and development of these trades and their specific characteristics. It is important that we should also look at the future of seaborne trade, by examining the past development of trade in general and seaborne trade in particular, to have a better idea of the factors that have been essential for the development of seaborne trade until today and those that might shape the trade of the future. In this chapter we will look at three aspects of maritime transport demand. First, we will examine the main influential factors for the future of global seaborne trade. Second, we will discuss in more detail one of the influential factors, which is the shipping cost for the development of seaborne trade. Finally, we will evaluate a new concept, which is maritime dependency factor, to analyse seaborne trade with regard to its impact and importance for national economies.

4.1 The evolution of and recent changes in maritime trade

The ancient "Silk Road" linking China with Central/West Asia and Europe was evidence of the early form of international trade. Yet such an "animal convoy" type of link means also the limited size of trade and exclusivity of its beneficiaries. In 2015 international merchandise trade was 58.4% of the world GDP. Today, throughout the world, foreign-made products are among the daily consumption of ordinary households. The process which has made the world economy as it is today is still going on. The international trade has integrated more and more countries together to an ever-deeper degree. Such a process, therefore, will also determine the long-term perspective of the maritime transport demand in the future.

How much is the world economy globalised?

People from different countries trade more now than they did in the past. A comparison between the foreign trade of a country and its production or GDP is a commonly used measurement of how much an economy is exposed to international trade. In other words, it measures the level of economic globalisation because the ratio reflects the level of reliance of a country's economy on other countries. In other words, it measures a country's integration with the rest of the world. Such a reliance increases if the country's foreign trade grows faster than its production does and vice versa. It is the same for the world as a whole, which means that if the global trade growth outpaces global production growth, the economic globalisation deepens. From 1950 to 2018 the world's merchandise exports grew at an average rate of 5.5% per annum, while the world merchandise production grew on average at 3.4% per annum. In Figure 4.1 we see that, during a period of almost 70 years, the two average growth rates have produced a vast difference in the total amount of value. While world production is ten times as big, global trade expanded more than 38 times. For comparison, we include the index of seaborne trade growth for the same period in Figure 4.1. Seaborne trade has also registered a faster growth rate than world production, though not as fast as that of export. During the same period, seaborne trade measured in tons of cargo loaded grew from about 500 million tons in 1950 to more than 11 billion tons in 2018.[1] This represents an increase of almost 20 fold and at an average annual growth rate of about 4.7%.

There are a number of reasons why seaborne trade in volume has not increased as fast as merchandise trade in value. The most important reason is what we explained in Chapters 2 and 3 – that international trade increase during the last more than half a century has mostly been in manufactured products with high unit value. Furthermore, a large portion of the value of manufactured goods is based on intra-regional trade in Europe and North America and is therefore carried mostly by other modes of transport than shipping. Maritime transport, being cheap but slow, attracts mainly low-value cargo with large volume and over long distances. In the 1980s, for example, the average annual growth

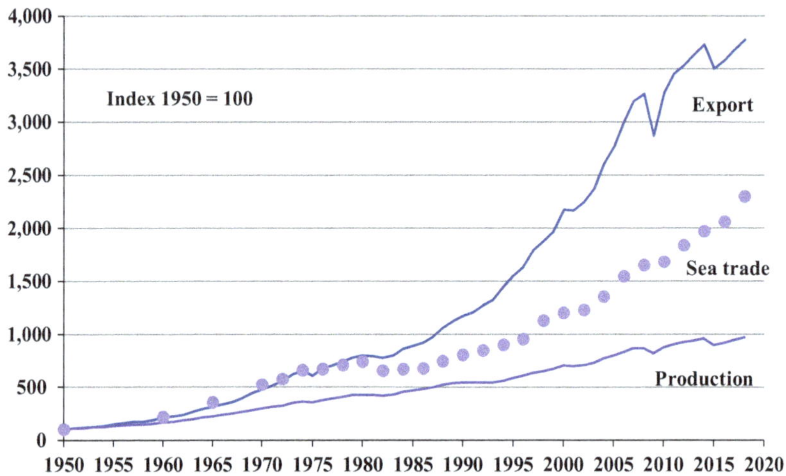

Figure 4.1 World merchandise export, seaborne trade and production growth 1950–2018 (Index, 1950=100).

Source: Shuo Ma based on data from WTO and UNCTAD.

Note: the indices represent merchandise export and GDP production, both in value terms, of agriculture, fuel and mining, and manufacturing sectors in the world. Seaborne trade is not measured in value but in tons of cargo loaded. The average growth rate is 5.5% per year for merchandise export, 4.7% for seaborne trade and 3.4% per year for production.

rate of seaborne trade was merely 1.1%, because of the decline of oil transport and relatively slower growth of trade in other natural resources. From the year 2000 the trade in natural resources and raw materials increased rapidly. It was mainly driven by the new demand of iron ore, coal, oil and other raw materials from the emerging economies, in particular China.

As a result of the faster growth of international trade compared with that of production, the foreign elements, either in the form of imports or exports, gain importance in many national economies. Usually, small economies are more dependent on foreign trade than large economies. Some small economies, such as Singapore, the UAE or the Netherlands, are like international trade hubs, in which the amount of trade crossing their borders can be bigger than their GDP. In fact, during the last half a century, virtually all countries have experienced such economic globalisation. For example, the ratio of merchandise trade as percent of GDP between 1960 and 2018 grew from 6.8% to 23% for the USA, from 30% to 68% for Europe, from 9% to 42% for China, from 9.6% to 38% for India, from 19% to 33% for Japan and from 9.6% to 78% for South Korea. Globally, the ratio of world merchandise trade to GDP was only about 11% in 1950 but by 2018 it became about 50%.[2] Figure 4.2 shows this development between 1950 and 2018.

It is essential to be aware of the differences between the numbers of international trade and that of GDP. Although both may be in the same currency unit, one is based on cross-border transaction values while the other is based on value-added. So one should be cautious when comparing trade with GDP. Trade numbers can be easily inflated in the global value chain, when the trade of intermediate goods is common and for trade hubs where re-export is the main activity. The same product can be counted several times when it, as intermediate goods, crosses borders from one stage of production to the next. This is the reason why some countries can have foreign trade bigger than GDP. The World Trade Organization and OECD calculate and publish trade statistics based on value-added rather than transaction values as one of the efforts to improve the accuracy of trade statistics. The trade to GDP ratio is an indicator of the exposure of an economy to its international trade. It is nonetheless safe to say that the world economy is more globalised and countries are more interrelated and interdependent

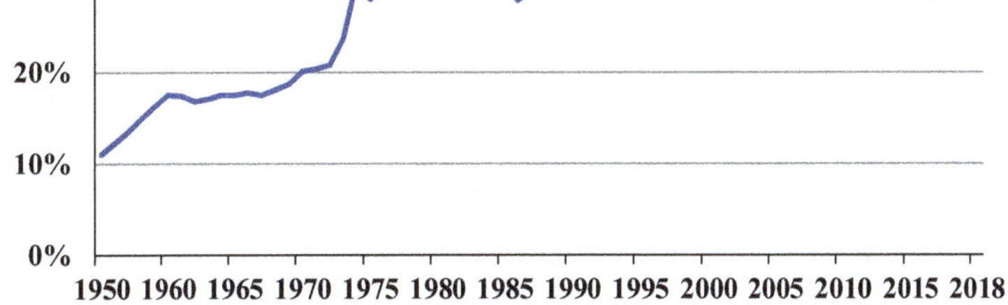

Figure 4.2 Share of world merchandise trade in world GDP, 1950–2018.

Source: Shuo Ma, based on data from OECD and the World Bank.

Note: GDP and trade are in current US$, so are affected by exchange rate and commodity price fluctuations. While trade numbers do not include services, GDP numbers do.

with each other than ever before. To a considerable extent, maritime transport has benefitted from the economic globalisation and, at the same time, it has also enormously contributed and been playing a central and decisive role to make the economic globalisation possible. We will discuss this subject in more detail later in the chapter.

What were the driving forces for international trade to grow faster than world GDP?

As we have mentioned in the previous chapters regarding why countries trade with each other, there are mainly three reasons for international trade to increase faster than the global GDP, which are:

1 The participation of more countries in global production and consumption markets through trade, or expansion of modern industrialisation and consumption to new and less developed countries;
2 The continuous reduction of tariff or non-tariff-related trade barriers;
3 The improvement of transport, particularly maritime transport, both in terms of cheaper prices and better quality.

Will these factors continue to develop in the same direction so as to drive trade and maritime transport demand to a higher level in the coming decades? There is not a straight answer. It is always difficult to make such predictions with so many variable factors and a lot of uncertainties. Yet, in shipping, many decisions are long term by nature. For example, when a decision has to be made on building a ship with regard to the type, the size, the time of order, etc., some sorts of forecast have to be made because the ship will have a life span of some 25 years. The same goes for many similar situations in shipping, such as whether a port expansion project should go ahead or whether a logistics centre is to be built.

We should not look for a precise prediction of market demand or supply; our objective is to have a general idea about the future trends, about the grand direction of the market development and about the potentials of the future growth. By "future", we refer to a very long-term perspective of 30 to 50 years. Obviously a discussion of such a long trend would be more meaningful if it is based on the critical influential factors rather than on the concrete traffic levels. Let's take a closer look at how more maritime transport demand is created by the participation of more countries in the global production and consumption markets. We first need to have a brief historical review of the world production and consumption market.

In 1840 the world seaborne trade was believed to be merely 20 million tons,[3] in 1950 the number was about 500 million tons and in 2018 it was more than 11,000 million tons. Seaborne trade development over the past two hundred years also mirrors perfectly the great economic evolution of mankind. According to Maddison,[4] the average income per capita was not very different between countries around the world. As shown in Figure 4.3, whether people lived in Africa or Europe, America or Asia, they had a similar per-capita income level at about US$400–500 per year. This is because the way of living and of production was more or less the same. This situation, however, started to change in the 18th century when the Industrial Revolution began in the UK. As the industrialisation progressed, it triggered a tremendous increase in productivity. Subsequently, the Industrial Revolution expanded from the UK to Europe, North America and later Japan. The income level in these countries continued to rise at a fast speed. It was the turning point in history that transformed the world economy completely and the world was no longer the same. For about two centuries since then, the amount of wealth created in this part of the world was much bigger than what had been accumulated for thousands of years before.[5] As a result, the "great divergence" happened and the world was divided into two parts: the industrialised West and the rest.[6, 7] Figure 4.3 shows the income level measured in US dollars per capita of some major economies. It can be observed that the divergence of income between countries began more noticeably in the wake of the Industrial Revolution in the 18th century.

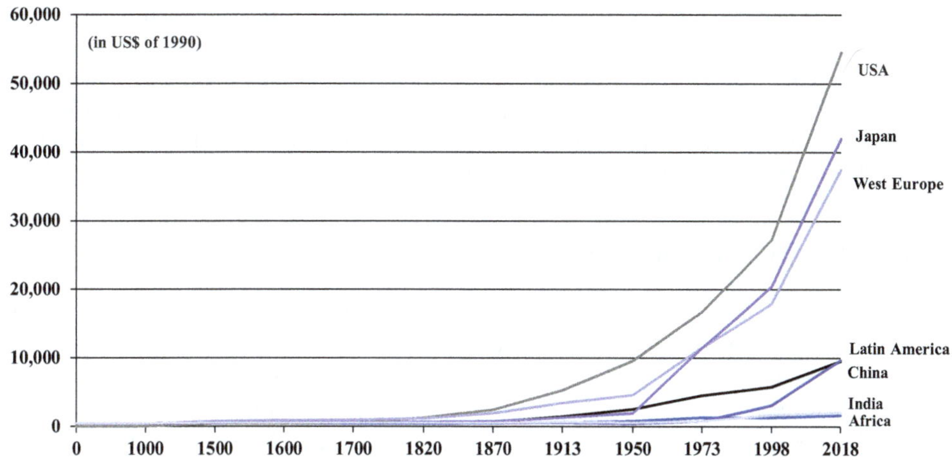

Figure 4.3 "The big divergence": income per capita of selected countries and regions (in 1990 US$).

Source: compiled based on Maddison (2006) and IMF (2016).

Note: there wasn't much difference of income level between countries until the 18th century, when industrialisation began in the West. The curves reflect the per-capita income evolution of selected countries and regions of each period, but not the actual trends, as samples are taken with different intervals. Countries and regions with low income bases like Africa, India or China have a much faster growth rate during the recent decades than those with high income levels like Japan, Europe or even the US.

The main reason for us to discuss such a long-term historical development of the world economy is that trade, including seaborne trade, only happens when some essential conditions are in place. For example, trade will flourish when productivity is high enough so that people produce more than their own need and trade the surplus with others. Trade will expand when people are rich enough to consume foreign goods produced in faraway places. Trade will grow when transport technology is advanced enough so that products can be traded at low cost, in significant quantity and over long distances between countries. Without industrialisation, none of these conditions would exist. So in the 18th and 19th centuries the Industrial Revolution did create these favourable conditions for Europe, North America and Japan and therefore the international trade of those countries boomed. For example, between 1870 and 1950, the income per capita of the US increased 3.8 times, while its foreign trade increased 25 times. For Western Europe during this period, the income level increased by about 58%, while its trade increased 6.8 times.[8] With regard to manufactured goods, the majority of trade has been between the industrialised nations. As regards basic commodities, the trade pattern is one-way traffic from non-industrialised countries to industrialised countries.

The history shows that the industrialised countries will prosper and become rich and those non-industrialised countries will stay where they had been, with much slower economic progress. The Industrial Revolution started in the UK, spread quickly to the rest of the Western world, while most of the other countries remained unindustrialised and were therefore weak and poor. One may argue that the industrialisation spread successfully to the entire West but not the rest of the world because of the cultural closeness between the Western countries. However, Japan's rise disapproved this theory. While other Asian countries remained agricultural with stagnating low income per person, Japan embraced industrialisation in the second half of the 19th century and became much richer and more powerful than other Asian countries. Once industrialised, profound changes would happen to the society, such as rises in population, urbanisation, wealth, consumption and trade. So, the conclusion is that industrialisation allows countries to develop fast, become rich and trade more.

Is the Industrial Revolution over?

If the extraordinary growth and development of international trade in the past is attributable to the industrialisation, much of the answer to the question about the growth of trade in the other countries will be whether or not these countries embark on industrialisation as well. The historian Leften Stavrianos argued that "Industrial Revolution" was not an accurate expression. The industrialisation that started in the 18th century was not a sudden short-lived change. It is a process which is still going on today. And it has been making similar and big changes to those countries that start to embrace it. What happened recently in China or India is just the continuation of the same process of industrialisation. It started some 200 years ago in Europe and later spread to North America, Japan, Korea, Brazil and now China and India. In the process, all these countries have experienced similar growth in population, wealth and trade.

The best example of the effect of such an industrialisation process is probably what is called "convergence" or "re-convergence". As the "rest" of the world also industrialises, the gap of income per person, or the divergence between them and the industrialised "west", starts to reduce. Such a phenomenon is already reflected in Figure 4.3; that from the 1950s China, India and Africa began to have a faster economic growth as well as growth in the level of income per person than the rich world. To make the point clearer, we take the ratio of personal income, based on the same data measured in 1990 US dollars, between four pairs of economies: the USA versus China, Europe versus India, the USA versus Latin America and Europe versus Africa. As shown in Figure 4.4, up to 1820, the ratio of personal income between the USA and China, for example, was about 1, which means the two countries had the same level of income per capita. Then the divergence started to happen as the USA was industrialised while China was not. The gap reached the highest level in 1950 with a ratio of 21 to 1, which means that on average an American was 21 times richer than a Chinese. To a lesser extent, the same thing happened between Europe and India. Then, from 1950, personal income increased faster in China than in the USA. Therefore the gap started to reduce. From the late 1970s, the Chinese economy started to accelerate its industrialisation process by economic reform and opening up to the outside world. The country experienced a fast development of foreign trade, investment and industrial expansion. As a result, China entered into a period of rapid economic catching up with annual GDP growth at close to 10% for over 30 years. At the same time, the income per capita level soared. The GDP per capita ratio, in purchasing power parity, between the USA and China reduced to about 4 in 2016. As for India, which started the economic reforms in the 1990s but also had spectacular economic growth, it has reduced its personal income gap with Europe from 14 times in 1973 to about 5 times in 2016. The African personal income level was about one-thirteenth of Europe's in 1998 and the ratio was reduced to one-tenth in 2016. The Latin Americans have had, by and large, the same growth rate as the North Americans, so the ratio between them has remained somewhat constant.

Will the process of "convergence" continue in the future? Most scholars and many international institutions seem to think so. There are, however, people with more pessimistic views about the future convergence who point out that the rapid improvement of personal income level in some resource-exporting-dependent countries is not sustainable.[9] The experience shows that one of the critical issues is whether the catching-up countries or the "rest" of the world can successfully integrate

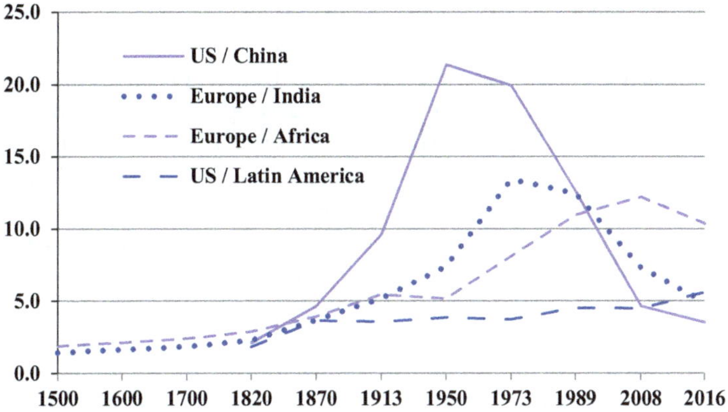

Figure 4.4 Ratio of GDP per capita of selected economies 1500–2016.

Source: Shuo Ma, based on data from OECD (2009) and Madisson Project.

Note: data selected are for the year indicated, so the curve does not represent the GDP per capita levels of the years in between. Different intervals are used for each period. The GDP per capita numbers between 1500 and 1998 are in 1990 US dollars and those for 2016 are in current US dollars based on purchasing power parity.

themselves into the global industrial production, consumption and trade. Should the large emerging economies, such as China and India, with between them about 35% of the world's population, continue to develop, the impact on the world economy and the global shipping market would be significant and profound.

4.2 The future of maritime transport demand

In Chapter 2 we discussed the correlation between GDP per capita and seaborne trade. By examining the situation of the world's major economies in 2018, as well as the historical statistics of Japan and China during the period of industrialisation, we found that in every case there was a very high correlation between the level of GDP per capita and that of seaborne trade. The statistics of the WTO on trade as well as those of the UN on seaborne trade have all shown that the increase of merchandise trade and maritime traffic have been driven by those fast-growing emerging economies.[10] As long as the catching-up or re-convergence process of the developing countries, including the large economies such as China and India, continue, which is likely, the international seaborne trade will continue to grow in the future.

How big will the maritime transport demand be in the future?

There are several projections about the future merchandise trade and maritime transport demand, some of them more optimistic than others, but all have favourable views of the future. The WTO estimates that the elasticity of the world trade growth to the global GDP growth is in the region of 1.5.[11] From 1950 to 2018 world merchandise trade grew on average at more than 5% per year.[12] It is, however, unrealistic to assume that the recent past trends will continue by applying simple extrapolations about the future size of maritime transport demand. The growth rate of both the economy and foreign trade in China, which had been one of the main drivers of the global trade increase, started a decelerating phase from 2013. After a long period of fast development, a slowdown is inevitable. Macroeconomic models are often used by the IMF, the World Bank, OECD and others to make long-term projections, with assumptions on growth determinants such as labour force, capital, natural resources and technological progress. In view of numerous uncertainties, a scenario approach is generally used for long-term forecasts. Having examined all the influential factors, the WTO made a world export estimate for 2035 in two scenarios, optimistic and pessimistic. Based on a projected world GDP growth between 2.1% and 4.11% per year on average, world inter-regional merchandise export by the year 2035 would be between pessimistic US$13,163 billion and optimistic US$46,094 billion.

Figure 4.5 shows the steady increase of the world's seaborne trade per capita from less than 0.4 tons per person in 1960 to 1.6 tons per person in 2018, as represented by the grey bars in the figure. What is the main reason for this growth? The economic globalisation is the direct drive. The root cause is people's rising wealth. To the right of the figure is the global average GDP per capita in US dollars, which is represented by the black curve. The two developments are closely correlated. We may, therefore, conclude that the future of the seaborne trade demand depends not only on the growth of the world's population but also on the growth of GDP per capita of all countries. In an early discussion, in Chapter 2, on the correlation between seaborne imports per capita and the GDP per capita of a country, we concluded in Figure 2.2 that as the GDP per capita of the emerging economies increases, their seaborne trade will also increase. As these countries reduce the gap with the industrialised countries in personal income level, the gap in seaborne trade per person will narrow down in the same fashion. As of 2017, annual seaborne imports per person varied between 0.3 and 0.5 tons for

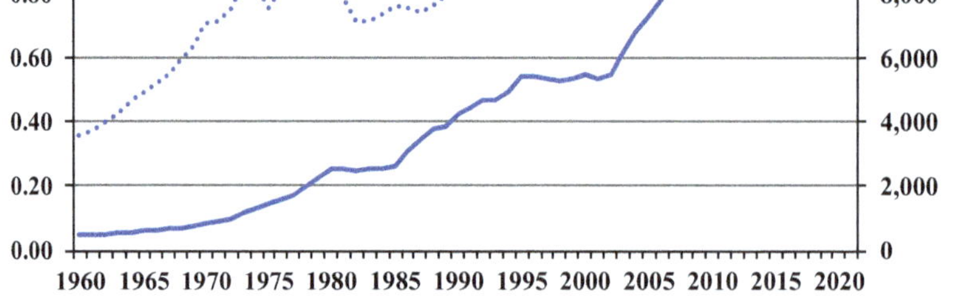

Figure 4.5 Rising seaborne trade per capita and correlation with GDP per capita growth.

Source: Shuo Ma, based on data of Clarksons Shipping Intelligence and the World Bank.

Note: this figure is about the world's average seaborne trade per capita and average GDP per capita from 1960 to 2018. So the future of the world seaborne trade depends on both the global demographic growth and the world economic development.

India and Africa, 1.3 tons for South-East Asia to 2.5 tons for North America, 4.9 tons for Europe and 6.5 tons for Japan. There is a solid reason to believe that the potential economic catching up in the poorer countries will be the driving force for more seaborne trade. If the majority of the global population could double their seaborne import level from the current about 1 ton to 2 tons per person, there would be more than 6 billion tons of new seaborne trade to carry.

For almost 70 years since 1950, the world seaborne trade has experienced a significant period of expansion. The global maritime traffic rose from about 500 million tons in 1950 to almost 12,000 million tons in 2019.[13] This represents an average annual growth of 4.7%, as shown in Figure 4.6. During this long period of about 70 years, the growth has not been consistent. There are two "golden" periods during which seaborne trade grew very fast. The first was between 1950 and 1970 when the maritime trade increased more than fivefold from 500 to 2,605 million tons. This means an average annual growth rate of 8.6%. The main reason for such fast growth is the industrial expansion or the re-building of Europe and Japan after World War Two. In the 1970s and 1980s the massive construction was over. The pace of infrastructure building and industrial production slowed down and, at the same time, there were two oil shocks. As a result, seaborne trade experienced a period of slow growth. Between 1970 and 2000 the world seaborne trade grew at an average annual rate of only 2.2%. The second period of maritime "boom" was between 2000 and today or, more precisely, between 2002 and 2008, which was probably the best time in the history of modern shipping. Although the period was short, the new demand came suddenly and in a very strong and persistent way. China was the main driver of this shipping boom. After the opening up of the Chinese economy to the outside world in the late 1970s, it took about 20 years before the country was ready with clear economic development directions and sufficient resources to enter into a fast track of construction and infrastructure building, unleashing a force never seen before on the world shipping market. China's joining WTO in 2001 was another boost for the development of the country's manufacturing sector.

Currently there are signs suggesting that the good time is over. During the period 2015–2016 the lowest record of the dry bulk freight market was registered. History shows that international shipping is a cyclical market with periodical ups and downs. The critical question remains as to where the maritime transport demand will be in the future. Market forecasts have had a poor record, whether it is about the overall economic and trade growth or the development of maritime transport demand. Few people had foretold the forthcoming up-rising freight market in the second part of 2002 and there are countless failed predictions for market recovery since its collapse in 2008. Research on the performance of more than 82 thousand political and economic forecasts made by hundreds of professional experts over 20 years shows very disappointing results.[14] However, as we explained earlier, many decisions in shipping are, by nature, of the long term. Regardless of its reliability, a forecast has to be made. When a decision on, for example, new ship investment is taken, a forecast has been made. Having more relevant, accurate and up-to-date information, using both quantitative and qualitative approaches and trying to build a system which can respond to multiple-scenario outcomes, is probably the most appropriate way to deal with the future market.

It is common and appropriate that a three-scenario model is used to foretell the future of maritime demand. Some recent forecasts for the maritime market in the future suggest the expected annual growth rate would be between 1 and 4%.[15] Despite many optimistic views of the future demand, a decelerated globalisation process and the rise of protectionism remains to be the possibilities ahead. There are many uncertainties about whether most developing countries could successfully catch up with rich countries through industrialisation. Also, the ever-increasing environmental pressure may mean a major change in the structure of world energy consumption and a decline in the demand for oil and coal. In view of the political, economic and environmental uncertainties ahead, it is wise to adopt a more conservative approach in the estimates. We take the world seaborne trade of about 11 billion tons of cargo in 2018 as a base and suggest three scenarios for the maritime demand in 2050: with an average annual growth rate at 1%, 2% and 3%, as shown in Figure 4.6. Respectively, the future

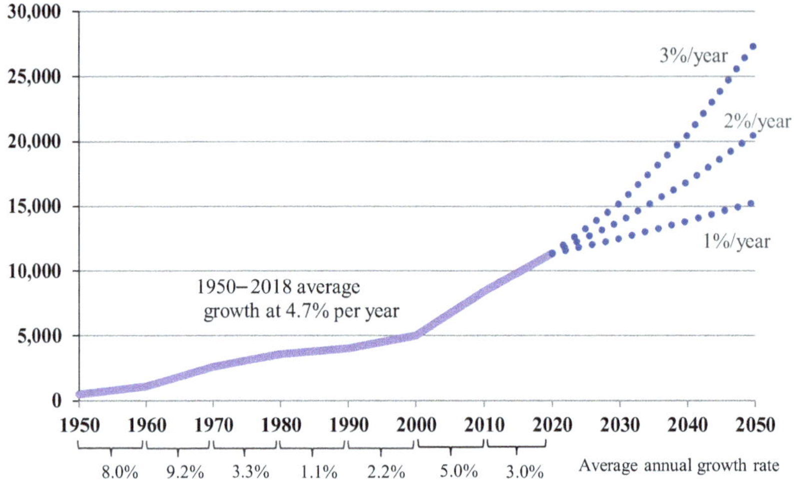

Figure 4.6 World seaborne trade 1950–2018 and projections to 2050 (million tons).

Source: Shuo Ma, based on data from UNCTAD. Note: as China contributed to the latest traffic boom since 2000, so new driving forces are needed to trigger the next boost for a more optimistic market. India remains a big hope and South and South-East Asia as well as Africa are also promising.

maritime trade in 2050 will be about 15 billion tons, 20 billion tons and 27 billion tons. The proportion of manufactured goods in the total global trade will remain by and large at the same level of about two-thirds as it is today. So, if the middle range of 2% annual growth is taken as an example, by 2040, or in nearly 20 years or within the usual life span of a new ship, the global seaborne trade could be 50% bigger than it was in 2018.

Is there a limit to the maritime demand?

This question may also be asked in another way as "what is the maximum amount of material a person will consume in a year?" There is not a straightforward answer to the question. But, as a rule, the higher the income level the bigger the proportion of spending will be on services. From Figure 2.3 in Chapter 2 we can see that the Japanese seaborne imports reached the highest level when the GDP per capita was at about US$36,000 around the year 2000. Higher GDP per head later did not lead to additional maritime imports. A similar situation can also be observed in Europe and North America. At a high personal income level, comparable with that of Japan, the international seaborne trade of Europe between 2000 and 2014 remained virtually unchanged and that of North America had only marginal increases.[16] The general cargo volume may have increased, but the import of raw materials declined. There is a clear limit to or a slowdown of growth of maritime demand for all countries.

There is, on the other hand, another aspect which is that the less-developed countries will reduce the gap with the rich countries by importing and exporting more. So the limit to the global seaborne trade might be the standard set by today's industrialised countries. Based on Figure 2.2, in 2017 the

EU, with about 500 million people, imported about 4.9 tons of cargo per person by ships, Japan, with 130 million people, imported 6.5 tons per person and North America, with 400 million people, imported 2.4 tons per person. If these numbers are taken as the upper limits, then we can have an idea about the maximum seaborne trade in the future. For the future maritime demand, let's make three assumptions about the global population, the global convergence of GDP per capita and the global average seaborne import cargo per person. With declining fertility, the UN's medium scenario forecast of the world population for 2100 is 11.2 billion.[17] Let's take this number for the world population and let's assume that the GDP per capita level could by and large be successfully converged globally by 2100. Adding to these assumptions, if we take a high level of personal income then, on average, 3 tons of seaborne cargo would be imported worldwide. This suggests that the maximum amount of seaborne trade would be in the region of 33.6 billion tons per year.

Based on the above medium scenario estimate, the outcome represents only a relatively high possibility of occurrence. Apart from the global population and economic catching-up-related uncertainties, the future maritime demand will be heavily affected by new environmental standards, particularly those for fossil fuels. In 2018 about 30% of world seaborne trade was of oil and coal. Japan, for example, imported by sea about 180 million tons of crude oil and a similar amount of coal in 2018.[18] With a population of 126 million, this represents 2.8 tons of fossil fuel per person. In other words, more than half of Japanese seaborne imports are fossil fuels. If crude oil and coal are excluded, Japan's seaborne imports would only be about 2.3 tons of cargo per person per year. So a reduction of trade in fossil fuels will undoubtedly have a big impact on future maritime demand.

4.3 The shrinking shipping cost and the effect on maritime demand

In Chapter 1 we generally discussed the role of maritime transport cost in trade, both from the perspective of freight as a percentage of trade value as well as of continuous decline of freight cost in absolute terms. During recent years, as shown in Figure 1.7, the ratio of global maritime freight to the value of world imports is about 5%. The freight of general cargo transport by containers, as shown in Figure 1.8, has been by and large constant in current US dollar terms. But when measured in constant US dollars, the freight has undergone a continuous decline. In real terms, the freight in 2018 is only about 10% of that in 1968. The maritime demand is influenced by freight in both *ad valorem* and absolute terms. But there are many variations and important situations hidden behind the global ratio of 5%. A simple comparison of freight evolution does not reveal the real value of transport derived by trade. We will, therefore, discuss this in more detail in this section.

What is the trend of freight as a percentage of the value of cargo?

In the very long term, the cost of transport has been in decline thanks to the technological improvement and massive productivity enhancement of the shipping industry. Not to compare with the era of sailing ships, the freight of transporting a container in the 1960s was much higher in constant currency than it was in 2018, as shown in Chapter 1. However, in the short term, and even in the medium term, the situation is more complex and the freight may be volatile. There are two ways to measure the maritime freight cost to trade: by freight per ton in constant currency or by freight in *ad valorem* equivalent in current currency. For example, between 1996 and 2006, as shown in Figures 4.7 and 4.8, the first shows the effect of specific market conditions on the maritime freight, while the second shows the influence by differences in the value of cargoes on the freight. While recognising the long-term decline of freight, we will examine the factors that affect the shipping freight as a cost to maritime demand.

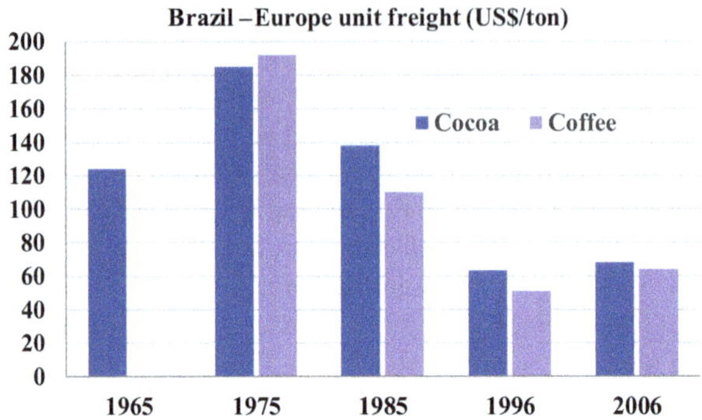

Figure 4.7 Freight by unit for cocoa and coffee, Brazil to Europe, 1965–2006.

Source: compiled based on data from UNCTAD and OECD.

Note: despite the long-term downward trend, in the short and medium terms, both freight per ton and freight *ad valorem* equivalent, in current US$ terms, can fluctuate in response to market conditions.

Maritime transport cost as a percentage of cargo's import value between the same countries varies greatly from one type of goods to another. Figure 4.9 shows such *ad valorem* freight for a selected group of the most traded products from China to the USA between 1991 and 2007. The percentage is about 10 times as high for stone and plaster as for cameras. Most of these goods were transported in containers. Shipping companies usually charge for the transport services based on a fixed rate per container (in 20 or 40 feet equivalent units), regardless of the content of the containers. Therefore, the freight makes up a high percentage of the value of cargo if it is low-value cargo, such as stone, and a low percentage if it is high-value cargo such as cameras. The *ad valorem* freight for iron ore from Brazil to China was about 40% between 1998 and 2007.[19] There are many other factors that have impacts on *ad valorem* freight.

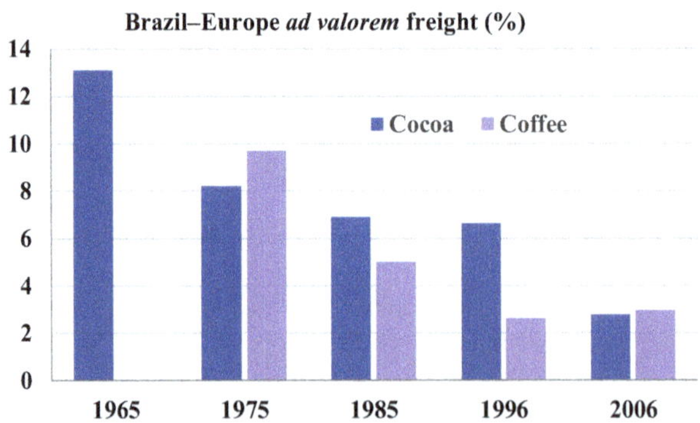

Figure 4.8 Freight by *ad valorem* for cocoa/coffee, Brazil to Europe, 1965–2006.

Source: compiled based on data from UNCTAD and OECD.

Note: the maritime freight ad valorem equivalent for basic commodities in current US$ terms can fluctuate in response to market conditions.

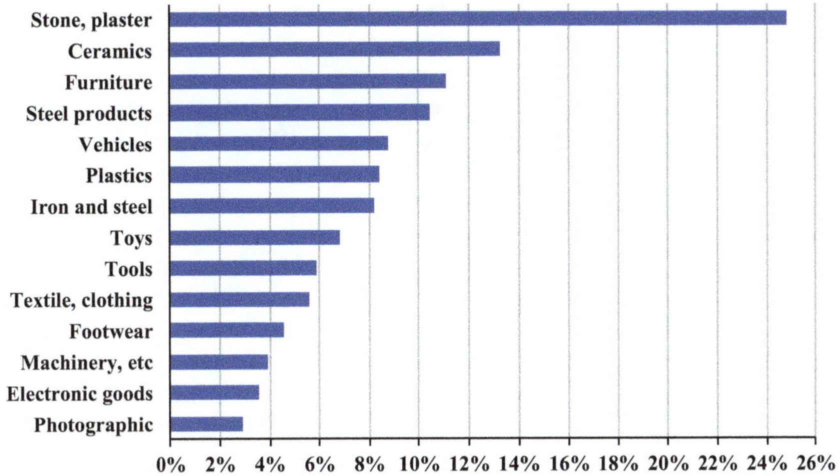

Figure 4.9 *Ad valorem* freight for main import goods from China to USA, 1991–2007 average.

Source: Shuo Ma, based on data from OECD.

Note: apart from steel products and stone/plaster which are transported in bulk, all goods are transported in containers, using FAK flat rate per container.

When using the evolution of freight to test whether or not the maritime transport cost has fallen over time, two very important elements have to be kept in mind. When examining unit cost in terms of freight per ton of cargo carried, the effect of inflation has to be taken into account. Using a currency in constant value is the key to obtaining a more accurate account. For example, the unit transport cost for many goods has been by and large constant in current US dollars since 1990. But this does not mean that there has been no transport cost reduction. On the contrary, with an adjustment of inflation effect, in most cases, sensitive cost reductions are observed. On the other hand, when using *ad valorem* freight, the relative change of the value of goods ought to be taken into account. Throughout the last couple of decades, a price drop often happens for most manufactured goods thanks to the benefits of productivity improvement and the global value chain. As a consequence, when this happens, the *ad valorem* freight will not change or goes up even when the actual freight reduces.

What are the determining factors for the level of *ad valorem* freight?

Apart from the long-term downward trend of shipping costs due to technological development and productivity improvement and, on the other hand, the short-term price fluctuation based on the market situation of demand and supply, the level of *ad valorem* freight is mainly determined by factors which can be divided into three groups. The first is related to the demand, which means the characteristics of cargo. The second is related to the supply, which means the characteristics of shipping services. The third is related to the market. We will explain briefly these factors in this section and some of the important aspects will be further analysed in more detail in the later chapters.

- ***On the demand side.*** There are mainly three aspects in this regard. First, the value of cargoes is a decisive factor. This is because maritime transport freight is by and large based on the volume/weight of the cargo rather than on the value of it. So the freight-to-value ratio is small for high-value cargoes such as electronic goods and other high-value manufactured products. The ratio is big for low-value cargoes, such as minerals and other raw materials transported in bulk. The second aspect is the average transport distance with the main trade partners. For example, the proportion of intra-regional trade is much higher for most Asian countries than for African countries. As a result, often, for the same products, Asian countries benefit from a lower *ad valorem* freight than most African countries. Another example is the import of iron ore to China. During the 10 years from 1998 to 2007 the average *ad valorem* freight for Australian imports was 25%, but for Brazilian imports it was 40%.[20] The third aspect is about the balance of trade. Natural resources such as energy and minerals are usually transported in one direction. So the cost of return journeys in ballast has to be covered by the freight. For general cargo, the chances of having two-way traffic are greater. But, as explained in Chapter 3, many container transport markets do not have balanced traffic. As a result, the freight level is generally lower on the trade lanes with a traffic deficit.

- ***On the supply side.*** There are also three aspects which are analysed as follows. The first is the type of shipping services. Some cargoes, like manufactured products, require more services such as cargo handling, care, delivery speed, etc., while others need less, such as minerals transported in bulk. Obviously, the level of freight will reflect the kind of service provided. The second aspect is about the type and size of ships. A specialised vessel can be more expensive, but also more productive and capable of delivering a better quality of service. Also, bigger ships can be operated with less cost per unit of cargo carried and can offer lower freight. This is the situation in some markets such as the Far East, Europe and North America. The large volume of the so-called North–North trade makes the employment of big ships possible. The third aspect is about port facilities and efficiency. Port activities are considered as an integral part of maritime service. Ports play a vital role in shipping performance, in terms of cost, delivery time as well as safety and security. Physical limitations may prevent big and specialised ships from coming. Sometimes considerable differences exist between ports in terms of the charges and tariffs for services. Inefficient port services may increase the cost of shipping to a very high level. So maritime freight levels are profoundly affected by port facilities and performance.
- ***On the market side.*** There are mainly three aspects in this regard. The first is about the situation of competition, especially on the supply side. With competition, mainly in shipping and port services, freight will be kept at a lower level than without competition. Two economic conditions are necessary for the shipping market to be competitive. The first is that the maritime market is open and free. The second is that the market is big enough for multiple service providers. When such conditions are not met, like in some developing countries, freight is usually pushed high by various sorts of monopoly. The second aspect is about social conditions. They include social stability, labour relations and safety/security issues. Maritime freight can be sensitive to events such as piracy, strike or pilferage. The third aspect is about environmental standards. Oil transport freight to the countries that have adopted regulations on double-bottom tankers or more stringent environmental standards will be higher. For example, the freight may also be affected by fuel cost if ships are trading in "special emission control areas".[21]

What does a simple shipping cost comparison miss?

The growth of trade is attributable to the fall of transport cost in absolute terms and in many cases to the declining proportion of transport cost in the value of traded products. But this tells only part of the truth. This is the reason that some researchers do not think that maritime transport cost is a contributing factor by claiming that, since the early 1970s, maritime transport freight has fallen very little, whilst international trade has expanded rapidly.[22] Some of the researchers examined difference periods to decompose the relative contribution of income rise, tariff, freight, etc., to trade and concluded that the income rise was the main driving force while the role of shipping cost reduction was not significant.[23] However, serious omissions may be responsible for such conclusions. There is clear evidence that maritime transport cost is a major contributing factor to the growth of global trade. To support this argument, three very important factors ought to be discussed, namely, the currency issue, the transport cost to income level ratio and the quality of the transport.

- ***Currency issues.*** Most of the transport cost comparisons, including the maritime transport cost statistics of the OECD or UNCTAD, collect cost data in current US dollar terms, without discounting adjustment for the effect of currency inflation.[24] However, for the period between 1950 and 2018, the average annual inflation rate of US dollars is about 3.5%. So, even if the price does not change from one year to the next, it is already in fact 3.5% cheaper. That is why, when measured in current dollars, as shown in Figure 1.8, the freight of transporting a 40-foot container from the Far East to the US West Coast was on the whole at around US$2,000 between 1968 and 2018. In constant dollars, however, there is a very significant reduction in transport cost over this period. Similarly, the Baltic Dry Index (BDI) is produced based on actual freight of current US dollars. So if the BDI is 1000 points today, which is the same level as in 1985 when the index began, it costs a fraction of freight of that year in 1985 dollars.
- ***Freight to income ratio.*** Even when the freight increased, or the *ad valorem* equivalent is high, such as the 40% *ad valorem* freight for iron ore transported from Brazil to China, the volume of trade may not be discouraged. This is because, if the price of the product remains unchanged, when the ratio of freight to income level decreases, i.e., freight increases more slowly than GDP per capita does, the consumers can afford to buy more transport services. If the income level is very low, no matter how cheap international transport is, people cannot afford to buy foreign-made products. For example, in 2016, to pay for a burger such as a McDonald's Big Mac, based on the minimum wage, a North American or a European or a Japanese person needs to work for less than 30 minutes, but a Brazilian person needs to work for 173 minutes, a Chinese person for 183 minutes and an Indian for 347 minutes.[25] So, if the price of a burger is replaced by the transport freight of an imported product, we will see that, even if freight remains unchanged, it will become relatively cheaper and more affordable so long as personal income level increases. There is the effect of "Engel's Law" on transport costs, which means that if the growth of income continues to outpace that of transport cost, which is highly likely, people will be able to trade more. So, for example, in 1968 the maritime freight of transporting a 40-foot container with electronic products from the Far East to the US West Coast was equivalent to about 30% of the average household annual income of US$6,698 in the US. However, as shown in Figure 4.10, in 2018 the freight was equal to only 3% of the American average household income of US$61,013.
- ***Quality aspects.*** A comparison is only meaningful if it compares like with like. But for a long time, many transport cost comparisons often ignored the quality aspect. So a claim that shipping cost did not contribute to the growth of trade between, say, 1970 and 2010 because the freight did not fall is mostly unjustifiable. The shipping services, particularly in the transport of manufactured goods, have changed so much during this period that they have become almost incomparable between themselves. The major areas of difference are in the quality of services, such as the speed of delivery, service reliability, sailing frequency, market coverage, safety and security standards, logistics and other value-added services. Typically, in the 1970s, a general cargo ship travelled at about 15 nautical miles per hour, while a container ship in the 2000s usually sails at more than 20 nautical miles per hour. A modern container ship can handle the same amount of cargo at a port in a matter of hours that a typical general cargo ship in the 1970s would need weeks to do. It makes little sense to draw conclusions based only on comparisons of the cost when cargo is

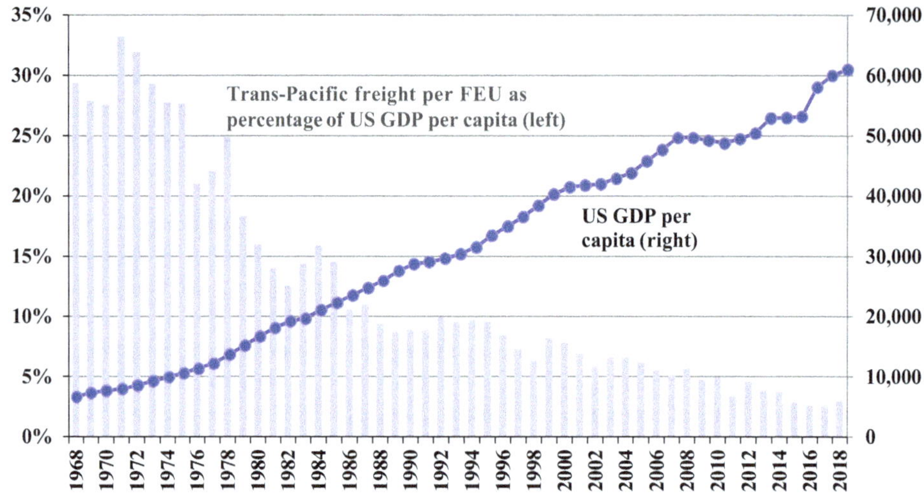

Figure 4.10 Trans-Pacific freight per FEU as percentage of US median household income, 1968–2018.

Source: Shuo Ma, compiled based on data from Lloyd's List, Clarksons and the US Census Bureau.

Note: it is a kind of "Engel Curve" on maritime freight, which means: as income rises, a decreasing portion of it is sufficient to pay for the freight of transporting a 40-foot container (FEU) from the Far East to North America. All data are in current US dollars.

delivered in less than half of the time in one case than in the other. In terms of value for money, international trade has benefitted enormously from better and cheaper shipping services and, for the global value chain, the contribution of maritime transport is mainly in the quality rather than in the cost of the service.

What is the role of distance in maritime transport demand?

For a train ticket or a bus ticket, the basic fare is normally determined by two elements: how many people and how far they want to travel. One of the main differences between trade and the transport of trade is that the former cares about the volume, in physical or monetary terms, while the latter cares about the volume and the distance. So far, our discussions on maritime transport demand have been focussing mainly on international trade. To capture the full picture of maritime transport demand, the aspect of distance has to be considered. To import the same commodity of iron ore to China, the freight is about 40% of the cargo's value if it is from Brazil, but only 25% if it is from Australia. This is because Brazil is far from China while Australia is close. So, for the same amount of cargo, more ship tonnage will be needed for Brazilian imports than for Australian imports. From the experience of travelling by plane, we observe many other effects of travel distance on transport. For example, a larger aircraft is deployed for long routes. Although at a given speed the transit time is proportional to distance, the fare does not have a linear relationship with distance.

If seaborne trade can be measured in volumes such as ton or cubic metre, then for the transport of such trade, ton-mile is the measurement to use. For a country, the seaborne trade is generally the quantity of cargo moved in and out of its ports. To know how much transport is involved, the volume of cargo should be multiplied by the distance. A combination of nautical miles to travel and the tonnage of cargo to carry will tell you how much maritime transport is needed. So, in principle, to transport 10 tons of cargo for 1 mile implies the equivalence of transporting 1 ton of cargo for 10 miles. For example, if the US imports more oil from Venezuela than from Kuwait, given all the other factors such as terminal productivity or ship's speed remain equal, more maritime transport capacity would be needed for the smaller traffic from Kuwait due to the difference in distance.

The fast expansion of international trade, as we have discussed previously, has included not only more countries but countries that are far from their trade partners. As a result, the average distance of trade has increased. This is precisely what has happened over the last couple of decades, particularly since the 1990s. Figure 4.11 shows the seaborne trade changes in both ton and ton-mile between 1970 and 2018. Compared with the situation in 1970, the average distance travelled per ton of seaborne trade increased in 1975. But then, by 1985, it fell back to about the level of 1970. From 1985 it started to increase consistently. In almost 50 years from 1970, the maritime transport of this seaborne trade in ton-miles grew by 6 times, while the global seaborne trade in tons only grew by 4.5 times. The annualised growth rates between 1970 and 2018 were 4% and 3.5% respectively, and between 1995 and 2018 were 5.1% and 4.2% respectively.

The divergence of development in tons and ton-miles of seaborne trade is a reflection of the evolution of the world economy. In the 1970s the Atlantic Ocean was the centre of gravity of the global economy and trade, not only in terms of value with manufactured goods but also for natural resources and commodities. In 1970, for example, about 50% of crude oil imports and 40% of iron ore imports by sea went to Europe, as shown in Figures 2.8 and 2.11. A significant portion of the oil imports came from the Middle East and iron ore came from Brazil. In the 1970s between 40% and 50% of the seaborne trade in coal was imported by Europe and exported by North America. Since then, the global economic and trade centre of gravity started to shift from the Atlantic to the Pacific. The speed of change accelerated from the 1990s with the rise of China, as we have discussed

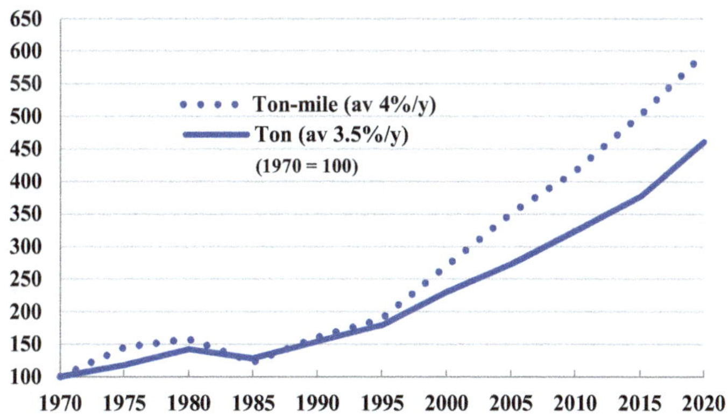

Figure 4.11 Seaborne trade growth index in ton and ton-mile, 1970–2018.

Source: Shuo Ma, based on data from UNCTAD and Clarksons.

Note: the rise of emerging economies and trade moving from the Atlantic to the Pacific are the main reasons for the increased gap between ton and ton-mile since 1995.

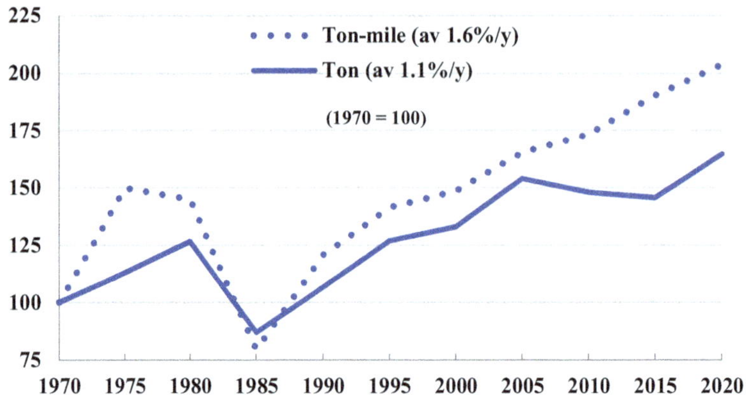

Figure 4.12 Seaborne oil trade growth index in ton and ton-mile, 1970–2018.

Source: Shuo Ma, based on data from UNCTAD and Clarksons.

Note: the enlarging gap since 2005 is mostly attributable to the increasing oil imports from West Africa and Latin America to the Far East.

in Chapter 2. One of the obvious consequences is the prolongation of the average distance of seaborne trade for both commodities and manufactured products. To illustrate this development, let's look at the ton and ton-mile evolution of seaborne trade of oil between 1970 and 2018. We see in Figure 4.12 that the oil trade in ton-miles grew much faster than that in tons from 1970 to 1975. This coincided with the increase in oil import market share of North America and Japan and a decrease of that of Europe. Consequently, the average transport distance increased. The two oil shocks led to a sharp decline in oil imports but there was a bigger drop in ton-miles than in tons. This can be explained by the gain of oil export market share of the production in the North Sea and Latin America, which are closer to the main consumption markets. The growing weight of the new economic powerhouses in Asia resulted in a continuous increase in the average distance of oil trade since 1985. It is interesting to note that, since 2005, the total tonnage of seaborne oil trade declined while the average ton-mile increased. The trade volume decline is mainly due to a reduction in exports by sea to Europe. However, this decline was partially compensated for by an increase in exports to the Far East, particularly China and India. The exporters were not only from the Middle East but also from Africa and Latin America, all of which further extended the average distance of maritime transport.

Consequently, as far as international shipping is concerned, the demand cannot be identified by the volume of seaborne trade alone. If, in Figure 4.12, a question is asked about how much tanker ship capacity is needed in 2018 as compared with 2005, the answer will be that we need more capacity even though trade has gone down in volume, as maritime transport demand is defined by ton-miles. So, even if the *ad valorem* freight for world seaborne trade did not change between, say, 1990 and 2018, it is a few percentage points lower because, during the 28 years, the global seaborne trade in ton-miles increased by 4% per year, while in tons it grew only by 3.5% per year. So more transport than trade has been accomplished. Because of a falling maritime transport cost, especially in terms of value for money, the adverse effects of longer distances than before on trade have been largely offset by cheaper and better transport services. The phenomenon of "shrinking distance" is evident.

4.4 The national maritime transport dependence factor

How do you measure the importance of seaborne trade in national economies?

The World Bank calculates and publishes "trade to GDP" ratio for each country, to reflect the relative importance of international trade in a country's economy.[26] This is the sum of exports and imports divided by GDP. If the trade of services is excluded, we will have the ratio of merchandise trade to GDP. Globally, such a ratio has grown from 11% in 1950 to 46% in 2018, as shown in Figure 4.2. Worldwide, national economies are more dependent on each other and the world economy is more integrated. However, the ratio varies significantly between countries. On the one hand, a large country with a big domestic market and GDP base tends to have a low ratio. In 2014, for example, China, which is the world's largest trading nation, had a merchandise-trade-to-GDP ratio of 41%. The rate for Japan was 33% and for the USA only 23%. On the other hand, small countries rely more on external sources and markets and sometimes the ratio can even be higher than 100% due to the fact that these countries have specialised positions in the global value chain or serve as trade hubs.[27] Singapore and Belgium are examples.

How vital is maritime transport to a country's economy? The most straightforward way to answer this is to look at the "seaborne trade to GDP" ratio of a country for a particular point in time. From the economic point of view, the importance of seaborne trade can undoubtedly be measured in different ways too. For example, to know exactly what the value of seaborne trade is, one should ideally make as detailed a segmentation as possible by the type of goods, the origin, destination, etc. For a country whose domestic production of food cannot satisfy the local needs, the importance of seaborne imports of grain is obvious. The same is true for energy products and critical materials or components. Directly related to such strategic imports, what the country exports may have the same importance because of the earnings to be made for imports. This is particularly true if the country has limited or no alternative goods or services to export. As a principle, the economic importance of a seaborne trade item depends on the situation of substitution of the products concerned. Often a distinction can be made between trade for necessity and trade for benefit. We, however, will discuss the subject in general terms without going into any specific circumstances. We use seaborne trade in value or STV to GDP ratio as a benchmark for the national dependence on seaborne trade. We call the exposure of a national economy to international shipping as the *Maritime Dependence Factor* or *MDF* which is expressed as a percentage: MDF = STV/GDP.

Several precautions have to be called upon when comparing seaborne trade with GDP and using the ratio as the benchmark for the maritime dependence of a country. I would like to mention two of them. One is about the conversion of a country's GDP from the national currency into US dollars. There are usually two ways to do this, either by using the official exchange rate or by a method called purchasing power parity, which reflects more accurately the value of the currency. International trade, seaborne or not, is usually in US dollars based on the official exchange rate for both importers and exporters. So, to calculate the MDF, the exchange-rate-based GDP is used. Therefore, there is the impact of exchange rates. The second precaution is about the distortion caused by the different ways in which GDP and trade are calculated. National GDP is calculated based on value-added, while international trade is calculated based on cross-border transactions. That's why we see some countries having international trade bigger than the GDP. As we have discussed previously, the fast growth of the global supply chain and intra-industry trade has resulted in a multiplication of physical cross-border transactions and caused inflation of trade statistics. Whilst the total value-added may be unchanged, the cross-border trade may have happened multiple times. For maritime transport, the cross-border cargo transactions are more important than the amount of value-added created in the processes. Nonetheless, the accuracy is inevitably affected when such a method is applied to the countries with different levels of involvement in the globalised production processes. One of the corrective measures is to consider the level of trade in intermediate products in the calculation of the MDF.

How much is a country's seaborne trade as a percentage of its GDP?

The first difficulty encountered is related to the extraction of seaborne trade from total trade in goods, because often they are not accounted for in the same unit. On the one hand, international merchandise trade is usually measured in value terms, without the distinction of the part transported by ships. For global trade, such statistics are published by international organisations such as the UN, the World Bank and the World Trade Organization. On the other hand, when it comes to the global seaborne trade, it is usually measured and published in volume terms, e.g., in tons, teu, barrels or cubic metres. Such statistics can be found from national governments or private companies or institutions, many of them in the UK, such as Fairplay or Clarksons. Some advanced countries do collect the information of total trade in weight and seaborne trade in value, but such data are rarely available for most other countries. For the sake of comparison, a unique unit, either volume or value, has to be used. There is, therefore, an issue of conversion. Since GDP, which is used as the denominator for the MDF, is always expressed in value terms, seaborne trade should be converted from tons into US dollars.

How much cargo in value out of a country's merchandise trade is transported by sea? In the absence of official data at the global level, statistics have to be collected from each country individually. For some regions, such as the EU or countries such as the US, data on international seaborne trade in value is available. For many other countries, estimates have to be made, taking into consideration some critical factors. Such factors are mainly related to different modes of transport, namely, road, rail, sea, air, inland-waterways and pipelines. So we will examine specifically three aspects: the geographical conditions of the country; the level of intra-regional trade that the country has, mainly when land-based cross-border transport is available with the trade partners; and the amount of international air freight the country has. The total value of seaborne trade in 2015 was estimated to be US$13.7 trillion, out of the total value of the world's merchandise export of US$18.6 trillion. If we take both import and export cargoes of all countries to compare with the GDP, the value of global trade transported by sea was US$27.5 trillion in 2015, which is about 35% of the world GDP. This reflects the importance of maritime transport in the world economy or global MDF. Figure 4.13 shows the evolution of the world MDF between 1960 and 2015. The value share of seaborne trade in total trade has not changed from around 65% over the last half century. Therefore, the profile of Figures 4.2 and 4.13 is similar. Although the deeper economic integration and fast growth of air transport in Europe and North America have led to a share reduction of seaborne trade, the effects have been rather limited. Europe and North America's declining weight in global trade has been in favour of Asia, which relies heavily on maritime transport. The combined share of Europe and North America in world trade declined from above 50% in the 1960s to about 33% in 2015, if intra-EU trade is excluded. At the same time, the global share of Asia rose from 15% to 36%.

When it comes to the MDF of individual countries, identifying accurate data is more challenging because of the lack of official statistics. Using both data on a country's bilateral trade and the geography of trade partners can estimate the possible land-based modes of transport used. About half of international trade in North America and more than two-thirds in Europe is intra-regional trade. Given the geographical conditions of these two regions, a majority of the intra-regional trade is transported by land-based transport modes. For example, about 90% of trade between the US and Canada and 78% between the US and Mexico is transported by land.[28] About half of Asian trade is intra-regional

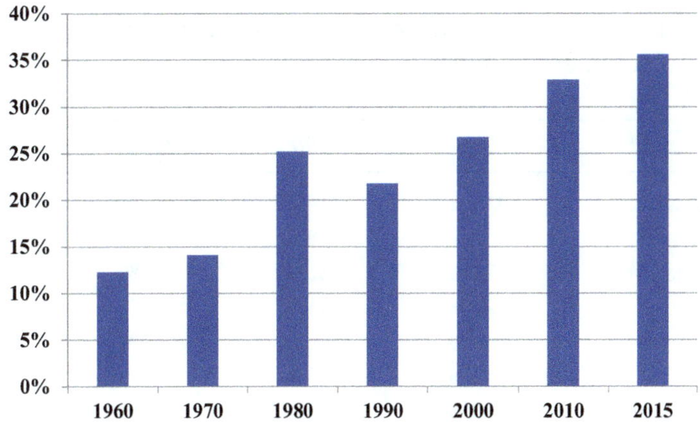

Figure 4.13 World seaborne trade to GDP ratio (%), 1960–2015.

Source: Shuo Ma, based on data from the World Bank, WTO and other sources.

Note: seaborne trade includes imports and exports in US dollars. World GDP is based on exchange rate.

and the proportion is still rising. But, contrary to Europe and North America, the vast majority of intra-Asian trade is moved by ships, as most Asian countries are separated by seas. For the rest of the world, the intra-regional trade has smaller proportions in their respective total trade in goods.[29] As far as European trade is concerned, we count only extra-EU trades, for which about 50% in value was seaborne in 2016, as shown in Table 3.3.

Globally, the air transport of cargo has been growing faster than sea freight during the last couple of decades. In terms of volume, air freight is still tiny. In 2015, for example, a total of 51 million tons of cargo was transported by air, which is about 0.5% of sea freight. However, in terms of value, the market share of air freight in 2015 was as big as almost 17% of the world merchandise trade, with a total value of US$6.4 trillion.[30] Precious stones, live animals, perishable products, high-value electronic products and parts, watches and fashion clothes, etc., are typical cargoes transported by air. The percentage of air freight in total trade is higher in the rich countries of North America, Japan, Europe and the Middle East than in poorer countries. In the US, for example, about 20% of imports and 30% of exports were transported by air[31] during recent years. Table 4.1 shows the estimate of the relative importance of seaborne trade in the national economy or the MDF of 36 selected economies. This is the ratio between the value of seaborne trade, both imports and exports, of the country and its nominal GDP in US dollars. We have taken four periods from 1960 to the latest year for which data is available. Though the method emphasises the value of seaborne trade, it should not lead to any conclusion that basic and low-value commodities transported by ships are not important for a country. The table includes all major economies, for which necessary data is available, of every continent of the world and combined they represent more than 80% of world merchandise trade by sea in 2015. The 28 EU member states are taken as one entity, excluding the internal trade within the EU. Although big differences exist among the European countries in terms of exposure to maritime transport, the overall dependence is low. Seaborne trade includes both import and export and also re-export of goods for those countries with active activities in export processing and cargo transit. This is the situation in places such as Belgium, the Netherlands, the UAE, Singapore and Hong Kong.

Table 4.1 MDF (value of seaborne import & export/nominal GDP) of 36 selected economies 1960–2015.

		1960	*1980*	*2000*	*2015*
1	Singapore	315%	314%	236%	202%
2	Vietnam		38%	72%	137%
3	Malaysia	93%	80%	154%	102%
4	Thailand	27%	41%	86%	90%
5	South Korea	9%	50%	49%	62%
6	Ghana	48%	45%	76%	58%
7	Saudi Arabia	90%	74%	49%	55%
8	Ivory Coast	45%	50%	49%	55%
9	Morocco	32%	26%	52%	51%
10	Chile	21%	30%	36%	46%
11	South Africa	42%	46%	34%	46%
12	Philippines	19%	38%	82%	40%
13	Israel	22%	62%	45%	40%
14	Turkey	5%	12%	24%	39%
15	Mexico	10%	14%	32%	37%
16	Norway	40%	47%	46%	37%
17	Indonesia	42%	39%	61%	36%
18	Bangladesh		15%	23%	34%
19	China	7%	17%	32%	33%
20	India	8%	11%	17%	33%
21	Peru	29%	32%	24%	32%
22	Kenya	33%	38%	31%	32%
23	Iran	28%	23%	33%	28%
24	Australia	23%	26%	28%	28%
25	Canada	13%	22%	34%	27%
26	Egypt	37%	29%	16%	26%
27	Japan	17%	21%	15%	26%
28	Pakistan	28%	29%	23%	25%
29	Colombia	21%	22%	19%	24%
30	Nigeria	22%	55%	52%	22%
31	Russia			29%	22%
32	Venezuela	37%	41%	36%	20%
33	Argentina	8%	19%	14%	19%
34	Brazil	14%	15%	13%	15%
35	extra-EU (28)	13%	14%	14%	15%
36	United States	3%	8%	10%	12%
37	**World**	**12%**	**25%**	**27%**	**36%**

Source: Shuo Ma, based on data from the World Bank, WTO, national statistics and estimates.

Note: seaborne trade includes import and export. The 36 countries represent over 80% of the world merchandise trade by sea in 2015.

What are the determining factors for the level of MDF?

There are mainly three aspects that explain the level of seaborne trade in value terms of a country relative to its economy. They are the size and type of the economy and the geographical features of the country. We shall examine these factors as follows.

- ***Size of the economy***. Countries with an open but small economy tend to have high MDF, while those with big GDP usually have low MDF. Proportionally, trade, as well as seaborne trade, places a heavier weight on small economies. The US economy in the 1960s was highly self-reliant with virtually every product of manufactures and raw materials. Later, the US turned more and more to the cheaper external supplies of oil and manufactured goods and exported more of its surplus of grain, coal and manufactures. Although the US has always been a big seaborne trader, when compared with its colossal GDP the ratio is small. On the other hand, some small economies, including those in Africa and Asia, may not have a very significant seaborne trade, yet their relatively small GDP makes them more dependent on maritime transport. In most cases, seaborne trade has increased faster than GDP since 1960. However, there are cases in which the rates decreased. When a country's seaborne trade is dominated by raw materials, the price fluctuation has an impact on the ratio. The use of nominal GDP can also give the countries whose currency is undervalued a higher MDF than if purchasing power parity-based GDP is used. For example, with PPP-based GDP, the MDF of Japan and Europe may most probably be higher whilst that of India, China and some other developing countries may be lower.
- ***Type of the economy***. The countries serving as transit platforms of trade for neighbouring countries usually have high ratios and this is the case of many hubs of international shipping lines like the Netherlands, Belgium, Singapore and Malaysia. If those economies are at the same time small, the ratio may well be more than 100%. The countries that are deeply integrated with the global value chain, such as Korea, China and some other Asian countries, will have high MDF. If an economy is relatively closed with a low level of foreign trade, the MDF is low. The MDF is also low for a country with an economy based on tourism rather than manufacturing. As an economy matures, the share of service will be bigger in terms of GDP and the ratio of seaborne trade to GDP of the country will be lower. Rich and industrialised countries trade more between themselves. But those countries relying mainly on the export of commodities would trade less with similar countries.
- ***Geographical features***. This is probably the most important factor, because the questions about Table 4.1 that cannot be answered by the above two economic reasons, may find their explanations in the geography of a country. The overwhelming reason for Asian countries to have high seaborne trade to GDP ratio is because most countries are separated from their main trade partners by sea. It is not only the case for island countries such as Japan, Indonesia or the Philippines, it is also the case for China, Vietnam or Thailand. As we have explained above, the situation of alternative modes of transport is very different for intra-regional trade in North America, Europe and Asia. Land-based modes of transport exist in regions like South America, the Middle East or Africa as well, though the intra-regional trade is of low level in these regions. One of the main reasons that the Russian MDF is relatively low is because it uses pipelines for most of its export of oil and gas.

The MDF is probably the best and the only possible way to establish a relationship between a country's seaborne trade and its GDP. Ideally, seaborne trade should be calculated according to the value-added of the country. The relatively recent development of intra-industry trade has made the ratio less accurate in revealing economic dependence. The impact of the shipping market changes would typically be more prominent for the countries with high MDF than for those with low MDF.

4.5 Summary

We have in this chapter discussed the long-term development trends of maritime transport demand, which is directly related to the future of trade. It is a general understanding that the biggest contributing factor for the growth of trade is the rise of income in the process of industrialisation and economic catching up of emerging countries. The industrialisation started more than 200 years ago in Europe and it is still going on presently in the rest of the world. In 1950 the US GDP per capita was about 22 times higher than China's. Then China started its industrialisation process and accelerated from the late 1970s. As a result, the gap of GDP per capita between the two countries reduced to about 4 times by 2015. Similar stories have happened in many other countries too. Between 1950 and 2018 the world production grew by 10 times, but the world export grew by 38 times and the world seaborne trade grew by about 23 times. Such a development pattern is expected to continue in the future, though not necessarily at the same speed.

We have also looked at the future development of seaborne trade based on a three-scenario forecast. There are sufficient reasons to believe that the average annual growth rate of 4.7% between 1950 and 2018 will not continue. The three scenarios represent low-, medium- and high-growth situations at, therefore, 1%, 2% and 3% per year. Correspondingly, the world seaborne trade will be growing from more than 11 billion tons in 2018 to 16 billion, 20 billion and 27 billion tons of cargo in 2050.

The role of maritime transport cost in the development of trade was discussed based on some previous research work by other researchers as well as on the analysis of the changes in international shipping services and costs. The effects of the shipping costs were examined from three angles: from the demand-side, supply-side and market-side. We also analysed some important aspects of maritime transport cost that are often overlooked. The first is the currency issue, which means that direct cost in current currency value may be misleading. The second is the purchasing power issue, which refers to the "Engel's Law" on transport cost, i.e., that the proportion of income spent on transport declines. The third is the issue of transport quality, which means that the implicit shipping cost decreases, even if the explicit cost does not, when the quality of service has improved and, at the same time, the average distance travelled per ton of seaborne trade has also increased. So the contribution of maritime transport to the growth of trade is bigger than many people think.

We finally introduced the concept of MDF, or maritime dependence factor, which is a measurement of the relative importance of seaborne trade in value terms in a country's economy. This is an attempt to link the seaborne trade of a country and its GDP. Although not a perfect measurement of the maritime reliance of a country due to transaction-based trade data, the MDF does reveal the relative importance of seaborne trade. Globally, the world economy is more dependent on maritime transport now than before, which led to the MDF rising from 12% in 1960 to 36% in 2015. The MDF of individual countries varies significantly according to their size, type of economy and their geographical features.

Notes

1 UNCTAD (2018) and previous issues.
2 OECD (2006) and World Bank (2015).
3 Stopford M. (2009).
4 Maddison A. (2006).
5 Stavrianos L. (1998). Stavrianos says (Chapter 26) that the lifestyle had remained the same for thousands of years in all parts of the world until science and industrial revolution, that started in the West, changed the world completely.

6 Ferguson N. (2011).
7 Pomeranz K. (2000).
8 Maddison A. (2006).
9 IMF (2015, 2016). See also "World economic outlook updates" January 2016. The collapse of commodity markets in 2014/2015 left many resource-export-dependent countries in Africa, Latin America and elsewhere in great difficulties and some of them saw their GDP decline.
10 WTO (2013a) and UNCTAD (2015).
11 WTO (2013b).
12 WTO (2018).
13 UNCTAD.
14 Tetlock P. (2005).
15 See the two recent market forecasts of maritime demand: in a report by Lloyds Register and University of Strathclyde (2013) on "Global Marine Trends, 2030", three scenarios were used to predict the future of maritime demand. Stopford of Clarkson Research (2016), in a speech at Fathom Shipping in September 2015, said that seaborne trade import annual growth rates would be between 1.1% and 0.28% for non-OECD countries from 2015 to 2065.
16 UNCTAD (2015).
17 UN (2015). It states in the report (p. 3) that "with 95% degree of confidence that global population will be between 8.4 and 8.6 billion in 2030 and between 9.5 and 13.3 billion in 2100. … Later in the century, global population is likely to continue to rise, but there is roughly a 23% chance that it could stabilize or begin to fall before 2100."
18 Clarksons (2018).
19 OECD (2010).
20 *Idem.*
21 A study of the Danish government showed that the total cost of a North Sea Emission Control Area would be Euro 282 million in 2030 for the shipping services. Source: Danish Ministry of the Environment (2012), "Economic impact assessment of a NOx emission control area in the North Sea", No. 1427.
22 Hummels D. (2007).
23 Baier S. and Bergstrand J. (2001). Baier and Bengstrand argued that 67% of trade growth was attributable to income growth, 25% to tariff reduction and 8% to transport cost declines. Jacks D. and Pendakur K. (2010). Jacks and Pendakur claimed that the GDP growth was an overwhelming cause of trade increase. O'Rourke K. and Williamson J. (2002). These authors also found that 65% change in trade is explained by the GDP growth.
24 OCED (2011).
25 *The Economist* (7 January 2016).
26 See https://data.worldbank.org/indicator/NE.TRD.GNFS.ZS.
27 WTO (2015). In 2014 30 countries had merchandise imports and exports more than national GDPs. There are among them rich countries such as Singapore (trade to GDP ratio of 252%) and Belgium (173%), or poorer countries like Vietnam (160%) and Cambodia (145%). The common characteristic is that they are the countries with small GDP.
28 US Department of Transportation, Bureau of Transportation Statistics, various years.
29 WTO (2015). The shares of intra-regional trade in 2014 were as follows: North America 50.2%, Europe 68.5%, Latin America 25.8%, Africa 17.7%, Asia 52.3% and Middle East 8.8%. The structure has been relatively stable for the last two decades.
30 IATA (2016).
31 US Department of Transportation, Bureau of Transportation Statistics, 2015.

References

Baier S. and Bergstrand J. (2001) "*The Growth of World Trade: Tariffs, Transport Costs, and Income Similarity*", Journal of International Economics, Vol. 53, No. 1 (February 2001), pp. 1–27.

Clarksons. (2018) "Shipping Intelligence Network", Database.

Danish Ministry of the Environment. (2012), "*Economic Impact Assessment of a NOx Emission Control Area in the North Sea*", No. 1427.

Ferguson N. (2011) "*Civilization, the West and the Rest*", Penguin Books, London.

Hummels D. (2007) "*Transportation Costs and International Trade the Second Era of Globalization*", *Journal of Economic Perspective*, Vol. 21, No. 3, pp. 131–154.

IATA. (2016) "*Economic Industry Performance*", International Air Transport Association, Montreal.

IMF. (2015, 2016) "*Where are Commodity Exporters Headed?*" Chapter 2 of *World Economic Outlook*, 2015.

Jacks D. and Pendakur K. (2010) "*Global Trade and the Maritime Transport Revolution*", The Review of Economics and Statistics, Vol. 92, No. 4 (November 2010), pp. 745–755.

Lloyds Register and University of Strathclyde. (2013) "*Global Marine Trends, 2030*".

Maddison A. (2006) "*The World Economy*", Development Centre Studies, pp. 241, 358.

O'Rourke K. and Williamson J. (2002) "*After Columbus: Explaining Europe's Overseas Trade Boom*", The Journal of Economic History, Vol. 62, No. 02 (June 2002), pp. 417–456.

OECD. (2006) "*The World Economy*", Development Centre Studies, Paris.

OECD. (2010) "*Maritime Transport Costs Database*", OECD Statistics, Paris.

OCED. (2011) "*Clarifying Trade Costs in Maritime Transport*", Trade Committee WP, TAD/TD/WP (2008)10/FINAL, pp. 22–24.

Pomeranz K. (2000) "*The Great Divergence: China, Europe and the Making of the Modern World Economy*", Princeton University Press, Princeton, NJ.

Stavrianos L. (1998) "*A Global History: From Prehistory to the 21st Century*", 7th edition, Pearson, London.

Stopford M. (2009) "*Maritime Economics*", 3rd edition, Routledge, London.

Tetlock P. (2005) "*Expert Political Judgement: How Good Is It? How Can We Know?*", Princeton University Press, Princeton, NJ.

The Economist. (7 January 2016) "*Big Mac Index*", and ConvergEx Report "Marning Markets Briefing", August 13, 2013.

UN. (2015) "*The 2015 Revision of World Population Prospects*", UN, Department of Economic and Social Affairs, Population Division, ESA/P/WP.242, New York.

UNCTAD. (2015) "*Review of Maritime Transport*", UCTAD/RMT/2015.

UNCTAD. (2018 and previous issues) "*Review of Maritime Transport*", UNCTAD/RMT/2018.

US Department of Transportation, Bureau of Transportation Statistics. (2015) *State Transportation Statistics 2015*, U.S. Department of Transportation, Washington, DC.

World Bank. (2015) "*World Development Indicators*", Retrieved from http://data.worldbank.org/indicator/TG.VAL.TOTL.GD.ZS.

WTO. (2013a) "*Trends in International Trade*", Part B of the World Trade Report 2013, WTO Publications, Geneva, Switzerland, pp. 44–111.

WTO. (2013b) "*Trends in International Trade*", Part B of the World Trade Report 2013, WTO Publications, Geneva, Switzerland, pp. 55–57.

WTO. (2015) "*International Trade Statistics 2015*", WTO Publications, Geneva, Switzerland.

WTO. (2018) "*International Trade Statistics 2018*", WTO Publications, Geneva, Switzerland.

Part II

The supply

Chapter 5

Productivity and structure changes in maritime transport

It was concluded in the previous chapter that one of the major causes of the extraordinary growth of international trade is the decline of maritime transport prices, especially in terms of value for money. It means that the price a customer pays for transport services with a comparable quality has been decreasing. Though prices do fluctuate in the long term and in a competitive market, which is very much the case of international shipping, the price is determined by cost. So, over a long time, the cost of providing a specific type of maritime transport service has declined. What are the root causes for this fall in the transport cost? Under what conditions did the cost decrease happen? What are the driving forces for such condition changes? In this chapter we will discuss these questions by looking at the structural evolution that occurred in the maritime transport industry and by analysing various issues related to maritime transport productivity: its nature, the reasons and the impact on international seaborne trade, both in the short and long term.

5.1 Maritime transport productivity

On 25 January 1736 the Swedish East India Company's 490-ton-capacity merchant ship *Friedericus Rex Suecia* left the port of Guangzhou, China, with a crew of 100 men for a homebound journey. The ship had been at the Chinese port during the previous months for loading porcelain, tea, silk, etc. About six months later, on 31 July 1736, the ship arrived at the port of Gothenburg, Sweden. Counting the time spent in ports and at sea, the ship could complete just a bit more than one such voyage per year.[1] On 21 July 2014 the Danish shipping company's container ship *Mary Maersk* sailed from Algeciras, Spain, for the Far East with 17,603 teu containers on board. The ship had a carrying capacity of 194,000 deadweight tons and a crew of 20 (possibly with as few as 13 people). It would take about 34 days for the ship to complete a voyage from Europe to the Far East calling at several ports on the way. A rough comparison suggests that, on the same shipping route, each seafarer working on *Friedericus Rex Suecia* would transport about 6 tons of cargo per year, while each crew member working on *Mary Maersk* should be able to complete approximately 80,000 tons of cargo per year, or some 13,000 times more.

The contribution of maritime transport to the growth of the world's trade and global supply chain comes mainly from the progress in productivity. Productivity is commonly understood as the ratio of output to input. Based on the framework of the OECD's manual on productivity measurement,[2] we will examine different aspects of maritime productivity in more detail.

What is included in maritime transport output and input?

Generally, maritime transport output can be expressed in physical terms such as gross output or financial terms like value-added. For maritime transport of merchandise trade, the gross output is cargo carried from A to B and the value-added is the difference between freight and expenses. So, for example, maritime labour productivity can be measured as tons of cargo carried per person per year or value-added per person per year. In this chapter we use cargo carried as output to discuss and compare maritime transport productivity from various angles. The amount of cargo carried by ships from one place to another is expressed in maritime transport as "ton-miles". So ton-mile is the unit of measurement for maritime productivity.

When measuring the amount of cargo carried by a ship during a year, the time used can be divided mainly into two parts: the time spent at sea and the time spent in port. In other words, transport starts and ends at the port: it is when cargo is loaded and when the cargo is discharged. The time spent by a ship for cargo handling varies enormously. In the above example of the Swedish merchant ship *Friedericus Rex Suecia*, the ship spent more than three months at each end for loading and discharging cargo. For a voyage between the Far East and Europe, the port to sailing time was 1:1. The proportion can be bigger for ships trading over shorter distances.

When it comes to input of maritime transport, capital and labour are the most used factors. For example, capital productivity in shipping is usually measured by fleet productivity in terms of the number of ton-miles completed by each deadweight ton of ships in a year.[3] Labour productivity is measured as the number of ton-miles per seafarer employed. In this chapter we use the factors of maritime transport as input, i.e., labour and capital stock. With regard to capital input, we will measure fleet productivity or ship productivity in terms of deadweight tonnage. Based on ton-miles performed per deadweight ton of commercial ships, capital productivity has not changed much for a long time. In 1965, for example, the world fleet productivity was at 28.67 thousand ton-miles per deadweight ton, while in 2015 the figure was at 31.01 thousand ton-miles per deadweight ton, or an improvement of 8% in 50 years.[4] By labour, we restrict this to seafarers only working on board ships in this chapter. Shore-based staff and reserved seafarers are not included. The responsibilities of seafarers have evolved a lot over time. They are much less involved in commercial activities now than they used to be in the past. The transfer of such duties to the shore-based staff has led to an improvement in the productivity of the people working on board.

Although labour productivity and capital productivity are separately measured, each of them reflects the joint effect of many factors, such as labour, capital, scale economies, technological changes, efficiency improvement, organisational and management changes, capacity utilisation and the balance between demand and supply. Labour and capital productivity are also affected by the changes in intermediate inputs. This is mainly about outsourcing and insourcing during the whole production process. For example, the labour productivity of a port is affected by the degree of outsourcing of intermediate service inputs such as equipment maintenance.

What are the changes in maritime labour productivity?

Labour productivity is measured as the ratio between the output and the number of seafarers involved. Such a ratio can be based on a certain fleet or a particular ship and expressed as ton-miles completed per person per year (ton-miles/person/year). According to some research, the long-term maritime labour productivity has improved steadily over the last couple of centuries. To begin with some early achievements. For example, it was estimated that the fleet labour productivity of the Netherlands-based seafarers was about 25,164 ton-miles per person in 1532, 34,884 ton-miles per person in 1636 and 58,104 ton-miles per person in 1780,[5] as shown in Table 5.1. So maritime labour productivity increased steadily during the sails period. This represents an average annual growth rate of merely 0.3% between 1532 and 1636, and 0.4% between 1636 and 1780. Such performance is not very impressive.

The calculation of labour productivity for a national fleet has drawbacks and can hardly be very accurate. There are many influential factors, such as the type of ships, the size of ships, the distance of trade, etc. So the ratio can only be estimated grossly as an average. However, despite the lack of accuracy, such a proxy can still provide meaningful and sufficiently convincing evidence of productivity improvement. If we focus on maritime labour productivity of more recent times, we have several ways of measurement. We can take the total amount of cargo transported in terms of ton-miles completed in a year, then divide it by the total number of seafarers to have an average ton-miles per seafarer per year. The advantages of this method are that it reflects the general situation of the entire maritime sector. But the obvious difficulty with this approach is that the accurate number of total seafarers is hard to find.

While the output in ton-miles of cargo transported is relatively accessible, it is not the case for the exact number of seafarers. The Baltic and International Maritime Council (BIMCO) and the International Shipping Federation (ISF) started to publish, every five years, a study on the global demand and supply of seafarers in 1990.[6] The global need for seafarers is estimated based on two main factors, namely, the number of seafarers required per ship and the number of ships in operation. Furthermore, to estimate the manning level, in addition to the number of ships, distinctions are made based on the size, type and age of commercial vessels as well as the country of registration. In the end, the final estimates of crew sizes are obtained by multiplying applicable back-up ratios. Let's look at the BIMCO's world maritime manpower update data regarding the evolution of the maritime labour productivity of the global fleet between 1990 and 2015. The labour productivity increased from over 16 million ton-miles per person to more than 37 million ton-miles per person in the space of 25 years. This represents an annual growth rate of 3.4% on average. It is a giant improvement in labour productivity from the 17th century to the 21st, with about one thousand times difference.

Although differences exist between the size, type, age and the flag of ships to measure the evolution of labour productivity over time, the total number of ships can reasonably be taken as a proxy representing the global size of seafarer input. This is because, on the one hand, the variations over time are gradual and relatively small and, on the other hand, and more importantly, factors such as size,

Table 5.1 Maritime labour productivity ton-miles transported per person.

Year	*Ton-miles per person*	*Average annual growth rate*
1532	25,164	
1636	34,884	0.3%
1780	58,104	0.4%

Source: based on Van Zanden L. (2009).

Note: this was the case of Holland with wooden sailing ships. Productivity improved by 0.3% and 0.4% per annum on average for the two periods.

type and age are the contributing factors for the changes in labour productivity to be measured and explained. According to some research, the differences in crew size between the main types and various size ranges of ocean-going ships serving international trade are relatively small.[7] More significant differences are found in two areas: the registry and age of ships. Under some registries, requirements exist with regard to the number of people working on ships. When it comes to the age of ships, the crew size is much affected by the technical evolution of the ship. Usually, new ships require a smaller crew. It is typical that a newly built ship, regardless of the size, will need about 20 people working on board, while an old-fashioned bulker or general cargo ship built in the 1970s or before would have about 40 people working on the ship.

If the objective is to have a general idea of the maritime labour productivity evolution rather than to have a precise account of demand/supply balance, we can work out an estimate of general average manning level for all commercial cargo ships, taking into account the average crew size per ship and the effect of technological evolution of ships. Then using such a number multiplied by the number of ships will allow us to get the total number of seafarers and thus the labour productivity for the year. Considering that, on the one hand, the crew size, based on the BIMCO study, is normally smaller for ships less than 1,600 grt and, on the other hand, the crew size is always smaller for newer ships, our estimate of average crew size for all ships from 1970 to 2015 was 18 people. Figure 5.1 shows the evolution of maritime labour productivity between 1970 and 2015, which is estimated based on the data from the BIMCO Manpower Update, ISL and Clarksons.[8] In 45 years, maritime labour productivity increased from 12.6 million ton-miles per seafarer in 1970 to 33.4 million ton-miles per seafarer in 2015, or an increase of 2.6 times at an average growth rate of 2.19% per year. This growth rate is much higher than in the past. It is interesting to note that during the same period of 1970 to 2015 the general labour productivity of all sectors in the OECD countries increased on average by 1.75%

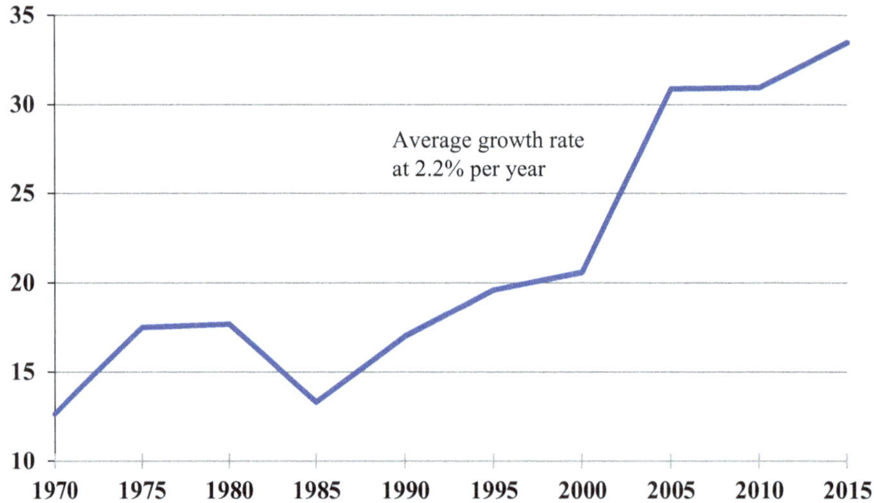

Figure 5.1 Global maritime labour productivity (million ton-miles of cargo transported per seafarer per year), 1970–2015.

Source: Shuo Ma, based on data from BIMCO, ISL and Clarksons.

Note: the number of seafarers is calculated taking into account the number, size, type, age, country of registry and backup ratio of commercial ships.

per annum. This is quite a significant difference that demonstrates a net positive contribution of the maritime industry to global labour productivity.

Although maritime labour productivity has been increasing in the long term, the evolution does not follow a linear trend and, in the short term, the development may go in the opposite direction.[9] This is because of market fluctuations which resulted in an imbalance between the demand and supply. For example, when the need for transport surges, such as the situation in the early 1970s and 2000s, the freight would be higher which leads to an effort by the shipping companies to load more cargo and reduce the transit time with the existing supply. As a consequence, productivity rises. In the long term, new ship capacities will be added to adjust to the demand increase. But often an over-supply will happen either due to a decrease in demand or excessive increase in supply. Such a situation happened in the early 1980s and the late 2000s and ship capacities were not fully utilised, which implies a reduction in productivity.

What are the changes in maritime capital productivity?

Capital services, or maritime transport in the context of this book, are defined as the flow of services from capital goods, e.g., ships, into the production process. Capital services in production analysis are assumed to be proportional to the capital stock and this is also known as capital utilisation. Such capital stock is usually referred to as "productive stock".[10] With regard to maritime transport, the productive stock of ships taken as the input of productivity is measured in the unit of *deadweight* (dwt). Or it is, in effect, the productivity of an asset. When it comes to capital services, which are the output of capital productivity, ton-miles of cargo carried per year is still used.

Unlike labour productivity, over the last couple of decades the capital or ship productivity of the world fleet in terms of ton-miles of cargo transported per deadweight per year has not changed much. The development of ship productivity between 1970 and 2018 is illustrated in Figure 5.2. There is a process of factor substitution of maritime labour for capital. New ships are built bigger, are increasingly more sophisticated and equipped with more advanced technologies. While modern ships are safer

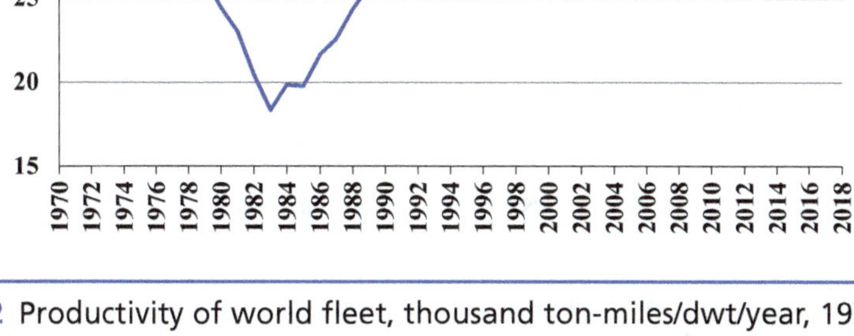

Figure 5.2 Productivity of world fleet, thousand ton-miles/dwt/year, 1970–2018.

Source: Shuo Ma, based on data from UNCTAD, Clarksons and ISL.

Note: the fleet productivity decreased in the 1970s and early 1980s as a result of structural changes in seaborne trade and other factors.

and more efficient, they are also more costly and need fewer people. The size and quality changes of an asset, such as technological progress embodied in transportation capital goods, are reflected in the productive capital stock of ships. The issue of ship prices will be dealt with in later chapters. There are many other reasons for the limited changes in capital productivity. For example, more specialised ships are less flexible for carrying different types of cargo, which usually results in carrying less cargo per year or low overall productivity. But, at the same time, the quality of services is superior. The main contributing factor for the ups and downs of the fleet productivity is the shifting of the market balance between demand and supply. The cargo demand can rise or fall a lot within a short period, but the ship supply cannot. In the 1980s, for example, the depressed shipping market with low freight rate led to a drop in fleet productivity.

One may argue that there is a difference between physical ships and the capital invested in them. To measure capital productivity we should have a closer look at the investment side. If the same ship can be built more cheaply and other factors remain constant then, in a year, the same amount of ton-miles of transport can be performed with less capital involved. It will lead to an improvement in capital productivity. Over the years the shipbuilding industry has made enormous progress in terms of reductions in cost and time and of improvement in quality for building new ships. Take, for example, a bulk carrier of 30–45,000 deadweight, commonly known as a "Handysize" ship. In 1965 the average and representative price for such a ship was 4.3 million US dollars. In 2018 the price was 21 million US$ apiece, which is about five times as high as the price some 50 years ago. During this period, the representative price of this type of ship fluctuated up and down with the highest price at 39 million US$ in 2007.[11] Such a very high price is an exception, which is attributable to specific market situations. Overall, the evolution of the ship price followed an upward trend. But, for a more accurate comparison, the effect of inflation of the US dollar should be factored in. Figure 5.3 is about the development of the new ship price of a Handysize bulk carrier between 1965 and 2018, in both nominal US dollars as well as in constant US dollars of 1965 after the price adjustment with the US dollar deflator. The conclusion should not come as a surprise – that to build the same ship, it costs much less today than it did in the past. Based on Figure 5.3 the price of a new Handysize bulk carrier

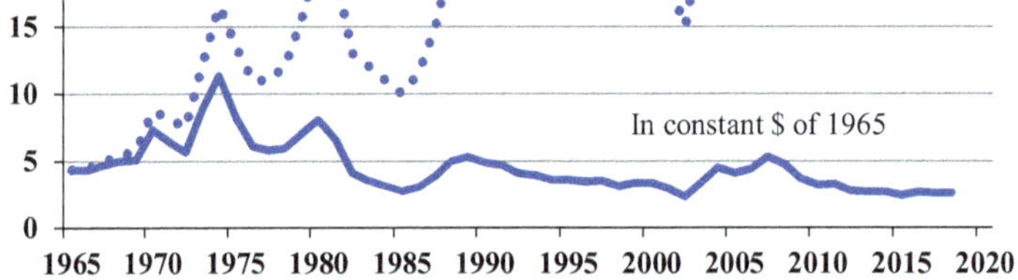

Figure 5.3 New ship prices of Handysize bulk carrier in million US$ (in current and constant 1965 US dollars), 1965–2018.

Source: Shuo Ma, based on data from UNCTAD and ISL.

Note: the price fluctuation in nominal US$ reflects market imbalance. In constant US$ of 1965, the actual price in 2018 is 60% of that in 1965.

in 2018 was equivalent to 2.3 million US dollars of 1965, or a reduction of price by 56% in the last 50 years. If this discounted price is taken for the measurement of capital productivity, then even under the assumption of constant fleet productivity in terms of ton-miles of cargo transported per dwt per year between 1965 and 2018, there is an improvement of capital productivity by 43%. Compared with a 260% increase in labour productivity between 1970 and 2018 the increase in capital productivity is very modest. The reasons will be discussed in the next section.

The price changes are only one aspect; the quality of ships is another, which is commonly overlooked. Although the ships, for example Handymax bulkers, are of similar size, the quality of the new ships is usually better than the old ones. Such improvement may or may not be reflected in ton-miles of transport service performed. It may be demonstrated as better safety, cheaper maintenance or extended operation time. Another aspect to look into is that the changes in maritime capital productivity are positively correlated with the evolution of freight. When the freight is low, the capital goods, i.e., the ships, are less efficiently used, by having, for example, ships not fully loaded and by slow steaming. The ships as capital goods will also lose productive capacity as they age and spend more time in repair and maintenance.

What are the changes in maritime multifactor productivity?

The two inputs, labour and capital, may to a certain extent be interchangeable or have trade-off effect. For example, ship automation often results in an increase in labour productivity but, at the same time, a decrease in capital productivity. The level of productivity may also be influenced by the level of intermediate inputs. Faster sailing speed would normally lead to a higher amount of cargo being carried by a ship in a year, which means a higher level of labour productivity. At the same time, more input is needed on increased fuel consumption.

Total factor productivity (TFP) is measured as the production function covering a set of endogenous variables of factor inputs, such as labour and capital or, alternatively, it can be estimated based on cost function of factor inputs that are exogenously determined by the market. In the long run and within a competitive market, the level of freight should be equal to the marginal cost. Therefore, the growth index of output as the ton-miles completed and that of input as freight will shed light on the changes in TFP. As discussed in the previous chapters, the maritime freight productivity, measured as ton or ton-miles of cargo transported per a unit of freight, has been increasing over the past decades, particularly when the factors such as currency devaluation and quality of services are taken into consideration.[12]

Multifactor productivity compares the changes of output with the changes of combined labour and capital inputs and other factors including intermediate inputs. When all factor inputs are considered, it is also referred to as total factor productivity (TFP). The growth of TFP is defined as the residual growth in output that is not explained by the increase in factor inputs. In maritime transport, multifactor productivity has been growing. It is believed that the TFP of the British tramp shipping sector grew by between 0.76% and 1.64% per annum on different shipping markets during the period from 1871 to 1889. Then, on the same shipping markets, the TFP growth increased during the period from 1889 to 1911 by between 0.84% and 1.94% per annum.[13] More recent research found that the TFP of container ships has grown continuously.

5.2 Drivers of shipping productivity improvement

The growth in productivity, particularly for labour, in the maritime transport sector since 1960 has been extraordinary. There have been different explanations regarding the reasons for the growth. Maritime technology, innovation and operational improvement have certainly played important roles in enhancing productivity. The contributions from other elements, such as capital investment in larger ships, faster sailing speed and more efficient port operations, are significant too. In this section we will examine the main factors that have contributed to the productivity changes.

Why is "economies of scale" the most important driver of the productivity growth?

The single most important contributing factor for labour productivity growth is the continuous increase in the ship's size. For the last 100 years between 1915 and 2015 the average size of commercial ships has increased almost six times if all ships of 100 gross register tons and above are counted.[14] Should only the deep-sea ships serving intercontinental trade, such as container ships, tankers and bulk carriers, be considered, the size increase is even bigger. The size of the crew working on board commercial ships capable of trading on long-haul deep sea international shipping routes is a relatively fixed factor, regardless of the size or even the type of the ship. However, the output in terms of ton or ton-miles is directly and positively correlated with the size of the ship. As a consequence, the effects of scale economies are very big. Driven by competition, large vessels are favoured for the sake of lower average operational costs.

During the last century, the size of commercial ships trading in coastal as well as intercontinental markets continuously increased. Compared with the situation in 1915, the average size of all ships of 100 grt and over increased by 24% before World War Two in 1939. Such growth accelerated after the war. From 1950 to 1975 the average size of ships doubled. Then, as an impact of economic stagnation in the wake of the two oil crises, the average ship size dropped. Starting from the 1990s, average ship size began to increase again, driven by the employment of ever bigger bulk carriers in response to the growing demand for raw materials and larger container ships which have replaced smaller general cargo ships. Figure 5.4 shows the dynamism of the ship size development between

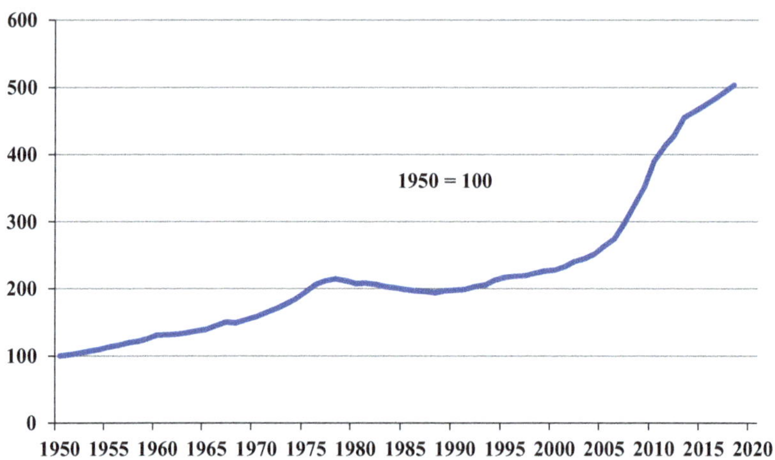

Figure 5.4 Index of average ship size of world fleet 1950–2018, 1950=100.

Source: Shuo Ma, based on data from *ISL Shipping Statistics Yearbook*.

Note: the ships included are those of 100 grt and over. The average ship size decreased from the late 1970s due to downgrades in tanker ship sizes and other factors.

1950 and 2018. So that, in 2018, the average size of commercial ships of 1,000 grt and above was five times as big as in 1950.

If the changes in average ship size between 1970 and 2015 are calculated, we will have an average annual growth at 2.03%. It is interesting to notice that during the same period, maritime labour productivity increased on average by 2.19% per year. Other factors, such as the shortening of transit time, have certainly also contributed to the productivity improvement but, in view of the magnitude of the evolution, most of the improvement is attributable to the effect of scale economies of ships.

Larger ships have not only been the main source for the rise of maritime labour productivity, but it has also led to an improvement of capital productivity, though at a lower rate. The effect of increasing returns to scale is also very evident in the shipbuilding industry, in respect of both the size of shipyards and especially the size of ships. For shipbuilding, the average cost decreases when the ship's size increases. The size of container ships has been growing at a rapid speed, mainly driven by the pursuit by the shipping companies of cost advantage. The situation is the same for the other two major types of ships: bulk carriers and oil tanker ships. For example, the price of a new ship is market-driven rather than cost-based and it is therefore fluctuating. We can have a fairly good idea of the effect of the increasing returns to scale if we compare the unit price in US$ per dwt of the ships of different sizes at the same point in time. Figure 5.5 shows the indices of the average prices between 1965 and 2015 of two types of vessels of various sizes: bulk carriers and oil tankers. The prices are in current US dollars per deadweight tonnage. The three most commonly available sizes of ships are selected for each type of ship. The smallest size, Handysize, is set as reference (100%). The figure shows that the price per dwt for a 70,000 dwt Panamax bulk carrier is about three-quarters of that of a 30–45,000 dwt Handysize ship and a VLCC tanker is about 60% cheaper per dwt compared with a small Handysize tanker ship. Due to the fact that the average ship size of the world fleet has been growing, both labour and capital productivity in the shipping industry have risen, though the labour productivity increased at a much faster pace.

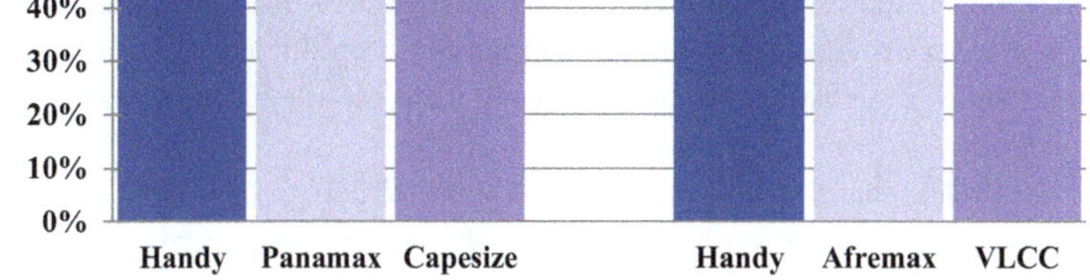

Figure 5.5 Index of ship price in US$/dwt, 1965–2015 average, Handysize=100%.

Source: Shuo Ma, based on data from UNCTAD and ISL.

Note: for bulk carriers, Handy (30–45,000 dwt), Panamax (70,000 dwt), Capesize (120–170,000 dwt); for tankers, Handy (30–50,000 dwt), Afremax (87–110,000 dwt), VLCC (250–300,000 dwt).

Bigger ships are more economical to operate. But the increase in ship size is constrained by several factors. The evolution of the ship's size is in effect a perfect reflection of the history of the changes in these constraints.

- The first and the most critical constraint on a ship's size is the demand for transport. The size of the trade is the fundamental determining factor of the size of ships. Larger ships are only economically justifiable when they are fully loaded with cargo. So having sufficient volumes of trade on a sustainable basis is a precondition for big ships. The development of large oil tanker ships in the 1970s was a direct response to the growth of demand. The more recent example of very large ore carriers (VLOC) of 400,000 dwt was related to the continuous high demand for Brazilian iron ore from the emerging economies in Asia, particularly China.
- Second, the size of the ship is constrained by the technical possibilities regarding both shipbuilding capability and propulsion constraints. These robust limitations are more in theory than practice because today's technology is more advanced and capable of meeting the commercial requirements. So, the technical limits are higher than other limits.
- Another constraint is financial. Large vessels are more expensive to build and they also carry more financial as well as commercial risks. Small ships are more flexible commercially in terms of suitable cargo and destinations, big ships are less so.
- An essential element that prevents ships from being big is physical limitations. Navigational channels, ports and cargo-handling equipment can become constraints for big ships. To overcome them takes time and costs money.
- The interface between ship and shore is often one of the most critical factors to determine the largest size of ships. It is a topic of a later chapter that reducing the time spent at the port is vital for the productivity of ships. So if a ship is too big, it will be uneconomical to operate due to the disproportionally long time spent in port.
- A relatively new factor to consider today is an environmental constraint. Some ships such as chemical cargo carriers or oil tankers are more environmentally sensitive. Big ships are more risky for the environment than small ships.

What are the other main contributing factors to productivity improvement?

The increasing returns to scale for ships is not the only contributing factor for the improvement of maritime productivity. Much of the freight reduction can also be attributed to the impact of cheaper ships and more efficient marine engines. Another important area of improvement is, of course, the transit time. Faster transport is always leading to an increase in productivity but often at a higher cost. The reduction of transit time has been achieved mainly thanks to the increase in sailing speed and the reduction of port time.

It would take a sailing ship about 40 days to travel from Liverpool to New York in the early 19th century.[15] With new technology adopted in shipbuilding and ship propulsion, the speed of ships increased quickly. Towards the late 19th century, the time was reduced to 8–9 days.[16] Today, modern container ships are designed to sail at more than 20 nautical miles per hour, which means a trans-Atlantic journey can be as short as 5 or 6 days. Ship speed is positively correlated with ship productivity. However, technical conditions are usually not the main determining factor for the speed of ships. The actual speed is mostly based on a set of economic considerations, such as freight market, fuel cost, the value of the ship and cargo, etc.

For the same reason, time spent at ports has also been massively reduced over the years. It was typical when cargoes were loaded and unloaded manually at the port that a ship would stay at a port for months before setting off to sea. Today, in a modern seaport, tens of thousands of cargoes can be handled within 24 hours. In Chapter 10 we will have more discussions regarding ports.

The navigational conditions for ocean-going ships have also played an important role in the development of maritime productivity. For example, the opening of the Suez Canal in 1869 shortened the distance massively for the seaborne trade between Asia and Europe. The Panama Canal opening in 1914 did the same for the trade between Asia and the Americas. Consequently, more cargo can be transported with the same amount of ships and seafarers.

5.3 The great maritime transport revolution: specialisation

Adam Smith attributed the productivity rise or "the greatest improvement in the productive powers of labour, and the greater part of the skill, dexterity, and judgement"[17] to the effects of the division of labour, or specialisation. As specialisation has led to fundamental changes in every aspect of the economy, maritime transport has also been reshaped by this single most important phenomenon. Today, this process is still going on.

How are ships specialised?

Driven by the rapid growth of seaborne trade and market competition in the 19th century, continuous efforts were made by shipowners to reduce the cost of transport. Consequently, a lot of changes and innovation happened to ships and shipping firms. Such changes were in virtually every aspect of the industry, from the business model to shipping organisation and operation, from the types of ships to the types of ports. As a result of growing trade and the development of technology, a kind of separation or a division took place between the transport of small parcels of general cargo on some busy trade lanes on the one hand and the transport of a large amount of goods, often a full shipload, on the other hand. Such a separation evolved gradually into what we call today *liner* and *tramp* shipping. Such division allowed ships to be built for a specific type of cargo and transport aiming at better productivity and efficiency.

Before the mid-19th century merchant ships were multipurpose, which means that the ships were capable of carrying cargoes of all kinds. Gradually, they were separated to specialise in the transport of a specific type of cargo. It is believed that the first bulk carrier appeared in the UK in 1852 and the first oil tanker in 1886.[18] If most of the merchant ships were of the multipurpose type in the past, the vast majority of ships serving international trade are today specialised ships. These ships are purposely designed to carry a kind of cargo with specific transport features, which are so specific that in most cases the ships cannot transport other types of cargo. For example, tanker ships cannot be used to carry dry cargoes. Similarly, container ships cannot transport un-containerised goods. Such ship specialisation has led to the emergence of distinct shipping markets. Even though, in the long term, different markets are integrated and interrelated, in the short and sometimes medium terms, the markets may evolve differently, each to their own. There are about 12 major types of cargo ships which can be broadly divided into three groups. In 2015 there were globally about 46,500 cargo ships of 300 grt and over with a total capacity of about 1,654 million deadweight tons.[19] There is a big difference between the three groups of ships in terms of average ship size, as shown in Figure 5.6. The 12 types of ships are as follows.

Group A: dry bulk cargo ships

- *Bulk carriers*: including bulk carriers of various sizes from 30,000 dwt to 400,000 dwt ships to transport mainly minerals and agricultural products.
- *Special bulk carriers*: including cement carriers, chip carriers, or oil/bulk/ore carriers, etc.

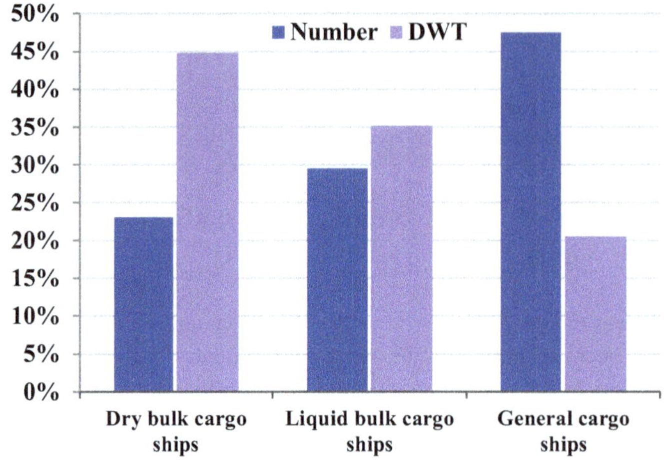

Figure 5.6 Main groups of merchant ships in number and deadweight percentage, 2015.

Source: Shuo Ma, based on data from ISL (2015).

Note: this includes ships of 300 grt and above.

Group B: liquid bulk cargo ships

- *Crude oil tankers*: including ships of various sizes ranging from small tankers to very large crude carriers of more than 300,000 dwt.
- *Product oil tankers*: these ships are mainly to transport processed oil product, such as diesel oil or gasoline.
- *Chemical product ships*: these ships are to transport chemical products.
- *LNG/LPG cargo ships*: these ships are designed to transport liquefied gases.

Group C: general cargo ships

- *Container ships*: including a big range of ship sizes.
- *General cargo ships*: they are usually small vessels with several decks capable of transporting a variety of goods in small quantities.
- *Ro-ro ships*: these ships are mainly to transport commercial vehicles, like buses or trucks, or ferry ships carrying cargo loaded on trucks.
- *Pure car carriers*: these are the specialised ships for carrying passenger cars.
- *Reefer ships*: they are the ships for perishable products, such as meat, fruit or vegetables.
- *Special ships*: they include ships with heavy lift capacity for project cargo.

With the specialisation of ships it is often difficult to discuss the shipping market as a whole. Over time, different technical, commercial and operational characteristics have emerged for each market. However, some of the specialised ships are in small market segments. The most important distinction has to be made between the three largest categories, namely: dry bulk carriers, oil tankers and container ships. The three markets share between them about 45% of the world total fleet in number of ships and 80% in deadweight tons.

What are the bases for the specialisation of ships?

Today, most merchant ships are specialised according to cargo types. Therefore, tanker ships are built for oil, bulk carriers for cargoes like iron ore or grain and container ships for general cargo such as toys or furniture. So when a new cargo appears, a specialised ship may be developed for it. This was the case for car carriers or liquefied gas carriers. Another factor to consider when a new type of ship is developed is the quantity and sustainability of the demand. When the seaborne trade of liquid cargo was in small amounts, drums were used to transport it in general cargo ships. Some small quantities of liquid cargoes are still transported this way. So the continuous growth of seaborne trade in volume has been a vital driving force for the specialisation of ships. In the dry bulk sector, a cargo-based speciality has happened concerning the size of ships. Small bulk carriers specialise in transporting commodities such as grain, while large ships are dedicated to the transport of iron ore. The following two conditions are to be considered when determining which type of ship is needed.

- ***The relationship between the amount of cargo and the capacity of the ship.*** The first condition to consider is whether or not the type of cargo to transport is big enough to occupy the total carrying capacity of the ship. This is because, for safety reasons, there is a minimum size of ocean-going merchant ships. Depending on the type of ships, this may vary between 3,000 and 10,000 deadweight tons. If the cargo size is big enough, the specific transport requirements of the cargo, such as departure and destination ports, or time of transport, can be satisfied by the ship. As a result, big ships are built for carrying iron ore and smaller ships are built for grain. Various sizes of tanker ships are constructed for different demand for the trade of oil. If the cargo size is not big enough to fulfil the entire vessel, the cargo has to share the space with other cargoes. Suitable departure and arrival ports as well as the sailing time, acceptable for all cargoes, have to be found. In the first case, the type and size of the ship can be purposely built to meet the quantity and other transport requirements of the cargoes.
- ***The way cargo is stored and loaded/unloaded.*** The second factor to consider is about how cargoes are stored in the ship and handled at ports. The evolution of ships from general and multipurpose types to specialised vessels always starts by addressing the obstacles to productivity improvement. As discussed above, the most remarkable growth in productivity of ships has been through the increase in ship's size and the reduction in transit time. In both areas, one of the main obstacles was in the interface between ship and shore or, in other words, the cargo-handling process in ports. In the past, even a small merchant ship would spend about half of its time in ports. When ships are bigger, they have to spend a more substantial proportion of the total time in ports. So time in port has been the main obstacle to the improvement of ship productivity. It is interesting to note that the features which differentiate ships from one type to another, such as a container ship, a ro-ro ship or a tanker ship, are in the way cargoes are handled at ports rather than the way ships navigate at sea.

How are the other aspects of shipping affected by specialisation?

Together with the specialisation of ships comes the specialisation of ports. It is difficult to say where between ship and port the specialisation process took place first. It must have happened at the same time. Just like most merchant ships, which are specialised, modern ports have also evolved from multipurpose berths to specialised terminals. Some ports are specialised in one commodity, such as crude oil or iron ore. For those ports capable of handling different types of cargos, cargo handling is separately done within the port for different types of cargoes and ships at dedicated terminals for containers, oil, dry bulk and ro-ro ships, etc.

Beyond ships and ports, specialisation has also affected maritime services and support activities. Not only have some general functions like finance or technical support sometimes been done by external specialist service providers, but also many core activities are becoming targets of specialisation. For example, the technical management of ships is usually an integral function within a shipping company, but it can now also be undertaken by a specialised ship management company. There has even appeared a new specialisation in ship owning, such as a Canadian company, Seaspan, does by acquiring a series of ships and leasing them to shipping companies to operate on a long-term basis. Today, shipping business has been fragmented, with an increasing number of functions completed by specialised companies that used to be undertaken internally by a company as an integral part of its business. The days have long gone when a shipmaster was indeed a "Master" in its full sense, so that, as soon as the ship left the port, he would assume not only the operational responsibility for the vessel but also the technical, and even the commercial responsibilities including the negotiation and conclusion of commercial contracts.

What are the benefits of maritime specialisation?

Maritime specialisation did not happen by itself in a natural course of evolution. It has been driven by market forces, by competition and by people pursuing better economic and commercial outcomes. So, for a shipowner, specialisation must bring additional economic yield and improve competitiveness. The benefits of maritime specialisation are many, particularly in the following areas:

- ***To increase ship productivity***. As discussed above, an essential source of ship productivity growth is from an increase in ship's size or from increasing return to scale. Without specialisation, the size of the vessel cannot be very big. This is mainly because when different types of cargoes are moved by the same ship, cargoes have to be loaded and stored separately. To do this, packaging is needed. But when shipments are packaged in cases, boxes, bales or barrels they prevent ships from being very big for several reasons. For example, packing creates broken spaces in the ship and packages, in wood boxes or carton cases, are not strong enough to be piled high within the ship.

With the specialisation of ships, usually only one type of cargo is transported by a ship so things are different. Cargo does not need to be separated. For cargoes of a homogeneous nature, such as raw materials and natural resources like oil, coal or mining products, there is no need for packaging. Cargo can be stored, loaded and unloaded in bulk, which means in loose form and in large quantities. The introduction of standardised and much larger steel containers and specialised container ships have solved the problems of not only slow handling but also storage efficiency. As a result, small unspecialised ships were replaced by larger specialised ones and the ship productivity increased continuously.

- ***To increase port productivity***. Merchant ships spend a considerable portion of their total operating time in ports. When ships are built bigger, the time in port becomes proportionally longer. So time in port is a major constraint preventing ships from being too big. Without specialisation, cargo cannot be handled efficiently at the port. For example, to handle general cargoes on and off a conventional ship, lifting facilities either of the ship or from the shore side are used at a typical rate of 1 or 2 tons of cargo per move. That would lead to a daily rate of about several hundreds of tons of cargo even with multiple gangs of stevedores working simultaneously on all ship holes.

When handling specialised ships with a single kind of cargo, dedicated cargo-handling facilities can be installed. For raw materials, cargo handling can be done continuously by using pumps, shore-based conveyor belts or grabs with big capacities. Even for general cargo, unitisation of packaged goods in standardised steel containers has massively improved the cargo-handling speed. A typical container gantry crane can move 20 or more containers per hour. Each container can carry 10 to 25 tons of cargo. If multiple cranes are used for the same ship simultaneously, a lot of cargo can be handled quickly. So specialisation has enabled ports to be much more productive.

- ***To improve service quality***. As mentioned in Chapter 3, many discussions of shipping's contribution to the world economy have not taken into account sufficiently the very important aspects of the changes in service quality. It is the same situation concerning ship productivity issues. So, in many ways, the value of the analysis on maritime productivity evolution suffers as it is not based on the comparison of like with like. For example, when examining the evolution of fleet productivity, it is observed that, measured in ton-miles completed per each deadweight ton of a ship, productivity has not shown a rising trend over the last couple of decades. However, we should still say that ship productivity has improved because, during this period, the quality of shipping services such as safety has much improved.

One of the most important areas of maritime transport quality is the reliability of the services. Shipping quality includes safety-related and time-related aspects. As we will discuss in more detail in the later chapters, particularly in Chapter 9, modern international shipping is much safer than before. Ship- and cargo-related accidents still happen but the safety performance measured as ship and cargo losses and damages per ton-mile of cargo transported continues to decrease. Specialised transport of general cargo by container ships has raised enormously the safety standard for this category of cargo, which is of high value and which used to suffer from a high rate of loss or damage. The safety performance can and should be extended today to the area of the marine environment protection, which is an aspect of quality shipping and has gradually become a centre of global concern.

With regard to the time-related quality standards, the first aspect to mention is the speed of ships. The average speed of ships has increased, particularly for container ships mainly because the shippers with high-value cargo much appreciate faster services. A higher service frequency in the liner shipping services is another quality improvement. In some busy shipping lanes, such as the one between the Far East and Europe, a shipping line provides a daily service.[20] The reliability of shipping services has also improved, in terms of predictability of delivery time and conditions as well as of punctuality of services. The extent of improvements varies among the service providers and there is enormous room for improvement. But in view of the extraordinary growth of seaborne trade and service, it is evident that the shipping services are more reliable than before. Maritime transport is also now provided with better information services. It is now common in liner shipping that customers are able to track the positions of the shipment in real time.

What are the costs of maritime specialisation?

Having gone through the major benefits of maritime specialisation, one may wonder, if it is so good to specialise, why there are still ships which are not specialised and why many activities in shipping businesses are not done by specialists. It must be because the benefits of specialisation are not big enough to offset the associated costs. We should, therefore, look into the main costs of maritime specialisations. These are mainly in the following areas.

- ***Cargo restrictions***. By the very meaning of the word, cargo-based specialisation means that the ship is supposed to transport a specific type of cargo. The exclusivity has a cost. Because the cargo demand moves up and down, a restrictive cargo base would represent a risk for the ship. A crude oil tanker cannot be used to transport grain or containers. The more types of cargo a ship can carry, therefore, the less the risk. Consequently, for the specialised dry bulk carriers as well as oil tankers, in a vast majority of cases the transport is only one-way with the return voyage in ballast. Many efforts were made to address this shortcoming and improve the flexibility for cargo. The typical example is the building of ships that can carry ore or oil in bulk (OBO), but such ships have not been popular. The lack of productivity improvement in terms of the ton or ton-miles of cargo carried per deadweight tonnage of ships can be largely attributed to the effect of cargo restriction as a result of ship specialisation.

- ***Port constraints***. Specialised ships usually require the port to specialise too at both the landside and waterside. On the landside, dedicated facilities and equipment for cargo handling are needed to handle specialised ships. To serve specialised ships, significant investment is also needed regarding other related facilities. These include storage facilities such as tanks, silos, yards and specialised warehouses. Many ports are reluctant to specialise due to the loss of flexibility in handling other types of goods. So a long-term, stable and sufficient cargo flow is usually the pre-condition of port specialisation. On the waterside, navigational restrictions often exist at many ports. This is mainly because, as a result of specialisation, average ship size grows. Many ports are not capable of receiving large vessels. The building of deepwater ports and the dredging of navigational channels demand considerable capital investment. It can turn into a risky business for those ports that compete with nearby ports, which may make a similar investment, thus creating a situation of oversupply.
- ***Higher investment***. Compared with conventional multipurpose ships and ports, specialised ships and ports are undoubtedly more costly. This is because, on the one hand, it is more expensive to build specialised ships, such as container vessels, than conventional break-bulk general cargo ships. And it is more costly to build a specialised terminal for containerised cargo than a general cargo berth. For example, it was reported that in 2014 the port of Dubai installed big container gantry cranes at the cost of US$28 million per unit.[21] Loading and unloading of bulk cargoes such as oil, minerals or grain also need specialised equipment. Building a dedicated fruit terminal, for example, can cost between 5 and 20 million US dollars. Sometimes new sites have to be found to build bigger ports with deeper water draft and more space. The high cost combined with low flexibility represents a high risk.
- ***Special expertise required***. Specialised ships and ports need to be operated by specialists. So, apart from the physical, financial and operational aspects, there is also the human dimension to consider. One of the major difficulties encountered when measuring productivity is the fact that both output and input never stay constant over time. In the maritime transport sector, not only does the quality evolve, but it also changes at a different pace. Historically, a close correlation was observed between maritime labour productivity and the quality of seafarers in terms of numeracy and literacy.[22] The technical development of maritime transport, including in the area of the ship and port specialisation, has been heavily dependent on the availability of highly qualified people. These include able seafarers and dockworkers who have been adequately educated and trained. But education and training take time and are expensive.

What are maritime productivity "trade-offs"?

The above discussions show that the gains from maritime productivity in one area are usually not to be made without losses in another area or areas. From the macro-economic perspective, a high level of specialisation might result in an excessive concentration of an activity which could lead to a situation of monopoly. Even at the company level, specialisation has some drawbacks. For example, large and specialised ships may lead to an improvement in labour productivity, but they may also cause lower loading factors, as the chances of not having sufficient and suitable cargo to carry will be bigger. This is particularly common for return voyages. Such a phenomenon has been clearly demonstrated by the differences between higher maritime labour productivity and lower fleet productivity. The lack of flexibility as a consequence of specialisation affects not only the demand side but also the supply side. Once specialised, the skill set might be locked and it would be more difficult for companies to adapt to market changes. So a careful weighing of the perspectives of benefits and losses is an important prerequisite when a decision is made on whether or not one should go for specialisation.

As discussed in earlier chapters, maritime transport has a derived demand from international trade. So the specialisation of ships is a direct response to the changes in seaborne trade, both in terms of new categories of cargo and the volume of goods traded. It appears clear that specialisation is a response to the volume growth of trade. Although, to a lesser extent, a reverse logic is also true in that specialisation of shipping has contributed to the growth of trade through a reduced transport cost. Another essential condition for specialisation to happen is a healthy and efficient market with transparent and predictable rules and regulations. In other words, in the absence of sufficient demand and an efficient market, the external transaction cost will be high, which in turn will discourage shipping specialisation.

5.4 A revolution in modern shipping: containerisation

Probably the most significant productivity enhancement in the recent history of modern shipping is from containerisation. General cargo transported by ships had always been by the package. But maritime containers are a different type of packaging: they are big, robust, reusable and, most of all, standardised. The invention of the metal boxes, or shipping containers, revolutionised the maritime transport industry, helped create the global supply and transformed the world economy. In this section we will examine some of the most essential aspects of containerisation.

How was the maritime container invented?

The original idea did not come from anyone in the shipping industry. It came from a truck driver or, more precisely, a self-made entrepreneur of the trucking business in the US with the name of Malcom McLean.[23] When his cargo, e.g., cotton in bales, was stuck at the port waiting to be handled on and off ships, he was thinking of alternative solutions. But, instead of trying to reduce the time by getting more dock workers or extending the working hours, he was more interested in an ultimate solution, which would be radically different from the conventional practice and which would allow a speedy cargo handling on and off the trucks and the ships at both loading and discharging ports. His original idea was to lift the entire vehicle with the cargo onto a vessel and lift it off the ship at the other end of the journey. McLean soon realised that it would make little sense to load the engines, chassis and wheels on-board vessels, as it would mean that the trucks could not be used and they would take up ship's space and add weight. So he came with the idea of cargo boxes detachable from the trucks: the shipping containers.

The advantages obtained by containerisation stimulated other people to follow McLean's example. But they built containers that suited their individual needs and the containers were in different designs, particularly for the corner fittings that cranes at ports lifted containers with. Containers were specific to each company and they were not interchangeable. It took a long time before a solution was finally found in 1961, when the US Federal Maritime Board and McLean set up the specifications of standard shipping containers. In 1965 the global standards for sea container design were established by the ISO, to be used by all countries and shipping companies. Having cleared the barrier of standardisation, the growth of containerisation went into full swing and the international liner shipping industry was never the same again.

What are the main impacts of containerisation?

After containerisation, the general cargo was not as general as before. The liner shipping carries non-specific cargoes of different type, size, weight, etc. So they are called general cargoes. But, thanks to maritime containers, many of such differences disappeared. Shipments are stored in steel containers of the standard type, size and weight. The standardisation of general cargoes has changed liner shipping completely. Because manufactured goods are transported by liner shipping, the containerisation has massively increased the quality and efficiency of the cargo flows internationally and, as a result, has contributed to the economic globalisation.

The containerisation has had a broad and deep impact on the liner shipping, particularly in the following three aspects: transport speed, cargo safety/security and transport connectivity. The first change is speed. But the container did not change the speed of ships, it changed the cargo-handling speed at ports. Using specialised equipment, the loading and discharging of containerised cargo is fast. It allows the ships to spend much less time in ports. Consequently, much bigger ships are used, which leads to a significant reduction in the average cost of the operation. The second aspect is the improvement of cargo safety and security. With the better protection of steel containers, cargoes are less likely to be damaged, stolen or lost. Improved safety and security lead to the reduction of insurance cost. The third aspect is about transport connectivity. The shipping containers are at the centre, based on which ships, trains, trucks, barges as well as terminals and cargo-handling equipment are purposely designed to carry standard containers. It is much easier and faster to shift the cargo from one mode of transport to another. After the introduction of containers, intermodalism developed fast with seamless delivery of cargo from door to door. Intermodal transport has extended the logistics and supply chain of many manufacturing businesses to a global scale.

Without containerisation, the world would not have such an integrated manufacturing system with the best input from different countries and run not only by large multinational firms but also by many small and medium-sized companies. The efficient international transport of general cargo by containers has allowed hundreds of millions of workers and consumers to benefit from participation in the global supply of low-cost foreign-made products. According to a research paper,[24] the benefit for the development of trade from containerisation is overwhelming. For example, five years after the adoption of containers, the dock labour productivity in seaborne trade between some industrialised countries rose by more than 17 times, the inventory cost reduced by 50% and the marine insurance cost was down by more than 80%. For the 22 industrialised countries over 20 years, containerisation boosted trade by 790%, while membership of GATT was associated with a 285% increase in trade and a bilateral free-trade agreement was responsible for only a 45% rise. The growth of world trade was attributable much more to containerisation than to all the trade agreements on tariff reduction put together.

What are the lessons learnt from the birth of the container?

The birth of maritime containers led to fundamental changes in the liner shipping industry and the world economy. Many lessons can be learnt from such revolutionary innovation. We want to discuss four important ones.

- ***It is about problem-solving.*** Many people are interested in innovation in the shipping sector. However, most attempts do not lead to the expected outcomes. This is partly because the focus is placed on innovation itself rather than on solving the key problems in innovative ways. McLean did not want to innovate, what he was interested in was to find a complete or ultimate solution to a critical issue, i.e., using containers as a solution to the problem of slow cargo handling in port. I want to emphasise the two words "complete" and "critical". Because when a *critical* problem is solved *completely*, the solution must be innovative. McLean began with identifying slow cargo handling as the critical problem and then, instead of improving the situation marginally, he tried to solve the problem completely. So a maritime innovation happens when a critical problem is solved completely.
- ***It requires a total commitment.*** Trying unusual methods to solve critical issues entirely is risky. To identify the critical problems may not be very difficult. Even finding innovative solutions is not necessarily the most challenging part. What is extremely hard to find are the individuals who have the ability and the quality to turn great ideas into concrete products and services that change

people's lives. In the 1950s the US federal regulations prohibited trucking companies from owning ships. So McLean sold his highly profitable business, which was one of the largest trucking companies in the US, to test out his ideas. He bought and converted a second-hand ship and ventured into a business that he knew little about. When asked later whether he had thought about ways to keep his trucking asset away from the risks of the unknown adventure, McLean's response was firm: "You've got to be totally committed".[25]

- ***The power of outsiders.*** It might not be a coincidence that a revolutionary innovation such as containerisation came from an outsider unfamiliar with the shipping business and its traditions. The theory of "disruptive innovation" suggests a total departure from the current system and the traditional ways of working. A disruptive innovator should be someone who does not have a limit to imagination or concern about the traditions and who can think out of the box. And such a person is more likely to be an outsider. The key methods used in disruptive innovation are usually also very new, for which shipping experts may not have any advantage. Shipping managers and executives could learn from the story of containers and try to lead the next round of maritime innovations empowered by digital technologies.
- ***The breakthrough is in ports, not in ships.*** It is interesting to note that the container innovation happened when tackling the problem of cargo handling at ports rather than the problem of cargo transport at sea. The ship–shore interface was the most critical barrier to the development of shipping and ships. The maximum size of general cargo ships is confined to about 10,000 dwt by the speed of cargo handling in ports. When general cargo has been containerised, fast cargo handling in ports leads to an increase in the optimal ship size. Virtually all the difference between specialised ships is in the way cargo is handled in ports rather than in the way it is carried at sea. Today, the ship–shore interface remains one of the most critical areas of shipping productivity, efficiency, safety, security and environment protection.

5.5 The limit to productivity growth and the future trend

By operating bigger ships and using specialised vessels, the labour productivity of maritime transport improves. But the improvement often causes other costs to rise. For example, new ships with more advanced equipment could save labour cost. But they would usually be more costly to build and thus the capital productivity decreases. Higher ship speed would allow more cargo to be transported, but the fuel cost would increase. The effort to improve ship productivity would be subject to the economic law of diminishing return. In this section we will assess the effectiveness of the improvement measures and discuss possible future development.

Is there a limit to maritime productivity growth?

The average cost will decrease when a bigger vessel is employed. But when a variable factor such as ship size starts to increase, even if other factors remain constant, the performance will improve. But as the size continues to increase, the improvement will begin to reduce and eventually stop. So the answer to the question of whether a limit of maritime productivity increase exists is *yes* under certain conditions. Such conditions are that other factors, such as the technical and organisational settings, are fixed. In other words, changing a single variable factor, while the basic organisational and technical structure remains constant, means the marginal effect will decrease. For example, when the ship's size increases, while all other factors such as ship operation, cargo handling, etc., remain unchanged, the productivity will also rise, but to a declining degree. In economics this is called the effect of "diminishing return", which means that when an increasing amount of a variable factor is applied to a given quantity of a fixed factor, the marginal outcome and the average outcome will eventually decrease.

Let's take an example in a port to show how the law of diminishing return works for the port operation. Assuming the number of stevedores is a variable factor, increasing the number of people working in a gang will affect the overall labour productivity in terms of the amount of cargo handled. However, before long, the additional output for every extra stevedore added will diminish. And, up to a point, if the number of stevedores continues to increase, the average output per person will also start to decline. This situation is illustrated in Figure 5.7, which is about a case of gang size for cargo handling of a conventional breakbulk general cargo ship at a port using the ship's derrick. With one person, only 10 tons of cargo are handled per day. If the second stevedore is added, the two men handle 30 tons of freight and, with the 3rd person joining, a total of 60 tons of freight is handled. And the productivity continues to rise for each additional person added. But the amount of extra cargo handled by the last person added starts to decrease from the 6th stevedore. However, the average output, that is the amount of cargo handled per person, is still improving. So every person is more productive with an additional person joining. This situation starts to change when the 8th stevedore is added and the average output starts to decline. For any economic activity, the different production elements are mixed in a particular proportion. If the quantity of one aspect is increased while that of the other aspects remains unchanged, it means that the ratio of production factors has changed. It is such a proportional change that leads to diminishing return.

We can look at another example of ship productivity. Let's assume a situation with a ship carrying 5,000 tons of cargo for 1,000 nautical miles and one single variable factor, the ship's speed, is changed while all other factors remain constant. By increasing the speed the total sailing time will reduce and the ship can transport more cargo during the same period. However, faster sailing speed does not affect time in port. So the total operating time is only reduced to the extent of the sailing time reduction. As the sailing speed increases further, the proportion of time in port becomes more prominent and the benefit in terms of additional ton-miles performed per each unit of speed increase gets smaller. The effect of diminishing return is evident. Table 5.2 shows this phenomenon when the speed increases

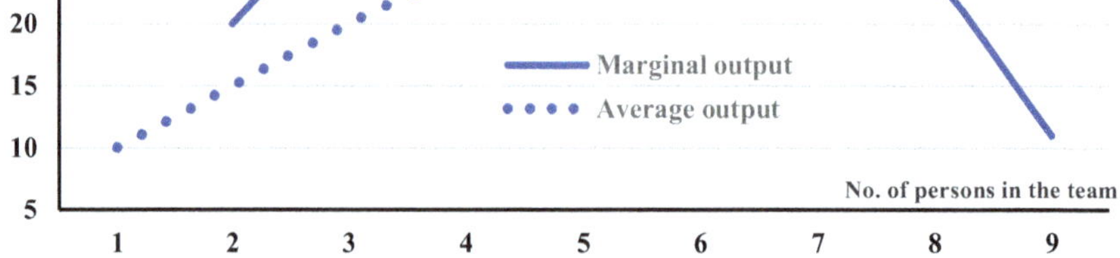

Figure 5.7 Effect of diminishing return on cargo handled with number of stevedores in a team.

Source: Shuo Ma.

Note: the extra output for an additional person starts to decline from the 6th stevedore and the average output starts to decline from the 8th stevedore. So the team productivity is the highest with seven persons.

Table 5.2 Diminishing return with speed increases, for a ship carrying 5,000 tons of cargo over 1,000 miles.

Speed (knot)	*8*	*9*	*10*	*11*	*12*	*13*	*14*	*15*
Sailing days per trip	5.2	4.6	4.2	3.8	3.5	3.2	3.0	2.8
Port days per trip	4.0	4.0	4.0	4.0	4.0	4.0	4.0	4.0
Total time per trip	9.2	8.6	8.2	7.8	7.5	7.2	7.0	6.8
000 ton-miles per day	543	579	612	642	669	694	717	738
Speed change	–	1	1	1	1	1	1	1
000 ton-mile/day change	–	36	33	30	27	25	23	21
Diminishing return		6.7%	5.7%	4.9%	4.2%	3.7%	3.3%	2.9%

Source: Shuo Ma.

Note: this is only a technical comparison in theory. For an economic evaluation of speed changes, factors such as the benefits from faster turnaround time and the cost of extra fuel consumption have to be taken into account.

from 8 to 15 knots. In the beginning, an extra knot leads to an increase of 36,413 ton-miles per day on average, or 6.7% more. But for every additional knot of speed increase, the extra ton-miles realised are smaller, for example increasing from 14 to 15 knots results in an additional 20,981 ton-miles performed or only 2.9% more.

What are the differences between incremental and structural changes?

The history of modern shipping indicates that there are two types of productivity improvement: incremental enhancement and structural changes. The above discussions are mainly concerned with the first type of improvement. The productivity increases with larger or faster ships. But the scope of improvement is limited due to the effect of the law of diminishing return. To break such limits, there need to be structural changes. These are fundamental changes usually triggered by new technological development. If this is about a complete change it is often referred to as destructive innovation,[26] which means replacing the existing system with totally new organisational and technical settings. Moving from wooden to steel ships is such a kind of structural change. Other examples should also include the shift from sails to steam and diesel engines or containerisation.

It appears likely that the effect of diminishing return has manifested for most variable factors such as specialisation and gigantism of ships. Consequently, it is becoming increasingly difficult to further increase ship productivity. The maritime business model currently used, both technically and organisationally, was established a long time ago. The last big structural changes, such as diesel engines, bulk shipping and containerisation, happened more than half a century ago. Since then, every effort has been made to explore the potentials of the business model and the technologies it is based on. Each new generation of engines has been made more fuel-efficient than the earlier ones and vessels are built bigger. But all such efforts seem to have reached their limits. From the 1990s the fuel efficiency of marine engines has not changed much and the economic benefit from operating larger ships has also been shrinking.

What are the areas of further improvement in shipping productivity?

There is certainly no straightforward answer to such a question because no one knows where, how and led by whom the next structural changes in maritime transport will happen. Looking back at the important past innovations in the shipping industry, one could draw some lessons concerning the basic characteristics of the fundamental changes that could revolutionise the shipping sector.

Merely looking for big structural changes is unlikely to result in finding any. The revolutionary changes always happened unintentionally in the process of solving fundamental problems and deficiencies, which have been the bottlenecks to good maritime transport services. For example, containerisation is considered as a revolution that has changed the liner shipping industry completely and increased productivity to a new height. But it was invented as a result of an effort to solve the problem of slow cargo handling in port. So, the right questions to ask should be, for example, "what are the biggest problems that have led to bad customer experience?" and "what are the biggest bottlenecks and the most serious problems faced by the shipping industry?". Not only should the problem areas be thoroughly explored and identified, but it is also necessary that solutions which can radically and fundamentally change the situation should be attempted. These are not the measures that would allow incremental improvements; they are the solutions that should lead to a destruction of the existing structure and system and their replacement by a new system.

Another characteristic of significant innovation which can boost maritime productivity many-fold is that such changes are always triggered by new methods, technologies and business models from outside the shipping sector. For example, the introduction of a proven technology applied in another industry to the shipping industry could trigger fundamental changes. Steam and later diesel engines are examples of such "imports" from outside sectors to shipping. Before containers were introduced to the liner shipping sector, they had already been used in other modes of transport. Now looking at the shipping industry of the present day, one may pose these questions. Will the "unfriendly" user interface in the liner shipping sector have the fate of being revolutionised by an unknown external "invader", similar to that in the hotel sector, taxi sector, music sector, etc.? How far and fast will the development of automation-related technology affect the shipping sector? What would the position of shipping be if the relationship between production, trade and transport was reshaped? There are many more such questions that can be asked and what will happen as the next big structural change to the shipping industry may still come as a total surprise to everyone. One thing is certain and that is that the potential for incremental improvement in productivity has been almost exhausted. With increasingly more integrated world economies, current shipping services are seen by many as an obstacle to their business development. A radically different business model of the maritime transport sector seems to loom ahead.

5.6 Summary

In this chapter the issue of productivity of maritime transport has been discussed. It has been concluded that maritime labour productivity, in terms of the number of ton-miles of cargo transported per person per year, has been increasing since the 1950s. Between 1990 and 2015 maritime labour productivity rose by 230%. This is mainly attributable to the two most important developments in modern shipping history: one is about the increase of ship size and the other is about ship specialisation. To cope with the fast expansion of international trade and fierce competition, shipping companies have ordered new ships of larger sizes. The immediate benefit of having larger ships is low operating costs per ton as a result of size economies of scale. The capital productivity, measured as the number of ton-miles of cargo carried per deadweight ton of ships, has registered, however, much smaller changes, because of high shipbuilding cost and the low space utilisation rate of large and specialised ships.

One of the main reasons for productivity improvement comes from the increase in ship size. Many costs, such as shipbuilding cost, do not change proportionally when the size of a ship changes. Some other expenses are virtually fixed, such as manning or management cost. So the average cost tends to decline when the ship's size increases. The effect of economies of scale has been the main driving force for shipping companies to cut costs. The average ship size of the world fleet increased fivefold between 1950 and 2018. Another important reason for the productivity rise is specialisation. Merchant ships are purposely built for particular types of cargo. As a result they are less flexible but more productive. The specialisation of vessels has led to the specialisation of ports and other maritime services.

Containers are the most significant game-changer in modern maritime transport, particularly for the liner shipping sector. Containerisation has also brought the productivity of liner shipping to a new level. Thanks to shipping containers, the international carriage of goods is faster, safer and intermodalism-friendly. As time in port is dramatically reduced due to containerisation, ships can be built larger, which in turn leads to further productivity improvement. The average size of container ships has kept increasing. As a landmark maritime innovation, shipping containers offer us lessons which may be valuable for future development.

The development of ships in the direction of gigantism and specialisation has drawbacks too. While at the beginning of the processes benefits are greater than costs, the further development in size and speciality will create fewer benefits but more cost. In maritime transport under the current maritime technology, there have been clear signs of diminishing return of productivity improvement from virtually all contributing factors, but particularly the size of ships. So more specialisations and further increases in speed or size of ships are increasingly leading to smaller productivity gains. Such a development trend can only be reversed and the productivity significantly enhanced when structural changes take place in the maritime sector that will fundamentally alter the business model and technological settings. Such development will mostly happen in the most severe problem areas of maritime transport services and it will most probably be triggered by external forces, models and technologies.

Notes

1 Hermansson R. (2003).
2 OECD (2001).
3 UNCTAD (2009).
4 UNCTAD (1972, 2015).
5 Van Zanden L. (2009).
6 BIMCO/ISF (1990, 2005, 2010, 2015).
7 SIRC (2006).
8 ISL (1979, 2015).
9 Harley C. K. (1988). Ocean freight rates and productivity, 1740–1913: the primacy of mechanical invention reaffirmed. *Journal of Economic History* 48, 851–876. And Angier, E. A. V. (1920). *Fifty Years' Freights, 1869–1919*, Fairplay, London.
10 OECD (2001).
11 UNCTAD (2010).
12 Hummels D. (2007).
13 Mohammed S. and Williamson J (2003).
14 ISL (1979, 2015).
15 North D. C. (1968).
16 Oxford Economics (2016).
17 Smith A. (1776), p. 8.
18 Stopford M. (2009), pp. 23–29.

19 ISL (1979, 2015), pp. 12–15.

20 Lloyd's List (5 March 2015). In September 2011 the shipping line Maersk of Denmark started a daily liner service between the Far East and Europe. The service is provided on daily basis at a fixed departure time. However, due to the market conditions and circumstances, the daily service discontinued.

21 *World Maritime News* "Three of World's Largest STS Cranes Arrived in Khalifa Port". The crane weighs almost 2,000 tons and is 126 metres high, 65 metres outreach and capable of lifting 90 tons. (http://worldmaritimenews.com/archives/102830/three-of-worlds-largest-sts-cranes-arrives-in-khalifa-port-uae/).

22 Lottum J. and Zanden L. (2014).

23 Levinson M. (2006).

24 Bernhofen D., El-Sahli Z., and Kneller R. (2013).

25 Levinson M. (2017).

26 See Joseph Schumpeter (1994 [1942]) who developed the concept of "creative destruction"; and other related concepts developed by other people such as "destructive innovation" by Aghion and Howitt (1990) and "disruptive innovation" by Clay Christensen (1995).

References

Bernhofen D., El-Sahli Z., and Kneller R. (2013) "*Estimating the Effects of the Container Revolution on World Trade*", Working paper 2013.4. Department of Economics, Lund University.

BIMCO/ISF. (1990, 2005, 2010, 2015) "*Manpower Update*", Baltic and International Maritime Council.

Harley C. K. (1988) "*Ocean Freight Rates and Productivity, 1740–1913: The Primacy of Mechanical Invention Reaffirmed*", Journal of Economic History, Vol. 48, pp. 851–876. And Angier, E. A.V. (1920). Fifty Years' Freights, 1869-1919, Fairplay, London.

Hermansson R. (2003) "*Den stora Svenska Aventurer*", Breakwater Publishing A.B., Gothenburg.

Hummels D. (2007) "*Transportation Costs and International Trade in the Second Era of Globalization*", Journal of Economic Perspectives, Vol. 21, No. 3 (Summer 2007), pp. 131–154.

ISL. (1979, 2015) "*Shipping Statistics Yearbook 2015*", Institute of Shipping Economics and Logistics, Bremen, pp. 12–15.

Levinson M. (2006) "*Box – How the Shipping Container Made the World Smaller and the World Economy Bigger*", Princeton University Press, Princeton, NJ.

Levinson M. (2017), "*The Now Ubiquitous Shipping Container Was an Idea before Its Time*", Zocalo Public Square, 16 June 2017. Retrieved 10 June 2019 from www.smithsonianmag.com/innovation/shipping-container-idea-before-time-180963730/.

Lloyd's List. (5 March 2015), "*Premium 'Daily Maersk' Service Abandoned*".

Lottum J. and Zanden L. (2014) "*Labour Productivity and Human Capital in the European Maritime Sector of the Eighteenth Century*", Explorations in Economic History, Vol. 53, pp. 83–100.

Mohammed S. and Williamson J. (2003), "*Freight Rates and Productivity Gains in British Tramp Shipping 1869–1950*", Working paper 9531. National Bureau of Economic Research.

North D. C. (1968) "*Sources of Productivity Change in Ocean Shipping, 1600–1850*", The Journal of Political Economics, Vol. 76, No. 5 (September-October 1968), pp. 953–970.

OECD. (2001) "*Measuring Productivity – OECD Manual on Measurement of Aggregate and Industry-level Productivity Growth*", OECD, Paris, p. 52.

Oxford Economics. (2016) "*Trade Winds – Shaping the Future of International Business*", for HSBC. p. 7

Schumpeter J. A. (1994 [1942]) "*Capitalism, Socialism and Democracy*", Routledge, London, pp. 82–83.

SIRC. (2006) "*An Analysis of Crewing Levels: Findings from the SIRC Global Labour Market Survey*", SIRC, Cardiff.

Smith A. (1776), "*An Inquiry into the Nature and Causes of the Wealth of Nations*", Retrieved from www.freebooks.com, p. 8

Stopford M. (2009) "*Maritime Economics*", 3rd edition, Routledge, London, pp. 23–29.

UNCTAD. (1972, 2015) "*Review of Maritime Transport*", UNCTAD/RMT/2015, Geneva, Switzerland, pp. 6, 15.

UNCTAD. (2009) "*Review of Maritime Transport*", various years. and Stopford M (2009) "Maritime Economics", 3rd edition, Rouledge, London and New York.

UNCTAD. (2010) "*Review of Maritime Transport*", various issues, UNCTAD/RMT, Geneva, Switzerland.

Van Zanden L. (2009) "*Roots of Growth and Productivity Change in Dutch Shipping Industry, 1500–1800*", Explorations in Economic History (October 2009), p. 8.

World Maritime News. (2014, January) "*Three of World Largest STS Cranes Arrived in Khalifa Port*". Retrieved from http://worldmaritimenews.com/archives/102830/three-of-worlds-largest-sts-cranes-arrives-in-khalifa-port-uae/.

Chapter 6

Optimisation of a ship's carrying capacity

We discussed, in Chapter 5, the issue of maritime transport productivity. The discussions were mainly based on the amount of transport in terms of ton-miles performed per active seafarer working on board a vessel or per deadweight tonnage, dwt, of a ship. Since the size of the crew is, by and large, not a variable factor for the size of a ship, the larger the ship is, the higher the labour productivity will be. The other measure, dwt, is a measurement of a ship's cargo-carrying capacity. In 2019 a total of 61.5 trillion ton-miles of international seaborne trade was transported. One question that remains to be answered is how many dwts would be needed for such a demand. The exact amount of ton-miles each dwt of a ship's cargo-carrying capacity can transport in a year depends on mainly five factors, namely ship's size, ship's speed, time in port, the ratio between operation and maintenance, and the loading factor. The change in each element affects the benefit and cost of ship operation. There is, therefore, a need for an optimisation, which means the need to find the best level of each influential factor so that the ship's cargo-carrying capacity is optimised. It is for this reason that a good knowledge of the impact of these influential factors is important. In this chapter we will discuss each of these factors so as to analyse the economic significance of them. We set profit maximisation as the objective for the optimisation of a ship's cargo-carrying capacity. From a financial point of view, profit is the residue of revenue minus cost. Therefore, the optimisation can be obtained by either a maximisation of income or minimisation of cost or both. A timeframe to be used for profit maximisation should be as long as practically applicable. The calculation unit is US dollars per ton of cargo, ship's tonnage (dwt) or teu, whichever is applicable.

6.1 Optimisation of a ship's size

As discussed in the previous chapters, there has been a trend of employing ever-larger ships. The average ship size has steadily grown over the last couple of decades for the world fleet as a whole. The growth has been extraordinary for container ships and dry bulk carriers where the record for the largest ships has continuously been broken. The driving force behind this is the benefit from scale economies. The questions that remain to be answered include the following: if big ships are advantageous why are small vessels still used? Why were bigger ships not built earlier? What is the limit to the size of ships? What are the most suitable ship sizes for different markets? The optimisation of ship size is by and large cost-based as, usually, revenue per unit is not affected by the change of ship size, or one can say that size elasticity for income is zero. So the ship size is optimised when the total cost is minimised.

What are the relevant factors regarding the ship's size?

It is generally believed that the amount of cargo to transport per year is the first and the most significant determining factor for ship size. If such a demand is big enough on a long-term basis and, at the same time, the requirement of transport frequency is satisfied, the building of large ships, as well as the construction of adequate port facilities, are justified.[1] Some other factors also have an impact on the optimal size of the ship. So, the ship's size is determined by the following four major elements.

- ***The volume of the demand.*** The demand is not the total seaborne trade in and out of a market. It refers to a specific kind of cargo to be carried by the ships concerned between specific markets attainable by the shipping company in question. So the cargo segments include, for example, crude oil, iron ore, coal or containerised goods. The cargo base should not only be big enough for the ship during the total operation period, but it should also assure a service frequency required by the customers. In liner shipping, in addition to trade growth, another main reason for the increase in the size of container ships is the effect of the cooperation between shipping lines in the form of shipping alliances or merger and acquisition. Such consolidations have massively enlarged the shipowners' cargo base, which in turn enables the use of larger vessels.
- ***The costs at sea.*** This is about the unit cost either per deadweight ton of ship or ton of cargo, depending on whether it is from a cost perspective or revenue perspective. Ideally, there should be the exact amount of cargo for every deadweight capacity but, in practice, this is not always the case. The costs at sea include all expenditures incurred during the time the ship is sailing, such as capital cost, manning cost, insurance, repair/maintenance costs and fuel cost. All the costs at sea are for shipowners only. Although cargo owners incur a capital cost as well when the cargo is in transit at sea, however, unlike for a shipowner, such a cost is not affected by the change of ship size. The capital cost for ships is, on the other hand, directly affected by the size of ship. Obviously, the larger the ship is, the higher the capital cost. This is also true for fuel and maintenance costs, but it is much less true for crew costs.
- ***The costs in port.*** A ship may come to a port to change crew, to take bunkers and other provisions, or to do ship maintenance. But the main purpose of a merchant ship calling at a port is to load and unload cargo. So, except for fuel cost, all costs at sea described above are payable while the ship is in port. And, in addition, port charges and cargo handling costs also occur in port. Although the unit cargo-handling cost will not change with the change of ship size and port charges are usually a flat levy collected per port call, the larger the ship is, the more cargo it loads and therefore the longer time it spends in port. Some of the costs in port are time-based, such as capital cost and crew costs. Such costs are therefore directly affected by ship size.
- ***The costs of risks.*** We said that, ideally, the unit in the calculation of costs at sea could either be a deadweight ton of ship or a ton of cargo. This is because every deadweight capacity is expected to be loaded with cargo when the ship is at sea. But, in reality, such an ideal situation is rather an exception. For various reasons, ships' capacity is rarely fully utilised. Trade fluctuation and imbalance between markets often results in ships carrying less cargo than their capacity. However, unless more transhipment is used or more ports are called, bigger ships are more likely to suffer from cargo shortfalls. Bigger ships have more port restrictions and they also pose more problems when it comes to capacity adjustment, shifting tonnage among different routes. So, it is safe to say that, as a rule, the bigger the ships are, the higher the risk of low capacity utilisation rate will be.

Why are size elasticities different for costs at sea and for costs in port?

Ship size is optimised when the total cost per ton is minimised. Two of the four influential factors are cost-based: the costs at sea and the costs in port. But they have the opposite reaction to the change of ship size. Generally speaking, the costs at sea and ship size have a negative correlation, while the costs in port and ship size have a positive correlation.[2] In fact, it is this negative correlation between the costs and the ship size that has been the driving force for shipowners to build ever bigger ships. On the other hand, it is the positive correlation between costs in port and ship size that has prevented ships from being built too big. But there are two fundamental reasons for the costs to react differently to the change of ship size at sea and in port and for the two kinds of cost to have different size elasticities for the following reasons.

- ***Some costs at sea are fixed when the ship's size changes.*** The costs at sea consist mainly of three parts: capital costs, crew costs and fuel costs. As we discussed in the previous chapter, for deep-sea ships, crew size is by and large constant regardless of ship sizes. Therefore, the total crew cost can be treated as a fixed cost at sea. As a result, the bigger the ship is, the lower the crew cost per ton will be. The same principle applies to the expenses of shore-based personnel and administrative overhead. Because manning is a major cost item, such a feature offers a significant cost benefit in favour of large ships.
- ***Some costs at sea do not change proportionately when the ship's size changes.*** Other costs at sea are not fixed to the size of ships, but they change disproportionally, or less than proportionally to be more precise, with ship size and this is the case with total capital costs for ships, insurance costs, maintenance cost and fuel costs. Capital cost for cargo will not change when ship size changes. Capital costs for the ship, on the other hand, change with ship size. But it changes less than proportionally. As illustrated in Figure 5.5 of the previous chapter, compared with the cost of a Handysize bulk carrier in US\$/dwt, a Panamax ship is 24% cheaper and a Cape-size ship is 43% cheaper. For tanker ships, a VLCC is only about 40% of the price per dwt of a Handysize tanker. A similar situation is also true for container ships. When it comes to insurance cost, maintenance cost and fuel cost, such a less than proportional increase can also be observed. Consequently, there is a clear economic incentive for using big ships.
- ***Costs in port are mostly variable to the ship size.*** Contrary to the costs at sea, most costs in port are either cargo-based or time-based, which are variable to the change of ship size. Let's take total cargo-handling cost as an example. This is a cost which is basically proportional to the quantity of cargo handled. Therefore, the larger the ship is, the more cargo is loaded and the higher the total handling cost will be. The same principle is applicable to storage cost, cargo dues, etc. However, for ships of any size, cargo handling cost per ton remains unchanged. So more cargo does not lead to a higher unit cost in port. What it does lead to is more time. This means at a given cargo-handling rate, the larger the ship, the longer it takes for cargo handling. And the time changes over-proportionally to the quantity of cargo handled.
- ***Time cost in port may change exponentially.*** It is, therefore, the extra time caused by cargo handling that has been the principal reason for diseconomies of scale of ships. In port, capital costs for ship/equipment and cargo, crew cost, insurance cost, etc., are all time-based costs and are affected by ship size. Let's take a closer look at the three major time-based, or rather ship-size-based, costs, namely, capital cost for ships, capital cost for cargo and crew/others cost. Time spent in port by the ship and cargo is proportional to the amount of goods to be handled. At a given cargo handling rate R, e.g., in terms of tons/day or teu/hour, and with a ship size S, the total time on cargo handling in port T is

$$T = 2S / R \tag{6.1}$$

If multiple ports are called, T represents the addition of cargo-handling time of all ports. We assume that the ship's cargo-carrying capacity is fully utilised, so one deadweight ton is equal to one ton of cargo on board. If return cargo is also included, as in liner shipping, cargo handling time is doubled, since at ports each deadweight capacity has one ton of cargo to load and one ton to unload, so S is multiplied by two. If time unit is daily, then the time costs for crew/others $TC_{c\&o}$ and for ship and equipment TC_{ship} can be calculated by T multiplied by crew/others' daily capital cost $C_{c\&o}$ or ship's daily capital cost C_{ship}. Capital cost for ships can be estimated by using the value of the ship V_s and the bank interest rate I_s.

$$TC_{c\&o} = T\,C_{c\&o} \quad or \quad TC_{c\&o} = (2S / R)\,C_{c\&o} \tag{6.2}$$

$$TC_{ship} = T\,C_{ship} \quad or \quad TC_{ship} = (2S / R)(V_s\, I_s) / 365 \tag{6.3}$$

When it comes to the capital cost for cargo in port, time in port is affected by how much cargo is on-board ship. We limit cargo capital cost only to the cargo on board. Then, while one unit of cargo is being handled, a time cost occurs to all other cargo on board. If the cargo is handled at a constant rate R, the average waiting time for all cargo to discharge is $S/R2$. With S multiplied by 2 for both loaded and unloaded cargo, the average waiting time for cargo on board is S/R. As cargo can be of different kinds, f_i is the daily capital cost per ton or teu for cargo i and n is total units of cargo on board. The total time costs for cargo TC_{cargo} can be calculated as the aggregation of hourly capital cost per unit of all cargo multiplied by time T which is shown as follows:

$$TC_{cargo} = \sum_{i=1}^{n} f_i(T) \; or \; TC_{cargo} = \sum_{i=1}^{n} f_i(S / R) \tag{6.4}$$

If cargo is homogeneous with the same hourly or daily unit value f, n equals to S, the total capital cost in port for cargo on board will be:

$$TC_{cargo} = S^2 f / R \tag{6.5}$$

The time costs for ship, crew, insurance, etc., are usually borne by shipowners, while the time costs for cargo in port are covered by cargo owners. The total time costs in port will be:

$$TC = TC_{c\&o} + TC_{ship} + TC_{cargo} \tag{6.6}$$

When ship size increases, the costs at sea will increase less-than-proportionally; however, the costs in port will increase more-than-proportionally. This is mainly because time in port grows with ship size and the capital cost for cargo increases more than proportionally to ship size. The time in port may be proportional to ship size if the cargo-handling rate remains constant. But it can be less-than-proportional if higher cargo-handling rate can be achieved on bigger ships.

How to find the optimal ship size?

Taking all the four influential factors together, namely cargo volume, costs at sea, costs in port and costs of risks, into consideration, we should be able to propose the most suitable ship size. The best way of doing this is to use a practical example to demonstrate the relationship between these variables and the optimisation process.

We take container shipping as an example. Let's simplify the case by making two bold assumptions that the cargo base is not a constraint and the ship's carrying capacity is fully utilised on both ways with no commercial, operational or technical risk. In such a special case, the optimal ship size is determined by a minimisation of the total cost, which includes costs at sea and costs in port. We take a Trans-Pacific liner shipping service between the Far East and North America, calling four Asian ports and two North American ports. The costs at sea include mainly four parts: (1) capital cost for ship and containers, which is basically calculated by taking the purchasing value of the ship and containers multiplied by the bank interest rate for the sailing period; (2) crew and other operation costs such as insurance, maintenance, etc. These costs have low-cost elasticity for ship size, so we take them as fixed costs; (3) fuel costs for ships. This cost is positively correlated with the ship's size and speed. The level of cost also depends on bunker price and to some extent the age of the ship; (4) capital cost for cargo which relies on the value of cargo and the bank interest rates.

As discussed above, the ship's sailing time is not affected by the size of ship and, therefore, all time-based costs, such as crew and capital costs, are either fixed or change less-than-proportionally with ship size. As such, average cost decreases when ships get bigger and the effect of economies of scale is evident, which is illustrated in Figure 6.1. When it comes to costs in port, apart from cargo-handling charges, most of the other costs are time-based and are thus affected by the ship's size and the amount of cargo to handle. An effect of diseconomies of scale can be observed. While for cargo owners the cost at sea is not affected by the ship's size, the capital cost for cargo at port increases very sensibly when ships are bigger. But such a change of cost may not always be taken into consideration by shipowners in their search for optimal ship size. In Figure 6.1 we see two optimal ship sizes: the lower total cost curve is for the shipowner only because it does not represent cargo's capital cost in port. The higher total cost curve is for both the ship's and cargo's costs in port. As a result, such as in this particular case,

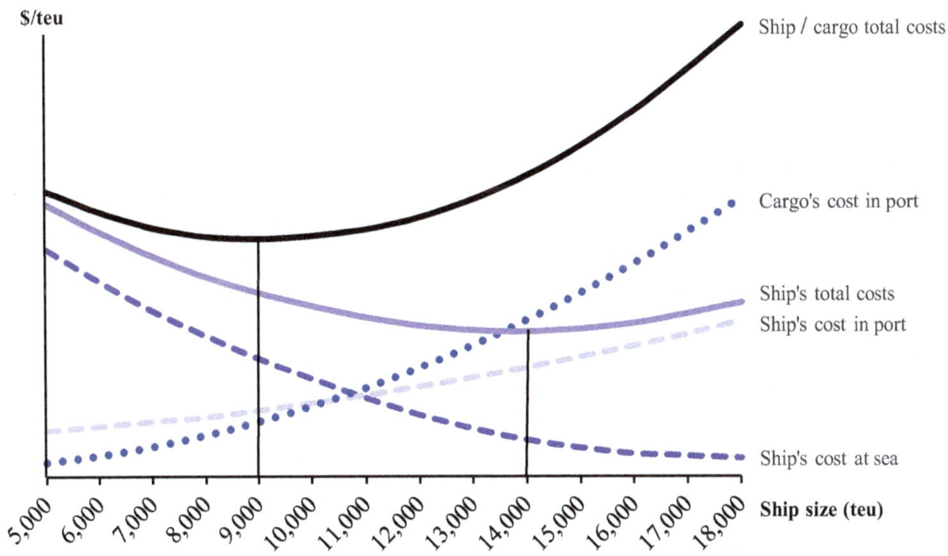

Figure 6.1 Optimal ship size for ship and ship/cargo interests (daily unit cost based).

Source: Shuo Ma.

Note: two other aspects, cargo volume and risks, are not considered. The actual cost levels are affected by various conditions. The curves and optimal points are indicative only.

when only shipowner's costs are considered, the optimal ship size is bigger than when both the ship's and cargo's costs caused by ship size changes are taken into account, which means the optimal ship size is smaller.

What is the dynamic nature of the influential factors on ship size?

The determination of optimal ship size is more challenging to do since most of the determining factors such as those discussed above are not static. The changing characteristics of these factors result in optimal ship size being a relative concept. Or, in other words, an absolute and exact optimisation is virtually impossible. Based on the characteristics of changes and the types of impact, these factors can be divided into three groups: trade-related, port-related and ship-related.

- Trade-related factors include cargo volume and evolution, travel distance, cargo value, interest rate, etc. Although assumptions are made for the above discussions that available cargo is sufficient and stable, in reality there has never been a guarantee of such conditions. When cargo volume drops, large ships will suffer more than smaller ones. Distance has a big impact on the optimal ship size because of the changing ratio between sailing time and port time. The longer the distance is, the bigger the proportion of the cost savings at sea will be. So in the liner shipping market there is usually a positive correlation between distance and ship size. Large ships may need extra time in port, which will, in turn, cost more for high-value cargo than for low-value cargo. Cargo's capital cost is also determined by the level of the internal rate of return or the bank's interest rate, which is volatile and unpredictable. In the 1990s the typical borrowing interest rate of US dollars could be more than 20%. When the commercial bank interest rates are low, as was the situation in the 2010s, the capital costs for both ship and cargo are also low, which means that the optimal ship size will be bigger.
- Port-related factors include the number of ports, port efficiency, cargo handling productivity, etc. Costs in port, or more exactly the time-costs in port, are actually the decisive costs for ship size. Such costs are in the form of capital costs for ship and cargo, which are primarily determined by port service efficiency and by cargo handling productivity. Service efficiency refers to the technical, administrative and commercial procedures, formalities and services related to ship, cargo and crew. So the total number of ports to call, including transhipment ports, and the efficiency of each port have a big impact on port costs. The above argument that the bigger the ship the longer the time in port is based on the assumption that cargo handling speed remains constant. In reality, a considerable difference exists between ports in terms of efficiency and productivity. At some ports, if the cargo-loading conditions permit, a big container ship can be served by as many as seven cranes simultaneously.[3] It is an undeniable fact that the extraordinary improvement in cargo-handling productivity in many ports has been one of the most important contributing factors for the continuous increase in the average size of container ships. Cargo-handling costs are not included because these costs are not affected by ship size or the length of time spent in port.
- Ship-related factors include ship's value, fuel cost, crew cost, insurance, maintenance and other costs. A very large container ship can cost about US$200 million each and, with an interest rate at 8%, the cost of interest is more than US$43,000 per day. The costs of crew, insurance and to some extent maintenance are time-based. Yet, the prices of ships are famously volatile and totally dictated by the law of demand and supply. This will affect directly cost-based optimal ship size. Because the unit cost of fuel is reduced by using bigger ships, a change in fuel prices will alter the optimal ship size.[4] Figure 6.2 shows that the fuel consumption per 1,000 dwt is lower as the size of ships becomes bigger. With large container ships it is usual that more transhipment has to be used due to the reasons of, e.g., a bigger quantity of cargo needed, a desire to reduce ship's costs and the technical constraints of some ports. But transhipment will increase the cost of cargo, both in transport and time-based.

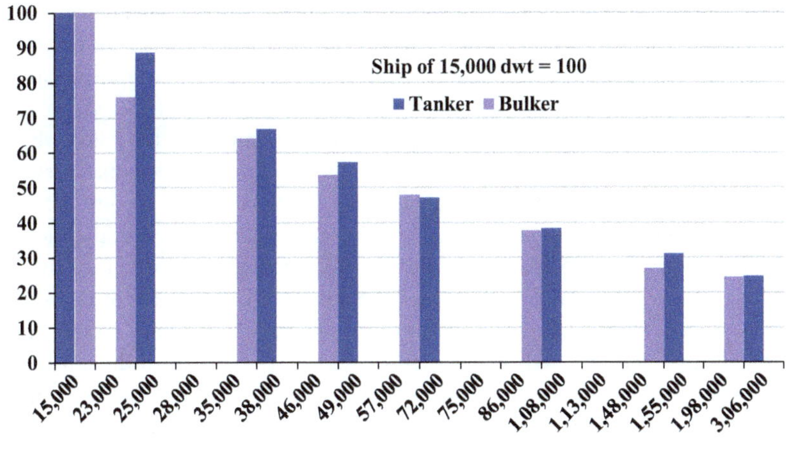

Figure 6.2 Daily fuel consumption per 1,000 dwt at 14 knots (ship of 15,000 dwt = 100).

Source: Shuo Ma, based on the data from Clarksons (2016).

Note: the index is about the average daily fuel consumption of tankers and bulk carriers of all age groups ranging from 15,000 to 306,000 dwt. The consumption index is based on tons of fuel per day per 1,000 dwt at a speed of 14.5 knots.

6.2 Optimisation of a ship's speed

The faster a ship sails, the more cargo it can transport in a year. Ship's speed is a technical issue as well as an economic one. Technically, diesel engines allow a modern vessel to attain a speed that could never be matched by a sailing ship. From the economic point of view, time is an expensive factor, which should, for the benefit of both ship and cargo owners, be reduced as much as possible. But, when the reduction of time not only brings benefits but also generates costs, time management is a matter of optimisation rather than minimisation, in the same way as for ship size. But, unlike ship size, for which the optimisation process is done by minimising the total cost, the optimal speed will be achieved when profit is maximised. This is because the ship's speed affects the level of revenue directly, while the ship's size affects the cost only.

What are the main factors affecting the ship's speed?

As far as ship speed is concerned, there are three groups of stakeholders, namely shipping companies, shippers and society. For each group, the optimal speed may be different based on different roles played by shipping. For shipping companies, transport cargo is the main business and therefore the goal is profit maximisation, or to generate revenue at the lowest cost. For shippers, maritime transport is a service input for their production or consumption and therefore the goal is cost minimisation. The shippers' cost includes mainly the freight and the time cost. For society, in addition to the interests of both shipping companies and shippers, the externalities of maritime transport, in terms of the environmental cost, should also be taken into account. By and large, the international shipping market is free and competitive. As such, the level of freight, particularly in the medium and long term, is determined by the demand and supply of the market. Therefore, freight level reflects the needs of society. It goes up when there is insufficient supply and down when there is not enough demand. In a perfectly competitive market, cost minimisation is the only way for a shipping company to maximise its profit. If the costs include those for shipping companies, shippers and society, profit maximisation is also the objective for society.

Within the technically achievable scope, ship's speed has an impact on the following three aspects: revenue, transport time and cost. For example, if speed is high, more revenue is made, less time is spent and more cost on fuel will occur. At a given freight rate, the lower the total costs are, the higher the profit will be. For shipping companies, speed-related costs include two parts: the fuel costs, which are affected directly by the ship's speed, and the capital/operating costs, which are time-based costs for both ships and cargo. As far as cargo's interests are concerned, the impact of ship speed is on the so-called *inventory cost*. Like the capital costs of ships, the cargo's inventory cost is determined by the value of the cargo and the level of the interest rate. When it comes to the environmental cost, the impact of ship speed can be measured by the emission level of greenhouse gases and their prices. Taking the above elements into account, the optimal ship speed is determined mainly by six factors, which are: the freight level, the fuel price, the value of the ship, equipment and other fixed costs, the value of cargo and the environmental cost. Among these six factors, as shown in Figure 6.3, freight is revenue-related and the other five are cost-related.

How do you calculate the optimal ship speed?

With an objective of profit maximisation, the optimal ship size can be calculated by taking into consideration the level of revenue on the one hand and the total costs for the interest of ship, cargo and the environment, or the five types of costs shown in Figure 6.3, on the other hand. Based on the costs to the shipping company and other stakeholders, the speed optimisation can be expressed by using the following formula:

$$Max\ P_d = F_d - C_d \tag{6.7}$$

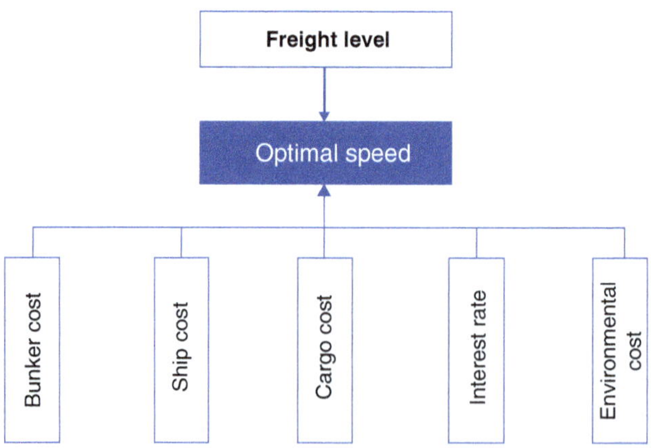

Figure 6.3 Influential factors on a ship's optimal speed.
Source: Shuo Ma.
Note: freight is revenue related, while all other factors are cost related.

where P_d is the daily profit, F_d is the daily freight income and C_d is the daily total cost, which includes costs for the ship, cargo and the environment. The daily freight is the freight income per unit divided by the total sailing days, which is derived from the distance divided by the ship's daily speed. The total cost includes the five parts shown in Figure 6.3. The level of fuel consumption per day as a function of ship speed varies from ship to ship and is affected by many other factors such as hull design, load, wind and water conditions. The relationship between fuel consumption and ship speed is not linear, and the "cube rule" is generally taken as a proxy of the relationship.[5] With regard to the capital cost of cargo, the situation of general cargoes with different values has to be taken into account, though the same interest rate may be applied. When it comes to the environmental cost, we use the amount of CO_2 emitted per ton of fuel consumed multiplied by the applicable price of CO_2. So the formula for the optimal ship speed can be extended as follows:

$$Max\ P_d = F\,Q\,l / \left[d / (s\ 24)\right] - pks^3 - C_o - V_s\,I / 365 - \sum_{i=1}^{n} V_{ci}(I) / 365 - gks^3\ C_e \qquad (6.8)$$

where P is daily profit, F is freight rate per ton, Q is ship's cargo carrying capacity in dwt, l is loading factor, d is distance, s is speed in nautical miles per day, p is bunker price per ton, k is technical constant, ks^3 is the proxy of fuel consumption to the changes of ship's speed, C_o is ship's daily operating cost, V_s is the total value of the ship and equipment, I is capital's annual interest rate, V_{ci} is the value per ton of cargo i, n is total number of tons of cargo, g is the ratio of CO_2 emitted per ton of fuel consumed, C_e is cost per ton of CO_2.

Although both shipowner and shipper are affected by the ship's speed, the impacts are different. Because ship's speed affects the time cost for cargo, the high-value cargo benefits more from a speedier transit than the low-value cargo and shippers are consequently willing to pay a higher freight as long as such extra expense is lower than the inventory cost saved. The environmental cost, as an externality, is in most cases still not an explicit cost, though it looks likely to be so in the future.

What is the impact of the influential factors on the ship's speed?

Although the optimal ship speed is affected by six factors, two of them are of particular importance: the freight rate and the fuel cost. In a competitive market, the maritime freight rate is determined by the balance between demand and supply. Given the natures of the demand and supply, freight is famously volatile, especially in the transport of basic commodities in bulk. At a time of low freight, which reflects a situation of over-supply, ship owners will use various methods to save cost. Speed reduction is one of the most effective methods. Similarly, when the freight is high, the optimal speed would be higher. With regard to fuel cost, which is a variable cost to speed, this is directly linked to the international oil market. The fluctuation of bunker price has a big and direct impact on the optimal speed, based on the "cube rule" generally applicable to the relationship between the fuel consumption level and the speed. We will take a closer look at these two factors.

It is better to examine the effects of the two factors on ship speed in the context of a particular scenario by using formula 6.8. The basic scenario chosen is as follows.

> A container ship of 8,000 teu capacity with an average loading factor of 85% trading between Shanghai and Rotterdam; the value of the ship is US$100 million and the operating cost is US$8,500 per day. The average value of the cargo is US$60,000 per teu. The annual capital interest rate is 5%. For every ton of marine fuel consumed, 3 tons of CO_2 are emitted at the price of US$25 per ton. We should also fix one of the two factors under investigation when analysing the other. So, when discussing the effect of freight, the fuel cost is set at US$300 per ton and when discussing the effect of fuel cost, the freight is set at US$600 per teu.

- ***The impact of freight.*** Although the liner shipping market is not claimed to be a perfectly competitive market as the tramp shipping market is, the liner shipping freight is still generally determined by the balance of the market demand and supply, especially in the medium and long term and on the major international shipping routes. Between March 2014 and March 2015, for example, the Shanghai Containerised Freight Index changed from close to 1,100 points to about 400 points[6] and the freight between China and Northern Europe was as low as US$211 per teu in early March 2016,[7] while the rate was US$1,795 per teu in the first quarter of 2005.[8] Figure 6.4 shows the results of the calculation with the freight ranging from US$200 to US$2,000 per teu, the market and ship conditions as described above and the fuel cost at US$300 per ton. So, at the freight level of US$300 per teu, the optimal speed is at 14 nautical miles per hour (kn) and at this speed the maximum profit, or the minimum loss in this particular case, is made. The optimal speed is positively correlated with the level of freight. When the freight reaches US$1,000 per teu or higher, the ship should sail at 25 kn or the top speed. The break-even point for the liner shipping company in this particular case is at US$500 per teu. The break-even point is much influenced by the size and the loading factor of the container ship. Bigger ships are more resilient to freight fluctuation than smaller ones. But smaller ships are more likely to enjoy a higher cargo loading factor as discussed previously. Obviously, when other conditions change, such as ship operating cost, fuel cost, cargo value or even interest rate, the optimal speed will be affected.
- ***The impact of fuel cost.*** Among the running costs of a ship, fuel cost has become the biggest cost item due to the continuous rise of the oil price since 2000. During the period between 2005 and 2015 the price of the marine bunker (MFO180 CST) varied between US$250 and US$700 per ton. The price of the marine bunker is not determined by its own demand and supply but by the

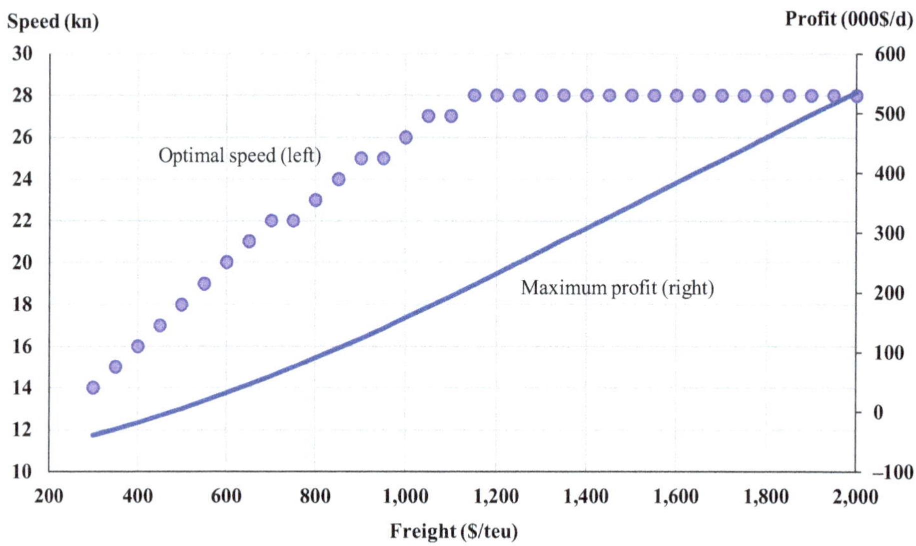

Figure 6.4 Optimal speed and maximum profit at different freight levels, fuel cost at US$300/ton.

Source: Shuo Ma.

Note: the optimal speeds calculated are for a specific case as described. The break-even point is when the freight is at US$500/teu. The ship should go at full speed when the freight is at US$1,000/teu or higher.

world's oil market, which always fluctuates. Figure 6.5 shows a calculation made for the fuel cost ranging from US$60 to US$860 per ton with the market and ship conditions as described above and the freight rate at US$600 per teu. The results of the calculation shows that the optimal ship speed and the fuel cost are negatively correlated, which means that the lower the fuel cost is, the higher the optimal speed will be. So if fuel cost is at US$100 per ton, the optimal speed will be above 25 kn or the full speed. When the price of fuel rises to US$300 per ton, the optimal speed is reduced to 19 kn. In this particular case, the break-even point is when the fuel cost is at US$650 per ton.

Some of the six factors are more or less predictable, at least in the medium and short terms, such as ship's cost and cargo's cost. Other factors, such as freight rate, fuel cost or interest rate, are difficult to forecast. The influential factors are interrelated, though they may also change independently in the short term. For instance, in 2005, high freight rate coexisted with high fuel cost, while in 2014, low freight rate coexisted with high fuel cost. The impact of one factor on the optimal speed is different from that of another. Consequently, the importance varies between the factors. The environmental cost has not yet played a significant role in determining the optimal speed, even though some shipping companies claim emission reduction is a chief objective of slow steaming. The primary driving forces or the most important influential factors are undoubtedly the levels of freight and fuel cost.

6.3 The impact of time in port

How much cargo a ship can transport in a year also depends on how much time the ship transports, i.e., navigates on the sea, and how much time it does not. Such non-navigation time may be for ship repair and maintenance or for anchorage due to operational or commercial reasons or most likely for

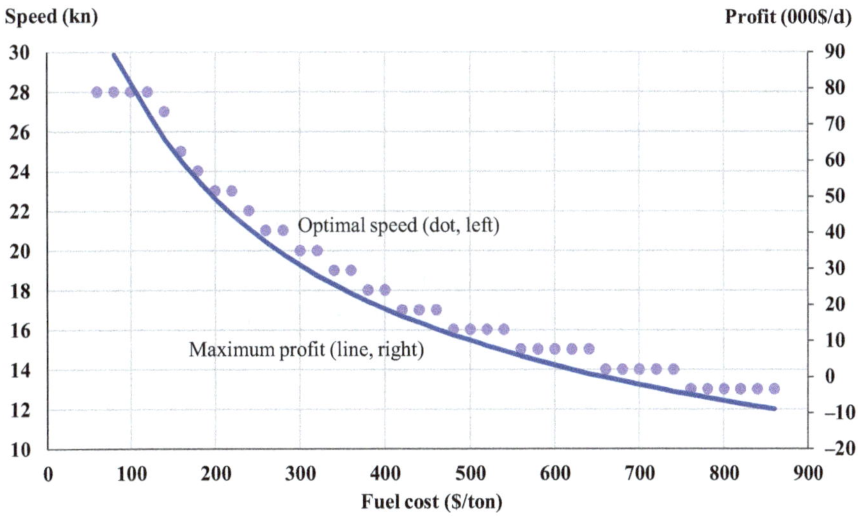

Figure 6.5 Optimal speed and maximum profit at different fuel cost levels, freight at US$600/teu.

Source: Shuo Ma.

Note: these optimal speeds are for the specific case described. The break-even point is when the fuel cost is at US$750 per ton and ship sails at about 14 kn.

cargo handling in port. Unlike the issues such as ship size, speed, maintenance or loading factor, the matters related to time in port are usually not in the control of shipping companies. And it is most probably for this very reason that an increasing number of shipping companies have entered into the port business.

Why is the time in port so crucial for shipping?

A ship needs to spend time in port for various reasons. First, port calls are necessary for matters related to the ship itself. A ship needs to re-fill with bunkers at ports, before or during a voyage. This is not only for operational reasons but may also be for economic reasons by carrying more or less cargo based on the difference in bunker prices at different ports. Similarly, a ship calls at a port to change crew and to make provision of consumables for both ship and crew. The most time-consuming activity in a port is certainly not ship-related, but cargo-related. Cargo handling takes most of the time of ships in port. The bigger the commercial ships are, the longer time they will need for cargo handling. A very large oil tanker or bulk carrier may load or discharge more than 300,000 tons of cargo. And a 20,000 teu container may need to load and unload in a single port a total of more than 10,000 teus with possibly as much as 100,000 tons of cargo. Unless it is a very efficient port, a ship can easily take one or several days in port for cargo handling.

The time spent by a ship in port also includes that between the moment of the ship's arrival and the start of cargo-handling operations, as well as that between the end of cargo handling and the departure of the ship from the port. The total time spent is also referred to as *dwell time* in port. The navigational conditions are different in each port. If time in port starts when the ship arrives at the anchorage and is ready for cargo handling, it may take a long time for the ship to position itself safely at berth for cargo-handling operations to begin. A port may be located upstream on a river or behind locks. Many ports have complicated and restrictive navigational channels and areas where ships have to be assisted by tug boats and pilots and move slowly. Such time spent to get the ship in and out of a port may sometimes be longer than the time needed for both ship service and cargo handling. Time is also needed for administrative formalities and procedures and this time may also vary enormously between countries.

If a ship spends 25% of its time in port in a year, its annual cargo-carrying capacity reduces by the same percentage. Take two identical ships of 50,000 dwt for example. If one ship spends 73 days in a year in port and the other ship spends 110 days in port in a year, then the first ship will have 10% more time for transporting cargo than the second ship. The cargo-carrying capacity of a ship is negatively proportional to the time spent by the ship in port. It can be written as:

$$C_a = C_d\left(365 - T_p\right)/\,365 \tag{6.9}$$

where C_a is actual carrying capacity of the ship in dwt or teu, C_d is the designed capacity of the ship in dwt or teu and T_p is the time, in number of days, spent by the ship in port during a year.

So if a ship spent 183 days per year in port, it would lose 50% of its cargo-carrying capacity. Or, in other words, it can be considered as a cost increase to the same proportion with the exception only of fuel cost. A shipping company's profit margin could be severely affected by excessive time spent in port. It is therefore in the interest of shipping companies to control and reduce the ship's time in port as much as possible.

Why does time in port differ so much between countries and ports?

In a modern and efficient port, the port dwell time for a ship may be shorter than 24 hours, while at other ports a similar type of ship may have to stay for weeks. Such differences are attributable to natural factors such as navigational conditions; technical/operational situations such as port facilities and equipment; and organisational issues such as administration/institution-related issues, including rules, practices, procedures and formalities. We will discuss these in more detail.

- ***Natural conditions.*** Navigational conditions have a big effect on a ship's time in port. A tidal port may end up with ships sometimes spending a long time waiting for the right moment to enter or exit a port. Sailing over a long distance from anchorage upstream in some river ports, often with shallow, narrow, crowded and restrictive waters, can also be very time-consuming. A port with direct access from the sea has, therefore, a distinct advantage. Easy access from the sea, together with the increase of average ship size, has resulted in a trend of port relocation from upstream to downstream or even offshore.[9]
- ***Technical/operational situation.*** Port facilities and equipment are other determining factors for time spent by a ship in port. Port facilities include under-water as well as shore-based infrastructure, which takes a long time to build and requires big capital investment. Depending on natural conditions, the construction of a port may involve initial and maintenance dredging work which is usually costly. A specialised port terminal may cost tens of millions of US dollars. Following the specialisation of ships, ports today consist of specialised terminals rather than the "one-type-fits-all" berths in the past. Specific shore-based facilities and equipment are needed for loading and unloading specific cargoes. Thanks to port specialisation, the productivity has been greatly improved and the time for cargo handling is much reduced compared with the situation in the past. But in many less-developed countries, port efficiency is still far from being satisfactory due to insufficient investment in both facilities and equipment and management skills. It was revealed in a survey that in the 2000s the average time in port in less-developed regions was more than two weeks compared with the average time in most developed areas. Even within the same region, big differences still exist between ports.[10] The hardware is only a partial cause for the differences in time in port and management and human factors are as or even more important. The specific knowledge and skills of port workers can play a decisive role.
- ***Organisational issues.*** Ships can be held up and the cargo-handling process can be slowed down by inefficient organisational and institutional arrangements. Safety and security procedures, customs formalities and other administrative requirements can all be time-consuming. At some ports these activities are undertaken efficiently, but at many other ports these are the main obstacles to the speedy turnaround of ships and cargo. It was found that in some ports the relaxed rules and regulations have led to shippers using port areas as free storage for their cargoes.[10] As a consequence, the already limited space is quickly full of cargo and the ships cannot be handled quickly. Customs and other administrative procedures and formalities can be a main cause for delays. Data technologies provide certainly partial solutions, but the organisational and management streamlining remains to be the key factor. A port operating on a 24/7 basis can sensibly reduce the ship's time in port. It is a general belief that to improve port efficiency, the priority should be given to the improvement in organisational and management efficiency, not only because it is more effective and less costly in terms of capital investment in hard currencies, but also because modern port facilities and operation systems can only deliver the expected outcomes when efficient organisation and good management are in place.

What are the costs and benefits of the reduction of time in port?

Unlike the issues of ship size or speed, there is probably not an equivalent concept of "optimal time in port". And for both ship's and cargo's interest, the shorter the time in port the better. Yet, when the interests of ports are included, the conclusion will be different. For a port operator, providing services generates an income and also a cost. When treated as a commercial activity, the optimal amount of port facilities should be when the marginal revenue is equal to the marginal cost. The situation in ports is more complicated so Chapter 10 is devoted to port-related subjects. The issue of optimal port facilities can also be seen as an issue of optimal waiting time in port by ships and cargo. If we put the role of organisation and management aside and assume that the more port facilities a port offers, the less a ship's waiting time will be and the lower the berth occupancy rate will be, but the higher the cost will be for the port, then the optimal port waiting time is when the total cost for the port on the one hand, and for ships and cargo on the other hand, is at the minimum.

The amount of time during which a berth is utilised by a ship divided by the total available time is called *berth occupancy rate*. For a port, the ideal situation is that its facilities are fully utilised with no resources wasted. This would mean a berth occupancy rate at 100% or as high as possible. However, for a shipping company, the ideal situation is that there will always be a vacant berth available when the ship arrives at the port, or a berth occupancy rate as low as possible. The critical issue is to find the optimum occupancy rate between these two extremes. The problem has been studied by many researchers and practitioners alike. The question is quite complex with many influential factors, but the following two elements are the most important to take into consideration.[11]

- ***Ship arrival pattern***. If a ship's arrival at port is stochastic, the average waiting time will be longer over a period of time. So big data technology, better planning, communication and coordination can help increase the berth occupancy ratio without creating additional waiting time.
- ***The number of berths to use***. In a port with one berth and average berth occupancy rate at 50%, the possibility of a ship waiting for a berth is 50%. But in a port with two berths and 50% occupancy rate, the chance of a ship waiting for a berth when both berths are unavailable is reduced to 25%. So the more berths a common user terminal has, the shorter the average waiting time for ships will be.

For shipping as a whole, the objective should be to minimise the total cost of both ships/cargo and ports. It would usually be better to keep a low average waiting time even at the expense of a low berth occupancy ratio. This is because, grossly speaking, the time cost is cheaper for ports than for ships and cargo. For example, a container terminal may cost about US$100 million to build, but a container ship and containers may be worth over US$200 million. If the value of the cargo is included, the total value could much higher. So the value ratio ship/cargo to port would 3–5 to 1. So port congestion may cost a country much more than unutilised port facilities do.

Often, the biggest challenge is not that time in port is too long, but the fact that time in port is unpredictable. For shipping, such a situation can lead to difficult and costly consequences. Ships are employed usually with strict and tight schedules, such as the case of liner shipping, or with multiple cargo fixtures in time sequence. If the length of time in port is a matter of certainty, it will always be possible for the shipping companies to arrange the ship deployment accordingly. So, to cope with the situation of the unpredictability of time in port, shipping companies often have to protect their interest by means of insurance or a compensation clause, e.g., demurrage, or by avoiding using the port altogether.

6.4 The impact of a ship's operation to maintenance rate

Ships should be maintained in optimal condition for safe and efficient operations. Although much such maintenance is carried out by engineers on board ships, periodically ships have to suspend transport operations to undertake maintenance in a port or a ship repair yard. This is particularly the case for old ships. Such downtime undoubtedly has an impact on the cargo-carrying capacity.

What are the requirements for the ship's repair and maintenance?

There are two main categories of ship repair and maintenance: planned and unplanned. They can also be called preventive and corrective maintenance. Planned ship repair and maintenance are usually undertaken according to standards which are laid down by various organisations such as the IMO, flag states, classification societies and insurers. There are overlaps but each regime has specific emphases. Most such requirements are mandatory and often considered as minimum standards. Shipping companies have their own repair and maintenance policies and some of them are more stringent than the mandatory requirements. Adequate planned maintenance can reduce operational breakdowns and damage, thus minimising unplanned maintenance.

As a part of planned maintenance, many ships follow a dry-docking cycle of, for example, every two and a half years. Technical surveys and necessary repair and part replacement will be undertaken based on the requirements of the classification society for the ship to remain in the class. All commercial ships are also subject to periodic surveys demanded by the classification societies. Any ship may also meet the situation where unexpected repair and maintenance are needed, as a result of breakdown or damage in port or at sea.

Many ships practice a "planned maintenance system" which usually is a computer-based system for ship managers to carry out repair and maintenance regularly according to ship manufacturers' and classification society's requirements. The general philosophy is to take preventive measures by undertaking repair and maintenance systematically and predictably. So the planning and documentation of ship repair and maintenance should be made. It is also a mandatory requirement by the International Safety Management Code – the ISM Code – of the IMO that ships should have a planned maintenance system.

What is the impact of the ship's age on its cargo-carrying capacity?

Ships in their operational life should be in good technical condition or seaworthy. It is defined in the IMO's SOLAS regulation on Goal-Based Standard that a ship's

> specified design life is the nominal period that the ship is assumed to be exposed to operating and/or environmental conditions and/or the corrosive environment and is used for selecting appropriate ship design parameters. However, the ship's actual service life may be longer or shorter depending on the actual operating conditions and maintenance of the ship throughout its life cycle.[12]

The operational life of a ship depends on the ship's type and construction, its operational environment and its maintenance conditions.

Ship maintenance and repair can generally be grouped into three types. The first is routine maintenance which consists of work undertaken by the crew and that can be done without interrupting the ship's operation. The second type is intermediate maintenance which is performed by specialists, usually at berth, when the ship is at a port. This is done either as a scheduled work required by the company and classification society or in response to a survey or technical problems. The third type is periodical dry dock maintenance, which is carried out by a ship repair yard. It usually involves comprehensive and most intensive maintenance. Depending on the conditions of the ship and the class requirements, it is common that after the first 10 years of service, ships are taken to the dry docks at about a two-year interval for steel renewal and other maintenance operations. The amount of steel replacement varies but, in general, it rises with the ship's age. The dry docking usually takes 1 to 2 weeks and the cost varies depending on steel price, the type of ship, the period and the repair yard. It is common that such dry docking is performed approximately every 30 months. However, after 15 years, the downtime for dry-docking will become two or three or more times longer due to the more extensive repair and maintenance work involved.[13]

6.5 The impact of loading factor

The amount of cargo a ship deadweight capacity can carry in a year depends on whether the full capacity of the ship can be utilised each time it performs the transport. There are, however, many reasons for such an ideal situation not to happen. The reasons include the variation of cargo load, the competitiveness of the shipping company, the type and amount of cargo the shipping company has, the ship's type, the ship's size, etc. Or, in other words, the level of loading factor is determined by both the demand and the supply.

How does demand affect the level of loading factor?

Insufficient cargo demand is the direct cause of ships leaving a port not fully loaded. It happens when there is an over-supply. There is also an important demand-side factor related to the trade imbalance. Unlike passenger transport, which in a majority of cases includes two trips, go and return, of the same person, all cargo transport is of a single voyage. With the specialisation of ships, it is often by design that some ships transport cargo in one direction only. This is the case of crude oil tankers and many dry bulk carriers, particularly the big ships. However, as explained in the previous chapter, the economic gains from ship specialisation outweigh the losses from the ship's low loading factor. In other words, the market generally accepts a freight paid to the shipping companies that is meant to cover the cost of both ways.

For liner shipping the situation is different and the ships are usually designed to carry cargo both ways, although, in reality, the situation is often different. The so-called general cargo ships are built to be operated in any market in the world. The ship's type is standard and the size, constrained by the time needed in loading and unloading cargo in port, is small. As such, in a majority of cases, the ships are sufficiently fully loaded with cargo for every journey. For container shipping the situation is different. Driven by the economic globalisation and international supply chain, while the total volume of general cargo expanded rapidly, such expansions have been uneven geographically. For many years, Asia, particularly the Far East, has exported more general cargo to the rest of the world than it imported. Consequently, container ships, which have replaced most conventional general cargo ships, are commonly designed based on one-way trade, or "head-haul" traffic, at least on the main East–West shipping routes. This means that the size of container ships is largely determined by the cargo volume of one trade direction. Given the thin profit margin of the shipping industry due to fierce competition, the competitiveness of a shipping line often depends on the level of loading factor of the return voyages.

How does supply affect the level of loading factor?

From the ship side, the loading factor is mainly affected by the specialisation and the size of ships. The more a ship is specialised, the narrower the cargo base it will have and the harder it becomes to maintain a high loading factor. So general cargo ships usually have a higher loading factor than tankers or bulk carriers. Ships continue to become more specialised simply because the gains from specialisation outweigh the losses from the low loading factor. Attempts have been made by some shipping companies to increase loading factor by building ships that can carry both crude oil and ore, or OBO type of ships, but such ships have not been proven very successful.

It is argued that there is an effect of diseconomies of scale of loading factor, which means that the larger the ship is, the more likely it is that the ship has a lower level of loading factor. This is particularly true for container ships due to the fluctuation of trade. Ships transporting cargoes in bulk have a bigger chance of leaving the port fully loaded. There are many reasons for this, such as the limited cargo base a shipping company has. While small ships can more easily adapt to the market changes, for example if there is cargo shortage in a port it could go and load cargo at another port, large ships suffer more from the technical limitation of ports that can accommodate big ships. Today, container ships are very big. The largest ships are capable of carrying more than 20,000 teus and at a port, as many as 4,000–5,000 teus are expected to be loaded. Such a need for a huge amount of cargo in a short period of time presents a serious challenge to the port and the local transport systems. When seaborne trade changes in direction or volume, big ships are always more difficult to adapt than smaller ones.

What are trade-offs between the type, size and loading factor of ships?

Two aspects of the ship are directly interacting with the loading factor: the ship's type and the ship's size. As explained above, there is a reverse relationship between cargo-based ship specialisation and loading factor, i.e., specialisation of ships will usually result in a low loading factor, as seen in Figure 6.6. This is different when compared with the impact of ship specialisation on time in port, in which case specialisation leads to a reduction of time in port per unit of cargo handled. Container ships normally have a higher loading factor because, on the one hand, the specialisation is not focussed on a particular cargo but on a big category of different goods, or general cargo. On the other hand, the trade of containerised cargo is more affected by customer preference and global supply chain. As a result, there is a bigger chance of having a return cargo in liner shipping than the transport by tramp shipping of natural resources and basic commodities.

The impact of the ship's size on the loading factor is more related to the market situation and the company's commercial/operational capabilities. Generally speaking, the larger a ship is, the more difficult it is to load the ship fully. This is also true for container ships. This effect is illustrated in Figure 6.6, where we can see that the cost related to loading factor increases as the ship becomes bigger. However, in comparison with the big benefit from the reduction in unit cost, the ship owners are ready to pay for the cost of low loading factor. It is, therefore, crucial to maintain a reasonable loading factor while operating large vessels. This has become one of the main objectives of many shipping companies in cooperating between themselves in the form, for example, of liner shipping strategic alliances.

Due to the fact that the actual loading factor of ships is in most cases lower than 100%, the measurement of ton-miles cannot accurately capture the exact amount of transport capacity needed. Or, in other words, if the ship's capacity is utilised only in one instead of two directions, the actual mileage travelled for every ton of cargo carried should be multiplied by two.

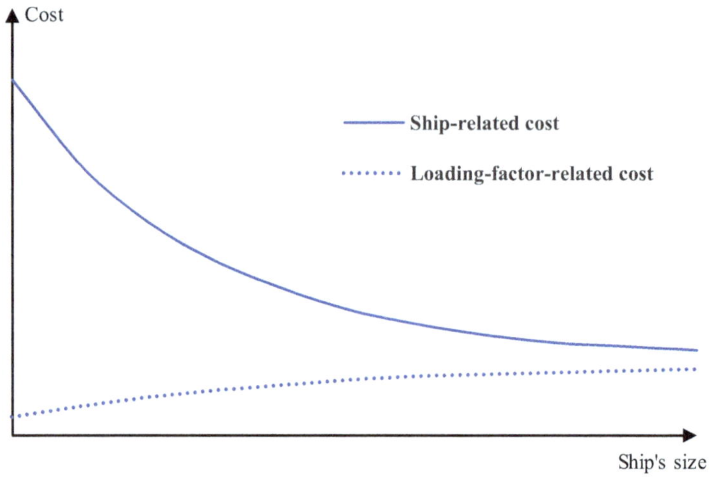

Figure 6.6 Size versus loading factor – the impact of ship's size on costs.
Source: Shuo Ma.
Note: the benefit from scale economies in the form of low unit cost for ships is often more than sufficient to offset the loss from low loading factor.

6.6 Summary

For a given amount of seaborne trade to transport, the number of ships needed depends on a number of factors. In this chapter these factors are discussed for the purpose of optimal use of the ship's cargo-carrying capacity. The first factor to be decided on is the size of the ship. The optimal size depends on the volume of demand, the costs at sea, the costs in port and the costs of risks. Out of the four influential factors, the costs in port is the most critical constraint on ships being too big, because big ships incur extra system costs at ports as well as time costs to ship and cargo. So the most suitable size of a ship is when the total cost is at the minimum. Such optimal size varies when the determining factors, such as port efficiency, change. The second aspect discussed is the optimisation of the ship's speed. The optimal speed depends on six factors, namely the freight level, the bunker price, the value of the vessel and cargo, the interest rate and the environmental cost. The freight rate and the bunker price play the largest role in the determination of the optimal speed. The third aspect examined is time in port. The time a ship spends in port is affected by natural conditions, the technical situation and optional features of the port. It is in the general interest of maritime transport as a whole that time in port should be reduced to as short as possible, even when a costly investment is needed. Appropriate ship maintenance planning and management can affect a shipping company's bottom line. Competition between shipping companies in this respect is focussed on the dry-docking and optimal use of the ship's capacity. Whether or not a shipping company can load the ships fully has direct effects on its profitability and thus its competitiveness. There is a trade-off between the size of the ship and the average loading factor. Generally, the benefit from the ship's size outweighs the loss from low loading factor.

For a given ship's cargo-carrying capacity in dwt, the actual ton-miles performed depend on the above five factors. Globally, the performance of the world's fleet between 1970 and 2010 was at the level of about 10 tons of cargo per deadweight on average for container and general cargo ships, about 7 tons of cargo for oil tankers and 5 tons for dry bulk carriers.[14] The container fleet was more productive because of faster sailing speed, shorter time in port, shorter average distance and higher loading factor thanks to more available cargo in both directions.

Notes

1 Jansson J. O. and Shneerson D. (1982). In this paper the authors argued that, given a suitable trade, optimal ship size is a function of costs in port and costs at sea.
2 Some researchers argue that at low range of ship size there is no evidence of diseconomies of scale in port, which means that the costs in port will not grow with bigger ships. See: Cullinane K. and Khanna M. (1999).
3 One of the world records is held by the Port of Qingdao when, at 01:50 am on 28 November 2006, the last container was loaded on board container ship *COSCO Beijing* after a total of 16 hours of cargo handling with 4,588 teu unloaded and 5,651 teu loaded, averaging 640 teu per hour (source: http://qdchinanews.com/FocusNews/News/2011/0719/8796.html).
4 It is argued that during the period of the 2010s, when the price of oil dropped from more than US$100/b to about US$40/b, the reduction of unit costs would be from about 20% to 10% between a ship of 20,000 teu and 13,000 teu (source: Lloyd's List, "Ultra large containerships still cost-effective, says OOIL", *Containers*, 8 August 2016).
5 The relationship between fuel consumption and ship speed, such as the "cube rule", comes from tests and experiments. So, strictly speaking, for every ship the ratio is different. When a ship moves ahead, the water and air resistances are determined by speed, ship displacement, shape, materials, current, wind and other factors. With better ship design and materials used, the ratio may be lower. For more detail see: Evens J. and Marlow P. (1990) *Quantitative Methods in Maritime Economics*, Fairplay Publications, UK, pp. 79–91; Dykstra D. L. (2005) *Commercial Management in Shipping*, Nautical Institute, The UK, pp. 264–287.
6 The data is taken from Shanghai Shipping Exchange at http://en.sse.net.cn/indices/ccfinew.jsp (retrieved 15 August 2016). This index is composed from 15 container liner shipping services from China to various destinations. The index was established on 1 January 1998 and set at 1,000 points.
7 Lloyd's List (11 March 2016).
8 UNCTAD (2007).
9 The port of Shanghai has for a long time suffered from difficult access by ships to its port areas along the Huangpu river. So it built a container port on an island with a 32-km bridge linking to the mainland in 2004/2005.
10 World Bank (2012). In sub-Saharan Africa the average port dwell time was more than 16 days.
11 Thoresen C.A (2014).
12 IMO SOLAS Convention.
13 Gratsos G. A., Psaraftis H. N., and Zachariadis P. (2009).
14 UNCTAD (2011).

References

Clarkson (2016) "*Shipping Intellence Network Timeseries*", Clarkson, London, UK.

Cullinane K. and Khanna M. (1999) "*Economies of Scale in Large Container Ships*", Journal of Transport Economics and Policy, Vol.33, Part 2, pp. 185–208.

Dykstra D. L. (2005) "*Commercial Management in Shipping*", Nautical Institute, London, pp. 264–287.

Evens J. and Marlow P.. (1990) "*Quantitative Methods in Maritime Economics*", Fairplay Publications, London, pp. 79–91.

Gratsos G. A., Psaraftis H. N., and Zachariadis P. (2009) "*Life Cycle Cost of Maintaining the Effectiveness of a Ship's Structure and Environmental Impact of Ship Design Parameter's*", Retrieved from http://nee.gr/downloads/176Life.cycle.cost.pdf

IMO SOLAS. "*Convention, Regulation II-1/3-10, Goal Based Standard Tier I – Goals*", Paragraph 5.

Jansson J. O. and Shneerson D. (1982) "*The Optimal Ship Size*", Journal of Transport Economics and Policy, Vol.16, No.3 (September 1982), pp. 217–238.

Lloyd's List. (2016a) "*Ultra Large Containerships Still Cost-effective, Says OOIL*", Containers, 8 August 2016.

Lloyd's List. (2016b) "*Asia-Europe Rates Slip Perilously Close to All-time Lows*", 11 March 2016.

Thoresen C.A.. (2014) "*Port Designer's Handbook*", 3rd Edition, ICE Publishing, London, p. 349.

UNCTAD. (2007) "*Review of Maritime Transport*", UNCTAD/RMT/2007, Geneva, p. 73.

UNCTAD. (2011) "*Review of Maritime Transport*", UNCTAD/RMT/2011, UN Publication, p. 82.

World Bank. (2012) "*Economic Premise Why Cargo Dwell Time Matters in Trade*", No. 81, May 2012.

Chapter 7

The main forms of shipping operation

There are billions of tons of seaborne trade that are to be transported internationally on the one hand, and tens of thousands of commercial ships to assume the transport on the other hand. In this chapter we will examine how the demand for maritime transport is satisfied by the supply of it. There is more than one way of transporting the trade and the differences have resulted in the shipping sector being separated into distinct markets. Each market has its own characteristics in various aspects, from operational to technical, organisational and commercial sides. We will discuss the special features of the main forms of shipping activities to see how they are organised and operated. As the maritime transport market is demand-driven, especially in the long term, we should first of all look at the demand side to consider the nature of seaborne trade and the requirements for maritime transport. This will help us understand why shipping services are organised and operated in the way they are now. It will also allow us to have an idea about where the industry might be heading from the organisational point of view. As demand changes, the way such new demand is satisfied should be different as well.

7.1 Types of seaborne trade and the transport requirements

The demand from seaborne trade for transport varies greatly. Some of the needs are big, others are small; some needs are occasional, others are frequent; some needs are urgent, others are not as time-sensitive. Yet these features of demand for transport will define the types and forms in which shipping services ought to be operated. So we will examine the demand for maritime transport in the following three aspects: the stage of the production process, the volume of the demand and the value of it.

What is the relationship between shipping and production phases?

As discussed in Chapter 2 and Chapter 3, seaborne trade is divided into two big groups: primary materials and manufactured products. Sometimes a country uses imported primary materials to produce manufactured products for export, even if the importers and exporters are different companies. In such a situation, the two groups of seaborne trade can be seen as going through different phases of production linked by maritime transport. At the end of the first production phase, raw materials such as crude oil, coal, mining and agricultural products are traded and moved by ships for processing. Then, as the second production phase, such materials are processed and used in manufacturing consumer goods. After that, some goods are exported to end-users. This is the case for some manufactured products and also for some primary materials, such as crude oil, coal or grain, that usually need to be processed into consumable products like chemicals, oil products, processed cereals, etc., before being exported to the end-users.

The development of the global supply chain has led to the situation whereby manufacturing is completed across a number of countries. The production is therefore divided into several phases to form a global supply chain. While this phenomenon has been discussed in the previous chapters, the very profound impact of such internationalised manufacturing on maritime transport has not. Traditionally, most manufacturing activities of a product took place in a single location or between factories in proximity without a need for international shipping. So maritime transport happened either before the industrial production processes or after them. This means transporting raw materials before the manufacturing activities began or to transport finished products after the activities are completed. However, at the present time, most international trade consumer goods are products of a global supply chain or an internationalised production system. Consequently, maritime transport has entered into the manufacturing processes by moving intermediate goods between countries. This pattern of international production and trade, as discussed in Chapter 3, has registered very rapid growth in recent decades. Figure 7.1 shows such a situation of more production phases which are linked by maritime transport. On the left we can see the traditional pattern of localised production whereby only finished goods are transported by ships to end-users. As more production phases are included in the globalised production system, the quantity of seaborne trade increases, even if the amount of finished products and the total value added do not. So development of globalised production and that of maritime transport have formed a *virtuous circle* whereby more efficient shipping allows and encourages manufacturing activities to be more global and, in turn, more globalised production provides extra seaborne trade to the shipping industry, giving it room for further cost reduction and thus reducing further still the transaction cost of the global supply chain.

By comparing seaborne trade before, during and after manufacturing processes, we notice two changes. The first is about the unit value and the second is about the size and form of shipment. The price of natural resources is by and large determined by the market forces, though the scarcity of supply and the existence of monopolistic powers, such as OPEC, play an important role as well. All manufactured products are made from raw materials, which constitute the base to which more value is added. So, by definition, primary materials have the lowest unit value. Obviously the products that reach the final consumer have the highest unit value, although such value varies enormously between products.

With regard to the changes in shipment size and form, this is a lot to do with the homogeneity of the cargo being transported. For raw materials, there is only a limited and known number of kinds, each usually being traded in big quantities. In their homogeneous natural form, the raw materials are loosely stored and transported in bulk without packing. Manufactured products, on the other hand, are different. With a highly diversified demand, there are so many kinds of products that the shipment of a product is generally in a small quantity. The forms of manufactured goods are also in a big variety, which makes it impossible to store and transport them in bulk.

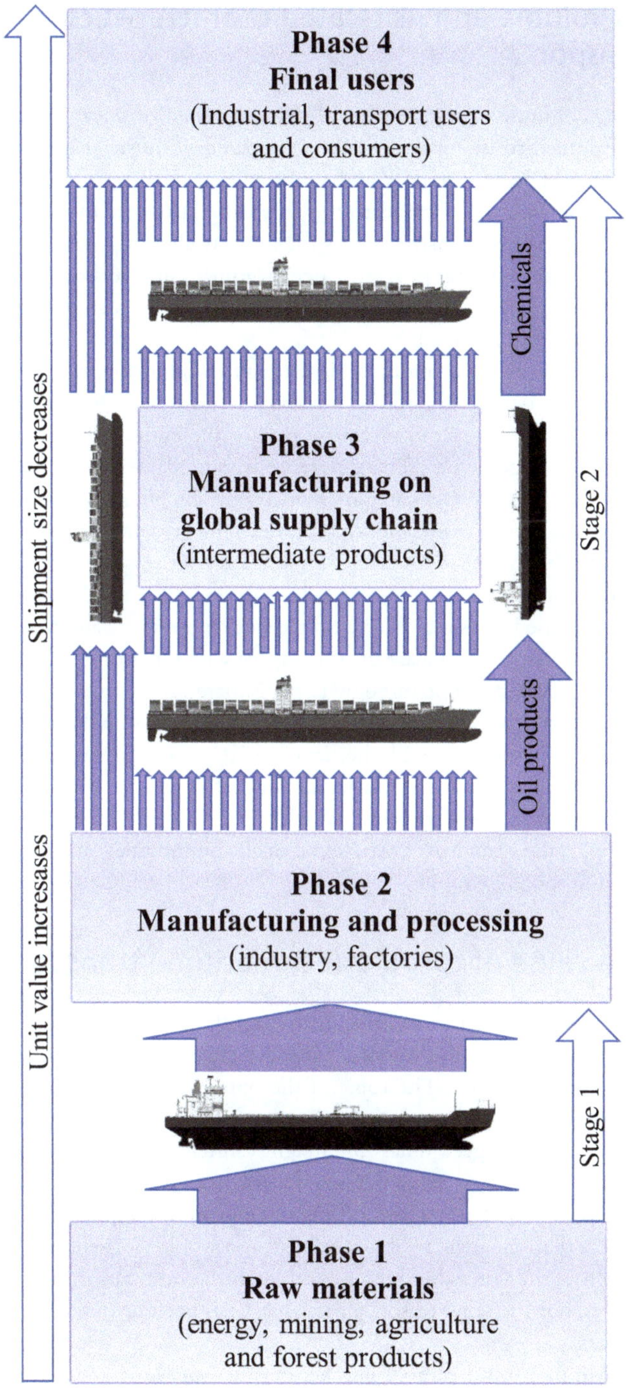

Figure 7.1 Seaborne trade at two transport stages.

Source: Shuo Ma.

Note: from primary materials to manufactured good, unit value increases and shipment size decreases.

Why is cargo volume and its related characteristics so critical for maritime transport?

The technical and economic characteristics of shipping require ocean-going vessels to have a minimum size. Ships need to be relatively large, compared with the situation of other modes of transport, for sailing over long distances and withstanding challenging navigational conditions. Therefore matching the amount of cargo to the ship's size is one of the key aspects in maritime transport and one of the major decisive factors for the way shipping services ought to be organised. Accordingly, given the minimum size of ocean-going ships, seaborne trade can broadly be divided into two groups: the shipment that is large enough to fill a ship's capacity and the shipment that is less than the full shipload.

In the case where the cargo quantity is big enough to fill a ship, it is a single-user transport, whereby the cargo owner uses the ship for his own sake. If, however, the cargo in question is not big enough for a ship, the cargo owner can of course pay for the entire space. But usually he needs to share the ship with other cargo owners. This difference is so fundamental that it leads to a division of modern commercial shipping into two categories: the tramp shipping and the liner shipping.

The size of shipment defines the relationship between the demand and the supply, that is, in other words, between the shipper and the transporter. This is because if the amount of cargo is big enough to fill the whole ship, the ship will have a sole user and the cargo owner will have more say regarding the way the transport is organised. He should, for example, decide on where and when the ship should go. On the other hand, if the cargo has to share the ship's space with other cargoes, the question of "when" and "where" cannot be decided by one cargo owner. It is therefore up to the shipping company, based on the demand of the whole market, to choose when and where the ship should go. The "tramp/liner" relation has a lot of points in common with the "taxi/bus" relation in urban transport. The importance of cargo volume is in its decisive role in the specialisation of ships and ports. This is because the large volume provides a basis for frequent transport, which, in turn, justifies investment in specialised ships and port facilities. This is the main reason why some small commodities, such as cocoa beans or sugar, can hardly benefit from specialised ships.

How does the value of cargo affect maritime transport?

From Figure 7.1 we can observe that as cargo moves up the supply chain the unit value increases. Such unit value has an impact on the way shipping services are organised, particularly in respect of a ship's sailing speed or transit time. The topic of the optimal speed of ships has been discussed in Chapter 6. For a shipping company, higher ship's speed incurs a higher bunker cost. So a shipping company will not increase the speed unless the freight can recover the extra cost. The time cost for cargo is determined by the cargo's value per unit in, for example, US dollars and the time cost of the dollar, or the interest rate. The owners of high-value cargo will, therefore, be more willing to pay for faster transport than the owners of low-value cargo would. So, generally speaking, the higher the value of the cargo is, the faster the ships are, although the best transit time varies depending on specific circumstances. For the same reason, air transport has been favoured for very high value and time-sensitive products.

For the users with high-value cargo, a number of other special arrangements and services is also made available by shipping companies. Such services include cargo insurance, information services on the tracking of cargo flows, etc. As shipping speed rises, time spent on cargo handling at ports becomes the main obstacle for the reduction of the transit time. As a solution to the problem, containerisation was introduced in the 1950s, which has completely revolutionised the liner shipping industry. By the same token, it is expected that the higher the unit value of the cargo, the smaller each shipment or ship size should be because, for big vessels, extra time is usually required for cargo accumulation and handling at port. But thanks to the low interest rate, the time cost for both cargo and ships is low. At the same time, progress has been made on port efficiency, so the average size of container ships has been growing.

What is "industry-controlled shipping"?

A trade will not be completed until the goods are moved from the seller to the buyer. So transport is always an integral part of trade. Historically, shipping was indeed a part of trade and was always directly operated by the traders. The shipowners were the traders too. Traditionally, a shipmaster, representing the trader/ship-owner, would, in addition to being the captain of the ship, directly engage in buying and selling the goods when the ship arrived at a foreign port. Taking the transport of crude oil as an example, at the beginning of the last century, about 90% of oil trade was transported by ships owned and operated by traders, oil producers or oil companies. Since then the so-called *independent* tanker owners, or specialised common-user shipping companies, emerged and steadily increased their market share. By 1950 the oil transport market was split equally between trader owners and independent owners and, by 2010, over 80% of the oil was transported by independent owners.[1]

Today, most seaborne trade is transported by specialised third-party common-user shipping companies. So, in addition to the two principal ship operation systems, i.e., the tramp shipping and the liner shipping, there is another category of shipping that can be called *industrial shipping*. It is special in the sense that the demand and the supply belong to the same company and shipping is a company's internal function. Transporting large volumes of the same cargo is different from transporting small quantities of different goods because the size of each consignment is not the only element to consider when choosing the most appropriate way to organise shipping services. A cargo may sometimes be so large that it needs more than one ship and over an extended period. In such a case, the cargo owner may be interested in examining the shipment requirement with regards to its *frequency and regularity*. So there are four possibilities, as shown by the four cases in Figure 7.2: (1) the demand for transport is frequent and regular; (2) the demand is frequent but not regular; (3) it is regular but not frequent or (4) it is neither frequent nor regular.

In the case where the transport need is frequent and regular, one should compare the situation against the operational and commercial aspects of shipping services, such as the size of ship to consider, the distance to travel and the port turnaround time. This is because it may be possible that the demand is big enough to sustain one or more ships being fully employed for an extended period of time. For example, a company has a demand of 5 million tons of oil per year to import with a delivery frequency of one shipment per month in equal quantities. This demand could keep one or more tanker ships fully employed. So the importer could acquire one or more vessels and undertake the transport of his cargo by his own ships.

	REGULAR	NOT REGULAR
FREQUENT	1	2
NOT FREQUENT	3	4

Figure 7.2 Frequency and regularity of big shipments of bulk cargo.

We call this model of transport "industrial shipping" or "industry-controlled shipping", although many other terms can also be used. Such terms include "integrated shipping" or "in-house shipping,", which signifies that shipping is an integral part of a company's internal business functions; or "dependent shipping", which emphasises the relationship between the shipping entity and its parent company. The tanker companies that are not owned by states or oil companies are called "independent tanker owners".[2] This can also be called "trader shipping", "shipper shipping" or "non-3P shipping". The latter name refers to maritime transport as part of the logistics system. In logistics, the term "third-party logistics" (3P logistics) refers to logistics services carried out by common-user service providers rather than by the seller or the buyers themselves.

With "industry-controlled shipping", the cargo transported and the ships deployed are not freely traded in the shipping market. The companies which control and operate their own shipping capacities are usually big firms in resource exploitation or heavy industry sectors. Taking BP, a major oil company, as an example, in 2016 it had a fleet of 84 ships, of which 44 were operated and 40 were time-chartered by the company. It also had another 34 vessels on order.[3] Apart from companies in the energy sector, big firms in other sectors such as steel mills, grain importers, forester product exporters, etc., also undertake maritime transport themselves. This kind of practice is also common for some specialised sectors such as the car and heavy machinery industries. The Shanghai-based port equipment maker ZPMC, for example, owns a fleet of more than 25 specialised ships of 60,000 to 100,000 dwt. Many of them are submersible vessels suitable for carrying completely assembled container gantry cranes and heavy steel structures and components.[4]

What are the primary operational forms of shipping?

To sum up the above discussions, seaborne trade can be transported in one of three ways, namely tramp shipping, liner shipping and industry-controlled shipping. Which way is used depends on the characteristics of the cargo and the cargo owner's choice. The cargo volume, the frequency and regularity of shipment are decisive factors too.

- If the cargo to transport is of full shipload and also the shipment is regular and frequent over a long period of time, then the cargo owner has several options. He may use tramp shipping for multiple voyages or hire a ship for a period of time or acquire a vessel to organise the maritime transport himself. Whether shipping service is operated by the seller/buyer as an internal function or is purchased by them from a shipping company remains an option based on their business strategy.
- If the cargo to transport is of full shipload but the transport needs are irregular and/or infrequent in the long run, then the cargo owner should use tramp shipping for one voyage or consecutive voyages or for the period suitable for the cargo concerned.
- If the consignment is of less-than-full shipload, then the cargo owner should consider packing the cargo and using liner shipping transport. In the case of bulk cargo, tramp shipping remains as a possibility, though it is only occasionally that suitable combining cargoes can be found.

Using liner shipping and short-term tramp shipping is usually not a matter of choice for a cargo owner whose cargo shipment is too small to fill the ship or the need for transport is only occasional without long-term regularity. But whether or not a big shipper will opt for industrial shipping is a more complicated question. The factors to consider include a long-term cost comparison, in-house expertise, risk management and control, competition strategies, etc. The cost consideration is obviously the main concern for such decisions. Operating maritime transport in-house could be more cost effective when compared with chartering ships on the market, even if this means the need for the necessary expertise within the company. From the viewpoint of risk management and control, operating shipping internally can enable the company to not be directly exposed to freight fluctuations. For some special ships, risks may also be related to service availability and, by having an internal fleet, this risk is reduced. Integration of shipping into the product offering can also be an effective marketing strategy. The crane maker ZPMC sells its equipment with delivery and installation. Such value-added services helped them to become a market leader. But, on the other hand, there are drawbacks to self-owned ships too. Special expertise, technical management, demand fluctuation, etc., represent challenges and risks, particularly for a limited scale of operation. It is common that big trading companies choose a combined arrangement of a self-owned fleet supplemented by chartered ships.

Consequently, the total seaborne trade can be divided into three groups based on how maritime transport is organised, as shown in Figure 7.3. In 2018 about 16% of global seaborne trade was containerised cargo carried by the liner shipping sector. And a part of the other dry cargo, which made up 9% of the world total, was also in the liner shipping market carried by conventional general cargo ships or specialised vessels. So the estimated amount of seaborne trade in terms of tonnage for the liner market is approximately 20%.[5] The rest is by and large bulk cargo, liquid and dry. Some of the bulk cargo is transported as industrial shipping by the traders themselves, but it is difficult to estimate the exact amount. For crude oil, an estimate suggests that roughly 20% of tanker ships are owned and/or operated by cargo owners.[6] In the dry bulk sector, a similar or lower percentage would also be right. For specialised ships, the proportion may well be higher than 20%. On the whole, about 20% of the global seaborne trade is moved by industrial shipping. Therefore, approximately, the remaining 60% in terms of tonnage is the seaborne trade for tramp shipping.

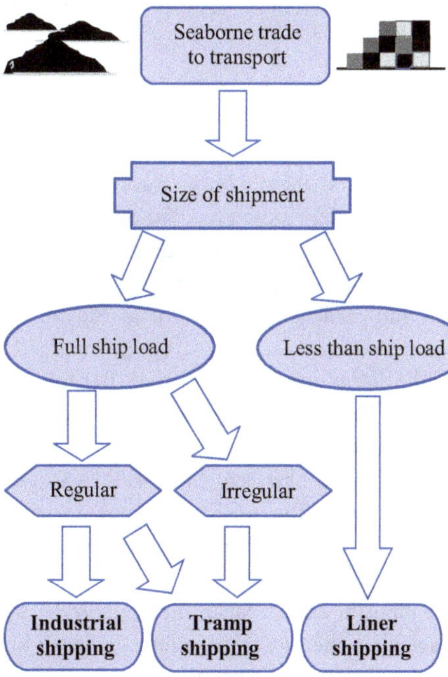

Figure 7.3 Cargo type and shipping patterns.

Source: Shuo Ma.

Note: industrial shipping is an option for cargo owners even if their cargo shipment is regular and of full ship load.

The future development of the three main operational patterns of the shipping service, based on our previous discussions, would follow a trend that the share of the tramp shipping sector, transporting bulk cargo, would stabilise in the long term. This is mainly because, on the one hand, less oil and coal will be traded and transported by sea due to consumption pattern changes driven mainly by environmental concerns. Alternative energy, domestic production and land-based transport will grow. On the other hand, the high-level dry bulk imports largely fuelled by China have started to decrease, although the import from other emerging economies, such as India, will eventually grow on a fast-track. The part of industrial shipping will also be smaller in the future, while, at the same time, the share of containerised cargo for liner shipping will increase. Since industrial shipping is an internal function of the shipper companies, our discussions will concentrate on the tramp and liner sectors only; the two types of maritime transport traded openly on the international markets.

7.2 The main features of tramp shipping

Of a total of about 12 billion tons of global seaborne trade in 2018, approximately 60% or 7 billion tons were transported by tramp shipping. Generally speaking, this is a maritime transport service made to suit cargo's need, based on the type and quantity of cargo to transport as well as the routing and timing of shipment. When shipping started to emerge as an independent and third-party common-user service in its own right, tramp shipping was the first form of operation. Liner shipping appeared later in the middle of the 19th century when better and more reliable ships became available.[7] Obviously, in the beginning, there was only a single type of ship which was capable of carrying all sorts of cargoes. Then ships started to specialise and maritime transport was subdivided into different segments of tramp, liner and industrial shipping.

What types of cargo are transported by tramp shipping?

Today, tramp shipping is used to transport mainly bulk cargo, but also specialised cargoes. Bulk cargo refers generally to the cargo in a completely loose type without packing, which can be loaded, stowed and unloaded easily and quickly by using specialised equipment in or out of vessels in a continuous manner. There are different types of bulk-cargo-handling equipment commonly used in ports, such as pumps, grabs, conveyor belts and off-loaders that work by sucking or screwing. The typical bulk cargoes are, for example, oil, grain, coal, ore, etc. The overwhelming strength of bulk shipping is the extremely low unit cost achieved through economies of scale. Because of the physical features of bulk cargo, ships can be built very large. For instance, the biggest oil tanker to date is more than 500,000 dwt and the biggest dry bulk carrier is 430,000 dwt. The specialised cargo includes liquefied gases, vehicles, project cargo, forest products, etc. The term "neo-bulk" is also used to cover a special type of cargo, which is homogeneous in nature and identical in appearance but not in loose form and has to be loaded and unloaded individually, piece by piece, in or out of the ship. The cargoes in this category include logs, steel products, bagged cargo like cement, fertilizer, cocoa, coffee, etc.

Three elements should be mentioned to explain the extraordinary size of bulk carriers and the consequent economic advantage: first, there is an enormous need for bulk cargo in the market. The market need for cargo like oil, coal or iron ore has always been in great quantity, which requires a transport capable of satisfying the need. The huge and stable need not only justifies specialised bulk carriers but also purposely built terminals in ports. Second, bulk cargo is primary raw materials that are homogeneous in nature, which makes the transport in loose form possible. Third, because of the loose and homogeneous nature, bulk cargo can be handled rapidly at ports using specialised equipment. Terminals specialised in handling bulk cargo, liquid or dry, have normally the following characteristics.

- ***Deepwater draft.*** As the size of bulk carriers is usually large, deep draft at ports is necessary. This may vary between 12 to 17 metres, sometimes deeper, according to different types of bulk cargo and ships.
- ***Specialised handling equipment.*** The equipment is purposely built to handle the cargo with high productivity. A dry bulk terminal, for example, can normally load, or even unload, a bulk carrier with a rate of 10,000–20,000 tons per day or more and even faster for liquid cargoes.
- ***Large storage area and facilities.*** Oil tanks, grain siloes or big storage areas, open or closed, are often symbols of bulk terminals.
- ***Good onward transport connection.*** Bulk cargo is normally raw materials with a low unit value. In the same way as for sea transport, the overland transport of bulk cargo also needs to be of low cost. Therefore, bulk terminals are very often well connected with the railway system and sometimes also have inland waterway transport possibilities to transport the cargo to and from the port.

What are the operational features of tramp shipping?

The most fundamental difference between tramp shipping and liner shipping is that the former is "one ship, one cargo" while the latter is "one ship, many cargoes" and the former does not have a "fixed schedule and planned ports" of call, while the latter does have both. This difference is fully reflected in the operational features of the two shipping service models.

In tramp shipping, a ship sails based on the cargo commitment of the trade interest. Such a ship is built by the owner with a view that the size and other specifications are what will be required by the demand of trade on the market. In practice, the shipowner and the trade interest will look for each other at a shipping market, often through a broker. So the time of shipment as well as the names of the cargo loading and discharging ports are decided by the cargo's side, although, technically and operationally, the ship is always under the command and responsibility of the shipowner. The shipowner pays all the expenses for the ship, its crew and the insurance, but also for the costs of bunker and other consumables. For cargo handling at ports, however, the responsibility and cost can be borne by either the cargo owner or the shipowner and therefore this has to be agreed upon specifically by both sides in advance.

As discussed above, bulk cargo is the most common type of goods transported by tramp ships. All seaborne trade goods other than small shipment parcels, or general cargo, are cargoes for tramp shipping. These include many specialised goods such as chemical products, liquefied natural gas, refrigerated cargoes, livestock, forest products, cars, bagged minerals/construction materials/agricultural products, etc. Based on the characteristics of each kind of cargo, as well as the amount of trade and the shipping routes concerned, tramp ships are divided into some categories for each of liquid and dry cargoes. Such specialisation includes mainly four to five groups based on ship size. Typically, the size categories of tramp ships are ranging from about 30,000 to 350,000 deadweight tons for liquid cargoes and from about 30,000 to 400,000 deadweight tons for dry cargoes. As a rule, the bigger the volume of trade is, the longer the distance of travel should be. And the lower the value of cargo is, the bigger the ship size will be. Therefore, the biggest dry bulk carriers of 400,000 tons are used to transport iron ore from Brazil to China.

What are the organisational features of tramp shipping?

Many tramp shipping companies do not have many ships. The nature of tramp shipping allows shipload transport to be made at any time, to and from any place. From a ship's point of view, individual and often independent transport arrangement is the essence of tramp shipping. There are numerous reasons and situations whereby a large shipping company with multiple ships is needed. But there are also a lot of opportunities in the market for small, even single-ship, companies to exist. For example, in the Greek port city of Piraeus, there are more than 360 shipping companies and most of them are tramp shipping companies.[8] Such a situation is quite similar to that in the trucking business of freight transport or barge companies in inland waterway transport. In all these sectors, an organisationally small company could enjoy numerous advantages in being flexible and responding quickly to the market demand.

Since it is "one ship, one cargo" transport, the shipping organisation is also relatively simple and straightforward. The shipowner is usually directly involved in the fixing of the ship for cargo transport and, once this is done, he just needs to look for the next cargo to load. An agent can be appointed to help when the ship arrives at the port. So it is typical that a tramp shipping company has a small number of people working in the office. Certainly, being very small has some disadvantages too. For example, if some big customers have a very large amount of cargo to transport they will prefer a shipping company with many ships rather than many companies each with just one or two ships. In such a case, the small shipping company could join a *shipping pool*, which consists of ships from different member companies and thus could have a combined total tonnage big enough for large shipments.

What are the contractual features of tramp shipping?

The formal transport contract between a shipowner and a customer is called a *charter party*. As a contract, it defines the terms and conditions based on which ship is to be used. While the shipowner is called an *owner*, the user of the ship is called a *charterer*. A charter party is a free contract, which means that the clauses and the texts are all subject to negotiation and agreement between the two parties.

Both the owner and the charterer must agree on and sign a charter party in advance for each shipment. Such processes may easily become very time-consuming. So the industry has developed some standard forms of the most commonly used charter parties for trades and operational arrangements. Consequently, for each shipment, the two parties will concentrate on the main terms and conditions such as the freight and the terms of cargo handling, while leaving, or making minor changes to, the other clauses with the standard forms, which are well-known and agreeable to both sides. In this way, one can save a lot of time and create better certainty for the benefit of both sides, particularly when market situations change quickly. It is common that chartering brokers are involved in the conclusion of charter parties, though the final agreement depends upon the market conditions and the bargaining power of the owner and the charterer.

To employ a ship for the transport of a particular cargo, the standard charter party mostly commonly used is BIMCO's *Gencon* form. The following are the essential aspects which are typically the key elements for negotiation and agreement in such a charter party:

- The specifications of the ship.
- The description of the cargo to be transported.
- The date on which the ship is ready for loading and the loading and discharging ports.
- All matters concerning the cargo handling at the loading and discharging ports.
- The freight and the terms of payment, including brokerage fees.

What are the commercial features of tramp shipping?

The tramp shipping market is an open, free and competitive market with a large number of shipowners and charterers across the world. A shipowner provides the ship to meet the need for cargo transport and, in return, receives payment for the service. The payment, by the name of freight, is made based on the amount of cargo loaded on-board ship at the rate agreed between the two parties when the charter party is negotiated. For this reason, the ship's captain signs a document called a *bill of lading* as the receipt for the type and amount of cargo. The tramp shipping freight rate fluctuates according to the balance between the demand and the supply of the market. As a derived demand from trade, which changes constantly, it is hard to predict the total need for cargo transport. The level of freight is therefore rarely a reflection of the cost for the shipowner.

Under the charter party, the charterer has an obligation to pay for the agreed amount of cargo for transport. It is difficult, in practice, to load the exact amount. So it is common that a tolerable margin is allowed. Should the cargo actually loaded be more than the agreed amount, it is less problematic since the shipmaster can certify for the calculation of the freight. In case the available cargo is less than the agreed amount, the charterer should usually pay for the full agreed amount. It is possible that a lump sum payment arrangement is agreed on, in which case the actual amount of cargo loaded will not be used for the freight calculation.

In addition to the payment of the freight, the payment for two related services, cargo handling and brokerage, has also to be agreed on in advance. So the freight can include cargo handling at both loading and discharging ports, or just one of the two ports, or none of the two ports. With regard to the broker's payment, it is normally paid as a percentage of the total freight.

7.3 The types of ship chartering

A charter party is a contract for the use of the ship concluded between a shipowner and a charterer. But a shipowner does not have to own a ship to perform the transport. It can charter a ship to do that. There are also variations of how the ship is employed under a charter party with a different split of responsibilities between the two parties. Three major types of charter party can be identified, namely voyage charter, time charter and bareboat charter.

How are the different types of ship charter used?

As there has not been a rigorous definition of tramp shipping, we should understand that all those that do not belong to industrial shipping and liner shipping fall within the sphere of tramp shipping. Cargo can only be transported by one of the three shipping arrangements. However, a ship can service more than one market at different times. A ship can be chartered for one specific cargo transport and the same ship can also be hired or chartered for a period of time by another shipowner in industrial shipping or liner shipping. In this case, the charterer is a shipowner. Vice versa, an industrial shipowner can also charter-out his ship to a tramp shipping company or a shipping line or another industrial shipowner. For liner shipping, most ships are container carriers which can be chartered between shipping lines but it is difficult to use these in industrial shipping. Ships are therefore frequently chartered between shipping companies of the same type, i.e., between tramp companies or between shipping lines.

The charter party used between shipping companies is normally not for any specific cargo shipment but for a period of time. As such, the charterer gets more involved in the operational activities of the ship. This is because the shipowner provides only the ship, not for carrying specific cargo or for calling at a particular port. The charterer has the power to command the ship by giving operational instructions to the shipmaster on cargo shipment and voyage-related matters during the charter party period. The charterer can also have more control of the ship by chartering it *bare* from a shipowner. This means that the ship is chartered as a hull, without even a crew, and all operation-related activities such as insurance and ship maintenance are the responsibility of the charterer.

Apart from tramp shipping companies, time and bareboat charters are also frequently used by ship-leasing companies. Some of them are also involved in ship operation, but some are limited to ship leasing or long-term time charter businesses only. Their customers include both shipping lines and tramp shipping companies and the contracts, whether it is a bareboat charter, time charter or leasing, are always long term. The three types of charters, namely voyage charter, time charter and bareboat charter are illustrated in Figure 7.4 and explained below.

What is a voyage charter?

Voyage charter is the backbone of tramp shipping because it is about the transport of a specific cargo from A to B. Under a voyage charter, the shipowner undertakes the responsibility to provide a specific vessel at the charterer's disposal for the carriage of an agreed type and amount of cargo at the time and between the ports requested by the charterer. Payment is made at rates and conditions negotiated, mutually agreed upon in advance and based on the quantity of cargo actually loaded within the range allowed. An alternative way of payment is by "lump-sum", which means to agree upon a total figure rather than any rate.

During a voyage charter period, the ship is, technically and operationally, under the full control of the shipowner who bears all costs incurred to the ship, the crew and the voyage concerned. These include capital cost as well as crew wages, stores, provisions, insurance, bunkers, canal tolls, harbour dues, etc. However, cargo handling and the related costs have to be negotiated and agreed upon between the two parties and the responsibilities have to be clearly specified in the charter party. The charter party can be for a single voyage or for a number of consecutive voyages. This is normally the transport for the same kind of cargo moving between the same ports and under the same conditions and the freight.

For a single voyage charter, both ship and cargo are specified. In the case where a charterer has a very large amount of cargo to transport that requires many consecutive voyages of multiple ships, the charterer may have a voyage charter without named ships, specifying only the total amount of cargo, the size of the shipment, the total number of voyages and the interval between them. It is therefore up to the shipowner to select suitable ships to perform the voyages. This type of voyage charter is

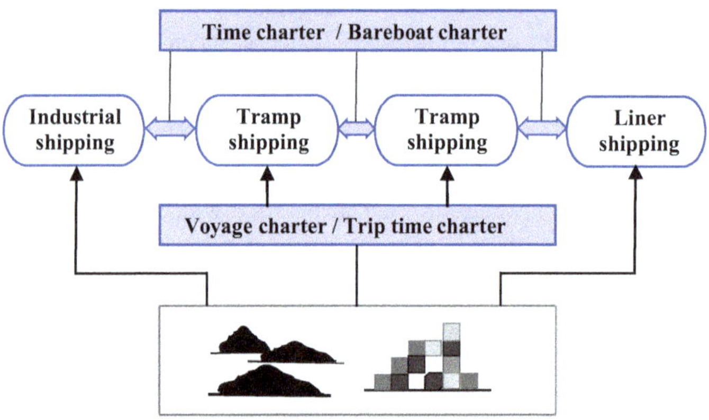

Figure 7.4 Chartering options and inter-changeable uses of ships.

Source: Shuo Ma.

Note: the size of both industrial and liner shipping can be increased or decreased by chartering ships in or out in the tramp shipping market for a period of time.

generally known as a *contract of affreightment* (COA). This kind of arrangement gives the benefit of flexibility to shipowners who can use their ships according to various positions, whilst it offers the benefit of simplicity to charterers without the transport of cargo being adversely affected. So COA is a common and popular form of voyage charter.

What is a time charter?

When ships are chartered for a period of time, it is called a time charter. This type of chartering is often used among shipping companies. Under a time charter, the charterer uses the specific vessel for a period of time specified in the charter party, usually with no restriction to the geographical area of trading, unless the shipowner indicates otherwise. The period agreed upon varies from several weeks to several years, or even the entire economic life of the ship. For such very long time charters, though not very common, the effect of cost changes are considered and reflected in the terms of payment. The payment by the charterer is known as hire, expressed in a certain amount of dollars per day. The charterer may use the ship to transport his own cargo, in which case he pays also bunkers, port and canal dues and cargo-handling costs. Or he can charter the ship out for voyages. The ship's operating costs such as the salary of the crew, insurance and maintenance cost are still paid by the shipowner in addition to the capital cost.

The duration of a time charter can also be based on the time needed for the trip. This is a variation of a time charter and is generally called a voyage (or trip) time charter. Here the charterer hires the ship for the time needed to perform the voyage concerned. Compared with a voyage charter, the charterer pays daily hire based on the time during which the ship is employed by him, instead of freight based on the amount of cargo moved. The charterer fulfils the responsibility of a time-charterer, which is greater than that of a charterer in a voyage charter. To some extent a trip time charter is similar to a lump-sum-freight voyage charter in that the payment is not based on the quantity of cargo transported, with the exception that the voyage costs, such as bunker, are paid by the charterer for the former but by the shipowner for the latter.

The market of voyage charter, trip-time charter and short-term time charter is called the *spot market*. The spot market refers to short-term contracts which reflect the actual situation of demand and supply and thus the fluctuation of the freight market. Every year there are tens of thousands of *ship fixtures*, or charters, concluded in the market. As bareboat charter and time charter are mostly used between shipping companies or between financial institutions and shipping companies, the number of concluded charters is small. The majority of tramp ships are on the spot market under voyage charters for cargo shipment, as shown in Figure 7.5. Container ships are not used in the tramp shipping market as they are for liner shipping only. So there is not voyage charter for these. However, between shipping lines, and between specialised ship finance/asset management companies and shipping lines, many ships are traded under time charters. The duration varies from a few months to multiple years.

What is a bareboat or demise charter?

A bareboat charter can also be considered as a kind of time charter because the ship is put at the charterer's disposal for a period of time. But in this case the charterer will take over a "bare" boat, which cannot be operated as such. The ship under the bareboat charter is just a hull with an engine. This means that the charterer should find a ship crew and pay for it. The charterer also needs to pay for the ship's maintenance and insurance costs as well as fuel costs, port costs, etc. The shipowner pays only the capital cost and transfers both the technical and operational control of the ship, during the

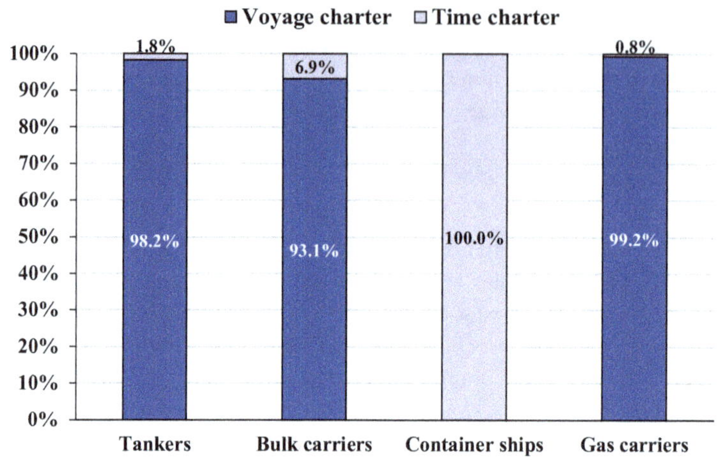

Figure 7.5 Types of charter (ship fixtures) concluded, 2013–2016 (in %).
Source: Shuo Ma, based on data from Clarkson (2016).
Note: a majority of tramp ships are employed on spot market under "voyage charter". Container ships are all under time charter due to the nature of liner shipping.

charter party period, to the charterer against the bareboat hire payment. So a bareboat charter is also called a demise.

Under a bareboat charter, the ship is in the complete control of the charterer who can operate the ship as if it is his own. The charterer can either use the ship for their own purposes or put it on the market for chartering to new charterers. An important source of demand for this kind of tramp shipping service comes from liner shipping companies. When their own tonnage capacity is inadequate to meet the market needs, shipping lines can supplement their fleet by chartering in ships from the tramp market.

Some shipowners are actually financiers who want to invest in ships but are not interested in being involved in ship operation or do not have the necessary knowledge to do so. On the other hand, some charterers wish to acquire ships without bearing the financial burden or who do not have access to the capital needed. So, in such cases, bareboat chartering is the best fit. The charterer who has the full control of the ship is also called a *disponent* owner. Sometimes a bareboat charter is concluded between the owner/financier and the charterer/disponent owner before the ship is constructed. Such a contract is seen as a guarantee for future revenue from the ship and it is also a way to ensure the suitability of the ship for the charterer's needs.

The above three different types of tramp shipping or chartering arrangements highlight the variable nature of maritime demand for tramp shipping services. Long-time charter or demise charter is often used by big trading and industrial groups and as part of industrial shipping capacity or by financial institutions. The commercial risks are believed to be lower for long-term time charter or demise charter than for short-term time or voyage charter. This is because, for the former, the level of hire is more closely linked to the cost of ship operation while, for the latter, the payment is totally subject to market forces. Obviously, the volatility of the spot market also offers an opportunity for speculators to make quick extra profit for either the shipowner or charterer.

7.4 The main features of liner shipping

It is believed that liner shipping as a distinct sort of shipping organisation appeared by the middle of the last century when steamships started to enter into commercial shipping service to offer a better, faster and more reliable transport. Shippers with a cargo of small quantities but usually of higher value preferred to use this kind of shipping service. Today, with about 20% of the global seaborne trade in ton and less than 20% of the world's fleet in deadweight tonnage, it is estimated that more than half of the world's total freight income from sea transport is earned by the liner shipping sector. The liner shipping system consists of several subsystems. There are certain common features between liner shipping and tramp shipping, but there are also fundamental differences between them.

What are the operational features of liner shipping?

Liner shipping is a kind of transport similar to public passenger transport by airlines, trains or buses. It share the same characteristics as common-user transporters. So a liner ship does not serve one customer, but many of them. To do this, the shipping company usually needs to know where most customers come from and go to. Then, accordingly, liner shipping companies provide a transport service with fixed sailing schedules, fixed ports of call, named vessels and, in most cases, standard prices. Not only should these be fixed, but they are also published, making them known to all present and potential customers alike. As far as shippers are concerned, the issues related to schedules and ports of call are not subjects for negotiation, except for special circumstances where, for example, specific arrangements need to be made for a big and strategically important customer. Obviously, shipping lines do adjust their services to the changes in trade and general customer need. The operational system of a liner shipping company usually includes a series of ships sailing on the same route to maintain the desired service frequency. In liner shipping, cargo handling at ports is included as part of the liner shipping service.

The routeing and scheduling of a liner shipping service is a decision of the shipping line. The number of ports of call is decided based on factors such as the availability of cargo and the required transit time. Typically, in a round trip, or a "loop", between intercontinental markets six to ten ports will be called. Scheduling and the calling interval between services is another important decision. However, today a *fixed-day-weekly-service* has become the norm of the liner shipping industry. This is because such a service fits well with the planning of most industrial production and trade. So an even shorter interval is often not appreciated and accepted by the customers. Due to the uncertainty of many influential factors, keeping to a tight schedule has been a challenge for many liner shipping companies. Some customers, particularly those with time-sensitive cargoes, have a high demand for the reliability and punctuality of the service. There are different operational patterns for the liner shipping services, which will be discussed in the following section.

Given the nature of and the need for general cargo, liner shipping has also been extending its operations to cover a wider range of services. These include port terminal operations, inland transport services, warehousing and distribution activities, etc. With the level of containerisation in liner shipping transport at more than 90%,[9] the management and operation of the container fleet has also become an important area of control for the liner shipping industry. As liner shipping extends into logistics, maintaining inland clearance depots (ICD) is also part of routine operation.

What are the organisational features of liner shipping?

A liner company has a large and complex organisational structure. Compared with tramp shipping companies, liner companies are generally extensive networks. There are many reasons for this. First, to provide a regular liner service, the shipping company often needs several ships with similar specifications. Within the organisation, sales and cargo services are always needed to ensure a continuous traffic supply for the fleet. Shipping lines generally have to deal with a large number of clients even for one single voyage. This requires a lot of staff spreading out in all major markets covered by the company. Shipping lines incur a high cost on marketing, sales and company overhead. In liner shipping, multiple ports are called to deliver and receive cargoes. So an agency network has to be established at all ports of call to provide services to ships as well as cargo. Information management and coordination efforts are more important in liner shipping than in tramp shipping due to the high value and time sensitivity of manufactured goods. With the containerisation of most liner shipping services, the speed of cargo movement is higher than before. The organisation of port terminals and cargo distribution activities is increasingly included as part of liner shipping services. The scope of liner shipping networks has extended beyond ports.

In response to the needs of the global supply chain, liner shipping companies cooperate between themselves. The network and coordination systems between and among different shipping lines need to be established. Commercially, the liner shipping services are more structured and thus may be seen as more rigid and risky. This is because ships have to sail on planned schedules whether the ships are fully loaded or not. Most of the costs incurred in liner shipping are therefore fixed costs which do not change with the amount of cargo transported. To keep the service level and at the same time to reduce the cost, shipping lines look for competitiveness from scale economies by deploying larger vessels and cooperating between themselves. Today about 85% of the liner shipping capacity is controlled by a small number of liner shipping alliances. Such joint ventures increase the complexity of liner shipping organisations. They also create a concern of excessive concentration of the sector at the expense of competition.

What are the contractual features of liner shipping?

In liner shipping, the transport contract between a cargo owner and a shipping line is called a *bill of lading* (B/L). A B/L is not only used as a transport contract but also as a receipt of cargo and a document of title. Such triple functionality is a distinctive characteristic of B/L. As a transport contract, the bill of lading defines the responsibility and liability of the carrier and the shipper by the clauses printed on the back of the document. As a receipt of cargo, the bill of lading is signed by the shipmaster on behalf of the shipowner, with a clear indication of the quantity and the appearance of the cargo loaded. In practice, this task is often delegated to an agent. With the signed bill of lading, free of remarks, the shipper will be able to get cargo payment from the bank, because, in modern international trade, the transaction is usually made through the bank credit system. As a document of title, a bill of lading represents the ownership of the cargo and it can also be transferred to another person by an endorsement of the holder of the original bill of lading.

Shipping lines define and decide on the terms and conditions of a liner shipping service and preprint them on the bill of lading. Unlike a charter party, the clauses of a bill of lading are not negotiable. This is understandable because it is impractical to negotiate with shippers for there are too many of them, even for a single liner voyage. Each shipping company has its own bill of lading, although the majority of shipping bills of lading follow similar formats and clauses. Typically, bills of lading are prepared based on international rules and practices such as The Hague Rules or Rotterdam Rules. Some shipping lines offer a door-to-door transport service and in such a case a combined bill of lading may be issued, which extends the responsibilities of the shipowner beyond ports.

What are the commercial features of liner shipping?

The pricing system of liner shipping is complex and different from tramp shipping in many aspects. In the past, shipping lines used to use a commodity-based tariff system, which is sometimes also called a value-based tariff. It is a kind of pricing system with detailed commodity classifications. The tariff is measured on weight (in tons) or dimension (in cubic metres) of cargo. So, for the same unit of measurement, the tariff varies from one product to another according to the unit value of the commodity. The tariff is set at a level deemed as "what traffic can bear". By using a commodity-based tariff system, high-value cargoes cross-subsidise low-value cargoes and, as a result, more cargoes can be transported. This concept of pricing was necessary when, at the beginning of liner shipping development, sufficient traffic volume was needed but a uniform tariff would often be too high for many low-value cargoes.

The liner shipping freight rate is usually much higher than that of the tramp shipping sector. For instance, the price for the transport of one ton of coal from North America to Europe would be around US$10, but it could be about US$100 to transport a ton of general cargo by liner shipping. There are many reasons for such a difference. The quantity economies are certainly more in favour of bulk cargo than small parcels of liner cargo; regular and frequent liner shipping services are suitable for general cargoes but they are also more costly to operate; shorter transit time with faster ships is also required in liner shipping; the liner shipping freight also includes more services such as port charges, cargo handling and storage. Normally liner freight is paid before the transport is completed.

During the history of liner shipping there have been many changes. The most significant one is what we discussed in Chapter 5: containerisation. Invented in the US in the 1950s, the shipping containers have gradually dominated the transport of general cargo and become almost a synonym of the liner shipping of today. Containerisation is widely considered as a revolutionary development of the maritime transport sector. This is because it has not only improved productivity and efficiency exponentially, but it has also completely changed every other aspect of liner shipping, from safety to intermodalism. The impact of containerisation is well beyond maritime transport. Thanks to maritime containers, the logistics sector is not the same anymore and the cargo transit between countries is much faster, cheaper and more reliable. In the end, the international supply chain and economic globalisation are possible.

With the general adoption of containerisation by the liner shipping industry, the commodity-based tariff system was replaced by a flat rate per container regime which is called a freight all kinds (FAK) tariff or box rate. This means that the price charged is based on the number of containers transported irrespective of the type of cargo in the container. This is, in essence, a non-discriminatory market-based tariff.

7.5 The main liner shipping operational patterns

Unlike tramp shipping vessels that go anywhere at any time, regular liner ships are following pre-fixed maritime routes linking various ports on pre-determined schedules. Liner shipping routes can be discussed from two aspects: the geographical market coverage and operation patterns.

What are the main geographical markets of liner shipping?

As explained above, the layout and the development of the liner shipping markets are directly related to the international trade patterns of manufactured goods. Liner shipping routes can first of all be divided into two levels: long-haul trade and regional trade. The former usually refers to intercontinental markets and the latter is about intra-regional liner markets. Each of the two markets consists of several distinguished routes or networks covering different geographical regions. Intercontinental liner services are generally divided into three sub-categories, namely the East–West markets, the North–South markets and the South–South markets (Figure 7.6).

- ***East–West*** markets. The majority of general cargo flow is presently concentrated on markets among three industrialised regions: *East Asia, Europe and North America*. Thus the markets are called the East–West shipping routes, which are of three separate liner trades, namely *the Trans-Pacific trade, the Far East/Europe trade* and *the Trans-Atlantic trade*. These East–West markets have by far the largest liner trade. With the effect of the economic globalisation, the global share of this market has gradually declined from close to 50% in the 1980s and 1990s, to less than 30% in the 2010s. However, the East–West liner shipping markets remain as the leading and most influential markets for mainly two reasons. The first is the high level of transport need in terms of ton-miles. The Far East and European shipping route, for example, is one of the largest and longest routes in the world. The second reason is the relatively high unit value of cargoes carried. Such features have resulted in the ships trading on the East–West routes being large and fast. There are also some secondary East–West liner trades, such as the ones serving the Middle East or the ones serving the Indian subcontinent.

- ***North–South*** markets. While the terms of East and West carry mostly geographical and cultural meanings, those of North and South have more geopolitical significance. It is in this context that the liner trade between the North and the South refers to the container traffic mostly between the industrialised and rich countries in Western Europe, Japan and North America and that of the developing world of Asia, Latin America and Africa. These shipping routes include therefore those between each of Europe, Japan and North America and each of Africa, Latin America and developing Asia. The biggest changing factor in this traditional notion is the rise of the newly industrialised countries or the so-called emerging economies. Most such countries are geographically in the North, such as China and, to some extent, India. So for some references, the North–South liner trades include the Chinese trades with Africa or Latin America. Some people define such liner services as the South–South trades. With a faster economic development in many emerging economies of Asia, Latin America and Africa, the growth rate of East–South trade has been faster than the traditional East–West liner trade.[10]

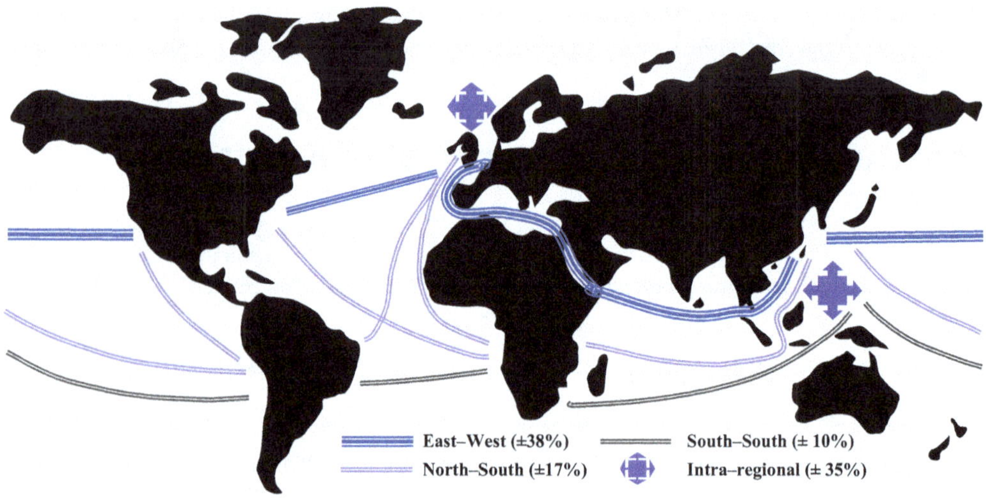

Figure 7.6 World's main liner shipping markets.

Source: Shuo Ma, based on data from UNCTAD (2016), Clarkson (2016) and ISL (2016).

Note: the shares of each market change as the pace of economic development and the situation of global production vary between countries over time.

- ***South–South*** markets. The definition of these markets also has its political origin, in the sense that it refers more to the trade between developing nations rather than the one within a geographical dimension only. As a consequence of the rapid economic development and the development of a globalised industrial production and supply chain in more and more formerly poor countries, as described in Chapter 3 and Chapter 4, the general cargo trade between emerging economies has recorded steady growth. An increasing number of countries in Africa, Latin America and elsewhere are trading more with the newly industrialised countries in Asia, such as China and India, than with Europe or North America. Such South–South trade at the early development stage has been by and large "one-sided" in that most manufactured products are imported from Asia to Africa and Latin America in exchange for primary materials exported from these countries.

Intra-regional liner shipping services have registered a very rapid growth since the 1990s. This was mostly driven by the development of the global supply chain in Europe and, particularly, in Asia due to the extraordinary economic growth of the region.

- ***Intra-Asia liner services.*** The most striking difference between Asia, Europe, America and Africa is the fact that most Asian countries rely predominantly on maritime transport for the bulk of their foreign trade. This is partly because of the specific geographical characteristics of the region in that, on the one hand, many countries are composed of islands, such as Indonesia, Japan and the Philippines. On the other hand, land transport is either too long, like the distance between Malaysia and China, or too expensive, like that between Bangladesh and China. It is also partly because of the geopolitical conditions, such as, for example, that South Korea is separated from China by North Korea and therefore does not use land-based transport modes. Another reason is that many countries that share common borders are not big trade partners. And, instead, these countries have their trade partners in remote countries separated by sea. The intra-Asia liner trade is the world's largest container shipping market in terms of the total number of teu traded.[11] The average size of container ships employed in this market is even bigger than that for some intercontinental markets.
- ***Intra-Europe liner services.*** This is the second largest intra-regional market after Asia. Most European countries are well connected by an efficient land transport system. Most trade between, for example, France and Germany, is transported by land transport. However, intra-Europe container liner shipping is still an active market, particularly the services for British, Scandinavian and Mediterranean markets. Compared with the intra-Asia services, more ro-ro ships are utilised in the intra-Europe market.

What are the main operation patterns in liner shipping?

Shipping companies are operating on the above-mentioned routes with services in a number of operational patterns. A pattern refers to the way the individual markets are served. A suitable pattern is chosen according to the geographical conditions, the type and volume of trade, the situation of ports of call and the characteristics of the ships employed. Often, the balance of trade also plays an important role. Presently, there are many variations of liner service patterns. We will discuss the three most common ones, which are called "End-to-End", "Hub-spoke" and "Pendulum" services.

- The ***End-to-End*** type of liner operation is the most common and traditional way of organising liner shipping services between the two markets. Explicitly, ships in an end-to-end arrangement serve only the two markets by loading all cargoes in one and discharging them in the others, as shown in Figure 7.7. The performance and profitability of the lines are much affected by the stability of the traffic and the balance of the two directions. A liner service between Western Africa and Western Europe is an example of an end-to-end service. The end-to-end service is straightforward and relatively easy to manage. The number of ships needed depends on the distance, the speed of the ships and the time in port. There is a disadvantage of the end-to-end liner pattern when the size of the ship is large and cargoes are scattered among many ports, because calling more ports increases not only the total cost and transit time but also the risk of delays. The order of the ports of call can be a very tricky issue to handle because multiple factors, such as the volume of cargo to load and to discharge, ship stability, port equipment allocation, etc., have all to be considered in order to minimise cargo handling and time in port. The trade imbalance is also a challenge for container shipping companies because carrying empty containers generates no income but is a high cost and takes time. Another difficulty operators may have to face is the double calling of the same ports in a loop due to the scheduling and also on-board storage requirements.

- The ***Hub-spoke*** pattern refers to a practice called transhipment, which means transporting cargo using more than one ship. The main purpose of transferring cargo from one ship to another is to serve a larger market without the main-line ships calling too many ports. Instead of calling at every port, big and costly ships serving long-haul markets only load and discharge cargo at a limited number of ports. Such ports are called hubs or transhipment centres, to and from which relay shipping services are arranged to cover more ports. These are smaller feeder vessels which go back and forth between the hub port and other ports. The feeder ports usually have less traffic or are located away from the main maritime routes. The hub-and-spoke liner shipping pattern is illustrated in Figure 7.8. The port of Singapore, for example, is a well-known hub port with very high transhipment traffic to and from the other ports in the region, such as those in Malaysia, Indonesia, Thailand, Vietnam or the Philippines. The disadvantages of the hub-spoke system are the higher port cost and longer transit time for the shipping companies and the shippers alike. Transhipment means more cargo handling and port charges, more ship costs for feeder vessels and more time spent in the process. So, for many shippers, having a direct liner service is an important criterion for their selection of ocean carrier and port of call. Transhipment was not a popular practice in the era of conventional general cargo transport by tweendecker ships. This is mainly because of the low productivity and high cost of cargo handling associated with this type of ship.
- The ***Pendulum*** liner shipping operation started to become popular in the mid-1980s. In this type of liner service, ships move between more than two markets. This can be compared with a combination of two or more end-to-end services. The market in the middle serves as the fulcrum. The ships, after discharging all or partial cargo at the port(s) in the market on their way, will load cargo for another market and continue to sail forward. The ships swing to either side of the fulcrum like a pendulum, linking together not only the two end markets but those in the middle. Such a kind of operation is used on the many major East–West liner shipping routes, such as the example in Figure 7.9 in which the Middle East serves as the fulcrum between the Far East and Europe. Cargoes from Asia for the European market, as well as the Middle East and African markets, are loaded. At the port of Salalah the cargoes for the Middle East and Africa are discharged and the cargoes from these markets for Europe are loaded and the ship will continue on its journey to Europe. There are a number of advantages of the Pendulum pattern. It increases cargo load by serving additional markets; it improves revenue by using each slot more times; and it saves cost by the possible elimination or reduction of double-called ports. Pendulum services can also help shipping lines to deploy larger container vessels with more competitive unit cost. When such a concept and practice are further explored, more long- and short-haul routes can be combined to take advantage of the fast growth of the intra-regional markets in Asia and Europe. For a Far East and Europe liner shipping service, South-East Asia or South Asia can be a fulcrum, so a long-haul container ship transporting cargo from Japan/Korea/China to Europe can unload cargoes for South-East Asia in Singapore or for South Asia in Colombo and take on their European export before continuing to sail for Europe. As a result, the loading factor can be sensibly improved and the utilisation of the ship's space can be multiplied.

Figure 7.7 "End-to-end" liner shipping services.

Note: this is the most commonly used liner service pattern, calling a group of nearby ports at each end.

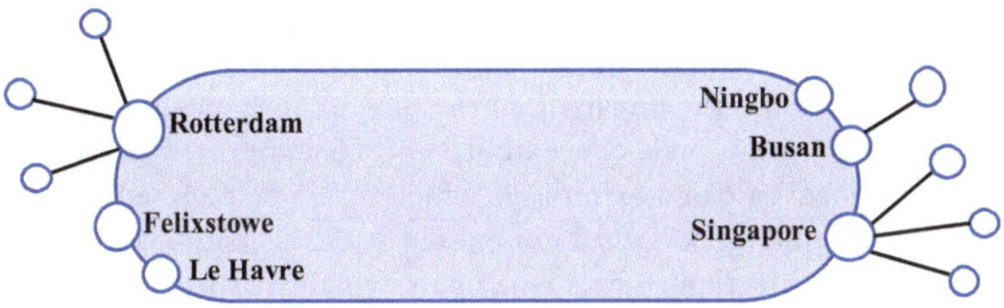

Figure 7.8 "Hub-and-spoke" liner shipping services.

Note: this pattern is often used when the long-haul ships are large and the secondary ports are many and not on the shipping route.

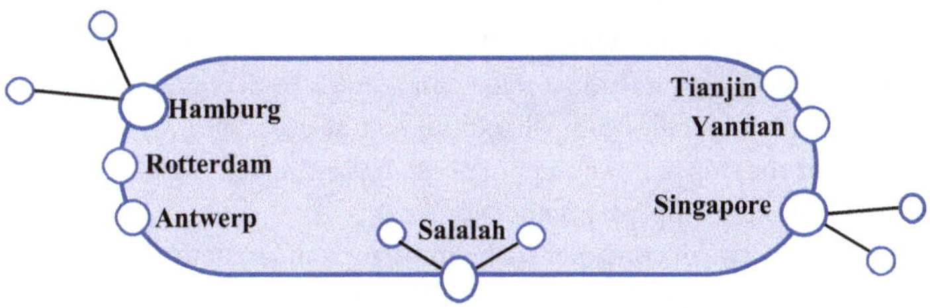

Figure 7.9 "Pendulum" liner shipping services.

Note: ships on route may call at the mid-way ports to improve space utilisation and revenue.

There are, apart from the above three patterns, a number of other liner service patterns, such as "double-dipping", which is a kind of pendulum service, and a "round-the-world" service, which was first introduced by two then leading shipping lines, Evergreen of Taiwan and US Line of the USA. Later on, another shipping line also started but now the "round-the-world" services have been discontinued.

7.6 The main operational challenges facing liner shipping

Liner shipping has probably been the most dynamic sector in commercial shipping for more than 50 years, since the beginning of containerisation. Containerisation has changed the liner shipping sector completely by enhancing productivity, reducing cost and improving connectivity. It has led to the very rapid development of the services and, at the same time, it has also brought serious challenges to the liner sector. If we concentrate only on the operational aspects of liner shipping, the most important challenges are often found in the areas such as trade imbalance, coping with the demand and the number of ports of call.

What are the problems with empty containers and how to deal with them?

The key element of containerisation is the creation of a cargo unit for transport and handling at a port. While it has brought so many great improvements and highly positive changes, it has also created a problem, which is the box itself. At the time of pre-containerisation, when general cargo was transported by break-bulk conventional ships, cargoes had simple packing using a wooden box, or a cardboard case or a nylon sack, which would be disposed of locally after usage. The problem of repositioning packing had not existed as the packing materials were not meant to be reused. With the introduction of steel containers, which are specially designed and built at a high cost, the one-time-use packing materials became packing equipment that is expected to be used and reused for many years.

The issue of trade imbalance has always been with liner shipping long before containerisation. The problem is, however, more serious with containers because additional costs are added to the loss bill. A conventional liner ship which sails full in one direction but only with a half load for the return voyage will incur a loss of 50% income on the return voyage. However, in the age of containers, a ship in a similar situation will have to carry the empty containers back. So the shipping lines not only incur a loss of income, but also a cost of repositioning empty containers. The repositioning cost includes four parts: (1) container-related costs which include the capital cost and repair cost; (2) storage and land-transport-related costs which include storage cost at ports or depots and hauling cost to the port; (3) port-related costs, which includes cargo-handling cost at ports; and (4) ship-related costs, which include the time cost for the ship and the shipping cost. It is estimated that the total repositioning cost is in the region of US$500 per empty container.

There is a difference between container traffic imbalance and trade imbalance. While trade imbalance is measured in value terms, seaborne traffic imbalance is measured in volume. Because of this difference, the situation is more complicated. This means that even if a perfectly balanced trade exists between two countries, an imbalance of container traffic may still happen. For example, an Asian country may have to export millions of shoes in exchange for a commercial aircraft from the US. Or tens of thousands of containerised cargoes are exported from Asia to Africa in exchange for mostly raw materials which are not transported by containers. A balanced container trade in volume is an exception rather than a norm. Traditionally, industrialised countries have always had a container traffic surplus with the countries of Africa, the Middle East or Latin America, whose exports have mostly been natural-resource-based. However, the situation became more serious with the development of a global supply chain and the greater concentration of industrial production in a handful of countries. Asia has, for the past half a century, been the home for a very large portion of the global production and thus had a big and consistent surplus of containerised cargo over most other regions, including Europe and North America.

We can measure the container traffic balance of a region or a country by the ratio of export to import teus in a year. If the trade is in a perfect balance then the ratio is 100% and the ratio is more than 100% if export containers exceed import ones, or less than 100% for an opposite situation. For many years Asia, in particular the Far East, has exported more containerised cargo than it imports. It runs a big container traffic surplus with Africa and Latin America and also Europe and North America. Figure 7.10 shows the container traffic balance of these four regions. It is to be noted that although Europe, as well as North America, have a container traffic deficit with Asia of almost 60%, their overall container export and import are more balanced. This is because they have a balanced trade between themselves and even a surplus with other regions. Africa and Latin America used to have more balanced trade, but as they import more containerised goods from Asia the overall ratio has declined.

If about 50% of the containers a ship carries on one of every two intercontinental voyages are empty, the cost can be very high. One estimate puts the total cost of container repositioning at 15 to 20 billion US dollars per year for the liner shipping industry.[12] So, how to deal with the issue of empty containers? Over the years various attempts have been made to reduce or control the cost. The methods used included making foldable containers, employing dedicated slow and cheap vessels to move empty containers, or even using cheaper containers in the Far East and disposing of them after a single usage. Yet, so far, none of the methods is satisfactory and the industry still has to shoulder the high cost. The seriousness of the problem has evolved to the extent that the capability of securing more return containerised cargo becomes one of the decisive factors in market competition.

The scale of operation is an important factor because it has been revealed that among all empty containers, about two-thirds are so-called "structural imbalance", which is generated by the imbalance of containerised cargo flows, but the remaining one-third of empty containers is related to individual carriers. This means that a shipping line serves more shippers with cargoes in one direction but not

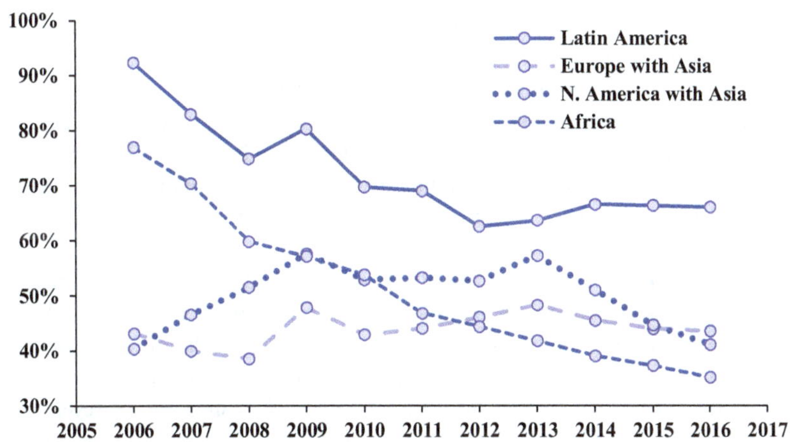

Figure 7.10 Export-to-import container traffic ratio of selected markets, 2006–2016.

Source: Shuo Ma, based on data from UNCTAD (2016, 2015) and Clarkson (2016).

Note: these are export-to-import container ratios. So 100% means a perfectly balanced trade. The European or North American trade is relatively balanced but they have a big container traffic deficit with Asia. Africa has a low ratio with most of the trade partners.

enough shippers with return cargoes and another shipping line may just have a different or reversed situation. So the larger the scale of operation is, the better the chances are of minimising the transport of empty containers. This has been one of the reasons behind the formation of liner shipping alliances, in which there is usually a provision for the members to use each other's empty containers. In 2015 a leading consulting company, Boston Consulting Group, launched a web-based public service portal named *xChange* to help shipping companies, container leasing firms and logistics enterprises with a platform to share information and to exchange empty containers.[13]

What are the impacts of supply rigidity?

Another operational challenge facing the liner shipping industry is the difficulty for the supply to cope with the demand changes. On one hand, the demand for liner shipping transport is constantly changing in the medium term, but the liner shipping supply, on the other hand, has some built-in rigidities that prevent it from changing and responding quickly and easily to the changes. Unlike in tramp shipping, where a ship is chosen just to suit the cargo to be transported, liner shipping ships have to be ready without knowing how many shippers will come and use them. Once the ships are in place, this is very hard to adjust. Such rigidity comes from mainly two sources, the first is the size of ships and the second is the fixed service intervals.

- ***Multiple expensive ships of the same size***. Liner shipping is like "public" transport offering standard services. In a typical intercontinental container liner service, the company needs to have a series of ships of very similar specifications, such as the type, size or ship speed. Once the ships are in operation, this is very difficult to change. However, cargo demand is not a fixed factor. So when there is a shortage of demand, all the ships will still have to be employed, which will undoubtedly affect the liner company's bottom line. If the cargo demand increases, it is equally hard to adjust the capacity up, because it is extremely difficult to change the size of all ships. To increase a ship's size means a considerable capital investment. Ships or a series of ships are designed and built for a specified market over many years. Shipping lines with limited market coverage cannot deploy their ships of different sizes among various markets. The experience of rapid world container traffic development, especially the extraordinary and continuous increase in container trade in Asia, has shown that the ship capacity is often considered insufficient long before the time that the economic life of the ship is over. Yet no shipping line can afford to upgrade a whole series of ships every three years. Consequently, in anticipation of such a situation, container liner ships are often built with spare capacity.
- ***Fixed-day weekly service standard***. Over the years, the modern commercial liner shipping, in response to the market requirement, has followed a standard that is called "fixed-day weekly service". This has been accepted by the majority of the shippers as the norm of the liner industry. This means that, from a port, the departure and arrival of a liner shipping service are always on a fixed day of the week. Any different intervals, either longer or shorter than seven days, are typically rejected by the customers. Such a "rigidity" has left very little room for manoeuvre for liner shipping companies when there is a change in demand. Apart from replacing the fleet concerned with larger ships, the only other alternative is to add an entirely new weekly service. But that may not be a suitable solution if the increase in demand is more incremental and modest, for example, by 10% or 15% rather than by 100%.

To cope with the changes in demand, the size of the operation is important. A large shipping company which has services in multiple markets requiring different ship sizes will have the advantage of redeploying ships among the markets according to the level of demand. This is also one of the motivations for the liner shipping companies to increase the size of their operation.

Why do ports remain the biggest sources of challenges?

The operational relationship between a port and a container ship is multi-fold. Some of the aspects of this particular relationship will be discussed in Chapter 10 which is dedicated to ports. In this section we will look at two port-related challenges for liner shipping. One of them is about the choice of the port of call and the other is about delays and uncertainties of port services.

The issue regarding the port of call is an essential but complicated one for any liner company. It becomes an even more difficult question when new ships are built ever larger. Because big ships are more valuable, the total transit time should be as short as possible and the number of ports should be kept to a minimum. However, larger vessels need more cargo to load, which means that more ports ought to be called. One of the solutions is to use a "hub-and-spoke" pattern. A port may be served by feeder ships for either technical/operational or economic reasons. Physical and equipment constraints may prevent ports technically from receiving large mainline vessels. Inefficient and unreliable port operations can also make shipping lines serve the port with small and cheaper feeder ships rather than with expensive mother ships. But transhipment has a major drawback for shippers, which is the expensive operation in terms of feeder transport cost, additional cargo-handling cost and longer transit time. To avoid the high cost of feedering practice, shippers prefer direct calls. For a shipping line, upgrading a feeder port to a port of direct-call will increase its own cost. So it is based on the result of a cost comparison between direct call and feedering for both the shipping line and shippers that a choice will be made. The cargo volume and the port efficiency are the two decisive factors in such a calculation.

From a shipping line's point of view, the number of direct-call ports depends on a series of interrelated variables such as transport distance to each port, ships' cost, hub and feeder port cost, ships' size and speed, freight level and the volume of cargo traffic, etc. The most important deciding factor is the volume of cargo in teus that the line is able to consolidate to sustain the weekly services to and from a port on a trade route. This number of teus per week and its expected future development will determine the size of ships to be used and the number of weekly services to offer. Based on the weekly volume and the applied freight level by the line, the total revenue per week can be calculated. Hence, what the shipping line should do is to minimise its cost by selecting the appropriate speed of ships, the number of direct-call ports, including the hub ports, and the right number of ships in a string of liner service.

Shipping lines cannot include as many ports of call as they want in a trade route even when the volume of traffic to and from those ports grows to a sufficient level for direct calls. This is mainly because of the concern of total transit time. Despite possible cost savings, adding more ports to a liner route does not increase any carrying capacity for the demand but it does increase the tonnage requirement of the shipping line as more ports of call mean more ships and longer time for the round trip. For instance, adding two more ports of call may require eight ships instead of seven per loop and extend the time for a round trip by one extra week. The extra cost of additional ships could indeed be offset by savings from the feedering. However, the consequent longer transit time could make it very hard for the line to compete in the marketplace where the ever-higher-value containerised cargo is becoming increasingly time-sensitive. So the alternative is either to use transhipment or to open new weekly services.

There is an issue of the delays and other uncertainties. For a fixed-day weekly liner shipping service, the regularity and punctuality is one of the essential operational features. But such quality of service is far from being guaranteed and it has been constantly compromised by various circumstances of unreliability. The overall performance of the liner industry has been mixed. According to a British shipping consultant company, the average liner shipping schedule reliability rate of all major service providers on the main East–West routes was in the region of 50%–60%. The schedule reliability rate may vary greatly from period to period, port to port and shipping line to shipping line. When the demand is high, the reliability rate tends to be low due to congestion in ports. The best performers recorded can achieve a service reliability rate of about 80%.[14] The major source of uncertainties is from delays in port. It is found in a study that weather and navigation-related reasons count for less than 10% of all causes. More than 90% of delays and unreliability of liner shipping on the Far East–Europe route are attributable to port-related reasons.[15]

When looking into the port-related reasons, one realises that congestion is the biggest source of delays. This happens when a ship arrives at a port but has to wait for a berth in a queue. But congestion is a symptom rather than a real cause. The shortage of facilities, either infrastructure or superstructure, is often one of the root causes of the problem. Sometimes, proper maintenance may be the main reason, which might lead to unexpected breakdowns, more time spent on repair or waiting for spare parts. Administrative services can also have an impact on the turnaround time of a ship in port. If labour productivity is below expectation, delays will happen.[16] Labour productivity can also be affected by problematic social relations. Therefore, ports play a vital role in the assurance of quality service for the liner shipping industry.

7.7 Summary

In this chapter we examined the structural change that happened in the production processes which had a profound impact on maritime transport. Traditionally, ocean-going ships carry raw materials from overseas to industrialised countries for processing and manufacturing. Then finished products are transported again by ships to the final consumption market. The internationalised manufacturing and global supply chain have changed this pattern completely. A product is manufactured across multiple countries sometimes separated by oceans. So shipping has entered into the production processes. As a result, for making the same products, more maritime transport is needed. At the same time, shipping ought to provide faster, more frequent, secure and reliable services.

Maritime transport can be operated in one of the three models: industrial shipping, tramp shipping and liner shipping. The choice of model depends on the characteristics of transport demand. Two such characteristics of cargo shipment are of particular importance: the size and the regularity/frequency. Large shipments that can occupy the full shipload are transported under tramp shipping. It is also possible that cargo owners own and operate ships directly to transport cargo for their own sake. In this case, it is called industrial shipping. For small parcels, also named as general cargo, liner shipping is the common form of a shipping operation. As the industrial shipping, which makes up approximately 20% of the world's total seaborne trade, is not a commercially traded shipping service, our discussions in this chapter have focussed on the features of tramp shipping, which is about 60% of the market, and liner shipping, which is about 20%.

Most of the global seaborne trade is moved by tramp shipping. Typically, cargoes transported by tramp shipping are in bulk and divided into two big groups: liquid and dry. The liquid cargo includes crude oil, product oil, chemicals and other liquid cargo. The dry cargo includes iron ore, coal, other minerals, grain, etc. Under tramp shipping, the ship can be "rented" for a definite period, but most tramp shipping contracts are for carrying specific cargo. Operationally speaking, a tramp ship is serving at a point in time one customer. Therefore, the time of shipment and the location of loading/discharging ports are decided by the cargo's interest. Since it is a "one ship, one cargo" operation, a tramp shipping company is usually small with a simple organisation. In tramp shipping, the transport contract is called a "charter party", which defines the responsibilities of the shipowner and the charterer. Standard forms of charter parties are commonly used. There are three types of charter party: under a voyage charter, the ship is fully equipped and operated by the shipowner to transport a specific cargo for the charterer; under a time charter, the ship is manned, insured and given to the charterer to operate for a period of time; under bareboat or demise charter, the ship is given to the charterer as a hull without crew or insurance for an extended period of time.

With regard to liner shipping, the type of cargo includes all kinds of manufactured goods, either finished or semi-finished. Like public transport such as a bus or a train, a liner ship carries cargoes of many clients. The shipping lines decide on the routes, the ports and the sailing schedules. The shipping company provides more services than in tramp shipping. Operated as a network, a liner shipping company often has a more sophisticated organisation and extended geographical coverage. The contract of transport is called a bill of lading, which also has the role of cargo receipt and the document of title representing the ownership of the cargo concerned. Today, liner shipping has been highly containerised. With containers, the freight applied is the so-called FAK rate, which is a flat tariff per container. The liner shipping services are organised under some operational patterns. Apart from a classical "end-to-end" type of ship operation, a popular liner shipping pattern is called the "hub-and-spoke" in which transhipment is used.

Over the last couple of decades, liner shipping has undergone some profound changes, moving from conventional general cargo ships to the container vessels and from small and slow ships to large and faster container carriers. In this process there are a lot of new challenges emerged in the liner shipping industry. Three major challenges were discussed. First of all, containerisation and economic globalisation have increased the number of empty containers. The repositioning costs for the liner sector are as high as some 20 billion US dollars per year. Another challenge is the ability to adjust the supply of ships to the constant but unpredictable changes of cargo demand. The third challenge is about ports because the number and the choice of ports are tricky issues for the shipping lines and, at the same time, ports are the origin of delays and unexpected expenses.

Notes

1 Ranheim E. (2008).
2 The professional shipping organisation "Intertanko" defines "Independent tanker owner" as "independent tanker owners and operators of oil, chemical and gas tankers, i.e. non-oil companies and non-state controlled tanker owners". Source: Intertanko official website (www.intertanko.com/About-Us/).
3 BP Shipping (2018).
4 ZPMC (2018).
5 UNCTAD (2016).
6 Ranheim E. (2008).
7 Alderton P. (2011).
8 UNCTAD (2016).
9 In 2016 among the world fleet of liner shipping in terms of deadweight, 83% were container ships and 10% were multi-purpose ships (Clarkson, 2016). But container ships have a much higher productivity and there is a higher proportion of liner cargo that is transported by container ships.
10 UNCTAD (1995–2016).
11 According to Clarkson's data (Clarkson Shipping Intelligence), about 40% of all imported container trade in 2015 was intra-regional trade. The intra-Asia market is the biggest intra-regional container trade market.
12 Sanders U. et al. (2015) and BCG Report, 17 November 2015. It is found in the BCG report that about two thirds of empty containers are trade-related structural imbalance and one third of them are carrier-specific.
13 See BCG, "BCG launches platform that could save the container industry billions of dollars", https://finance.yahoo.com/news/bcg-launches-platform-could-save-050100678.html.
14 According to the British maritime consultant company Drewry, the average of the container line schedule reliability rate was at 63% at the beginning of 2016 (see Lloyds List, "Box carrier schedule reliability falls to 12-month low", 17 March 2016). The average rate was 53% in 2006.

15 Notteboom T. (2006).

16 It is reported that the average schedule reliability was 55% during the US West Coast labour dispute at the beginning of 2015 (Lloyds List, "Box carrier schedule reliability falls to 12-month low", 17 March 2016).

References

Alderton P. (2011) "*Sea Transport, Operation and Economics*", 6th Edition, Thomas Reed Publication, London, p. 202.

BCG. (2015) "*Think Outside Your Boxes: Solving the Global Container-Repositioning Puzzle*", BCG Perspectives, Boston, MA.

BP Shipping. (2018) "*Our Fleet*", www.bp.com/en/global/bp-shipping/our-fleet.html

Clarkson (2016) "*Shipping Intelligence Network*", Type of fixtures. Clarkson, London, UK.

ISL. (2016) "*ISL Shipping Statistics*", Institute of Shipping and Logistics, ISL, Bremen, Germany.

Lloyds List. (2016) "*Box Carrier Schedule Reliability Falls to 12-month Low*", 17 March 2016.

Notteboom T. (2006) "*The Time Factor in Liner Shipping Services*", Maritime Economics and Logistics, Vol.8, pp. 19–39.

Ranheim E. (2008) Intertanko, "*Market Actor and Behaviour*", CBS, Oslo, February 2008.

Sanders U. et al. (2015) "*Think outside Your Boxes: Solving the Global Container-repositioning Puzzle*", BCG Report, 17 November 2015.

UNCTAD. (1995–2016) "*Review of Maritme Transport*", issues of the multiple years. UNCTAD, Geneva, Switzerland.

UNCTAD. (2016) "*Review of Maritime Transport*," 2015, UNCTAD/RMT/2016, United Nations Publication, UNCTAD, Geneva, Switzerland, pp. 7–26.

ZPMC. (2018) "*Shipping Services*", www.zpmc.ae/maintenancetroubleshootingdetail.aspx?ProductID=0102509b-10cd-48c8-ad20-ddecc4dfdda3

Chapter 8

Ship finance and the economics of risk

Ship finance has specific importance mainly for three reasons. First, ships are expensive or, in other words, shipping is a capital-intensive sector. This often represents an obstacle to start a business or to expand it. Second, the ship prices are, in the short and even medium term, disconnected from the cost of building the ships. They are determined by the market forces. As such, ship prices fluctuate, sometimes violently. Third, due to the above two features, financial risk is always associated with shipping. In this chapter we will examine such specific characteristics of ship finance.

8.1 The financial characteristics of ships

As for most modes of transport, the initial cost of acquisition of the transport vehicles or assets, such as a ship, a lorry or an aircraft, is always prominent in proportion to the total cost of running the business. As far as commercial shipping is concerned, such capital cost to overall cost proportion varies from one type of shipping organisation to another. In liner shipping, due to the higher cost of setting up and maintaining a network of commercial and operational activities as well as faster ships and broader service coverage, such a proportion is usually lower than in tramp shipping,

What is the level of capital requirement of ships?

It was reported in 2011 that the Danish shipping company Maersk Line signed a contract with a Korean shipyard to build ten large container ships of about 18,000 teu for a total cost of US$1.9 billion, or US$190 million per ship.[1] More sophisticated ships, such as LNG vessels, often cost more than US$200 million apiece to build. Even a small vessel, of around 30,000 deadweight tonnage, would cost around US$20 million. Shipping is an asset-based business and the cost of ship acquisition is usually very high. The total amount of funding invested in new ships increased from about US$20 billion per year in the 1990s to more than US$100 billion in the years before the financial crisis in 2009. The amount is significant because the demand has been increasing and the existing tonnage needs to be replaced, given that an ocean-going ship typically has a service life of about 25 years. Therefore, each year, about 4% of the current fleet needs to be replaced, in addition to the net world tonnage growth, which has been at about 3% on average for many years. This represents a total of about 4,000 new merchant ships each year. The total amount of asset of the existing fleet of merchant ships, including those under construction, has exceeded US$1 trillion.[2]

The cost of a ship can be roughly divided into the following four groups:

1 ***Material and energy costs.*** Among these costs, steel costs are the most important. Other costs such as the cost of paint or energy cost such as electricity are also included.
2 ***Engine and equipment costs.*** These are the costs for the main engine and the auxiliary engines and generators as well as the equipment for ship control, navigation and communication, etc.
3 ***Labour costs.*** The labour costs are very important, not only because they occupy a large portion of the total shipbuilding costs but also because they are the main source of cost differentiation between countries. These costs should be adjusted for productivity.
4 ***Administration and overhead costs.*** Apart from general administration costs and rent, the costs of ship design, research and development are also included.

The cost of a new ship is much affected by the cost of steel in the international market. However, it is not a coincidence that most of the leading shipbuilding countries are also big steel producers. The strength of the shipbuilding industry in a region requires the existence of a well-developed industrial base. Yet the biggest cost difference in ships comes from the labour-related cost, which can be calculated based on a combination of salary/benefit and productivity. For a long time, the Japanese shipbuilding industry has managed to maintain a good market share despite high salary/benefit costs thanks to the superior productivity of the labour force and to automation. The high cost of new ships is also accounted for by the extended building process over several stages and a long period of time. It takes typically two years to build a new ship, although it may take less time for those ships of a standard design.

The capital investment sometimes includes equipment beyond ships. Take container vessels for example. Steel containers for carrying cargo should also be acquired. It is common that two to three or even more times the number of containers are needed for every container capacity of the ship. Similar to the cost of ships, the cost of containers is also subject to the price of steel. A representative price for an ordinary 20-foot container, a teu, would be in the region of US$2,000 and, if it is a 40-foot container, US$3,000. Therefore, for example, if half of the container fleet are 20-footers, the other half 40-footers and the container-to-slot ratio is 3, then for a 10,000-teu container ship, the total cost for containers would be US$52.2 million. This may already be more than 50% of the cost of the ship itself.

Why does the price of ships change in such a volatile way?

As discussed above, ships are very costly to build. But it is difficult to provide price tags for the ships, even as an approximation. This is because the prices of new ships are extremely volatile. The degree of price fluctuation is unique for ships. A lorry may see its price move up and down from one year to the next. But it would be within a moderate range and largely in line with the cost changes. An aircraft such as a Boeing 737–600 cost around $40 million in the year 2000 and the cost rose to about $57 million in 2015. The price changed moderately and gradually during this period without any remarkable ups and downs. But the situation for commercial ships is entirely different. The degree of changes in the price of ships, both up and down, can be 100% to 200% or even more within a relatively short period of time.

As a perfectly competitive market, the price of new ships is determined by the market forces of demand and supply. This also implies that, in the short term, the price is much less cost-based than in most other sectors. The cost of ship construction in the short and medium term follows the general trends of labour and steel costs in the shipbuilding countries. When new orders decline, the prices of new ships drop while the costs of shipbuilding do not. Figure 8.1 shows the development of the prices of selected types of ships, namely tankers, container ships and bulk carriers, from 1980 to 2017. There are some variations concerning different sizes but, generally, the prices of other types of ships evolved in a similar way. From 1980 to 1985, for example, the prices of virtually all types of ships went down between 30% and 50% due to weak demand and an oversupply of ships, before swinging back during the next five years. From 2002 a sudden, strong and persistent increase in demand led to a rise in ships' prices to a very high level. Because of the exceptionally strong increase in the demand for iron ore from China, the newbuilding price of Cape-size bulk carriers experienced a more than 313% rise between 2002 and 2007.

There are a number of reasons that can be cited to explain the volatility of ships' prices. First of all, the international shipping market, particularly in the tramp shipping sector, is competitive and, therefore, the price is determined by the demand and supply. Second, the maritime transport demand in general, and that of the primary commodities transported in bulk in particular, is not stable. The volume fluctuates in response to various factors, such as economic situation, government policy and even weather conditions. But we may find other markets also under these two conditions of competitive nature and changing demand, yet no similar price volatility is observed. There are some additional and shipping-specific reasons that help explain the unique situation of ship prices. The following three are the most important ones.

- Shipbuilding capacity is usually inflexible to adjustment when the demand changes. Many shipyards can only produce a few ships at the same time and shipbuilding takes a long time. All this limits the ability of yards to adjust. So when the demand reduces, to keep the yards in operation in the short and sometimes medium term, orders are still accepted even with very low prices. For the same reason, but in the opposite direction, when the demand rises, shipyards have only a limited ability to increase the production, which drives the prices up.

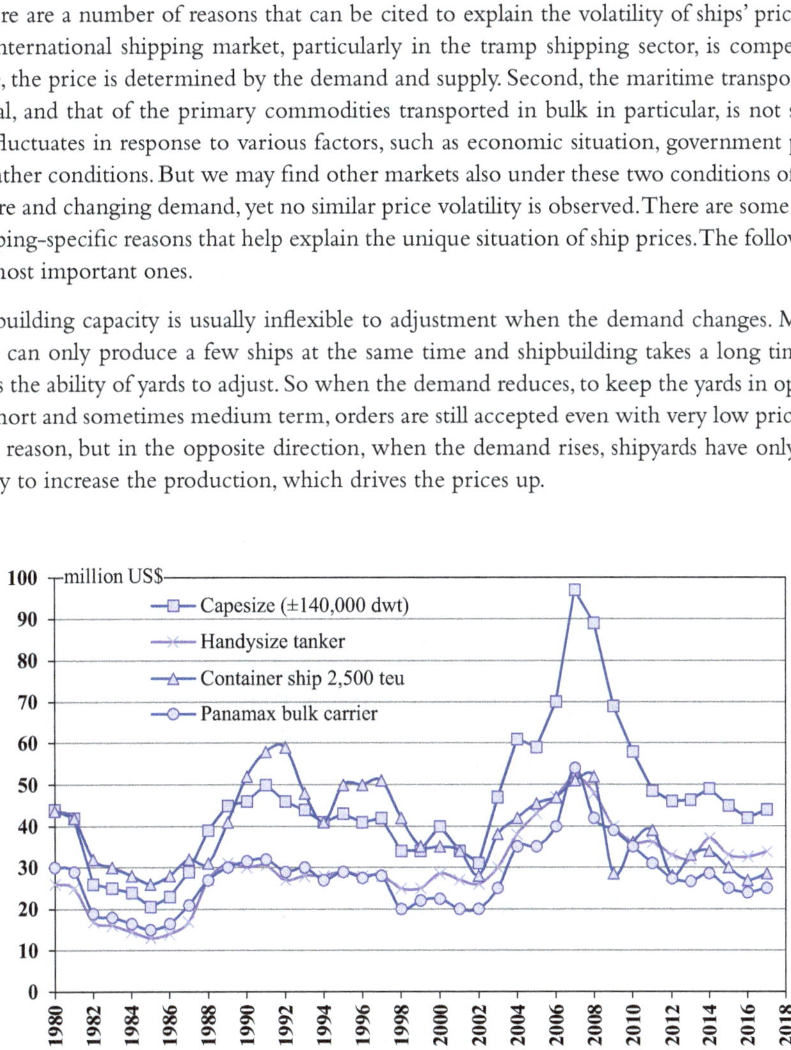

Figure 8.1 Price development of new ships, in million US$, 1980–2017.

Source: Shuo Ma, based on data from UNCTAD, Clarkson and ISL.

Note: this figure includes the representative new-building prices of selected ship types. The price movement of other types of ships followed similar patterns.

- Another reason relates to public intervention. Though the shipbuilding market is generally free and competitive, it is also socially influential as a supplier in the areas of employment as well as a large number of related sectors. It is, therefore, not uncommon among most shipbuilding countries, and has been so for a long time, that when the demand is weak, yards get financial support for them to survive rather than to reduce or close the production.[3] Such subsidies help ship prices go further down before a reduction of supply finally happens.
- The freight market fluctuates violently when the level of demand changes. This is especially the case in the bulk transport market, such as the demand for coal, iron ore and grain. The freight may be so high that shipping companies are willing and able to acquire new tonnage at very high ship prices. So, in the short term, the demand for new ships may be price inelastic.

What are other special characteristics of ship investment?

Investment in shipping has a high uncertainty of the ship's price. However, this has not been a main cause of discouragement for the investors. On the contrary, often overflow of capital into financing ships is the origin of extended low freight in the market. People are interested in investing in ships or lending money to ship investors for numerous reasons. Apart from general commercial motivations, there are some special reasons unique to international shipping, particularly the following three.

- The economic risk associated with an investment in ships is, to a large extent, mitigated by the nature of international mobility of ships. Unlike a factory, ships can go to where the business is worldwide if the market they were meant to serve is not good anymore. This advantage is most evident when the ships invested in are of standard types with a broad scope of usage. So highly specialised ships for small market segments may be riskier to invest in.
- Another factor which contributes to the mitigation of investment risk is the existence of a well-developed sales-and-purchase market of used commercial ships. Although the price of second-hand ships moves in many ways hand-in-hand with that of new ships, selling or buying a second-hard vessel is easy and may sometimes even be profitable.
- Merchant ships are much less restricted by national rules and legislation. This is because about 75% of the global fleet in deadweight tonnage is under so-called "open registry". This allows many ship investors to avoid restrictions or exposures imposed by national rules and to have more flexibility and freedom for financial operations. Because shipping is a business conducted on international waters, a shipping company or the operational base can be located anywhere in the world. Switzerland, for example, hosts some big shipping companies owned by foreigners.

8.2 Sources of ship investment

As discussed above, in 2018 the total asset value of the world commercial fleet was about US$1 trillion and the fleet continues to grow at about 3% per year on average. Ship finance has evolved from self-financed out of an individual's savings to a more sophisticated system with specialised financiers, banks, financial institutions and a market place through which private and public funds are channelled to the building of ships. Basically, in the 19th century, most of the commercial ships were financed by owners' own capital.[4] Then the stock company became more popular in the area of ship finance. There are many ways to finance ships. But if our discussion is focussed on the ownership of the ship, then the financing required for such ownership should be divided into two parts: the owner finances their ship with their own money, or the owner finances their ship with other people's money that is lent to the owner. The former is called equity financing and the latter debt financing.

What are the main forms of equity financing?

Equity represents the capital right of the business. The holders of the equity are owners of the business concerned. Generally, they exercise the control of the business proportional to their holdings of the shares and are entitled to profit earning in the form of dividends as well as liable for claims to the limit of their investment. Equity financing is, therefore, about holding or trading total or partial ownership of the ship for funds. Equity financing can take a number of forms, among which the four most important ones are briefly explained below, namely self-financing, private equity financing, public equity financing and secondary equity financing.

- ***Self-financing.*** This is to use one's own savings or the earnings from current or past businesses or sales of stocks or shares to invest in a ship. It also includes, of course, people from the family, friends, business partners or individuals close to each other who come together to pool funds for ship finance. A management buyout is also a kind of self-financing. This form of financing is common for small start-up shipping companies. The advantage of this kind of financing is its simplicity. However, the large amount of money involved in the purchase of a vessel is generally beyond the financial capability of most owners. In this case, other ways of equity financing can be considered.
- ***Private equity financing.*** This is to obtain funds from private investors, financial institutions, funds or foundations, etc., without going through a public exchange. Such private financial institutions can often mobilise a large sum of funds for an extended period. Some banks can also become equity investors either because they see shipping as a viable sector for investment or they turn from creditors to equity owners. Insurance companies or pension funds may also be interested in becoming ship equity firms. The objectives of private equity investors are usually to have long-term business opportunities and financial gains.
- ***Public equity financing.*** This is about the issuing of shares at a stock exchange to finance ships or shipping companies in the capital market. The word *public* means that the ownership of the company or ship in the form of shares is offered to anyone, meaning the public, in exchange for funds. Such public offerings are traded in the established stock exchanges, such as New York, London or Hong Kong. This form of ship financing became more popular in the 1990s. A shipping company wishing to raise capital from the public stock exchange should make an *initial public offering* or IPO, which means that the company goes public by offering shares at the market for trading for the first time. To do so, the company has to provide information about the company itself, the financial performance and the commercial activities. It should also decide on the share price at issue. Usually, the share price at issue, which is determined by the company, is set at a discount so as to ensure a full subscription of the initial offers. New York remains the leading market, thanks to the strength of the capital market in the US, while Hong Kong and Oslo are also main markets for shipping IPOs. Although public equity financing has become more popular today for shipping, it still has a small market share. Such a situation can be attributed to several reasons, mainly the following. To issue shares at a stock exchange costs more than the issue of debt bonds due to the requirements of stock market procedures. Such a system cost can be more easily absorbed by large IPOs but shipping companies, particularly in tramp shipping, are usually too small. The second reason is the reluctance of some shipowners to use this method due to the fear that it may undermine their control of the business by diluting the voting power of the company. The third reason is probably related to the perceived risks by the public because of income volatility in shipping.
- ***Secondary equity financing.*** This is about a new equity offering by a shipping company that is already publicly traded at a stock exchange. It is also called *seasoned* equity financing or simply capital-increase or followed-on offering. This is normally a relatively easier and less costly operation than an IPO. It is also an effective way of securing additional funding for a company's development programme. For example, in 2016, the Greek shipping company Costamare raised US$72

million through 12 million common shares to the public at US$6 per share at the New York Stock Exchange. Costamare had already been a listed company at the Exchange.[5]

The main advantage of private or public equity financing for new ships is to solve the problem of the lack of investment capital without having the excessive financial burden of debt servicing. Or, in other words, it can also be seen as a way of spreading out risks. On the other hand, however, this particular aspect can also be a disadvantage of this kind of funding because if the shipowner is so confident about the prospective profitability and has the skill to operate profitably, opting for equity financing means sharing the business success with other investors. Another disadvantage is that, depending on the share structuring, a publicly traded company can affect the decisions of the shipowners with regard to development objectives and priorities. In a way, every ship is financed at least partially with equity or funds out of a shipowner's own financial resources, as a "down payment". It is rare that a shipping company can acquire a ship with 100% borrowed capital.

What are the main forms of debt financing?

Debt financing remains the most popular and the primary source of capital investment in ships. This is also called *loan* funding, which means that the shipowner borrows part of the money needed for purchasing the ship at an agreed rate of interest and with other debt repayment conditions. As discussed above, the freight market volatility was one of the reasons for equity financing not being an attractive prospect. Freight rates may fluctuate significantly during a relatively short period. However, the main reason why it still attracts so many investors is the fact that the long-term average profitability of shipping is more comparable with most other economic sectors. The freight market is cyclical, which equalises the ups and downs of the market. Shipping companies have to make an extra profit while the market flourishes in order to pay for the inevitable losses of the bad times. So, in spite of its short-term speculative nature, the shipping sector is seen, by many long-term investors, as a good business opportunity.

With a better knowledge of the sector, there are commercial banks, institutional investors and individuals who are interested in lending funds to shipowners or shipping companies. As of today, debt financing provides about 60%–70% of the total ship investment.[6] From the shipowner's point of view, debt financing is only a type of temporary external funding, which must be paid back by them. In other words, debt financing is a solution to the problem of initial capital availability for the shipowner. In time, it will be the same as self-financing equity funding when all debt service has been paid back. There are numerous debt financing instruments. Looking at the kind of creditor and the way lending is arranged, four major categories of debt financing can be identified, namely bank loans, shipyard credits, bond issuance and private borrowing. We shall examine each of them in this section.

- ***Bank loans***. This has been the biggest source of ship finance. There are many commercial banks interested and specialised in providing loans to shipping companies. Traditionally, most of them are European banks but, since around the year 2000, commercial banks from Asia have started to be active and have expanded their market share quickly. Bank loans, compared with other types of debt financing, have the advantage of being simple, flexible and often a quick way for shipowners to obtain the necessary funding. The process starts with the bank carefully assessing the request from the shipping company. In addition, the bank will also know other essential information, for example on the general performance of the shipping company in the past and the quality of the management, which may include the profitability of the company and its safety record. The bank will also evaluate the specific ship concerned in terms of the market conditions, freight earning perspectives and re-sale value. The experience and reputation of the potential borrower regarding the debt service and the company's current loan-to-asset ratio are of critical importance to the bank. Should the bank consider the loan request as acceptable, a loan agreement is usually negotiated between the bank and the shipping company around the important issues, such as the size of the loan, the interest rate, the repayment period and the security.

Typically, and in normal circumstances, the amount a commercial bank will lend to a shipowner will be about 50% of the ship's value based on the above-mentioned conditions, in particular the reputation of the company and the level of debt and security provided. With reliable security or a long-term commercial engagement of the ship, such as a long-term charter party, the bank may be willing to further increase the loan up to 80% of the total value or even higher.

Interest rate is another major area both parties will negotiate on. This is the cost of capital loans for the shipowner. The interest rate may be at a fixed percentage during the entire period of the loan or, more commonly in shipping, it may be allowed to float in line with the changes of the market interest rates. The London Inter Bank Offered Rate (LIBOR) used to be a benchmark and a base for medium-term loans made to the shipping industry. Typically, a bank may charge its interest at 0.5% to 2% above the LIBOR depending on specific conditions. As is the nature of the world financial market, the LIBOR or an alternative benchmark rate can change greatly over time.

The term of a bank loan, or the repayment period, may vary, for example, between 5 and 15 years depending on different agreements between the shipowner and the bank. Usually, the repayment is made in equal instalments over the loan period. Sometimes the choice of currency may also be an issue. In order to avoid the effects of currency exchange fluctuation, a shipbuilder may prefer the national currency in which most of the costs are paid. Because the US dollar is still the dominating currency used in shipping for both most expenditure and income, a loan made in any other currency than the US dollar may present a risk for a shipowner. To overcome this difficulty, a multi-currency loan can be made.

Security is always an integral part of a ship loan from commercial banks. For any loan project, a credit evaluation must be made of the borrower. Subsequently and based on the risk involved, the bank usually requires security to be provided to minimise the risk, particularly in case the shipowner defaults. This can be an asset or simply a mortgage on the ship. It can also be a guarantee provided by an individual, a company, a financial institution, another bank or a government.

- ***Shipyard credit***. This is sometimes also called *export credit*. A government may provide a credit system through the country's shipbuilding companies. The shipyard credit started in the late 19th century in the UK and it had expanded to nearly all European yards in the 1930s. However, the real development of the modern yard credits system started in the early 1960s in Japan when the Japanese yards introduced an export credit scheme that offered the shipowner credit on 80% of the purchase price over 8 years at 5.5% annual interest on the security of a first mortgage on the ship. The shipbuilders from other countries followed more or less this example. In 1969 the OECD set up a standard level of export credit that all signatories agreed not to exceed ("OECD understanding on export credits for ships 1969"). With the aim of safeguarding the environment of fair competition, eliminating subsidies and streamlining the government-backed shipyard credit systems, the OECD formula has been revised several times and is only applicable to the ships for export.[7] In the three major shipbuilding countries of the Far East, this is done through export credit agencies or government banks: the Export Credit Bank in Japan and Export-Import Banks in Korea and China.
- ***Bond issuance***. This is about borrowing money from the public. Shipping companies or operators, which issue corporate bonds based on their credit or that of their parent companies or principals, can attract investors seeking long-term stable returns. Shipping companies can also issue bonds, which is a debt security with a specific maturity date and fixed interest rate, in the capital market to raise funds for ship investment. This method was not commonly used due to, on the one hand, a lack of knowledge or awareness on the part of potential investors and, on the other hand, the

requirement of a good reputation of the company, which means that only the well-established shipping firms had the option of issuing bonds. Such a situation has started to change recently and an increasing number of shipping companies have opted for bond financing.

One of the most important conditions for bond financing is to obtain an acceptable credit rating from one of the specialised credit rating agencies. The ability to borrow and the rates of interest are related to the credit rating of the borrower. The creditworthiness of a company is measured by credit rating agencies with a system of investment grades going, for example, from triple "A" to "D" in multiple levels. Take one such system as an example. Triple "A" is the highest grade with an extremely strong capacity to repay the debt in full, but, while "BBB" has an adequate capacity to pay interest and repay principal, adverse economic conditions or changing circumstances are more likely to lead to a weakened capacity for the borrower to do so. Grades from "BB" to "C" are generally considered as speculative grades, which means that there are large uncertainties or major exposures to adverse conditions. The grading is made primarily on the past, present and expected future financial viability and performance of the organisation. The criteria for credit rating normally include the following key financial ratios: profitability (gross earnings interest coverage), funds to total debt, cash flow to total debt, debt to gross earnings, return on capital and total debt to total capital. The bonds issued by the companies with a high credit rating, at "A" or triple "B" categories, are considered as low-risk bonds with low interest rates and are called *investment-grade bonds*. The bonds issued by those companies with a low credit rating, for instance, lower than triple "B", are considered to be of high risk and thus come with high interest rates and are called *high yield bonds*.

- ***Private borrowing***. Like private equity financing, investment funds can also be secured through a private placement of debt directly with private funds, insurance companies or financial institutions. Such private placements have the advantage of having fewer procedural requirements and are, therefore, preferred as an efficient, less expensive and quick method of ship finance. Commonly, an investment bank is used to handling such private placement of debt by preparing the documentation and making presentations to the potential investors.

Commercial and investment banks involved in ship finance are traditionally from Europe. This is partly due to tradition and partly related to the highly specialised knowledge and expertise required. However, after the financial crisis of 2008/2009, Asian banks started to be interested in the market and are taking an increasingly larger market share. It is highly possible that Asian banks will become the major sources of ship finance in the future.

What are other forms of ship financing?

Apart from equity and debt financing, the two main forms of ship investment sources, there exist some other variations and modalities of ship funding which are used by the investors and shipping companies as alternative methods or supplementary ways to secure the financing of ships. Most of the variations are designed to overcome the difficulties, or to take advantage of the specific financial environment, or to suit the particular needs of the stakeholders. We will examine some of such major alternative methods as follows.

- ***Syndication***. As the size of investment in ships is normally large, a bank may be unable or unwilling to take on the whole transaction alone. It is therefore common that several banks pool funds together to spread out the financial liability and risks. This kind of syndication of loans is more of a standard practice in shipping financing. Depending on specific circumstances, syndication may turn out to be a complex and time-consuming operation. It is preferable that the number of banks involved is limited and the participating banks share common philosophies and practices, while a strong and experienced bank leads the syndication. In Northern Europe, specialist ship mortgage banks are also important sources of ship funding through syndications.

- ***Mezzanine finance.*** This is a hybrid alternative of debt and equity financing often used for existing firms to finance the new development. This form of financing has been used in shipping activities though it is not a popular option. It is basically designed for high yield debts that also offer the lender the right to convert the debt to an equity interest in the company concerned, in case the loan is not repaid in time and in full. Often, mezzanine finance is used as a supplement to top up the basic debt. As it is shown on the company's books as equity, the arrangement may help the shipping companies obtain normal bank loans.
- ***K/G system.*** This is basically a fiscal regime of limited partnership of business entity which was commonly used in Norway (called K/S) and especially in Germany (called K/G for *Kommanditgesellschaft*). It developed quite fast in Norway in the 1980s and Germany from the 1990s until 2015. The Norwegians were particularly interested in tanker finance while the Germans had been active in investing in container ships. As the companies that arrange the K/G financing are prudent in selecting the ships for funding, the vessels financed normally already had long-term employment (charter parties) with established shipping companies. Under the K/G structure, a shipowner would sell and charter back a ship to a company purposely established to own the ship during the chartering period. Then negotiation would be held with banks to sell the equity to private individuals who use the investment to reduce their income tax liabilities. A specially authorised high depreciation allowance enables investors in the K/G system to reduce tax payments. This provides the investors with a good dividend income in addition to the tax relief. With regard to the shipowner, there are mainly two kinds of benefits: first, it will free up substantial financial resources as KG provides the total financing; second, the KG arrangement usually offers the shipowner who sold the ship at a lower rate, based on the required return on capital for the deal, the opportunity to charter the ship back. Some container shipping lines such as CMA-CGM, in the 1980s, built their vast fleet to a large extent on chartering ships with a K/G arrangement with the German "shipowners". The K/G system has high handling costs and charges. In the wake of the shipping market downturns after the 2009 global financial crisis, which led to numerous cases of default in ship finance, the K/G system was very much affected and was discontinued.
- ***Leasing.*** Until relatively recently, leasing in shipping has not been as widely employed as in many other sectors, such as civil aviation. Leasing, or finance leasing, is generally understood as a system whereby a lessor (owner) puts at the disposal of the lessee (operator) the physical asset (ship) for the employment of the asset during the lease period, which is relatively long. According to the lease contract, the lessee pays a rental to the lessor in exchange for the full operational control of the asset. Also, thanks to a purchasing option, the lessee can eventually take the asset (ship) over at the end of the lease by paying the lessor a price previously agreed upon.

  Many countries have specific regulations on the financial lease of vessels. The period of a lease could be extended as long as the vessel's economic life lasts. It is pre-agreed between the two parties regarding what to do with the vessel at the end of the lease. A lot of similarities exist between a financial leasing of ships and a bareboat chartering. It is common that a standard bareboat charter-party is used as the base of the lease contract. The main reasons for using leasing instead of chartering are in the areas of taxation and purchasing option. In some countries, to encourage investment, taxation regulations provide tax relief or allow accelerated depreciation to the lessor on the investment made in ships. As the lessor acquires the vessel for subsequent rental to the lessee, the lessor can, according to the regulations of some countries, claim full tax relief, if they have a large taxable income. This makes their investment in the asset (ship) cheaper compared with if they were to purchase the vessel and then charter it out. The lessor can then share such benefits with the lessee in the form of reduced rental in order to make the deal more attractive. From the lessee's point of view, leasing can also be cheaper than buying for the same reason of tax relief.

8.3 Investment risks and risk management

For commercial shipping companies, the purpose of investment in ships is to make a profit. As profit is the difference between revenue and cost, such profit-making depends on the future levels of revenue and cost. Therefore, the financial risks in shipping refer to the uncertainties of future revenue and cost. While risk-taking is a general feature for all business in a market economy, the international shipping industry is well known as a sector with special and high financial risks. Although different aspects of financial risk are closely linked and integrated, we leave the income-based risks and risk management to Chapter 12 on freight market analysis. Instead, we focus in this section on the investment-related financial risks. Or, putting it another way, we will discuss the risks for the investors other than shipowners or shipping companies. It concerns mainly debt financing, commercial bank loans in particular, which is still the most important way in which new ships are financed. For example, on 17 February 2017, a Korean court announced the bankruptcy of the 40-year-old Hanjin Shipping company. The bankruptcy led to heavy losses to the bondholders of up to US$1.05 billion with about 80% of the bonds belonging to privately placed debt offering and 20% to public bond sales.[8]

What are the characteristics of ship investment risks?

The investment risk in lending money by financial institutions, public or private, is referred to as credit risk. This means the lenders, whose objective in offering a loan for ship acquisition is to make a profit. But there might be a situation where the shipping companies fail to honour the full repayment of the loan and the interest according to the contract. The borrower, or the shipping company, is expected to generate a sufficient income that not only can cover the expenses of the operation but also repay the loan and interest, as well as creating sufficient collateral value for the loan guarantee. Yet such expected income is often made in a market full of uncertainties. In the case of an adverse situation, the company may become insolvent and the deal becomes a bad loan. Such a risk is therefore called default risk. It is essential that the lenders are not only fully aware of such a risk but also, especially, that they are able to evaluate and control it.

To identify and evaluate the creditworthiness of a borrower is the purpose of credit risk management on the part of the investors, usually through financial institutions. So necessary information and data should be collected, processed and analysed in order to assess the risk. The sources of credit risk are of many kinds that can be divided into the following two categories.

- ***External elements***. They include two aspects, revenue and cost. The first source of uncertainty is the level of freight. The maritime transport market in general and the dry bulk shipping market in particular are said to be highly competitive. The freight is determined by the balance of demand and supply. As the demand has a nature of volatility and the supply is well known for its rigidity in adjusting itself to the changes of demand, as a result the freight level fluctuates. The volatility of the maritime freight market will be discussed in more detail in Chapter 12. It is a common phenomenon that the freight level can change by 50% or even more within a short period of time. So the default risk is mostly attributable to the freight volatility.

  The cost represents another external source of risk. While some costs of operation are more or less predictable, such as capital cost or manning cost, many other costs are subject to significant changes, most of which are out of the shipping company's control. One such cost is fuel cost. The prices of marine fuel are closely related to the world price of crude oil, which is constantly changing. Without mentioning the oil crises in 1973 or 1979, in normal circumstances the bunker price may fluctuate by 20%–30% or more within a year. Other sources of cost-related risks include the price of marine insurance, interest rates, etc.

- ***Internal factors***. While the external elements are by and large unpredictable, the internal factors can often be monitored through a set of indicators. These factors reflect the characteristics of the shipping company in question from financial, strategic, organisational, managerial, technical, etc., aspects. Such internal factors can be used to define the creditworthiness of the shipping company. They range from the vision of the company, its long-term strategies and objectives, the quality of the leadership, the management team, the company's reputation in the market, including its relationship with key customers, to the optional details and everything in-between. The experience and track record of the shipping company, as well as its capability of dealing with adverse market situations and crises, is a very important aspect to look into as well.

  The company's financial health is another key internal aspect that determines the level of credit risk. There are a number of critical financial parameters indicating the strength or weakness of the shipping company. The gearing is the debt to asset ratio which is also referred to as leverage. High gearing means bigger risks given the uncertain nature of the freight market. The second most important financial indicator is probably the profit margin in gross terms achieved by the shipping company measured as EBITDA, or *earnings before interest, taxes, depreciation, and amortisation*, over total revenue. The next key parameter would be the liquidity or the level of cash flow from the earnings, which can be measured as retained cash flow against debt, especially the short-term debt. The probability of default, thus the credit risk, is high with high gearing, low profit margin and low liquidity, and vice versa.

What are the critical factors for investment risk evaluation?

The inherited credit risks in bank-loan-based ship finance as described above may be considered worth taking because of the corresponding rewards one expects to receive from the market. Or, in other words, investing in a project with a high probability of default is only justifiable with a bigger reward for the non-default outcome. Likewise, investment projects with a low probability of default, or less risky investments, can only give a low reward. For example, in a bank loan, rewards can be reflected in loan conditions such as the level of interest rate or length of the repayment period.

There are some specific approaches suggested by researchers as well as credit rating agencies regarding the credit risk evaluation of bank loans to shipping companies.[9, 10, 11] These methods examine the issue of credit risk from different angles, but they also have similarities and common features. The factors used for the evaluation fall within the external or internal environment of ship operation, as we discussed above. The financial performance of the shipping company in question, which is reflected by various ratios and indicators, is certainly the main area to look into. The company's characteristics from both managerial aspects such as strategic decisions and the effectiveness of the operations are another important aspect to examine. The specific business of the company often has a big impact on the level of credit risk. A loan to a shipping company that has secured substantial long-term transport contracts is considered less risky. Depending on the market perspectives at the time, the particular shipping sector the shipping company operates in, e.g., tanker, bulk carrier, container, or the type of ship the company intends to acquire, e.g., VLCC, Cape-size, Handymax, will also represent different levels of credit risk.

To evaluate the creditworthiness of the shipping companies and the loans to be made, many banks use a system similar to that used by the rating agencies, such as Moody's or Standard & Poor, to rate the bonds and industry debts.[12] As discussed earlier in this chapter, such rating agencies have

Table 8.1 Financial credit rating standards of Moody's and Standards & Poor

Rating categories		*Cumulative Historic Default Rates (%)*		*Credit worthiness rating decriptions*	*Decision and recommendation*
Moody's	*S & P*	*Moody's*	*S & P*		
Aaa	AAA	0.52	0.6	Extreme strong capacity to meet financial commitments	Investment Grade
Aa	AA	0.52	1.5	Very strong capacity to meet financial commitments	
A	A	1.29	2.91	Strong capacity to meet financial commitments	
Baa	BBB	4.64	10.29	Adequate capacity to meet financial commitments	
Ba	BB	19.12	29.93	Vulnerable with risk of default in adverse conditions	Non-Investment Grade
B	B	43.34	53.72	Highly speculative and high default risk in adverse conditions	
Caa - C	CCC - C	69.18	69.19	Highly vulnerable and substantial risk of non-payment	

Source: Moody's Investers Services https://www.moodys.com/researchandratings/market-segment/home; Katz L.F. (2008) "Rating Agency and Their Methodologies" http://www.standardandpoors.com

Note: Shipping companies are routinely rated by the Credit Agencies. Adverse market conditions affect the overall rating. In December 2016, for example, Moody's rated Maersk, the container shipping giant, at "Baa".

developed comprehensive and sophisticated systems by including both internal and external risk factors to evaluate the creditworthiness of the shipping companies. Take one of the leading container shipping companies, Maersk, for example. In December 2016 one of the leading credit rating agencies, Moody's, gave the shipping company a new rating at "Baa2", which is at the lower end of the so-called "investment grade" as shown in Table 8.1. It was reported that Moody's commented that the grade

> reflects our expectation of reduced diversification following the results of the strategic review, as well as the deterioration in Maersk's credit profile amid weak market conditions, particularly in container shipping and drilling, which we do not anticipate to be reversed shortly.[13]

So from such a statement we can see that both the internal decision of the shipping company to separate its business units as well as the changes in the external market environment played a role in the level of credit rating. Table 8.1 summarises the systems used by two rating agencies. The categories range from a high triple "A" to a low "C", which indicate the probabilities of default. The higher the rating, the lower the credit risk and thus the better the loan conditions that can be expected.

8.4 The financial performance of ship investment

The financial performance of ship investment is usually measured in "return on investment" (ROI). Shipping is well known for its modest average financial return over the long term. Although the average long term ROI is low, the standard deviation is high, which means that the level of return moves up and down violently, particularly in the spot market for ship chartering. Yet, despite the relatively low average profit margin over time, the shipping sector still remains attractive to many investors. In this section we will discuss some of the specific characteristics regarding the financial performance of shipping investment.

What is the average return on investment in shipping?

As discussed earlier, the two determining factors for the profitability of a shipping company, i.e., cost and revenue, are unstable or even volatile over time. This is particularly true for tramp shipping. As a result, the ROI fluctuates enormously from one period to the next. It is, however, generally believed that over a long period the average ROI of the shipping industry is not high.

The long-term profitability for any enterprise operating in a competitive market is called *normal profit*. This is defined as the minimum profit that is necessary to ensure that the enterprise keeps providing productive operations. The level of normal profit depends not only on the competitive nature of the market but also on the level of financial risks associated with the sector concerned. The higher such risks are, the larger the normal profit needs to be. Under the notion of normal profit, the *opportunity cost* is the cost of not undertaking an activity. Normal profit exists when resources available to the enterprise are used most efficiently. This means that, in a competitive market, resources are best utilised and enterprises are earning normal profit. In other words, on the one hand, opportunity cost makes sure that resources are attracted to the sectors where higher-than-normal-profit is available and, on the other hand, market competition makes sure that no higher-than-normal-profit exists in the long term.

The low ROI of the shipping industry has been the subject of research and reports. For example, it is revealed that over a period of more than 25 years, the average rate of return on various investments was 7.2% for dry bulk shipping and 4.9% for tanker shipping. However, during the same period of time, the average return on investment was 14.1% for S&P 500, 9.6% for corporate bonds and government bonds and 8.5% for the London interbank offered rate, which is considered to be one of the least risky loans.[14] To conclude, we can say that, in the long term, shipping underperforms most other sectors in terms of return on investment.

Why does lower-than-average profitability in shipping still attract investors?

Opportunity cost means that the best investment choice is the one which would cost the most if not taken. So such an investment should be the best choice and therefore the opportunity cost is the cost of the second-best choice. The question is why international shipping, particularly tramp shipping, is still chosen by so many investors. What are the attractions of the shipping industry when a long-term average return on investment has been 25% lower than that of government bonds, which guarantee not only a higher yield but also much lower risk? The answers to these questions are related to the nature of volatility of the freight market and thus the revenue.

Let us make a comparison between the US government bonds and the dry bulk shipping industry. Between 1928 and 2016 the annual ROI of the US 10-year government bonds registered a modest variation with a standard deviation of lower than 0.1,[15] the ROI for S&P 500 had a standard deviation at 0.15 between 1975 and 2004, but, during the same period, the ROI for dry bulk and tanker shipping combined had a standard deviation at 0.55.[16] So the ROI is much more volatile in the shipping industry than in the S&P 500 and the long-term bond market. Such volatility means that there are times when the shipping industry generates a much higher ROI than the bond market does and there are also times when the ROI is much lower in the shipping sector than in the bond market. So this feature brings an opportunity for those investors who are interested in making a profit by investing and divesting in the tramp shipping market at the right times.

It may not be considered appropriate to use the example of a lottery in the explanation of the unusual attractiveness of investment in tramp shipping, because the former is basically a matter of value redistribution while the latter is nonetheless a business of value creation. But both share, in the end, a common speculative nature, even if the average yield is low or even negative. People are attracted to shipping investment not by the average yield, but by the possibility of super high returns. Take, for example, the dry bulk freight index, BDI, which started at 1,000 in 1985, moved between 600 and 2,000 points until 2002 and then it went up to as high as more than 10,000 points in 2007/2008. The extremely high freight level from late 2002 to mid-2008 allowed shipowners to make a huge profit. Such a possibility of an extraordinary award, which is believed to happen periodically in maritime transport, represents an irresistible attraction to many risk-prone minds and has become an integral part of the nature of the shipping sector.

Why can ship asset operation be the main activity in shipping?

Closely related to the freight market fluctuation and the consequent financial attraction of investment in shipping, the trading of ship assets has also become a business in its own right. As discussed earlier in this chapter and as shown in Figure 8.1, the prices of new ships as well as used ships are volatile, due to the freight market changes and the price-inelastic supply of new ships. So, if the prices can change up and down by as much as 200% or even 300% over a relatively short period of time, this gives a very strong incentive to investors to specialise in ship trading. It happens frequently that the market value of a new ship moves up or down by 30% to 50% or more within a year. Figure 8.2 shows the price movement of a 5-year-old Panamax bulk carrier. Even if the extraordinarily high ship price between 2005 and 2008 is not considered, the price changed with a very large margin within a short period of time. As building a new ship normally takes about two years, in a rising market an investor may already make a handsome profit by selling the contract of the ship before the completion of construction.

Given that the profit to be made from ship "asset trading" is based on market fluctuation, the timing of the investment is a decisive factor. Therefore, people buy ships when the price is low and sell them when the price is high. Such an approach is referred to as a strategy of anticyclical investment. The booming new building market in the wake of the maritime freight market collapse in 2008/2009 can be considered a round of investment of such a speculative nature. This strategy is only valid if the market develops in a cyclical pattern. Such an assumption is of course far from being certain. In the very long run, the shipping freight market, and the prices of new and second-hand ships, do move up and down periodically. Yet the interval between cycles varies enormously.

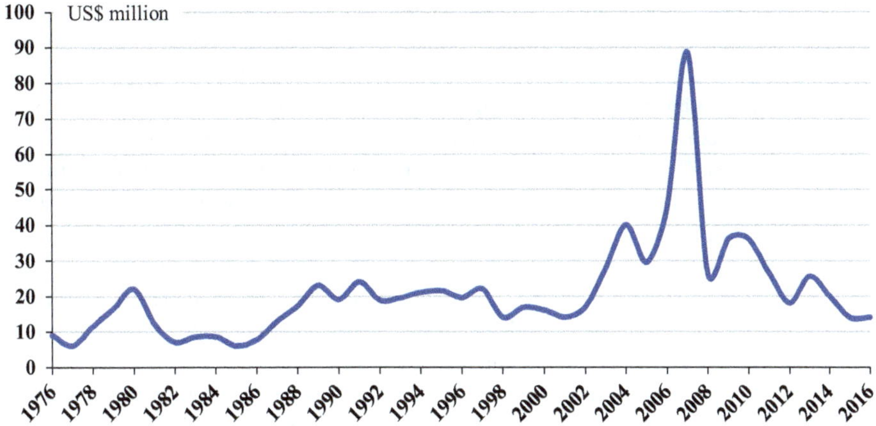

Figure 8.2 Prices of 5-year-old Panamax bulk carriers, annual average 1976–2016 (in million US$).

Source: Shuo Ma, based on data from Clarkson.

Note: the price of the second-hand bulk carriers is totally dictated by the market demand and supply. The price is thus highly volatile. The standard deviation of price movement during this period was 14.2.

As there is no way for people to know whether and when the market rises or falls, ship "asset trading" is a high-risk business. So any investor wishing to become a ship asset trader should be prepared to take financial risks. Being high-value assets, ships are expensive to maintain. If ships are not bought for operation, selling them quickly might be essential because an investor can easily be losing money in a descending market. It may be true that only at the rock bottom of the shipbuilding market, when the price may be even lower than the scraping price, is when it could be the moment for a "safe" buy.

8.5 Investment in second-hand ships

International shipping is blessed with a large, well-developed and active second-hand ship market. Every year, thousands of used ships are sold and bought on the sale and purchase market, representing tens of billions of dollars. It is even uncommon that a ship is with one single owner for its whole economic life and it is not rare that a vessel's ownership changes multiple times, even within a short period of time. The finance and commercial risks for second-hand ships are similar to those of new buildings, but with some special characteristics. There is no shipyard credit available for used ships, so the buyer has normally to rely on their own capital reserves or to seek loans from commercial banks.

What are the main reasons for selling and buying used ships?

People sell and buy used ships for various reasons. The motivations for shipowners operating in the sale and purchase market are not merely economic, they are more complex than that. From a seller's perspective, shipowners do not necessarily change their ships just for the sake of finding a newer model. They usually find old ships unfit when the trade has changed, the market has shifted, or fuel or maintenance costs have been too high. Another situation frequently seen is selling ships in emergency situations such as a cash flow crisis. At the time of market downturn, for example, during the period of economic turmoil, shipping companies may encounter difficulties with regard to cash flow. Selling ship assets in such cases is often the only option for them to keep the business going. This is therefore also called "distress sales", which often means that ships will be sold at a price below their market value. Of course, there is also the case of ship asset speculative trading, when the primary purpose for investors to buy and sell ships is to make a profit.

From a buyer's point of view, to acquire a new ship the shipping company has to be financially strong and be willing to bear the burden of high capital cost for an extended period. Alternatively, the shipowner may wish to turn to the second-hand ship market, where usually less investment capital is needed. A shipping company interested in purchasing a second-hand ship may have other motivations. The most important motivation is probably direct and quick access to tonnage to meet the current transport requirement. So, instead of waiting for one or two years' lead-time for a new-build, a second-hand vessel can be used almost immediately. This last feature is of particular importance for tramp shipping given the volatility of the freight market. There are obvious disadvantages in filling the gap with used ships. For example, ships cannot be tailor-made, the operating cost may be high and there might be hidden defects in the ship.

How is the price of second-hand ships determined?

The straight-line depreciation method means that at a given economic life of the ship, say 25 years, a constant discount rate will apply. If the value of a new ship on the one hand and the value of the scrap ship on the other are taken, we will then have a straight-line second-hand ship valuation with a constant value discount rate over time. Obviously, such a simplistic valuation does not exist in the real ship sale and purchase market and there is indeed a lot of room for ship "asset trading" excitement.

The value of second-hand vessels is determined by market forces or the balance of demand and supply of the vessels in the market concerned. So, on the demand side, the influential factors include trade policies, trade volume, production patterns, etc., and, on the supply side, factors such as the new building price, the scrap price, the freight level, the operation costs, etc., are to be considered. However, for an investor who is interested in buying a second-hand ship, they should pay attention to two fundamental aspects which are the expected net earnings and the re-sale value of the ship.

- ***The expected net earnings*** are the future income after deducting the costs. We can take freight earnings as the income for the period in which the ship is in possession of the investor. To make net earnings, all relevant costs should be deducted from the freight income. Such costs include, first of all, the capital investment itself. The price of used ships diminishes as the vessels age. Other operating and voyage costs such as cost of manning, insurance, repair, fuel, port services, etc., are also included. These costs may vary and thus affect the level of net earnings to be made. For example, if a major repair at the dry dock is expected soon, the cost should then be taken into account in the valuation of the second-hand ship.

  Because a used ship is immediately available, the ship's value is directly affected by the current freight market. But, in the same way as for new ships, the future market situation and the expected earnings are to be considered as well. However, future earnings are uncertain. It is, therefore, the actual freight level and immediate earnings that play the most decisive role in the valuation of second-hand ships. As we have discussed previously, since the freight rate is so volatile, the second-hand ship prices fluctuate also with significant margins. What is interesting to note is that when the freight rates are very high, the price of second-hand ships can be higher than that of the new ships. This happened during the boom years between 2003 and 2008, especially in the dry bulk sector. The freight rate was so high that, in order to acquire ships as quickly as possible, shipowners were prepared to pay higher prices for a second-hand ship than a new ship which can only be available some two to three years later. If a ship has an economic life of 25 years, using the straight-line depreciation method, the value of a 5-year-old and 10-year-old ship should be, respectively, up to 20% and 40% lower than that of a new ship, taking a positive scrap value into account. But during 2003 and 2008, as shown in Figure 8.3, the annual average prices of new 175,000 dwt Panamax bulk carriers are lower than the prices of 5-year-old and 10-year-old ships. The price of a 5-year-old Panamax ship was higher than that of a new ship for most of the time between 2003 and 2011. By the end of 2007, a 5-year-old Panamax ship was 62% more expensive than a new ship and even a 10-year-old ship was more expensive than a new bulk carrier of the same type.

- ***The expected ship's scrap price.*** A second-hand vessel can be re-sold or employed by a shipowner until the end of its economic life. In the latter case, the residual or scrap value of ships should be considered in the evaluation of a second-hand vessel. The ship scrap value is also based on demand and supply. While the supply of ships to demolish is easy to see, the driving force behind the demand for ships is not as clear. The final customer of scrapped ships is the steel industry. So there are two major contributing factors for the scrap value of a ship, the freight level on the supply side and the steel market on the demand side. At the time of a second-hand vessel acquisition, it is difficult to estimate its residual value, given the volatility of both the freight and steel markets.

  The freight rate and volume of ships for demolition follow a negative correlation. This means that the higher the freight rate is, the fewer ships are for demolition and, subsequently, the higher the scrap

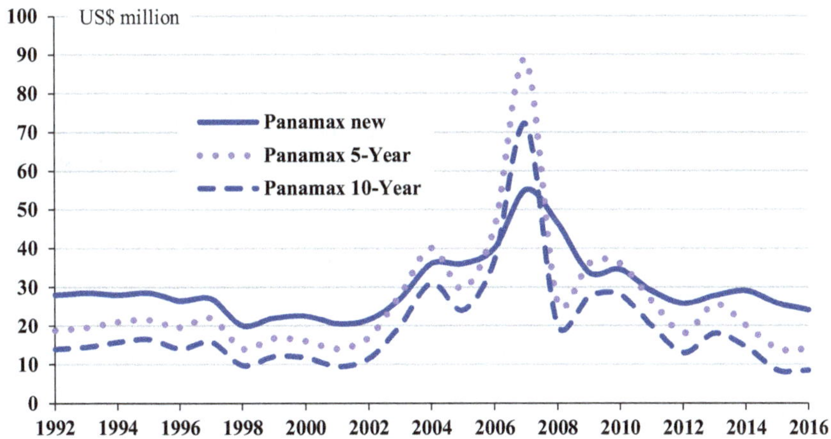

Figure 8.3 Prices of new, 5-year-old and 10-year-old Panamax bulk carriers (in million US$).

Source: Shuo Ma, based on data from Clarkson and ISL.

Note: the freight from 2003 to 2008 was very high. So the price of second-hand ships was expensive. Outside this high freight period, i.e., before 2002 and after 2008, the prices were in normal shape.

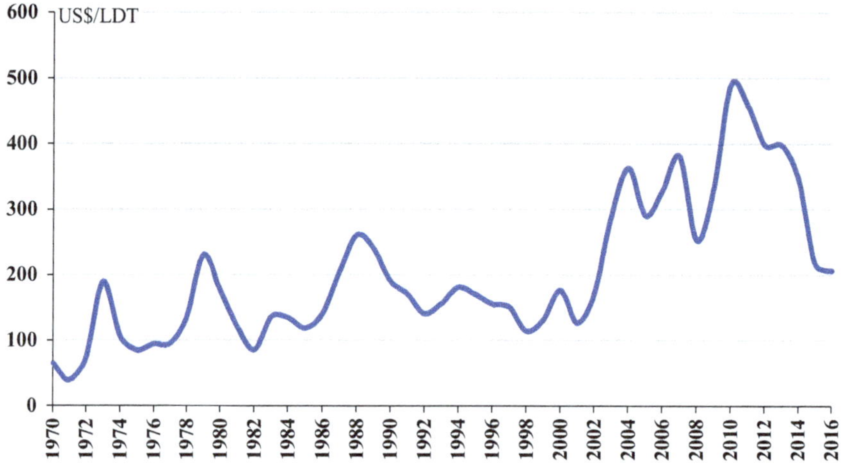

Figure 8.4 Prices of ships for demolition (average VLCC 1970–2016 (US$ per ldt)).

Source: Shuo Ma, based on data from Clarksons.

Note: the price of ship scrapping is directly affected by the freight market. At the height of the market, fewer ships are for demolition and the price is high.

price will be. It is also true in the opposite situation. From 2003, for example, the freight was high, so the ship-scrapping volume was very low. As the demolition yards were competing for ships to scrap, the scrap price was much higher than the usual US$100 to $200 per LDT (light displacement ton) range. The price was further pushed up from the demand side as the price of steel soared. As a result, the scrap price reached the highest ever level of US$500 per LDT[17] in 2010. On the other hand, when the freight market is down and the steel price is low, the value of ship scrap will be very low, and this is what happened in 2017 when the scrap price was less than US$200 per LDT.[18] Figure 8.4 shows the price evolution of scrap ships from 1970 to 2016. We can see that over time the prices changed a lot with a standard deviation at 14.2. When the freight market was high, such as the case after 2002, fewer ships were demolished and the price went up. But when the freight was as low as in the 1980s and since 2015, more ships were taken out of service and many were demolished, which drove the scrap price down.

Since the 1990s, ship scraping activities are primarily concentrated in Asia, particularly South Asia, like India, Bangladesh and Pakistan. It is a labour-intensive sector. In recent years, environmental concerns have developed rapidly regarding ship demolition activities. Various solutions are being discussed and debated by the world maritime community to control the related pollution of coastal zones where shipbreaking takes place and to cover the costs of ship recycling. The IMO has investigated the environmental impact of ship demolition activities for many years. In May 2009 the IMO adopted the Hong Kong Convention (The Hong Kong International Convention for the Safe and Environmentally Sound Recycling of Ships) to regulate the safety and environmental aspects of ship demolition activities.

8.6 Summary

In this chapter we have examined the issues related to shipping finance. If a sector's capital intensity is measured as the amount of capital required per employee created, international shipping is a *capital intensive* sector. The tendency is that the capital intensity increases further due to the continuous growth of average ship size and sophistication, on the one hand, and the reduction of crew size thanks to a higher level of automation on the other hand. Eventually, for a totally autonomous "crewless" ship, the capital intensity would be pushed even higher. Ocean-going ships are not only expensive but the prices also fluctuate. One of the most striking characteristics of international shipping is the volatility of ship prices. This is mainly because of two reasons, the first of which is the competitive nature of the market and the fluctuating demand, and the second is the lack of price elasticity for both demand and supply.

Capital investment for ships comes mainly from two types of sources: funds owned by the investors themselves, referred to as equity financing, and loans borrowed from others, referred to as debt financing. Each of the two types of funding sources has some variations. Debt financing, particularly commercial bank loans, has been the primary source of ship finance. Most shipowners are not in a position to finance ships with their own means, but at the same time they wish to maintain full control of the company and the ships. In this case, getting a loan is the most obvious option. Apart from commercial banks, loans can also be obtained from the government, yard credit, financial institutions and individuals.

Investment in commercial ships carries financial risks. These are mainly due to the uncertainties of the future revenue and the cost of ship operation caused by the changing nature of many internal as well as external factors. It is therefore very important that, before committing to a loan, the lender undertakes a careful assessment of potential risks against default risks. The assessment should be undertaken on the external elements such as the changes in revenue and cost. It should also be done on the internal elements, which include the quality of the organisation and management of the borrower, the corporate strategies and the capabilities of dealing with adverse situations. Such internal characteristics determine the creditworthiness of the shipping company.

In the long term, international shipping's financial performance in terms of return on investment is lower than in many other sectors. The ROI of shipping is even lower than that of low-risk investment in government bonds. The reason that such below-industry-average profitability has not discouraged the interest of many investors is mainly related to the very nature of volatility in the ROI. Many investors are attracted by the high market volatility and are aiming at the extremely high profitability period which happens periodically in shipping. The changing freight market also leads to changes in the price of ships, either new or second-hand. So buying and selling ships, which is referred to as ship "asset trading", can sometimes generate more and faster profit than ship operations. Ship asset trading has become the main business for many investors.

A well established and functioning second-hand vessel sale and purchase market is one of the specific characteristics of international shipping. It is rare that a ship is owned by one single shipowner for life. Given the long lead time of building a new ship, buying a second-hand ship is of particular interest during the time of high freight. Yet the short supply of second-hand ships when the market is at its peak can make the second-hand ship cost more than a new ship of the same type.

Notes

1 Porter J. (2017).
2 Clarkson and Marine Money (2016). At the beginning of 2015, the total amount of global ship assets, include those in the order book, was US$1.2 trillion. But at the beginning of 2016, the amount had shrunk to less than US$1 trillion.
3 OECD (2002).
4 Stopford M. (2009), *Maritime Economics*, 3rd edition, Routledge, London, p. 271. "According to records for ships registered in the City of London in 1848, out of 554 vessels, 89% were owned by individuals, 8% by trading partnerships. … Only 18% of the vessels were mortgaged."
5 Lloyd's List, "Costamare to raise up to $72 m via public share offering", 30 November (2016).

6 Tufton Oceanic Ltd (2016). By the beginning of 2016, the total value of the world's existing fleet and ordered ships was about US$1 trillion. Out of this sum, 24% was from equity financing and most of the remaining 76% fell into the category of debt financing of different forms.
7 OECD (2008). According to the OECD, official export credits may provide up to 80% of the new building's contract value with a repayment period of up to 12 years in equal instalments. With regard to interest rate, Commercial Interest Reference Rates were also introduced in the Sector Understanding on Export Credits for Ships (2002).
8 Lloyds List (2017).
9 Grammenos C.T. (2010). Grammenos suggests a framework of bank credit risk analysis based on the six "Cs" of credit, namely Character, Capacity, Capital, Company, Conditions and Collateral.
10 Kavussanos M. (2016). Kavussanos says, based on an empirical study, that Capital, Company and Capacity factors are more important than Character, Conditions and Collateral factors when assessing default risk in corporate bank loans.
11 Mitoussi et al. (2016). The authors found that loan amount, loan tenor, balloon-loan ratio, the level of fleet finance, leverage and employability and the shipowner's experience are good estimates for evaluating the performance of shipping loans.
12 See above, Note 8, p. 794.
13 Hadhi A. (2017).
14 Stopford M. (2009).
15 Federal Reserve of St. Louis (FRED), US treasury 10-year bond at the end of each year.
16 Ibid. 14.
17 Clarkson's Shipping Intelligence Network.
18 Lloyd's List (2017).

References

Clarkson and Marine Money. (2016) at "*Marine Money Ship Finance Forum*", London, 27 January.

Grammenos C.T. (2010) "*Revisiting Credit Risk, Analysis and Policy in Bank Shipping Finance*", in "The Handbook of Maritime Economics and Business", 2nd Edition, edited by C.T. Grammenos, Lloyd's List Publication, London, pp. 777–810.

Hadhi A. (2017) "*Moody's Downgrades Maersk on Weaker Credit Profile*", Lloyd's List, Containers, 21 December 2016.

Kavussanos M. (2016) "*Default Risk Drivers in Shipping Bank Loans*", Transportation Research Part E, Vol. 94, pp. 71–94.

Lloyd's List. (2016) "*Costamare to Raise up to $72 m via Public Share Offering*", 30 November 2016.

Lloyd's List. (2017) "*Scrap Rates Continue to Fall amid Increased Demolition Sales*", Lloyd's List Asia, 10 February 2017.

Lloyds List. (2017) "*Hanjin Shipping: Rest in Peace*", 21 February 2017, World Maritime News, "Hanjin's Bondholders to Suffer Big Losses", 20 February 2017.

Mitoussi K., et al. (2016) "*Performance Drivers of Shipping Loans: An Empirical Investigation*", International Journal of Production Economics, Vol. 171(2016), pp. 438–52.

OECD. (2002) "*Arrangement on Officially Supported Export Credits*", Annex on "The Sector Understanding on Export Credits for Ships (SSU).

OECD. (2008) "*Sector Understanding on Export Credits for Ships (SSU)*" OECD Council Working Party on Shipbuilding (WP^) 2008).

Porter J. (2017) "*Maersk Lines up World's Biggest Ever Ship Order*", Containers, Lloyd's List, 21 February 2011.

Stopford M. (2009) "*Maritime Economics*", 3rd Edition, Routledge, London, pp. 271, 320–324.

Tufton Oceanic Ltd. (2016) at "*Marine Money Ship Finance Forum*", London, 27 January 2016 Clarkson's Shipping Intelligence Network.

Part III

The market

Chapter 9

Maritime operational, regulatory and technological systems

The international maritime transport is an integral part of international trade, as we discussed in the chapters of Part 1. Over many years, the industry has evolved into a complex international maritime transport system consisting of numerous categories of activities or subsystems that are interconnected and interdependent. The relationship between the subsystems is different from one case to another. If ship operation is considered as the core of the maritime transport industry, there are several other groups of activities or systems which provide conditions for the core ship operation activity to be carried out properly. Some such systems are more closely linked to ship operation, others are more general, providing broader supportive activities. In this chapter we will discuss the major systems and the activities which constitute the business conditions and environment in which the international maritime transport of cargo operates. Our focus will be on the three most important ones: the operational, regulatory and technological systems of maritime transport. We will first discuss the specific characteristics of each system: the key factors, the standards and the requirements to follow, etc. Then we will analyse the relationship between each of the main subsystems and ship operation.

9.1 The ship operation system

International maritime transport is about moving cargo from one country to another by ship. So ship operation undertaken by shipping companies is at the core of the shipping business. Historically, a substantial portion of ship management was or had to be entrusted to the shipmaster, due to the absence of communication between the ship and shore once the ship sailed off on the oceans. Nowadays, ship management has become largely a shore-based activity undertaken by professionals in shipping companies, thanks primarily to information and communication technology advancement and, in particular, to satellite communication. With the ship operation as the core, all other activities of the subsystems are subordinate and supporting systems provide necessary conditions or services to the core in order to complete the transport. Let's begin with the core function, ship operation.

What are the main functions included?

The organisational structure may vary from one shipping company to another. It differs also according to the type of shipping market in which the company operates. Generally speaking, in a typical shipping company, there are several shipping-specific functions, but the two most essential are the following two categories: the commercial and technical management of ships. The exact activities and the extent of responsibilities change very much between tramp and liner shipping. It varies also between a small single-ship company and a big multiple-ship corporation.

The activities related to commercial management normally include all those concerning the sales in the market, finance, revenue and customers, etc. Some of such activities involve important financial management tasks, for example on ship acquisition or sale and purchase. Some activities are more routine and operational, for example the chartering of vessels. The commercial functions of a shipping company also include tasks in relation to ship operations such as voyage cost estimates, freight calculation and collection, giving instructions to the shipmaster, the appointment of port agents, etc.

Technical management of ships includes a wide range of activities. First of all, one of the most essential responsibilities of technical ship management is to make sure the ship is in good technical condition or is seaworthy, which means that the ship is safe to sail in difficult navigational conditions. The tasks involved include regular inspections undertaken on board ship to make sure the vessel is fully maintained to comply with all relevant national and international rules and regulations. On board ships, the technical management tasks include navigation and machinery aspects for the objectives of safety, reliability, compliance and efficiency. The technical management of ships is affected by many factors, such as the type and age of the vessel, the size and composition of the crew, the type of cargo to carry and the voyage to undertake, etc.

One of the main aspects of the technical management of ships is crew management. This includes activities related to the recruitment, training and service schedule, etc. Regarding crew recruitment, nationality, qualifications and experience are important aspects to consider. Very often, special expertise and qualifications are required for people working on a particular type of ships, such as an oil tanker, a chemical carrier or an LNG ship. So there may be a need to organise training programmes for the crew to acquire specific knowledge or skills. Another complex area of work is the planning, scheduling and repatriating of crew, which may involve international travel. There are two major international conventions that are relevant to crew management: one is the STCW Convention of the IMO and the other is the Maritime Labour Convention of the ILO. The STCW Convention is about professional qualification requirements for the training, certification and watch-keeping of seafarers and the MLC covers the working and living standards and conditions for seafarers working on board ships.

What are the specific economic characteristics of ship operation systems?

The development of ship operation, particularly the technical management of ships, has followed two directions: concentration and standardisation. By concentration we mean that, thanks to the advancement of information and communication technology, there has been a shift of the work from ships carried out in a decentralised way to shore carried out by shore-based professionals. Increasingly the tasks for the ship's crew to undertake are purely related to navigation, leaving the main maintenance of the ship and the management of crew to the shore-based staff. The second development, which is linked to the first, is the standardisation of ship operation procedures and standards. The main reason for this is the introduction of quality assurance concepts and methods into ship management and operation.

The ship-operation-related quality assurance system is more than the application of general quality assurance schemes such as the ISO-9000 series. The International Maritime Organisation (IMO), in 1994, adopted a specific piece of regulation called the International Safety Management Code, or ISM Code, and incorporated it into the Safety of Life at Sea or SOLAS Convention. The creation of the ISM Code was directly triggered by the human-error-related accident of the ro-ro ship *Herald of Free Enterprise* in 1987. The Code provides the maritime industry with an international standard for the safe and environmentally responsible management and operation of ships. Now virtually all commercial vessels involved in international trade are required to apply the ISM Code. To comply with the Code, shipping companies must have a functioning safety management system, with specific responsibilities, procedures and tasks ensured at both company and ship levels. A study which was undertaken ten years after the adoption of the ISM Code showed that if the Code is treated as an effective method in line with the company's objective of efficiency through a safety culture, tangible positive benefits were evident.[1]

As a consequence of a more concentrated and standardised ship management and operation, there has been an increasing number of shipping companies that have opted for a policy to outsource this task to specialised ship management companies. The third-party ship management business has a relatively short history. It appeared in the general extension and movement of shipping activities from Europe to Asia. The globalisation of the shipping industry in the 1970s after the first oil crisis meant that competition on cost intensified, which led to more use of the open registry, substitution of traditional seafarers for cheaper, multinational crew and a more adjusted level of maintenance. For example, in the 1970s many European shipping firms set up Asian branches in places like Hong Kong and Singapore to take advantage of abundant and inexpensive seafarers from Asia. Later on, the business expanded from crew management to more comprehensive ship management services and from manning agents of parent companies in Europe to independent third-party ship management companies. However, to be closer to European shipowners, cities like London and Limassol in Cyprus have attracted many ship management companies. The specialised third-party ship management companies combine specialised management skills with economies of scale. The high value of this new service was recognised and appreciated by the shipping companies who were interested in a quality ship management service at a competitive cost. In 1991 the International Ship Managers Association (ISMA) was created, with an ISMA Code of Ship Management Standards established. The ISMA Code has comprehensive coverage of both technical and commercial aspects of ship management and operation. As of 2018, some 5,000 ships and almost 250,000 seafarers are managed by the members of the Association, which is now called "InterManager".[2]

What are the development trends and challenges of the subsystem?

Ship management and operation is the centre of maritime transport. It is, therefore, the shipping industry's core business. When a customer is looking for a maritime transport service, such service is recognised by the quality of ship management and operation. It is also a critical aspect of business for the investor who is interested in a good return on the investment, because whether the company makes money or not depends to a large extent on the quality of ship management and operation.

In the future, it is highly likely that standardisation will continue in the area of ship management and operation. It will mainly be the case in technical management, but also in some aspects of the commercial management of ships. Such development has led and will continue to lead to the following trends.

- The first is the *loss of company identity*, which means that the company- and country-based differentiation disappears and, instead, companies and their services become more standardised, homogeneous and globalised. The sources of production input are consequently also homogeneous and globalised. For example, the same type and source of international seafarers are employed, irrespective of the country or company to which the ship or shipping company belongs.
- The second trend is *automation and artificial intelligence*. This is probably the biggest eventuality that will probably happen sooner than most people think and which will reshape ship management and operation profoundly. Although the process might be gradual and the impact could well be partial, the technological development will certainly make ship management and operation of the future very different from what we have known until now. On some recently built ships, the average crew size has decreased from typically about 30 to less than 20. When activities and operation models are standardised, it will be possible and easier to automate the processes. Even though totally crewless ships may not be a reality soon, the replacement of humans by automation in ship operation will continue. This subject will be discussed in more detail in Chapter 16.

In the future, all decisions of ship management and operation may be divided grossly into three parts: the first is about the decisions without fixed patterns. These include business strategy, direction, management of people, investment, etc. Shipowners or senior executives are more likely to be the ones to make such decisions. The second part is about those decisions with known patterns and requiring predictable physical activities and outcomes, for example collecting data on board ship, processing them and taking predictable actions accordingly. The third part is about the decisions mixed between the two. While the automation potential is low for the first part of decisions on ship management and operation, the automation potential is high for the second part. The situation for the third part of the decisions is midway in the short and medium terms, but, in the long run, depending on the development of artificial intelligence technology, it is highly likely that a good part of the decisions will also be automated.

9.2 The legal and regulatory system

International shipping is, without doubt, one of the most internationalised economic activities. This is mainly because ships are largely operating on the open sea which is international territory. Although the history of the "freedom of the seas principle" may go back to the 16th and 17th centuries, today the freedom of navigation is specified in the United Nations Convention on Law of the Sea of 1982.[3] According to the Convention, all vessels enjoy the freedom of navigation in the contiguous zone, the exclusive economic zone, the continental shelf and the high seas. In other waters, ships have rights of access, innocent passage and transit passage. The freedom of the seas does by no means imply an absence of regulation. However, the shipping rules and regulations are international rather than national. Although the first pieces of shipping-related rule and law can be traced to as early as the 15th century,[4] the real development and expansion of maritime regulation is something remarkably recent.

What are the goals and coverage of the maritime legal and regulatory framework?

In areas of ship safety and marine environment protection, cargo transport on domestic waters, for example coastal shipping or inland waterways shipping, is regulated by national legislation. It is expected that international shipping is subject to the same standards. This may be difficult to do because national standards can be quite different from one country to another. A unique system of rules and regulations needed to be established for ships from all countries to observe. To do this, international organisations in the maritime transport sector at both professional and governmental levels have been created. The most important one among them is the International Maritime Organisation, the IMO.

Broadly, maritime-related regulations can be divided into three categories covering technical, economic and social aspects of international shipping. The technical regulations primarily concern the problems of ship-related safety and pollution matters. As a transport activity on the high seas, international shipping presents a high level of safety risk to the people and property concerned. Recently, technical regulations have been more focussed on matters in connection with the protection of the marine environment. The economic regulations are to regulate maritime transport according to some specific economic principles such as fair competition (anti-trust) or free market access. The social regulations are the international legal framework for the working and living conditions of seafarers. There are two groups of institutions that make rules and regulations, the professional bodies and government or inter-government institutions. We can also examine the regulations at either national or international levels.

What does the technical regulatory framework look like?

By technical regulation, we refer mostly to safety-related standards, rules and regulations. Two levels of regulations should be distinguished based on the nature of regulators. The first is official regulations exercised by governmental or inter-governmental authorities and the other is professional regulation carried out by the shipping industry itself. We will discuss them as follows.

- ***Technical regulations at the official level.*** There are a number of international organisations involved in formulating regulations regarding the technical aspects of maritime transport. The most important of all is evidently the IMO (International Maritime Organisation). Other organisations, which cover a broader scope of sectors including maritime transport, are the ISO (International Organization for Standardization) for equipment (e.g., containers) and quality standards and the ITU (International Telecommunication Union) for telecommunication, etc.

  The IMO was established in 1948.[5] With 172 Member States, the IMO is a specialised agency of the United Nations with purposes of

  > providing machinery for cooperation among Governments in the field of governmental regulation and practices relating to technical matters of all kinds affecting shipping engaged in international trade; to encourage and facilitate the general adoption of the highest practicable standards in matters concerning maritime safety, efficiency of navigation and prevention and control of marine pollution from ships.

  Such a technical role of the IMO is reflected in the conventions adopted in the field of maritime safety and marine environment protection. Among some 26 IMO Conventions, the most important are SOLAS (International Convention for the Safety of Life at Sea 1974), MARPOL (International Convention for the Prevention of Pollution from Ships 1973, 1978 and 1997) and STCW (International Convention on Standards of Training, Certification and Watchkeeping for Seafarers, 1995 and 2010). The IMO conventions can generally be divided into three groups, concerning respectively maritime safety and security, the prevention of marine pollution, and liability and compensation. A number of other conventions falling outside these three categories deal mainly with trade facilitation, tonnage measurement, unlawful acts, etc.[6]

  To comply with the IMO safety and environmental regulations, ships and ship operation should meet the required standards. The compliance incurs a cost, but it is wise to see such expenses as an investment because, in the long term, the proper utilisation of resources, financial or human, pays back. In other words, to ensure the required safety and environmental standards is economically viable. The IMO has adopted since 2002 a methodology, known as formal safety assessment (FSA), in the rule-making and rule-amendment processes. The FSA is a new approach, based on risk analysis and cost–benefit evaluation, to make sure that the regulations are not only technically sound but also economically justifiable.

- ***Technical regulations at the professional level.*** Technical regulations are established at the professional level by the industry for the wellbeing of the sector as a whole. The best example in this respect is the classification of ships. Every ocean-going ship is technically verified and certified by a classification society at every stage from the construction to the entire operation. Classification societies were originally started with the insurance practices in the later part of the 18th century as the insurers needed to know the technical conditions of the ship for coverage. Since then, to have a ship insured, one has to keep ships in class with a classification society based on its rules. As classification societies are usually not governmental organisations, most leading maritime countries have their own society, but they all serve the common market. So the harmonisation, coordination and standardisation of the rules of different classification societies were necessary. In 1968 the International Association of Classification Societies, IACS, was established and today, with 12 member societies, it represents more than 90% of the world's commercial fleet. Over the years, IACS has developed a variety of common technical rules and requirements according to which ships are built and operated. The classification certificate is the authority document showing that the ship is properly built and maintained in good technical condition.

What does the economic regulatory framework look like?

Some regulations on shipping are established for economic purposes by either national governments or inter-governmental organisations. This is because governments consider international shipping as a specifically important sector for a country's economic development, thus seeing the necessity to regulate the sector in order to direct its development in a specific manner. We here look at the economic regulations on shipping from national and international perspectives. Some countries adopt supportive policies for the shipping sector with measures such as financial subsidy to shipbuilding or ship operation, tax relief for ship operation or services, cargo reservation or cargo preference in favour of national ships. On the other hand, many other countries take a liberal attitude by having regulations aiming at safeguarding a healthy market order in terms of free and fair competition. We will briefly examine the economic regulations in the sphere of fair competition.

- ***Economic regulations at the national level.*** Although there are many countries with commercial fleets trading internationally, we will focus on the three major entities, namely the EU, the USA and China. This is because they are not only very active but also more influential in exercising economic regulations on international shipping due to their market share in both seaborne trade and shipping service capacity.

  The European Union's economic regulations on maritime transport focus on the application of the free movement of services and to ensure that competition rules are complied with. At the European Commission, the Directorate-General for Competition is responsible for the enforcement of EU competition rules. Exemptions from the EU rules were repealed and, from September 2013, maritime transport has been subject to the EU's general competition law,[7] according to which, apart from technical cooperation that improves service quality and reduces the cost for consumers, any agreement that restricts competition like price-fixing or capacity control is not allowed. In November 2002 the EU concluded its investigation by giving clearance to the acquisition by Wallenius Line and Wilhelmsen of the car carrier business of Hyundai Merchant Marine, subject to a commitment to discontinue a cooperation agreement, including price-fixing, with a major competitor.[8] Another more recent case is an antitrust investigation opened by the European

Commission (EC) against 14 liner shipping companies suspected of price-fixing practices by making price announcements known as General Rate Increase announcements. In July 2016 the EC concluded the investigation by accepting the binding commitment of the companies under investigation to stop such practices.[9]

In the US, the Federal Maritime Commission is responsible for economic regulations, based mainly on the Ocean Shipping Reform Act (OSRA) of 1998. According to the OSRA, ocean shipping carrier agreements are still exempted from antitrust rules, in spite of several attempts to repeal the immunity. For the cases where the requirements for the antitrust exemption are not met, the antitrust laws will apply and the Department of Justice undertakes investigations in the law enforcement processes. A recent case involving price-fixing and bid-rigging practices was in international shipping services for roll-on roll-off cargo of the United States. Three shipping companies were found guilty and were sentenced to pay criminal fines of more than US$136 million and four corporate executives were sentenced to prison terms.[10] In 2018 new antitrust amendments were introduced to the US Shipping Act.[11] This is a response to the recent trend of liner shipping consolidation and ocean shipping alliances. The new amendment further empowers the Federal Maritime Commission to monitor potential anti-competition behaviours of ocean carriers and maritime transport operators. The aim of the amendments is to protect US ports and port service operators.

As China has become a major global maritime power for both seaborne trade and shipping services, its economic regulations have started to have a bigger impact internationally. Two ministries are involved in shipping-related economic regulations: the Ministry of Commerce and the Ministry of Transport. The most well-known case is probably the rejection in 2014 by the Ministry of Commerce of the application for an intended shipping alliance called "P3 Network" by Maersk Line, Mediterranean Shipping Corporation and CMA CGM, the world's three largest container shipping lines. The decision was made after both the EC and the US had given the green light for the proposed alliance to go ahead. The Chinese rejection was based on the conclusion of the investigation that "the establishment of the network centre may lead to the formation of a compact association by Maersk, MSC and CMA CGM, and have effects of excluding or restricting competition on the container liner shipping market for the Asia–Europe route" and

> The participating undertakings have failed to prove that the beneficial effects of the concentration on competition significantly outweigh the adverse effects, or the concentration would comply with the public interests. Therefore, the Ministry of Commerce has decided to prohibit the concentration of undertakings, in accordance with Article 30 of the Anti-monopoly Law of the People's Republic of China.[12]

The plan for the alliance was dropped after the Chinese decision.

- ***Economic regulations at the international level.*** The organisations which have been active in regulating maritime transport are the intergovernmental agencies such as UNCTAD (United Nations Conference on Trade and Development) and WTO (World Trade Organisation).

  UNCTAD was established in 1964 and it was the only UN agency with a standing committee on shipping. The general objective of the *Shipping Committee* was to promote the participation of developing countries in maritime transport. During the period between the 1960s and the mid-1980s, UNCTAD was particularly active. It produced several international conventions: the most important one is the UN Convention on a Code of Conduct for Liner Conferences. This convention had an objective to increase the participation of the developing countries in maritime transport by breaking the protectionist liner conferences. It was for the first time that a cargo-sharing formula was proposed (the 40:40:20 principle). Although this Convention has been adopted by many countries of both new maritime nations and the traditional maritime powers, in practice the Convention has not been successfully implemented. As both the political and economic environment has changed, especially after the late 1980s, UNCTAD's role in the maritime transport regulations has diminished dramatically. After UNCTAD IX (1996), the Shipping Committee was dissolved.

The involvement of WTO (formerly GATT) in maritime transport regulations started at the end of the "Uruguay Round" in the 1980s and early 1990s. It came with the inclusion of the service sector (GATS) in the GATT discussions and negotiations in the last round of trade negotiations. Presently, despite the strong interests of many countries in its inclusion, the maritime sector has not been included in the WTO due to disagreements between major maritime countries. In GATS negotiations, maritime transport covers a broad scope of activities. In addition to international shipping, auxiliary services, such as port activities and intermodal transport, are also included. If the sector was subject to WTO rules, the impact could be far-reaching in view of the general WTO principles that will be applicable such as Market Access, which makes cargo protection illegal; National Treatment, which means that foreign companies are to be treated the same way as national ones; Most-Favoured Nation, which means no discrimination is allowed between foreign companies. Based on negotiations between member countries, commitments are made under GATS. There are so far 56 WTO members who have made commitments to different degrees regarding international maritime transport, auxiliary services and access to port facilities.[13]

What does the social regulatory framework look like?

At the social level, the regulations on international shipping are first of all established by various flag States or port States. Apart from the government, a number of NGOs have also been involved in this aspect. We shall focus on the two most important organisations in the following discussions. The first is the ILO or the International Labour Organisation, which is a part of the United Nations, and the second is ITF, the International Transport Workers Federation, which is a trade union association. The rules and regulations by national institutions are not covered.

- ***Social regulations at the inter-governmental level.*** The International Labour Organisation (ILO), which started in 1919, is one of the oldest UN agencies. Up to 2006, the ILO had produced more than 30 important conventions dealing with the working and living conditions of seafarers on board ships. These conventions were consolidated in 2006 into one single piece of regulation, named the Maritime Labour Convention or MLC 2006, which came into force in August 2013.

  The new ILO Convention modernises the international seafarer-related standards to consolidate and update earlier ILO Conventions and Recommendations under five titles, namely: minimum requirements for seafarers to work on a ship; conditions of employment; accommodation, recreation facilities, food and catering; health protection; compliance and enforcement. The MLC 2006 promotes compliance by ship operators and owners by giving governments sufficient flexibility to implement its requirements in a manner best adapted to their individual laws and practices. It strengthens enforcement mechanisms at all levels, including provisions for complaint procedures available to seafarers, the shipowners' and shipmasters' supervision of conditions on their ships, the flag States' jurisdiction and control over their ships, and port State inspections of foreign ships. Together with the SOLAS, MARPOL and STCW conventions of the IMO, the MLC of the ILO is considered to be the fourth pillar of international maritime legislation.
- ***Social regulations at the non-governmental level.*** The most influential international organisation at this level is the ITF (International Transport Workers' Federation) which represents the interests of the national trade unions in the transport sector. The ITF was created over a hundred years ago. It now has about 700 trade unions representing some 4.5 million transport workers in around 150 countries. Although it covers all modes of transport, maritime transport is the original and also the most essential aspect of the ITF's activities. The ITF has an objective to ensure safe ships and decent

working conditions for seafarers, to raise standards and protect seafarers' rights. The ITF receives the complaints from member seafarers and negotiates with the employers on behalf of the seafarers. For the purpose of protecting the rights of the seafarers working on ships under open registry, the ITF has some basic agreements for use between a maritime trade union and a shipping company.

9.3 Enforcement and implementation of regulations

Making the right maritime regulations is one thing, implementing them effectively is totally another. It was once said that "better a first-class implementation for a second-class strategy than vice versa".[14] The challenges and problems regarding implementation are more acute for maritime regulations as the enforcement is outside national boundaries.

How are rules and regulations implemented and enforced?

The effective implementation of an established maritime regulatory system is more critical at the international rather than national levels. This is chiefly because the enforcement mechanism at the international level is generally either much weaker than at the national level or absent altogether. Maritime transport is an activity taking place outside the scope of national jurisdiction. International institutions, either governmental or professional, are capable of making regulations, but the implementation and enforcement responsibilities are those of the national authorities. Usually, an enforcement system should include agencies such as police and court, but, for shipping, this is very much missing at the international level.

Let's take the technical regulations as an example. By design, the IMO has no power to enforce its conventions. The enforcement of IMO conventions depends on the governments of Member States. A convention becomes binding upon governments which have ratified it, which means that it has to be accepted formally by individual governments. Then the governments are called contracting Governments and they are the flag States for the ships under their registration. The flag States are responsible for the enforcement of the provisions of IMO conventions as far as their own registered ships are concerned and they also set the penalties for infringements where these are applicable. Therefore, concerning ships and their personnel, the flag State holds primary responsibility for enforcing conventions. *The contracting Governments also have certain limited powers in respect of the ships of other Governments.*[15] This is the case when foreign ships enter the territorial seas of a country; the state is then a "coastal state". For the foreign ships visiting a country's ports, the state is called a "port state". Both coastal states and port states are allowed to ensure that the passage or visit of foreign ships is not presenting any danger to their countries.

- ***Flag State implementation.*** The United Nations Convention on the Law of the Sea or UNCLOS defines the meaning of flag State as

> every State shall fix the conditions for the grant of its nationality to ships, for the registration of ships in its territory, and for the right to fly its flag. Ships have the nationality of the State whose flag they are entitled to fly.[16]

The flag State has the responsibility and obligation to "exercise its jurisdiction and control in administrative, technical and social matters over ships flying its flag, these include maintaining a register of ships, their masters, officers and crews and taking the necessary steps to ensure safety at sea, including regular surveys".[17] The flag States should "ensure compliance of their vessels with international rules and standards, through the adoption of the necessary implementing legislation and effective enforcement irrespective of where a violation occurs". The UNCLOS (article 94) further defines the obligations of flag States as of taking necessary measures for ensuring that their ships are in conformity to "generally accepted international regulations, procedures and practices", which should include the major ship safety-related regulatory instruments of the IMO. So the enforcement of international maritime safety and marine pollution prevention regulations falls within flag State jurisdiction. The IMO's Flag State Implementation Sub-Committee was set up in 1992 and produced the guidelines. In 2014 the IMO's Maritime Safety Committee and Marine Environment Protection Committee adopted amendments to the main conventions to make the following mandatory audit scheme from 2016:

> the use of Code for the implementation of Mandatory IMO Instruments (III Code), which provides the audit standard and provides flag States with guidance for the implementation and enforcement of IMO conventions and auditing of the flag States to the treaties concerned.[18]

- ***Port State control.*** A port State is a country whose ports are called by vessels of other countries. According to UNCLOS, a port State has a certain power to legislate for foreign vessels in its territorial waters with regard to maritime safety and marine environment protection matters. Safety and environmental problems may arise when foreign ships are not in compliance with the rules and regulations of the country they visit. Such a situation sometimes may become more acute with an increasing number of ships being under open registries. Consequently, many port States became more proactive by exercising port State control over foreign ships visiting their ports so as to ensure that the relevant international regulations ratified by the port State are duly respected. Whenever there is clear evidence to believe that the certificates and documentation are incomplete, invalid or the conditions of the ship or its equipment do not sufficiently comply in accordance with the requirements, the port State officers have the power to prevent the ship from leaving the port. So, as shown in Figure 9.1, port State control is meant to enforce the requirements of the international conventions on foreign ships.

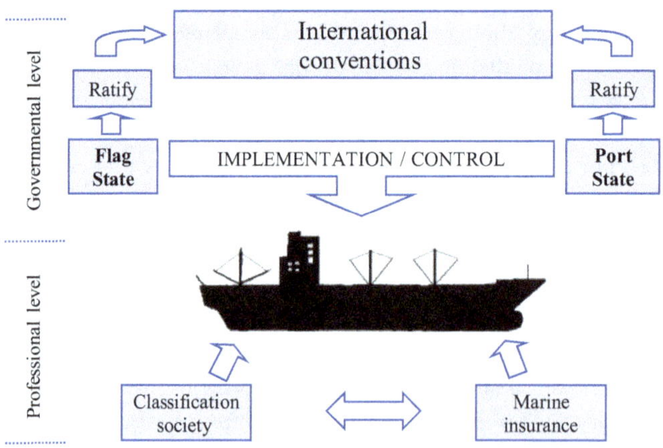

Figure 9.1 Implementation of international maritime conventions.

Source: Shuo Ma.

Note: usually the flag state works closely with classification societies, which will participate actively in both the formulation and implementation of the regulations.

Many international conventions, e.g., SOLAS, require ship inspections to be done to ensure that the ship condition and equipment comply with the requirements of international regulations. Such inspections are often done by port State control officers. Although port State control inspections are intended as a supplement to flag State implementation, in reality port State control has been proved to be a more effective enforcement mechanism, like a "safety net" to catch substandard ships. As port State control expanded, it was evident that regional cooperation in ship inspection was necessary so that inspections could be more targeted and unnecessary repetition avoided. In 1982 14 countries in Europe set up the Paris Memorandum of Understanding on Port State Control, or the Paris MOU, to coordinate port State control activities and to share information among the countries. Following the example of the Paris MOU, another nine regional MOUs were also established in the Mediterranean, Asia, the Indian Ocean and Latin America, etc.

What would the future development of technical regulations be?

Although the system of international maritime rules and regulations started to emerge less than one hundred years ago, their development has been on a fast track during recent decades. They have evolved into a complex system with both national and international institutions involved. The future development trend of the maritime regulatory framework can be summarised as follows.

The rules and regulations related to safety and environment protection, particularly those of the IMO, remain at the core of the maritime regulatory framework and serve as a foundation for the international maritime transport industry. As far as the IMO technical regulations are concerned, we observe some new development trends, such as the following.

- ***Standards and coverage***. Starting from the basic ship safety standards, the first version of the SOLAS Convention was adopted in 1914 in response to the *Titanic* disaster. Since then, five versions were adopted and numerous amendments have been introduced to the Convention, which has now become a comprehensive and complex regulation package with 14 chapters covering the full range of ship safety areas. By and large, the same responsive and reactive approach has still dominated most of the changes developed and introduced in the Convention. On the other hand, the amendments are needed to cope with new situations. Consequently, with further changes still happening, the standards of the regulations have become more stringent and the coverage wider. The maritime community, influenced by public opinion, has also become increasingly more sensitive to and less tolerant of shipping accidents causing life losses and environmental disasters. This usually leads to the creation of new conventions or changes in the existing ones. For example, the maritime regulatory coverage has expanded with the introduction of the anti-fouling systems convention (2001), the ballast water management convention (2004) and the ship recycling convention (2009).
- ***Effectiveness***. At the IMO, two aspects have specifically been addressed to enhance the effectiveness of safety and environmental regulations. One is to ensure that appropriate and adequate implementation mechanisms and measures are put in place by flag States. In this regard, the mandatory audit scheme for all member States introduced from 2016 is a new approach to monitoring the proper exercise of the flag States' obligations required by the conventions and, at the same time, to standardising the flag State implementation processes based on good practices. The other aspect is about using new concepts of rule-making and rule-changing processes. It is about the change from the traditional reactive and prescriptive approach to a new philosophy and method based on risk analysis. Typical examples include the "Goal-based" standards and regulations and the application of "Formal Safety Assessment" (FSA) in the rule-making and rule-changing processes.
- ***New emphasis***. The IMO's safety and environmental regulations were mostly made by identifying the technical shortcomings, deficiencies and loopholes and thus developing standards and requirements to fix them. This approach has been pragmatic on the whole, but it has also encountered

some major challenges. The first is that such "problem fixing" and reactive methods may easily miss the root cause of the case and a holistic view of the system shortcomings; second, segmental fixes do not allow the convention to evolve as a whole and to cope with rapid technological changes; third, most safety and environmental problems are not caused by technical reasons or technical reasons alone. The causes are more complex and most of them are related to the human factor, ship management and operation. Some new developments in the IMO technical regulations started to address these challenges. For example, the application of FSA enables rules to be made based on risks analysis, instead of on the prescriptive cure of direct problems. The "goal-based" regulatory framework allows appropriate solutions to be identified and tested under specific conditions. More and more regulations are introduced to focus on the human factors, overall management and operation procedures.

What would the future development of economic regulations be?

With the end of the policies in favour of cargo reservation and sharing symbolised by the "40:40:20" cargo-sharing practice promoted by UNCTAD and implemented in some developing countries without satisfactory results, the tendency of economic regulations is clearly in the opposite direction, which is the promotion of free and fair competition. Traditionally, the international shipping industry was granted, by most countries, exemption from anti-trust or competition laws. The main reason for such special treatment was the very high risks associated with the international shipping sector. It was generally accepted that such protection was necessary to keep sufficient shipping companies in the business with the desired level of services.

However, as we have discussed previously, there has been an enormous improvement of ship safety thanks to technological development and proper rules and regulations. So the justification for the exceptional treatment of maritime transport gradually disappeared. In 2006 the EU Council passed the regulation to repeal the existing rules which had allowed practices such as price-fixing and capacity control by liner shipping conferences.[19] Subsequently, the guidelines were adopted on the application of Article 101 (1) of the EU Treaty regarding the competition in the maritime sector.[20] From September 2013, Article 101 (1) has been fully applicable to shipping. Maritime transport is now treated the same as any other sector.

In the USA, the Shipping Act of 1984 permits conference agreements. Currently, the US legislation in respect of maritime transport is found in the Ocean Shipping Reform Act 1999, in which antitrust exemptions for liner shipping conferences remain. In China, the international shipping sector has not been separately treated as far as competition law is concerned. So the Anti-Monopoly Law of China is applicable to the maritime transport sector.

What would the future development of social regulations be?

The ILO's Maritime Labour Convention 2006 (MLC) is a milestone. The shipping industry for the first time has a consolidated and comprehensive international set of social standards for seafarers' working conditions. International shipping has become, therefore, the only sector in the world that has a common scheme and framework for all areas of employment. Since the entry into force of the MLC, the Convention has started to be implemented globally by the shipping industry as a whole. The role of each individual shipping company, or the employers, remains the key to making sure that the compliance is respected on board ships. Both the flag State and the port State are charged with the task of enforcement.

One of the challenges in the future will be the use of autonomous ships. The size of the ship crew has continuously been reduced and replacing labour with modern ships and advanced equipment

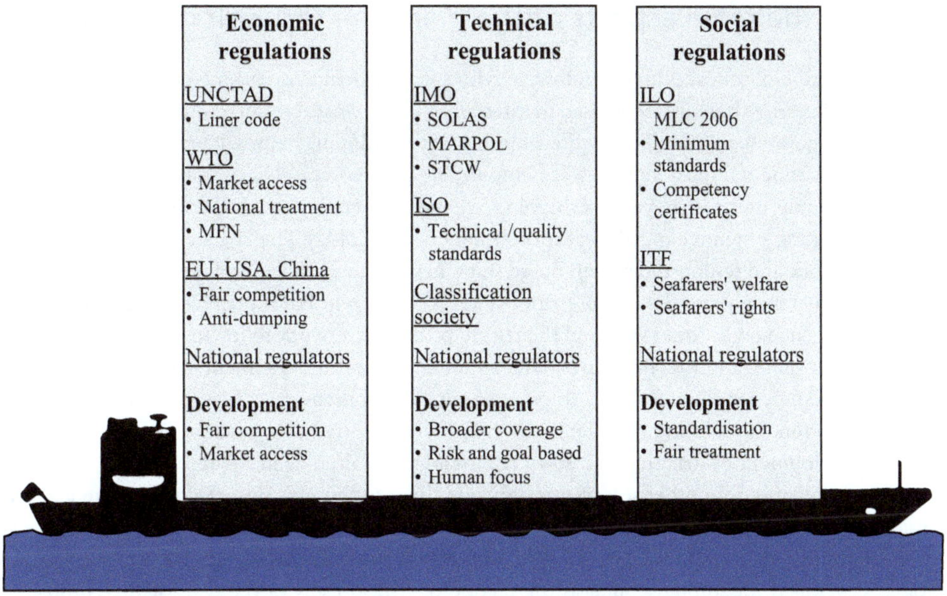

Figure 9.2 Regulatory framework of maritime transport and development trends.
Source: Shuo Ma.
Note: most of the international regulations on shipping have been established since the end of World War Two.

has been going on for a long time. However, this time it is different. The process has accelerated in recent years and the prospect of *crewless* ships becomes increasingly clear and certain. Should a gradual reduction of crew size be the form of transition towards total automation? How soon will this happen? There is no ready answer to these questions. But the changes will be radical and the impact will be huge. Many new issues with regard to employment on board ships need to be dealt with.

International maritime transport is still one of the freest and most open businesses in the world, even though there are always more rules and regulations with which the shipping industry ought to comply. Compared with other economic activities, the rules and regulations are unique and different. But the specialisation and differences are not that shipping is more or less regulated, but that it is regulated by international rules made by international organisations, either inter-governmental or professional, and that the implementation and enforcement of the regulations fall on national authorities. Figure 9.2 is a summary of the regulatory framework for international shipping from a technical, economic and social perspective.

9.4 The technological system

The evolution of the shipping industry has very much been driven by technological progress and advancement. As far as maritime economics is concerned, the technological environment is an important background for most economic parameters and conditions for basic analysis. In this section we will examine the most significant technological developments and their impact on the international shipping industry.

What are the main aspects of the maritime technological system?

Modern maritime transport is an economic activity supported and conditioned by ship-related technologies which can be broadly recognised in three areas, namely naval architecture, marine engineering and maritime communication. Throughout the history of shipping, technology remains the foundation for all maritime transport activities. It is also the most important determining factor for development. For example, in the early years of shipping, when steam engines were introduced to replace sails, the entire shipping system changed to adapt to the new technology. The changes included a new distribution of work and responsibilities on board ships, new training and apprenticeship schemes for the skills needed, fuel supply and ship maintenance systems at port, etc. For more recent examples, we have seen profound changes in ship safety and the nature of on-board work following the improvement of ship–shore communication technologies. Due to technological development, specialised ships, such as oil tankers, container ships or LNG ships, are built. As a consequence, new activities, such as port services, education and training of seafarers, even entirely new transport systems, emerged and grew.

The development of maritime transport technology has often been the result of the adoption of existing technologies from other sectors and applying them to shipping. For example, steam and diesel engines had been in use in other sectors before being introduced in ships. The same can also be said for telecommunication technologies. However, there are also dedicated equipment and specific technologies developed for shipping, such as the technology specifically developed for the construction of ships. The application of the technologies already employed in other sectors to ships requires many adjustments and adaptation, which can be technically challenging for shipping companies. The satellite telecommunication is another example of an existing technology which was introduced to shipping with an adaptation for the specific need of ships sailing across the oceans.

The shipping industry is deeply influenced by the technological development in the shipping sector as well as outside of the shipping sector. The relationship between technology and shipping is two-fold. One the one hand, technology provides solutions to virtually all challenges to the shipping industry. The challenges may be related to the need to increase productivity and efficiency of ship operation; they may also be related to safety and environment protection improvement. The emergence of new technologies can often have a profound impact on shipping and sometimes they may even reshape the landscape of the sector altogether. For example, the current digital technologies like artificial intelligence, automation, internet of things, big data, etc., will almost certainly change the shipping sector fundamentally.

What are the differences between technology evolution and revolution?

Economic analysis is usually made based on some assumptions, such that the basic technological foundations and conditions are fixed factors. To optimise production processes, managers are most concerned with the technical and business environment. For instance, in the short term, the technological setting of production is assumed to be stable. Many costs, such as the manning cost, insurance cost, maintenance cost, etc., do not vary in the short term due to the fact that the technical conditions of the ship are fixed. But, in the long run, everything is variable. All existing business models or technologies will evolve and change.

There are two types of maritime technological changes, either incremental improvement and gradual changes or fundamental innovation and complete changes. In other words, the former changes are evolutionary, while the latter changes are more revolutionary. Evolutionary changes always happen. When a new technology is developed, more improvement can be made at an early stage with a rising marginal effect. For example, ship productivity rose rapidly when general cargo ships evolved from a single deck to multiple decks, or from loose units of bales or boxes to palletised units, or from ship derrick crane to shore-based lifting equipment. As people become more skilful and technology matures more efficiency improvement can be made. However, should similar efforts be made continuously for further improvement, the marginal outcomes will start to decline. This means that the effect of diminishing return starts to kick in. Then any significant change in productivity and efficiency can only happen with more fundamental and radical changes. New business models or technologies will replace the old ones. Such changes are also referred to as destructive innovation. The invention of sea containers is a case in point. Their introduction triggered a complete change of every aspect of liner shipping with an enormous improvement in the productivity and efficiency of the shipping system. Since the beginning of containerisation, container ships evolved from non-cellular to cellular ships, from single to double bridge design and from small to large ships. The same technological cycle has happened several times in the history of shipping, i.e., that significant improvement is made for a period then additional yield starts to fall even if bigger efforts are made. The productivity improvement of this kind is normally incremental or marginal because it is based on the existing basic technological concepts and conditions. In other words, to have a more significant enhancement of productivity, one needs to have more revolutionary innovation in technology or a totally new business model.

Figure 9.3 is a gross summary of the major regulatory and technological milestones in maritime transport for the last 100 years. The list, though not exhaustive, includes those developments which had a very significant impact on the safety and environmental performance of world shipping. Thanks to such regulatory and technological progress, the nature of deep-sea shipping has fundamentally changed. We will further discuss such performance in a later section of this chapter.

9.5 Three maritime technological revolutions

Although it is one of the oldest economic activities, maritime transport has never stopped evolving technically. The technological changes have always been driven by market competition, leading people to take risks, usually by introducing and adopting the latest technologies and business models in the shipping sector. In this way, the changes in maritime technology can be considered as the same process of global technological change as in other industries. The tremendous maritime leaps forward and technical restructurings are the reflection and application of industrial revolutions in general.

What are the three maritime technological revolutions?

Maritime transport has gone a long way to become what it is today since its original state about two hundred years ago. Thanks to the technical progress, the shipping sector is so efficient that it plays a vital role in linking the world together by moving more than 10 billion tons of merchandise a year between countries. Over this long period, technical and organisational improvement has not been a linear process at a constant speed. We can recognise two maritime revolutions in the past, based on the changes that have fundamentally impacted and reshaped the maritime transport industry and massively enhanced the productivity and efficiency of the shipping sector. And the third revolution in the shipping sector has just started, which may have an even more significant impact on the future of the shipping sector. There are common features as well as differences between the three waves of revolutionary changes in maritime transport. They are briefly discussed below.

- ***The first maritime revolution.*** The first maritime revolution happened in the 19th century in the wake of the Industrial Revolution in the UK and Western Europe. It was during this century that a number of new technologies were introduced to the shipping industry, although the transformation took many years to complete because time was needed for the technology to be accepted,

REGULATORY SYSTEM	Selected milestones	TECHNOLOGICAL SYSTEM
	1910	
1914 SOLAS Convention	1915	
	1920	1922 Echo-sounding for water depth
	1925	
1930, Load Lines Convention	1930	
	1935	
	1940	1940s Welding in shipbuilding
	1945	1944 DECCA position fixing
1948, Establishment of the IMO	1950	1940s LORAN radio navig. system
	1955	
	1960	1960s Computer-aided-ship-design 1960s VHF radio ship-to-ship comm.
	1965	1965 Onboard radar mandatory
1972 IMO COLREGS Convention 1973 MARPOL Convention	1970	1969 Automatic Radar Plotting Aid
1974 SOLAS Convention	1975	
1978 STCW Convention 1982 Port State Control, Paris MOU	1980	
	1985	
1992 Double-hull tankers of MARPOL	1990	
1993 ISM Code	1995	1994 GPS (Global Position System)
	2000	1999 GMDSS 2000 Voyage Data Recorder
2006 ILO MLC 2006	2005	2004 (AIS) Auto Identification
	2010	2012 ECDIS (Electronic chart)
2017 MASS	2015	AI and digital disruption
	2020	

Figure 9.3 Regulatory and technological milestones in maritime transport, 1910–2020.

Source: Shuo Ma, based on data from IMO, Allianz and LR.

Note: the regulatory and technological milestones in the figure, which are not exhaustive, represent the main developments that have an important impact on the safety and environmental performance of ships.

adopted and to improve. The revolution was triggered by three totally new and disruptive technologies in ship construction, ship propulsion and telecommunication. The final result was revolutionary. The changes in the shipping industry during this period were greater than those of thousands of years previously.[21] In the area of shipbuilding, steel replaced wood to be used to build ship hulls. So ships were much stronger and larger. With regard to the ship propulsion system, two technological breakthroughs made the difference. Steam engines and screw propellers replaced sails. Consequently, ships could navigate faster and in any wind conditions with more controllable speed. When it comes to telecommunication, overland and cross-ocean cables were laid in the late part of the 19th century linking the major trade centres in the world, so trade and transport could be arranged in advance. As a result, shipping was gradually separated from trade, to benefit more from specialisation and scale economies. With the first maritime revolution completed by the end of the 19th century, the shipping of the first generation era began. Based on the new technological settings, modern organisation and operation structures, both for on-board ship and shore-based activities, were established. So the first maritime revolution is the result of the combination of many technological breakthroughs, but mainly the three mentioned above which were inter-related and emerged during the same period.

- ***The second maritime revolution.*** This happened after World War Two, particularly in the 1950s. Different from the first revolution, the second maritime revolution was not only about the introduction of new technologies but was also about the fundamental changes in the production method and business model. Specialisation, standardisation and scale economies are the best characteristics and features which explain the second maritime revolution. Better marine engineering technology led to continuous improvement in engine reliability and fuel efficiency. But the real driving force behind the tremendous increase in shipping productivity was without any doubt the specialisation of ships and the subsequent growth of average ship size, as explained in Chapter 5. Ships were no longer built to carry all types of cargoes. Instead, each category of cargo was transported by purposely designed and built ships. Oil was carried by tanker ships, iron ore by large dry bulk carriers and grain by smaller bulk ships. For general cargo, which had previously been moved by small multipurpose twin-deck vessels, the revolution is even more spectacular with the introduction in the 1950s of standard steel containers. Containerised general cargo was transported on specialised cellular container ships in big quantities and loaded/unloaded rapidly at ports. Consequently, the transport of general cargo by liner shipping became many times more productive and efficient. As discussed in Chapter 1, the average freight cost in inflation-discounted US dollar terms for transporting a 40-foot container from the Far East to North America in 2018 was less than 10% of that of 1968. Considering the much superior quality of the shipping service in 2018, as compared with that of the post-second-World-War era in terms of delivery speed, service frequency, punctuality and safety, the extra customer value is massive and the changes are revolutionary. Since then, shipping has been in its second generation.
- ***The third maritime revolution.*** This is about the digitalisation in maritime transport in an inter-connected digital world. The forthcoming maritime revolution has now just started and has not yet got into full swing. Like the first revolution, the third maritime revolution is also a part of the general revolutionary transformation triggered by new technologies. This is the result of the cumulated development of several existing digital technologies with some crucial breakthroughs, for example in the areas of artificial intelligence (AI), blockchain or internet of things (IoT). The widespread disrupting effect will be on virtually every aspect of the maritime transport sector. The basic feature of the third AI-driven maritime revolution is the application of advanced digital analytical methods and techniques, including machine learning, to interpret events so as to support and automate the decision-making process and actions. When digitalisation extends beyond the existing activities and operations to include all observable objects and processes, a huge amount of data will be collected and transmitted by high capacity and speedy wireless technology to the unlimited and low-cost cloud-based storage facilities for processing using smart algorithms by extremely powerful computing capabilities, wonders will happen.

The third maritime transport revolution relies on the application of digital technologies and new business models, most of which may have been employed in other sectors. Some shipping-specific technology and innovations will also be developed and a lot of radical changes, which are more than usual organisational adaptation and structural adjustment, are necessary. Some of the changes have already begun. For example, crew size reduction has happened with the use of new control and automation technologies and equipment on board ships. With the rapid development of big data, artificial intelligence, IoT and other technologies, this process looks set to accelerate. It is difficult to foretell how fast the disruptive changes will evolve, but high-level autonomous and even totally crewless ships are almost certain to be the mainstream mode of maritime transport in the future. The transition will most probably be in phases. Similarly, other technologies such as 3-D printing in shipbuilding and maintenance or fuel-cells and other new energies will also be the broad technology basis of the third generation shipping. Like the revolutions that preceded it, the third maritime revolution also has the potential to massively enhance productivity, improve the quality in terms of safety as well as reliability and reduce the cost. The impact of digitalisation on shipping will be discussed in more detail in Chapter 16.

What are the differences between the three maritime revolutions and generations?

Comparing the three maritime revolutions on the basis of great technological leaps forward, there are several similar as well as different characteristics. We will discuss the following eight most important aspects of the differences, which are also illustrated in Table 9.1.

- ***Time frame***. Obviously, the time frame is different. For example, the first maritime revolution took place in the 19th century in the wake of the Industrial Revolution and it lasted for about 50 years. The second maritime revolution was in the middle of the 20th century after World War Two. A maritime revolution can be divided into two periods: first, it will take a decade or two for technology improvement, then it is followed by a period of wider application to explore the potentials of the technology. So the full potential of the third digitalisation-driven maritime revolution will most probably not be realised in the short term.
- ***Background***. A maritime revolution is always triggered by the evolution of demand and the market pressure to change the existing technology. It is always a part of the general and broader economic development and technological progress. The first maritime revolution was part of the Industrial Revolution. After the two world wars, there was a rapid economic and business expansion in the US, Europe and Japan, which were the driving forces behind the second maritime revolution of the productivity rise and a new generation of shipping. Currently, the third maritime revolution is a part of a new wave of digital disruption happening in virtually all economic sectors including the shipping sector.
- ***Ship characteristics***. Using today's ships as a benchmark, the ships after the first maritime revolution were small and sailed slowly, typically at less than 10 knots. They were general cargo ships that carried all kinds of cargoes. As a result of the second maritime revolution, specialised ships became the mainstream ocean-going ships and containerisation revolutionised general cargo transport and the liner shipping sector. Ships were faster and the average ship size continued to grow. In the future, ships may not be bigger but they will most probably sail faster, thanks to cheaper and cleaner energy and more efficient propulsion systems. Semi or totally autonomous ships will be a reality.
- ***Productivity level***. The level of shipping cost is determined, to a large extent, by the level of productivity, which has been discussed in Chapter 5 previously. The biggest outcome of a maritime revolution is increased productivity. As a result, sea transport cost as a percentage of the value of the imported goods has followed a long-term declining trend. Today maritime freight is about 5% of the cargo's import value globally.[22] It is expected that the third maritime revolution will dramatically boost shipping productivity and reduce the transport cost, thanks to cheaply produced ships, autonomous ships and new sources of clean and low-cost ship energy.

- ***Service model***. The services offered by the first generation of shipping were of a small scale in terms of seaborne trade and shipload sizes. After the second maritime revolution, in pursuit of scale economies, specialised third party common carriers expanded their business with big and specialised ships providing standard and undifferentiated services. The situation might be very different for the shipping services of the third generation. Smaller ships might be favoured and more differentiated and tailored services will be offered thanks to the shrinking of factor costs as a result of AI, automation and new sources of energy.
- ***Organisational features***. The relationship between trade and shipping has changed and will continue to change from one generation of shipping to the next. Transport is an integral part of trade. The two activities had been more integrated until the first maritime revolution took place. Then the transport was separated from trade in favour of specialisation and scale economies. Maritime transport has been dominated by large and independent shipowners and common-user shipping companies. In the future, for the third maritime revolution, digital platforms and trade ecosystems will be created and, consequently, shipping may well be re-integrated with trade and logistics.
- ***Leading players***. By leading players, we refer to those who lead disruptive changes and the maritime revolutions. Naturally, shipowners or shipping companies are thought to be such leaders. But, since shipping has a derived demand from trade, traders were the main drivers of the first maritime revolution. They were the most eager and willing risk takers to trade more by reducing the transport cost. While, in the second maritime revolution, the competition within the shipping industry made the shipowners also the main players. It is expected that the third maritime revolution will be led by those who control the data and the digital international trade and logistics ecosystems.
- ***Dominating technologies***. The driving technologies for the first maritime revolution were shipbuilding, steam engines, propellers and cable communication. The technologies and know-how such as diesel engines, satellite communication, computer-aided ship design and operation, ship specialisation, standardisation, containerisation, etc., have together contributed to the formation of the second generation of shipping. It is premature to tell the exact new technology which will play a dominating role in the forthcoming maritime revolution. It will most probably be a combination of many digital technologies with AI as the core.

The main features of the three maritime revolutions and the three generations of shipping discussed above are summarised in Table 9.1.

Table 9.1 Three maritime revolutions and generations of shipping.

	First maritime revolution and first generation of shipping	*Second maritime revolution and second generation of shipping*	*Third maritime revolution and third generationof shipping*
Time	Second half of the 19th century	Around the middle of the 20th century	First half of the 21st century
Background	Industrial Revolution	Industrial expansion and globalisation	Digital revolution
Ships	Small, slow, multipurpose ships	Large, fast, specialised ships	Fast, autonomous ships

continued

Table 9.1 *continued*

Productivity	Small scale and low productivity	Higher productivity	Very high productivity
Services	Small scale and undifferentiated	Large scale and undifferentiated	More variations and differentiated
Organisation	Shipping less integrated with trade	Shipping separated from trade	Shipping integrated in logistics and trade
Controlled by	Traders and shipping companies	Shipping companies and ship users	Trade and logistics ecosystem operators
Technology	Steel ships, steam engine and propeller	Specialisation, telecommunication	Digitisation, AI and automation

Source: Shuo Ma.

Note: the third maritime revolution has not fully started. But the development of trade and technologies has paved the way for the new disruptive innovations to happen and a new generation of shipping to come.

When and why does maritime revolution happen?

Although the three maritime revolutions happened many years apart, they have many common features, particularly with regard to when and why a radical and disruptive change takes place. In fact, there are many factors and conditions which together will trigger an extraordinary change. But the following three are the essential and necessary elements that need to be in place each time such a change takes place.

- ***New and expanding demand.*** When new trade emerges and expands, shipping supply will have to adapt to cope with the requirements. There may be different reasons for this. But one of the common economic reasons is the effect of diminishing returns. In the 19th century the need for more trade provided the marker for the first maritime revolution. And the revolution reduced the cost and improved the quality of transport, which in turn enabled a fast-growing trade of imported raw materials and exported manufactured goods. With the first maritime revolution, the world's seaborne trade increased from about 20 million tons in 1840 to about 200 million tons in 1900. In the 1950s, before the second maritime revolution began, the demand reached a new high in terms of volume, diversity and geographical coverage. In 10 years, the seaborne trade volume grew from about 500 million tons in 1950 to over 1 billion tons in 1960 and 2.6 billion in 1970.[23] Now, in a more globalised world economy, seaborne trade entered into a new era of expansion. The shipping industry was able to meet the growing demand not necessarily only in terms of ton-miles completed, it was also in terms of the quality of services, such as the speed of delivery and safety standards. New services with extra value were offered, such as door-to-door packages, customer convenience, or more integration with logistics and trade.

  Disruptive innovations in shipping will happen when expanding and new demand require better and cheaper shipping services. The effect of diminishing return means that, under the existing technological setting, the additional benefit from quality improvement or cost reduction per unit of effort input is getting increasingly smaller. The marginal economic outcome of unity input is shrinking towards zero. Between the established suppliers, quality differentiation disappears and the service becomes increasingly standardised. The focus of competition will shift from new features and better quality to mainly price. Only radical and disruptive innovations can break such a deadlock by replacing the existing system and resetting the technology base.

- ***Technological breakthroughs***. Disruptive changes happen when new technologies are available. The actual time of fundamental change depends on when suitable technologies and business models are developed. As discussed above, technological breakthroughs triggered the two maritime revolutions in the past. So the need from trade is the stimulus for shipping to change and the relevant technologies provide the conditions for the change. Although new, such technologies often have proven to be valid and working in other related sectors. When introduced to the shipping sector, time is needed for adaptation so the new technologies can be applied in the specific shipping environment. The replacement of the old system by a new one is never risk-free and often involves a long period of a trial-and-error process. After the first steam-engine-powered ship appeared, it took more than 100 years before the last sailing ship disappeared. Today, after more than 60 years of containerisation, there are still conventional general cargo ships in active commercial operation.
- ***Competition and entrepreneurship***. To succeed in disruptive innovation and the replacement of an existing system with new ones in shipping, the role of entrepreneurship is indispensable and decisive. A relatively recent example is that of Malcom McLean, an American entrepreneur who invented sea containers in 1956, pioneered the first containerised transport and started a revolution in liner shipping. The example also shows that the leader of maritime innovation may come from outside the shipping sector. McLean was working in a trucking company and he tried to solve a problem he encountered as a user of the shipping service. Bringing in a totally new method and business model to change and replace the existing system is hard and risky. There will certainly be technical difficulties, but the biggest barrier comes from the resistance of people to change. So strong leadership, such as a fully committed shipowner, is paramount for the success of disruptive innovation in maritime transport. It is for this reason that newcomers or outsiders who encounter fewer oppositions often have a better chance to succeed.

When and where will the third generation of shipping take place?

The third generation of shipping will again be the result of the application of new technologies to the shipping industry, ranging from new ways of ship construction to automatic decision making and to new energy for ship propulsion. The biggest change of all will be the application of the digital technologies of the fourth industrial revolution.[24, 25, 26] Although robotics and artificial intelligence have existed for many years, it is thanks to some recent technological breakthroughs in the areas such as deep learning, AI, big data, computing power, mobile data transmission, cloud computing, etc., that a great transformation of all economic activities is about to happen. It will not only be a game-changer but a true revolution. Maritime transport, like so many other sectors, will not be the same any more. What will be the impact of the forthcoming digital revolution on maritime transport and what will the third generation of shipping look like? We will discuss this subject in Chapter 16. Here, we will give brief answers to the question at both theoretical and practical levels.

- ***The theoretical answer*** is that any activity requiring predictable decisions can be undertaken automatically using AI technologies. Or, as described by an AI expert, "if a typical person can do a mental task with less than one second of thought, we can probably automate it using AI either now or in the near future".[27] So we can say that, with the exception of those tasks relying on personal interaction or decisions of creative nature, any activity that has one best way to be done will be suitable for automation.

- ***The practical answer*** is more complicated as it involves some conditions that are not yet available for disruptive changes to happen. For an automation system to work there should be rule-based working procedures. Most of the activities in shipping are operational by nature, needing standard and predictable actions. So there is no reason why they cannot be automated. Some of the activities in shipping have already been automated and are without human intervention, such as online booking, freight payment, unmanned engine rooms, automated container terminals, etc. Now this process is accelerating and broadening. The real purpose and the most important effect of replacing people with machines are not only to reduce cost but to improve service quality and to create new value for customers. For those remaining activities which could be but have not been automated, one of the biggest and most crucial barriers is about the digitisation of these activities followed by data generation and data collection. Data has now become a new and most precious resource, if it can be systematically and comprehensively collected, filtered, categorised, labelled and processed for specific purposes. When this happens to the shipping sector in a generalised manner, then, with appropriate algorithms and computation power as well as modern robotics technology, the new age of maritime transport will begin.

Although we call it a third revolution, it may take a relatively long time to complete. In the same way as for the previous maritime revolutions, time is needed for the technologies to develop and improve as well as for the business to adapt and adjust to the new business model. The restructuring of the shipping industry will take place sector by sector according to the following conditions.

- ***It will happen when and where the necessary data exists.*** The amount of data needed for automation depends on the complexity of the operations. For example, cargo-handling operations at a container terminal are much less complex than the navigational operation of ships on the high seas. So automation will take place for the activities for which data is already available. The sales, booking, cargo tracking and freight payment operations in liner shipping will be automated earlier than the chartering and related activities in tramp shipping. For such relatively simple operations, it will be easier to acquire the necessary data as well as to label and process it for automation purposes.
- ***It will happen when and where the bottlenecks are.*** One of the best ways to identify bottlenecks is to hear complaints from all sorts of stakeholders, from customers to staff and even the public. Such complaints may be related to concerns on cost or quality of services or practices causing the concerns. For example, the complexity of the interface between customers and shipping companies in terms of purchase of service, transport documentation and formalities, etc., has been considered as a major bottleneck to the transport of international trade. And shipping companies have taken the risk of changing the current system with new digital technologies such as blockchain. Other quality issues such as schedule reliability, safety, or cost issues related to insurance and labour cost can also be serious causes of concern.
- ***It will happen when and where new value and better customer experience can be created.*** Value can be created by a new service or by a combination of new and existing services. The big data technology may enable shipping companies to know their customers better, to anticipate their needs and to provide customised services. A re-integration of maritime transport into international trade may create new values and improve customer experience.

The stakes and consequences of the forthcoming maritime revolution will be overwhelming. Many activities will shrink or be eliminated or replaced by automation, while some new tasks, most probably fewer in number, will be created. With a re-set of the basic maritime technologies, the fundamental concepts, standards and business model will be totally different from the ones of today. Without exception, every maritime sector will be affected: from ship operation, either on board or in the office, to port operation, shipping services such as shipping intermediates, insurance, legal service, classification, etc., even to maritime safety administration and maritime education and training. The maritime transport business model will be reshaped.

9.6 System improvement and impact on shipping performance

Modern maritime transport has witnessed vast improvements in all three areas, namely ship operation, regulations and maritime technology. As we have examined in this chapter, thanks to such improvements, international shipping has become safer, cleaner and more efficient. The productivity and efficiency performance of the world fleet has been analysed in the previous chapters. In this section we will evaluate the impact of the operational, regulatory and technological progress on maritime safety and marine environmental protection. The progress can largely be attributed to the combined improvement in operational, regulatory or technological systems. We will analyse the general outcomes of ship safety and environmental records over a period of about 50 years from 1970.

How effective are system improvements in maritime safety?

In 2018 a total of 31 merchant ships in the world were lost due to accidents. It was, until then, the best safety performance ever achieved.[28] This is a tiny proportion in comparison with the world's fleet of about 50,000 merchant ships, or about one total loss out of 1,600 ships. If only dry bulk carriers are counted, the ratio was one total loss out of 228 ships in 1970. During about 50 years between 1970 and 2018 the number of total losses in the world fleet was in a general decline, though with fluctuations in the 1980s and 1990s. By just looking at the numbers of total loss alone, we cannot have a clear grasp of the real changes in ship safety performance. This is because the business is different. Seaborne trade has increased and so has the number of ships. We therefore examined the safety performance of the world dry bulk fleet during this period by calculating the ratio of the total ship losses per year and the total number of bulk carriers. Bulk carriers are not only the largest group of the world fleet, but they also have serious safety concerns. We compare the total losses with the total numbers of ships rather than the deadweight tonnage because the average ship size has kept increasing. Usually, the probability of total loss is lower for larger vessels. As shown in Figure 9.4, the ratio fluctuated between 1 and 4 total losses per year for every 1,000 ships for the period of 1970–2000. From the 2000s, maritime safety improved more rapidly. In 2018 the safety performance of the bulk carriers was more than ten times better than in 1970.

Taking the total losses of bulk carriers per year and comparing them against the total amount of bulk cargo transported, we can appreciate the safety performance of maritime transport in the business of dry bulk cargo trade. Such a comparison gives us an idea about the tremendous progress made since the year 2000. This is because the volume of dry bulk cargo trade expanded extraordinarily rapidly from the early 2000s from over 2 billion tons in 1999 to more than 4 billion tons in 2011. However, this fast increase in shipping business did not lead to a rise in ship total losses. On the contrary, the number of total losses of bulk carriers decreased during this period. This may be an important piece of information for marine cargo insurance. Figure 9.5 shows the annual total losses of bulk carriers per every billion tons of dry bulk cargo transported. As far as the reasons are concerned, references can be made to Figure 9.3. The regulatory measures taken and the technological progress made prior to and during the 2000s had certainly a very positive impact on ship safety performance. The improvement of bulk carrier safety is proof of the effectiveness of the operational, regulatory and technological systems.

Generally speaking, maritime safety performance has almost reached the point where the marginal cost and even the average cost of additional measures for further improvement start to rise. The law of diminishing return means that under the existing organisational and technological frameworks, any new effort will be very costly and not as effective. It also means that new developments require structural changes.

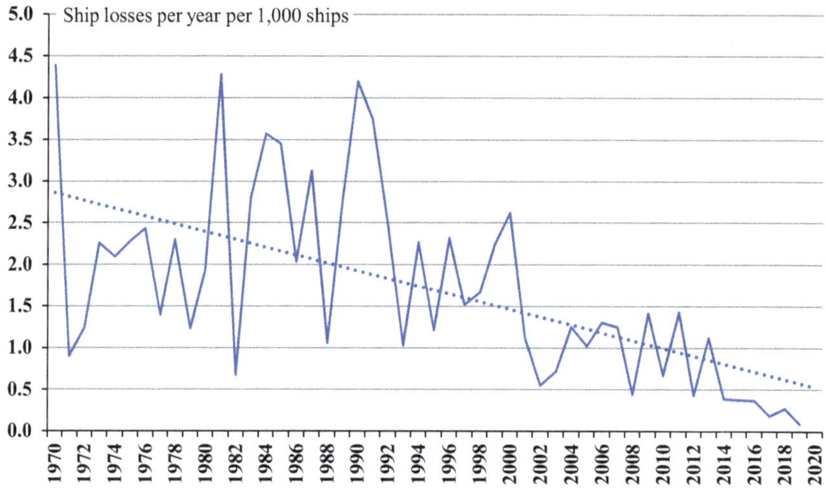

Figure 9.4 Total losses of bulk carriers per 1,000 dry bulk carriers per year, 1970–2018.

Source: Shuo Ma, based on data from Clarksons and UNCTAD.

Note: the safety performance of dry bulk carriers has been steadily improving for about 50 years from, on average, 3 total losses per year for every 1,000 ships in 1970 to below 0.5 total losses per year per 1,000 ships in 2018. Such improvement is demonstrated more from the 1990s.

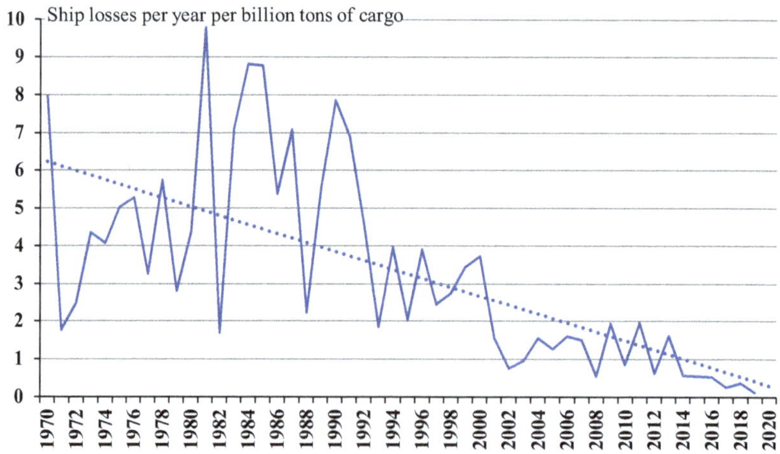

Figure 9.5 Number of total losses of bulk carriers per billion tons of dry bulk cargo transported per year, 1970–2018.

Source: Shuo Ma, based on data from Clarksons and UNCTAD.

Note: the figure is about the annual total losses of bulk carriers per billion tons of dry bulk cargo shipped per year. The number decreased from about 6 losses per year on average per billion tons of bulk cargo carried in the 1970s to less than 1 loss per year in recent years.

How effective are system improvements in marine environment protection?

Although the first ship safety convention, SOLAS, was introduced in the 1910s, the International Convention for the Prevention of Pollution from Ships, MARPOL, did not enter into force until 1973, more than 60 years later. Since then, ships' environmental performance has become one of the main concerns of the global maritime community. Because of the existence of externality, the International Maritime Organisation, IMO, has been the main rule-making body to ensure that the marine environmental impact originating from ships is properly regulated and internalised. The enforcement of the rules falls under the responsibility of the flag State and port State.

Apart from air emissions from ships, maritime safety and environmental challenges are similar and inseparable because they are often caused by the same accidents. So the efforts made to improve ship safety will usually have a positive effect on the ship's environmental performance. The MARPOL Convention deals with different types of pollution from ships. Oil spills have been the main source of marine pollution ever since oil became the main cargo of seaborne trade and the fuel for ships. We use the data of ITOPF on oil spills of the world's tanker fleet between 1970 and 2018 to analyse the tanker fleet's environmental performance over time.[29] Due to the fact that, during this period, the global seaborne trade of oil and oil products evolved and so did the world's tanker fleet, our analysis is based on the amount of total oil spills per year out of the total cargo transported by the world's tanker fleet. Figure 9.6 shows the tons of oil spilt for the spills of 7 tons or more per billion tons of crude oil, oil products and chemicals transported by the tanker fleet per year. The record of oil spills from ships reflects the history of major marine accidents. In 1979, for example, the accident of the tanker ship *Atlantic Empress* resulted in an oil spill of 287,000 tons. Big marine accidents with oil spills of similar magnitude happened in 1983 with tanker ship *Castillo De Bellver* and in 1991 with tanker ship *ABT Summer.*

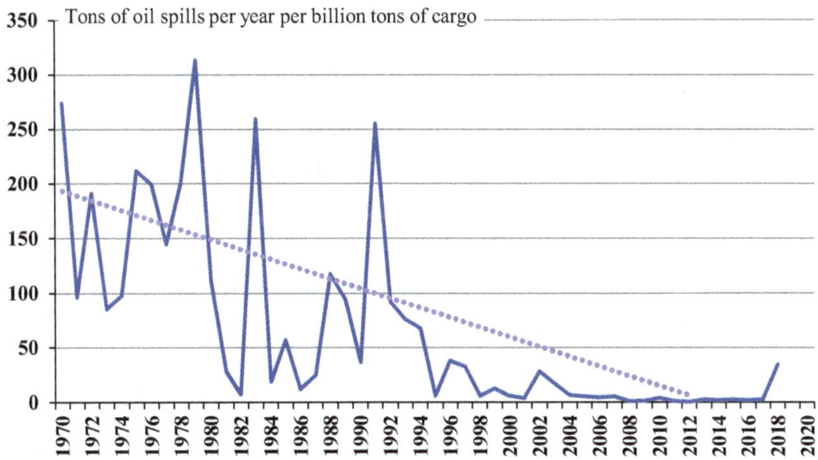

Figure 9.6 Tons of oil spills (≥7 t) per billion tons of oil transported per year, 1970–2018.

Source: Shuo Ma, based on data from ITOPF and UNCTAD.

Note: the figure is about the ratio of the amount of oil spills per year to every billion tons of crude oil, product oil and chemicals shipped per year. The number reduced from about 200 tons on average in the 1970s to less than 10 tons on average since 2004.

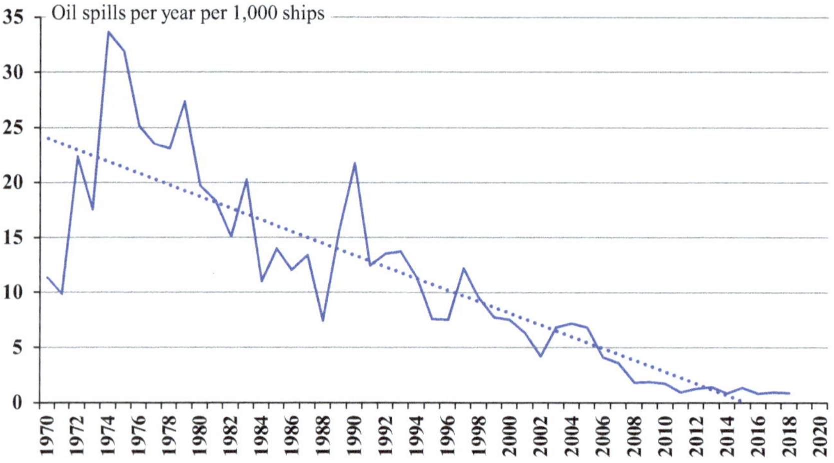

Figure 9.7 Total number of oil spills (≥7 t) per 1,000 tanker ships per year, 1970–2018.

Source: Shuo Ma, based on data from ITOPF and Clarksons.

Note: the figure is about the ratio of total number of incidents with oil spill of more than 7 tons to every 1,000 tanker ships of 10,000 dwt or above. The environmental performance improved from, on average, more than 20 spills per 1,000 tankers per year in the 1970s to about 1 spill per 1,000 tankers per year in the 2010s.

Preventing big disastrous accidents with a large quantity of oil spills is certainly a main task of the world maritime community. At the same time, the negative environmental impact of small but more frequent spills is significant as well. So the number of oil spills should be reduced. Figure 9.7 is about the annual number of oil spills of 7 tons or more per 1,000 tanker ships from 1970 to 2018.[30] The number of oil spills reached the highest level before the first oil crisis in the early 1970s. It coincided with the adoption of the MARPOL Convention at the IMO. Since then, the number of oil spills has continued to decline steadily, even with a growing tanker fleet. For the decade from 2008 to 2018, the total oil spills of 7 tons or more has been in single digits.

It is hard, even impossible, to attribute the improvement of safety performance to a single factor. It is the result of the combination of multiple factors, especially the tremendous progress in the three systems that we have analysed in this chapter, namely ship operation, regulations and maritime technology. A conclusion can be drawn that, on the whole, the measures taken on the improvement of ship safety and environmental performance have been effective. However, for any further improvement, new and totally different technological settings and business models have to be used. With the application of digital technologies and AI in the shipping sector, we can only expect the safety and environmental performance of the global shipping industry to improve further. In Chapter 16 we will discuss this subject in more detail.

9.7 Summary

The modern shipping industry consists of some basic systems. We have examined the three most important ones, namely the operational system, the regulatory system and the technological system.

These systems affect many aspects of maritime transport and the systems evolve when the internal and external environment changes. The ship operation system includes commercial management, crew and technical management. The ship operation activities have become more concentrated and standardised. The concentration has led to more tasks being shifted from ship to shore and from being multifunctional to specialised. The standardisation has led to the fast development of professional ship management companies and pursuit of competitiveness from economies of scale. Consequently, there is a tendency of losing individual identity and it is also possible that standardised operations will be automated.

With regard to the legal and regulatory system, we have looked at the technical, economic and social aspects: for each aspect, rules and regulations are made at national and international levels, by either governmental bodies or professional institutions. Concerning the technical aspect, the international regulations dominate, which focus mainly on maritime safety and marine environment protection. The IMO and the IACS are the main players at the governmental and professional levels respectively. When it comes to the economic aspect, which focusses on fair competition, the national and regional authorities are the main regulators. The most active ones are the USA, China and the EU. Regarding the social aspect, which aims at safeguarding seafarers' rights, working conditions and social welfare standards, both national and international organisations are involved. At the international level, the ILO's Maritime Labour Convention 2006 provides a fundamental regulatory framework in this regard. The enforcement and implementation of the rules and regulations are as important as the making of them. The maritime regulations are implemented by the countries concerned as the flag States or the port States. The future trend of technical regulations is to focus more on the effectiveness of the rules and human factors. As far as the future trend of economic regulations is concerned, all remaining protectionist measures have been gradually removed and the sector is based on the principles of a free and competitive market. The global social standards, such as the MLC-2006, have been adopted by more countries, including those in Asia, which remains the main source of international seafarers.

We also discussed the technological system in this chapter. There are three main aspects of the maritime technology system, namely naval architecture, marine engineering and maritime communication. The development of these technologies has made, over more than one hundred years, the modern shipping we know today. Over this period, international shipping has experienced two big revolutionary changes. One was in the middle of the 19th century, which transformed shipping from wooden vessels with sails to steel ships with engines and propellers. The other was in the middle of the 20th century, which restructured the shipping industry with ship specialisation and a massive increase in ship size. Currently, a third maritime technological revolution is underway, which will, like the previous maritime revolutions, reshape and disrupt virtually every aspect of the shipping sector. This is the so-called digital revolution or the third generation of maritime transport. The new data-based technologies, such as artificial intelligence based on big data, deep learning, supercomputing power and fast data transmission and processing capabilities, will soon be utilised to disrupt the existing business model, technological setting and operational structure of the shipping industry. The third generation of maritime transport could be reintegrated with trade in an international trade ecosystem. The shipping services will be even cheaper and tailored to the individual customer's needs with autonomous vessels built by robots and powered by cheap and clean energy. Such days have not arrived yet, but the future is becoming ever clearer and increasingly obvious.

We assessed the impact and the effectiveness of the progress in the operational, regulatory and technological systems on the performance of the global fleet in terms of ship safety and environment protection. On the safety aspect, from the statistics between 1970 and 2018 of the total losses per year of bulk carriers, we found that, both in terms of the number of losses per 1,000 ships and per billion tons of dry bulk cargo carried, the safety performance improved remarkably. In the 1970s, the average total losses per 1,000 bulk carriers was 2 ships per year and the total losses per 1 billion bulk cargo carried was 4.3 ships on average. From the 2010s until 2018 the two numbers were 0.6 and 0.8 ships on average respectively, or 3 and 5 times better. On the environment aspect, we examined the data between 1970 and 2018 on oil spills per year and found that, both in terms of the total amount of oil spills per billion tons of oil transported and the number of spills per 1,000 tanker ships, the environmental performance also improved significantly. In the 1970s the average oil spills per year were 181 tons per billion of oil transported and 22.6 spills per 1,000 tanker ships. From the 2010s up to 2018, the two numbers were 5.5 and 1.1 respectively, or improvements of more than 30 and 40 times.

Notes

1 IMO (2005).
2 ISMA (2018).
3 It is widely considered that the book *Mare Liberum*, written by Dutchman Hugo Grotius in 1609, was the first text in which the principle of "freedom of the seas" was formulated. The UNCLOS was adopted in 1982 and came into force in 1994. Until 2016, a total of 167 countries had joined the Convention.
4 Farthing B. and Brownrigg M. (1997).
5 In 1948 an international conference in Geneva adopted a convention to formally establish the IMO. The IMO Convention entered into force in 1958 and the new organisation met for the first time the following year. Retrieved July 2019 at www.imo.org/en/About/HistoryOfIMO/Pages/Default.aspx.
6 Based on information taken from the IMO official website: www.imo.org/en/About/Conventions/Pages/Home.aspx.
7 The EU competition rules are contained in Article 101 (1) of the Treaty on the Functioning of the European Union. The EFEU came into force on 1 December 2009.
8 Benini F. (2003). From the investigation conducted by the European Commission, it was found that deep-sea car transport is a highly concentrated sector and the four largest shipping companies had, jointly, a price-fixing agreement.
9 EC (2016).
10 US Government (2015).
11 US Government (2018).
12 MOC (2014).
13 WTO (2010).
14 Owen A. A. (1993).
15 IMO (2019).
16 UN (1982).
17 UN (1982) "*United Nations Convention on the Law of the Sea*", UN, New York.
18 IMO, "IMO Member State Audit Scheme", www.imo.org/en/OurWork/MSAS/Pages/AuditScheme.aspx.
19 EU (2006).
20 The Treaty on the Functioning of the European Union (TFEU) came into force on 1 December 2009, following the ratification of the Treaty of Lisbon.
21 Stopford M. (2009), pp. 3–46.
22 UNCTAD (2007).
23 UNCTAD (various years).
24 World Economic Forum (2017).
25 Manyika J. et al. (2017).
26 Purdy M. and Daugherty P. (2016).
27 Andrew Ng (2016).
28 Allianz (2019). In 2018 the number of total losses was 46 ships, of which 11 were fishing vessels, 2 were barges and 2 were dredgers and 31 were cargo-carry ships.

29 ITOPF (2019).
30 Clarkson Shipping Intelligence (2019).

References

Allianz. (2019) "*Safety and Shipping Review, 2019 – An Annual Review of Trends and Developments in Shipping Losses and Safety*", Allianz Global Corporate & Speciality, p. 12.

Andrew N. (2016) "*What Artificial Intelligence Can and Cannot Do*", Harvard Business Review, 9 November 2016.

Benini F. (2003) "*Current and Future Competition Policy Issues in the Maritime Sector*", EU Competition DG, Transport Unit, pp. 5–6.

Clarkson Shipping Intelligence Network. (2019) Data is from the Clarkson Shipping Intelligence shipping statistics, Clarkson, London.

EC. (2016) Press release, "*Antitrust: Commission Accepts Commitments by Container Liner Shipping Companies on Price Transparency*", IP-16-2446, 7 July 2016.

EU. (2006) "*Official Journal of the European Union*", L 269: 1., 28 September 2006, COUNCIL REGULATION (EC) No 1419/2006, pp. 1–3.

Farthing B. and Brownrigg M. (1997) "*Farthing on International Shipping (Business of Shipping)*", 3rd Edition, Lloyds of London Press Professional Publishing, London.

IMO. (2005) "*Assessment of the Impact and Effectiveness of Implementation of the ISM Code*", MSC 81/17/1, 21 December 2005.

IMO. (2019) "*IMO Conventions, Introduction*", Retrieved from www.imo.org/en/About/Conventions/Pages/Home.aspx.

IMO. "*IMO Member State Audit Scheme*", Retrieved from www.imo.org/en/OurWork/MSAS/Pages/AuditScheme.aspx (accessed 2 September 2018).

ISMA. (2018) Data from ISMA/InterManager Retrieved from www.intermanager.org/members/.

ITOPF. (2019) "*Oil Tanker Spill Statistics 2018*", ITOPF Limited, London, January 2019.

Manyika J., et al. (2017) "*A Future that Works: Automation, Employment and Productivity*", Mckinsey Global Institute, January 2017.

MOC. (2014) (The Chinese Ministry of Communication) Announcement No. 46 on "*Decisions of Anti-Monopoly Review to Prohibit Concentration of Undertakings by Prohibiting Maersk, MSC and CMA CGM from Establishing a Network Centre*", 20 June 2014.

Owen A. A. (1993) "*How to Implement Strategy, in Managing Changes*", 2nd Edition, edited by C. Mabey and B. Mayon-White, Paul Chapman Publishing, London, p. 144.

Purdy M. and Daugherty P. (2016) "*Why Artificial Intelligence Is the Future of Growth*", Accenture.

Stopford M. (2009) "*Maritime Economics*", 3rd Edition, Routledge, London, pp. 3–46.

UN. (1982) "*United Nantions Convention on the Law of the Sea 1982*", Article 91.

UNCTAD. (2007) "*Review of Maritime Transport*", UNCTAD, RMT, United Nations, Geneva.

US Government. (2018) "*The Frank LoBiondo Coast Guard Authorisation Act of 2018*", in Title VII "Federal Maritime Commission Authorisation Act of 2017", amendments to the Shipping Act (46 U.S.C. § 40101-41309).

US Government. (2015) Press Release of the US Department of Justice "*Three Ocean Shipping Executives Indicted for Fixing Prices and Rigging Bids*", 6 October 2015.

World Economic Forum. (2017) "*Realizing Human Potential in the Fourth Industrial Revolution*", REF:040117, WEF white paper, Geneva, Switzerland, January 2017.

WTO. (2010) "*Maritime Transport Services*", Background Note by the Secretariat, S/C/W/315, WTO, 6 July 2010.

Chapter 10

The economics of port services

Ports are places where ships can anchor, berth, load and discharge cargo, have maintenance and load supplies. Ports are the interface between sea and land transport. Ports have two basic functions on each ship and cargo side. Even though loading and discharging cargo have long been widely recognised as the major roles of ports, the other most fundamental function of a port is to provide ships with a safe anchoring and berthing place. In other words, ports are, first of all, built to safely accommodate ships and then to handle cargo on and off ships. In this chapter we will discuss the main aspects of a commercial port and the relationship between ports and various aspects of maritime transport in order to appreciate the unique and decisive role ports play in the shipping sector.

10.1 Port systems

Ports are an integral part of shipping for obvious reasons. On the one hand, ports are built to accommodate and handle cargo on and off ships, so, without ships, there is no need for ports. On the other hand, ports are the homes of ships, so, without ports, ships have nowhere to go and nowhere to load and discharge the cargo. Ports, however, have their own special characteristics and we will look at the essential ones.

How is the port location chosen?

As mentioned above, maritime ports have two basic functions: to accommodate ships and to handle cargo on and off ships. A port should, therefore, be located where these two functions are best accomplished. So, there are two levels of location decisions. The first is about cargo or the general market to be covered by the port and the second is about ships or the exact physical place for the port.

- ***Market to serve.*** This is an economic and commercial decision about which market the port serves. A vast majority of the world's ports are public ports, which are built and owned by local governments. Ports ought to be of a certain size in order to be economically viable so that facilities can be built at the port as well as for the transport connections both on the landside and seaside. Consequently, the "density" of ports along a coast is, first of all, an economic issue based on total traffic, the type of cargo, shipping cost, port costs and land transport cost. The purpose is to minimise the total cost. For economic reasons, ports should be close to the cargo, which means production or consumption centres. So in a region with a large volume of maritime traffic, numerous ports may be built relatively close to one another. This is the situation in the Netherlands/Belgium, the Pearl River delta, or Southern California. Because ports are owned and built by governments rather than commercial companies, sometimes social/political considerations may also play an important role at both municipal, regional or national levels. Between the two basic port functions, accommodating ships and handling cargo, the decision on which market to serve is by and large driven by the cargo factors.

- ***Site to choose.*** This is mostly a technical and operational decision about the exact port location, which is the most suitable for transport-related matters. That includes all physical conditions with regard to safe and efficient ship accommodation, landside transport connections, space needs, environmental considerations, etc. Compared with the past, when ships were small and the volume of cargo was low, less space was needed and the environmental cost was negligible. So, many ports were built close to city centres. The new trend we have seen is that ports are moving away from city centres. Port construction includes landside facilities such as terminals, berths, storage and yards as well as the waterside facilities such as land reclamation, dredging and the building of breakwaters. Consequently, the building of a port is generally costly and takes a substantial amount of time to complete. The exact location ought to be chosen taking into account the factors of both waterside conditions, e.g., open space, water depth, current, tide, weather conditions, etc., and landside conditions, such as land and expansion potentials, and transport connections, such as railway or inland waterways. If a port is in such a location where navigational water has natural depth and is well protected from the sea, the port is a natural port. Otherwise, major construction and dredging works are required and the port is a man-made port. A port built along the coast and that has direct access to the sea is a seaport and a port that is alongside a river is a river port. If it is exposed directly to the sea, a seaport often needs a breakwater for protection. River ports, though protected from the ocean, may have more chance of encountering the problems of siltation or complicated navigational channels. A tidal port means that the water draft is affected by the level of the tide and sometimes safe berthing requires the protection by locks.

What are basic port functions with respect to ships and cargo?

As illustrated in Figure 10.1, port functions can be broadly divided into two categories: ship related and cargo related. The ship-related functions are in two groups of services, namely navigational services and technical services.

- When a ship arrives, it normally needs assistance to get in and out of the port safely. The anchorage area is a protected water space for ships while waiting for berthing. In restricted channels and areas close to or in the port, not only are navigational aids such as lighthouses and buoys needed but often a pilot and tugboats are also required, especially for big ships or ships and seafarers that do not frequently call at the port. At some ports, ships have to pass locks to offset, for example, tidal effect, although with seagoing ships becoming ever larger, more terminals are built outside locks.
- Ships also get technical services from ports. These include ship repair, maintenance and surveys. At a port, ships get all necessary supplies, such as fuel, lubricant, spare parts and paint, as well as provisions of crew subsistence like food, vegetables, fresh water, etc.

Another category of basic port functions is for cargo. These are divided into the following four types of operations: ship operation, cargo-transfer operation, storage operation and reception/delivery operation.

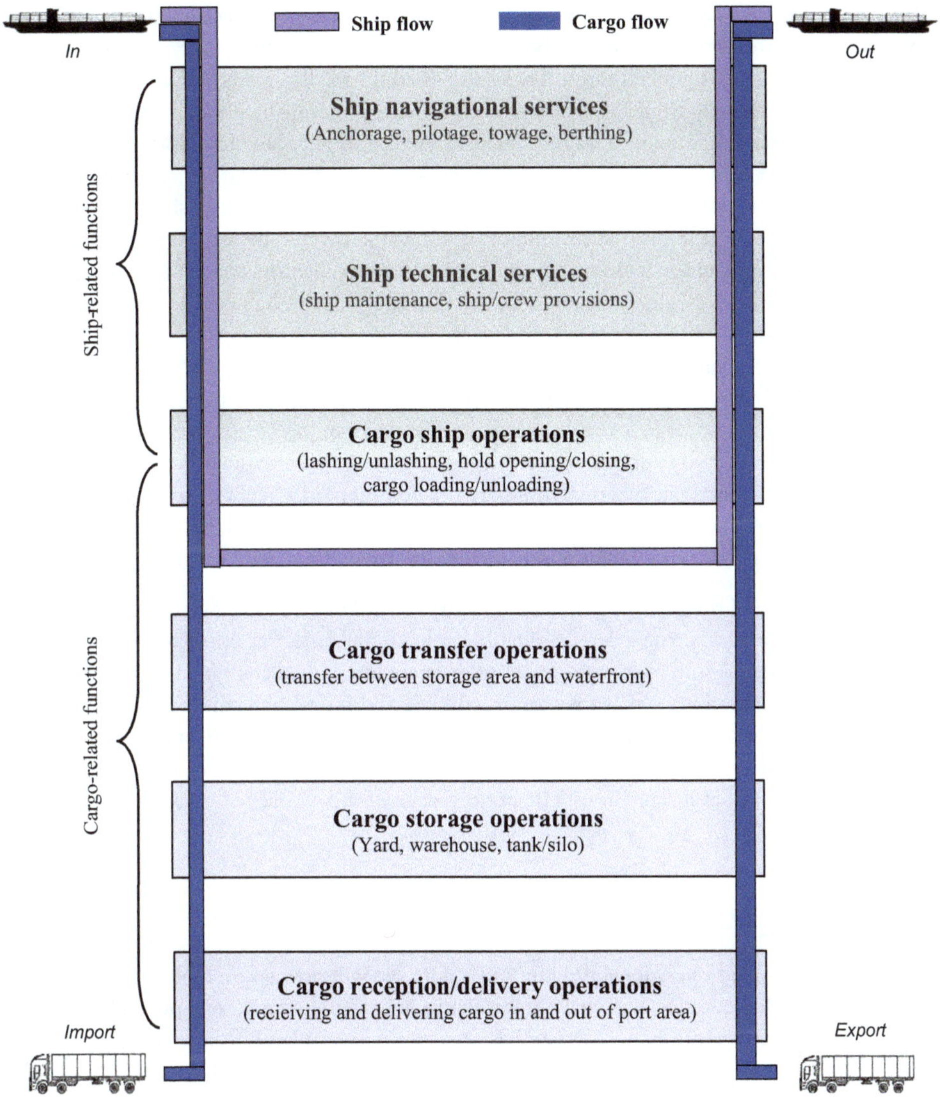

Figure 10.1 Basic port functions of cargo and ship flows.

Source: Shuo Ma.

Note: ports may be of different types, such as container ports, oil, bulk or ro-ro terminals. But the basic functions are the same.

- ***Cargo ship operations***. These include the loading and discharging of cargo on and off ships. Depending on the kind of cargo and ship, loading and unloading are done in several ways. For liquid cargo, pumps are used and for dry bulk cargo, grabs or screws are commonly used. When it comes to general cargo, lift-on lift-off (lo-lo) or roll-on roll-off (ro-ro) are the two main forms of cargo handling. Though ship's cranes can be used in some cases, for the large and specialised ships calling at container ports it is shore-based cargo-handling equipment that is generally used.

- ***Cargo transfer operations.*** These refer to the operations to move cargo back and forth between the waterfront and storage areas. This can be done using pipelines for liquid cargo or conveyor belts for dry bulk cargo. For general cargo, trucks, trailers and straddle carriers are usually used. In the past, such operations might not always have been necessary because cargo might be directly loaded from trucks or railway wagons to ships or discharged from ships to land transport vehicles. In more and more ports, automated transfer vehicles are now employed in container terminals.
- ***Cargo storage operations.*** Before or after being loaded to or unloaded from ships, cargo usually is temporarily stored in the port. Such temporary storage lasts typically for a few days, maybe in a shed, a warehouse, or a tank, a silo, or an open yard. Necessary facilities and equipment are required to move or reposition cargo. Safety and security measures need to be taken. It is in the interest of a port to optimise the use of storage land and facilities. So quick cargo turnaround time is often one of the key performance indicators.
- ***Cargo reception/delivery operations.*** These are at the gate separating the port area from the inland transport connections. Cargo is usually transported in and out of the port by road or railway. The reception and delivery operations are critical because cargo registration takes place at the gate. Although, at some ports, manual operations are still common, new technology such as image recognition, internet of things and automation are more and more adopted, which not only increase productivity and reduce cost, but also improve accuracy and the quality of service in general.

No matter what type of port, be it a general cargo port, a dry bulk cargo terminal or a container terminal, the above four basic cargo-related operations remain the same. For some freight such as liquid cargo or a ro-ro terminal, ship operation, and transfer operation, can be combined. Another important feature of the four operations is that they are interlinked and interdependent for the completion of cargo-handling operations in the port. This implies that the change in one operation will affect the others. An effort to improve one single operation can easily be fruitless unless corresponding improvements are also made in other operations. The performance of the whole system is determined by the weakest link.

10.2 Port and state

After discussing the main operational functions of a port, we will now take a look at who carries out these functions. Such a question is probably meaningful only in the context of a port. This is because, apart from commercial companies, the state has an active role to play. Furthermore, physically, it is relatively easy to identify a port, but organisationally it is far from clear what a port is. In many places the basic port functions are carried out by different organisations that are independent of each other. A port is, first of all, a physical land and water area on which port facilities are built and equipment installed. The ownership of such a property is a good indicator for defining a port. Yet an owner may or may not assume all or even any operational activities. The relationship between ownership and port operation varies enormously from one port to another. It is thus necessary to examine the different types of ports from this point of view.

Why do ports play an important role in a country's trade and economic development?

The importance of international trade for the economic development of a country has been discussed in the first two chapters. As the vast majority of international trade measured in tonnage is transported by sea, the critical role of shipping is prominent and the role of port services, as an integral part of shipping, is vital. According to a World Bank study, if the most efficient port is given a score of 100 and the least efficient one a score of 0, then a 10% increase in the average efficiency score of a country's port sector will lead to a reduction of the maritime transport cost of the export by 2.3% and subsequently an increase in export by 1.8%.[1] Taking China as an example, in a space of 30 years between 1978 and 2007, the country's position in global international trade rose from 27th place with about 1% of the world total to 2nd place with about 8% of the total world trade in value.[2] A large part of this extraordinary development of trade was attributable to the massive improvement of the shipping and port services in the country during this period. It is revealed by research that the efficiency improvement of the shipping and port sectors of the country was responsible for about 25% of the growth in foreign trade. And, given the high level of the Chinese economy's reliance on trade, the contribution of the efficiency improvement in the shipping and port sector to the annual GDP growth in 2007 was as high as 0.68 percentage points.[3]

Another aspect of the critical role of ports for a country's trade and economic development is based on a fundamental difference between international shipping and national ports. Generally speaking, shipping is international, open and free, while ports are national, more closed and regulated by each country. The best example of that difference is the existence of global markets in shipping for ship registration, seafaring, etc., but an absence of them for ports. For international shipping, there are common legal and regulatory frameworks, such as the Rotterdam Rules or IMO Conventions, global pricing systems such as the World Scale or measures such as the BDI. But in the port sector, none of the above exists. Every port has to follow different national rules and has its own price structure. This is because shipping is carried out in international waters while ports are operated within national boundaries. The so-called "cross traders", such as Greece, Norway or Hong Kong, own enormous shipping fleets, the majority of which serve the trade of other countries rather than that of their own. For ports, however, although it is now possible to open ports to international terminal operators, the efficiency of ports depends mostly on that of the infrastructure and superstructure of the country.

This is why countries with internationally competitive trade always have an efficient national port sector, but they do not necessarily have a strong maritime transport sector of their own. Such a difference has important policy implications for governments that wish to have active trade. Shipping service can be "outsourced", but port service cannot. It is, therefore, argued that a country should make port development and efficiency a development priority while they may rely on the international market for better and competitive shipping services.

What is the difference between a public and a private port?

Most ports in the world are public ports. Here the term "public" has two meanings. The first is about the people ports serve. A port may have just one single user or it may have many users. In this latter case, the people the port serves are the public or common users. A port is a type of basic transport infrastructure, the same as a road or an airport, which is open and accessible to all users. Common user ports normally are owned by the public sector, either local or central government. So the second meaning of public refers to the ownership of a port in terms of coast, land and water area. By the same token, single user ports are usually owned by firms. Such ports generally belong to large corporations with functionalities tailored to the specific needs of the firm. Large producers and traders of raw materials, such as iron ore, coal or oil, often build and operate their own port facilities. Such private ports provide exclusive services for the owner companies themselves. It is very rare to see a totally privately owned port operated as a common-user service provider.

From the 1980s a wave of institutional reforms began in virtually every corner of the world.[4] Port operations were decentralised, commercialised and privatised. The widely adopted modality is that, on the one hand, a port authority is always a public representative of the government that owns and manages the land, coast and other property and assets of the port. Port authorities are at the same time in charge of safety, security and environmental-related matters. On the other hand, port operations are either transferred to the publicly owned stevedoring companies or given in concession to the private sector, national or international or mixed, to run.

What are the characteristics of a "landlord" port and an "operating" port?

In publicly owned common user ports, the government is usually represented by the port authorities. There are two distinguishable types of port authorities, namely landlord ports and operating ports, based on the nature and degree of their involvement in port operation activities.[5]

- ***Landlord ports***. For this type of port authority, the power is limited to the decisions concerning the ownership and management of the port asset. Such responsibilities include land development and use, the reservation of space for the port areas and the construction and maintenance of port infrastructure. The port authority is, however, not involved in port commercial operations. The operational activities are left to individual companies, either public or private or combined. Those companies are also responsible for the installation and operation of port facilities and equipment necessary for providing services to ships and cargo. The port authority often gets into long-term contracts of lease or concession on the use of quay and land to port service operators, usually for an extended period. The port authority is also responsible for other so-called public goods such as safety, security and environment protection in the port area, as well as other issues of the general interest of the port such as planning, dredging, land development, hinterland transport connections, administrative services and even the marketing and promotion of the port.
- ***Operating port***. In some countries, the port authority, in addition to owning and managing the port asset, is also directly involved in port operation. Such port authorities are called operating ports or service ports. This means that the port operational functions, such as cargo handling, warehousing or navigational services, are undertaken by the port authority rather than by a company. There are different reasons for a port authority to be like this. For example, there may be a situation where no suitable company is available to undertake port operations due to a lack of financial or technical capability. Or the government does not wish to open the port business to foreign operators. Or it may consider that it is more appropriate for the sake of public interest that the port authority should itself engage directly in port operations so as to ensure the kind of services to both ship and cargo as well as for the general national interest. So, an operating port authority is also called a "service port".

Most port authorities in Asia, North America and Europe are landlord ports. Operating ports are mostly found in Africa, Latin America and some parts of Asia. From the 1980s, there was a wave of institutional reform of the port sector, which covered almost the entire world. One of the main characteristics of such reform is to change the nature of port authorities from operating ports to landlord ports.[6] This movement is also labelled as the commercialisation of ports, which emphasises the economic functionalities of port services and treats port activities as businesses rather than administrative services. Consequently, operating ports are today a shrinking minority and a vast majority of ports in the world are operated as commercial entities.

Why is "public finance" often required for ports?

As described above, in many countries port activities are considered as public services. Ports are therefore expected to play a social role. The understanding of such a social role may differ between countries, but it usually means that the transport safety of strategic materials and trade should be assured. Some basic services, such as safe port access by ships and cargo, should be provided at an affordable price, even if a subsidy is needed. Although the emphasis is still placed on operational efficiency and financial viability, full cost recovery is not necessarily the only goal of a port authority, either in principle or in practice. As a result, many ports are not operating on pure market principles. Given the high investment cost and a long pay-back period, a public subsidy on the infrastructure is very common in the port sector around the world.

The cost of building a port varies according to the type and size of the port as well as the geographical, technical and economic conditions. If land reclamation and capital dredging are needed, the construction cost will be very high. To build a container terminal in the 2010s, for example, the cost may be in the region of one hundred million US dollars or even higher.[7] It is therefore typical that public funds need to be made available. The investment covers the construction of port infrastructure, which includes land reclamation, dredging, the building of the navigational system, a breakwater, quay walls, pavement of yard, etc. Sometimes, such public funding does not need to be repaid.[8] In some countries, the government is responsible for all "underwater" facilities and the operators are responsible for cargo-handling equipment and cargo storage facilities. A survey of 11 European countries revealed that the construction and maintenance of breakwater, lock, maritime access, quay, open yard and hinterland access are all under the responsibility of port authorities.[9]

There are mainly three kinds of funding sources for port investment: self-funding, loans and grant. Self-funding usually comes from savings or the stock exchange; loans come from financial institutions such as banks or through the issuance of bonds; grants are given by the government, either local or central. The involvement of government finance may be considered as a source of unfair competition between ports. It would be difficult for a port which has to pay back even partially the investment in basic infrastructure to compete with another port which does not need to pay for the infrastructure financed by the government. This situation is more a subject of debate or dispute between countries which are in the same region but with different port development policies, such as is the case for some ports in the UK and those in continental Europe.[10]

10.3 Port and shipping

As described previously, maritime transport has a derived demand from trade and, by the same token, ports have a derived demand from maritime transport. The same idea can be expressed in a different way, i.e., that merchandise trade will not be completed until the cargo has been transported by ships, and shipping won't be completed without the cargo having been unloaded by ports. A port is not only an integral part of shipping, it also plays a very important role in the development of shipping. From an economic viewpoint, such a role is mostly demonstrated in the areas of cost and quality of shipping services.

How do ports affect shipping cost?

The cost of using a port is affected by many factors. We can examine such a cost from two aspects, i.e., the cost of the services to ships and the cost of the services to cargo. A certain amount of time has to be spent by ships and cargo in the port, regardless of whether this is due to port services to ships or to cargo, and the differences among various port authorities. We can call such time ship or cargo turnaround time or dwell time and broadly define it as the period between the moment when a ship or cargo enters the port and the moment when it leaves the port.

From an economic point of view, two types of cost are incurred by port users. One is the explicit cost in terms of port charges, which are either related to services rendered to ships or to cargo. The other is the implicit cost in the form of time cost. A common mistake made by people is to ignore or underestimate the importance of time cost and to think that port charges are the only important element that determines the port cost. For ship and cargo owners, the time element can be more important than port charges when calculating the total cost at a port. It is more so given the continuous increase in the unit value of both ocean-going ships and internationally traded cargo. On the one hand, more time is spent by ships and cargo in ports because of the growing size of ships and for other reasons. Time in port may cost more for the users than for the port. It can also be more costly than the port charges they pay for services. It is also easy to incur extra time cost because the cost is sometimes hidden and unexpected delays can always happen.

The investment in port infrastructure needs to be recovered by charging port dues from the users. This cost is usually paid based on the ship's tonnage. In the port of Rotterdam for example, port dues for ships are ranging, according to the types of vessel, from 0.4 to 0.5 US$ per gross registered tonnage of the ship.[11] Other ports in Europe apply more or less a similar level of port dues for ships and for cargo. In some countries, such as those in Asia, port dues are charged per registered tonnage per day. Other costs in relation to navigation in the port area are for services such as pilotage, towage, locks, etc. The level of these costs depends both on ships' characteristics and the local navigational conditions. Ships are also expected to pay for the use of a berth. This cost is usually calculated based on the size of the ship and the amount of time the ship is at the berth.

The explicit port cost for cargo has two parts: port dues for cargo and the costs related to cargo handling. The port dues for cargo are sometimes referred to as wharfage and are charged based on the volume of cargo. The exact amount, again, is different from one port to another. In the Port of Rotterdam, it is about 0.6 US$ per ton.[7] When it comes to cargo handling, the payment should be made to the service providers. Here a huge gap exists between ports in terms not only of the sophistication of port facilities and equipment, and the skill and cost of labour, but also the efficiency of the organisation and the operation. As a result, the cargo-handling cost varies enormously from one port to another. According to a World Bank report, cargo-handling charges in the Caribbean ports were two to three times higher than in similar ports in other regions.[12]

If most of the shipping costs are the fixed costs regardless of the amount of cargo carried, the cargo-related port costs are a variable cost. Based on an example at the Port of Rotterdam, for a container ship of about 75,000 gt calling at the port with a total of around 5,000 teus of cargo, the total port dues are in the region of US$43,000.[7] If US$120 per teu as container-handling cost is added, the total amount would be about US$640,000 to be paid by the shipping company and the cargo interest. Such a container ship will call at several ports on a round trip, so the total port-related costs will be at a very high level. For a shorter haul service, the port cost would proportionally contribute an even larger part of the total cost. So, depending on the length of the voyage and other factors, the port-related costs may constitute between 20% and 50% of the total shipping cost. Port costs and fuel costs are always the two major elements of a shipping company's operating costs. Because the price of fuel is fluctuating according to the global oil market, the proportion of the two costs are continually shifting. For example, for global container shipping during 2007 and 2012, the port cost and fuel costs were in an equal percentage. Then, with a decline of bunker price and an increase of port costs, the port, terminal and canal costs were 3.6 times that of fuel cost.[13]

What is the role of a port in the quality of shipping services?

One of the most important quality aspects of shipping services is transit time. In this regard, the length of time is only one element, the predictability of schedule is another. In many cases, slower shipping service with more reliable timekeeping is considered to be better than a faster service but with an inconsistent schedule. This is because unpredictability represents a commercial and operational risk to the stakeholders on the transport chain from shippers to shipping companies and ports. The risk is bigger if the transport is concerned with a global supply chain. A study reveals that, in some ports, the dwell time for cargo can be as long as 16 days on average.[14] Another study shows that for a Far East–Europe liner shipping service, about 21% of the total transit time was spent in ports. This means that about the same percentage, i.e., 21%, of all time-based costs, such as capital cost and crew cost, are also spent in port. Depending on the types of shipping, port costs contribute between a third and a half to the total shipping costs. And, more importantly, over 90% of the time lost due to schedule unreliability was attributable to ports, while weather and ship mechanical problems accounted for less than 6% of the reasons for unreliability.[15] Among the reasons for unreliability, the biggest is port congestion, which usually leads to long unexpected waiting time for ships and cargo. This is followed by the failure of the port in delivering the expected productivity performance.

Another important aspect of quality shipping is related to accidents. Maritime transport remains an activity with safety and environmental risks. Port is a place where many such accidents will happen. This is because ports often have a high density of ships. Many ports have restricted navigational waters and limitations in depth or width. The concentration of many ships of various sizes and types, sailing at different speeds, increases the chances of collisions. So, compared with the open seas, more safety and environmental accidents are likely to happen in the port areas. In Europe, out of a total of 1,460 cargo ship casualties and incidents recorded by EMSA in 2017, more than 50% of them happened in the port area when ships were anchored or alongside, on arrival or departure.[16] According to ITOPF, about 80% of oil spills are of less than 7 tons and 80% of such smaller spills happen in the port area from operational accidents during loading, discharging and bunkering.[17]

In conclusion, ports play a vital and decisive role in shipping, as shown in Figure 10.2. It is worth focussing on port operations for the effectiveness of cost and quality control at shipping companies. It is more frequent to experience unexpected costs from port operations rather than from ship operations. This is partly because as much as 90% of time losses due to schedule unreliability happen in ports. These losses may come from port congestion as well as technical, operational, safety and environment-related incidents in the port.

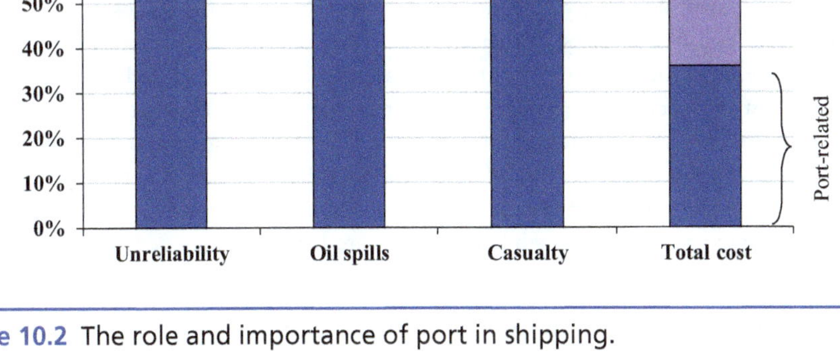

Figure 10.2 The role and importance of port in shipping.

Source: Shuo Ma, based on data from EMSA, ITOPF and other sources.

Note: about a third of shipping costs are port related, either as payment or time spent in port; more than a half of cargo ship casualties in Europe happen in the port area; about two thirds of all oil spill accidents happen in the port area; and about 90% of delays are port related.

10.4 Port operation and the development of ships

The importance of port for shipping operation and development can hardly be overestimated in the area of the ship's size and type or even in the way the entire shipping is operated. It is argued that the ship–shore interface has been the most critical element in the development of ships. In this section we concentrate on two aspects of ships, type and size, to examine what their relationship is with the ship–shore interface or the port operation.

Why is the specialisation of ships mostly driven by the port operation?

A question may be asked about whether ports follow ships or ships follow ports and the expected answer will be that ports follow and serve ships. However, when it comes to the types of ships, most of the specialised vessels are created as solutions to the problems of port operation. The transport of cargo by ships consists basically of two distinctive kinds of activities: getting the cargo on and off the ships and moving it from A to B. The costs involved in these activities are referred to as port cost and shipping cost respectively.

The relationship between ship type and shipping cost is quite different from that between ship type and port costs. While most shipping cost stays, by and large, constant between different types of ships, the port cost varies a lot from one ship type to another. The reasons are related mainly to the cargo for transport. Let's take a look at the shipping costs and port costs more closely.

- ***The shipping costs*** are the costs of transporting cargo by a ship and they consist primarily of capital cost, manning cost, insurance cost, maintenance cost, fuel cost and management cost. Among them, the capital cost will change between different types of ship in most cases. For instance, a crude oil tanker ship will cost less to build than a LNG carrier of a similar size and the price of a roll-on roll-off vessel is very different than that of a bulk carrier of the same tonnage. But the variations of other shipping costs are much more limited or, in many cases, they are negligible between different types of ships. For example, the crew structure and size are similar for all types of ships. Though some special requirements may exist regarding the training and qualification of the crew, the manning costs do not differ much between the types of ships. When it comes to insurance and maintenance costs, the cost differences are also rather moderate. The fuel cost is not a cost affected by the type of ships. So, on the whole, the effect of ship type on shipping cost is limited.
- ***The port costs*** include two parts, those related to vessels and those related to cargo. As far as the type of ship is concerned, the ship-related costs can be considered as mostly fixed, though some additional cost may occur, for example, on navigational safety. But when it comes to the cargo-related port costs, the situation is very different. The costs are for cargo handling and storage operations. Obviously, different types of cargo are often handled in different ways and with different equipment incurring different levels of cost. For example, containerised cargo is handled with ship-to-shore gantry cranes, while oil and gas are handled and stored using totally different facilities.

Based on the above discussion, what is a very important point to observe is that it is not the shipping operation, but rather the port operation, or more precisely the cargo handling, that is the cause of the specialisation of ships. This is because the transporting by ship of different cargo does not necessarily lead to much significant differentiation in operation and cost. So, for a long time, multi-purpose general cargo ships were the sole type of commercial vessels. But, as the diversity and volume of seaborne trade increased, the situation became more challenging at the port rather than on the sea. One of the most critical operations was loading and unloading of cargo on and off ships. Given the physical specifications and constraints of the ships and ship- or shore-based lifting equipment, cargoes could only be handled in small lots. The cargo-handling operation was expensive and time-consuming. It also prevented the ships from being large. So there was an incentive to increase cargo-handling productivity by using dedicated terminals with specialised equipment. Consequently, new types of ship emerged. The ro-ro ships provide probably the best example in this regard. Vehicles can certainly be lifted on and off ships, but it is slow, expensive and exposed to more damages. So "roll-on roll-off" is the solution. Such ship specialisation only saves port cost because, no matter how the goods are loaded and discharged, there is no difference in the shipping cost. Improving cargo-handling productivity at the port has been the same motivation for building bulk carriers and container ships.

Figure 10.3 illustrates the fact that the differentiation of various types of ships is more apparent and reflected in cargo-handling operations at the port. Specialised ships lead not only to higher productivity in port operations but also to the improvement in ship space utilisation. Nonetheless, the essential functions of the vessel at sea, such as the navigation or propulsion systems, remain by and large the same regardless of the ship's type. On the other hand, cargo-handling method in ports varies a lot for different types of ships. So, cargo handling or the interface between ship and shore is the main driving force for ship specialisation.

Why is the effect of the ship's size different for shipping costs and port costs?

If the specialisation of ships has been to a considerable extent driven by the need for more efficient port operations, cargo handling at ports has also played a decisive role in ship size. The time needed for ship berthing varies a lot between a river port and a seaport, a port with locks and a port without locks. But it is cargo handling that takes most of the time a ship spends at a port. For example, a conventional general cargo ship carrying bagged cargo can only be loaded or discharged at a rate of about 250–300 tons per day per ship's hole. Even when working at four holes of the ship simultaneously, the typical cargo-handling rate will be in the region of 1,000 tons per day. A ship with 10,000 tons of cargo will spend ten days to discharge the cargo and probably another ten days to load the backhaul cargo. Such a cargo-handling rate prevents the ships from being large as the ratio of sailing time to port time will be out of proportion, which makes big ships uneconomical to operate.

The total cost of shipping can be divided in different ways depending on the purpose of analysis. If the size of ships is a variable factor, we can examine the impact of ship size changes on the shipping cost and port cost. In order to do this, the shipping cost should be divided into two categories: the costs for ship and cargo at sea and the costs for ship and cargo in the port. So let's look at the two types of cost in more detail.

- ***Costs for ship and cargo at sea.*** These costs have two parts. The first is related to operations. It includes all the expenditures for a shipping company during the time the ship is sailing at sea. They include, for example, capital cost, manning cost, fuel cost and insurance cost. As far as cargo is concerned, the operation-related expenses at sea are not significant because at sea very limited services are needed for cargo. The second part of the costs incurred to ship and cargo at sea is related to time. The expenditures are primarily on the capital cost of the ship, the equipment such as containers and the cargo. The capital cost is mainly affected by three factors: the length of the time spent at sea, the applicable interest rate and the value of the ship and cargo.
- ***Costs for ship and cargo in ports.*** In the same way as the costs at sea, the costs in port also have two parts, one of which is related to operations and the other is related to time. As far as the operation-related costs are concerned, they are paid by shipping companies or cargo interests during the time in the port. The expenditures include port dues for ships, payments for navigational services, cargo-handling charges, etc. When it comes to the time-related costs in port, similar to the

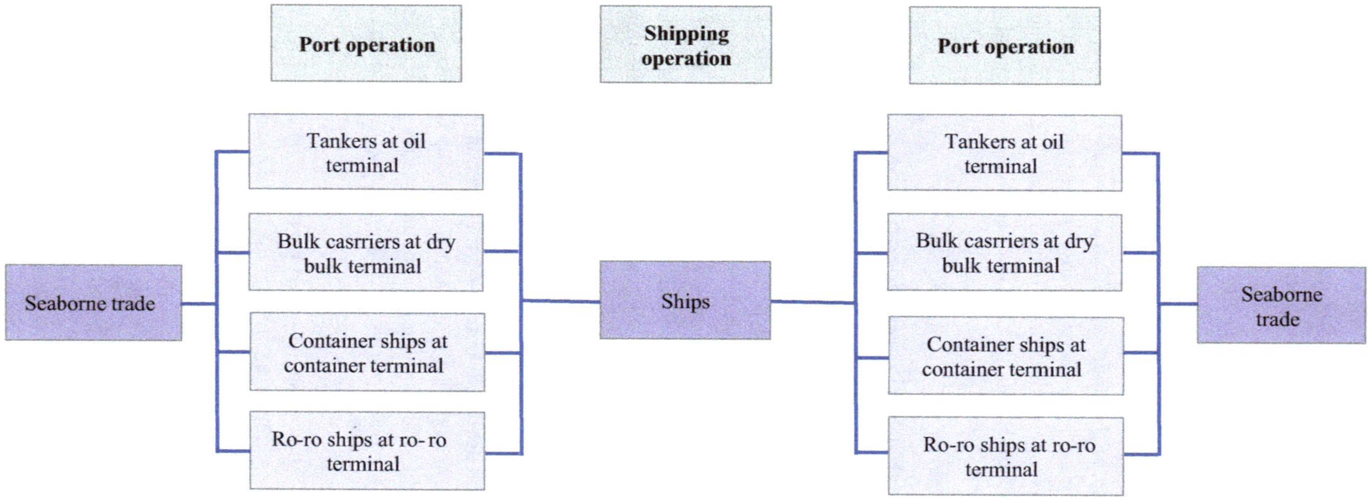

Figure 10.3 Cargo handling at the port as the driving force for ship specialisation and operational differentiation.

Source: Shuo Ma.

Note: from navigation and propulsion points of view, the differences are limited between types of ships. Ships are specialised to save costs from cargo handling in ports.

situation at sea, it is about the capital costs of the ship, equipment and of the cargo incurred during the time in port. At a given value of the ship and cargo and the level of the applicable interest rates, this cost depends on the amount of time spent in the port.

When the size of ships increases, both the costs at sea and the costs in port are directly affected. However, they do not change in the same way. There are two fundamental differences between the reactions of these two costs to the changes in the ship's size. Figure 10.4 illustrates such differences through an example of a given market between two ports for a type of cargo and of ships ranging from 10,000 to 90,000 dwt. Taking the costs for a ship of 10,000 dwt as 100, we can see the differences between the ways the two costs, those at sea and those in port, change when the ship's size increases. We make two observations. The first is that the costs at sea change much less than the costs in port. The second is that the two costs change in opposite directions. As the ship's size increases, there are economies of scale for the unit cost at sea and diseconomies of scale for the unit cost in port.

- ***The unit cost at sea and the ship's size are negatively correlated.*** When ships become larger, up to a point, the unit cost of transport will be lower. By unit cost, we refer to the total transport cost at sea per ton of cargo, or per unit of carrying capacity such as dwt or teu. This is because most shipping costs are either fixed to the ship's size or increase to a lesser extent when ships become bigger. For example, the costs such as manning cost are by and large fixed regardless of the ship's size. When ship size increases, other costs such as capital cost, fuel cost, etc., increase more slowly and disproportionally. There is a strong effect of scale economies concerning the shipping cost at sea. As discussed previously, the economies of scale in shipping cost has been the major driving force for the continuous increase in the average size of the world fleet and for the massive improvement in labour productivity.

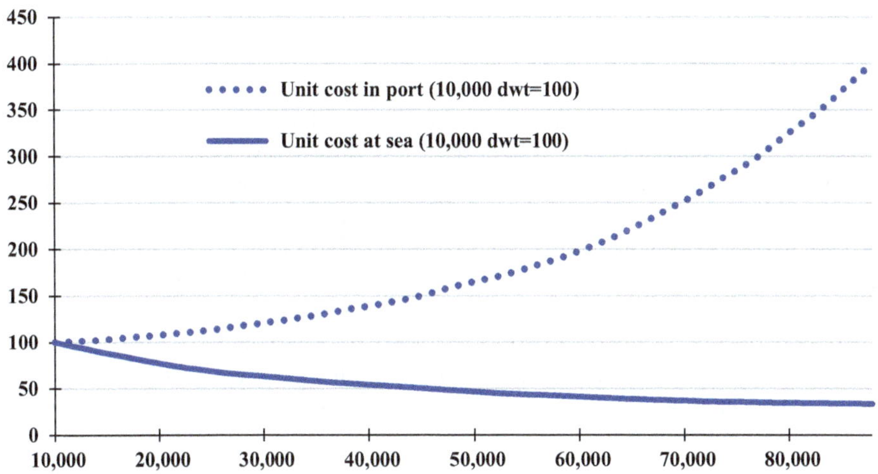

Figure 10.4 Economies of scale at sea vs. diseconomies of scale in port (ship of 10,000 dwt = 100).

Source: Shuo Ma, calculated based on various sources.

Note: the figure shows that, when ship's size increases, there is an effect of scale economics for cost at sea, but an effect of scale diseconomies for cost in port. The level of the cost is affected by numerous factors.

- ***The unit cost in port and the ship's size are positively correlated.*** The effect of changes in the ship's size on the cost in port is different. Contrary to the cost at sea, for the cost in port there is an effect of diseconomies of scale when the ship size increases. When the ship is bigger, more cargo can be loaded. However, almost all operation-related and time-related costs are variable when the size of the ship increases. The cargo-handling cost changes proportionally with the amount of cargo handled. Another major difference is about time cost. While the transport time at sea is not affected by the amount of cargo loaded on board ship, the time in port is directly and almost proportionally affected by the amount of cargo loaded. As explained above, 20 days would be needed to load and discharge 10,000 tons of breakbulk cargo carried by a conventional general cargo ship. Such a long time in port generates a very high time-related cost to both ship and cargo.

Why is cargo-handling productivity one of the decisive factors for the ship's size?

The specialisation of cargo-handling operation at ports has revolutionised the shipping industry by massively increasing cargo-handling speed. At a dedicated container terminal, a ship-to-shore gantry crane can move, in normal circumstances, 25 containers per hour. A big container vessel can be served simultaneously by several cranes, which combined can handle 100 or more containers per hour per ship. Supposing the containers are a mix of 20-footer and 40-footers with an average weight of 15 tons, then about 1,500 tons of cargo can be loaded or discharged per hour. With 16 working hours a day, the daily output will be 19,000 tons. This is almost 20 times more productive than a conventional vessel. In some big ports, a much higher productivity can be achieved. In the port of Singapore for example, as many as 300 containers per hour per ship can be loaded or unloaded, which represents 4,500 tons per hour.[18] With 20 working hours per day, 90,000 tons of cargo can be loaded or discharged per day. Increasingly large gantry cranes capable of moving two fully loaded 40-foot containers are installed in big container ports. Such equipment leads to a further increase in cargo-handling speed. A dry bulk terminal with specialised equipment can unload as quickly as 10,000 tons of iron ore per hour and the loading of dry bulk cargo normally takes even less time. Coal and especially grain, transported in smaller bulk carriers, generally need more time for cargo handling. At a specialised oil terminal, the cargo-handling rate can reach 100,000 tons of crude oil per day or even higher.

By examining what has happened in the shipping industry during the last half century, one realises that many new technological innovations have taken place in the area of port rather than sea. Or, in other words, the new methods introduced are often to improve cargo- handling operations rather than transport activities. Containerisation was invented originally to speed up cargo handling at ports and was not intended to improve navigation or ships themselves. Ro-ro technology did not really change the method of sea transportation, but it did bring profound changes to port operations. Similarly, the transport cost of primary materials has been dramatically decreasing due to the use of large tankers and bulk carriers. But this was possible only when efficient cargo handling at ports was in place with specialised facilities and equipment.

Cargo-handling speed is one of the critical constraints on the increase of ship size. The biggest ships usually are defined by the highest cargo-handling rates achievable at the ports to which the ships are deployed. We can see this effect in Figure 10.5. This shows a sample set of ten types of vessels based on the fastest cargo discharging rate and the largest ships available in the market. The two variables, cargo-handling speed at port and ship size, are positively correlated. Based on Figure 10.5, the changes in ship size are 77% explained by the changes in cargo-discharging rate. There is a close relationship between the average cargo-handling speed and the optimal size of ships. The container shipping industry has consequently always been working hard to increase the speed and productivity of port operations because people understand that port is source number one of all the delays and uncertainties in

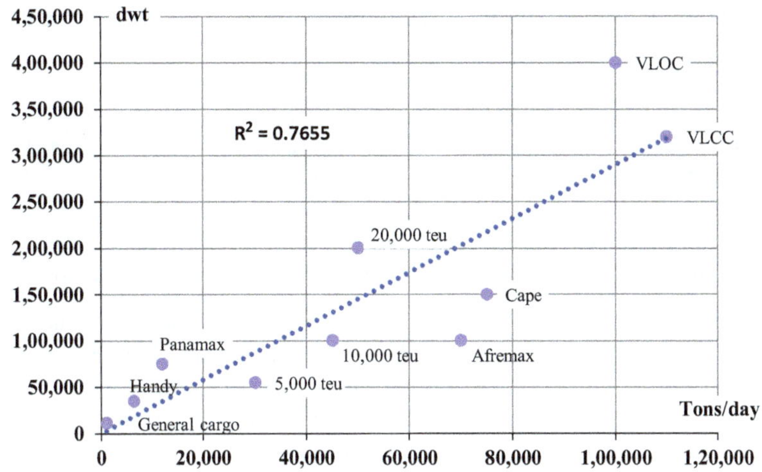

Figure 10.5 Correlation between cargo-handling speed and ship size.

Source: Shuo Ma, based on various sources.

Note: the samples taken represent ten types of ships based on the highest unloading cargo-handling rate per day and the largest vessel size in dwt.

liner shipping operations. Higher cargo-handling speed requires specialised and dedicated terminals with ample space for storage. The concept of general berth and quay has given way to that of specialised terminals, which include not only the waterfront but also vast landside areas.

While port specialisation proves to be highly beneficial, one has to be fully aware of the drawbacks of it. Two disadvantages can be mentioned about specialised cargo handling at ports. The first is the lack of flexibility. The specialisation is the opposite of multipurpose. A dedicated container terminal can handle only containers, often nothing else. As a result, specialised terminals are much riskier commercially than, say, multipurpose berths. The second is the high investment requirement in the areas of infrastructure, superstructures such as specialised equipment, as well as operational expertise and skills. But when the volume of trade increases to a high level, specialisation is an inevitable development direction for ports. Usually, the long-term benefits are several times greater than the cost related to higher risks.

10.5 Evolutions of ports

Over the years, ports evolve together with their internal and external environment and changes. The port sector readjusts itself continuously when economic and technical conditions develop. Broadly, there are the following three main types of port evolutions. The first is business or commercial evolution, which is about the change of basic port functions and services; the second is spatial evolution, which refers to the changes of the geographical dimension of ports and their operations; the third is social-technological evolution, which is about the changes in the relationship between people and capital or, in other words, between man and machine. The first evolution is on the issue of *what* activities a port does, the second evolution is about the issue of *where* a port does its activities and the third evolution is on the issue of *how* a port does its activities.

What are the changes in port business – the commercial evolution of ports?

We have explained the basic functions of a port in this chapter, such as providing ships with safe berthing and cargo-handling services. Over the years, port activities have evolved and expanded from these basic functions. Although the core of port functions has not changed, the development of international trade and maritime transport require more activities to be offered by the port. Such new functions are mainly in two categories, both related to cargo: one is cargo processing and the other is cargo distribution. The commercial function of ports has evolved over three phases or generations.[19]

- Traditionally, ports are only considered as an interface between sea and land for import and export goods. As such, cargoes are loaded onto and discharged from the ships once they arrive at the port. The cargo, once unloaded, should leave the port as soon as possible. Many of such cargoes are then processed in factories located inland. However, for two reasons, a port is a better place for such cargo-processing activities to take place. One is about cargo concentration. This means that, due to maritime transport, ports are the place to have the highest concentration of cargo along the entire transport chain. In order to benefit from the effect of scale economies, ports are therefore ideal places for some cargo processing and transformation activities to take place. Activities such as oil refinery or steel mills are examples. The other reason is about re-export activities. Export-processing industries are those activities generating a good income for the country by combining internal factors such as land, labour, energy, etc., with external elements such as materials, capital and market. Ports are the places with the shortest transport and lowest logistics costs for the combination.
- The development of the global supply chain requires regional distribution centres to be established for semi-finished and finished products. Such centres should be located in places where cargo is concentrated before being distributed both pre- and post-maritime transport. Naturally, ports are expected to play the role as a distribution hub and logistics platform. Most internationally traded cargoes, particularly containerised goods, are distributed after being discharged from ships. Ports are often the places with the most stakeholders of global supply chains. These include shipping companies, shipping agents, brokers, shippers, freight forwarders, banks, law firms, customs offices and many others. The concentration of such organisations provides a favourable environment for logistics and cargo distribution activities from and to the hinterland. Cargo processing and cargo distribution activities are not necessarily dependent on each other, but they may well be interrelated and support each other. Such logistics and distribution activities will attract more ships and cargo and strengthen the position of the port in the region.

From the value-added point of view, the new roles of ports and the expanding port activities beyond the traditional functions are highly beneficial for the port as a whole. This is because, by taking the business previously done by others outside the port area, the port expands its share in the total cargo value chain or supply chain. However, there are two points worth mentioning. The first is about the core and additional activities. Though the new roles of ports in the areas of cargo transformation or cargo distribution have drawn much attention recently, the core activities of a port have not changed and these are to provide services to ships and the loading/unloading of cargo. A port is called a port because of these activities. So cargo transformation or distribution will not be the core business. They are supplementary and additional services to the core activities. The second point is about the port and port community. A port is much harder to define than a shipping company. Unlike a shipping company, a port usually consists of many entities, private as well as public, which are often independent of each other. The port authority may well be the representative of a port. But the stevedoring company at the port may be a totally separate private entity responsible for cargo handling and other activities. The services to ships, such as bunkering, may again be provided by different companies. When it comes to the activities of cargo transformation and distribution, independent firms like, for example, oil companies or freight forwarders, are responsible. Together with all other stakeholders, all these organisations form a port community. So, similarly, the port stakeholders can also be divided into the core, which is the port authority and cargo-handling firms, and other members that have a close relationship with the port, such as bunkering and cargo processing activities. A port community also includes those entities with a looser and partial relationship with the port such as forwarders or banks.

Where do ports undertake the activities – the spatial evolution of ports?

The increased seaborne trade has led to the specialisation of ships and a continued increase in the ship's size. As a consequence, more specialised terminals are built to handle specific ships and cargo. And for such dedicated terminals more space is needed to accommodate the growing amount of cargo to and from large vessels. Additional warehouses and yards are required with often bulkier cargo handling and transfer equipment. Ports, as a result, expand either inland by occupying more space from the city or foreland by reclaiming land from the sea.

However, very soon, the port and the city find themselves in a competition for space, either land, coast or riverside. As a result, it is always the port that has to relocate. This situation is seen in many cities such as Shanghai and London. Today the commercial and residential area called "Docklands" in the east of London used to be part of the largest port in the world, the port of London. From the 1960s, the lack of space and water depth needed by large vessels, in particular container vessels, drove the port to move downstream to Tilbury and then to Felixstowe. By the 1980s, all of the docks were closed and the space of the old port of London was converted and redeveloped for commercial and residential uses. A similar story is repeated in other places too and it became a worldwide trend in ports from Asia and Africa to America and Europe. For example, the new terminals of the Port of Rotterdam or Antwerp are all built downstream towards the river mouth. In Shanghai, in order to accommodate new generations of large container ships, a huge container port was built 32 kilometres offshore on an island linked to the mainland by a bridge.

Ports of the world almost always carry the name of the city in which they are located. So we have the port of Mombasa, the port of Yokohama or the port of New York. Even though there is a tendency of ports moving away from city centres, a port is still a part of the city. This is one of the biggest differences between shipping and ports. Shipping is global and mobile in the sense that ships can go wherever the business is. But this is not the case for ports. Ports are local, immobile and cannot move their locations. Unlike a shipping company whose business does not necessarily depend on the economy of a particular place, the rise and fall of a port is very much determined by the economic situation of the port city and its hinterland. This situation started to change from the 1980s with the emergence of "international port operators", mostly in the container terminal sector. The basic game changer is the movement of institutional reforms in the port sector from the 1980s. The background of such changes is the effort of many governments to improve the efficiency of the port sector by way of deregulation, commercialisation and privatisation. Many countries have transferred port governance from the operating port system to the landlord port system. Port operations have not only been separated from port administration, but they are also carried out by professional port operators, including foreign-owned firms. As a result, an Asian port operator can take over a business on long-term concession in a European port. PSA of Singapore, Hutchison Whampoa of Hong Kong or DP World of Dubai, for example, have now expanded beyond their homeports to become global port operators with a global rather than local business scope. At the same time, many leading shipping lines have also entered the global container port terminal market.

How do ports undertake their activities – the social/technological evolution of ports?

Over the last half a century, the social aspects of ports have changed a lot for almost the same reason that has driven the commercial and spatial changes as discussed above, which is specialisation. Ports used to be a highly labour-intensive sector. This was because of the old fashioned cargo-handling operations at ports. When most merchant ships were multipurpose general cargo ships, which was the case before World War Two in many countries, cargo-handling equipment was simple and with limited capacity. Many ports did not even have shore-based cranes so cargo had to be loaded and discharged using ship's own derricks with typically small lifting capacity. Dockworkers were needed in big numbers on board ships as well as on shore. The transfer of cargo to and from the waterfront as well as in warehouses involved a lot of manual work. So it was common that a medium-sized port would have tens of thousands of port workers, either full time or casual. This is an important reason for the very close relationship between the port and city. Often, the port was one of the biggest job providers of the city.

The introduction of modern cargo-handling methods and equipment and the specialisation of ships happened at the same time. Dedicated terminals with specialised cargo-handling equipment had a significant impact on port labour, both qualitatively and quantitatively. The nature of the work changed from many manual porters to fewer crane operators and trailer or forklift drivers. More education and training are needed for dock workers to have the necessary skills. At the same time, using modern equipment, many fewer workers are required. For example, the number of port workers was massively reduced after the containerisation of general cargo transport. The substitution of port workers for more productive equipment has never stopped. This started in the Port of Rotterdam's ECT, where the first automated container terminal was built in the 1990s, and more and more ports have transformed port operation with automation. As a result, the port labour force is much reduced. For example, in one of the latest automated container terminals, the labour force was reduced by 85%. The terminal, capable of handling 2 million teus per year, requires only nine people.[20]

These dual effects, the need for more space due to the continuous increase in ship's size on the one hand and the introduction of more and more efficient work methods and equipment on the other hand, have led to a detachment of ports from cities. More and more cargo terminals have been moving downstream to the seaside. The physical separation of ports and cities is coupled with a reduction of the social interdependence between the port and the city, although the economic ties between them remain strong. With the new wave of the digital revolution driven by the application of digital technologies such as artificial intelligence and automation, the social and technological transformation of the port sector will certainly continue. The three directions of port evolution, commercial, spatial and techno-social, are summarised in Table 10.1.

10.6 Port competition

Port competition was not a major concern for most ports in the past. This is because the majority of the cargo of either import or export was for the city or the surrounding region. Ports were mostly apart from each other geographically and land transport was expensive and time-consuming. In the 1980s the situation started to change. Containerisation improved the transport efficiency on both the landside and the seaside. As every port's hinterland expanded, there was more competition between ports when their hinterlands overlapped. The liberalisation and institutional reforms in the port sector around the world require the ports to be more financially self-reliant and commercially viable. As a result, the notion of competition emerged in the port sector. In this section we will discuss the five main types of port competition: inter-port competition, intra-port competition, competition with other modes of transport than maritime transport, competition on supply chains and competition for value-added.

Table 10.1 Three directions of port evolution: commercial, spatial and techno/social.

Port evolution	*Past*	*Present*	*Future*
WHAT a port does – commercial evolution	Navigation/cargo-handling services	Navigation/cargo handling and cargo processing/ distribution	Navigation/cargo handling and cargo processing/ distribution
WHERE a port does it – spatial evolution	City centre	Downstream and seaside	Seaside and off-shore, away from city centre
HOW a port does it – techno/social evolution	Labour-intensive, close city–port relation	Specialised terminal with fewer and more skilful workers	Automated terminal with very few people

Source: Shuo Ma.

Note: commercially, a port evolves to do cargo processing and distribution; spatially, ports move away from city centres for more space and easy access from sea; techno/socially, future ports will be automated with very few people and a looser social relationship with city.

What are a port's hinterland and competition between ports?

A cargo inland finding itself between two ports may use either one. If both ports wish to have the cargo, they are in competition. Inter-port competition is the most common kind of port competition, when ports grow with more capacities and when ports have become more business-oriented commercial entities, maintaining the existing businesses may not be enough and developing new activities is often the objective of the organisations. Such new activities may well come either from the existing business of other ports which share the same hinterland or from new activities in which all ports serving the same hinterland are interested.

Port hinterland does not have a simple definition. It can be defined administratively by drawing lines along national or regional borders or defined geographically by mountains or rivers. One can also define it by dimensions in square kilometres of diameter from the port. But the most appropriate and accurate definition is "economic" hinterland. Theoretically, a port can have a hinterland as far as the land extends. But we usually do not call the San Diego area in southern California as the hinterland of the port of Seattle for containerised goods as it would not make economic sense. It is not because the distance is too far but, instead, because there are other ports that are better located to service the area. So economic hinterland is a relative notion which should be defined as a total cost comparison between competing ports. This means that, if an island has a single port, the whole island is the hinterland of the port. But if it has two ports, then the island is divided into two hinterlands, one for each port. However, the size of each hinterland is neither fixed for all cargoes nor for all time.

The way in which the hinterlands are divided between ports is very complex. Apart from distance, transport conditions, types of cargo, port situation, shipping services, safety, security and environmental performances, etc., are all factors. The service quality issues are among the main decisive factors for defining the hinterland of a port. Distance is not the most relevant factor when transport conditions and costs differ so much between any two points at the same distance. The existence of a navigable river, a railway link or a highway can extend the hinterland of a port farther up to a place close to a rival port which does not have the same transport conditions. High-value cargo certainly prefers a speedier transit such as a highway to a cheaper but slower river transport alternative to a competing port. A special cargo may choose a more distant port for reasons such as specific services at ports or better shipping connections. An improvement in either service quality or cost or both at a port will extend its hinterland further, provided the competing ports do not also improve. Similarly, a rise in cost or a drop in quality will reduce the port's hinterland. The above factors, combined, will determine the total cost, including time cost, and quality of service for the cargo to use the port, which in turn determines a port's hinterland.

When a port has an absolute total cost advantage over other ports for the areas very close to it, these areas are called the port's "captive" hinterland. Between two ports, the borders of the hinterland are where the cost for cargo to use either port is the same. Of course, the borders are not clear cut lines, but rather a zone or a broader region for which the cost differences between using the two ports are insignificant. The competing ports' hinterland overlaps. Such areas are called common hinterland or contestable hinterland, like central Europe for the competing western European ports from Le Havre to Hamburg or a landlocked country like Mali for the West African ports from Dakar to Lagos. So, as the influential factors are not static for a port, its hinterland is always a dynamic concept.

The focus of the inter-port competition is on ship and cargo traffic and it is done by offering services with extra value to customers. Such extra value takes the form of either cheaper cost or better quality for the services offered to ships and cargo. The value a port provides is the value-added to the cargo after port services. Thanks to port service, a shipping company can earn freight incomes and cargoes can be sold in the market. However, for a port, its competitiveness does not depend entirely on the factors under its own control. Let's look at the two sources of port competitiveness as follows.

- ***The internal sources of competitiveness.*** These sources, which are in a port's control, include the physical conditions such as water depth, quay length, yard space, facilities and equipment, sea access, etc. They also include the costs, i.e., the structure and level of prices. They include operational efficiency, for example port turnaround time, the types and quality of services provided and other aspects such as safety, security and environmental performance.
- The external sources of competitiveness. These sources, which are out of a port's control, include the general economic situation of the city, region and hinterland, the government port-related policies, the services of shipping companies and agents, logistics and land transport services, transport infrastructure and services, customs and administrative services. Some of these will be discussed further below.

It is difficult to indicate precisely the relative importance of each source for a port's competitiveness. Because, in a similar external environment, there are situations in which significant differences exist in terms of competitiveness between neighbouring ports. While we can also find cases where a port attracts or loses traffic and customers purely due to changes that are out of the port's own control. However, the large size and robust growth of seaborne trade in the hinterland are indeed determining factors and prerequisites for being a competitive port.

What are the advantages and disadvantages of the competition within a port?

As we discussed above, a port is not one organisation but a mix of many independent organisations. Within a port, the same kinds of services may be provided by more than one operator. Competition may exist between operators in the same port. Such services include cargo handling, storage and warehousing, pilotage or tugboat services. In the port of Hong Kong, for example, different container terminals compete for cargo and shipping lines. In a typical "landlord" port, any of the above services may be offered by different companies, even international ones. For users, such kinds of intra-port competition and, as a result, more choice, are welcome. The biggest constraint on intra-port competition lies in the division of business sizes. With increasingly more specialised port operations, most of the activities, from cargo handling to warehousing, have an optimal size of operation which is much bigger than in the past. Related to this, inter-port competition has intensified globally because of the containerisation of liner shipping and liberalisation of the port sector. The pressure on cost has led port operators to explore more benefits from scale economies by business consolidation. Consequently, we see more mergers or acquisitions and less intra-port competition, even at some very big ports.[21]

Today, large shipping lines are increasingly interested in direct involvement in container terminal operation activities. The Maersk Line of Denmark, Mediterranean Shipping Corporation of Switzerland, CMA-CGM of France or COSCO Shipping of China all have substantial businesses in terminal operations in many ports all over the world. In large ports, container terminals may be leased on concession to shipping lines for exclusive usage. This may be extended to the liner shipping alliances, each of which includes several liner companies. It may not be seen as traditional intra-port competition for traffic because the leased terminals are for exclusive use only, while the terminals run by the port operators are common user facilities. Most ports do this for the reason of attracting or maintaining the shipping lines to the port.

How is a port affected by the competition between modes of transport?

As an integral part of shipping, ports are affected by competition between maritime transport and other modes of transport. During the 20th century, the land transport infrastructure in Europe, Japan and North America improved tremendously. At the same time, the rising living standard stimulated the mass production of vehicles, as well as modern organisation and management of land transport systems, in these countries too. The fast development of land transport by road and rail represented severe competition for maritime transport. Such a trend has expanded to other regions as well. For example, the volume of containerised cargo transported by train between China and Europe increased from 114,000 tons in 2013 to more than 510,000 tons in 2016.[22] This cargo, although small compared with about 52 million tons of seaborne trade between China and Europe in 2016, is a loss of business for both shipping and ports. In many places, e.g., the UK, the US or Western Europe, coastal shipping has lost market share due to competition from road and, to a lesser extent, rail transport. Pipelines are competition for shipping and ports with regard to the trade of oil and gas. Air transport competes with sea transport for high-value cargo over long distances.

The overwhelming strength of shipping is in its low-cost transport of a large quantity of cargo over a long distance across oceans. But shipping has also a number of weaknesses in comparison with other modes of transport. If the competition is from road or rail, then maritime transport loses mainly on the following two aspects, speed and flexibility, though both have connections with ports.

- ***The slow speed***. Although oil tankers or dry bulk carriers have slow speed, container vessels may travel at 25 nautical miles per hour or about 46 km per hour. This is approximately half of the speed of a truck or a freight train. The slowness of shipping is not only about the sailing speed, it is also about the time in port. As ships load more cargo than either rail or road, it takes a longer time for loading and unloading. It is also more time-consuming preparing ships for cargo handling. As longer time is costly for high-value cargo, so maritime transport is more suitable for low-value goods for long-distance transport which is less sensitive to time and more sensitive to cost.
- ***The lack of flexibility***. Ships can only reach as far as where ports are. But ports are usually not the origins or destinations of the cargo. While trains, trucks or pipelines can reach the origin or destination of the cargo, ships cannot. So it is almost impossible to have door-to-door transport by

using ships only. Therefore, despite the high cost of road transport, the total transport cost is often still lower when the cost of more cargo handling and extra time spent are taken into consideration. This is one of the main reasons for cargo to turn to land transport, especially for the transport of general cargo over a short distance. Another weakness is about risks. Because of long distances and much bigger volume, the maritime transport services are less frequent and more vulnerable when it comes to reliability.

What is the position of ports in the competition between supply chains?

Ports are not only a part of the transport system, they are also a part of international supply chains. So, when different supply chains are in competition, ports will take the consequences. The once-leading ports in the world, such as Venice, lost to the competition from new ports, such as Amsterdam, not necessarily because of any pure port-related factors. Their decline had more to do with the change of the international supply chain. A similar situation has been happening almost all the time. The port of Kaohsiung of Taiwan was among the top five container ports in the world in the 1990s. But, as a result of the competition of global supply chains, Kaohsiung port experienced a continuous decline of traffic. The competition between North American ports provides another case in point. The development of the East Coast ports, such as New York-New Jersey, is less affected by the competition between ports than by the competition between supply chains. It loses to the West Coast ports, like Los Angeles, because the supply chain, of which the West Coast ports are a part, prevailed.

So, to some extent, the competitiveness of so many Chinese ports is attributable more to the success in the competition between global supply chains than to the performance of the ports. Of course, excellent port services are also important for the success of a supply chain. In this sense, the fate of the ports is not always in the hands of the ports themselves. This is because ports, unlike ships, are not mobile. Ports have a passive position and they usually take the consequences of the competition between supply chains, despite the fact that their role is indispensable in global supply chains. The opening of the new Panama Canal has strengthened the competitiveness of the supply chain for Asian exports to the US via the ports of the East coast such as New York-New Jersey. Likewise, the moving of some manufacturing activities from the Far East to South Asia will benefit the port of New York-New Jersey which is a part of the global supply chain from South Asia to North America via the Suez Canal.

How is a port affected by the competition for value-added?

The commercial evolution of ports discussed earlier in this chapter reflects the business expansion of ports by doing more than the basic activities of navigational services to ships and loading/discharging services to cargo. But such development is at the expense of other contributors in the value chain. For example, the processing, distribution and logistics services of import and export cargo are traditionally done outside the port by other companies. If port companies start to take such activities from others, it is a competition for value-added. From the origin to the final destination, value is created and added to the product by various economic activities. These include product processing and manufacturing as well as transport and logistics. The total value added is the price of the final product and the whole process is called a product value chain. On the value chain, firms, such as logistics companies, shipping lines and ports, compete for a bigger portion of the total value added by doing more activities.

Shipping companies are the main customers of ports. But, at the same time, shipping and ports can be potential rivals as well because both of them are on the same value chain. Apart from some big cargo owners who operate both shipping and port activities for their own interests, common-user shipping companies and public ports concentrated on their own business and cooperated closely. But such a situation started to change in the 1980s for two reasons. On shipping's side, continuous consolidation of the container shipping business resulted in some mega shipping lines; on the port's side, commercialisation and privatisation opened a door for outsiders to get into port businesses. For example, the port of Singapore, one of the world's biggest container ports, and Maersk Line of Denmark, one of the world's leading container lines, were close business partners for many years with Maersk contributing about 10% of the annual container traffic of the port of Singapore in the late 1990s. Then, on 18 August 2000, Maersk Line announced that the transhipment business of the company would move to a terminal operated by themselves in a Malaysian port 27 miles north of Singapore in which Maersk Line had a 30% stake.

It is generally believed that the competition in the shipping sector is much tougher and more intense than that in the port sector. This is because shipping competition is global while port competition is local, restricted to the region. The barriers for customers to shift between competitors are usually lower in shipping than in ports. Consequently, in most cases, the marginal value added is bigger in ports than in shipping. A study by researchers from the National University of Singapore and the Georgia Institute of Technology revealed that the profit margin was at least four times higher in container terminal operation than in container ship operation.[23] So, as it was not possible to operate a terminal of its own in Singapore, Maersk Line went to a Malaysian port which offered such a possibility. Driven by the deterioration of the freight market in the wake of the 2008 financial crisis, shipping lines tried to save cost by a consolidation. By the end of 2017, for example, the top six shipping lines had a combined market share of more than 67.8% of the world's total container terminal capacity in teu.[24] The biggest shipping lines, which controlled almost the entire world liner shipping market, were operating in three super powerful alliances. Such alliances are capable of reducing their port cost sensibly by squeezing the value-added margin of the ports.[25] The effect of the reinforced competition for value-added from the shipping lines on ports led to the situation that, under the pressure from a few large and strong liner shipping alliances, service contracts had to be renegotiated. As a result, many ports experienced, simultaneously, an increase in the volume of traffic and a decline in revenue.[26]

In the competition for value-added, ports have a few advantages but, at the same time, some disadvantages. One of the advantages of a port is that it is the place with the biggest concentration of cargo in the supply chain. However, ports are not in a position to control trade and transport. Financially, shipping companies and logistics service providers are usually more powerful than ports. To build a container terminal may cost less than to build a big container ship. Technically, to operate a port terminal is usually less complex than to run a shipping company. As a result, many shipping companies get into port activities but it is rare to see ports offering shipping services.

We can summarise, in Table 10.2, the five types of port competition. They have different objectives and in each case the competitors are different too. But port service efficiency remains the most essential source of port competitiveness.

Why is government policy important for port competition?

Port competition is sometimes subject to government regulations and policy. When port services were considered as pure public goods with little consideration for commercial objectives, competition might sound an incompatible and irrelevant concept. Port services should simply be made available when ships and cargo come. New port facilities would be built often by the public authority when the existing ones have become inadequate and the port has become congested. So, when such a policy changed, the competition began to become increasingly an important preoccupation of port managers.

Table 10.2 Five types of port competition – objectives and competitors.

Port competition	*Objectives*	*Competitors*
Inter-port competition	To increase business share in the market	Other ports sharing same hinterland
Intra-port competition	To increase business share within the port	Other operators in the port
Transport modal competition	To increase shipping share in total transport	Road, rail, river, pipeline and air transport
Supply chain competition	To be in more global supply chains	Other supply chains the port is not in
Value-added competition	To increase share in the product value-added chain	Other providers of value-added activities

Source: Shuo Ma.

Note: a port can compete alone, such as inter- and intra-port competitions. It can also compete together with shipping companies, such as competition between transport modes. Port efficiency is always a determining factor for every type of competition, though location is also a critical factor for supply chain competition.

When talking about port competition, the free choice of ports by cargo is an important issue. Apart from physical access to ports such as the availability of transport, access may be restricted by government regulations. Even a cargo in the immediate hinterland may not have free access to use the port simply because the cargo and the port are in different countries or sometimes in different administrative regions. In some places where some relatively small-sized countries are sharing the coastline, competition between ports may be conditioned by the policies of the countries concerned. Today, most countries do not specifically impose restrictive rules to prevent cargo of the country from using particular ports.

True port competition should be free of any public intervention on the commercial decisions of the port. It is, however, not rare that such intervention exists in some areas such as the pricing of port services or decisions on employment. The justification for such intervention is often related to the port facilities as public goods and social externalities. Not only is coastline usually owned by the state and in short supply but also the construction of port facilities often benefits from public funds. So the government does not want to see that the rise in prices of port services hurts trade and the economy. And with public money invested, they also want the port to be a stable employer of the local community.

10.7 The pricing for port service

The pricing of port services is very different from that of shipping services. One of the main reasons is that the nature of competition is not the same between them. While the competition in shipping is mostly global and almost perfect, the competition in ports is different: it is localised, complex, diverse and far from perfect. Sometimes port competition is even absent. As we have discussed above, the relationship between the government and ports is very close, with the usually direct involvement of the government in ownership of the land, the establishment of rules and regulations and investment in port infrastructures. This specific characteristic is the foundation of the discussions on port pricing.

There are three reasons why port competition is usually not perfect. The first is because the market entry and exit are not free mainly due to the public ownership of land. The second is that the services are never the same between two ports because they are location related. The third is that the number of ports that can be chosen by a customer is always limited and localised due to land transport constraints and scarcity of coastlines. Based on the nature of competition, there are three basic philosophies or approaches to port pricing: input-based, outcome-based and market-based. We will discuss each of them in more detail.

What is input-based port pricing?

Input-based is also a "cost-based" port pricing. Under this concept, port services are priced according to the cost of operations. Clearly, cost-based pricing can only be exercised when perfect competition is absent. This, however, does not preclude certain degrees of inter-port competition. But, as costs are different from one port to another, particularly in view of the specific geographical conditions of each port, cost-based pricing implies that, for similar services, the price may be very different between ports.

When a port is in control of the pricing for the services it offers, it can choose to apply a cost-based approach. There are two key issues with this pricing method. The first is whether the cost is used as a proxy of price, in which case the objective is to recover the cost or the cost is treated as the minimum level of pricing. As such, in the case of a monopoly, the objective is to charge as much as the demand can bear. The second issue is whether or not the cost to be recovered should be the total cost, including capital investment by the government in infrastructure.[27] The situation of monopoly and setting the price as high as the market can bear will be discussed under market-based pricing below, where we will look at the issue of pricing for cost recovery.

It is common in many ports that the investment made by the government in the basic construction of the port infrastructure is not expected to be paid back. Such costs may be on initial capital dredging, site planning, land reclamation, the building of breakwater, quay-wall, road, yard, etc. However, when the infrastructure is financed by a loan, the cost has to be recovered by the income. The non-refundable investment distorts the free market and creates unfair competition because, in this case, a determining factor for being successful in port competition will become the amount of public money a government is willing to provide for free in favour of particular ports. In order to guarantee fair competition, even if public funding is made available, it is important that the pricing should be on the basis of the full cost recovery.

Cost-based pricing usually falls under the responsibility of the department of finance of a port. It is an inward-looking approach with little consideration of the customer value created by port services and offering little incentive for the effort to cut costs and improve efficiency. Ports applying pure cost-based pricing are often those in monopolistic positions and they will end up with low efficiency and high cost. Most of such ports can, however, survive thanks, on the one hand, to government subsidies and, on the other hand, to the users in the captive hinterland who do not have any choice but to use the port.

What is outcome-based port pricing?

In the wake of the increasing pressure of marine environment protection, many ports in the world adopt a kind of pricing called "green tariff".[28] This is a performance- or outcome-based port pricing. Ports commonly use pricing as a tool to achieve specific objectives. Such objectives can be anything from the maximisation of income, value-added, the volume of a particular type of cargo or a category of ships to the minimisation of cost, turnaround time, or in the areas of safety or environment protection or accidents. For this reason it is sometimes also called a "strategic port pricing", meaning using the pricing as a mechanism to achieve a particular outcome.[29]

As an outcome-based pricing philosophy, the issue of price elasticity of demand is crucial. For example, a port may reduce its tariff in order to attract more ships or cargo. But the effect of such price reduction depends on many factors and different stakeholders. Regarding the level and changes of port tariffs, a shipping company and a shipper will react differently; a liner shipping company and a tramp shipping company will also react differently; the value of cargo plays a significant role and the situation of alternative services is extremely important as well. For a user to change the port for its cargo or its ship, it often involves other costs and uncertainties. For these reasons, to implement strategic port pricing, the knowledge of customer value obtained from having the port service is of great importance. An appropriate level of punitive tariff on storage charges aiming at a faster cargo turnaround time at the port may be set if the cost of alternative storage is known. In container shipping, the cost of handling transhipment cargo is similar to that of non-transhipment cargo, but many ports apply differentiated pricing between them because transhipment cargo is more "foot-loose".

Unlike cost-based pricing, which aims at cost recovery, outcome-based pricing aims at the improvement of port performance. In a port using outcome-based pricing, the responsibility of pricing belongs often to the operational, commercial or marketing departments. The decision may also be taken by the public authorities if it is a port built with public funds. The objective of the government may be to promote trade and thus to impose an upper-limit or maximum level of the port tariffs.

What is market-based port pricing?

The competitive nature of the market determines the way the price of port services is set. For many ports operating in a competitive environment, the pricing, or at least a part of it, is market based rather than cost or outcome based. In such a competitive market, a port competes with other ports providing the same services and it does not have the control of price. The balance of demand and supply in the market will determine the level of the price. In the real world, a perfectly competitive market is not common in the port sector. As we said above, port services are, by definition, location dependent and provided by different ports that are not totally identical. As a result, a port can easily have a captive hinterland, in which cargoes have no other choice but to use the port.

Market-based port pricing is also value-based pricing. When a port is operating in a competitive market, it has to improve the quality and/or reduce the cost of its service in order to survive or to develop. Numerous studies show that the most efficient ports providing the highest value for money to the customers are those operating in a highly competitive environment.[30, 31] The root causes of a high price, often driven by high cost, long turnaround time as well as low quality and unreliable services, are often found in the lack of competition.[32, 33] In such ports, the responsibility for pricing falls to marketing managers and people who understand the value of the services and the cost of them.

10.8 Summary

This chapter focusses on ports, an indispensable component of maritime transport. The basic fact that ports are always within national boundaries while shipping is, most of the time, in international territory makes the port sector far more diversified than the shipping sector. A port is very closely attached to its location, not only in the sense that the port often carries the name of the place but also that the demand for the port services relies on the economic development of the hinterland and the supply of the services depends on the local human and capital inputs. Ports serve two basic groups of customers: ships and cargo. While the services to ships can be divided into navigational and technical aspects, the services to cargo consist of four groups of operations, namely ship operation, transfer operation, storage operation and reception/delivery operation.

Because ports are close to cities, occupying a scarce resource of coastline, and, at the same time, because port services are often considered as public goods with economic and social externalities, the national or regional governments are commonly directly involved in port-related affairs. The vital role played by a country's port sector in the promotion of trade and economic development has been well documented. However, excessive government involvement causes port inefficiency. Since the 1980s there has been a wave of institutional reforms in the port sector throughout the world by which port operations are transferred from administrative entities to commercial companies, private or public, national as well as foreign. More and more ports have become landlord ports, with the role of port authority restricted to the owning and planning of the port assets.

We have examined the importance of ports for the development of shipping from the cost and quality perspectives. Port-related costs can be as high as a third or even a half of the total shipping cost. As far as the quality of shipping is concerned, the port has been the most critical part of the operation because it is responsible for up to 90% of delays, most accidents and cargo loss and damages. Many great innovations in shipping are originated in ports out of the efforts to solve cargo-handling-related problems. By observing specialised ships, we can realise that the real differentiation between the ships is in the way cargo is handled in ports rather than the way cargo is transported at sea. We have also made an important observation that, with an increase of ship's size, there are economies of scale for the cost at sea, but diseconomies of scale for the cost in port. Because of this particular feature, cargo-handling speed plays a decisive role with regard to ship's size.

Over a long period, ports have evolved very much commercially, spatially and socially/technologically. From a commercial point of view, ports have expanded their functions beyond cargo handling to cargo transformation and distribution; spatially, ports are moving away from city centres, as more space and better access to the sea are required; socially and technologically, due to the employment of modern cargo-handling equipment, a smaller but more skilful labour force is needed. More and more ports have built automated terminals. We also examined various aspects of port competition. There are five types of competition in the port sector. Inter-port competition is between neighbouring ports having a common hinterland. The intra-port competition is between operators within a port. The competition between different modes of transport is the one in which port is a part of shipping in competition with other modes of transport. The fourth type of competition is between different supply chains, of which ports are a part. The fifth type of competition discussed is the competition for value-added.

Finally, we also discussed the pricing issues. We divided the port pricing into three types, namely input-based, outcome-based and market-based. The port cost is often used as the base of input-based pricing. One of the most critical issues is whether the full cost, or partial cost, which means that the government subsidy in port infrastructure is excluded, is used in the pricing. The outcome-based port pricing can also be called performance-based port pricing because it is used to achieve specific performance objectives. Such objectives can be the increase of value-added for the port or customers, the improvement of productivity and efficiency, the reduction of cost or turnaround time, etc. The third type is market-based port pricing, which is the one applicable when the port is operating in a competitive market. In this case, the port does not have full control of the price. The only way to improve profitability is to provide a better value-for-money to the customers. This means better quality and/or lower prices. So it can also be called value-based pricing.

Notes

1 Herera Dappe M. and Suarez-Aleman A. (2016).
2 WTO (various years).
3 Ma, S. (2009).
4 Haralambides H. and Ma S. (1997).

5 Baudelaire J.-G. (1986).
6 Ibid., note 4.
7 Rijksdienst voor Onderneme d Nederland (2015). It is reported that in 2014 the Port of Tema, Ghana, obtained a loan of US$1.5 billion for the port expansion project.
8 Ibid., note 1.
9 IAPH (2010).
10 OCED (2011).
11 Port of Rotterdam (2017).
12 Cubas D., Briceno-Garmendia C., and Bofinger H. (2015).
13 Baker J. (2017a).
14 Roballand G., Refas S., Beuran M., and Isik G. (2012).
15 Notteboome T. (2006).
16 EMSA (2018).
17 O'Brien M. (2014).
18 It is reported that on 8 September 2008 the Port of Tianjin, China, completed loading and unloading 2,555 containers on the container ship *COSCO Yokohama* in 6.6 hours, which represented an average cargo handling rate of 387 containers per hour per ship (see: http://news.enorth.com.cn/system/2008/09/15/003682029.shtml).
19 UNCTAD (1992). "Port marketing and the challenge of the third generation port", TD/B/C.4/AC.7/14, UNCTAD GE-92-50020. In this study, the ports are divided into three generations. The ports of the first generation are those traditional ports concentrating on navigational services to ships and cargo-handling services to cargo; the second generation ports are those which also undertake cargo transformation activities such as oil refinery; the third generation ports are those that play a role as a trade and transport platform for logistics services.
20 Port Technology (2017).
21 *World Maritime News* (1 August 2016). It was reported in 2016 by the British shipping consultant company Drewry that a number of major merger and acquisition deals were in the pipeline and there were more to come.
22 *The Economist* (2017).
23 Kleywegt A., Goh M. L., Wu G., and Zhang H. (2002).
24 See "Alphaliner Top 100 Container Shipping Lines". By the end of 2017, the combined market share of the top 15 lines was 81% of the total teu capacity. Source: https://alphaliner.axsmarine.com/PublicTop100/.
25 Joerss M. et al. (2015).
26 Baker J. (2017b).
27 Haralambides H. and Veenstra W. (2002).
28 Virtually all major ports in Europe use some kind of differentiated tariffs by offering incentives to the users who employ more environmentally friendly practices. By typing "port green tariffs" into Google, 3.6 million hits are listed, featuring on the first pages all major ports throughout the world.
29 UNCTAD (1995).
30 Cubas D., Briceno-Garmendia C., and Bofinger H. (2015).
31 JOC (2013).
32 Raballand G., Refas S., Beuran M., and Isik G. (2012).
33 Dappe M. and Suarez-Aleman A (2016).

References

Baker J. (2017a) "*Container Carriers See Reversal of Bunker Costs and Terminal Fees*", Lloyd's List, 16 October 2017.

Baker J. (2017b) "*HPH Reports Volumes Up, Revenues down – Terminal Operator Warns Uncertain Times amid Consolidation and Alliance Changes*", Lloyd's List, 19 July 2017.

Baudelaire J.-G. (1986) "*Port Administration and Management*", Published by IAPH, Tokyo, pp. 199–202.

Cubas D., Briceno-Garmendia C., and Bofinger H. (2015) "*OECS Ports – An Efficiency and Performance Assessment*", Policy Research WP 7162, World Bank, January 2015.

Dappe M. and Suarez-Aleman A. (2016) "*Competitiveness of South Asia's Container Ports – A Comprehensive Assessment of Performance, Drivers and Costs*", Directions in Development, World Bank, Washington, DC.

EMSA. (2018) "*Annual Overview of Marine Casualties and Incidents 2018*", European Maritime Safety Agency, Lisbon, Portugal, pp. 49–57.

Haralambides H. and Veenstra W. (2002) "*Port Pricing*", in "The Handbook of Maritime Economics and Business", edited by C. Grammenos, Lloyds of London Press, London, pp. 782–802.

Haralambides H. and Ma S. (1997) "*World-wide Experiences of Port Reform*", in "Transforming the Port and Transport Business", edited by H. Meersman, published by ACCO, Leuven, Belgium, p. 121.

Herera Dappe M. and Suarez-Aleman A. (2016) "*Competitiveness of South Asia's Container Ports*", World Bank, Washington, DC, pp. 84–86.

IAPH. (2010) "*Ports and Economics*", Port Planning and Development Committee, International Association of Ports and Harbours.

JOC. (2013) "*Key Findings on Terminal Productivity Performance across Ports, Countries and Regions*", JOC Port Productivity White Paper, July 2013, JOC Group.

Joerss M. et al. (2015) "*Landside Operations: The Next Frontier for Container Shipping Alliances*", Travel, Transport and Logistics, April 2015, McKinsey & Company.

Kleywegt A., Goh M. L., Wu G., and Zhang H. (2002) "*Competition between the Ports of Singapore and Malaysia*", Retrieved from www.researchgate.net/publication/265114505_Competition_between_the_Ports_of_Singapore_and_Malaysia

Ma S. (2009) "*The Impact of Shipping and Ports on China's 30-year Rapid Economic Expansion*", (in Chinese with English abstract). published on China Navigation, Shanghai, China, March 2009, pp. 82–86.

Notteboome T. (2006) "*The Time Factor in Liner Shipping Services*", Maritime Economics and Logistics, 2008, 8, pp. 19–39.

O'Brien M. (2014) "*Oil Spills in Ports (2006)*", ITOPF 22 May 2014, Retrieved from www.itopf.org/knowledge-resources/documents-guides/document/oil-spills-in-ports-2006/

OCED. (2011) "*Competition in Port and Port Services*", DAF/COMP(2011)14 Directorate for Financial and Enterprise Affairs Competition Committee.

Port of Rotterdam. (2017) "*Port Tariffs 2017*", Port of Rotterdam.

Port Technology. (2017) "*Asia Enters Fully Automated Terminal Era*", Port Technology, 15 May 2017, Retrieved from www.porttechnology.org/news/asia_enters_fully_automated_terminal_era

Raballand G., Refas S., Beuran M., and Isik G. (2012) "*Why Does Cargo Spent Weeks in Sub-Saharan African Ports? Lessons from Six Countries*", The World Bank, Washington, DC, 204333.

Rijksdienst voor Onderneme d Nederland. (2015) "*Sector Report, Port Development Ghana*", April 2015.

The Economist. (2017) "*New Rail Routes between China and Europe Will Change Trade Patterns*", Business, The Economist, 16 September 2017.

UNCTAD. (1992) "*Port Marketing and the Challenge of the Third Generation Port*", TD/B/C.4/AC.7/14, UNCTAD GE-92-50020.

UNCTAD. (1995) "*Strategic Port Pricing*", UNCTAD/SDD/PORT/2, GE.95-50533, UNCTAD, Geneva.

World Maritime News. (1 August 2016) "Drewry: Container Port Operators Eye Mergers and Acquisitions" Retrieved 18 September 2018 from http://worldmaritimenews.com/archives/198481/drewry-container-port-operators-eye-mergers-and-acquisitions/

WTO. (various years) "*World Trade Statistics*", WTO, Geneva.

Chapter 11

The economics of supporting services for maritime transport

To provide international maritime transport, shipping companies rely on many other services. Some of these services, such as ship finance and ports, have been discussed in the previous chapters. In this chapter we will examine the other essential services, which are supportive by nature, represent significant parts of the total cost of a shipping company and, at the same time, have big influences on the performance of a shipping company. We will first look into the manning market, focussing on the demand and supply of the seafarers. Then we will discuss the features and the impact of ship registration, which is very special for international shipping. We will have a discussion of the marine insurance market. We will also look into shipping services provided by agents, brokers and forwarders. Finally, we will examine the bunkering market. Through the discussions of this chapter, we would like to provide an overview of the market system of the major supporting services for maritime transport. The emphasis is on the features of the services, their evolution, the aspects of supply and demand, the cost implications, their role in the operation of ships and the development trends.

11.1 Seafarer service market

Seafarers, or ship crew, are generally divided into two groups of people who work on board ships under the overall leadership of the captain: the deck department and the engineering department. Crew members working in the deck department include, ranked from high to low, chief officer, second officer, third officer and some ordinary seamen. Crew members working in the engineering department include the chief engineer, second engineer, third engineer and some ordinary seamen. The captain, the deck officers and the engineers are collectively called "ship officers" and are holders of an official certificate of competence. The ordinary seamen, or able seamen, are called ratings, who do not have the same qualification. Seafarers operate ships and also carry out daily ship maintenance and help with cargo handling at ports. In this section we are going to discuss the international seafarer market: the demand and supply of seafarers, the size of crew for a ship, the training of seafarers, the cost of ship manning and the duties of seafarers.

What is the general situation of demand and supply of seafarers?

As discussed in Chapter 5, for a long time the size of the ship crew did not change significantly with the size or even the type of ships. For most deep-sea ships, the number of officers is almost constant regardless of the ship's size or type. In 2016 there were about 50,000 merchant ships of 1,000 gross tons (gt) and above carrying international trade.[1] A ship should have at least seven officers on board and, for deep-sea ships of 1,000 gt and above, the average number of officers is nine across major types of ships.[2] Consequently, there should be a total of about 450,000 officers needed on board ships. Adding to this number is a backup and other off-duty shore-based crew of about 250,000, so we should come to a roughly estimated demand of about 700,000 officers.[3] Such an estimate is close to the numbers suggested by two reports which are often used by the industry as basic references.[4] When it comes to ratings, the number may vary slightly between ships but is usually between 9 and 11. Therefore, taking shore-based backup seamen into account, a total of about 800,000 should be a rough estimate of the demand of the global fleet for ratings. So, with about 50,000 deep-sea ships, approximately a total of 1.5 million seafarers is needed. Unlike in the past when over 100 men would work on a sailing ship or about 40 people on a conventional general cargo vessel, today it is typical for a modern vessel trading on international routes to have a crew of fewer than 20 seafarers.

Traditionally, seafarers were recruited from the countries where ships were built and operated. So the Dutch seafarers were working on Dutch vessels and British seafarers were working on British ships. But this situation has entirely changed since World War Two. Seafaring has become a highly internationalised profession. Today a handful of countries provide most of the global seafarers. For countries like Japan, Norway or Germany, all of which are big shipping countries controlling a massive number of commercial ships, yet their ships are mostly operated by a foreign crew. The international seafarers are mostly coming from Asia and the East European countries. The Philippines, for example, has a relatively small fleet of ocean-going ships, or about 0.1% of the world total in terms of deadweight tonnage, but the largest group of seafarers or about 16% of the total global seafarers.[5]

Why is the situation like this? What are the contributing factors for a country to be a major seafarer supplier? Should the capability in other maritime activities be relevant factors for the country's seafarer base? Is the level of the labour cost of the country, or its GDP per capita, also a relevant factor? We therefore examined these factors by collecting related data as shown in Table 11.1. We can here observe the relationship between the three variables. The two columns on the left are the top ten seafarer supply countries by numbers of officers and ratings combined and the share of the total world seafarer supply. The two columns in the middle are the ranking of the controlled fleet in dwt and the corresponding market share of the ten countries. The two columns on the right are the global ranking and the GDP per capita in US dollars of the ten countries.

Let's look at the correlation between seafarer supply and controlled fleet. Based on the data of Table 11.1 we have Figures 11.1a and 11.1b. For the top ten biggest seafarer suppliers, with the coefficient of correlation R^2 at 0.17, there is a lack of correlation between the two variables. Though in two cases, China and the UK, we see a level of positive correlation, for all the other eight countries there is a lack of correlation. The East European countries and India have relatively weak positions in terms of controlled fleet, but this does not prevent them from being leading suppliers of seafarers. It is particularly striking to see the case of the Philippines, which controls about 0.1% of the global fleet, but the country provides almost 16% of the seafarers in the world. Let's now look at the correlation between seafarer supply and GDP per capita. This time we can see in Figure 11.1b that there is a closer relationship. The two variables are negatively correlated which means that the richer the countries are, the less likely they will be big suppliers of seafarers. Except for the UK, the world's ten biggest seafarer suppliers are those countries with a GDP per capita ranging between US$2,000 and US$12,000. The average world GDP per capita is about US$11,000. So neither the poorest nor the wealthiest countries are the primary suppliers of international seafarers. It implies that when a country's GDP per capita reaches a certain level, e.g., US$12,000, it may start to lose the competitive edge in the international seafarer market.

Table 11.1 Relationship between seafarer supply, controlled fleet and GDP per capita (2015).

	Seafarers		*Fleet*		*GDP/capita*	
	Rank	*Of total (%)*	*Rank*	*Of total (%)*	*Rank*	*US$*
Philippines	1	15.8%	47	0.1%	125	2,924
China	2	12.0%	3	9.1%	71	8,113
India	3	7.5%	17	1.3%	142	1,723
Ukraine	4	5.0%	40	0.2%	132	2,194
Russia	5	4.8%	20	1.1%	68	8,929
Poland	6	2.9%	45	0.2%	57	12,316
Romania	7	1.6%	64	0.1%	64	9,465
UK	8	1.5%	9	2.8%	19	40,096
Croatia	9	1.4%	43	0.2%	58	12,095
Latvia	10	0.9%	65	0.1%	52	14,060

Source: Shuo Ma, based on data from Drewry (2015), UNCTAD (2016) and IMF (2016).

Note: global ranking of seafarers by number includes both officers and ratings. Global ranking of controlled fleets in dwt include those under open registry. Global ranking of GDP per capita is in nominal US dollars. Total seafarers 13,80,000.00.

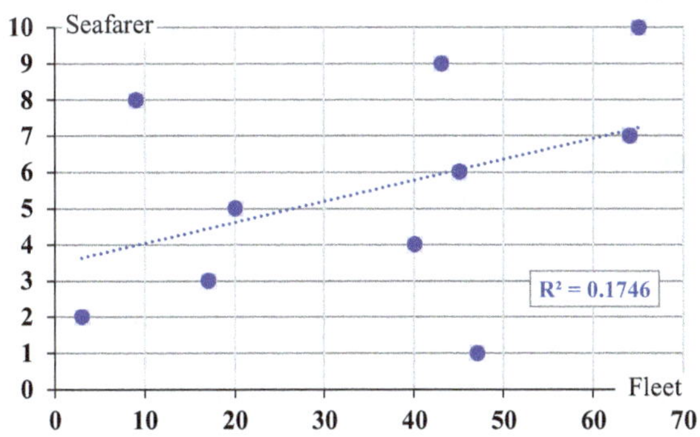

Figure 11.1a Correlation between seafarer and fleet supply.

Source: Shuo Ma, based on data from Drewry, UNCTAD and IMF.

Note: this is about the world's top ten seafarer supply countries and their rank of fleet supply. The two are not correlated.

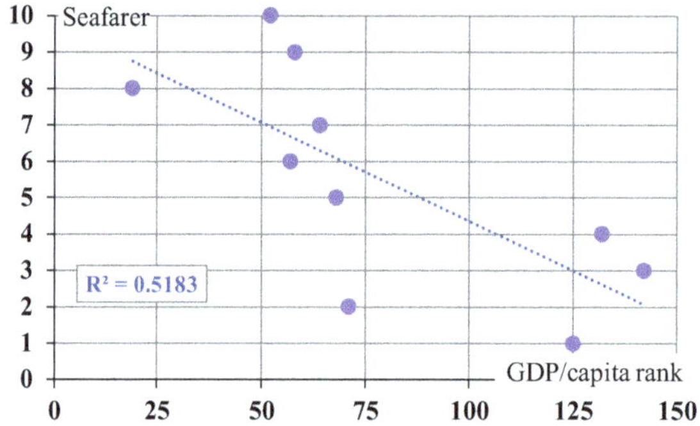

Figure 11.1b Correlation between seafarer and GDP/capita.

Source: Shuo Ma based on data from Table 11.1.

Note: this is about the world's top ten seafarer supply countries and their rank of GDP/capita. The two are negatively correlated.

What are the determining factors for the price and supply of international seafarers?

As we can see from Table 11.1, apart from the UK, none of the top ten seafarer supply countries is a traditional maritime power. And, except for China, none of the countries that control the largest fleets, such as Japan, Greece, Germany or the US, is a major seafarer supplier. It is generally believed that one of the chief reasons for many traditional seafarer supply countries in Europe, North America and Japan to experience a serious shortage of seafarers has been the high labour cost. A key question to be addressed is how the price of seafarers is determined. To answer this question, we will take a look at the following three aspects of the seafarer market: its scope, its competitive nature and its characteristics of demand and supply.

- ***The scope of the seafaring market is global.*** We have explained that the situation of work and employment on board ships are internationally standardised both on the structure of the organisation and on the types of skills required. The mobility of ships and the international nature of the shipping business, including the practice of open registry, have made the employment of foreign seafarers an easy process. As a result, for most shipping companies, the supply of seafarers is not a national but an international or global market.
- ***The seafaring market is competitive.*** We can examine the four basic features of a market to determine whether the international supply of seafarers is a competitive market or not. The first feature is about the freedom of entry and exit. Clearly, there are no legal, regulatory or administrative barriers preventing seafarers of any country from entering or exiting the international market, so it is a free market. The second factor is about whether or not the quality or ability of seafarers between different supply sources are the same and therefore substitutable or interchangeable. The answer is not straightforward because, arguably, differences do exist though the gap in differences has been diminishing. It is partly because of the skill improvement of some seafarers, e.g., those from some countries in Asia, and partly thanks to the quality and standardisation processes facilitated by the implementation of the STCW Convention and ISM Code. The third feature is about the awareness of the competing alternatives in the market. The international seafarer supply market is common knowledge among the shipping companies. The

fourth reason is about a large number of suppliers. As we see in Table 11.1, the biggest supply has a market share of about 16%, which is big but not dominating, and, within the Philippines, competition exists between manning agencies. So we can conclude by saying that the international seafarer market is highly competitive.

- ***The balance between supply and demand for seafarers.*** As a competitive market, the price is determined by the market forces or, more precisely, by the balance of supply and demand of seafarers. The price agreed by supply and demand is the equilibrium price. This means that if supply and demand are out of balance, the price will change, up or down, triggering the responding adjustment of supply and demand until a new equilibrium is reached. So the movement of seafarer price is basically determined by two factors: the stability of supply and demand and the responsiveness of supply and demand to the price changes. In economics, the former phenomenon follows the law of supply and demand, while the latter is referred to as price elasticity. If either demand or supply is unstable, the price will keep changing. But how much the price changes depends on the responsiveness of supply and demand to the price fluctuation. With very responsive supply and demand, the price will not change much as a new equilibrium will quickly be established. Since the level of remuneration is one of the most important reasons for the unattractiveness of working as a seafarer and because of a high cadet wastage rate and that there are alternative jobs for seafarers,[6, 7, 8] the supply of seafarers is price elastic.

In a competitive market the shipping companies always look for ways to reduce costs, including crew cost. The price of international seafarers is, to a large extent, influenced by the leading suppliers. Take the Philippines for example. With about 16% of the market share, the Filipino seafarer market sets the standard and has a big impact on the price of international seafarers.

The supply and demand of international seafarers do get out of balance from time to time. For example, some recent reports indicate a shortfall of ship officers since 2000 and the situation deteriorated in 2015. If such opinions are correct then there should be a rise in the price of seafarers because the market is competitive. This, however, has not always happened. We should not believe that such a shortfall will continue to grow to as high as more than 18% of the total supply by 2025, as estimated by some reports.[9] This is because, before such a big shortage of supply will happen, the market forces, price elasticity of the supply, the impact of automation and other new technology will have already reacted and adjusted so a new market equilibrium will be achieved.

What are the fundamental changes in the duties of seafarers?

If the organisational structure of seafaring has remained without a lot of changes for over half a century, then the nature of the work has evolved enormously. Such changes are usually the direct result of the new technologies and production models. Probably the most fundamental changes, which have long-term effects, are in the following two aspects.

- For ship management and operation, the ship-based crew relies increasingly on modern navigation technology and shore-based ship staff. This development means a higher level of integration of shore-based and ship-based management on the one hand and an increasing dependence on technology on the other hand. The skillset has to be adjusted and such changes make the seafaring profession less challenging, not well paid and unattractive to many people.
- The average ratio of port time to shipping time continues to decline, even though the average ship size has increased. This is because of the reduction of time in port thanks to specialisation of shipping as well as more efficient port equipment and operation. On the other hand, relatively fewer changes happened to ships' speed and the average distance travelled. These developments have an impact on the work rhythm and the level of stress for the seafarers.

How about the evolution and future trends of seafaring?

The ability, skills, nature and conditions of work on board ships have not stopped evolving. The major driving force behind such evolution has always been the technological development of the shipping industry. In the early age of shipping, the technology and navigational know-how were relatively simple. The skills were acquired mostly through on-the-job training. Usually a large number of seafarers was needed per ship. With a very long time spent on the voyage and on cargo handling at ports, combined with small cargo capacity and a high casualty rate, the shipping cost was high in comparison with the value of cargo. When modern steel ships powered by diesel engines were introduced, the situation for seafarers started to change. On the one hand, the crew size reduced but, on the other hand, higher skills were required. Longer training time and pre-education were needed. Shipping cost kept decreasing thanks to the productivity improvement resulting from larger and faster ships, more efficient port operation and smaller crew size. Table 11.2 and Figure 11.2 are indicative illustrations of the evolution of seafaring, in terms of crew size, driven by the development of maritime technology and, consequently, a declining trend of the ratio between crew cost and total shipping cost.

Presently, as indicated by Figure 11.2, we are still in the evolutionary process. At the current level of technology, 20 to 30 people are needed to work per ship and crew cost is still one of the major cost elements of ship operation. But, as the new technologies continue to be introduced to ships to make them safer, more efficient and more autonomous, the number of crew is further reduced. In May 2017 some fully autonomous cargo ships started operation in Norway.[10] It is believed that a new era of crewless ships has begun.[11] Although it may not happen in full-scale soon, the future development looks highly likely to be in the direction of a high level of automation. Future maritime transport will be very different to what we see today. Ships will be crewless and controlled from shore. The shipping service will be cheaper still with a very low ratio between the transport cost and the value of cargo carried.

11.2 Ship registration market

Ships have the nationality of the country in which they are registered. In Britain, ships were required to register by the Navigation Act 1660. As the ship should then fly the flag of the country of registration, the country is called the flag State. The registration gives the ships national protection and, at the

Table 11.2 Evolution of the seafaring sector.

	Past	Present	Future
Nature of skills	Simple	More sophisticated	Complex
Number of seafarers	Huge	Reduced	Unmanned
Shipping:trade ratio	High transport:trade value	Declining ratio	Very low ratio
Type of education	On-the-job	Vocational/ university	General
Place of control	Ship	Ship/shore	Shore

Source: Shuo Ma, based on data from Drewry (2015), UNCTAD (2016) and IMF (2016).

Note: As ships are more sophisticated and technology-intensive, the number of seafarers needed and the nature of their work change.

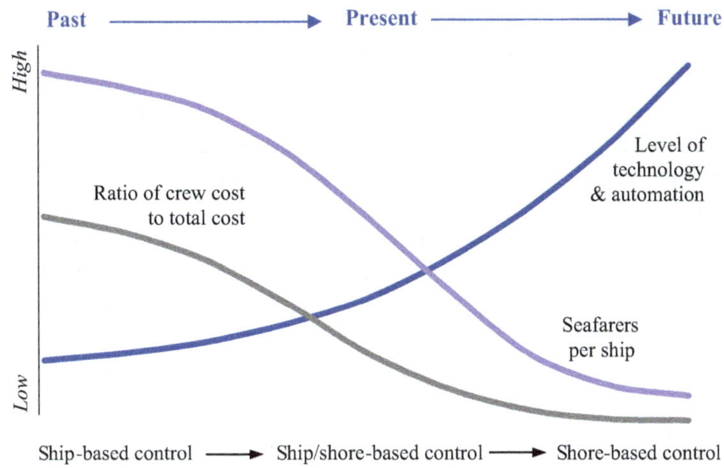

Figure 11.2 Evolution of technology, seafaring and crew cost vs. total cost ratio.

Source: Shuo Ma.

Note: the figure shows the indicative evolution of maritime technology, the number of seafarers per ship and crew cost to total cost ratio.

same time, the obligation to comply with the laws and regulations of the country of registration, as defined in article 91 of the 1982 United Nations Convention on the Law of the Sea. However, such national ship registration is more complicated for maritime transport, because shipping is by definition an international business and ships are operating mostly outside any national jurisdiction on international waters. So, on the one hand, ships trading in the same market may belong to different countries, therefore following different rules and regulations, and, on the other hand, it is possible for ships to choose or change the country of registration.

What are the differences between the national ship registrations?

A flag State has both administrative and political implications. So a ship carrying a national flag is affected by the political conditions of the country. It has the country's protection and assistance in international waters or in foreign ports. Ships are also affected when visiting foreign countries with which the flag State has political frictions. Although ships are operating in international waters, the different national registrations provide the vessels with diverse technical, social and economic conditions and standards.

- Regarding ***technical conditions and standards***, ships operated under a country's flag should comply with all rules and regulations of the flag State to ensure ship safety and marine environment protection. Given the international nature of maritime transport, ships must comply with the international rules and regulations adopted by the flag State. Such regulations cover a wide range of technical areas, for example the standards about ship construction and equipment, the seaworthiness of ships, ships' survey and certification, etc. Countries do not adopt the same international regulations, so ships under different flags may have different technical requirements.

- Concerning ***social conditions and standards***, several aspects of on-board employment are covered by the national rules and regulations. Such rules are on manning standards, seafarer qualifications as well as the working conditions and seafarer welfare treatment. Some countries impose restrictive requirements for the composition of the crew working on their ships. For example, no foreign officers can be employed on certain ships or there is a percentage limit for the use of foreign crew. Differences may also exist between countries in the areas of minimum salary levels as well as social welfare conditions.
- As far as ***economic conditions and standards*** are concerned, these are probably the most important considerations for shipowners when choosing ship flags. There are two parts of ship-registration-related costs, one direct, the other indirect. The direct cost is about registration fees. The direct cost is not a complex matter as it is usually an annual payment per tonnage. The indirect costs are the consequential expenses required under the registration. Such costs include tax liabilities, crew cost, ship maintenance cost, regulatory control cost, etc. Even access to funding may also be affected by ship registration.

How has ship registration turned from a public service into a commercial business?

Registration of a property, ships or otherwise, should normally be a purely administrative service provided by public authorities to the citizens or enterprises of the country. But, in international shipping, the registration of ships has become a commercial service offered by some countries to all clients, national and foreign alike. Such a practice, which is unique in international maritime transport, is called "open registry".

It is reported that open registry began in 1922 when two US passenger ships were transferred to the Panamanian register in order to serve alcohol to passengers during Prohibition.[12] Very soon, other benefits of registering ships abroad were realised by more shipowners, such as the avoidance of high labour cost and more demanding working conditions in US legislation such as the Seamen's Act of 1915. After World War Two, open registry became increasingly popular because shipowners from other parts of the world, especially Europe and the Far East, also found the practice attractive as a means to save on tax payment by shifting ships away from national registries.

For the countries offering open registry, they received an annual tax income without much cost. So it was a very good business. As the demand for open registry increased after World War Two, more countries, especially some small developing countries, also opened up their ship registration to foreign ships. According to the International Transport Workers' Federation, there are some 30 countries that are considered to have, to a different extent, an open ship registry. But this market has been concentrated on a few big flags, such as Panamanian and Liberian.[13] The Liberian registry was founded after World War Two in a structure of joint-venture between a US company and the Liberian government, as an alternative to the Panamanian flag. For most of these small countries, international ship registration has become a substantial source of income.

Turning public service, such as the registration of ships, into a commercial business has been embraced by the shipping industry enthusiastically. There is indeed a weak link between the country of open registry and the ships that fly its flag but that rarely or never visit the ports of the country. Compared with most traditional maritime countries, the exercise of flag State duties and obligations in respect of the enforcement of national or international laws and regulations was done in a less rigorous manner by open registry countries, particularly at the beginning of the development. However, the shipping industry's self-discipline has a positive effect. Most of the shipowners believe that it is in their own interest not to compromise safety by ignoring regulations or not to save cost by running sub-standard ships. Statistically, as we will discuss in the next section, the ships under many

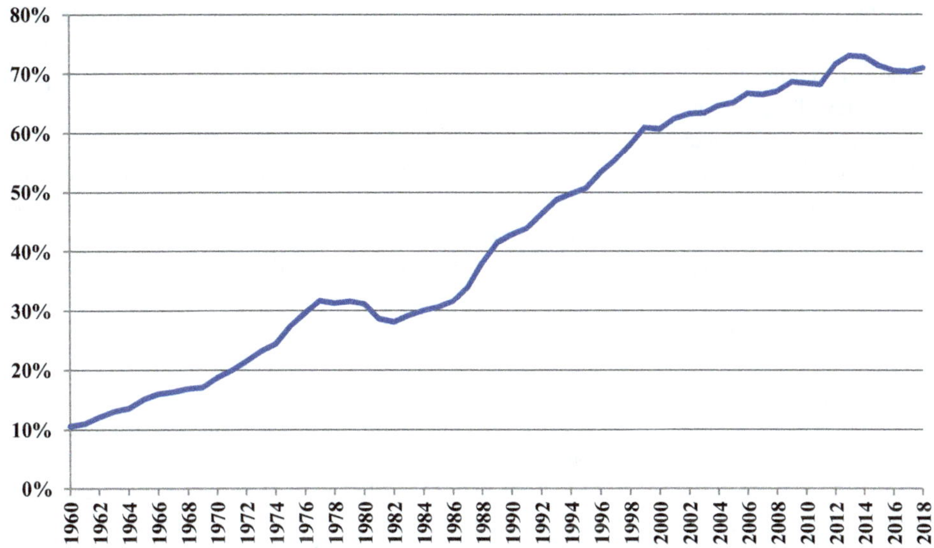

Figure 11.3 Growth of open registry 1960–2018, percentage of world total fleet in dwt.

Source: Shuo Ma, based on UNCTAD, ISL and other sources.

Note: the curve represents the share of foreign flagged ships of the world total fleet. These are the ships owned and commercially controlled in a country other than the country of the flag.

open registries have had good performance in terms of compliance with the international rules and regulations. Because shipping is not undertaken within national boundaries, and the countries offering open registry do not require the shipowners to pay income tax, this is very attractive. Consequently, the fleet of the open registry has continued to grow with more and more shipowners registering, including those of most reputable companies from traditional maritime countries. Figure 11.3 shows the percentage growth of the fleet under open registry compared with the total world fleet in dwt from 1960 to 2018. In about 60 years, over 70% of the world's commercial ships are flying flags other than those of the countries of the shipowners and operators. The market share of open registry may continue to increase in the future.

What are the economics of open registry?

There are various reasons for shipowners to register their ships in an open registry country abroad, but the main motivation is economic. The financial benefits to gain by choosing open ship registry rather than national registry are substantial. The following is the examination of the main economic benefits and costs of open registry.

- The tax-related advantage. This is the single most important benefit for most shipowners when choosing open registries for their ships. The world average corporate income tax stood at 23% in 2017. Although a few countries have zero or very low corporate income tax, this tax is high for most ship-owning countries. In 2017, for example, the total corporate income taxes were at 29% for Greece, 30% for Japan, 25% for China, 30% for Germany and 38% for the US.[14] If the ship is registered in Panama, or in one of the other main open registry countries, no corporate income tax needs to be paid. After the initial registration fees, shipowners only pay an annual tonnage tax. This is a considerable incentive for shipowners, who are mostly operating in a highly competitive international market, often with narrow profit margins. If some of them have changed to open registry, others will follow.

- The countries of the open registry are mostly small nations, which are less likely to be in politically sensitive positions with other countries, especially the major seaborne trade countries. The open registry provides, therefore, a valuable alternative solution when political sensitivity or conflict or hostility between countries or groups of countries could present a threat to the crew, ship or cargo. Sometimes, when choosing a foreign flag, a ship may gain access to financial sources or certain types of cargo reserved to specific flags. For example, after joining the EU, Malta, as an open registry country, may see its flag becoming more attractive to those shipowners who are interested in getting into the EU shipping market.
- Freedom is the fundamental base of maritime transport for the simple reason that shipping activity is undertaken on international waters. However, national ship registry often comes with restrictions that undermine freedom. The typical example is the employment restrictions imposed on shipowners under many national flags. Owners want to choose freely any suitable crew available in the market. Shipowners will not always take the cheapest labour in the market, either national or international. It is not in their interest to leave the ship and cargo, worth many hundreds of millions of US dollars, in the hands of an incompetent crew. Since the cost of seafarers depends on the labour market of the country of the seafarer, seafarers of low cost are not necessarily seafarers of low quality. When the open registries allow the shipowners the freedom to choose the best value for money option for seafarers, shipowners will opt for open registry.
- Another aspect of the economic value of open registry is about its simplicity and easy accessibility. The flag State control is kept at the basic level for most open registries. For a ship to change to the Panamanian registry, for example, it does not require a new safety survey if valid certificates are available, including existing tonnage certificates and survey certificates of all major classification societies.[15] Panama even allows dual registration of foreign ships if this is also allowed by the other country concerned, although, according to the UNCLOS, ships shall sail under the flag of one state only. To sum up, open registries, as a commercial service, offer as far as possible the services that customers may wish to have.

What are the controversies of and the future of open registry?

From the early stage of the open registry development, various attempts have been made by governments or non-governmental organisations to either compete with open registries or to eliminate them altogether. From the government side, incentives are offered to shipping companies to prevent them from transferring their vessels from national flags to foreign flags. Some traditional maritime countries have even mimicked open registry practices by creating off-shore registries, or the so-called second registry, under which vessels pay a tonnage tax only. The organisations that are the most hostile to open registry are the trade unions, ITF (International Transport Workers' Federation) and also the UNCTAD (the United Nations Conference on Trade and Development). The opinion of these organisations is that the open registries are simply a way for shipowners to escape their responsibilities and obligations that they otherwise have to assume with a national registry with respect to safety requirements, taxation and the protection of seafarers' rights, working conditions and welfare.

One of the criticisms that is most commonly heard on the open registry is that these flags provide an opportunity for those shipowners who wish to escape safety obligations to save cost by operating substandard ships. However, there has not been sufficient evidence in support of such

Table 11.3 Flag performance (in excess factors) of main open registries, Paris MOU.

	Panama	*Liberia*	*Marshall Islands*	*Malta*	*Bahamas*
2008–2010	-0.30	-0.12	-1.42	-0.99	-1.51
2009–2011	-0.69	-1.38	-1.31	-1.01	-1.50
2010–2012	-0.85	-1.57	-1.38	-1.11	-1.64
2011–2013	-0.55	-1.53	-1.31	-1.05	-1.59
2012–2014	-0.45	-1.45	-1.58	-1.22	-1.74
2013–2015	-0.46	-1.25	-1.66	-1.16	-1.74
2014–2016	-0.45	-1.15	-1.73	-1.21	-1.80

Source: based on Paris MOU, Flag Performance Lists, 2010–2017 (www.parismou.org).

Note: the flag performance is measured based on the number of inspections and detentions over a period of three years. Those with excess factors below 0 are considered as quality flags and are in the White List. The smaller the excess factor, the higher the quality of the flag.

criticisms. Judging from the recent Port State Control statistics, the situation is more complex. The Port State Control is an effective means of verification of whether or not international rules and regulations are adequately enforced by the ships of foreign flags visiting the port. The two largest Port State Control authorities consist of the countries of the Paris MOU and Tokyo MOU. A very large proportion of global seaborne trade is carried to and from the ports covered by the two MOUs and is therefore subject to the Port State Control inspections. The ship inspection results are published annually. The countries of registration are ranked in three categories to indicate the flag performance of compliance. The first category is called the "White List" and consists of the countries perceived as quality flags; the second category is called the "Grey List", which are the countries whose ships performed poorly in the Port State Control; the last category is called the "Black List", which includes the flags with high risks. Table 11.3 shows the flag performance of the five leading open registries published by Paris MOU for the period from 2008 to 2016. All five flags are in the White List for the whole period. The indicator of performance is called "excess factor", which is based on the inspections and detentions of ships. The higher the factor is, the riskier the flag will be. If a flag has a factor below 0, it enters into the White List. As far as compliance with the international rules and regulations is concerned, open registries have generally performed well. From 2008 to 2016, as shown in Table 11.3, all five leading open registry flags were below 0. A similar performance has also been reported by Tokyo MOU, in that these open registry countries are consistently ranked among the very good flags, even out-performing many traditional maritime countries.[16]

11.3 Insurance service market

The maritime transport of cargo across oceans has always been an activity with risks. There are many types of risks, the risks of ship or cargo loss or damage are the major ones. Such safety-related risks have been part of the features and main concerns of international shipping, particularly when maritime technology was not as sophisticated as it is today. Marine insurance is an activity dealing with risks of hazards from shipping activities. The business of marine insurance is as old as shipping itself.

How are the risks covered by marine insurance?

In this section we concentrate only on marine insurance associated with ship-related risks. The first thing to do when managing maritime risks is to assess the risk or risk evaluation. Risk is about the uncertainty of hazards. So the assessment consists of the measurement of both the uncertainty and the hazard. Let's take a look at the basic principles and features of ship- and shipping-related uncertainties and hazards.

It sounds like a paradox to talk about measuring uncertainties because uncertainty by definition implies immeasurability. So only by introducing the notion of probability can uncertainty be made measurable. It is therefore not to tell with any precision which hazardous event will happen and when, but it is, rather, to calculate the likelihood, or probability, for such an event to happen during a specific period of time. For example, a maritime safety risk assessment may suggest that, in the next 24 months, the probability of having five accidents of ship collision with a loss for each of US$1 million for the global fleet of container ships is 50%. Such measurability of risks is based on the statistics of past safety performances over a long time. As long as the basic technical and business conditions remain constant, accidents will always happen. Take the total loss of ships of the world fleet of commercial ships as an example. From 2012 to 2015, between 54 and 60 ships were lost each year.[17] When assessing the risks of ship loss for 2016, a similar number of losses would be expected to happen. This means that accidents reoccur at a certain rate or a range of rates in spite of the diversity and differences of the causes for each accident.

We know that a certain number of accidents will happen, but what we do not know is when and to whom they will happen. In other words, although accidents always happen, individually affecting a particular person, ship or company, the risk of an accident is for the whole population of the crew, ships or companies. This certainty of occurrence of hazards for a population versus the uncertainty of occurrence of hazards for an individual is the foundation for marine insurance. Assuming ships have an equal chance to suffer from a loss, then the risk is the ratio of expected losses to the total population. If 50 total losses are expected for a fleet of 50,000 ships, the probability of total loss for each ship is 50/50,000 or 0.1%. The idea of insurance is to cover the loss of 50 ships by spreading the cost over the whole population. So insurance is, in essence, a kind of mutuality through which individual losses are mitigated by each ship bearing a fraction of them. Marine insurance is the system through which the loss-sharing is organised by diverting the loss from the individual to the whole group who participate in the insurance.

What are the differences between Hull & Machinery and P&I insurance?

There are three categories of maritime-transport-related insurance, two of them concerning ships and one concerning cargo. The first ship-related insurance is called Hull & Machinery Insurance, which is insurance for physical loss and damage of the ship. The loss or damage may be caused by collision, fire, grounding, explosion or natural causes such as bad weather, earthquakes, tsunami, etc. Many Hull & Machinery Insurance policies cover only up to 75% of the actual liability of the shipowner. It is believed that letting shipowners bear the other 25% of losses means that they might be more cautious with ship operations.

The shipowners, however, will cover this 25% by the arrangement of other insurance. They started to organise between themselves in the 19th century an insurance system for mutual protection. It is done through P&I (Protection and Indemnity) insurance. When an accident happens, often not only the shipowner will incur losses or damages but other parties may also do so. This can be damage to another ship, port facilities or the pollution of the environment. But the liability to others is not covered by Hull & Machinery so P&I insurance is intended to cover the third-party liability risks. The P&I insurers are called P&I clubs because, unlike the Hull & Machinery insurance, P&I insurance is based on mutuality between shipowners in order to cover the third-party liability risks and to protect the members from the losses that are excluded from Hull & Machinery insurance.

While Hull & Machinery insurance is a commercial activity, a P&I club is operated on a not-for-profit and cooperative basis with the finance provided by "calls". A common pool is set up with contributions from club members. In case of large claims that cannot be covered by the pool, supplementary "calls" will be sent to members asking them to pay more. If, by the end of the year, the pool has a surplus, a refund will be made to the members or they will be asked to pay a lower subscription the following year. The larger the pool, the more capable a P&I club will be to deal with big claims. So, as a way to spread out the risks, P&I clubs need to reinsure in the insurance market the risks of big third-party claims.

How does the insurance cost change over time?

In 2017 the total premium of ship- and cargo-related marine insurance was about US$28.5 billion. Of this total, about US$16.1 billion or 57% was for the cargo insurance, US$6.9 billion or 24% was for the Hull & Machinery insurance and about US$1.8 billion or 7% was for the protection and indemnity insurance or the P&I insurance.[18] To put these numbers in perspective, the total capital value, as of the start of 2016, of the world merchant ship fleet, including the order-book, was estimated at US$922 billion.[19] Based on the total premium of US$8.6 billion for H&M and P&I combined, in 2016 the cost of ship-related marine insurance was therefore about 0.1% of the value of all ships. This percentage happened to be very close to the ratio between the number of total ship losses and the total number of merchant ships for the same year, which was approximately 50 to 50,000. Certainly, many other factors should be taken into consideration. For example, the total loss of ships is only one of many risks covered by marine insurance.

For shipowners, the marine insurance cost varies from one ship to another. A variety of factors, such as the type and size of the ship, the age and trading areas of the ship, will impact on the premium level. The insurance cost is a part of a ship's operating costs, which include also the manning cost and the maintenance cost. The share of insurance cost, both H&M and P&I, of the total operating cost dropped from 14.3% in 2004 to 11.7% in 2016.[20] Not only has the relative cost of insurance fallen but the absolute amount has also reduced. The total amount of premium for H&M insurance decreased from US$8,300 million in 2011 to about US$7,000 million in 2016.[21]

What will the future of marine insurance be?

There are a number of influential factors on marine insurance cost. The future of marine insurance will most likely be affected by three important changes, which are the rising risks and cost regarding marine environment protection, the business- and supply-chain-related risks and the digitalisation of the shipping sector. Among these three, the most important is digitalisation.

Unlike the situation in the past, today shipping is not a dangerous adventure any more. The safety performance of ships continues to improve, from about 1 total loss per 100 ships in 1910 to about 1 in 1,000 ships in 2016.[22] This tremendous progress achieved in about 100 years is attributable to two main factors. The first is the new technology introduced to the shipping industry in the areas of shipbuilding, ship propulsion, communication and control. The second is the international rules and regulations on maritime safety and environmental protection. These developments explain the long-term downward trend of marine insurance premium per deadweight of ships. However, as ships are getting technically more sophisticated and regulations are more stringent and demanding, seafarers are under ever-increasing pressures. It is claimed that today almost all accidents are caused by human errors.[23] So the effort of safety improvement has been shifted to human elements. Specific regulations are in the areas of seafarer training like the STCW Convention, or working conditions like the MLC2006, or ship management and operation like the ISM Code.

It looks almost certain that the future of marine insurance will not only continue to decline but that it will also be reshaped by the application of new digital technologies in the shipping industry. The ultimate solution to human-error-related risks, which are responsible for most accidents, is the introduction of autonomous ships in the future. When ships are operated autonomously by algorithm, human-related accidents will be massively reduced and safety performance will be improved. Obviously, however, other risks of a different nature, such as cyber risks, will emerge. The big data technology will allow the causes of accidents to be identified and anticipated with more accuracy and speed. The internet of things (IoT) technology will make most technical faults detectable in advance so preventive measures can be taken in time. The blockchain technology will not only improve the efficiency of transactions but also reduce maritime fraud. All the above, which are just some examples, will have a very profound impact on marine insurance. We will discuss the impact of digitalisation on shipping in Chapter 16.

11.4 Intermediary service market

We have discussed the demand for maritime transport, which is about international trade and seaborne cargo, and we have also looked into the supply of maritime transport services, which include various aspects of ships and shipping services. Taking the total amount of cargo per year and dividing it by the total capacity of ships, we can roughly find that every deadweight would transport about 5.5 tons of seaborne trade each year. This means that, given that ships are not always fully loaded, a ship performs roughly about six trips per year on average. So, every year, there are a lot of transport transactions between demand and supply, particularly in liner shipping. However, in most cases, maritime demand and supply do not always meet directly in the market. They meet most of the time via intermediaries.

What are the main roles of shipping intermediaries?

There are three main reasons why shipping intermediaries are needed and these are related to information, facilitation and logistics services. More precisely, the three types of functions of shipping intermediaries are: to satisfy the clients with necessary information on the market; to facilitate the arrangements related, directly or indirectly, to the transport of cargo; and to undertake various kinds of services for clients, such as the preparation of transport documents, booking of the space and the collection of payments.

Information service

The world shipping market consists of many individual markets and each has its own features and characteristics. First of all, the geographical location makes them different from one another. The African market is definitely different from the Latin American market. Similarly, even in countries on the same continent, maritime transport markets and business environment can be very different. This is mainly because the transport-related laws and regulations are different between countries. The economic, social and cultural backgrounds are so different from one place to another that the same business is not done in the same way everywhere. Consequently, knowledge of the local market is essential for doing business. The other aspect is about market contacts or the network of business contacts. In liner shipping markets, for example, the number of shippers is always very large. It is difficult for a shipowner to keep close contact with all shippers in every market or to develop relations with new customers. Therefore, the use of intermediates is necessary to enlarge the market coverage of the shipping companies.

Technical and facilitation service

Technical know-how and professionalism play a vital role in carrying out a business. Today, maritime transport has become a highly developed and specialised market with a high degree of sophistication and complexity. Take the example of a shipowner who wishes to purchase a second-hand ship. They may not have the necessary knowledge to identify and evaluate the vessel. They need to call a specialised shipbroker. Shipping intermediates not only have the commercial knowledge of the market but many of them also have special technical and managerial know-how. For instance, in a ship-chartering business, a shipowner often needs expert help in financial, legal and technical aspects to conclude the contract. In tramp shipping, in-depth knowledge of the market, the charter-party and the ship and cargo are of great importance. Technical know-how needs to be supplemented by market negotiation techniques, skills and experiences. Intermediaries often play an indispensable role both in concluding a transport contract and helping to find solutions to problems and disputes.

Logistic and administrative services

Shipping intermediaries are often requested by shipowners or shippers to provide a variety of logistic services to shipping companies and cargo owners. Such services may include the preparation of transport documents, like transport contracts, insurance arrangements, customs clearance and other procedures and formalities required by the authorities. They sometimes also provide their clients with advice regarding transport routeing and connections. They make necessary arrangements for cargo storage, distribution and door-to-door transport services. Many shipowners rely on intermediaries for the arrangement of port services.

What are the main types of shipping intermediary services?

We can make a distinction between three major groups of intermediaries, namely shipbrokers, shipping agents and freight forwarders. As they work in different markets serving specific clients for different purposes, their functions are often different from each other, even though they have common features too. The following is a discussion of the three groups of shipping intermediaries.

A broker is someone who acts between two parties for pre-defined tasks. A shipowner may need to establish a good relationship with its clients on different occasions. Such occasions may be the purchase of a ship, or the charter of a ship for a voyage or for a period of time, or service arrangements at ports. Although there are many different kinds of shipbrokers, two of them are more commonly used. They are sale/purchase brokers and charter brokers.

- ***Sale/purchase brokers*** specialise in the trading of new and second-hand ships. Buying a ship involves a highly complex decision-making process. Specialised knowledge is needed in the financial and technical areas, for example the financial conditions offered by shipbuilders or sellers and the technical aspects of the ship such as ship specifications and physical condition. They should also have the commercial knowledge on the shipping freight market and its development. A sale/purchase broker should offer services especially in the following areas:
  - To provide information on the reported ship's sales in the recent past. This includes the ship's particulars, the names of the seller and the buyer, price and condition, etc.

- To provide information on the relevant vessels on the market for sale. Again, this should include technical conditions of the ships and their location, names of the sellers, the price offered and other financial conditions, etc. Information on alternative suppliers should also be provided for comparison.
- To provide information and analysis on the market in which the vessel will be operated. This includes freight rates and future trends.
- To provide information on the second-hand market, its development trends and also ship scrapping markets.
- To assist its principal in negotiating the conditions of sale/purchase contract.

- ***Chartering brokers*** specialise in the negotiation of charter parties. Compared with sale/purchase brokers, there are more chartering brokers. Chartering brokers are mostly for tramp shipping and, usually, shipowners and charterers each use their own brokers. Therefore, the contacts and negotiations are often between two brokers each representing the shipowner and the charterer. A chartering broker may also help in the settlement of any dispute. Given the large number of charterers and shipowners and the diversity of situations, chartering brokers usually specialise and concentrate on specific market segments and client bases.

A *ship agent* is someone acting on behalf of a shipowner. There is no clear cut and exact border between a broker and an agent, and the two terms may sometimes be used interchangeably. However, while a shipbroker is working between two parties, a shipping agent is normally representing his principal to deal with various parties. And while a broker's work often ends with the conclusion of the business, an agent's work normally lasts for multiple transactions over a long period of time. Amongst various kinds of shipping agents, two are of particular importance, which are port agents and liner agents.

- ***A port agent*** is generally appointed by a shipowner to represent the owner at the port of call. Port agents are widely used in tramp shipping. The agent assists the shipmaster in all respects including the contacts with local authorities and service providers and the matters related to cargo loading and discharging. A port agent also assists with ship's berthing, the payment of port charges, the supply of ship's provisions such as fuel, fresh water, etc., the processing of port and cargo-handling documents and other activities required by the master and crew at the port. In voyage chartering, cargo-handling cost may be either the owner's or the charterer's responsibility. Whichever party is in charge, the agent must take care of cargo-handling matters with the port authority and stevedoring company. Because of the complexities with respect to cargo-handling matters and the possibility of delay for the ship, a shipowner, if he has to accept the charterer-appointed port agent, may wish to appoint a protecting agent, who will then assist the shipmaster and look after the interests of the shipowner.
- ***A liner agent*** is working as a general agent for one or several shipping lines within a geographical area. The activities carried out by a liner agent are usually much wider than those of a port agent. A liner agent normally enters into written contracts with its principal for an extended period of time. In addition to the activities of a port agent, a liner agent also carries out some other activities, for instance the arrangement of pre- and post-sea transport connections for cargoes, container equipment control and maintenance, freight collection, transport documents, processing and signing of bills of lading on the shipowner's behalf, vessel booking and even sales and marketing for the liner shipping services.

A *freight forwarder* differs from a shipbroker or a shipping agent in many ways. Unlike shipping agents who represent shipowners, freight forwarders represent shippers. They are the organiser of the transport of goods. However, in the absence of an internationally accepted definition, the term "freight forwarder" is sometimes confusing. This is because a freight forwarder may act on behalf of their principal but may also act on their own account. They are transport companies and they are organisers of transport. We distinguish these two kinds of freight forwarders by whether they act on behalf of an exporter/importer as forwarding agents or whether they act in their own name as Non-Vessel-Operating Common Carriers (NVOCC).

- Traditionally, a *forwarding agent* operates on behalf of the exporter or importer. Their work includes the arrangement of loading/discharging of goods, cargo storage, land transport, etc. Today, a forwarding agent may have more responsibilities. They typically are involved in activities ranging from space booking or customs clearance to providing services covering the total transport, distribution and logistics process. A forwarding agent may study the provisions of trade documents and all government regulations and advise the principals on the choices of route.
- *NVOCCs* are shipping companies without ships. When a freight forwarder acts in his own name, the activities undertaken may be very similar to that of a forwarder acting as an agent. However, the big difference is that, when acting as a principal, the NVOCC takes full responsibility for the transport concerned. The company often provides services of cargo consolidation, i.e., the grouping of small parcels from different shippers into a larger consignment. As a principal, an NVOCC issues his own transport documents such as bills of lading. The Federation of International Freight Forwarders Association (FIATA) has a standard transport contract or bill of lading for door-to-door transport organised by freight forwarders.

From a legal point of view, all the above intermediaries have the same status, except for the freight forwarders who undertake activities in their own names, such as NVOCCs. Although differences exist between different national legal systems, some principles are generally followed. When acting as agents, sale/purchase brokers, chartering brokers, port agents, liner agents and forwarding agents, the following terms are frequently used when signing a transport document: "on behalf of …,", "in the name of …,", "for the account of …,", or "as agent only". As such, they accept liability for their own faults or omissions and those of their employees. The brokers or agents may also be exposed to claims from third parties for any loss or damage or personal injury. However, a broker or an agent generally does not accept liability for acts or omissions of the third parties, such as a shipping company, so long as they have shown proper care in the choice of such third parties. When a forwarder acts as a principal, such as the case of an NVOCC, the forwarder is an independent contractor who assumes responsibility in their own name, under the transport document issued by them. In this case, they become liable for the acts and omissions of actual carriers, warehouse operators, etc., whom they have engaged for the performance of the contract.

What are the costs and benefits of using shipping intermediaries?

The services provided by shipping intermediaries are basically to facilitate business transactions. Their services generate a cost as well. So the impact and the future development should be looked at from these two aspects, the value and the cost of the services.

Regarding the value of the services provided by shipping intermediaries related to information, facilitation and logistics, the benefits for customers vary a lot in the market. In shipping, a good broker is often referred to as a "first-class broker". Between brokers and agents there is a big difference in marketing and operation capabilities. A good agent with experience and business connections can enlarge the shipowner's market share in a competitive environment. In a shipping market where defaults, the breaking of contracts, frauds or other kinds of unexpected events and risks are unfortunately still common to see, relying on good brokers is of great importance. The role of agents is important for shipping lines because they are sometimes very influential in the shipper's choice of ocean carriers. Some agents have expanded to become logistics companies by organising door-to-door transport services.

The impact of shipping intermediaries on the cost of transport is twofold. On the one hand, by using a good broker or agent or forwarder, unexpected costs can be avoided or minimised for better cost control. On the other hand, using shipping intermediaries generates a direct cost. The payment takes the form of a commission or fees. A shipbroker, either for sale/purchase or for chartering, is normally paid a commission, which is a percentage of the contract price. The percentage of commission varies from 1% to 5%. It is rare to see the total commission being at more than 7.5% of the contract price. Liner agents, port agents and forwarding agents are usually paid with fees. The fees can be either per service or per annum. For freight forwarders who act as principals, the income is from the difference between the freight with the shipper and that with the shipowner.

How will shipping intermediary services be affected by digital technologies?

The impact of digital technology on the business of shipping intermediaries is direct and profound. This is because all three functions of shipping intermediaries, namely providing information, facilitation of transactions and logistics services, will all be directly affected, though to different degrees. In the early days, information on ships and cargo was provided and received when people met physically at a shipping market. The oldest and the most famous shipping market is the Baltic Exchange in London, which started at the beginning of the 19th century. It is a place where shipbrokers can meet face to face, exchange information and negotiate informally for the chartering and sale/purchase of ships. There are some 750 company members and 2,500 individual members at the Baltic Exchange, The broker, having surveyed the market, will inform his principal, owner or charterer, of the various possibilities. The owner or charterer will then make firm offers through the broker.

However, the Baltic Exchange model of providing intermediary service has not been followed by other shipping markets which were established at later times. This is mainly because, by the time those shipping markets, such as New York, Hong Kong, Tokyo, Hamburg or Singapore, took shape, the new telecommunication technology was developed. As a result, instead of gathering in a place physically, brokers communicated with each other by telegraph, telephone and later by telex and facsimile. It is not uncommon for some brokers and shipowners to have worked together for a long time without ever having the chance to meet with each other. There is thus no tangible market in those places. These kinds of brokers are also called "cabling brokers".

Today, information and telecommunication technology has revolutionised the way people obtain information and the way of doing business. For shipping intermediaries whose function remains as providing information, the new technological development in telecommunication will most probably ruthlessly alter the pattern of brokering and agency businesses. The biggest challenge is not only the widely and freely available access to complete and up-to-date information thanks to the changes brought about by the internet, but the real threat is also coming from the use of AI – artificial intelligence. For example, the latest AI system based on specially designed algorithms can look for, identify, select and process the most important and relevant data and information and present them in a timely fashion to the decision-makers. Eventually, some decisions on ship chartering may also be made by algorithms automatically. The changes and improvement in IT technology are incredibly quick. It is quite certain that the traditional functions of shipping intermediaries will be less and less needed. Although there still are problems related to security, reliability, etc., it is only a matter of time before the functions of shipping intermediaries are by and large automated and integrated into the trade/transport transactions.

What is less likely to be replaced by digital technology is the activity closely dependent on a personal relationship and interactions. For example, a shipbroker will always be essential in the settlement of a dispute. There are also exceptional circumstances where experienced experts rather than algorithms are in a better position to find a solution.

11.5 Marine fuel and bunkering market

The cost of fuel is always one of the largest cost elements for ship operations. But there is a big difference between fuel cost and other ship-related costs. Most ship costs that we have discussed so far are mainly time-based and are, therefore, fixed. This includes capital cost, manning cost, insurance cost and even maintenance cost. The marine fuel cost varies according to the characteristics of the ship and the market conditions. The level of marine fuel cost is mainly determined by the voyage and the speed of the ship.

What are the main characteristics of the marine fuel market?

The vast majority of merchant ships consume two main types of fuel for the main engines and the auxiliary engines which generate electricity for the ship. Both fuels come from the same source, crude oil. At the refineries, the crude oil is distilled to produce distillate fuels such as gas oil and diesel oil, which is used for the auxiliary engines. The residue left after distillation is the base to produce heavy fuel oil (HFO), to be used for the ship's main engines. Heavy fuel oils are black, thick and viscous. The quality of the residue oil depends on the quality of the crude oil. For the residue oils to be used by ships, they should be processed through cleaning, additives and heating to achieve required quality levels. The residue fuels are often blended with distillate fuels to produce what are known as intermediate fuel oils (IFO) or, as they are also called, heavy marine diesel oils. The intermediate fuel oils are classified according to their viscosity. The most commonly used marine fuels are with viscosities of 180 mm^2/s (IFO180) and 380 mm^2/s (IFO380). The biggest advantage of marine fuels is obviously their low cost because, typically, the price of marine diesel oil is 70%–80% higher than marine fuel oil. However, there are also disadvantages to using marine fuel oils. As the residue oils, the heavy fuels have sodium, vanadium and sulphur dissolved in them. So the use of heavy fuels creates more pollution in the environment and has a negative effect on people's health.

In 2016 a total of about 200 million tons of marine fuel oil and about 30 million tons of diesel oil were consumed globally by the international shipping industry. It is estimated that about 55,000 ships burn heavy fuel oil bunkers, of which about 30,000 vessels account for roughly 80%.[24] The main types of bunker are available at all main ports of international trade, usually through oil companies. The port of Singapore alone sold some 50 million tons of marine bunker in 2017.[25] However, the quality and price of marine fuels vary a lot between ports.

What are the economics of fuel?

Merchant ships have significantly benefitted from technological improvement in fuel efficiency. It is argued that in the early 19th century when coal was used to transport long-haul trade, more fuel was consumed than the cargo carried. This was because of the use of coal as fuel, the low fuel efficiency of the propulsion system and the small size of the ships. For example, in 1855, a typical liner ship with 750 tons of cargo, sailing at about 7.5 nautical miles per hour, would consume about 12 tons of coal. This means that about 63 tons of cargo were transported per ton of fuel consumed on a daily basis. By the beginning of the 20th century, although still using coal as fuel, the efficiency of a liner ship carrying about 7,500 tons of cargo was improved by more than three-fold to over 210 tons of cargo per every ton of fuel consumed. In 2015, in a sailing day, for every ton of marine fuel oil, about 700 tons of cargo is transported by a modern large container vessel, which can transport about 180,000 tons of cargo and at 23 nautical miles per hour. But if size-related efficiency gains are excluded, the improvement of fuel economy, which had a remarkable record between the 1960s and the 1980s, has stagnated for the last 30 years. The average fuel consumption of a bulk carrier of 60,000 dwt sailing

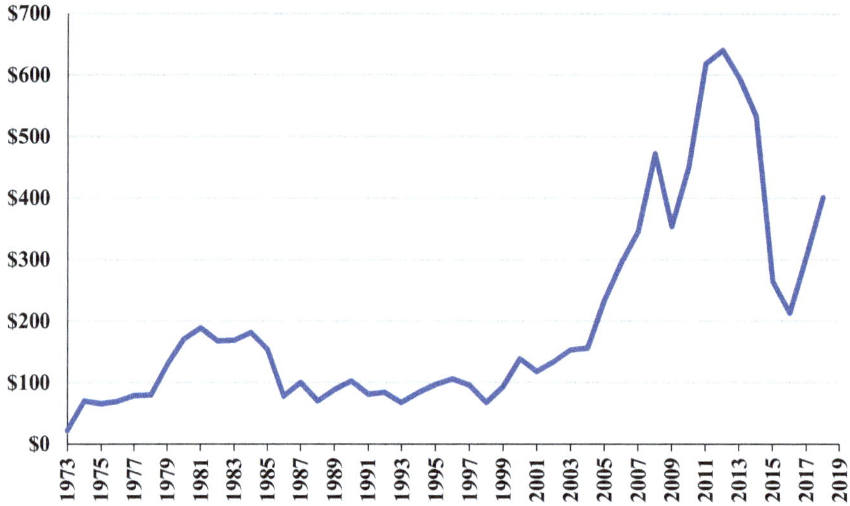

Figure 11.4 Marine bunker prices, in US$/ton of 380cst in Rotterdam, 1973–2018.
Source: based on data from Clarkson.
Note: the bunker prices fluctuate constantly and vary between ports. The prices in the figure are at the beginning of the year in the port of Rotterdam.

at 14.5 nautical miles per hour was at about 45 tons per day in the 1960s, about 40 tons in the 1970s and about 32 tons in the 1980s and has barely changed since then.[26]

The price of the bunker is closely linked to that of the international oil market. It is, therefore, constantly fluctuating. This cost item is very different from that of manning or insurance which are relatively stable and more predictable. Figure 11.4 is a record of bunker prices at the beginning of each year of the main type of marine diesel oil, 380 cst, at the port of Rotterdam from 1973 to 2018. We can see the effect of the oil crisis of 1973, when the price went from US$22 to US$70 per ton, and that of 1979, when the price increased from US$80 to US$170 per ton. The increase was even bigger between 2005 and 2013 when the price was over US$600 per ton. At that time, the bunker cost became the biggest daily cost element for a shipowner and overtook the cost of time charter hire. So, as soon as the freight dropped, bunker-saving measures, such as slow steaming, were adopted widely by most shipowners. The prices of marine bunkers vary a lot between ports and the prices at the port of Rotterdam are very competitive.

What are the challenges of new maritime energy?

The shipping industry is facing two of its biggest challenges which have long-term and far-reaching effects: one is digital disruption, the other is maritime energy. We will discuss the digital disruption in Chapter 16. The driving force behind the energy-related challenge are the concerns about air pollution and greenhouse gas (GHG) emissions from ships. The total shipping industry is responsible for about 3% of the global carbon dioxide (CO_2) emissions, of which about 2.6% are from international shipping. However, when it comes to sulphur oxides (SOx) and nitrogen oxides (NOx), the emissions from international shipping account for 13% and 12% respectively of global total SOx and NOx emissions.[27] In the city of Hong Kong, for example, ships were found to be the biggest source of air pollution and were responsible for more than half of SOx and a third of NOx emissions in the city, overtaking the emissions from all land-based transport.[28] The shipping industry and the governments have been under tremendous pressure from global public opinion to take more drastic action to control GHG emissions from ships.

In 2011, at the IMO's MEPC 62 meeting, a decision was made to amend the MARPOL Convention Annex VI by making the Energy Efficiency Design Index (EEDI) mandatory for new ships and the Ship Energy Efficiency Management Plan (SEEMP) mandatory for all ships. This was the first time for the IMO to introduce a specific and legally binding treaty aiming at climate change mitigation by technical (EEDI) and operational (SEEMP) measures. The EEDI requires, for individual ship design, a minimum energy efficiency level for different ship sizes and types in terms of CO_2 emission per ship's capacity-mile. The SEEMP provides a framework and a mechanism for ships to be managed and operated in an energy-efficient and cost-effective way. A decision was made in 2016, at MEPC 70, that as a part of the SEEMP, ships are required to record and report their fuel oil consumption to the flag State.

The air pollutants caused by ships are due to the quality of the marine fuel oil commonly used by ships which, for example, has high sulphur and nitrogen contents. So reducing such substances is the obvious solution. The IMO decided in 2016 to strengthen the requirement for emission control by introducing the new global limit for the sulphur content of ships' fuel oil from 3.5% m/m (mass by mass) to 0.50% by 1 January 2020. Under MARPOL Convention Annex VI, four sulphur Emission Control Areas (ECA), the Baltic Sea, the North Sea, the North American and the US Caribbean Sea, were established with tighter restrictions on the sulphur limit for fuel oil at 0.1% m/m since 1 January 2015. After the first year of implementation, it was reported that the performance of compliance in the European ECA was good. The additional bunker cost reached an amount between US$128 and $244 per ton of fuel. But because of the decrease in the market price of crude oil during this period, the shifting of ships' bunker from high to low sulphur content fuel was adopted by both the shipping companies and shippers rather smoothly.[29]

Three options are available to the shipowners in order to comply with the new IMO regulations, with different technical, operational and cost implications. The first is to take low sulphur content bunker fuels; the second is to install on-board emission-compliant engines or gas cleaning equipment such as scrubbers to remove sulphur dioxide from the exhaust; the third is to adopt alternative fuels, such as LNG, and make vessel modifications. The additional cost of low sulphur fuel will be borne by both shipping companies and shippers.[30] The use of scrubbers has not been popular due to concerns about cost and reliability. The cost of retrofitting is expensive. As far as alternative fuels are concerned, LNG has been selected by most ship companies that opted for this approach rather than renewable energies or methanol. However, to use LNG, the high ship cost and the shortage of bunkering capacities at ports remain a challenge.[31] According to the IMO's GHG emission control ambitions, international shipping will eventually be a carbon-free sector.

11.6 Summary

In this chapter we have discussed the economic and market characteristics of some main maritime services. We began with the seafarer market. One of the economic features of this market is that the number of seafarers per ship does not change much for different sizes of ships. We found that the biggest seafaring countries are not necessarily those that operate ships but those whose GDP per capita is between US$2,000 and $11,000. The seafarer market is a global, free and competitive market. The price of seafarers is determined by the law of supply and demand. While the demand for seafarers is not price-sensitive, the supply is more price elastic. So the market imbalance between the demand and supply of seafarers is a short-term rather than a long-term phenomenon. The development of seafaring has been and will continue to be affected by technological advancement. As a result, the crew size will continue to reduce and highly autonomous ships might be a reality in the not too distant future.

We have examined the market for ship registration. Although legally defined by the UN Convention on the Law of the Sea and generally perceived as an administrative procedure put in place by the public authorities, in effect most ship registration is done as a commercial service by a dozen countries of the so-called open registries. Presently, over 70% of global merchant ships are under the flags of open-registry countries, which do not have the financial and commercial control of the ships. Although the open registry practice started for the avoidance of regulatory constraints, the real cause of its extraordinary growth is tax-related advantages as well as the operational freedom and flexibility. On the whole, the safety performance in terms of ships' compliance with the international rules and regulations of the main open registries is not a matter of concern.

We have also discussed the marine insurance market. Ships are insured to cover the risks of loss or damage to the ships or to third parties. There are two kinds of marine insurance: one is called the Hull & Machinery insurance, which covers the ship's own loss, and the other is called the Protection & Indemnity insurance, which is a third-party liability insurance. As the safety record of the shipping industry continues to improve, the insurance premium as a percentage of the ship operating cost reduces.

With regard to the market of shipping intermediaries, such as shipbrokers, agents and freight forwarders, we have discussed the three basic services of information and advice, facilitation of negotiation and logistics and administrative support. There are two main types of shipbrokers: sale/purchase brokers who help shipowners with the selling and buying of ships; and ship chartering brokers who help with the conclusion of charter parties. There are two types of ship agents as well: port agents who are mainly working in the tramp shipping market and liner agents who work for shipping lines. Freight forwarders work in cargo's interest and there are also two types of them: forwarding agents and NVOCCs. The latter are not agents in the legal sense as they act as principals for transport, though they do not own and operate ships. As in the other sectors, the shipping intermediaries have been very much affected by the development of information and communication technologies. It is generally believed that more structural changes will happen in this area in the era of digital disruption.

Finally, we have analysed the bunker market. The cost of fuel has always been a major expenditure of ship operation. We looked at three aspects of marine fuels: the price of fuel, the issues of fuel efficiency and the environmental impact of marine fuel. The prices of the bunker are closely related to the global prices of crude oil, so they are volatile. Fuel efficiency had a steady improvement until the 1980s and, since then, very limited progress has been made. Presently, in the area of maritime energy, the biggest challenge is greenhouse gas emission control and the reduction of the environmental impact. About 2.6% of the global CO_2 emission was from the international shipping industry in 2018. Shipping's share of more harmful pollutants such as SOx and NOx is 13% and 12% respectively. In some port cities, ships are the biggest source of air pollution. Since the new millennium, the ship-sourced GHG emissions and air pollution have been the most actively debated topics at the IMO. The new regulations include the mandatory application of the technical measures (EEDI) for all new ships and the operational measures (SEEMP) for all ships. In addition, stricter requirements with specific target dates have been set regarding the sulphur content of marine fuels and GHG emissions.

Notes

1 UNCTAD (2017).
2 BIMCO/ISF (2015).
3 It is estimated that, due to leave, training, illness and other reasons, for every position on board a ship, about 1.8 persons for officers and 1.3 persons for ratings. Or, on average, 1.5 persons per position on board (Ibid., note 2).

4 Drewry Shipping Consultant (2015), p. 2.
5 Ibid., note 1.
6 Gardner B. M. and Pittit S. J. (1999).
7 Gekara V. (2009).
8 Nguyan T. T., Ghaderi H., Caesar, L. D., and Cahoon (2014).
9 Ibid., note 2.
10 It is reported that, on 16 May 2017, totally autonomous cargo ships carrying container, bulk and general cargo started operation on coastal routes in Norway. Source: accessed 13 January 2018, http://astat.autonomous-ship.org.
11 Blanke M. (2017).
12 Swaby A. (2014).
13 UNCTAD (2017). According to UNCTAD, the five largest open registry countries in 2017 are: Panama, Liberia, Marshall Islands, Malta and Bahamas.
14 OECD (2018).
15 Panama (2018).
16 Paris MOU (2018) and Tokyo MOU (2018).
17 ISL (2016).
18 IUMI (2019).
19 Hampson A. (2016).
20 IUMI (2012, 2017).
21 Drewry Shipping Consultant (2012).
22 Allianz (2012).
23 Rothblum A. (2006). The USCG Research and Development Centre indicates that the rate of human error varies from 75% for fire to 96% for collision.
24 Grati H. (2017).
25 Ship & Bunker (2018).
26 Stopford M. (2015).
27 IMO (2014).
28 OECD (2014).
29 Den Boer E., Ahdour S., and Meerwakdt G. (2016).
30 ICS (2017).
31 Lloyd's List (2018). The French liner shipping company CMA-CGM has ordered nine 22,000 teu container ships which will be powered by engines using LNG instead of heavy fuel oil. It is believed that each of these ships will cost an additional US$ 20 million.

References

Allianz. (2012), "*Safety and Shipping, 1912–2012*", Munich, Germany, p. 13.

BIMCO/ISF. (2015) "*Manpower Report – The Global Supply and Demand for Seafarers in 2015*", London.

Blanke M. (2017), "*A Pre-analysis on Autonomous Ships*", Technical University of Denmark.

Den Boer E., Ahdour S., and Meerwakdt G. (2016) "*SECA Assessment: Impacts of 2015 SECA Marine Fuel Sulphur Limits*", CE Delft, 16.7H83.43, April 2016.

Drewry Shipping Consultant. (2012), "*Ship Operating Cost Annual Review and Forecast 2012–13*", Drewry Shipping Consultant, London.

Drewry Shipping Consultant. (2015) "*Manning 2015 Annual Report*", Drewry Maritime Research, London, p. 2

Gardner B. M. and Pittit S. J. (1999) "*Seafarers and the Land Based Jobs Market: The Present UK Situation*", Marine Policy, Vol. 23, No. 1 (January 1999), pp. 103–115.

Gekara V. (2009) "*Understanding Attrition in UK Maritime Education and Training*", Globalisation, Societies and Education, Vol. 9, No. 2, pp. 217–232.

Grati H. (2017) "*Bunker Fuel in 2020*". Retrieved 23 February 2018 from ihsmarkit.com/research-analysis/imo.html and www.tokyo-mou.org/doc/Flag%20performance%20list%202016.pdf.

Hampson A. (2016), "*The Evolving Financing Landscape of Shipping since 2009*", Marine Money London Ship Finance Forum, 27 January 2016.

ICS. (2017), "*International Chamber of Shipping Annual Review, 2017*", ICS, London, p. 18.

IMF. (2016) "*World Economic Outlook, 2016*", IMF, Washington DC.

IMO. (2014), "*Reduction of GHG Emissions from Ships – Third IMO GHG Study 2014*", MEPC 67/ INF. 3, 25 July 2014, p. 14

ISL. (2016), "*Shipping Statistics Yearbook, 2016*", Casualty returns. Bremen, Germany. ISSN: 0721-3220, December 2016.

IUMI. (2012, 2017) "*Global Marine Insurance Report*", 2012 and 2017. International Union of Marine Insurance.

IUMI. (2019) "*Global Marine Insurance Report 2018*", and IUMI Stats Report 2018.

Lloyd's List. (2018), "*LNG Makes Power Play for Container Shipping*", Analysis, Lloyd's List, 23 January 2018.

Nguyan T.T., Ghaderi H., Caesar, L. D., and Cahoon S. (2014) "*Current Challenges in the Recruitment and Retention of Seafarers*", The Asian Journal of Shipping and Logistics, Vol. 30, No. 2 (August 2014), pp. 217–242.

OECD. (2014), "*Shipping Emissions in Ports*", International Transport Forum, Discussion Paper 2014-20, OECD, Paris, p. 11

OECD. (2018) "*Statutory Corporate Income Tax, 2017*", *OECD* Stat. Retrived 20 January 2018 from https://stats.oecd.org/index.aspx?DataSetCode=Table_II1.

Panama. (2018) "*Benefits and Advantages of Ship Registry in Panama*", Retrieved on 25 January 2018 from www.panama-offshore-services.com/benefits_and_advantages_of_ship_registry_in_panama.htm

Paris MOU. (2018) "*Paris MOU Flag Performance List*", Retrieved 25 January 2018 from www.parismou.org/detentions-banning/white-grey-and-black-list

Rothblum A. (2006), "*Human Error and Marine Safety*", Vol. IV, USCG Risk-based decision making guidelines, USCG Research and Development Centre.

Ship & Bunker. (2018) "*Singapore Sets New Annual Bunker Sales Record with over 50 Million MT Sold in 2017*", Asia Pacific News, 12 January 2018. Retrieved 23 February 2018 from https://shipandbunker.com/news/apac/751732-singapore-sets-new-annual-bunker-sales-record-with-over-50-million-mt-sold-in-2017

Stopford M., (2015), "*What Lies Ahead, Predicting the Future of Operating Environment*", Fathom Shipping, September 2015. Retrieved 3 March 2018 from www.fathomshippingevents.com/uploads/2/5/3/9/25399626/dr_

Swaby A. (2014), "*Why so Many Shipowners Find Panama's Flag Convenient*", BBC, 5 August 2014. Retrieved 21 January 2018 from www.bbc.com/news/world-latin-america-28558480.

Tokyo MOU. (2018) "*Tokyo MOU Flag Performance List*", Retrieved 25 January 2018 from www.tokyo-mou.org/doc/Flag%20performance%20list%202016.pdf.

UNCTAD. (2016) "*Review of Maritime Transport*", UNCTAD/RMT/2016, Geneva.

UNCTAD. (2017) "*Review of Maritime Transport 2017*", UNCTAD/RMT/2017, p. 28.

Chapter 12

The economics of the maritime transport freight market

The freight discussed in this chapter refers to the income received by the shipping companies from the users of the transport services provided. It is also the price paid by the users. This income is obviously meant to cover the cost incurred and to allow the shipping companies to continue and to develop the business. We will examine the structure and the basic functions of the maritime transport freight. As tramp shipping differs from liner shipping, we will have separate discussions on the freight of the two markets. The key to understanding maritime freight is whether the market is competitive or not. The freight market is periodically interrupted by expected and unexpected events, so it is hard to predict. One of the characteristics of international shipping is the volatility of the freight market in the short and medium terms, which has an important impact on the long-term profitability of the sector.

12.1 The structure and basic functions of maritime freight

Maritime transport activities generate costs at different stages, from ship acquisition to ship operation and voyage arrangement. The freight is the revenue received from the users to cover the costs and, hopefully, to make a profit. The aim of a commercial enterprise, such as a shipping company, is to maximise its profit, especially in the long term. To do this, the enterprise should either maximise the revenue or minimise the costs or do both. We will first look at the ways in which various aspects of maritime transport costs are paid.

How are the maritime transport costs divided?

We have discussed various aspects of shipping costs so far. In Chapter 8 the capital cost of ships was examined, in Chapter 10 the port cost was analysed and in Chapter 11 the manning cost, registration cost, insurance cost, brokers/agents-related cost, as well as bunker cost were discussed. These cost elements can be divided into three categories as capital cost, operation cost and voyage cost.

- ***The capital cost*** includes all cost with regard to the acquisition of the vessel. The cost of the ship, either new or second-hand, is referred to as capital cost and it is paid, in the case of a new vessel, over a period of time. Depending on the way in which the vessel is financed, i.e., by equity or debt funding, the capital cost is paid in the form of depreciation or the repayment of the loan and the interest. Apart from the purchasing value of the vessel, a number of other factors also have an impact on the level of the capital cost. They include the rate or period of depreciation, the loan ratio, the interest rate and the pay-back period of the ship loan.

- ***The operation cost*** refers to those costs that are spent to make the ship operational. To make a delivered ship operational or employable, the shipowner has to pay for the crew, insurance and maintenance. Equipping the ship with a full and competent crew is the first part of the operation cost. Shore-based personnel and management cost is also part of the operation cost. In addition, the ship should be covered by insurance, which is the second part of the operation cost. As explained in the previous chapter, this includes the Hull & Machinery insurance and the Protection & Indemnity liability insurance. The third part of the operation cost is related to ship maintenance. This cost is spent to keep the ship seaworthy and in the required technical condition. When the above three costs on manning, insurance and maintenance are paid, the ship is ready to be used.
- ***The voyage cost*** refers to the costs that are involved directly in a specific voyage. There are mainly two types of cost. The first is the bunker cost. This cost varies according to the voyage the ship is taking. The cost is affected by the length of the voyage as well as the price of bunker the ship pays. This last element, as described before, can vary significantly between different routes and ports. The second type of voyage cost is the cost of port and canals. The port cost has two parts. One is related to port charges paid to the port authorities on the use of the facilities and on the services. The other is related to cargo handling, which, in the case of a landlord port, is paid to a stevedoring company.

How are the different ship costs paid?

Unlike some people might think, the shipowner may not have to pay for all the cost incurred to the transport as described above. There are differences between tramp shipping and liner shipping transport, and within tramp shipping there are variations between the types of charter parties. Table 12.1 is an illustration of who pays for which cost between a shipowner and a charterer or a shipper. As we can see, a liner shipping company pays all three parts of the transport cost. However, in the case of a bareboat charter, the shipowner pays only for the capital cost, while the charterer pays both the operation and voyage costs. Under a time charter, the shipowner pays both the capital and the operation costs, leaving the charterer to pay the voyage cost. When it comes to a voyage charter, the situation is more complex with respect to the voyage cost. While it is always the shipowner who pays the bunker

Table 12.1 Cost sharing between shipowner and charterer by type of shipping.

	Tramp shipping			*Liner shipping*
	Bareboat	Time	Voyage	Liner
Capital cost	Owner	Owner	Owner	Owner
Operation cost	Charterer	Owner	Owner	Owner
Voyage cost	Charterer	Charterer	Chart/Owner*	Owner

Source: Shuo Ma.

* *For cargo handling at ports, the cost may be paid by the owner or the charterer according to the charter party.*

cost, the canal tolls and the ship-related port charges, the cost of cargo handling is up for negotiation with the charterer. As a result, either party can be responsible for cargo handling and paying for it.

As a shipowner bears different parts of shipping costs when he deploys his ship under different arrangements, he does not receive the same kind of payments, or freight, from his customers who may also cover different proportions of the costs. Therefore, the forms of the payments are different and the names used for the payments are also not the same. Three major distinctions are to be made in this respect: liner shipping tariffs, voyage charter freight and time or bareboat charter hire.

Why do the cost-sharing schemes differ?

The main reason why a shipowner sometimes is not paying every category of the cost is about the degree of involvement of the shipping company in the operation of the ship. A shipowner may wish to just be a "landlord" by limiting his involvement to the ownership of the vessel and letting someone else operate it. This is the case of bareboat charter whereby the ship is transferred from the owner to the charterer without crew or insurance. So the charterer will man, insure and maintain the ship and consequently is fully responsible for the operation cost and voyage cost. While the involvement of a shipowner is at the minimum in a bareboat charter, their involvement is at the maximum in liner shipping. To understand the reasons for the cost-sharing, we may again compare shipping with urban passenger transport. Bus companies, like shipping lines, are responsible for all costs. Taxis, like voyage charter, also pay all costs. But when renting a car, like time charter, the client will pay for voyage costs such as fuel and bridge toll. In the case of a car lease, like a bareboat charter, even the cost of maintenance and insurance will also be paid by the customer.

Voyage chartering is a kind of tramp shipping practice that is widely used in the sea transport of cargo in bulk. In this kind of shipping arrangement, the shipowner bears all the transport costs except for the cargo-handling charges, as who will be responsible for this work and pay the costs is negotiated for each contract. Who will pay for cargo handling must be clearly stated in the charter party. Sometimes shipowners pay the cargo-loading cost but not the discharging cost or vice versa. If a shipowner pays the cargo-handling costs, it is the same situation as in liner shipping practice and then the term of payment is stated in the charter party as the "liner term" freight rate. If the shipowner does not pay for the cargo-loading costs, which means the charterer pays, the corresponding freight rate will be stated as a "free in" (F.I.) rate. If the shipowner does not pay for the discharging cost, the freight is known as a "free out" (F.O.) rate. If the case is that the shipowner does not pay the cargo-handling costs at all, then a "free in and out" (F.I.O.) rate is applied.

12.2 The freight of the tramp shipping market

About 60% of the global seaborne trade in 2017 was transported by tramp shipping.[1] The amount of freight generated in this market does not represent the same proportion of the total freight revenue of the world's shipping industry. A distinction should be made between the voyage charter on the one hand and the time charter and bareboat charter on the other.

What is the basic structure of voyage charter freight?

As explained in Chapter 7, more than 90% of charter parties concluded for tanker ships and bulk carriers are voyage based. The payment of the freight is made based on the agreed amount of cargo carried from the pre-specified port A to port B starting on the date indicated in the charter party. The payment is thus in the form of, for example, an amount of US dollars per ton of cargo. The level of the freight varies based on the market conditions. We will discuss this aspect later in the chapter.

As the freight is collected according to the amount of cargo carried, to provide enough quantity of cargo on time is one of the major obligations of the charterer. Normally, this quantity of cargo is indicated in the charter. In practice, a tolerance margin of, say, 5% more or less of cargo at the owner's (or charterer's) option may be allowed. This is because often the amount of a bulk cargo can hardly be exact as per the charter party due to shrinkage or wastage. The shipmaster may also want to have the flexibility for technical or economic reasons. If the charterer fails to provide the agreed amount of cargo, he has to pay for the shortfall to the shipowner in the form of a "dead freight". It is also possible that the shipowner and the charterer agree on a lump sum freight payable regardless of the actual amount of cargo transported. This is a solution when there is a big uncertainty in respect of the amount of cargo.

As mentioned above, another special feature of voyage charter freight is about the cargo-handling terms. At the stage of charter-party negotiation, it has to be decided who, the shipowner or the charterer, is responsible for cargo handling at both the loading and discharging ports. In addition, a loading and discharging rate are also agreed on when the charterer is responsible for cargo handling. The time allowed for cargo handling is called "lay-time". Accordingly, a penalty and reward clause is also included. If the actual cargo-handling time exceeds the agreed lay-time, a penalty charge is to be paid by the charterer to the shipowner and this charge is called "demurrage". If the lay-time has not been used up, a reward is to be calculated according to the charter party and an award is given by the shipowner to the charterer, which is called "dispatch money". The level of demurrage is subject to negotiation between the two parties, but it reflects the opportunity cost rather than the actual fixed cost of the ship. So the higher the market freight, the higher the demurrage would be. The dispatch money, which is less affected by the opportunity effect, is usually half of the demurrage.

The payment for a voyage charter for oil tankers is different from that for dry bulk cargo. People use a special system in oil transport known as the "World Scale". The scale system was first introduced during World War Two. Compared with the dry cargo market, oil tankers are specially designed to carry large amounts of a single homogeneous cargo, which is oil or other liquid products. It is simpler for both the shipowner and charterer to have a scale, which will provide the same daily net return, i.e., freight income minus costs, for any tanker irrespective of the voyage performed. The system provides both parties with the flexibility of using alternative loading and discharging ports. In September 1969 the "Worldscale rate system" was adopted and in January 1989 the New Worldscale (NWS) was introduced.

The worldscale rate system consists basically of a series of dollar figures representing the freight per ton for virtually all possible voyages. The way such basic rates are calculated can roughly be summed up as follows: a nominal tanker of 75,000 dwt is, in theory, sent on an infinite number of round voyages sailing at 14.5 knots with a bunker consumption of 55 tons per day. Diesel fuel consumption for a purpose other than steaming is counted as 100 tons per round voyage and 5 tons per each port. It is assumed that the nominal tanker has a total of 4 days of port time and 12 hours for each additional port other than loading and discharging ports. The tanker receives US$12,000 per day as income. The Worldscale schedule specifies the price of bunkers in the calculation and the Worldscale Association collects information about the port costs for the nominal tanker in the various ports. By using the round voyage distances, it is possible to calculate the total costs for the nominal tanker ship and this figure is then divided by the total cargo that could be carried to get the flat rate for that particular voyage. Similar calculations have been made for over 320,000 voyages. The full collection of the flat rates is published as the New Worldscale 100. To illustrate how flat rates are presented in the New Worldscale Schedule, we can look at the example shown in Table 12.2. The port shown in capital letters is the discharge port, so the flat rate for a voyage from Adelaide to Kobe is US$13.15. This rate is called New Worldscale 100 (NWS100 or W100). Depending on the quantity of oil to transport and on the current market conditions, the charterer and the shipowner will agree on a percentage of the flat rate. For instance, they may agree on NWS50, which means

Table 12.2 An example of the Worldscale 100.

KOBE	*US$/MT*
Adelaide	**13.15**
Aden	**14.23**

Source: Worldscale 100.
Note: a percentage is negotiated, agreed and applied to the actual voyage undertaken.

that the freight rate is 50% of the flat rate in the New Worldscale Schedule. If the agreed percentage is NWS120, then 120% of the flat rate is applicable.

What is the basic structure of bareboat and time charter hire?

In bareboat chartering and time chartering, the charterer uses the vessel for a fixed period of time during which the said vessel is under the charterer's control and the charterer can use the ship for their own purpose. Therefore, the payment for bareboat charter or time charter is called ship hire. It is paid in terms of a certain amount of US dollars per day. In the case of the time charter, the shipowner covers the ship's capital costs and operating costs with this payment. In the case of a bareboat charter, the shipowner pays capital cost only. In both cases, the voyage cost is paid by the charterer.

The length of a time charter can vary from several months to several years or even longer. Bareboat charters are always long term, due to the deep involvement and large investment committed by the charterer. The level of hire for bareboat charter and long-term time charter tends to be low and more cost-based, e.g., based on capital and/or operating costs plus a profit. For time charters of shorter terms, such as those lasting less than a year, on the other hand, the level of hire is very much influenced by the current market conditions and it thus fluctuates a lot.

Although calculated on a daily basis, the hire is payable every month in advance. The time charter hire starts to be paid from the moment the ship is delivered to the charterer until the moment the ship is redelivered to the shipowner. Therefore, the places of delivery and redelivery are an item of negotiation and are stated in the charter party as well. The technical conditions of the ship are obviously an important factor affecting the bareboat or time charter hire. Among the different aspects of a ship's technical particulars, a charterer is often more concerned with the ship's sailing speed and bunker consumption for the reasons of maintaining a certain level of productivity and cost control. The ship's maintenance record is another area to look into. Even though the charterer does not pay for the ship repair if it is a time charter, they generally incur a loss should their chartered vessel be "off-hire" for repair.

On the tramp market, which is a competitive market, a shipowner generally has the possibility to put his vessel either on a voyage charter or a time charter employment. Which one to choose depends largely on the forecast of the market development trend. Generally speaking, in a rising market, it will be better if the shipowner uses his ships on short-term engagement, for example on a voyage charter, so it is possible to deploy the ship on higher freight for the following fixtures. By the same token, in a falling market, the shipowner should fix his ships on longer-term employment such as time charter in order not to suffer from a depressed freight market in the future. Understandably, a charterer will try to do the opposite. So it is fair to say that, thanks to the fact that freight level is unpredictable, shipowners and charterers are making different and sometimes opposite forecasts and, as a consequence, charter parties are concluded.

12.3 The freight of the liner shipping market

In liner shipping, ship companies provide much more comprehensive transport services than tramp shipowners do. The shipping services are offered on a regular basis between fixed ports to a large number of shippers with a great variety of cargoes. All costs related to the shipping transport, including cargo handling at ports, are covered by the shipping companies. It is not practical for the shipowner to negotiate a rate with each shipper, on each item of cargo and for each voyage. Therefore, a form of pre-fixed transport tariffs is used by shipping lines to collect their payment from the clients.

What is the structure of liner shipping tariff?

Liner shipping tariffs are normally published and are usually not negotiable, though in practice the shippers with a large cargo commitment may be offered reduced tariffs. The level of the pre-fixed liner shipping rates depends on a number of factors. The general market situation is one factor and the levels of service is another. For liner shipping, to provide a regular service with a fixed schedule, a ship may not be fully loaded each time due to reasons such as the fluctuation of transport demand. Tariffs should, therefore, be set at a sufficient level to compensate for the cost of unutilised space. This is necessary because it is in the general interest of trade to have reliable and stable liner shipping services and the shippers are willing to pay for the cost.

The types of cargo moved by liner shipping are mostly manufactured goods, either transported in break-bulk form by conventional general cargo ships or in containers by specialised cellular container ships. The general cargo in break-bulk is loaded onto ships in bags, boxes, bales, drums, etc., and often secured on pallets. These cargoes are stored in conventional twin-deck ships. For conventional general cargo ships and container ships, the tariff structure is also different. Broadly speaking, the liner shipping freight payment consists of three parts: the basic rates, the surcharges and the rebates.

- ***Basic rates*** are the central piece of the liner tariff. These are typically set up for different shipping routes and directions. During the pre-containerisation period, for the transport of break-bulk cargo, the basic rates often varied according to different kinds of cargo as well. This is called commodity rates. Each commodity has a specific rate for different shipping routes. Similar products can also be put together into groups and the whole tariff consists of a number of classes of products. The basic rates are relatively stable in the short term. They are only revised periodically, for example every six months, every year or even longer, depending on the market circumstances.

  The level of the basic rates of commodity-based tariffs depends on a number of factors. The specific requirements for the transportation of the cargo are an important consideration, which includes the quantity, the packaging conditions, the transport and handling specifications, etc. However, the transport costs, though remaining a fundamental element, are not the only decisive factor for tariffs. The value of the cargo is a major consideration when determining the commodity rates. The general rule is that the higher the value of the cargo is, the higher the rate will be and the more the shippers should pay. Consequently, low-value commodities are cross-subsidised by high-value ones and the total transport quantity is increased. The original idea for such differential tariffs was that to maintain frequent and regular liner services, sufficient quantity of cargo needed to be consolidated and this was only possible if low-value cargoes also used the service. Yet, most low-value cargoes could not afford the liner tariffs. So a differential tariff system was the only solution. Obviously, market competition is another important factor that affects the level of basic rates. The rates depend also on the situation of return cargo for the round trip.

  In the transport of containerised cargo, whenever the quantity of cargo is large enough for a full container load, the basic rate is calculated per container rather than per the type and weight of cargo. This kind of liner tariff is called the "box rate". Although the box rate can also be commodity-based, in the majority of cases it is a FAK (freight all kinds) flat rate per either a 20-foot or a 40-foot container. The FAK rate has dominated containerised shipping because the quantity of cargo is no longer a matter of concern for liner shipping companies. And also because the transport conditions and cargo-handling activities have been standardised for all cargoes in container transport. The discriminative commodity box rates have given way to the FAK rates for most shipping lines. This is a fixed box rate for a particular shipping route charged per container regardless of the contents of the container. Of course, different rates are charged for dangerous cargo, reefer cargo or other special containerised cargo for which particular care is required for the transport. The level of FAK box rates depends on factors like transport costs, competition in the market, the balance of trade, etc.

- ***Surcharges*** are collected by shipping lines to cover the additional, sometimes unexpected, expenses in relation to the carriage of the goods. In the transport of break-bulk cargo, while the basic rates are kept relatively stable, many kinds of surcharges are used to offset any unpredictable increase in costs. Surcharge for cargo that is over-weight and over-dimension, for instance, is collected to offset the additional costs related to the transport. Congestion surcharge is applicable to both break-bulk and containerised cargo, often temporarily, during the period of port congestion. Port surcharge is collected to cover high costs at some particular ports because of poor port efficiency or abnormal high port tariffs. Bunker surcharge, often referred to as BAF (bunker adjustment factor), is used to offset the effect of some sudden increases of bunker prices. Certainly, bunker surcharge can be a variable and temporary cost. Devaluation surcharge, or currency adjustment factor, is collected to compensate for the owner's losses due to the changes of currency exchange rates, often between the US dollar and another currency. Shipowners pass the extra costs onto shippers because it is argued that the impact of the cost increases is substantial.

  In the transport of containerised cargo, the costs of cargo handling make up a significant part of a shipping line's total costs and this expenditure varies greatly from one port to the next. Many container shipping lines use a surcharge called Terminal Handling Charge (THC) to cover this extra expenditure on cargo handling at ports.
- ***Rebates*** are the reduction of freight rates offered by shipping lines to some clients. This has been a common practice in liner shipping with the aim to increase the volume of traffic in a competitive market. The two major kinds of rebates frequently used are deferred rebate and quantity rebate.

  Deferred rebate is a loyalty rebate that is offered to the shippers that give the totality of the cargo under their control for the selected shipping routes and for a specific period of time to the shipping line. Quantity rebate is given to shippers with large quantities of cargo to transport during a specific period of time. For example, some shipping lines give quantity rebate to shippers whose cargo in one or a series of shipments exceeds a certain amount. In container shipping, quantity rebate is given to big shippers or their representatives in the form of "service contract", which means that the shipper will be able to enjoy a favourable rate as long as they can provide a certain number of containers to the shipping line during a fixed period of time, such as a year.

Liner shipping tariff normally covers only the ocean transport costs including cargo handling and port charges. Some shipping lines offer multimodal transport packages with a door-to-door and logistics service and therefore they will apply a total transport tariff, beyond the port-to-port transport. In the case of transhipment, shipping lines may collect a through-transport tariff too. This can be considered as an addition to an ocean transport tariff. Total transport tariff not only includes costs of various modes of transport but it also covers charges related to warehousing, documentation, formality processing and sometimes cargo distribution activities, etc.

12.4 The competitive nature of the freight market

Ideally, maritime freight will be at a level that is just covering the marginal cost of shipping and leaves the shipping company with a reasonable margin of profit for future development. However, while the transport costs of the world fleet as a whole remain more or less constant in the short and medium terms, the shipping freight rates are far from stable. The dry bulk freight market, for example, is volatile and can change by a 100%, up or down, within months. The pricing mechanism in shipping has almost never been completely cost-based. It is not difficult to imagine how risky for a shipowner as well as a charterer it is to operate in a market with highly volatile freights. In this section we will discuss briefly the determining factors that lead to the changes in freight rates over time.

Why does competition matter for freight level changes?

Who decides the level of freight rates? Cargo owners or shipowners? This question can only be answered by looking at whether the market is competitive or not. It means that the freight mechanism depends on the competitive nature of the market. If there is no competition on the demand side but a lot of competition on the supply side or, in other words, there are shippers who enjoy a monopolistic situation while many shipowners are competing for business, then the freight levels tend to be decided by the shippers. Similarly, if there is no competition on the supply side, then the shipowner will have dominant power to decide on the level of freight rates. When both demand and supply are in a competitive environment, then the freight level is decided by the balance of demand and supply in the market.

Therefore, before discussing how the freight market mechanism operates, we will first look at an example of a competitive market of maritime transport supply. A competitive market should satisfy the following four conditions.

1 ***Freedom of entry and exit***: any new company is free to enter the market and any existing company is free to exit the market if they wish.
2 ***Homogeneous service***: different companies provide a similar service with little difference in quality, so, for customers, the suppliers are interchangeable and compete with each other.
3 ***Well-informed customers***: cargo owners are fully aware of the existence of alternative suppliers and the difference in freight offered.
4 ***Large number of service suppliers***: the number of shipping companies operating in the market is large enough that the change in the production of one company does not have any impact on price.

If a market has not only satisfied the above conditions but met them completely, it is then a perfectly competitive market. Otherwise, it is an imperfectly competitive market. In a perfectly competitive market, the supplier is a price taker or, in the maritime context, the shipping company is a freight taker. This means that the supplier can change the level of its production or transport capacity, but such a change has no or little effect on the freight level. So the company has to accept whatever freight is offered on the market as shown in Figure 12.1b. The same can be said on the demand side.

In a competitive shipping market, the freight level is determined by the total demand and total supply at the equilibrium point *E*, with the corresponding freight at *F* and output at *Q*. If the demand and the supply change in a different direction or at a different pace, a new equilibrium has to be reached with a new freight level and output quantity. This is called the law of supply and demand as illustrated in Figure 12.1a. As far as a shipping company is concerned, the situation is different. Because it is in a perfect competition, the company has no control of the freight or, in other words, no matter how much or how little the company produces, there is no effect whatsoever on the level of the freight, because the company's total production capacity makes up only a very small fraction of

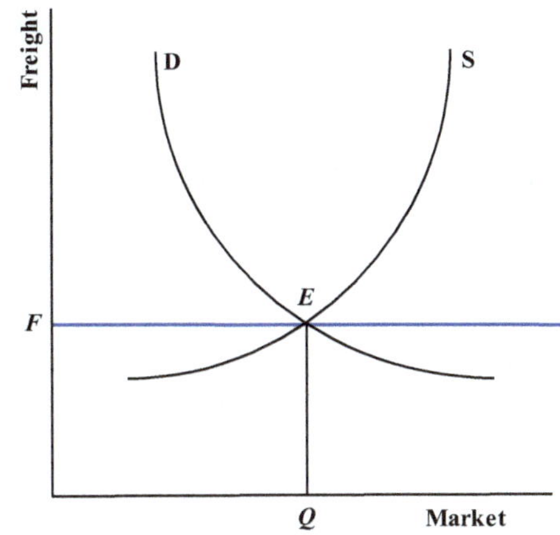

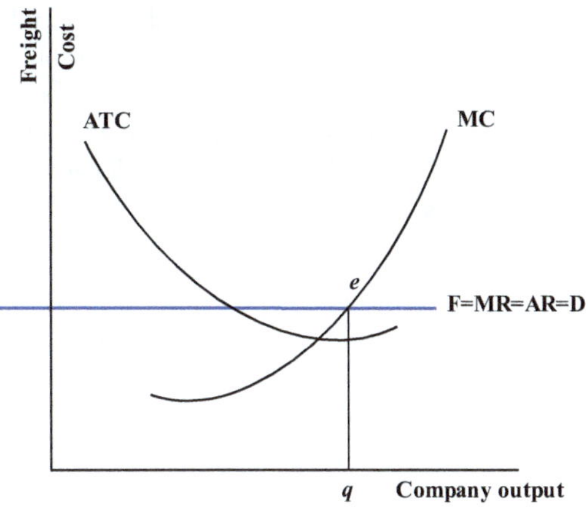

Figure 12.1a Short-run equilibrium of a competitive shipping market.

Note: the freight and the output levels are determined by the equilibrium of demand and supply at *E*.

Figure 12.1b Short-run equilibrium of a shipping company in perfect competition.

Note: the company has to take the freight and produces at *q* where the MC equals the MR at e.

the total supply. As a result, the freight determined by the market, as shown in Figure 12.1a, is imposed on an individual company, as shown in Figure 12.1b. This freight "F" is equal to the marginal revenue "MR", the average revenue "AR" and the demand "D" of the shipping company. The company's optimal production level is at *q* where its marginal cost is equal to its marginal revenue at point *e*.

Is tramp shipping a competitive market?

Using the four conditions for a competitive market to examine the two sectors of maritime transport, tramp and liner, we can find differences. Let's look at tramp shipping first.

1 ***Freedom of entry and exit***. The entry barrier for tramp shipping is low. This is because, on the one hand, most tramp shipping markets are internationally open, free and with little government intervention. On the other hand, the size of the business is highly flexible, which means it is fine to do business with one single ship or any number of ships. Even owning a ship is not necessarily a must, because a shipping company can operate with chartered ships only. To leave the market is just as easy. Apart from the flexibility for chartered ships, there is a very developed sale and purchase market to acquire or get rid of a second-hand vessel.
2 ***Homogeneous services***. As far as services are concerned, tramp shipping is highly standardised. The main types of cargo carried by tramp shipping are raw materials and commodities, which are of relatively low unit value and in large quantities. When it comes to the transport itself, it is mainly to move the cargo from port A to port B with little room for quality differentiation, particularly among established shipping companies.
3 ***Well-informed customers***. The information is presently something not in short supply and with easy access. Although proper channels and skills are necessarily needed, today if someone working

in shipping wants to be informed, they can easily get informed. Taking a particular tramp market as an example, market information on available alternative suppliers can be acquired through specialised agencies, brokers or consultants.

4 ***A large number of service suppliers***. In an economic sense, "large" means that there are so many suppliers that a single one of them will have no impact on the level of the price no matter how much change they make to their production level. This is the situation in tramp shipping, which is a global market with a very high number of suppliers competing with each other.

To sum up the above four points, we can say that the tramp shipping market is a highly competitive one and it can be considered as a market of perfect competition. In the dry or liquid bulk shipping market, there are thousands of shipowners operating and competing with each other. They provide an almost identical service, which is to move cargo by sea from one port to another. There are no restrictive regulations whatsoever that prevent newcomers from starting a business or existing ones from leaving the business. On the spot market or the short-term transport market, no shipowner alone is in a position to influence the freight rate by increasing or decreasing their activities. As we have seen in the previous chapters, the chartering market is a worldwide market thanks to highly developed shipping broker and agent networks and the use of modern telecommunication technology. Consequently, the majority of the shippers can be and are well informed of international freight levels.

Is liner shipping a competitive market?

Liner shipping is different from tramp shipping in many aspects, including in the characteristics of freight mechanism. If we use the same four competitive market conditions to analyse the situation of liner shipping, we will have the following.

1 ***Freedom of entry and exit***. Unlike in tramp shipping, the liner shipping market has higher entry barriers. Although administrative restrictions may not formally exist in most countries, the need for strong and specific technical, commercial and financial capabilities may well prevent many shipping companies from entering the market.
2 ***Homogeneous services***. Compared with tramp shipping, there are more variations in the quality and scope of services in liner shipping. Dealing with high-value cargoes for very diversified customer bases, there is a need for service differentiation, such as the ports of call covered and the speed and frequency of services. Most large liner shipping companies extend their service beyond ports to provide different levels of logistics and distribution services.
3 ***Well-informed customers***. This is probably the condition that both liner shipping and tramp shipping have satisfied. Today, information on market and services is increasingly open and accessible. There is no lack of information.
4 ***Large number of service suppliers***. In liner shipping, services are more fixed. The number of suppliers can be very limited in some shipping markets that do not have large amounts of cargo traffic, such as the routes between Africa and Latin America. In such cases, the level of competition can be limited.

As a result, the freight for liner services is relatively stable. Unlike the situation in tramp shipping, the liner shipping freight rates are modified, in the short term, not by market forces but rather by the shipping companies. Although, in the long term, liner freight is still dictated by the balance of market supply and demand. What are the reasons why liner shipping price does not change as much as that in tramp shipping in the short term? One of the main reasons is because the liner shipping market is less competitive. The service system is made up of separate shipping routes and the number of suppliers on some routes may be small. The recent development of the consolidation of shipping lines has further reduced the level of competition.

Despite all the above-mentioned facts about the lack of competition in liner shipping, this does not mean that competition is absent. In fact, in the middle and particularly in the long term, liner shipping is a competitive market. It is more appropriate to say that the liner shipping market is a *monopolistically competitive market*, which has the characteristics of a monopolistic market in the short run and of a competitive market in the long run.

12.5 Freight market evolution and cycles

Having discussed the competitive nature of the shipping market, we concluded that the price of maritime transport is determined by the demand and supply in perfect competition in the case of tramp shipping and not always in perfect competition for liner shipping. In this section we will look into the characteristics of the demand and supply of shipping services in the three main maritime transport markets, namely the dry bulk, the tanker and the liner markets. Then we will discuss the way the freight evolves over time as a result of the balance between demand and supply. We will see whether or not such evolution follows any regular market cycles.

How do the demand and supply of dry bulk shipping evolve?

The demand for dry bulk shipping comes mainly from the international trade of basic commodities and raw materials. As discussed in Chapter 2, three main dry bulk cargoes of iron ore, coal and grain dominate the dry bulk seaborne trade. The demand has steadily grown since the end of World War Two. But the growth rate varies from one year to the next and it is not easy to predict the future demand. Some commodity trade is affected by, for example, weather conditions, such as grain or coal for heating. Figure 12.2 is about the annual growth rate of the demand and supply of dry bulk shipping

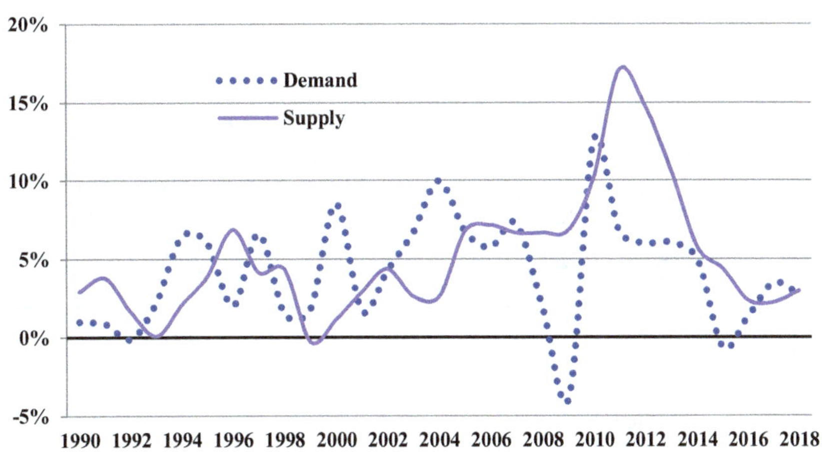

Figure 12.2 Annual changes (%) of demand and supply of dry bulk shipping, 1990–2018.

Source: Shuo Ma, based on data from Clarksons.

Note: the chart is about the annual percentage change of world seaborne dry bulk trade (iron ore, coal, grain and other bulk trade) in tons and the world's bulk carrier fleet in dwt.

from 1990 to 2018. The demand includes major dry bulk cargoes, such as iron ore, coal and grain, and minor dry bulk cargoes such as other minerals, cement, fertiliser, etc. The supply includes bulk carriers of all sizes. The growth of demand has been positive most of the time with an average annual growth of seaborne dry bulk trade by tonnage at 4.15% for this period of 38 years. However, the rate fluctuated enormously within a time span of 1 or 2 years. For instance, the demand increased by 2% in 1996, by 7% in 1997, 1% in 1998, then 9% in 2000 and again 2% in 2001. In 2009 the market was badly hit by the financial crisis. When we look at the supply curve which represents the annual growth rate of dry bulk carriers in terms of dwt, it is clear that it did not follow the same trajectory. It is interesting to notice that, several times during this 38-year period, the supply changed in the opposite direction compared with the demand. When the crisis hit the demand in 2009, the supply did not seem to be much affected. The reasons for the supply not being able to keep close pace with the changes in demand are many, which we will discuss later. The mismatch between the evolution of demand and that of supply would naturally cause the freight to keep changing.

How do the demand and supply of tanker shipping evolve?

The demand for seaborne crude oil and oil products depends on many factors, such as economic growth, the situation of alternative energy such as gas or coal, alternative transport such as pipelines, but, most of all, the price of oil. However, the oil price is a very complex matter, which is affected by a large number of factors from the geopolitical arena to the techno-economic sphere. As a result, the level of demand is constantly changing. Figure 12.3 shows the annual growth rates of demand and supply of the maritime transport service of crude oil and product oil from 1990 to 2018. During this period of about 30 years, the annual change rate for demand varies between +9% and -4.5% with very high volatility. There were more or less a total of eight cycles and the growth rate has rarely been stabilised for more than a year. However, on the supply side, the change in ship supply in terms of

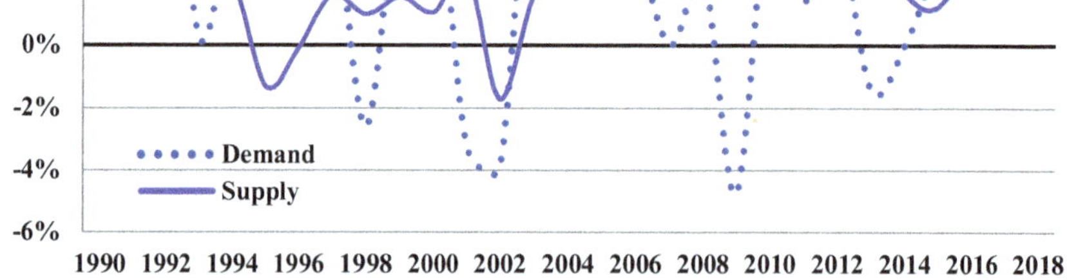

Figure 12.3 Annual changes (%) of demand and supply of oil shipping, 1990–2018.

Source: Shuo Ma, based on data from Clarksons.

Note: the chart is about the annual percentage changes of the world crude and product oil seaborne trade in ton-miles and the oil tanker fleet in dwt.

dwt has registered a much less fluctuating record. It does not follow the short-term ups and downs of the annual changes of demand, rather it reacts to the medium-term trend of the demand. The annual growth, over the same period, has a smaller cycle frequency, which means a longer period elapsed for a cycle to complete and a lower level of cycle amplitude, which means the difference between the highest and the lowest growth rate. While we will discuss the reasons for supply not closely changing to the tune of the demand changes, we can conclude here that the freight, as a result of the different growth rate of the supply and demand, will be more fluctuating.

How do the demand and supply of liner shipping evolve?

The evolution of the liner shipping freight market differs from that of tramp shipping. This is because the demand for the liner shipping services is mainly from manufactured goods, such as parts and semi-finished products in the production process or finished products. The demand for such goods is more stable than that for raw materials, as illustrated in Figure 12.4. From 1990 to 2018, the demand for container liner shipping service grew by about 8% on average each year. It shows hardly any cyclical character with the regularity of fluctuation. The annual demand growth was always positive at about 10% from 1990 to 2008, when the global financial crisis broke the trend and the demand dropped by -10% in 2009. However, as explained in Chapter 1, the negative effect of the 2008/2009 crisis was brief and the global trade recovered relatively rapidly in 2010. But, since then, the high growth rate of foreign trade did not reappear and an annual increase at about 4% became the new norm. This means that the days when world trade grows twice as fast as the world GDP seem to be over.

The supply of container shipping grew each year during 1990 and 2018, at rates much closer to that of the demand, with a noticeable exception in 2009 when the demand decreased dramatically and the supply continued to have a positive growth rate of about 6%. So, on the whole, with a smaller

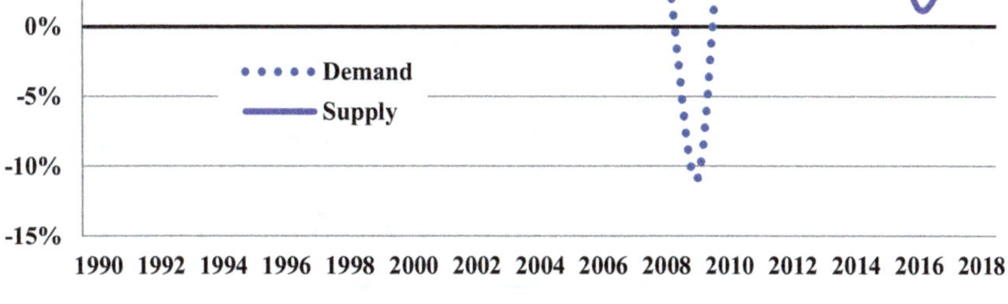

Figure 12.4 Annual changes (%) of demand and supply of container shipping, 1990–2018.

Source: Shuo Ma, based on data from Clarksons and UNCTAD.

Note: the chart is about the annual percentage change of the world containerised seaborne trade in tons and the container fleet in dwt.

differentiation between annual changes in the supply and demand, the freight market of container shipping is less volatile than that of either the oil or dry bulk freight markets.

What are the situations of the earnings for different shipping markets?

The main objective of studying the changes in the supply and demand for shipping services has been to achieve a better understanding of maritime freight or the financial earnings of shipping companies. Each time the demand changes, in the short and medium terms, the supply may or may not follow and change accordingly. In Figure 12.5 we see the evolution index of the average earnings from 1990 to 2018 of the three main types of ships: oil tankers, dry bulk carriers and container ships. The curves are the index of Clarksons average earnings during this period with the levels of the three markets in 1990 as 100. These Clarksons average earning indicators are the estimates in US$/day of voyage freight rates. The earnings for each route are calculated based on the total revenue, deducting current representative bunker costs, estimated port costs and the total commission, then the result is divided by the number of voyage days to obtain the average daily earnings. We can make three main observations based on the figure.

1 Among the three markets, the earnings of both dry bulk carriers and oil tankers are more volatile than those of container ships.
2 Taking into consideration the inflation factor of the US dollar, there is a general downward trend of the average earnings of all three types of ships.
3 There was a period from around 2003 to about 2008 when the freight was abnormally very high, especially for the dry bulk carriers, while, for the other periods, the three freight markets were not fluctuating as violently.

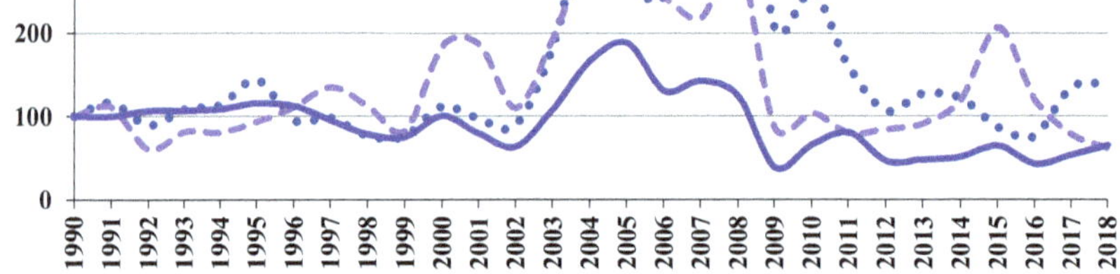

Figure 12.5 Index of Clarksons average earnings by ship types, 1990–2018 (1990=100).

Source: Shuo Ma, based on data from Clarksons.

Note: the chart is about the index of Clarksons average earnings, in current US$ per day, of the three main types of ships (tankers, bulk carriers and container ships) of all sizes and ages.

Are there freight cycles or market normalities and abnormalities?

It has long been claimed that long-term business growth follows a regular trend called an economic cycle which re-occurs every 50–60 years. Apart from such long waves, there are short cycles of 7–11 years. This means that economic development consists of alternating intervals between high and low growth rates. Since trade is an integral part of the economy, and shipping is an integral part of trade, it is believed by some that a similar cyclical movement of development exists in the maritime transport freight market too. The study of shipping market cycles takes into consideration not only the demand aspects, which are largely linked directly to the economic and trade cycles, but also the development features of the supply side. However, based on a large historical data set, the past shipping market cycles are too diverse and unstable to be a valuable guide.[2] By observing the dry bulk market freight evolution of the recent 33 years between 1985 and 2018, as shown in Figure 12.6, we can hardly find any clear pattern of change.

Since the "collapse" of the shipping market in 2008, which happened after more than five years of extraordinary boom, there was a great interest among many of those involved in shipping in the explanation of market cycles, in the hope of gaining an idea about the timing of the next round of high market. Yet the market kept being at a low level for more than 10 years without any sign of a new boom, despite the fact that the average interval of the past cycles did suggest that recovery should have happened. Therefore, the market cycle theory and the related discussions have not delivered real solutions and it has remained an attractive idea rather than a practically useful guide for the investment and business decisions of the maritime transport industry.

Consequently, the evolution of maritime freight level follows a general and long-term trend of a gradual decline, which is due to the continuous improvement of productivity of the shipping industry. At the same time, the freight market is affected occasionally by external events and special circumstances that are difficult to predict. Depending on the nature of the events, the impact on the freight market varies. For example, a change in the exchange rate between currencies, such as a very strong US dollar in the middle of the 1980s, may affect the liner shipping trade. A political crisis such as the

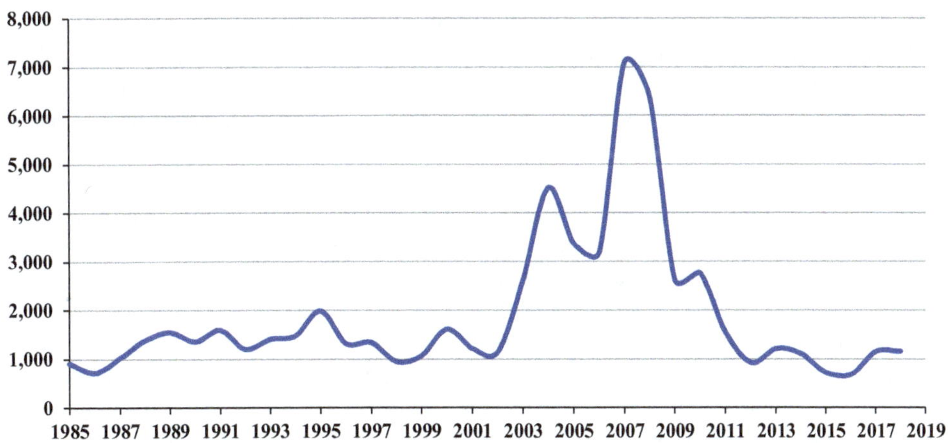

Figure 12.6 Baltic Dry Index, 1985–2018 (4 January 1985 = 1,000).

Source: Shuo Ma, based on data from Clarksons.

Note: the index is called the "Baltic Freight Index" from 1985 to 1999 and the "Baltic Dry Index" from 1999 to the present time. There are also indices for Handymax, Panamax and Capesize ships.

closure of the Suez Canal in 1967 would certainly have a bigger impact on the maritime freight. The occurence of such events is not normal and they are unpredictable. A major economic development may also have an impact of similar magnitude. In the wake of China's joining the WTO in 2001, the country's economic growth accelerated and foreign trade soared. China's share in world total trade rose from 4% in 2001 to almost 7% in 2005 and 12.6% in 2011. Given the size of the country's economy, the impact of China's trade expansion had a significant impact on the maritime freight market. As a result, the average Baltic Dry Freight Index (BDI), which represents the freight of the spot market of dry bulk cargo transport, went from 1,217 points in 2001 to 7,071 points in 2007.

12.6 Price elasticity and freight market volatility

The above discussion allows us to see the difference between tramp and liner shipping with regard to how the freight is determined. So we can draw a general conclusion that, in the long term, the freight is determined by the market forces for both tramp and liner shipping, whilst, in the short term, the tramp shipping freight is still totally market-driven, but the liner shipping freight is much less so because the supply offered by the shipping lines plays an important role.

Why is the freight elasticity of demand and supply important?

The law of supply and demand suggests that when the total quantity produced is equal to the total quantity demanded, the market is in equilibrium. Each time the demand or supply changes a new equilibrium should be achieved and this happens, in the competitive market, through the pricing mechanism. It means that the price is a messenger who tells, with incentive, the supply and the demand to adjust their quantity so as to achieve the equilibrium needed for a transaction. If the supply is more than the demand, there will be a competition among the suppliers, leading the price to move downwards. The reduced price carries the message for the supply to decrease and for the demand to increase. Thus a new equilibrium should be established. Similarly, when the demand is more than the supply, the price will rise, which sends the message to the supply to increase and the demand to decrease for new market equilibrium.

If the price message gets across, the quantity of supply and demand will adjust, the equilibrium will re-establish and the price will stabilise. Yet this is not always the situation, because the supply and the demand may not be very responsive to the price changes. In this case, the freight or price will continue to change, sending a stronger message, until the necessary quantity adjustment is made and equilibrium is achieved. How the supply and demand react to the changes in the price is called *price elasticity*, which is expressed as the ratio of the percentage change in quantity supplied or demanded to the percentage change in price. On a coordinate, the price elasticity of supply and demand is reflected in the slope of the curves: the bigger the price elasticity, the flatter the curve will be, and the smaller the price elasticity is, the steeper the curve will be.

Price elasticity of demand is influenced by the level of economic utility and the situation of substitution, while the price elasticity of supply is influenced by the cost structure and the situation of substitution. We should examine these influential factors in the tramp shipping sector to understand how the supply and demand of tramp shipping respond to the changes in the freight, or the price elasticity in tramp shipping.

What is the freight elasticity of supply in tramp shipping?

We need to examine two situations: when the freight increases and when the freight decreases. Usually, an increase in demand is the reason for the rise of tramp shipping freight. When this happens, the freight will rise and the supply of transport capacity should increase by having more ships, or there will be substitute transport. In tramp shipping, which mostly carries large quantity and low-value commodities in bulk over long distances, there is virtually no substitution for ships. The carrying capacity of vessels can be adjusted by, if possible, increasing the ship's speed and, to a lesser extent, by reducing the time in port and possibly by postponing planned off-service maintenance. When such limited supply adjustment measures have been exhausted, the only way to increase the supply in a meaningful way is to buy second-hand ships or construct new ships. Because tramp shipping is by and large a global market, this means that when the freight is high, few shipowners want to sell ships. There is also a big problem regarding building new ships because the normal lead time, which is the waiting time at shipyards, is about 1.5 to 2 years before a new ship can be delivered. So, it is not uncommon that, with a high freight level, the price of a not-so-old second-hand ship, say of 5 years, could be higher than that of a new vessel. Due to the above, the response of ship supply to the rise of freight is slow and limited. In other words, the maritime supply is freight inelastic.

When the freight decreases, the supply should reduce. But, again, it does not react very sensibly. Normally, slow steaming is the only short-term supply reduction method. The shipping supply does not decrease in response to the price reduction because of the special characteristics of the cost structure of shipping activities. As far as a shipowner in tramp shipping is concerned, most of the costs are fixed costs in the short term to the production level. Whether the ship is in or out of operation, or carries more or less cargo, the costs such as capital cost, manning cost, insurance cost, etc., are fixed and have to be spent, as shown in Table 12.3. If the ship is employed under a voyage charter, the cargo handling is the only variable cost according to the amount of cargo loaded. For a shipowner, the voyage cost as a whole will not be spent if the ship stops operation. Under a time or a bareboat charter, all costs are fixed for a shipowner. Consequently, when the freight is low, a shipowner does not lay up the ship in the short term. Instead, he will keep his ships in operation hoping for the freight to improve. This is true even though the ship is losing money. As a result, the short-term supply also is not price-elastic when the freight decreases.

When demand reduces, for the market to stabilise and regain its equilibrium the corresponding reduction of supply is needed. This may often mean laying up or demolishing ships. However, in the short term, laying up ships does not lead to any savings for shipowners because most costs are fixed. Or, in other words, a shipowner will only consider laying up a ship if the freight is lower than the variable cost. This is illustrated in Figure 12.7. In this case, a shipping company sets its production level to q where the marginal cost, MC, equals the marginal revenue, MR. Because of a drop in demand, the freight is reduced to F, which is lower than the average total cost, ATC, of the company. The company thus incurs a loss which is represented by the shaded area. However, the shipping company does not stop operation because the freight is still higher than the average variable cost, AVC. So, in the short term, although losing money by keeping the ship in operation, the company loses less because the

Table 12.3 Short-term cost structure for a shipowner by type of shipping

	Tramp shipping			*Liner shipping*
	Bareboat	*Time*	*Voyage*	*Liner*
Capital cost	Fixed	Fixed	Fixed	Fixed
Operation cost	–	Fixed	Fixed	Fixed
Voyage cost	–	–	Variable	Fixed

Source: Shuo Ma

Note: A time-charter shipowner does not pay voyage cost and a bareboat charter shipowner does not pay voyage and operation costs.

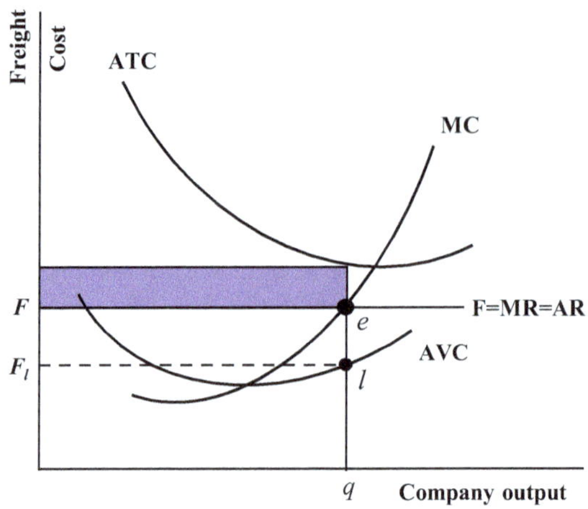

Figure 12.7 Economics of ship laying-up for a shipping company in perfect competition – short-term equilibrium.

Source: Shuo Ma.

Note: in the short term, even though the freight is below the average total cost, the company will not lay up the ship as long as the freight is higher than the average variable cost.

revenue F can, in addition to covering the variable cost, also compensate partially the fixed cost with the difference between the freight and the variable cost or the area $e - l$ multiplied by q. As there is a lack of reduction in supply, the freight will continue to decrease until it reaches F_l, the point at which the freight equals the average variable cost AVC at l, then the shipping company will consider reducing the supply by laying up the ship. Since the variable cost is only a small portion of the total cost, the freight needs to be very low to trigger a ship's laying up.

So, when the freight becomes lower, shipowners will first reduce ships' sailing speed to decrease the carrying capacity and to save on cost of fuel. Should the freight continue to drop, the least efficient ships in the fleet and the least competitive shipowners, whose average total cost is high, will be the first ones unable to continue. They will withdraw from the market by laying-up or scraping ships or leaving the business altogether and, as such, they are helping the market to regain its equilibrium. To conclude, we can say that the tramp shipping supply is not price-elastic. This is true in either the case of a price rise or the case of a price fall, although the reasons for freight inelasticity differ between the two cases.

What is the freight elasticity of demand in tramp shipping?

The demand for tramp shipping comes mainly from raw materials such as oil, iron ore, coal, other minerals and agricultural products. How sensitive are these demands to the changes of shipping freight? To answer the question we should look into two aspects, the economic utility of these cargoes and the situation of their substitution.

The economic utility of demand refers to the value or usefulness a consumer derives from a product or service. If a product or a service is necessary and essential for the customer to have, the economic utility of it is high, otherwise low. Therefore, compared with food, water, cloth, etc., which are essential to people's lives, goods such as toys, printing or most luxury products have lower economic utility. The tramp-shipping cargoes, like oil, iron ore, coal and grain, are usually called strategic commodities, given their importance as the primary sources for a country's population and economy. So, the demand for tramp shipping has generally a high economic utility.

Another important feature of the demand for tramp shipping is that most of these cargoes have no substitutes, especially in the short and medium terms. To examine the effect of freight change on demand, the issue of substitution should be analysed at two levels: the substitution for the cargo in question and the substitution for maritime transport. The current effort on the control of climate change demonstrates that crude oil can be replaced on a large scale. For this to happen, time is needed and both economic and political conditions should be right. The same can be said for coal, which people can substitute for with other energy sources such as natural gas. However, iron ore and grain are harder to substitute for. One can substitute Brazilian iron ore for Australian ore, and one kind of grain for another, but, as a whole, these commodities are by and large not substitutable. With regard to the substitution for maritime transport, apart from the transport of crude oil and natural gas which can sometimes be done by pipelines as an alternative to shipping, for most other tramp-shipping cargoes, maritime remains the sole mode of transport.

In view of a relatively high economic utility and generally a lack of substitution, we can conclude that the demand for tramp shipping is not price-elastic. When the freight changes, the demand for tramp transport is not much affected in the short and medium terms. One of the best examples is the very high freight in the tramp shipping market during 2002 and 2008. The Baltic Dry Index, for example, rose from about 1,300 to more than 7,000 points and for the Capesize ship freight the index was as high as 11,000 points in 2007. Yet such a high freight did not lead to the reduction of demand. During this period, the import by China of iron ore, the main cargo transported by Capesize bulk carriers, even increased.

So, with Figure 12.8, we can outline the following points as a summary of the above explanations about the reasons for the extraordinary volatility of the freight market in tramp shipping in general and in the dry bulk spot market in particular.

The market in tramp shipping in the short term

- To start with, the origin of the fluctuation comes from the very nature of the demand for tramp shipping, which is unstable due to the effect of policy changes, such as what happened in China in the 2000s or economic development, that affects the imports of basic commodities or the impact of natural conditions on, e.g., the trade in grain.
- Because the tramp shipping market is a perfectly competitive market, the freight is determined by the law of supply and demand. So the freight changes when the demand level changes.
- Such a change in freight will stabilise quickly if the demand and supply respond promptly to the price change by adjusting the quantity of demand and supply. But, due to the high economic utility of most tramp cargoes and the lack of substitutes, the demand is not freight-elastic.
- When the freight decreases, ship supply will not reduce in the short term because most of the ship costs are fixed. So, as long as the freight is higher than the variable cost, shipping companies will not lay up ships in the short term. So, the supply will not reduce when the freight decreases.
- When the freight rises, shipping supply can only be marginally adjusted by changing ship speed and time in port. New ships cannot be added in the short term. So the supply will not rise when the freight increases.
- As a result, the tramp shipping freight is highly volatile in the short term.

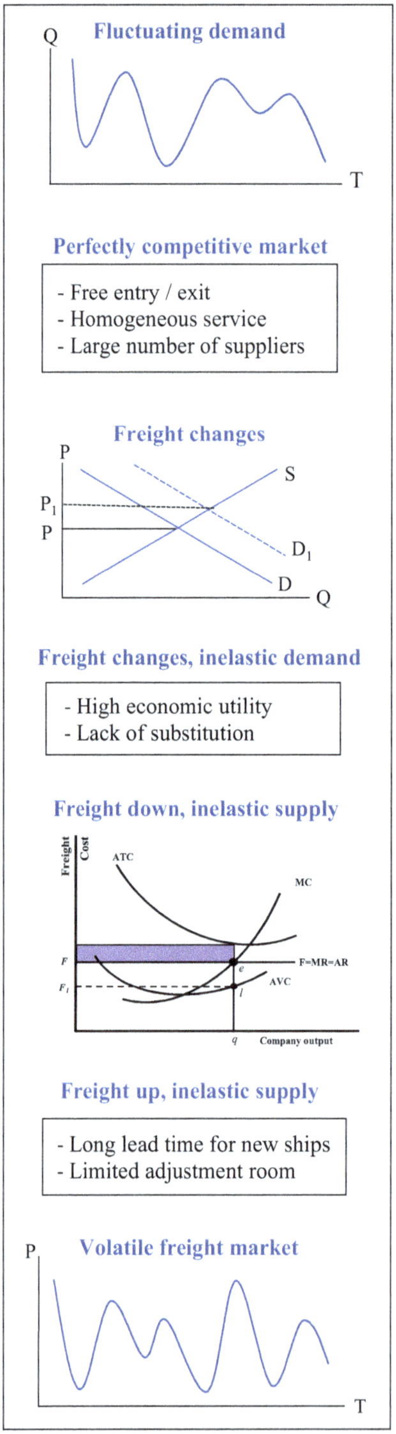

Demand by definition is fluctuating

The market is perfectly competitive

The prices (freight) change

The demand is not price elastics

The supply is not price elastic when the price goes down

The supply is not price elastics when the price goes up

So the freight continues to change, until it equals to variable cost or it is long enough for new ships to be built

Figure 12.8 Volatility of the tramp market.

Source: Shuo Ma.

Note: the figure shows the reasons for volatility of freight.

What is the price elasticity for liner shipping?

As far as the freight elasticity of supply is concerned, the situation of liner shipping is very similar to that of tramp shipping, i.e., the supply is not price-elastic. However, liner ships usually are not fully loaded, which allow the lines some room for adjustment to short-term changes of demand. Since the designed ship speed is higher for liner ships, the fuel consumption is high when ships are at full speed. If there is a substantial change of freight, liner companies may have more room to adjust the speed of ships. In case such adjustment is not sufficient and the freight continues to change, the liner shipping companies will face a similar situation as in tramp shipping and can hardly add or reduce the carrying capacities. It is even more difficult for them than for tramp shipping firms because, in liner shipping, fixed-day weekly calling has become the norm of the service. Therefore, unless all ships deployed in a weekly service are changed at the same time, the weekly carrying capacity will not change. But to do so is very difficult, costly and time-consuming.

When it comes to the freight elasticity of demand in liner shipping, the most important factor is the high value of the cargoes of manufactured goods transported by liner ships. The shipping freight is a very small percentage of the cargo's value. To transport a TV set worth US$1,000 from Asia to Europe, the freight cost is about US$6 or about 0.6%. In such a case, even a big change in freight will hardly be noticed and is highly unlikely to cause a significant change in demand.

As we have discussed, the demand for liner shipping, which covers a wide range of manufactured goods, does not change as much as with tramp cargoes, which are fewer in kind but big in quantity. When the volume of demand changes, the liner freight will rise or fall. But while such freight changes will affect the relative competitiveness of individual suppliers, they will have limited effect on the overall level of supply and demand in the short run.

12.7 Risk hedging and the future trading of maritime freight

The above analysis is about the freight market mechanism in the short term. The short-term tramp shipping freight market is so volatile that maritime transport is widely considered as a highly risky business. It may be particularly a challenge for those shipowners who are financially weak but have to operate on the short-term spot market. The freight market is cyclical and, in the long term, the market mechanism will bring the supply level in line with that of demand. This is because, on the one hand, no shipowners, no matter how financially strong they are, will be able to survive continuous loss and, on the other hand, in the medium and long term, when the demand has risen, the shortfall of supply will be offset by new ships constructed. Recent experience has shown that if the market is not recovering and the demand has always been at a prolonged low level, new ship orders will decline and more vessels will be laid-up or scraped. The market will be in balance in the long run.

What is the Baltic Dry Index (BDI)?

The maritime transport market is large and complex. It consists of various regional and sectional markets, which, although closely related to one another, have different features of development. Therefore, there wasn't a general indicator of the world shipping freight market. However, there was a need for a better understanding of the general trend of freight development. On 4 January 1985 such an indicator was created. The London-based shipping market – the Baltic Exchange – established a freight index, the BFI (Baltic Freight Index), which shows the daily weighted average freight rate level and daily weighted average trip time charter hire level of the short-term dry bulk cargo shipping market.

The Baltic Exchange was well placed to create such an index because of its dominating position in the tramp shipping freight market. It was believed that, at that time, about two-thirds of tramp market transactions were concluded at the Baltic Exchange. The BFI is a basket of dry cargo voyages and trip time charters, each of which is weighted within the Index according to its importance in the freight market. The composition of the Index is intended to be both wide-ranging and representative of the major sections of the dry bulk spot freight market. Each route has been carefully defined within narrow parameters and given an individual "weighting" factor so that its importance to the whole market is reflected in the final calculation of the Index.

The information is based on the actual freight rate levels of that day for the relevant Index voyage. The selection of routes that makes up the Index is based on several criteria. They include the percentage revenue value of the main commodities on the spot voyage market, the total number and frequency of voyage fixtures by each commodity, the balance of geographic origin and the ton-mile contribution. Some provisions are also made for the better balance of ship sizes. Initially, a total of 13 shipping routes representing the different markets, ship sizes and cargo types were selected to constitute the Index. The routes, their weightings and cargo sizes are regularly monitored, reviewed and modified to ensure that a fair, representative and accurate measure of the spot market is achieved. Each selected route is allocated a percentage weighting. The BFI is calculated daily from market information provided by the Index Panel – a group of London-based shipbrokers. Each panellist reports daily his view of the prevailing rate on each of the constituent routes. The Index was set at 1,000 on 4 January 1985. The Index's name was changed in 1999 to the Baltic Dry Index (BDI) with sub-indices covering the different sizes of bulk carriers.

Introducing an indicator system to reflect the dry bulk shipping freight market is not the only or even the main purpose of the Baltic Exchange and the BDI. The other objective is to use the index as a vehicle for the future trading of freight derivatives. The freight Index has also been an effective tool for the management and hedging of freight-related risks.

How do you manage freight market risks by trading on the future market?

The introduction of BFI provided the possibility of having a maritime freight future market. On 1 May 1985 the Baltic International Freight Future Market – BIFFEX – was opened. BIFFEX is an open exchange market at the Baltic Exchange which permits the buying or selling of BFI at certain specified future dates. In fact, the BFI is traded on BIFFEX for specified future settlement months (up to two years ahead). Trading on BIFFEX is the same as trading on any other futures market. Contracts are bought and sold freely on the market. The BIFFEX permits both shipowners and charterers to take out a suitable hedge in the market to protect themselves against the more volatile dry bulk freight market. A shipowner with a ship to be opened for charter in the future is concerned that freight rates will fall in the meantime. To calculate and avoid such a risk, the owner can sell freight future contracts for a voyage at the time near the period his ship will become available. If freight rates do fall to an extent that is more than his expenditure in future trading, he will be able to avoid the loss. If rates remain at the same level, his loss is the cost of trading only. If rates rise, he will make an alleged loss at the market and miss the extra profit. For a charterer, the situation will be the opposite. The BIFFEX also provides opportunities for speculators to make money if they can correctly anticipate the price movements.

However, there was always a problem of inconsistent changes happening between the shipping routes that constituted the BFI, which, consequently, affected the accuracy of the index and undermined the effectiveness of the contract used as a risk-hedging instrument. Such a shortcoming led to low and declining trading activities.[3] So the BIFFEX contract was discontinued in April 2002.

What is a Forward Freight Agreement (FFA)?

In addition to the lack of accuracy, the BIFFEX was also inflexible. It was a structured future trading system at the Baltic Exchange with restrictive time limits. In the 1990s a new form of freight future trading and risk hedging system emerged. It is an over-the-counter forward trading scheme for shipping freight which is called a Forward Freight Agreement – FFA. An FFA is very different from a BIFFEX contract. It is actually an agreement between two parties for the settlement of a freight rate at a specified future date with regard to a specific amount of cargo or a type of ship on one of the main tramp shipping routes of the dry bulk or tanker market. An FFA can use any market index, for example the Baltic Panamax Index or the Baltic Capesize Index. The difference between the contract price and the settlement price is settled between the two parties. The settlement price is calculated as the monthly average of the underlying route during the period concerned. It is common that the FFA traders use the BDI reported by the Baltic Exchange for the transactions.

An FFA is normally traded directly, or via a broker, between the two parties without passing through an exchange market. A shipowner wishing to protect his freight income from the risk of a falling market can sell through an FFA broker FFAs based on, for example, the quotations of Freight Investor Services (FIS) to someone who wants to take the risk. In case the freight does fall, the shipowner's loss in freight income will be compensated for by the gains in the FFA trading. Vice versa, in the case of freight rise, the extra income received by the shipowner will be offset by a loss in the forward position. For a charterer, the situation is the opposite. They will hedge their freight risk by buying FFAs from someone who wants to take the risk.

12.8 Summary

Maritime freight, which is the main income, occupies the central position in maritime economics because it affects directly a shipping company's financial performance. However, the freight changes are outside the control of the individual shipping companies because the shipping market in general and the tramp shipping market in particular are competitive. In this chapter various aspects of maritime freight are discussed. Shipping costs are divided into three parts: capital cost, operation cost and voyage cost. The proportion of the three parts vary according to the type, size, age and even the flag of the ship. These costs are mostly paid by shipowners but sometimes they are also paid by the users of the ship. The cost payment model reflects the degree of operational involvement of the shipowner and the charterer alike. For example, in a time charter, both operation and voyage costs are paid by the charterer rather than the shipowner. In the case of liner shipping, all costs are paid for by the liner company.

In tramp shipping there are a lot of voyage charter transactions. The voyage charter freight is calculated based on the exact amount of cargo loaded. The freight may or may not include the cargo-handling cost and the responsibility of cargo handling needs to be specified in the charter party. For the transport of liquid bulk cargo, such as crude oil, under voyage charter, a special freight system called the World Scale is normally used. The system offers flexibility in freight determination when changes of port are needed. When it comes to time and bareboat charters, the payment is referred to as hire and calculated based on the time during which the ship is made available to the charterer. In liner shipping, the freight is also called liner tariffs. With containerisation having been generally adopted as the standard line shipping model, the freight consists of the basic rate per teu or feu, the surcharges and the rebates.

The maritime freight market is by and large a competitive one. This is particularly true for tramp shipping as the market is totally free for newcomers to enter, the number of tramp shipping companies is very large and the services are highly standardised with very little difference between the transport services of different companies. The tramp shipping sector has been widely considered as one of the limited examples of perfect competition. The liner shipping sector is on the whole also competitive, especially in the long term and on the main shipping routes, but the number of service suppliers may be limited on some shipping routes. It is, therefore, not perfectly competitive. As a competitive market, the freight is determined by the market based on the law of supply and demand.

Despite the fact that the freight market has been proved to be cyclical, the lack of a minimum cycle regularity undermines the practical value of any cyclical analysis and prevents them from being a useful guide for decision-making. This is because there are too many randomly changing factors that have an impact on the development of shipping freight. A review of the market evolution during the recent years of the dry bulk, tanker and container shipping markets suggests that, instead of following any kind of cycle, the freight market evolution is characterised by a normal downward trend with occasional extraordinary developments caused by abnormal political or economic events.

The volatility of the freight market, particularly in the tramp shipping sector, is greatly attributable to the generally low price elasticity for both demand and supply. Consequently, the change of freight caused by the imbalance between demand and supply does not lead, in the short term, to corresponding changes in the quantity of demand for and supply of shipping services. There are two reasons which explain the lack of price elasticity of tramp shipping demand. One is the high economic utility of the tramp shipping cargoes and the other is that, in most cases, there is an absence of substitution. As regards the low price elasticity of supply, the reasons include the very high proportion of fixed cost in the total ship cost, as well as the long lead time for the building of new ships. As a result, the tramp shipping freight market is volatile. To manage and hedge the risks originating from freight fluctuation, shipowners and charterers can trade in freight derivatives such as the forward freight agreements.

Notes

1 UNCTAD (2018).
2 Stopford M. (2010). The study found that the shipping freight market has had many cycles since the 18th century. However, there is a serious lack of regularity between the cycles.
3 Nomikos N. K. and Alizadeh A. H (2009).

References

Nomikos N. K. and Alizadeh A. H. (2009) "*Managing Freight Rate Risk Using Freight Derivatives: An Overview of the Empirical Evidence*", Chapter 26 in "Handbook of Maritime Economics and Business", edited by C. Grammenos, 2nd Edition, Lloyd's List Publications, London, pp. 745–775.

Stopford M. (2010) "*Shipping Market Cycle*", Chapter 9 in "Handbook of Maritime Economics and Business", edited by C. Grammenos, 2nd Edition, Lloyds List Publications, London, pp. 235–258.

UNCTAD. (2018), "Review of Maritime Transport", UNCTAD/RMT/2018, UN, Geneva.

Part IV

The strategy

Chapter 13

The economics of maritime transport competition

In the last chapter we concluded that the shipping market is largely a competitive one. For the tramp shipping market, the competition is even considered to be perfect. The transport freight, consequently, is determined by the market forces. So a better understanding of international competition in the shipping industry is important at the company as well as the government policymaking levels. In this chapter we will examine various aspects of maritime transport competition, from its nature to its changing focus and from the internationalisation of the service inputs to the standardisation of maritime operations. Based on these discussions, we will analyse the strategic implications of maritime competition for shipping companies and policymakers alike.

13.1 The focus of maritime competition

What does maritime transport competition focus on? In his book on competitive advantage, Porter defines three basic ways for companies to achieve a competitive advantage, namely cost leadership, differentiation and focus.[1] The competition framework applies to maritime transport too. Shipping companies are competing on the transport cost or the quality of services. A competition on cost cannot be unrelated to the quality of services, because a service of unreasonably low quality would lead to high cost in the end. So the competition in shipping is rather on the combination of the two, known as "value for money". If the capability of a shipping company to offer a differentiated service comes from specific know-how that is difficult to acquire by others, the competitiveness of the shipping company is sustainable. Another aspect regarding the nature of maritime competition is about barriers to entry, or whether or not it is free and easy for new companies to join and compete.

What is cost leadership in international shipping?

The discussion on cost leadership in shipping should not exclude the quality aspect of services. This is because the leadership of transport cost is straightforward and it refers to the level of shipping freight. For a shipper, the transport time is also an important factor, but the time cost will be discussed as a part of service differentiation. A shipping company capable of consistently offering the same transport service at a lower cost than all its competitors is in the leader's position. The question is about how to define the term "same transport service". This may refer to decent or reasonable services. Cost leadership will be a meaningful advantage only if it is for a reasonable quality of service.

The meaning of good quality of service is different between tramp and liner shipping. In tramp shipping, the transport service is narrowly defined as moving a full shipload of the same kind of cargo in bulk from port A to port B. It is not operationally hard for a shipowner to deliver the service with a seaworthy ship and a competent crew. The quality of tramp shipping also depends on the reputation of the shipowner, which includes the aspects of integrity and sincerity. The reputation is also affected by commercial risks related to non-performance, fraud, dispute settlement, etc. For shipping companies, full compliance with the international rules and regulations on safety and environmental protection is considered to be a standard performance. In fact, what we will discuss in the following section is that most cost elements are the same for all shipowners. The main sources of cost differentiation are the cost of ship acquisition and, to a lesser extent, crew cost. Such cost advantages may be achieved from low purchasing prices or the effects of scale economies by operating big ships.

Cost leadership in liner shipping is harder to define because the services provided by different lines are more diversified. A typical liner shipping service will begin from the port where cargo is loaded onto the ship and end at the yard or warehouse of the port where the cargo has been offloaded from the ship. The cost includes cargo handling at both ports and the transport itself. However, apart from transporting cargo, other factors such as transit time also affect the cost of service. Employing larger specialised vessels may give the shipping company a cost advantage, provided the ships are fully loaded and efficiently handled at the port. Other cost advantages may also be sought from cheaper crews, open registry of ships or low fuel consumption. These and many other cost-saving measures are open to all shipping lines and the use of them will also have impacts on the quality of services.

What is service differentiation in international shipping?

Low cost is not the only interest of a customer; sometimes a shipping carrier is selected chiefly on the quality of service provided. In this case, differentiated services are the focus of the competition between shipping companies. The maritime service differentiation is usually reflected in the following two aspects: reduction of risk and addition of value.

- ***The reduction-of-risk-related service differentiation.*** This is about the reliability of the shipowner and the shipping services. It is basically about the assumption that "things are done as they should be". Many risks are in the form of non-compliance with the contract and with laws and regulations or failure to follow the instructions and procedures. The risk may be associated with technical issues, such as safety, commercial, operational and legal aspects. Although international shipping is becoming increasingly standardised, there are still a lot of uncertainties and, especially, many human errors. There are also substandard ships, shipping operators and incompetent personnel. So the risk-related service differentiation is between good shipping companies, sometimes referred to as first-class owners, with competent staff and poor performers which are referred to as riskier shipping companies.
- ***The addition of value-related service differentiation.*** This is the second category of service differentiation, which is about specific services provided by a shipping company from which the customers draw additional value. In liner shipping, faster transit time, higher service frequency, broader logistics services or better information are all examples of value-based service differentiation. The liner shipping companies have a bigger scope and more potential to offer differentiated services than the tramp shipping companies do. The capability of handling difficult transport and solving problems customers may have is also a source of service differentiation and thus of competitiveness. Even environmental performance may be considered as a service differentiation. An increasing number of transport users are concerned about the greenhouse gas footprint of their transport,

so a shipping company capable of offering a superior performance will be more competitive.[2] Value creation should be at the centre of the differentiation strategy. A sustainable differentiation strategy is one which is made based on the company's competitive advantage.

What are the skills and know-how required in shipping?

It is difficult to define precisely the knowledge required in the shipping industry because there are different types of tasks on board as well as ashore. As discussed in Chapter 11, the maritime human resource is highly internationalised in the sense that the expertise, mainly the ship-based workforce, is internationally available. This is also proof that many maritime transport professions, together with their knowledge and skills, are transferable from one country to another. The maritime jobs can be broadly divided into three categories: the first is about seafarers and dock workers, the second is about those working in supportive maritime services and the third is about managers and specialists working in shipping and port companies and organisations.

The US-based occupational information database "ONET" covers about one thousand professions in the US. For each job, the skills and knowledge required, as well as how the work is performed, are described. The database also provides the information about the education, training and experience needed for each type of work. The information is collected from surveys of incumbents, occupational experts and occupational analysis. But the information on occupational tasks, activities, knowledge, education and training is from the survey of job incumbents. The most important maritime jobs of the three categories are among these 1,000 or so occupations. For our discussion, we have selected twelve positions, four for each category, as shown in Table 13.1. For each job, information is given on five relevant aspects, namely: tasks to undertake, the knowledge required, skills needed, education level of the incumbents and the preparation required to do the job. The last column, the preparation required, is divided into five levels, called "job zones". Zone 1 refers to the occupations that need little or *no* preparation in terms of previous work-related skills, knowledge or experience. For these jobs, sometimes a high school diploma is needed. Zone 2 jobs need some preparation. High school education is usually required and some work-related knowledge, experience and skills are needed. Zone 3 is about jobs that need a medium level of preparation. This means training in vocational schools, related on-the-job experience and previous work-related skills and experience are required. Zone 4 refers to the jobs for which considerable preparation is needed. Most of these jobs require a bachelor's degree. A considerable amount of work-related skills, knowledge and experience is required. Zone 5 posts are those that require extensive preparation. Typically, graduate school education with, for example, a master's degree is needed and some require a PhD.

Although the table is made up of US-based data, it does reveal a lot of the general characteristics of basic maritime knowledge and skills as well as the levels of education, training and experience required to do the jobs. Although the aspects such as tasks, knowledge, activities and skills are usually job-specific, and therefore difficult to compare between occupations, the terms do reflect the nature of the jobs. We should look more closely at the types of education and preparation required for each profession. Evidently, a simple job requires less education and training in terms of work-related skills and experience.

As a whole, maritime transport is not a technology and knowledge-intensive sector. However, there are differences between the three main categories of maritime occupations. The jobs of ordinary seafarers and dockworkers are mostly routine and require a relatively low level of preparation. To be a ship officer, such as a captain or marine engineer, one has to have more knowledge and experience through multiple years of vocational post-secondary education and on-the-job training. Some maritime service positions such as agents and forwarders need some limited preparation and a majority of the incumbents are holders of a high school diploma only. The jobs of managers in shipping or logistics companies as well as maritime specialists such as jobs in marine insurance are more

Table 13.1 Maritime jobs, skills required and the knowledge intensity.

Maritime jobs – Category 1: seafarers and dockworkers – know-how required						
Job	**Task**	**Knowledge**	**Skills**	**Education**	**Preparation* (Job zone)**	**Knowledge intensity****
Ship captains	Steer/operate vessels, dock/ undock vessels, inspect vessels	Transport, safety, law, management, admin, mechanical	Judgement, decision making, complex problem solving, coordination	Post-secondary certificate: 52%, high school diploma: 22%	Job zone 3: Medium preparation, experience needed	Middle level
Ship engineers	Operate, maintain and monitor marine engines and other equipment. Maintain records	Mechanical, admin, management, engineering	Critical thinking, operation control, equipment maintenance	Post-secondary certificate: 50%, high school diploma: 33%	Job zone 3: Medium preparation, experience needed.	Middle level
Sailors	Stand watch, moor and unmoor vessels	Safety and security, transport, mechanical	Monitoring, control	High school diploma, post-secondary certificate	Job zone 2: Experience dependent: low (some)	Low level
Ship loader	Verify ship, operate ship load/unload equipment, record data	Production, processing, admin management, safety, mechanical, personal	Operation, control, monitoring, coordination	High school diploma: 82%, post-secondary certificate: 11%	Job zone 2: some preparation needed. Some experience needed	Low level

Maritime jobs – Category 2: maritime service providers – know-how required

Job	Task	Knowledge	Skills	Education	Preparation* (Job zone)	Knowledge intensity**
Brokerage clerks	Correspond with clients, document transactions, file	English language, personal service, mathematics, computer, economics, accounting	Communication, time management, critical thinking	Bachelor degree: 38%, High school diploma: 29%, Some college 20%	Job zone 3: Medium preparation. Experience needed	
Customs brokers	Prepare import/ export documents, Clear goods, pay, calculate duties	Transport, English, Clerical, law/rules, personal service	Communication, comprehension, problem solving	High school diploma: 45%, post-secondary certificate: 20%, bachelor degree 20%	Job zone 3: Medium preparation, experience needed	
Freight forwarders	Calculate weight, cost of goods, Inform clients, prepare docs, provide info.	Customer/personal service, transport, communication, language skills	Coordination, monitoring, reading	High school diploma: 45%, some college certificate: 20%, bachelor degree 20%	Job zone 2: Some preparation needed. Experience dependent: low (some)	
Cargo and freight agents	Advise clients on transport method and payment, track delivery, notify consignees	Transportation, personal service, English, Geography,	Communication, comprehension, critical thinking, service orientation	High school diploma: 93%	Job zone 2: Some preparation needed. Experience dependent: low (some)	

Continued

Table 13.1 *continued*

Maritime Jobs – Category 3: maritime managers and specialists – know-how required

Job	Task	Knowledge	Skills	Education	Preparation* (Job zone)	Knowledge intensity**
Transport managers	Plan, organise, direct activities of routeing, dispatching, tracking transport	Transportation, admin management, personal service, safety, HR	Communication, critical thinking, monitoring	Bachelordegree: 41%, high school diploma: 34%	Zone 4: Considerable preparation, experience dependent.	
Transport storage / distribution managers	Supervise activity of workers, plan, develop, implement warehouse, fleet, respond to clients	Transport, admin and management, customer service, English, Maths	Critical thinking, monitoring, coordination, communication	Bachelor degree: 50%, post-graduate certificate: 21%	Zone 4: Considerable preparation, experience dependent.	
Logistics managers	Collaborate with others, supervise logistics, create policies	Transport, admin and management, customer service, English, Maths	Reading, communication, coordination, critical thinking, monitoring	Bachelor degree: 60%, Master's degree: 17%	Zone 4: Considerable preparation, experience dependent.	
Insurance sales agents	Sell, interview, call	Customer/ personal service, sales/marketing, communication	Communication, writing capability	Bachelor degree: 46%, high school: 33%	Zone 4: Extensive experience dependent: high	

Source: compiled based on ONET database on the US market (2018).

**The last column is about the amount of preparation in terms of education, on-the-job training and experience needed for the job.*

***Five levels of preparation needed for the job:* 1 – none; 2 – some; 3 – medium; 4 – considerable; 5 – extensive.

knowledge-demanding. About half of the holders of such positions have done four years of university study with a Bachelor's degree. There is also a greater need for work-related skills and experience in these roles.

To conclude, we can say that there are two types of maritime transport knowledge and skills. The first is those simple knowledge and skills which are relatively easy to have. This type of work involves the standardised and mostly routine tasks of, for example, seafarers, dockworkers and freight forwarders. The other type is about a more sophisticated set of knowledge, skills and experience that is required for the jobs of managers and shipping specialists. These jobs require more creativity and analytical capability.

13.2 Internationalisation of maritime transport cost

Maritime transport competition is between shipping companies. The competing companies may come from the same country or, more often today, they come from different countries. Britain was in a dominating position for modern commercial shipping in the 19th century. In 1890 50% of the world's total ship tonnage was British and in 1900 Britain's share was lower, but still a remarkable 48% of the world's total.[3] It was only from the 20th century onwards that international competition with British shipping as a whole became more important than competition within British shipping.[4] In the 21st century, as a result of continuous consolidation during the last two decades, the competition is increasingly between shipping companies from different countries or regions. British shipping declined from almost half of the world's total in 1900 to merely 16% in 1960. The British maritime expert Sturmey, in his explanation of the main reasons for this, attributed the decline to the differentiation between countries such as the relatively high crew cost and government interference in some countries in support of their national fleet.[5] A question which remains to be answered is why shipping companies in high-labour-cost countries such as Norway or Denmark have been, until today, among the most competitive in the world. On the other hand, many of the most heavily subsidised shipping companies in rich and less-developed countries alike do not survive the competition. We will try to answer this question by looking at how the maritime costs have been internationalised.

Are the capital costs of ships different between countries?

The proportion of the capital cost out of the total cost for a shipping company is not fixed. This is because, on the one hand, the capital cost is affected by the type of ship, purchasing price, repayment conditions and a ship's age. On the other hand, some other costs are constantly changing such as fuel cost or insurance cost. Nonetheless, the capital costs of ships are always one of the biggest shipping cost elements. In the past, most traditional shipping powers were important shipbuilding nations. As recently as 1960, the USA, Japan and every major maritime nation in Europe all had a strong shipbuilding industry. But, since then, the shipbuilding sector started to concentrate in the Far East. The days have now long gone when shipping companies operated only the ships that were built by the yards of the home country. In Figure 13.1 we can see that the global deliveries of new ships have been highly concentrated. While Japan was the biggest shipbuilding country in the 1980s, another two East Asian countries, South Korea and China, increased their respective shares of the market steadily. By 2018 virtually all commercial ships were built by Japan, Korea and China.

The high-level consolidation of the shipbuilding sector means that the ship's capital cost is an international cost for all shipowners regardless of their countries of origin. Although Japan, Korea and China build more than 90% of all ships, the three countries combined only own about 25% of the global shipping fleet measured in dwt.[6] This means that about 70% of the ships they build are for foreign shipowners. There is not any country-based differentiation in the cost. The shipyards sell ships to

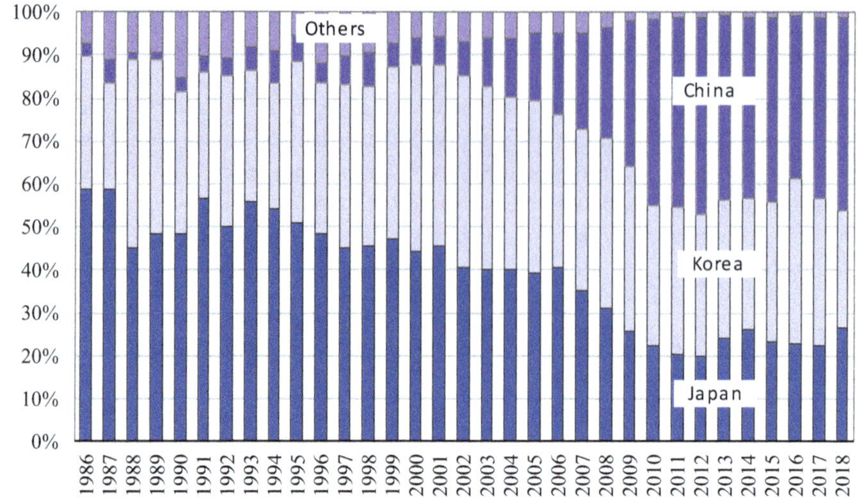

Figure 13.1 Concentration of shipbuilding industry, dwt delivered by countries, 1986–2018.

Source: Shuo Ma, based on data from Clarksons (2018).

Note: countries included under "others" on the top of the figure are in mostly Europe and Asia.

shipping companies at the same price regardless of the nationality of the shipowners. Some countries even offer incentives in the form of shipyard credit to foreign owners who place ship orders in those countries' yards as a way to support the countries' shipbuilding industries. To sum up, we can say that international maritime competition is not focussed on the capital cost of ships. A shipowner can have a competitive edge by ordering the ship at the right time, but that has no relation to the nationality of the owner. Most shipowners fund new ships through bank loans. The terms and conditions offered by the banks are related more to a shipowner's reputation than to nationality.

What are the differences in the ship operation costs between countries?

A ship's operation cost is another major category of cost which constitutes between 15% and 25% of total ship costs, depending on other variable factors such as the type of shipping market, liner or tramp, the age of the ship, the price of fuel, etc. There are three parts to the cost, namely the manning cost, the maintenance cost and the insurance cost. We will examine whether or not these costs vary between countries and therefore if they can be the sources for country-based competitiveness.

- ***Manning cost.*** As discussed in Chapter 11, to a large extent, most leading shipping companies trading on the international market use an international crew. Take container shipping as an example. In mid-2018 the top three shipping lines were Maersk of Denmark, MSC of Switzerland and CMA-CGM of France. They had a combined market share of about 46% of the world's total ship capacity in teu[7] but the vast majority of their seafarers were not Danish, Swiss or French nationals. As shown in Table 11.1, about 16% of global seafarers are from the Philippines. These seafarers predominantly work on foreign ships because the Philippines controls only 0.1% of ships in the world measured in dwt. For regulatory reasons as well as economic and social reasons, more national seafarers are employed on ships trading in domestic markets. For international shipping, the seafaring market is open and free. This is particularly true considering that almost 75% of the global fleet in dwt are under open registries which do not impose restrictions on the nationality of seafarers.

- ***Insurance cost.*** The UK remains the leading country for marine insurance with a market share of around 25%.[8] London is still the capital of the marine insurance business. The marine insurance sector is an open and competitive market in which shipowners are free to choose any company for their ship insurance services. Given the nature of the business, large insurance companies have the advantage of scale and, usually, insurance companies are linked together by reinsurance practice that enables insurance companies to reduce risks in case of large losses. Consequently, the income of marine insurance is more predictable. On the whole, marine insurance is a standard service with a similar fee structure for shipowners of any nationality.
- ***Maintenance cost.*** Though having some common characteristics with shipbuilding, ship repair and maintenance is far less concentrated. There are many ship repair yards in many countries. It is a competitive market in which there is no restriction on a ship's choice of its repair yard. There may be some limited cost advantages if the ships are repaired and maintained at national shipyards, but, by and large, the cost of ship repair and maintenance is an international cost which is the same for ships from all countries.

Are voyage costs of ships different between countries?

As discussed previously, the ship's voyage cost consists of two major parts: fuel cost and port cost. Port cost includes dues and fees for passing locks and charges paid by ships on canal tolls are also included. Let's begin with fuel cost. Would an oil-producing country's shipping company benefit from more favourable bunker suppliers? The answer is not really, and this is for three reasons. First, crude oil is in most cases an internationally traded commodity. Offering bunker supply at a reduced price to a national shipowner is a subsidy rather than any rational saving. Second, ships carrying international trade take bunker wherever they travel. Third, most countries that are strong in shipping, such as Greece or Japan, are not oil producers. Domestic shipping may be treated differently in some countries than international shipping. There are price differences when taking bunker at different ports, but such differences have little to do with the nationality of a shipowner or the flag of a ship.

Regarding port costs, which can usually be divided into port dues and cargo-handling charges, the situation is more complex. While most ports do not apply a differentiated pricing system based on the nationality of shipowners for foreign trade-related services, some ports do. From the 1980s, the world port sector underwent an institutional restructuring movement in the form of commercialisation, corporatisation and privatisation. In many countries the port sector is now open to foreign operators and shipping companies. In such a commercial and often more competitive environment, port operators gain more autonomy for setting up prices and standards for their services. It is, therefore, not common to implement favourable tariffs for some users based on non-commercial grounds such as a client's nationality. For the same reason as for the bunker cost, a ship carrying international trade incurs port cost outside its home country. With regard to the passage through canals, such as the Suez or Panama Canals, the same level of tolls is applied to ships of different national registrations. We may conclude by saying that, for ships, port and canal costs are international costs.

Why are most costs of a shipping company international costs?

We have examined all three main groups of ship's costs to see if there are country-based elements that give a shipping company cost advantages in international maritime competition. Our analysis shows that most of the costs are not country-based and are the same for all ship owners, as shown in

Figure 13.2. There are two main reasons for such internationalisation of shipping cost. The first is that many shipping activities have become separated from other activities and are being undertaken by a few countries. There is a high level of specialisation independent of each other. Every market is internationally open and those that are specialised in it are often highly competitive. For example, about three-quarters of total ships are registered in a few countries. Virtually all ship companies build their ships in just three Asian countries. The main reason for such concentration of a single shipping activity in a small number of countries is that these countries have a comparative advantage over other countries in carrying out the activity concerned. Such concentration has intensified with a free and open market on the one hand and competition on the other. The second reason is that international shipping happens on international waters rather than within the boundary of a country. It is about transporting cargo across oceans between countries, which, in a way, makes it difficult for ships to rely only on home-based inputs, but easy for them to access foreign inputs.

Shore-based staff, such as those working at headquarters, can incur a nation-based cost which varies from one country to another. However, even the administration and overhead cost can also be outsourced to ship management companies. Some shipping companies have relocated a part of their management and administration functions overseas to places such as Singapore or Malaysia. Even the level of tax is the same for companies in different countries because of open registries. Figure 13.2 is an illustration of the split of shipping costs between country-based and non-country-based costs. It is estimated that the majority of the costs, or about 90%, incurred by international shipping are the same for shipping companies of all countries. A small proportion of the operation costs, such as those related to overhead and administration, may be attached to the home base and vary from one country to another. However, the situation may differ for some ships that may be involved in domestic shipping. For the shipping companies that primarily carry trade for other countries, such as those from Norway or Greece, virtually all costs are international.

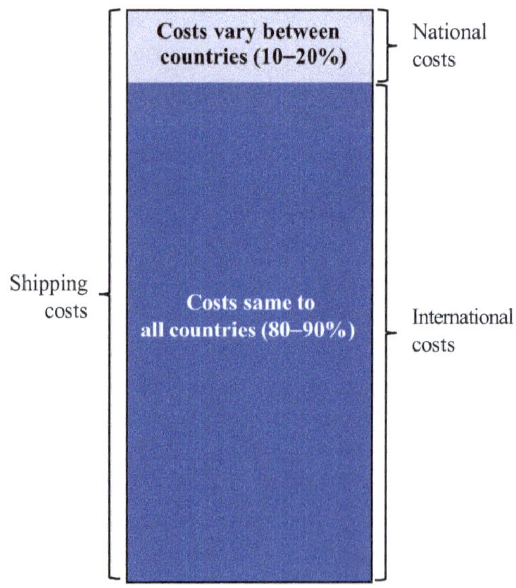

Figure 13.2 Shipping costs: country-based vs. non-country-based.

Source: Shuo Ma.

Note: while most capital and voyage costs are non-country based, some operation costs vary between countries.

13.3 Standardisation in maritime transport

Apart from the cost leadership strategy, another strategy of competition is focussed on service differentiation. This is to gain a competitive edge by providing services with distinguished quality features. According to the product life cycle theory, competition will be mostly on quality differentiation at the introduction and growth stages and, as the products or services mature, the competition is more on the cost aspect. Such a shifting of competition focus happens when the products or services of different suppliers are of similar quality and the production is more and more standardised. In this section we will examine the degree of standardisation of international shipping services.

Is international shipping technically standardised across all countries?

The technical conditions and standards of ocean-going ships are best examined from the ship safety point of view, i.e., from ship construction, ship operation and the control of ship safety performance. Thanks to international maritime rules and regulations, particularly those of the IMO but also ISO, today international shipping is becoming more and more technically standardised. We can examine the level of the technical standardisation from three angles: shipbuilding standards, ship management standards and ship safety administration standards.

- Most of the ships transporting international trade are not only built in the same countries but also according to the same safety and environmental standards in compliance with international rules and regulations established largely by the IMO (International Maritime Organisation), such as the SOLAS and LOADLINE Conventions. Based on the international conventions, specific technical rules and standards are established by the recognised classification societies[9] regarding the construction and maintenance of a ship's hull, main and auxiliary engines and electrical and automation installations. The compliance is verified by the classification societies as well as flag State authorities. Once a ship is built, the technical conditions should be maintained to the adequate level, which is usually described as being seaworthy. Periodic checks are undertaken by classification societies as well as flag and port States. Most ships are supervised by the members of the International Association of Classification Societies (IACS). Substandard ships will therefore not be able to have the necessary certificates for safe trading and they may even be detained at port.
- A ship built to adequate safety standards does not guarantee safety if it is not managed and operated safely. In 1994 the IMO adopted, as part of the SOLAS Convention Chapter IX, the "International Management Code for the Safe Operation of Ships and for Pollution Prevention" (ISM Code). For those countries that have adopted the SOLAS Convention, the compliance with the ISM Code is mandatory and shipping companies have to be audited by the flag State administration for compliance. The Code requires shipping companies to have a safety management system. This includes having a safety and environmental protection policy, allocating sufficient resources, designated persons and shore-based support to ensure the effective functioning of the safety management system and the implementation of the safety policy. Appropriate procedures, plans and instructions should be established for safe shipboard operations and emergencies. So, in the long run, the general application of the ISM Code has, to a large extent, standardised the technical management and operation of ships.
- The supervision of the technical conditions and safety standards of internationally traded ships and the enforcement of the international regulations in this regard are the responsibilities of the flag State through national maritime safety administration (MSA). How such a national responsibility toward the ships under its flag is carried out varies from one country to another and some

substandard ships continue to trade due to inadequate flag State control. This has created serious safety and environmental problems and has led to an increased emphasis on the role of port State control. However, to make sure that the responsibility of each country to implement international regulations in its capacity as the flag State has been standardised, there was the introduction of the mandatory IMO Member State Audit Scheme (IMSAS) in 2016. According to the IMSAS, each flag State is audited by an IMO-appointed audit team on the effectiveness of the safety administration and the implementation of the mandatory IMO instruments covered by the scheme.

When we say that international maritime transport is technically standardised, we do not refer to all ships and shipping companies. Shipping companies involved in transporting international trade can be divided into two groups: the established companies, which are usually big shipping companies with a good reputation, and the others. Most ships belong to the first group. Standardisation only applies to the established shipping companies and their ships. These companies are the mainstream of the shipping supply that transport most of the global trade.

How is international shipping standardised commercially and operationally?

In our discussion on the competitive situation of the shipping market, we explained that tramp shipping is a perfectly competitive market. One of the features of a competitive market is the homogeneous nature of the services. This means that in tramp shipping, the services are by and large standardised. The services include loading the cargo at one port, transporting it across seas and discharging it at another port. There are limited additional services that customers will need and a shipowner cannot differentiate itself from others. So, commercially and operationally, tramp shipping is largely standardised. The competition is, therefore, focussing on other factors rather than service differentiation.

The situation in liner shipping is more complex. The services are less homogeneous and there are more service options that customers want to choose from. In 1956 maritime containers were introduced to liner shipping and they later revolutionised the sector entirely. It has not only changed completely the way general cargo is handled in ports, making it so much more productive, time-efficient and safe, but it has also reshaped the total international transport and logistics chain. Cargo can be delivered door-to-door seamlessly through multimodal transport. Although invented in the US in the mid-1950s, the containerisation of general cargo transport did not take off until about ten years later and it took another 20 or so years until the mid-1980s for the majority of liner shipping cargo to be transported in containers. Today liner shipping is almost all by containers. Differentiation of liner shipping services can be found in the following areas.

- ***Service extension***. Maritime transport is a part of the transport and logistics chain for international trade. Many shipping lines expand their services to cover pre- and post-sea transport and logistics. By offering door-to-door service, a shipping company provides an added value for customers. Such a capability varies between shipping lines. The scale economies are an important factor and big companies have an advantage.
- ***Market coverage***. The more extensive a service network a shipping line has, the more cargoes it can attract. When choosing an ocean shipping carrier, a customer will give preference to the ones that are capable of covering all the destinations and markets in which the customer has businesses. Again, the size of the shipping company is a critical factor.
- ***Transit time***. In liner shipping, transit time is more important than in tramp shipping for mainly two reasons. The first is that the value of the cargo is generally much higher in liner shipping than in tramp shipping so the cargo is, therefore, more time-sensitive. The second is that, in addition to sailing speed, the number of ports of call and average time in port also has a bigger impact on the transit time.

- ***Schedule reliability***. The departure and arrival time of liner shipping is supposed to be punctual. But, in reality, this is rarely the case, though there is a gap between the best and worst performers. According to some liner shipping performance reports,[10] in the period of 2017–2018, the schedule reliability of the major liner shipping companies was between 70% and 90% on average. The unreliable schedule is a major deficiency of liner shipping because it increases risks and leads to higher inventory cost.
- ***Frequency***. This is another source of liner shipping service differentiation. For a customer, the higher the service frequency is, the lower the inventory cost will be. On many main East–West shipping routes, a shipping line will be considered as not competitive if it offers only a single weekly service. But offering multiple weekly services not only requires a lot of investment, it is also much harder to have enough cargo. So the size of the operation is important.

Although more room exists for service differentiation in liner shipping, the gaps between the leading shipping lines are reducing fast. This is mainly because the size of the operation is the most important factor for the above aspects of service differentiation. To further strengthen the size-based competitiveness, the leading shipping lines have joined forces by forming strategic alliances. By the middle of 2019, the top 10 liner shipping companies in terms of controlled dwt had a combined market share of over 83% of the total global teu capacity. The leading lines are further consolidated into three strategic alliances, as shown in Figure 13.3. They are named as "2M" with 33.5% market share, "Ocean Alliance" with 29.4% market share and "The Alliance" with about 17% market share.[11] The three Alliances have a combined market share of 80% of the world's total teu capacity. With such mighty sizes, the Alliances are capable of not only reducing costs but also offering services at a similar quality level.

In conclusion, we can say that, commercially and operationally, most tramp shipping firms and the leading companies of liner shipping are offering standardised services. This phenomenon is also referred to as commoditisation of maritime transport, which means that the differences in the quality of services between suppliers are insignificant. As containerised liner shipping matures, the business

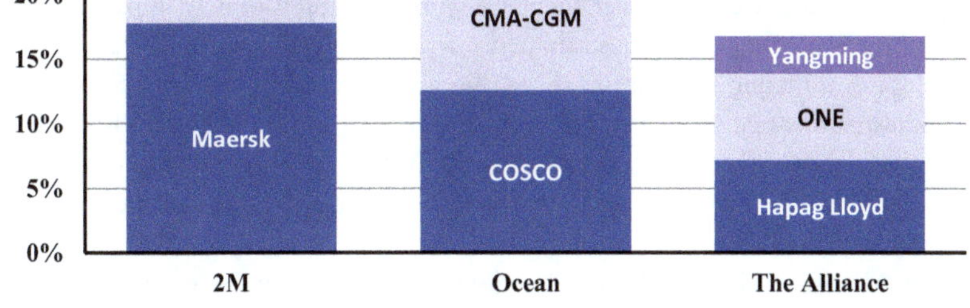

Figure 13.3 Market share in teu of three leading liner shipping alliances, 2019.

Source: compiled based on data from Alphaliner (October, 2019).

Note: the three Alliances have a combined market share of 80% of the world's total teu.

practices are more and more standardised. This is particularly true for the largest shipping lines which have consolidated, between themselves, into very large alliances that dominate the market. The general trend of consolidation in the liner shipping sector will most probably continue, though the composition of the alliances, as well as the individual members' market share, are constantly changing.

13.4 National competitiveness in different maritime activities

The competition in maritime transport is not focussed exclusively on the final output, i.e., the fast, safe and cheap delivery of cargo to the destination, it also happens in the process of the transport at each stage of input of the shipping production. This means that there are different sources of the activities which are product or service inputs to maritime transport, from shipbuilding to ship operation and from ship finance to seafaring. Such a process is common in other sectors too. But in international shipping, the various activity inputs are often coming from different countries. Such diversity is special and probably unique to maritime transport. In this section we first select some main shipping-related activities to see what the determining factors are for international competitiveness. Then we will examine the links between the selected activities.

What is the source of competitiveness for different shipping-related activities?

In an UNCTAD study on the participation of countries in international maritime transport, a total of nine activities were analysed.[12] In the following analysis we have selected seven maritime sectors and evaluate the relations between them to see whether the development of one sector will benefit from or depends on the development of any other sectors. The seven activities are shipbuilding, shipowning, ship registration, ship classification, liner shipping operation, ship demolition and seafarer supply. The main reasons for choosing these activities are threefold: the value generation capability, the employment creation potentials and the economic impact on the competitiveness of the transport. We now discuss them.

1 ***Shipbuilding***. As discussed previously, this is a highly concentrated sector with virtually all commercial ships built in three Far Eastern countries, Japan, Korea and China. They are also the countries with a strong heavy industry sector, such as steel production. They are the world-leading trade and shipping nations as well. However, their strength in the input of new ships is more attributable to the combination of a competitive labour force and sophisticated industrial base. They are in strong but not dominating positions in other shipping sectors. The decline of the European shipbuilding industry was mainly due to the high labour cost, although Europe has remained strong in much lower labour-intensity shipping activities. When it comes to shipbuilders, in 2018 the top builder Hyundai HI Group of Korea received 19.4% of all orders and the share of the top 10 shipbuilder groups was 63%.[13]
2 ***Shipowning***. Almost all ships under open registries are owned and controlled by shipowners in countries other than the flag States. Germany is one of the leading ship-owning countries but many German-owned ships are operated by the shipping companies of other countries. Many shipping companies employ a big fleet of chartered or leased ships along with their self-owned ships. Some ship asset management companies, such as Canada's *Seaspan* Corporation, or some financial institutions, such as commercial banks, are gaining popularity as a shipowning model.
3 ***Liner shipping operation***. Countries like Norway or Greece are not strong in container ship operations. Container ship operation has become an activity in its own right that can be in or move

to any place that suits the company, such as Marseille-based CMA-CGM or Geneva-based MSC, both of which are large liner shipping companies. Thanks to the internationalisation of most shipping costs, the high-cost locations have not been a hindrance to hosting large container shipping companies.

4 ***Ship registration***. This is probably one of the most extreme examples of how a country can be a provider of a shipping service input without having corresponding capacities in any other shipping-related sectors. The biggest countries of ship registration are Panama and Liberia and there are many other open registry countries. Yet almost all open registry countries are not found in any list of the major providers of other shipping inputs, such as ship operation or seafaring. It has been considered by some as an "easy" business with a low entry barrier so that countries with limited or no maritime expertise, such as Liberia, can venture into the ship registration sector relatively successfully.

5 ***Ship scrapping***. The ship demolition activities are labour intensive and have a significant impact on safety and the environment. So a country with a comparative cost advantage in these two aspects could be internationally competitive. For the same reason, this sector is "foot-loose" in the sense that when the labour and environmental costs rise in a country, the business may move to other countries relatively easily and quickly.

6 ***Ship classification***. The classification of ships is an activity closely related to shipbuilding and marine insurance. The technical conditions of ships are verified and classified by classification societies and therefore form the basis for marine insurance. As such, the business is highly technical and requires special know-how in ship design, construction, propulsion, engineering and operation. This sector is largely dominated by the traditional maritime countries of Europe, North America and Asia. Some big shipowning countries, such as Japan, Germany, Norway or the US, are also leading countries of ship classification, but others, such as Greece or Singapore, are not.

7 ***Seafarer supply***. International seafaring has become a more standardised activity with both established employment structures and a widely accepted code of practice on the one hand, and international rules and regulations, such as the IMO's STCW Convention, on the other hand. The traditional commercial functions of a shipmaster in relation, for example, to the negotiations for cargo, freight, bunker, cargo handling, etc., have been taken over by shore-based people. So the responsibilities of seafarers are almost exclusively technical and operational. It can be undertaken as a standalone profession and ships of the European and Japanese companies are commonly manned by international seafarers with mixed nationalities.

Can a country excel in one maritime activity without being strong in others?

As discussed above, there is a disintegration of shipping transport activities with regard to the sources of input. In other words, there is a clear international division of labour with a country or a small group of countries specialising in a particular maritime activity. The Philippines, for example, specialises in providing seafarers, Panama is the world's leader for ship registry, Greece has the largest controlled fleet of commercial ships and the UK dominates the marine insurance business. All these countries are the strongest in one or a few specific shipping sectors based on their respective comparative advantages, without, at the same time, being as good at any other maritime transport activities. Based on the 2018 statistics and a distinction between dependent sectors and correlated sectors, we analysed the links between the leading countries in some selected maritime activities. We calculated the market positions of the supplier countries that provided 90% of the service in each of the seven maritime sectors. Based on the country rankings, we studied the coefficients of correlation between the leading countries in each pair of maritime sectors. The findings are in Table 13.2. This shows the

Table 13.2 Country-based dependence between selected maritime activities – a correlation analysis, 2018.

Dependent sectors							
Shipbuilding	–	0.78	0.87	0.25	0.45	0.73	0.50
Shipowning	0.45	–	0.46	0.21	0.08	0.05	0.07
Registration	0.08	0.09	–	0.30	0.13	0.07	0.10
Classification	0.22	0.30	0.13	–	0.43	0.15	0.17
Liner operation	0.29	0.34	0.17	0.13	–	0.35	0.04
Ship scrapping	0.12	0.02	0.19	0.18	0.00	–	0.23
Seafaring	0.51	0.16	0.11	0.08	0.22	0.23	–
Correlated sectors	Shipbuilding	Shipowning	Registration	Classification	Liner operation	Ship scrapping	Seafarer supply

Source: Shuo Ma based on the data of UNCTAD, ISL, BIMCO/ISF, Clarkson, Alphaliner, etc.

Note: the coefficients of correlation indicate the dependence of the development of each sector (on the left) on the development of other sectors (at the bottom). When the coefficient is close to +1 or -1, the two developments of the two sectors are highly positively or negatively correlated. If the correlation is absent, the coefficient is close to "0". The table should be read from left to right.

coefficients of correlation (r) between a maritime sector, on the left, and each of six other maritime sectors, at the bottom. It measures if a country is a world leader in one of the activities shown on the left and to what extent the country is also strong in each of the six other activities.

- ***Strongly correlated cases.*** Out of 42 pairs, four cases have the "r" higher than 0.5 with the highest at 0.87. The four cases are all about shipbuilding as a dependent sector, and the four correlated sectors are "ship registry" r = 0.87, "shipowning" r = 0.78, ship scrapping r = 0.72 and seafarer supply, which includes both officers and ratings r = 0.50. The first two high correlations are because about 90% of ships are built by Japan, Korea and China and the three countries also register as well as own many ships. The last two high correlations are due to China, which is the world's largest shipbuilder, seafarer supplier and the fourth largest ship scraper.
- ***Weakly correlated cases.*** A majority of the pairs have weak correlation coefficients r between 0.0 and 0.4, which means the development in one sector is independent of the development in other sectors. The phenomenon is most markedly demonstrated in ship scrapping, where the correlation is low across the board with all other sectors. In reality, the leading country for ship scrapping, Bangladesh, does not appear among the top 20 countries of any of the other maritime activities we compared. Low coefficients are also found for ship registry and seafarer supply. For example, some of the biggest flag States are open registry countries, such as Panama or Liberia, which are not strong in any other maritime sectors.
- ***Negatively correlated cases.*** There are a few pairs with slight negative correlation coefficients. They are in the ship registration and seafaring sectors. These two sectors have very low entry barriers. Countries with high labour costs should lose their competitive advantage. Most open registries are small and low-income countries that do not have the financial, technical and human capability and resources to enter into other maritime sectors.
- ***Different coefficient for the same pair with a reverse order.*** In Table 13.2 we can find the same pairs twice with different order and coefficient. For example, shipbuilding/shipowning has r = 0.78, but shipowning/shipbuilding has r = 0.45. This means that to be a leader in shipbuilding, it is more important to also be a leading shipowning country, but to be a shipowning country, one does not have to be a shipbuilder. The comparison is more striking between r = 0.87 for shipbuilding/ship-registry and r = -0.08 for ship-registry/shipbuilding. This implies that there is a stronger dependence of shipbuilding on ship registry than the other way round. Similarly, it is more important to own ships for seafarer supply (r = 0.16) than to be a supplier of seafarers for owning ships (r = 0.07).

The above analysis should, however, be treated cautiously because of the huge difference between country sizes. In terms of territory, population or economy, the size of many provinces in China or states in the US is as big as many mid-sized countries. China is one of the biggest suppliers in many shipping sectors, from shipbuilding, ship finance and shipowning to ship operation, ship scrapping and seafaring. So, if Europe is taken as a single entity, the linkage between different shipping sectors will be much closer. Europe is a leading supplier of all of the above maritime transport activities except shipbuilding, ship registration and seafaring. For a country with a limited maritime tradition or industrial base to participate in maritime transport, ship registration, ship demolition and seafaring may be the suitable sectors of entry.

13.5 Quality versus cost – competition strategies

In the earlier discussions of this chapter on competition, it was concluded that the tramp shipping services provided by various companies are very similar. There is more service quality differentiation in the liner shipping sector, though the differences are becoming less significant among the leading shipping lines. We will focus in this section more on the quality of the liner shipping sector.

What are the values of shipping service for a customer?

People do not need transport, they need trade. But trade will not be completed without transport. To move trade from port A to port B is the basic value created by maritime transport. A trader will be interested in this value if it is higher than the cost. This value is affected by three factors, namely time, safety and reliability.

- The *time* used for the transport incurs an inventory-holding cost for the customer. So the level of the cost depends on the value and type of cargo transported and the cost of capital. It also depends on the interest rate for bank loans. Therefore the time value of transport can be accurately calculated. As cargo owners want to save time cost, fast transport creates an added value. However, when considering the cost aspect, the speed of transport should be optimal rather than the fastest. Generally speaking, shippers with higher-value cargo such as containerised goods are willing to pay extra cost for faster transport, while those with lower-value cargo such as raw materials prefer cheap and slow transport.
- *Safety* of transport is seen as an element of maritime transport value because of the high level of risks. For the last half a century, maritime safety performance has improved drastically, as explained in the previous section on marine insurance. Accidents and casualties have been on the decline and the transport has become safer. Therefore, the value of safety is more in the form of a cost-saving from otherwise unsafe transport.
- The *reliability* of transport is a related but different concept with regard to time and safety values. If time and safety are about quality standards, reliability is about the assurance of the qualities and the ability to honour all contract obligations fully. It refers, for example, to the punctuality of the shipping service or the safety standards and record. The service reliability is extended to also cover customer service in its broader sense, such as responsiveness and all services towards customers at every stage including pre-transaction to post-transaction.

What is the best "value for money" for maritime transport customers?

Customers get value from cargo transport in exchange for a payment. In a competitive market, a customer always looks for the highest value for the lowest cost. Therefore, a shipping company's competitiveness depends on its ability to provide their customers with the best value for money as compared with other companies. So a good knowledge of the exact relation between value and cost is important for a shipping company. For different customers, the value of international shipping is a variable factor and so is the cost which different customers expect to pay. This means that a shipping company may target a particular group of customers and develop services with the right value for money for them.

On 4 March 2015 the shipping newspaper, *Lloyd's List*, reported that the premium liner shipping service by Maersk, the largest shipping line, on the Far East–Western Europe route and called "Daily Maersk", was abandoned.[14] When the shipping line had introduced the service some 3.5 years earlier, it was considered as a big innovation in the liner shipping industry. The service deployed 70 large container ships offering a guaranteed departure/arrival time daily at main Asian and European ports. At the time, liner shipping suffered from poor schedule reliability records in that about half of the services did not arrive on time on the main East–West shipping routes. So the new Daily Maersk not only increased the service frequency but also offered guaranteed punctuality. The ships would leave the port at a precise hour and Maersk promised a fine of US$100 per container for a 1–3 day delay and US$300 per container for a 4 or more days delay. The shippers who used the premium service would have to agree to a "no-show" charge, which meant that the failure to provide the booked container for a shipment would also lead to the payment of a premium in the form of higher freight.

It was estimated that the Daily Maersk service would yield a very high benefit for the customers in terms of shorter transit time as well as much-improved reliability. Given the poor on-time performance of the liner services on major shipping routes at that time, the guaranteed daily cut-off liner shipping service was called an "ocean conveyor belt for the world's busiest trade lane".[15] The frequent and punctual services would allow the shippers to reduce expensive inventory cost. It is reported that about six months after the launch of the daily cut-off liner service, the average reliability hit 99%.[16] It was estimated that the benefit of a higher frequency from a weekly to a daily service would be a reduction of inventory cost for shippers by about 16% and that of improved punctuality from 70% to 99% would add another reduction of inventory cost by 9%, or a combined total cost saving by 25%.[17]

Why did such an "obvious" better service with a "substantive" customer benefit have to be abandoned? The direct cause was that the Daily Maersk service generated a high cost for the shipping line, but most customers did not want to pay extra freight for it. The main reason for the failure was that Daily Maersk did not provide the right value for money for most customers. The above estimate of 25% savings was incorrect because the exact inventory-holding cost depends on both average cargo value and the level of capital cost. Those highly time-sensitive cargoes, which are willing and able to pay a premium price for additional frequency and punctuality, are in a minority. At the same time, to maintain a daily cut-off service between the Far East and Western Europe is a highly complex and costly offering.[18] The daily cut-off service could not be offered unless an extra US$300–$500 per teu was paid.[19] The majority of shippers refused to pay the extra, so the service discontinued. The lesson learnt is that the additional value is not sufficient to offset the extra cost.

The competitiveness of a shipping company comes from the firm's ability to offer a service with the best value for money to its identified customers as compared with the competing services. For this outcome, the company has two main tasks. The first is to know the value the customers will have from the services provided and the second is to know how to offer the services at a cost that is sufficiently below the value. In Figure 13.4 the two curves represent the shipping company's service frontier and

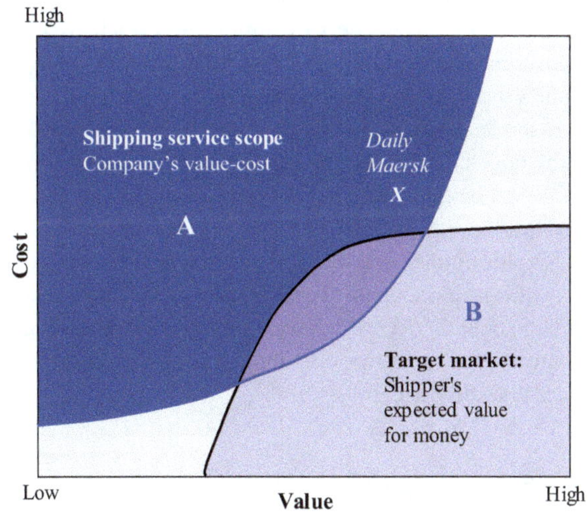

Figure 13.4 Optimal value-cost and value-for-money model.

Source: Shuo Ma.

Note: the two curves represent a shipping company's service frontier and a shipper's value-for-money frontier. The overlapped area represents the competitiveness of the shipping company.

the shipper's value-for-money frontier. For the shipping company, the overlapped area represents the service that can be sold to the shipper. The shipper is not interested in the services represented by the rest of area A. Similarly, from the shipper's point of view, the overlapped area is what it can get, and for the need represented by the rest of area B, that the shipping company is unable to provide. The bigger the gap between the cost to the firm and the value to the customers is, the more competitive the shipping company will be. In the above example, the Daily Maersk service is at point X, which is outside the customer's expected value-for-money zone. To sustain and to expand such competitiveness, a competitive strategy needs to be developed based on three fronts: to have a right service direction and pattern, to adopt the right technology and to have tight cost control.

How important are the service direction and pattern?

Maritime transport demand is diverse and constantly changing. In the early chapters of this book we discussed at length the development trends of global seaborne trade. A shipping company should monitor both the long-term perspectives and short-term changes closely, making sure that the right strategic decisions have been taken. Questions will be, for example, which markets to concentrate on, in terms of types of seaborne trade such as dry or liquid, container or specialised; or in terms of business scope, such as sea transport only or a full logistics and supply chain service coverage; or in terms of geographical focus, such as regional versus global focus. There are also other important issues which are of long-term and strategic importance for a company's business.

Successful shipping companies are often those with a good strategic plan. Specific marketing objectives are to be developed based on the market assessment and the competitive advantages of the shipping company. As shown in the above example, to have the right service standards with the best value for money for the target market is a very important strategic issue. That, in turn, helps the company build its brand and reputation in the market. When it comes to the question of business expansion, there are different ways of achieving growth objectives, whether in terms of absolute business increase or relative market share improvement. For example, a fleet expansion can be achieved by organic growth or by merger and acquisition. Investment in container port operations could be more profitable than an investment in ships, but it requires specific expertise and may represent a higher risk level. Let's take the time of ship acquisition as an example. It is an important but difficult decision to make. The long lead time for building new ships and the uncertainty of the freight market make ship investment a high-risk business.

Companies often need to be innovative in order to gain competitive advantages. An example is the Brazilian company Vale S. A., which took an innovative decision by building ultra-large ore carriers of about 400,000 dwt during the period of 2011–2013. To offset the cost disadvantage vis-à-vis the Australian competitors for iron ore export to China, the Brazilian company took a bold decision to build extraordinarily large bulk carriers which were more than twice as big as the largest bulkers to date. The strategy was a success and such large ore carriers have played a key role in the seaborne trade of iron ore between Brazil and the Far East.

Why is the right technology important?

The second determining factor for sustainable competitiveness is technology – the right technology and the excellent use of it. As discussed in Chapter 9, there are three dimensions of maritime technology, namely naval architecture, marine engineering and maritime communication. The external technologies can be applied to shipping production. The right technology and the good use of it mean that it can help improve value for money for the customers. Figure 13.5 shows how the proper application of the right technology can offer greater value for money for the customers and consequently sustain and expand the company's competitiveness. For any given client, there is a value-for-money frontier

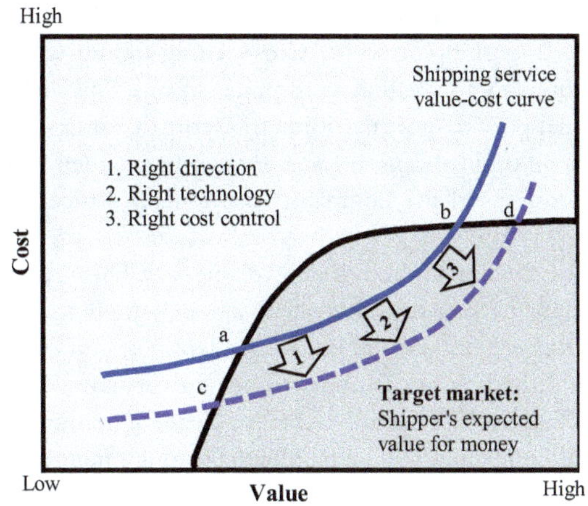

Figure 13.5 Sustaining and expanding competitiveness.

Source: Shuo Ma.

Note: a company's competitiveness is defined by the area above the "value-cost curve", which overlaps with the target market. The competitiveness can be sustained and expanded by the right strategies on business direction, technology and cost control.

line and area. For a certain value from transport, there is a maximum cost a shipper is prepared to pay. In the beginning, the customer will pay more for even a small additional value. When the main goal has been achieved, they will only be willing to pay a small extra amount for a higher value service. A shipping company incurs a cost when providing value service to customers. The blue curve is the company's value-cost frontier. The relationship between the cost incurred and the value provided is represented by the overlapped area between the shipping company's value-cost frontier curve and customer's value-for-money frontier curve. The intersection at *a* is the point of equilibrium between demand and supply corresponding to the minimum value service for the target customer and the minimum payment for the shipping company. Point *b* is the equilibrium of the supply's maximum value service and demand's maximum payment.

By deploying the right technology or adopting a better business model, the company can extend its value-cost frontier. When Maersk Line launched their 18,000-teu "Triple E" container ships in 2013, some technological innovations were used in the propulsion system, hull design and separation of engines and the deckhouse. As a result, compared with the previous generation of 15,000-teu vessels, the new ships can carry 16% more containers while being only about 5% wider, 0.5% longer and with no change in draft. The new generation of container ships, which improve economies of scale, the efficiency of energy and environmental performance (Triple-E), provide a service with new added value and reduced cost. The effects can be seen in Figure 13.5 as the shipping company's value-cost curve is extended from *a* and *b* to *c* and *d*. The company can serve a large customer base and its competitiveness is expanded and more sustainable.

How important is cost control?

In a competitive market, such as that of international maritime transport, the level of price is solely determined by the market. As far as an individual shipping company is concerned, for a given type of service, the only way to improve profitability is to reduce cost. This is more so because, as discussed previously, quality-wise maritime transport is largely standardised. The room for service differentiation is limited, even in the liner shipping sector. Cross-selling and up-selling are certain ways which may allow the shipping company to create new revenue streams. This includes expanding businesses vertically beyond traditional port-to-port maritime transport to, for example, offer logistics services. However, that may not be an optimal option for every company when such expansion means moving away from the core business of the company. So the main source of competitiveness remains cost control.

The shipping market is cyclical and often in a volatile way. This is particularly true in the new-build and second-hand ship markets as well as in the tramp shipping freight markets. The freight market and ship prices are closely linked and interdependent. The real competition begins when the freight market declines and the freight continues to be at a very low level due to the lack of price elasticity, as explained in Chapter 12. This is the time for cleaning up the excess supply through competition. The least efficient companies will be eliminated through merger, acquisition or bankruptcy. In this process, cost control plays a decisive role in a shipping firm's survival. Those who can manage the operation with a tighter and more effective cost control have a better chance to remain in the market. Competition in shipping often takes the form of a price war. Except for the firms enjoying external subsidies or protection, in the long term the winners are always those who are the best at cost control.

There are four main cost-saving areas that a shipping company should pay special and constant attention to and, depending on the type of shipping service provided, can make them the source of competitiveness. They are investment cost, labour/personnel cost, consumption cost and system cost. These are not only big cost elements, but they are dynamic by nature and can, to some extent, be controlled and changed by shipping companies.

1 ***Investment cost.*** This is about the cost spent on new or second-hand ships, containers, terminals, warehouses or other fixed assets. Given the volatile nature of the shipbuilding market, the timing of investment and funding methods are of particular importance and, at the same time, of high risk. The new AI-based risk management technology may be useful in the decision-making process.
2 ***Personnel cost.*** It is often difficult to have a flexible employment system that allows the shipping company to adjust the employment level and the type of seafarers close to the business needs and market fluctuations. But this is a critical pre-condition for effective cost control. The development in substituting labour for automation technology has accelerated in recent years as digitalisation expands quickly to virtually all sectors of maritime transport.
3 ***Consumption cost.*** In most cases, the largest consumption cost is fuel. There are several ways to save fuel cost. For example, the company can use more fuel-efficient engines; or it can benefit from low price fuels by having good deals from suppliers to avoid taking expensive fuel in certain ports; or it can optimise ship operation to save fuel; or it can reduce the ship's speed.
4 ***System cost.*** A substantial part of the cost is spent on purchasing services from outside to complete the maritime transport of cargo. Together, these services form the shipping system. Some of these costs can be relatively stable, such as ship registration cost, but many other costs need much more monitoring and control. These include port cost, agency cost, insurance cost, maintenance cost, etc.

The above four areas of cost control indicate that although most of the cost for shipping companies has been internationalised, which means that there is an equal playing field for all countries, it does not mean that shipping companies have the same costs. The differentiation of cost does not come from the nationality of the shipowner or the location of the company, it comes chiefly from the effectiveness of cost control. The companies which have a more successful cost control are normally those which have top management putting cost control as a management priority; they are those which have a culture and a strategy in favour of cost control; and they are those which often have dedicated cost control officers.

13.6 Market concentration and stages of national competitiveness

Regarding different maritime activities, there are two levels of market concentration. The first is at the company level. Aiming at the effects from economies of scale, maritime companies, particularly in the liner sector, have gone through a continuous process of consolidation in size. The second is at the country level. Due to the national competitive advantages, some maritime activities are increasingly concentrated in a small number of countries. In this section we will examine the country-based second-level concentration in selected maritime sectors. We will also study the background for the national competitiveness in each of the selected sectors.

How do you measure country-based market concentration?

In the previous section of this chapter we discussed the international division of labour for various maritime activities. The development of most activities has a weak correlation coefficient. Such a feature allows a deeper level of concentration of a particular shipping sector in a small group of countries. It is not straightforward to measure country-based market concentration accurately because almost all maritime activities are completed with elements from multiple countries. A new ship delivered by a country's shipyard may contain valuable parts from other countries. Some ship officers of a country may have been educated in another country. An open ship registration may also have very close ties with a foreign country. Many shipping companies have a highly internationalised share-holding structure and DNV-GL, the largest classification society, belongs to two countries.

However, despite all the complexities, we could still identify countries as the providers of each maritime activity and measure their market share. Based on the published statistics from several sources,[20] we calculated the country-based market share of the following seven sectors for 2018, namely seafarer supply (officers and ratings combined), shipowning, ship registration, liner shipping, classification, ship scrapping and shipbuilding. We then calculated the HHI (Herfindahl-Hirschman Index) for each sector as the measurement of the market concentration. The results appear in Figure 13.6. Of the seven maritime sectors, seafaring, shipowning, ship registration and liner shipping markets are with an HHI less than 1,500 and are therefore not concentrated. The classification market has an HHI of more than 1,500 and is moderately concentrated. Ship scrapping and shipbuilding are highly concentrated with an HHI of more than 2,500. The higher the level of market concentration is, the lower the level of competition in that market will be. In a perfectly competitive market, not only are there many suppliers, but the market share is also relatively evenly distributed among all suppliers. So, despite the continuous consolidation of the liner shipping sector and the extraordinarily large fleets controlled by countries like Greece and Japan, liner shipping and shipowning are still largely competitive markets. On the other hand, shipowners have less choice when it comes to the supplier countries in the sectors such as ship classification, shipbuilding or ship scrapping.

What is the situation of competition in selected maritime activities?

Are there dominating countries for each maritime transport sector? The answer is affirmative. But then how many of them are there and how strong are they? We shall try to answer these questions by taking a closer look at the market share of the leading countries in the following five maritime

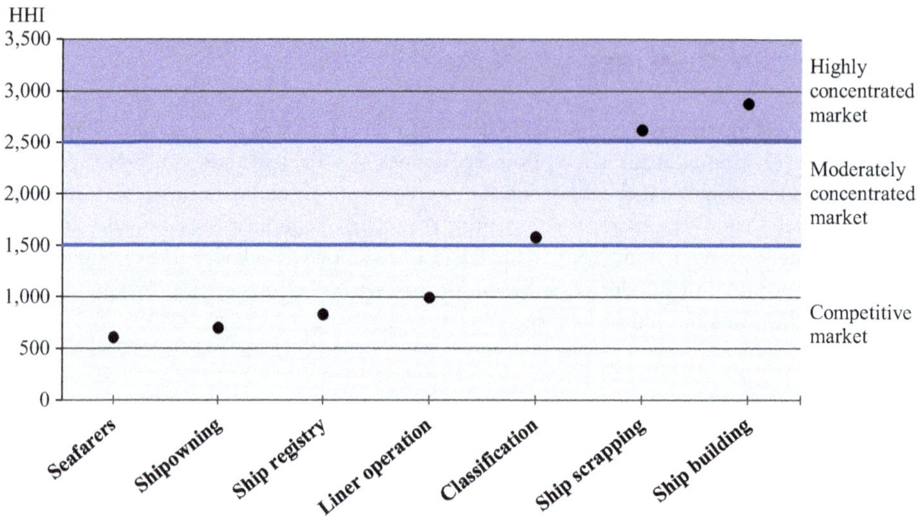

Figure 13.6 Country-based concentration of selected markets, Herfindahl-Hirschman Index, 2018.

Source: Shuo Ma based on the data of UNCTAD, ISL, Clarkson, Alphaliner and BIMCO/ISF.

Note: if the HHI is less than 1,500, the market is considered to be competitive. If the HHI is between 1,500 and 2,500, the sector is considered as moderately concentrated. If the HHI is greater than 2,500, the sector is considered to be highly concentrated.

transport activities: shipbuilding, shipowning, ship registry, liner shipping and seafaring. Figure 13.7 shows the market share of the top 50 countries in the five maritime transport sectors. We may examine the following three indicators on the situation of competition in the five activities.

1 ***The market share of the top 10 countries***. There are four sectors where the combined market share of the top 10 countries was more than 90% in 2018. They are ship scrapping – 99.7%, ship classification – 98.7%, shipbuilding – 97.7% and liner shipping – 90.2%. The top 10 countries' share was 77.6% for ship registration, 68.3% for shipowning and 60.5% for seafarer supply (officer/rating).
2 ***The market share of the top 1 country***. The general concept is that if the market share of a supplier is too big, e.g., one-third or more, it is considered to be in a position to influence the market. In 2018 Bangladesh's share of the ship-scrapping market was about 40%. China also had about 40% market share for shipbuilding. Denmark, the home country of Maersk Line, had an 18% market share in liner shipping in 2018 and DNV-GL, the Norwegian/German classification society, had a 21.3% share of the market. The biggest flag State, Panama, had 17.6% of the ship registration market and Greece's market share was 17.3% for shipowning.
3 ***The number of countries providing 90% of the service***. Shipbuilding is the most concentrated market because, in 2018, 3 countries, China, Korea and Japan, had more than 90% of the market. For the other sectors, the number of countries which provide 90% of the service is as follows: 4 countries for ship scrapping, 7 countries for classification, 10 countries for liner shipping operations, 23 countries for ship registration, 24 for shipowning and 35 countries for seafarer supply.

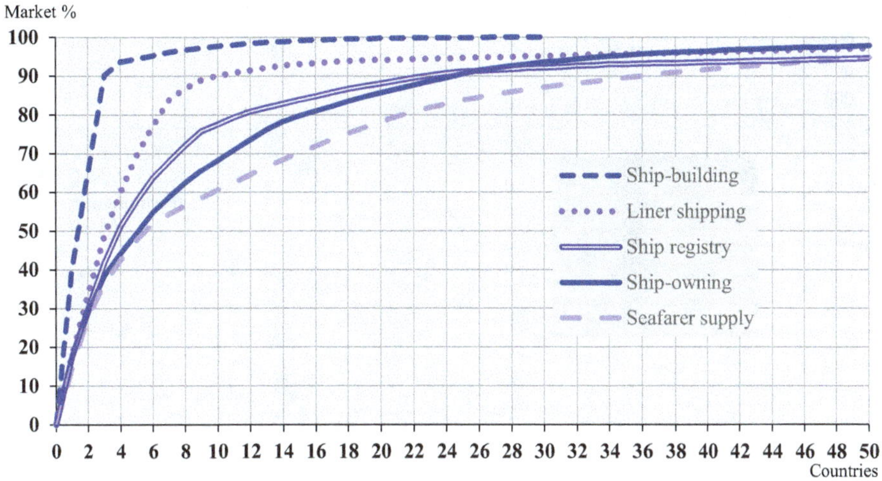

Figure 13.7 Market share of the leading countries in five maritime activities, 2018.

Source: Shuo Ma, based on the data of ISL, Alphaliner, UNCTAD and BIMCO/ISF.

Note: shipbuilding is the most concentrated sector with three countries building 90% of ships, while seafarer supply is the least concentrated sector with the top country's market share at less than 15%. In liner shipping, 90% of the capability is provided by 10 countries.

Ship classification and ship scrapping are relatively smaller markets in terms of total transactions and are not included in Figure 13.7. Both markets are highly concentrated. The 3 South Asian countries, Bangladesh, India and Pakistan, demolished between them about 80% of the ships. Together with China and Turkey, these 5 countries had about 99% of the global ship-demolishing market in 2018. For the classification market, the top 10 countries had 99% of the market in 2018.

How does GDP per capita affect a country's maritime competitiveness?

There are many reasons for a country to be a maritime sector leader. They may include tradition, special know-how and other intangible elements. One important factor is cost. European and North American countries used to be dominating powers in shipbuilding. The general belief is that the high labour cost was the main reason for the decline of shipbuilding in these countries. Some people believe that, given the high capital-intensive nature, international shipping should be the business of capital-rich countries. At the same time, some other people believe that, given the relatively low entry barriers and limited formal education and preparation for jobs requirements, international shipping should be the business of cheap-labour countries. We collected the official statistics on GDP per capita in 2018 for the top five countries in each of the seven selected maritime activities. The results appear in Figure 13.8.

Figure 13.8 reflects well the two basic features of international shipping that we have discussed in this chapter. The first is the disintegration and specialisation of different maritime activities. The second is the internationalisation of maritime transport costs. The combined market share of the top five

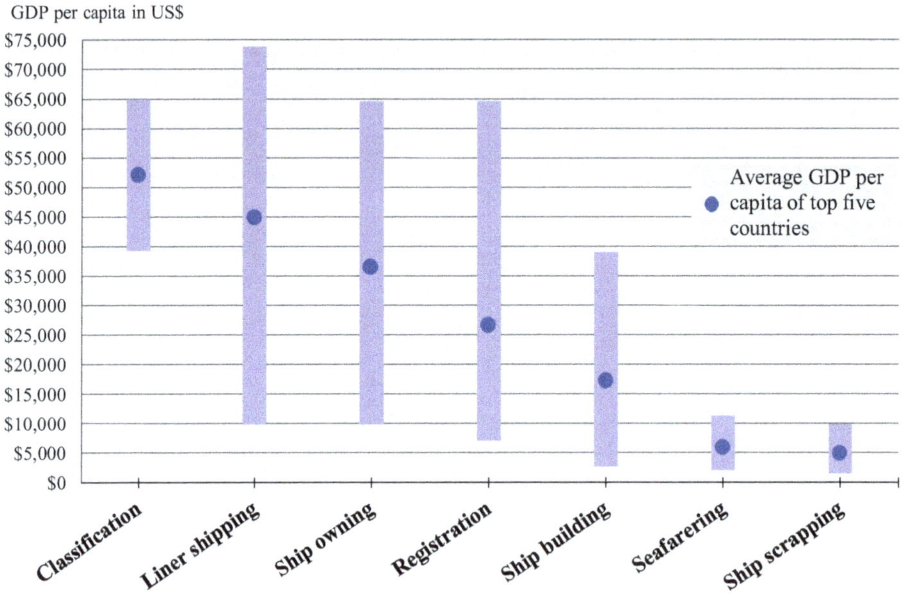

Figure 13.8 The range and average of GPD per capita of the top five supplier countries, 2018.

Source: Shuo Ma, based on the data of the World Bank, UNCTAD, ISL, Clarkson, Alphaliner and BIMCO/ISF.

Note: this figure is about the GDP per capita in nominal US$ in 2018 of top five countries for each sector. The combined market share of the top five is between 48% and 99%. There is a big difference in the average and the range of GDP per capita between sectors.

suppliers varies from the lowest of 48% for seafarer supply and 50% for shipowning to the highest of 94% for shipbuilding and 99% for ship scrapping. We make two observations in Figure 13.8 as follows.

1 The first observation is about the huge difference in the average GDP per capita between sectors. For example, there is a gap of more than 10 times from US$4,900 for ship scrapping to US$52,000 for liner shipping. Both low-income countries like Liberia or Bangladesh and high-income countries like Switzerland or Norway participate in different maritime transport activities as leading suppliers. This is possible because of the weak links between the activities, as seen in Table 13.2. A country can be a leader in one sector even with weak positions in other sectors. Ship classification has high entry barriers because it is a more knowledge-based sector, requiring extensive technical expertise in ship construction and engineering. The sector is suitable for high-income and industrialised countries. On the other hand, both seafaring and ship scrapping have low entry barriers and are labour-intensive, so low-income countries have a competitive edge in these sectors.
2 The second observation is the extremely wide range in GDP per capita between the top five countries of the same sector. It seems that GDP per capita is not a relevant factor because we find in the world's top five liner-shipping operators both countries with GDP per capita of less than US$10,000 and more than US$70,000. Differences as big as about six times are also found between the top five leaders in the shipowning and ship registry sectors. The explanation of this phenomenon is the

internationalisation of shipping costs, as discussed earlier in this chapter. As about 80%–90% of the cost has little relation with a shipping company's home base, the shipping activities organised from a high-cost country do not have any significant cost disadvantage. The gap will be bigger if more leading countries are included. Among the seven activities, three sectors are the most dependent on national GDP per capita, they are ship scrapping, seafaring and ship classification.

13.7 Summary

We have discussed various aspects of competition in maritime transport. The focus of the competition was examined from the aspect of cost leadership and service differentiation. We explained the meaning of good service in tramp shipping as well in liner shipping and discussed in more detail the concepts of service differentiation in terms of savings from a superior safety record or extra value from new or better service. We then examined the skill set for those working in the shipping sectors. We concluded that most jobs in maritime transport do not require a high level of education, technological skills and knowledge accumulation, while there is a small number of positions such as managers and specialists that require more creativity and analytical capability.

Most of the costs in maritime transport production are spent on purchasing product or service inputs on the international markets, from products like ships, containers and fuels, to services such as ship registration, classification, insurance, cargo handling, even seafaring. There are only some limited costs that rely mostly on the national market. So countries at quite different economic development levels such as Norway and Greece or Denmark and China can share similar maritime competitiveness in the same markets. Another important feature affecting maritime competition is the standardisation of shipping services. Technically, shipping has long been largely standardised and even commercially and operationally, among the established companies, the sector is much more standardised now than before, although in liner shipping there is still some limited room for differentiation.

Another important aspect of maritime competition is related to the fact that international competition is not only in the final transport service but also in various sub-markets of different inputs, ranging from shipbuilding, ship registration, ship financing, shipowning, ship operation to the manning and insurance services. What is interesting is that a country can be a leader in one type of activity without being good at any of the others. We call this disintegration of maritime competition. It is getting rare and increasingly difficult that a single country is capable of providing independently all maritime transport activities that are internationally competitive.

Shippers are looking for the best value for money. They will only pay for an improved service if the extra value is bigger than the additional cost. A recent premium liner service with high frequency and reliability had to discontinue because the additional cost exceeded the additional value. So a balance has to be sought. There are three ways for the shipping company to increase and sustain its competitiveness vis-à-vis rival companies for targeted customers. The first is by having a good strategic direction and service pattern; the second is to adopt appropriate technologies and the third is to have tight cost control.

In order to evaluate the situation of competition, we have also examined the market concentration levels in some selected maritime sectors. We calculated the HHI for these sectors and analysed their competition situations. We found that two markets are highly concentrated: shipbuilding and ship scrapping, ship classification is moderately concentrated and the other four sectors, liner shipping, ship registration, shipowning and seafarer supply, are competitive markets. We finally assessed the relationship between GDP per capita and the national maritime competitiveness in each of the sample sectors. We concluded that countries with high or low GDP per capita can all participate and be leaders in suitable maritime transport sectors. This is because of two reasons: the lack of interdependence between the development of different activities and that most shipping costs are internationalised costs.

Notes

1 Porter M. E. (1985).
2 Johnson J. (2017). "CMA CGM to power giant new container ships with LNG", *The Marine Professional*, 8 November 2017. By using LNG, the new ships can offer big environmental benefits including a 25% reduction in carbon dioxide emissions and 99% in sulphur emissions, despite a higher new building price, which is an additional US$20m per ship (*Lloyd's List*, 23 January 2018).
3 Hope R. (1990).
4 Sturmey S. G. (1962).
5 Ibid., pp. 383–403.
6 UNCTAD (2018), pp. 27–29.
7 Alphaliner (2019).
8 Oxera (2015).
9 More than 90% of the world's commercial ships in tonnage is covered by the 12 leading classification societies that are the members of the International Association of Classification Societies (IACS) (www.iacs.org.uk).
10 A number of research and consultancy companies, such as Drewry, SeaIntel or CargoSmart, monitor and publish liner shipping schedule reliability reports. "On time" vessel arrival means ships arrive at the port of destination on the scheduled day or on the day immediately before the day of arrival.
11 Ibid., 6.
12 UNCTAD (2011), pp. 144–167.
13 Clarksons Research (2019), p. 25.
14 *Lloyd's List* (May 2015). The CEO of Maersk Line, Skou, says: "we had a major attempt with the Daily Maersk product, achieving 95% on-time delivery of cargo – our experience was that we could deliver on our promises, but the customers were not willing to pay for it ... We had a lot of extra cost to deliver that level of reliability so we have changed our strategy."
15 *Lloyd's List* (September 2011).
16 Barnard B. (2012).
17 Zhang A. and Lam J. (2015), pp. 246–262.
18 Following the launch of Daily Maersk, some major shipping lines, working in Alliances, mimicked the practice by providing service with higher frequency, such as five days per week.
19 Maritime Denmark (15 January 2013).
20 The following sources are used for the market concentration analysis: UNCTAD (shipowning, ship scrapping), ISL (ship registration), Clarksons (shipbuilding), BIMCO/ISF (seafarer supply), Alphaliner (liner shipping) and the World Bank (GDP per capita).

References

Alphaliner. (2019) "*Top 100*", Retrieved 31 October 2019 from https://alphaliner.axsmarine.com/PublicTop100/.

Baker J. (2018) "*LNG Makes Power Play for Container Shipping*", Lloyd's List, Analysis, 23 January 2018.

Barnard B. (2012) "*Maersk Claims Absolute Reliability for Daily Maersk Service*", *Journal of Commerce*, 26 April 2012.

Clarkson. (2018) "*Shipping Intelligence Network*", Clarkson, London.

Clarksons Research. (2019) "*World Shipyard Monitor*", Vol. 26, No. 10 (October 2019), p. 25.

Hope R. (1990) "*A New History of British Merchant Shipping*", John Murray Publishing Ltd., London, pp. 306–325.

Johnson J. (2017) "*CMA CGM to Power Giant New Container Ships with LNG*", The Marine Professional, 8 November 2017.

Lloyd's List. (September 2011), "*Maersk Line Unveils Daily Revolution to Asia-Europe Service*", 12 September 2011.

Lloyd's List. (May 2015), "*Premium Daily Maersk Service Abandoned*", 4 May 2015.

Maritime Denmark. (15 January 2013), "*Maersk Lose Money on Daily Maersk*", Retrieved 26 July 2018 from www.maritimedenmark.dk/?Id=16492.

Oxera. (2015), "*International Competitiveness of the UK Maritime Sector*", Final Report by the Department of Transport, the UK, May 2015.

Porter M. E. (1985) "*Competitive Advantage, Creating and Sustaining Superior Performance*", Free Press, Macmillan, Maxwell Macmillan International, New York.

Sturmey S. G. (1962) "*British Shipping and World Competition*", The Athlone Press, University of London, London, pp. 1–12.

UNCTAD. (2011) "*Review of Maritime Transport*", UNCTAD/RMT/2011, United Nations Publication, Geneva, Switzerland, pp. 144–167.

UNCTAD. (2018) "*Review of Maritime Transport*", UNCTAD/RMT/2018, United Nations Publication, Geneva, Switzerland, pp. 27–29.

Zhang A. and Lam J. (2015) "*Daily Maersk's Impact on Shipper's Supply Chain Inventories and Implications for the Liner Shipping Industry*", Maritime Policy and Management, April 2015, Vol. 42, No. 3, pp. 246–262.

Chapter 14

Shipping and logistics

Maritime transport is a part of the logistics system for international trade. So we can consider it as a sub-system of trade logistics. The development of logistics has influenced shipping activities profoundly. Shipping companies have to consider logistics when making decisions in the areas of growth strategies, investment priorities, as well as commercial and technical operations. Some logistics firms expand their business to cover shipping and port services and, similarly, many liner shipping companies have turned themselves into logistics companies. So it is clear that, for maritime transport development and growth, one has to have a better understanding of logistics and the place of shipping in the logistics and supply chain. Such a better understanding of logistics will help the shipping companies appreciate the real needs of the customers.

14.1 A bigger and more complex system

The word *logistics* had long been used by the military exclusively and it had not been introduced and known to people in economic activities and the business world until the 1960s. The concept began to be known when industrial production and trade expanded in space and it was seen that, when competition intensified, there was a greater need to have a more efficient system regarding the movement and storage of resources before, during and after the production process.

What activities are included in logistics?

What is logistics? Some people define it very generally, e.g., that logistics is an activity of support; others give extensive and comprehensive definitions. There are almost as many definitions of logistics as the number of books written on the subject. In fact, to some extent, this also reflects the very characteristics of logistics, which has undergone a constant evolution during recent decades. A widely adopted textbook defines logistics management as follows:[1] "the process of planning, implementing and controlling the efficient, effective flow and storage of goods, services, and related information from point of origin to point of consumption for the purpose of conforming to customer requirements". As manufacturing activities became more global, logistics was extended to cover a wider range of interests and related activities from the late 1980s. Such an enlarged concept and practice is called *Supply Chain Management*. A typical definition of supply chain management is the following:

> the planning and management of all activities involved in sourcing and procurement, conversion, and all logistics management activities including coordination and collaboration with channel partners, which can be suppliers, intermediaries, third-party service providers, and customers.[2]

In the context of this chapter, the term logistics is used to embrace this broader scope of activities beyond the need of one single customer.

Logistics is about a *process* rather than a single activity. It is more than transport, covering a series of continuous and interrelated activities from planning to implementation and controlling. Therefore, logistics is concerned with more activities within an organisation, not just with cargo, but also with people and information. If maritime transport is about the movement of cargoes, logistics is not only about the movement but also the storage of goods. If the scope of maritime transport is from port to port, logistics is from the point of origin to the point of consumption. That is the reason why maritime transport is part of logistics and the supply chain.

Logistics activities are not new for a customer. It is the combination of some existing activities, such as transport or warehousing, but organised under an integrated concept as one single undertaking. The emphasis is on the optimisation of the whole process and the best overall result rather than that of any individual operation. So logistics, as described by many, is to get the *right goods* to the *right place*, at the *right time*, in the *right form* and at the *right cost*.

What are the basic concepts of logistics that affect maritime transport?

As a more comprehensive scope of the cargo distribution system, logistics has a lot of common features with maritime transport. At the same time, there are also some special aspects which distinguish logistics from shipping. The most important ones are the concepts of the total cost, customer service and third-party logistics. We will explain them below.

- ***Total cost.*** Logistics is an optimisation process which starts from the origin of resources and ends with the finished product in the hands of consumers. Therefore, the strength of logistics is in its integration of the entire cargo distribution, covering not only transport but also warehousing and inventory management and control. The optimisation can be performed at the sectional level. Different sections may have different goals. For instance, production logistics may emphasise the lowest per-unit production costs, while salespeople like to have a sufficient quantity of products to be put as near to the market as possible. Sectional optimisation is not reflecting the real significance of the logistics system. The correct method is to look at logistics problems at the organisation's top management level. This is because what is the best and optimal in one respect may not necessarily be the best and optimal in another. Integrated logistics means that the optimisation should not only be sought after at the sectional and operational level, but it should be especially assured at a global level for the organisation as a whole.

  The key element of integrated logistics is the *total cost* analysis. The objective of logistics is to minimise the total cost of the system rather than the cost of an individual activity. Any change made in one activity is likely to affect the cost of all other activities and therefore the total cost. An attempt to reduce the cost of individual activities may lead to an increased total cost. The total cost for a logistics system includes transportation cost, warehousing cost, order processing and information cost and inventory cost. It is obvious that those different costs are inherently interrelated with each other. The change in one will inevitably lead to changes in the others.

- ***Customer service***. Logistics is a central source of the competitiveness of companies in manufacturing or service, through either cost reduction or value creation. Directly related to value creation, customer service is about a service standard which, sometimes, is referred to as responsiveness to the need. Customer service can be broadly described as the measures regarding how well the logistics system performs in creating value-added benefits for the customers via better product or service in a cost-effective way. The level of customer service not only determines whether existing customers will remain the company's customers, but also how many of those who are not with the company will become customers. Thus the level of customer service has a direct and significant impact on the organisation's market share, total costs and profitability. Customer service should be viewed as an integral part of the design and operation of any logistics system. Though customer service is often associated with performance standards, it may also be defined either narrowly or broadly. For example, it may refer to some specific functions such as marketing officers or people responsible for public relations. It may also be treated as part of the corporate philosophy or values.
- ***Third-party logistics***. Logistics is needed in most enterprises and organisations. When a company carries out its logistics activities by itself, this is usually referred to as first-party logistics. Alternatively, the company may outsource its logistics operations to a specialised company in logistics services. Whether one should or should not outsource the logistics activities is not only an economic decision, it may also be for technical, operational or sometimes strategic reasons. International shipping is a logistics activity needed by importers or exporters. A big cargo owner may choose to carry out the shipping of the goods by itself internally. But, more often, it is much more economical to give this operation to a specialised shipping company to carry out. In this case, it is a third-party logistics service.

How big is the global logistics market?

Compared with maritime transport, global logistics is a much bigger market. In 2018 the total world logistics cost was about US$9.2 trillion.[3] This is about 11% of the global GDP of the same year. Based on the UN and IMF estimates, the maritime transport market in terms of total shipping freight is in the region of 5% of the total import value. Based on a gross estimate of about 68% of global trade in value moved by maritime transport and taking into account freight market volatility, the size of the maritime transport market would be in the region of US$600 to $800 billion, or about 7.3% of the global logistics market. In other words, the global logistics market is about fourteen times as big as the total international maritime transport freight market.[4]

There is a very big difference in the efficiency of logistics between various countries. In most industrialised countries, the total logistics cost as a percentage of GDP is about 8%–9%. But in many less-developed countries the percentage is typically between 12% and 17% and it can be as high as 25%.[5] Such a difference should not be entirely attributed to efficiency-related issues as it is also affected by the economic structure and level of development. For high-income countries, the service sector usually contributes the biggest part of the GDP. However, if the countries rely more on the industrial and manufacturing sectors, the percentage of logistics spending in GDP will be higher.

It is understandable that the logistics market is much larger than the maritime transport market, as international shipping is a part of the global logistics system. Figure 14.1 shows the estimates of the two markets and international shipping is only about 7.3% of the global logistics market. The cost of logistics is mainly spent on cargo transport and inventory. The inventory cost is primarily related to the time cost of cargo being in storage or in transit. As a time cost, the inventory cost is influenced by the value of goods as well as by the cost of capital, i.e., the interest cost. So, when the interest rate is low, the proportion of inventory cost out of total logistics will be lower than when the rate is high. The

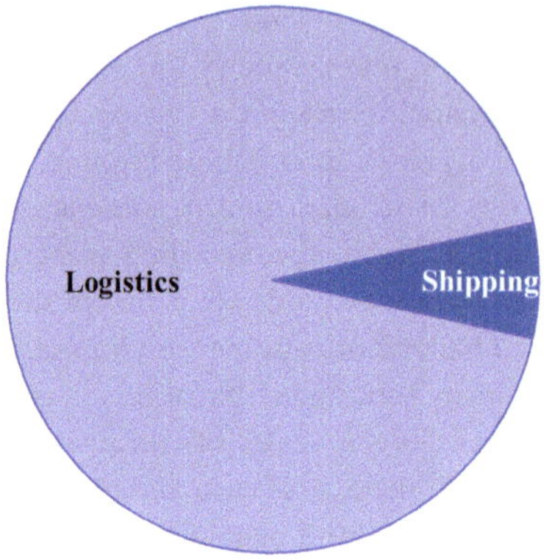

Figure 14.1 Logistics market vs. shipping market.

Source: Shuo Ma, based on various sources.

Note: the size of the international shipping freight market is estimated at about US$670 billion in 2018, which is 7.3% of the global logistics market.

differences between the logistics costs as a percentage of the GDP of countries are to a large extent due to high inventory cost, related to the time lost because of inefficient logistics services.

When we discussed the global supply chain, we described that globalised manufacturing today was only possible thanks to the logistics and supply chain system that links different stages of production together. Despite the challenges and difficulties, globalised production has kept growing. The business conditions make the distances shorter and the distinction between domestic and international distribution less important. Successful enterprises have realised that to survive and prosper in the business environment of today and tomorrow, they have to go beyond the country or region boundaries to where the best conditions are available and adopt a globalised production model for the lowest total cost. In this sense, a successful logistic is often a global system.

14.2 Relationship between international shipping and logistics

The customers of international shipping are also customers of logistics services. It is right to say that shipping has a derived demand from trade. People are interested in shipping because, without it, trade cannot be completed. In reality, shipping alone is not enough to complete the trade as shipping only takes cargo from port to port. But logistics will take the cargo from producers to consumers. So what traders need is logistics services, of which international shipping is a part. The relationship between international shipping and logistics can be examined from different perspectives. We will discuss the relationship from three angles: geographical distinction, cost contribution and time factor.

What is the geographical distinction between shipping and logistics?

The most striking geographical distinction between international shipping and logistics is that logistics is domestic while shipping is international. Or, with a more exact expression as shipping is a part of logistics, we can say that shipping is the international portion of a logistics service or that shipping is the link of national logistics systems. Certainly, cross-border trucking and rail transport, as well as the international air transport of freight, are also between countries, though the majority of international trade measured in tonnage is transported by sea.

Logistics is needed whenever and wherever trade happens, but maritime transport is only needed when a seller and a buyer are separated by the sea. As shown in Figure 14.2, maritime transport, as a part of trade logistics, links the domestic logistics markets. In such a logistics market, there is a wide range of activities of land-based transport, warehousing and distribution of cargo. In a global supply chain, there may be more domestic logistics markets involved. Figure 14.2 is an illustration of the logistics of manufactured goods involving a containerised liner shipping service. In this case, a container ship carries cargoes for many customers and therefore provides an international shipping link for many separate customer logistics systems. So, to conclude, maritime transport is the port to port and international portion of trade logistics, while the rest of logistics activities are land-based and domestic.

Traditionally, international shipping and domestic logistics are provided by separate companies. There are some good reasons for this. One of them is that specialised expertise and financial capability are needed to undertake maritime transport, which leads to specialisation. The shipping market is international and, at the same time, it is open and highly competitive. So it is common that international shipping companies transport the trade of other countries, as the liner shipping companies like Maersk Line of Denmark or Mediterranean Shipping Corporation of Switzerland do. Another reason is about the optimal size of a liner shipping operation, both for ships and shipping companies. For the reduction of cost and improvement of productivity, the scale of shipping production needs to be large. The optimal size of the shipping operation is often too large for serving the logistics needs of a single customer or one domestic logistics market. So it is difficult for a national logistics company to expand into the business of international shipping. However, a shipping company can grow beyond the port to provide its logistics services in domestic markets. This development will be discussed in the following section.

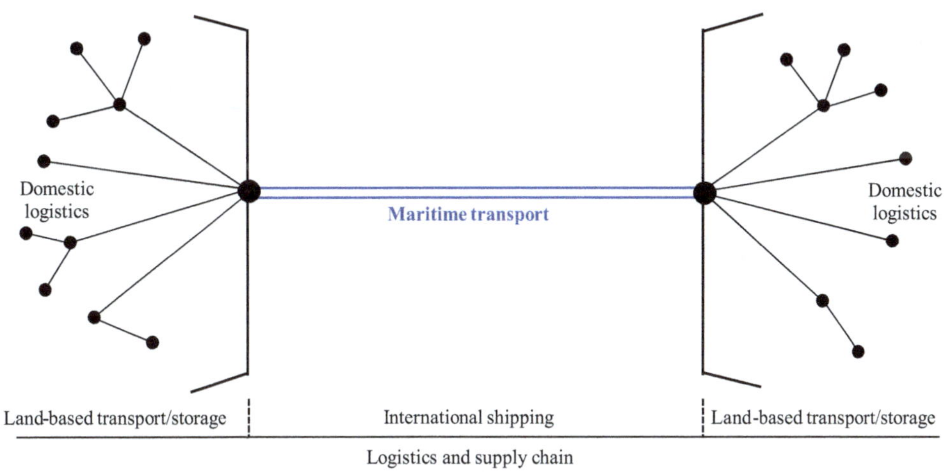

Figure 14.2 Geographical distinction of international shipping and logistics.

Source: Shuo Ma.

Note: apart from international shipping, most logistics activities take place on land as domestic cargo transport and storage.

What are the cost elements of shipping in logistics?

Logistics is defined as the efficient, effective flow and storage of goods. Such efficiency and effectiveness can be discussed from three aspects, namely cost, time and predictability or reliability. We will first examine maritime transport's cost efficiency in the flow and storage of goods by following the cost contributions to each stage of the "flow" and "storage" of goods. The contribution of maritime transport cost to the total logistics cost varies from one type of trade to another. International trade is grossly divided into raw materials, which include minerals, energy products and grain, etc., on the one hand, and manufactured goods, which include finished or semi-finished products, on the other. For the trade of raw materials, which is often transported in bulk, the cost of international shipping is a relatively high percentage of the total transport logistics cost. For the trade of manufactured goods, which is usually transported in containers, the proportion of maritime transport cost in the total transport logistics cost is small.

Figure 14.3 is an illustration of the contribution of transport and storage activities at different stages to the total cost of transport and storage. Sea transport freight in liner shipping has been, in current US dollars, at more or less the same level for the last 60 years between 1968 and 2018 on the main East–West shipping routes. If the inflation factor is considered, the freight in 2018 is about 20% of that of 1968 in constant US dollars. But, during the same period, other logistics costs have not had the same type of development. In the World Bank's Logistics Performance Index study, "international shipment" is one of the six aspects selected as key performance indicators.[6] The cost of maritime transport is the only part of the logistics cost that is international. All other costs are on domestic logistics, either at the exporting or importing country.

Compared with maritime transport, land-based transports, in terms of ton-kilometre cargo transported, are more expensive, although big variations exist between countries. The biggest advantage of

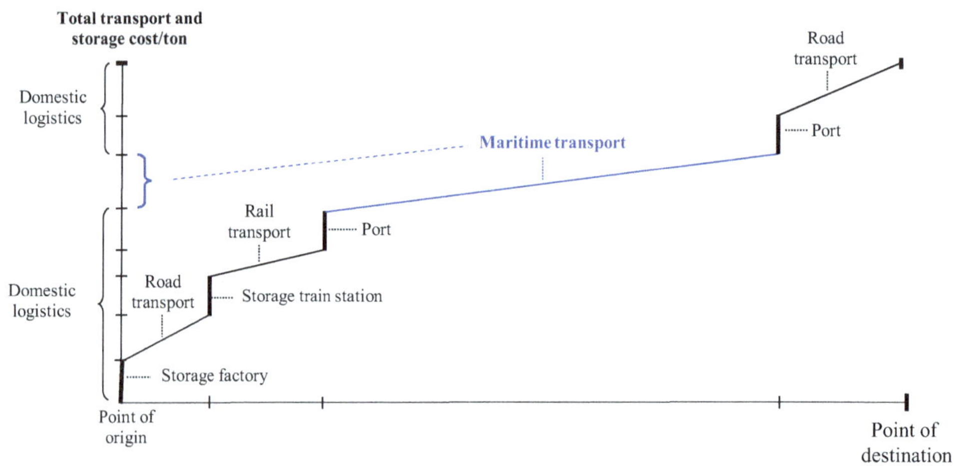

Figure 14.3 Cost contribution of maritime transport in total transport and storage costs – for general cargo trade.

Source: Shuo Ma.

Note: for trade of manufactured goods, the cost of maritime transport is generally small compared with the total logistics cost. It is to be noted that the total cost is on transport and storage only. It does not include inventory cost.

road transport is its flexibility and capability to reach the warehouses of the customers directly. But, due to the lack of scale economies and high labour intensity, the cost of transport is very high. In some countries the use of the port is expensive too. This includes dues paid on cargo and shipping and also the costs for cargo storage and handling.

Why does the time factor of maritime transport affect logistics?

For efficient and effective flow and storage of goods from the point of origin to the point of destination, one of the key indicators is total transit time used. An efficient logistics system can deliver goods in less time. The cost of time in logistics is in the form of inventory cost. This is mainly the cost of the capital which is tied up with the goods in the logistics system, so it is an opportunity cost as well. The cost of holding inventory may also include storage cost, though we have dealt with this separately.

For international trade, from the point of origin to the point of destination, different modes of transport are usually used. Time used for transport depends on the travel distance and the speed of transport. As far as maritime transport is concerned, the travel distance is normally long and the speed of transport slow. For example, a container ship leaving Shanghai for Rotterdam via the Suez Canal should travel about 10,500 nautical miles. If the ship sails at 20 nautical miles per hour, non-stop, the journey will take almost 22 days. The land-based transport in China or in Europe for moving the cargo between a customer's warehouse and the ports, by rail, road or inland waterway, may not take so long, because the distance is usually shorter and the speed of transport faster. However, along with the transport by various modes, there are a number of nodes at each end of the transport sections. Such nodes include warehouses, inland depots, train stations, ports, distribution centres, etc. Different activities are needed at the nodes such as cargo handling, regrouping, inspections, safety and security checks, customs clearance, or sometimes just waiting for transport vehicles or cargo accumulation. Time spent at these nodes varies, sometimes greatly, depending on the types of tasks to undertake and the efficiency of the logistics system.

Figure 14.4 shows an example based on time spent by different logistics activities between the point of origin and the point of destination for the trade of manufactured goods. In this particular case, three modes of transport are used and there are four nodes at which the cargo is kept in storage. The longest time is spent on international shipping. This time might be reduced if ships sail faster. But a slower speed may be preferable given the high fuel consumption involved and concerns about the total cost. When the fuel price is high, and the interest rates and, thus, the capital cost, are low, slow steaming may be justifiable. The time factor for domestic logistics is also variable between countries. Based on the World Bank's Logistics Performance Index of 2018,[7] within a 100-kilometre distance, the time needed to move the cargo between the factory and the port by land transport varies from 1 day to 18 days, reflecting a huge difference in logistics efficiency between countries. At ports, cargo can also be stuck for a long time due to complicated procedures and formalities. For import cargo, for example, in the countries with the most efficient logistics system, only one agency is needed and one form ought to be filled in, while in the countries with the least efficient logistics, more than ten agencies are involved and each of them requires a form to be filled in.

Another important aspect of time is about the predictability or reliability of a logistics service. This is related to the quality and quality assurance aspects of the logistics system. The logistics cost increases when the services are not consistent and predictable. In order to prevent stoppage of production or services, additional safety stock has to be made, which leads to high inventory cost. In a 2018 survey, when asked about the percentage of shipments that have met quality criteria, the responses of executives suggest that a wide range of performance record exists, from as high as more than 95% to as low as 40%. In many countries the rates are between 50% and 60%.[8]

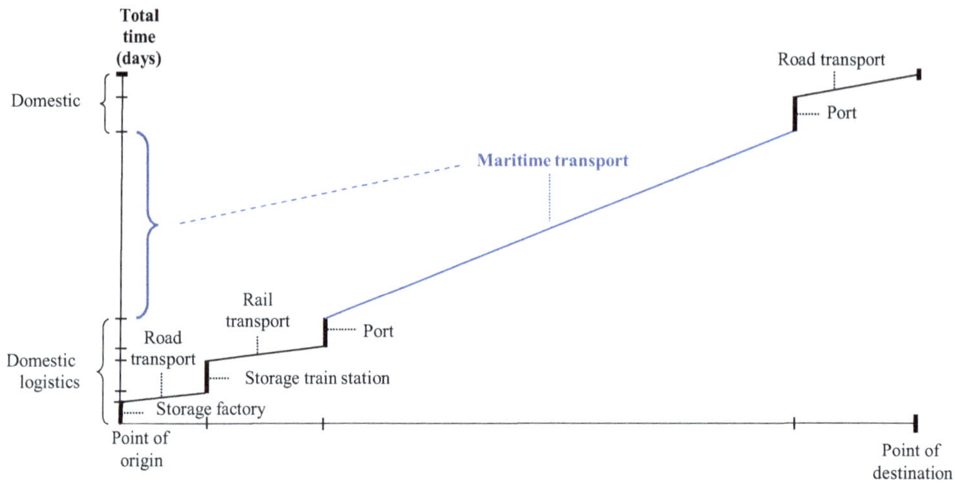

Figure 14.4 Time contribution of maritime transport in logistics – an example of general cargo trade logistics.

Source: Shuo Ma.

Note: for trade of manufactured goods, the time spent on maritime transport is generally large in the total time of logistics. The distribution of time spent reflects the contribution of each activity to the total inventory cost.

14.3 Dimension of maritime logistics

From a logistics point of view, moving traded goods from the origin to the final destination should be one single operation. But, in reality, most international trade is transported in a fragmented way, with a clear division between domestic logistics and international transportation. So integration of the two has been an intended goal for some logistics service providers and many shipping companies. In this section we will discuss maritime logistics from two angles. The first is about how logistics concepts and methods are applied within the shipping sector. Shipping companies have to address their own logistics-related needs. Then we will examine the prospects for shipping companies to become logistics service providers.

What are logistics issues within shipping companies?

Shipping companies, though a part of a broader trade logistics system, have their own logistics activities to operate. For example, they need to plan their services. They also need to manage the movement and storage of transport equipment, such as ships or containers, from one place to another to satisfy customer requirements and to reduce cost. Because there are more internal logistics decisions to make for liner shipping companies, we will discuss the logistics decisions regarding ships and containers in the liner shipping sector.

The planning of the liner shipping service pattern is a logistics decision. The purpose is to deploy suitable ships in a way so that the customers receive the best services at the lowest cost. Decisions have to be taken on, for example, the size, number and speed of ships, the ports of call and the service pattern. There are alternative patterns of liner shipping services, such as the "End-to-End", "Hub-spoke", "Pendulum" and "Double dipping" services.

- The ***End-to-End*** pattern is the most common and traditional way of organising liner services between the two markets. Explicitly, ships in an end-to-end arrangement stick to the trade between two markets. The performance and profitability of the lines depend on the stability of the traffic and the balance of the trade volume in both directions. The liner service between, say, Eastern Africa and Western Europe is an end-to-end transport service. The same can also be said of many other liner operations in other markets.
- The ***Hub-spoke*** pattern refers to transhipment practices. Instead of calling at every port, large or small, main-haul ships will only load and discharge cargo at a small number of transhipment ports or hubs. Then smaller feeder vessels go back and forth between the hub port and other ports in the region. Usually, those spokes have less traffic or are located away from the main maritime routes. With such transhipment, shipping companies can save costs while not losing traffic and service standard. The negative aspects of the hub-spoke system are the higher cost and longer transit time for the shippers at feeder ports.
- The ***Pendulum*** liner operation pattern means that the ships move between three, instead of two, markets with the market in the middle serving as the fulcrum of a pendulum. After discharging cargo at the last port of a market, the ship does not go back, but rather loads cargo and continues the journey forward for another market. Ships swing to either side of the fulcrum like a pendulum linking three markets, for example North America–the Far East–Europe. The main advantage of the pendulum concept is the possible elimination of double port calling. Ships' space is filled four times in a round voyage, instead of twice as in an end-to-end pattern. It can also help shipping lines deploy larger container vessels.
- The ***Double-dipping*** is a more recent concept in liner shipping. The purpose of this practice is to take advantage of the growing and usually higher priced intra-regional market by combining intercontinental legs with shorter haul regional trade. In 2017 the total intra-regional container trade surpassed the East–West trade and the intra-Asian container trade was as big as 75% of the East–West trade in 2018, up from 44% in 2001.[9] Double-dipping requires main-line ships to call a hub port in the middle of the voyage on both ways of a round trip. In a way, it replaces some ships in regional services with big main-line ships. For example, large main-haul container ships trading between Europe and the Far East can be involved in intra-Europe and/or intra-Asia liner markets by calling the hub ports both ways. As a result, the container slots are used more than once per voyage.

Container logistics has two major issues: container acquisition and reposition. Containerisation has brought to the liner shipping industry tremendous benefits from shorter transport time and higher cost efficiency to improved safety and security. But it has also created a new challenge, which is the container itself. Unlike the old-fashioned packing for general cargo in break-bulk format, which is disposable after usage, containers are to be reused. This situation would not be a big problem if the containerised trade measured in volume was balanced in both directions. Unfortunately, such an ideal situation rarely happens in reality. A very high proportion of containers moved by the liner shipping services are empty. As shown in Figure 14.5, for all containers loaded with cargo from Asia to North America and Europe, over 50% of them do not have return cargo and have to be transported back to Asia empty.[10] Such repositioning of empty containers is a very costly operation for the liner shipping industry. There are mainly two reasons for this to happen.

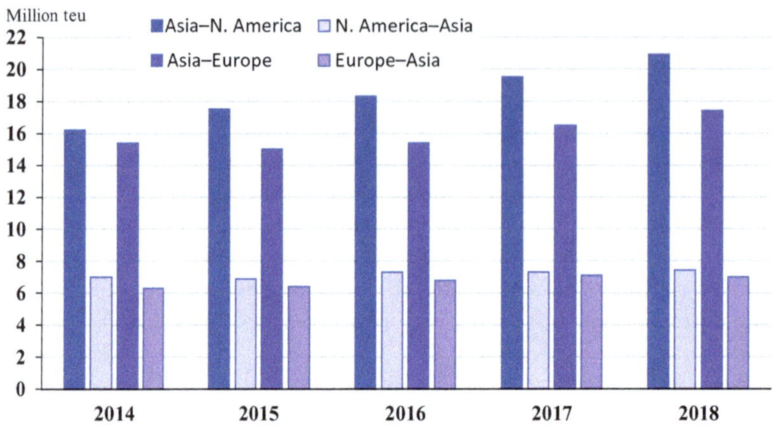

Figure 14.5 Container traffic imbalance on East–West markets 2014–2018, in million teu.

Source: Shuo Ma, based on data from UNCTAD and Clarksons.

Note: in 2018 the Europe–Asia container traffic was 35% of the Asia–Europe traffic and the North America–Asia container traffic was 40% of the Asia–North America traffic.

1 The first reason is about the global supply chain and the concentrated pattern of the manufacturing sector. Due to the attractive production factors such as labour and land, Asia has been the global centre of manufacturing. So, by design, a high volume of containerised goods is transported from Asia to the rest of the world. Many factories and manufacturing production are owned by multinational companies headquartered in Europe or North America, so trade in the capital may be more balanced between regions. However, the maritime trades in volume are not.
2 The second reason is about the differences in trade structure. For example, countries and regions in Africa, Latin America, Australia and the Middle East import a large quantity of containerised goods from Asia, but their exports are mainly raw materials transported by tanker ships or bulk carriers. The import from Asia by North America and Europe is chiefly containerised manufactured goods in big volume but relatively low value, but their export to Asia is mainly goods of higher value but low volume and these countries also enjoy a surplus of trade in service. As a result, there is consistently a big container traffic imbalance between Asia, particularly the Far East, and other regions, particularly North America and Europe.

Why is containerisation the driver of maritime logistics?

Maritime transport containers, which were first introduced in the 1950s, revolutionised the liner shipping industry and subsequently reshaped international trade logistics. Such a statement is based on the enormous improvement of transport productivity, particularly in cargo handling in ports and the efficiency of trade logistics in the form of fast and seamless transit between different modes of transport of goods from the origin to the final destination. Containerisation is the backbone and enabler of international trade logistics by integrating the transport and storage segments into a single logistics chain and by making the system safe and secure.

One of the most important reasons why international trade logistics was costly and time consuming had been the connections between different stages of transport which were generally inefficient. The low efficiency was caused mainly by two factors. The first was the inconsistency of packing in size, weight, shape and material used. The second was cargo handling at every interface between transport modes or between transport and storage. Such processes were usually slow and labour intensive. As described below, the introduction of containers has completely changed both aspects.

1 ***Cargo packaging***. General cargo includes various manufactured goods such as cloth, toys, furniture or electronic appliances. Given the enormous diversity, these goods are packaged in boxes, bales or wooden crates of different sizes and shapes. Consequently, there is a major problem for maritime transport when it comes to the storage of the goods in a ship's hole. The packages have to be stored and secured almost piece by piece by stevedores into the ship at the loading port and then, at the discharging port, they have to be taken out of the ship in the same fashion. Such operations, on the one hand, are labour intensive, slow and often cause injuries and cargo damage; on the other hand, there is always broken space which is wasted or unused. What is more problematic is that along the logistics chain from the origin to the final destination, such handling and storage deficiency happens at every stage: not only in ship's holes but also in trucks, railway wagons or warehouses. So low efficiency was a synonym for the international transport of general cargo and liner shipping.

   Though the introduction of pallets was an important improvement, it was the use of containers that put an end to the above-mentioned situation. The revolutionary change brought to liner shipping and international logistics by containerisation is the packing which is strong, standardised, big-volume and reusable. Cargoes of all kinds are stored and secured inside containers which are then sealed. In the beginning, shipping companies in North America were using self-designed containers that fitted the routes and trade they served. Based on consultations with stakeholders of sea, road and rail transport, in 1961 the Federal Maritime Board of the US set up the standard dimension of containers as 8 feet wide, 8 feet high and 10, 20, 30 and 40 feet long, which were acceptable for use by ships, trucks and the railway.[11] In 1964 similar container standards were adopted by the International Standards Organisation (ISO) and, subsequently, the ISO established international standards regarding the strength and lifting specifications of maritime containers. With containerisation, an efficient and seamless intermodal transport of general cargo became possible.

   With cargo stored inside closed and strong steel containers, the level of safety and security was improved considerably. As cargoes were better protected, both personal injury and cargo damage decreased massively and pilferage-related losses were much reduced.

2 ***Cargo handling***. Unlike bulk cargoes, either dry or liquid, general cargo could not be loaded and unloaded on and off ships or other transport vehicles easily and quickly. General cargo which was, as described above, in small and different packages, had to be handled manually. It was usually loaded on pallets of about one ton each which were loaded one pallet at a time by using forklifts or cranes of limited capacity. For loading the cargo onto a ship, a team of six stevedores or so was needed, with one crane operator either from the ship or shore and two or three persons on the shore-side as well as on board ship. Typically, a team could manage to handle 50–100 tons of cargo per shift. Or, on a per-ship basis, about 1,000 tons of cargo could be loaded or unloaded per day. It was common that ships spent several weeks at each port. A big general cargo ship trading on a not too long shipping route can easily spend more time per year in port for cargo handling than at sea for cargo transportation.

   Such a situation of slow cargo handling had not changed for centuries until containers were introduced. It was believed that Mclean, the container inventor who was a trucking entrepreneur, had the idea of maritime containers when his cargo was stuck at the port due to slow cargo-handling operations. He wanted to improve shipping efficiency for his cargo to reach remote markets by better integration of the then separated coaster shipping and trucking transport. He realised that the key challenge was at the interfaces and the solution was the standard cargo containers which fit both ships and trucks and which can also be loaded and unloaded efficiently.[12] When the first purpose-built container crane began its operation at the port of San Francisco, capable of handling 400 tons of goods per hour, the productivity was boosted more than 40 times the average performance of the pre-containerisation era.[13]

Logistics is about the movement and storage of goods from the point of origin to the point of destination. With containerisation, the logistics of the general cargo trade has become much more efficient. The speed of cargo movement has been faster, not because transport itself is speedier but because the time spent at the connection points is much shorter. Intermodal transport began to develop rapidly as a consequence of containerisation. Global retailers such as Walmart or Carrefour as well as many multinational manufacturing companies like Sony or IKEA were capable of building their vast, sophisticated and efficient global logistics and supply chain system. All of this was because of containers.

14.4 Value added, logistics integration and competition

The economic value of logistics or international shipping service can be judged by the recipients in terms of the difference between the benefits obtained and the cost paid. The bigger the difference is, the higher the value is. A negative value means that the cost is greater than the benefit and, in this case, the customer will not be interested in the service. In business, the value can also be defined as the price difference before and after the service. To create value, a company has to spend costs on labour, materials, equipment, energy and other intermediate consumptions, etc. The difference between the price and the cost is called value added. The total value added of a logistics system is, therefore, the difference between the value of the goods at the destination and their value at the origin. Every economic activity in the system, such as transport and storage, creates a value added to the goods and generates a cost to the customer. In this section we will examine the value added of international shipping in the context of the total value added of the logistics system.

How is the value of logistics services added to trade?

Most international trade of merchandise is concluded based on standard trading conditions called Incoterms or International Commercial Terms. These are the pre-defined commercial terms established by the International Chamber of Commerce (ICC) to facilitate the processes of international transactions. There are 15 such terms. The fundamental differences between them are not about the substance of merchandise traded but about the logistics of trade. More precisely, the Incoterms are about the specific stage along the logistics chain where the responsibilities, obligations, tasks and costs associated with the trade are transferred from the seller to the buyer. For this reason, each Incoterm defines the price of the goods at the specific stage of the logistics chain. Let's consider some examples of the three most frequently used Incoterms: EXW, FOB and CIF.

1 ***EXW (Ex Works)*** means that the goods are made available by the seller at its premises where its obligation ends. So the price of the goods is the one at the gate of the seller's warehouse, which means the price of the product without the added value from transport and logistics services.
2 ***FOB (Free on Board)*** means the price of goods is when the goods are loaded on board the ship at a port. So the price of the product includes the value of the logistics service up to this point. The buyer should then arrange and pay for the remaining logistics services, including international shipping.
3 ***CIF (Cost, Insurance and Freight)*** means the price of the product includes more logistics value added, particularly the service of maritime transport up to the point when the goods are unloaded at the discharging port.

According to the Incoterms, the added value by the logistics service can either be paid by the seller by including it in the price of the product traded, or by the buyer by paying it separately. Or, from the buyer's viewpoint, the logistics services are a part of the total value of the product that they have to pay for. If the cost of the logistics service is too high, which means the cost is higher than the value, then the trade will not take place. If, otherwise, the logistics cost decreases, leading to improved value for money, then more products will be traded. So cheaper transport and logistics services create a new trade.

What is competition for value added?

Like any commercial firm, the goal of a shipping company is to maintain long-term profitability. In a competitive market, the only way to achieve the goal is by offering the same service at a lower cost or offering more service at the same cost. Through competition between shipping companies, the best value-for-money service will survive. So offering more value-added service is a shipping company's competitive strategy.

The value of a traded product is higher at its destination than at its origin and the difference is the additional value created by the logistics services, including international shipping. The logistics value added is an integral part of the trade, regardless of who, the seller or the buyer, is responsible for undertaking the activities. Figure 14.6 is an illustration of logistics activities that add value to international trade. In this example, the product is 10% more valuable at its destination as compared with the value at its origin. The value of the product is 300 at its origin. Added value is created by some typical international trade logistics activities such as different modes of transport, storage and port operations. The numbers under each activity represent the amount of value-added created by the activity, which is a proxy for the firm's profit, depreciation and labour costs. In the end, the total value of the final product is at 330, which is also the price paid by the final consumer, of which 30 is created by the logistics.

Regarding the total value added created by logistics services, we have the following basic equation as:

$$\textit{Total Value Added} = \textit{Value Added per Unit} \times \textit{Total Units}$$

This means that, to increase total value added, one can either increase the total units, for example the volume of cargo transported, or increase the value added per unit of product, which is the amount of value-added activities for each unit of product. Along the logistics chain, activities are undertaken by different and independent firms. Some create more value added and others less. The value added created by international shipping for every unit of trade is relatively small compared with the total logistics value added. But it is possible that shipping companies may improve their profitability in terms of total value added by extending the services beyond maritime transport and by engaging in

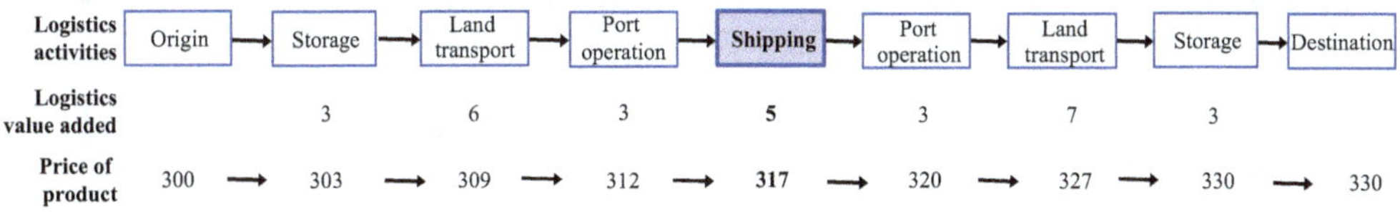

Figure 14.6 The value added of logistics activities and the position of shipping.

Source: Shuo Ma (2018).

Note: logistics activities add value to trade. The total value added of the logistics chain is the value difference between the product at its origin and its destination. In the above example, it is 30, or 10% of the value of the goods. Yet the part of maritime transport in the total value added is small.

logistics activities. Obviously, other logistics service firms, such as trucking, railway, air companies or warehousing firms, port operators, etc., can also penetrate shipping or businesses other than their own.

Apart from conventional competition between companies of the same sector for the same products or services, such as the competition between shipping companies or between ports, there is also another type of competition for value added. This is a competition between different businesses on the same value chain. For example, a shipping company competes with a land transport firm for cargo transport. Or a shipping company and a freight forwarder compete for cargo distribution. Or a shipping line and a port compete for terminal operation. On a value chain, different companies are partners, but they also can be competitors. A land transporter, as shown in Figure 14.6, instead of cooperating with a warehouse operator may compete with it by offering a storage service. This can also be called cross-sector vertical business integration.

What are the conditions for logistics integration?

However, such competition for value added has not happened in every direction, even if it is possible in theory and there are no administrative or policy-related barriers. Whether, within the trade logistics sector, different activities such as freight forwarders, a shipping company or a trucking firm can penetrate each other's business is far from being a simple matter and it depends on many conditions and elements. Four elements are of particular importance, namely the optimal size of operation, the sector's position in the logistics system, the level of technical/operational complexity and the financial capability/risks. We will focus on these four essential elements and their impact on seven selected trade logistics sectors, namely liner shipping, railway transport, freight forwarding (including road transport), port operation, air transport, storage/warehousing and e-retailer or e-commerce. The conclusion of the discussion is summarised in Table 14.1, which indicates the basic features and the general direction

Table 14.1 Vertical logistics integration - a sector domination and vulnerability analysis

Taker / *Target*	*Shipping*	*Railway*	*Forwarder*	*Port*	*Air*	*Warehouse*	*E-retator*	*Vulnerabilty rate*
Shipping		*	**	*	*	*	**	**8**
Railway	*		*	*	*	*	*	**6**
Forwarder	***	**		**	**	*	****	**14**
Port	*****	**	**		*	*	***	**14**
Air	**	*	***	*		*	***	**11**
Warehouse	*****	***	*****	***	***		*****	**24**
E-Retailor	**	*	*	*	**	*		**8**
Domination rate	**18**	**10**	**14**	**9**	**10**	**6**	**18**	**Target** / **Taker**

Source: Shuo Ma

Note: The 7 sectors are the main actors of international trade logistics. Those on the top row penetrate other sectors listed on the left column. Road transport is included in the business of forwarder. Retailors refer mainly to e-commerce companies. The points reflect the likelihood of the sector on top to extend the business into the sectors listed on the left.

of logistics integration, in terms of the vulnerability or the likelihood of a sector being the target of the integration or the likelihood of being the sector of domination of the integration. In other words, a sector can either be the initiator of the logistics integration or the victim of it. The stars reflect the likelihood that the sectors on the horizontal row on top would penetrate the sectors listed on the left, with 1 star being the least likely and 5 being the most likely.

- ***Optimal operation size***. For every economic activity there is always an optimal size of the operation, which is the scale of production or service that allows the effect of scale economies to be maximised. Trucking, for example, is usually a business of many small companies. Although big road transport firms exist, the type of production does not particularly favour very big operations. A similar situation may also be found for inland water transport as well as warehousing activities. On the other hand, liner shipping, air freight transport and railway transport require the size of operation to be sufficiently large. This is because, on the one hand, these logistics operations can benefit from an extensive network synergy and, on the other hand, there is a big cost advantage to be gained from scale economies. So we see many big shipping lines, airlines and railway companies, but not many trucking firms and warehousing companies. The port sector is special in the sense that a port is immobile and attached to a specific place. So the size of the port varies greatly due to its dependence on the development of the hinterland economic activities. The situation of e-commerce in logistics is new and evolving very rapidly. There are some very large internet-based e-retailers, such as Amazon or Alibaba, which have the ambition to include logistics as an integral part of their service offerings.

  It is difficult for two businesses to integrate if they have different optimal operational sizes, for example between a shipping company and a trucking firm. It is certainly harder for a sector whose optimal operational size is small to enter into a sector of a bigger optimal operational size than the other way round. For example, if a port wants to expand into the liner shipping sector, it will find that its existing business will be insufficient and it could not benefit from the current activities. But when a shipping line enters into port operation, it has a greater chance of keeping the port busy with its large shipping business. Therefore, it is more likely that the logistics integration moves in the direction of the sectors of big optimal operational size penetrating the sectors with smaller optimal size. This is why we have seen that e-retailers get into the warehousing business and shipping companies expand into terminal operations, but not the other way round.
- ***Position in the trade logistics system***. The trade logistics activities are provided by many different and independent firms and entities. Historically, trade and logistics were integrated. A trader used to be a shipowner, a warehouse keeper and a land transporter, all at the same time. Later, driven by specialisation, activities were separated and undertaken by different operators. When it comes to the logistics activities, an importer or exporter will approach either a freight forwarder or a sea or air transport company, but it will not contact a port or a warehouse operator. So the position of the seven trade logistics sectors in Table 14.1 can be divided into three levels: trade or e-commerce is at the centre of level 1; freight forwarders, maritime and air transport providers are at the second level; port and warehousing operators are at the third and lowest level. The logistics integration is moving in the direction of operational control from the higher to the lower level and from the centre to the periphery. In other words, it is more likely that a trading company operates its own shipping, a shipping company expands into the port sector and a freight forwarder gets into warehousing businesses rather than the other way round.
- ***Financial capability and risk***. This is another important factor affecting the direction of logistics integration. Some logistics sectors are more capital intensive than others. This is certainly true for shipping, aviation and, to a lesser extent, port and airport activities. As the size of financial exposure differs, there are different levels of risk between the sectors. Take maritime transport for example.

In normal conditions, to build a container terminal with one berth on leased land in a port will incur a similar cost as to build one big container ship. So, compared with a port operator, a liner shipping company is in a stronger financial position with a capability of mobilising a much bigger fund. As a result, it is much less difficult for a liner shipping company to expand into the port business than for a port operator to start a liner shipping activity. The situation is the same in the case of the storage and warehousing sector. Low financial requirement and commercial risks make storage an easy target for logistics integration.

- ***Technical and operation complexity***. Obviously, special technical and operational expertise and know-how are required in each logistics sector. Such requirements may be considered as barriers to entry. The level of technical demand and the degree of operational difficulties vary greatly between the sectors, though measuring them may not always be straightforward. As discussed in Chapter 13 and shown in Table 13.1, the barrier of entry is generally lower in the warehousing sector than in the maritime transport business. Similarly, it is difficult for a transport company to get into the e-commerce and retailer business. Even within maritime transport there are differences. For example, liner shipping is more complex than tramp shipping. Since the 1980s, thanks to the institutional reforms in the port sector in many countries, it has been possible for liner shipping companies to get involved in container terminal operations. Today many container terminals are operated by shipping lines. However, we have not seen development in the opposite direction. Maritime transport is an open and free market, but there have not been port operators expanding into liner shipping services. Certainly, out-sourcing or merger and acquisition can help with the situation of lacking expertise. But the commercial and market recognition, which is essential for business success, can only be obtained in the long term.

We can conclude the above discussion by looking again at Table 14.1. Based on the above four elements, which define the domination and vulnerability of the seven logistics sectors, we analysed and clarified the features of possible integration of international trade logistics. Domination rate is the measurement of the possibilities for a sector to penetrate other sectors, with 1 as the least possibility and 5 as the greatest possibility. Vulnerability rate is the measurement of the possibility of a sector to be operated by other sectors. The bottom row summarises the cumulative domination rates of the sectors, with the e-commerce and the shipping sectors being the most dominating, the freight forwarding, air and rail transport sectors being in the middle range and the port as well as the warehousing sectors being the least dominating. The column to the right summarises the cumulative vulnerability rates of the sectors, with the railway, shipping and e-commerce sectors being the least vulnerable, the air transport, forwarding and port sectors being in the middle and the warehousing sector being the most vulnerable and the least difficult to integrate.

14.5 Logistics strategy of liner shipping companies

The relationship between international shipping and logistics is a complex one. Not only has shipping experienced a shrinking portion in the total trade logistics value chain, but also shipping is increasingly affected by logistics decisions. In general cargo trade, instead of choosing a shipping service, customers are more interested in a logistics solution, in which international shipping is merely a small part. As discussed in the above section, shipping competes with other logistics sectors for value added. Therefore, one of the biggest challenging issues for a liner shipping company is about the logistics strategy. In other words, all liner shipping companies have to answer the questions about whether or not the company should develop and offer logistics services in addition to the shipping services and, if it should, more questions have to be addressed regarding the area, the method and the extent of penetration. We will discuss some of these questions from both economic and strategic perspectives.

How is shipping affected by logistics services?

Shipping, particularly liner shipping, is increasingly affected by logistics in many ways. Shipping lines may find that often the customers evaluate the liner shipping services in the broad context of logistics rather than based on the shipping service alone. The logistics influence can be examined from the following three aspects, namely customer service package, system responsibility and value added.

1 ***From a customer service package viewpoint***: this is about what service a customer needs. An importer or exporter wants to have goods reach their destination quickly, safely and cheaply. It is the whole end-to-end package rather than an individual segment of service that counts. So it is a logistics service, not a shipping service, that they need. Consequently, good liner shipping service alone is often not sufficient to secure business, if the shipping is not a part of a competitive logistics service package. For example, an importer trading between Asia and the East Coast of the US may prefer giving the cargo to an ocean carrier serving a West Coast port then using the railway land-bridge to the East Coast, rather than giving it to a shipping line with direct service to the East Coast ports, even though the total transport cost of all the waterway alternatives is lower. This is because the combination of sea/railway intermodal transport is more attractive from a logistics point of view due to shorter transit time and the subsequent savings on inventory cost. So, as a partial solution provider, the performance of shipping is much dependent on logistics solutions.
2 ***From a system responsibility viewpoint***: cargo can be moved from the origin to the destination using numerous separated services from road transporters, storage operators, ports and shipping lines, etc., either under separate or single responsibility. In the latter case, one company assumes the responsibility for the entire logistics even though it may not provide all the services. As containerisation has become a dominating form of liner shipping transport, a seamless connection between modes of transport has been a reality and the single arrangement has become a preferred option. So, many freight forwarders become logistics organisers, taking the full responsibility for and control of the logistics. They, instead of importers or exporters, select ocean carriers for the section of maritime transport. As a result, freight forwarders consolidate cargo shipments and are much more powerful than individual shippers. They negotiate contract terms with shipping lines, storage operators, port operators, etc. Shipping lines may not even know who the importers and exporters are. It is also possible that shipping lines turn themselves into logistics companies by assuming the overall responsibility for logistics services.
3 ***From a value-added viewpoint***: for an importer or exporter of manufactured goods, maritime transport is important, but only because shipping is part of the entire logistics system. International shipping has been increasingly standardised and more and more commoditised, even in liner shipping. From a value-added point of view, it is not necessarily the most critical part of the whole logistics chain. The real challenge is what people call "last-mile logistics", which refers to the final phase of the delivery process from a warehouse or distribution centre to the final consumer. It is usually about a short distance of delivery, but it may take up to 30% of the total logistics cost, or much more than the cost of the transport by ships over thousands of miles. This is partly because of the complexity of small and differentiated packages being delivered within time constraints and with challenging transport conditions. On the other hand, the standard transport by ships of cargoes in containers to/from large depots or distribution centres can normally be completed quickly and cheaply. As a result, the organiser of last-mile logistics often has the most influence on the entire logistics, including the part of international shipping.

What are the economic considerations for logistics integration?

In the above discussion we argued that the maritime transport sector could expand its activities into other sectors of the trade logistics system. But whether a liner shipping company should do this or not is also an economic issue which can be evaluated from different perspectives for different types of activities. A shipping company, like any other companies, is interested in having more value-added activities. An economic analysis of a shipping line's decision on logistics integration has two main dimensions. One is about the service cost and the other is about the degree of competition.

When it comes to the cost of providing a logistics service, who should be the service provider is an extremely important issue. The chosen company should be the one capable of providing the right service at the lowest average cost. In a competitive market, the average revenue cannot be influenced by individual service suppliers. The profitability of a service provider depends on the average cost of production. So a shipping line should consider undertaking a logistics activity only if it can beat the existing suppliers on cost. For example, a shipping line should offer storage services only if it can do so more cheaply than a warehousing company. According to the previous discussions, for international services such as trade logistics, most production factors, such as labour or capital, are international, so the majority of the costs are similar between producers. A liner shipping company can only be able to achieve a lower production cost from superior and more efficient management, from an advantage in scale economies, from the use of better technology as well as skills and synergy between different systems and activities.

It may be contradictory to assume that, for economic reasons, trade logistics services are better to be consolidated and offered by a single or few operators and, at the same time, to give the credit to specialisation for productivity improvements. If trade logistics was divided into specialised activities in the past, why should it now be economically justifiable to undo the specialisation? The explanation could probably lie in the changes in the technological conditions, business environment and operational nature of individual logistics activities. The technical settings, including means of communication, are certainly different now than before, though the progress differs from one sector to another. The size of production has also much evolved. For example, shipping was separated from trade because shipping operations should be large to reduce the average cost. But such large operations were too big for one trader so shipping had to be separated from trade to become a common user service. Now, liner shipping is highly concentrated with the top five lines controlling about 70% of the global teu capacity. So, when a single shipping line controls more than 10% of the global capacity, a more integrated logistics operation can lead to more synergy and rationalisation. The expansion of shipping lines involved in container terminal operations provides a typical example in this regard. When the calling of ships from a single shipping line at a port was infrequent with a limited amount of cargo carried, it was too expensive for the shipping company to have its own exclusive port facilities. But now a big shipping line can have more than one ship calling per day at the main port, which is sufficient for a satisfactory occupancy of its own terminal.[14]

Another economic reason for integrated logistics operations is about the level of competition. As a rule, whenever a market is highly competitive, the price of services is close or equal to the marginal cost. Whenever competition is insufficient, the price and profit will be higher. Therefore, there is an incentive for the sectors with a higher level of competition to move to the sectors with a lower level of competition. This is the case of container shipping and container terminal operations. The liner shipping market is generally more competitive than that of the port sector. So many shipping lines invest heavily in container terminal operations in order to have better returns on the capital invested. This is also one of the main reasons why we rarely see ports entering in the shipping sector. Shipping agent is another sector that may have a low level of competition due to the fact that the market is localised and restrictive. Shipping lines will often sell their own services when the volume of business reaches the threshold. Ports and shipping agents may also compete with each other. But their competition is localised. That is why a big gap exists between ports of different regions in terms of productivity and the poor performers always survive so long as they are not the worst in the localised competition. In shipping, the competition is international, thus only the globally most efficient companies survive. So when a shipping line enters into port terminal or agency businesses where the regional competition is not the toughest, the chance of success is generally high.

What are the strategic considerations for logistics integration?

For a liner shipping company, whether or not it should expand its activities beyond traditional shipping to become a logistics service provider is a complex issue and a decision of multiple dimensions. It has a strategic dimension, which means that it may or may not be the cost and other economic reasons for the shipping company to become a logistics firm. The CEO of Maersk Line, the largest liner shipping company, said that "the future will be very much about scaling the land side of the equation". And, as such, Maersk would "push the parts of its business not to do with the ocean, but with trucks, supply chain management and running warehouses".[15] It is interesting to note that Maersk Line sees more synergy of its liner shipping business with logistics services rather than with other shipping operations, such as the tanker or dry bulk sectors, which have been downgraded in the company.

The evolution of the development strategies of a shipping conglomerate such as Maersk provides a very interesting case study with regard to the future of liner shipping in general and the relationship between liner shipping and logistics in particular. Maersk used to have a very comprehensive business scope covering almost the entire maritime value chain from shipbuilding to ship operation in all three sectors of liner, tanker and dry bulk transport, to port terminal operations and logistics services. It had also diversified beyond shipping into energy, retail and financial sectors. However, the Maersk group recently adopted a different strategic direction by disengaging from other sectors and concentrating on logistics and liner shipping business.

There are many reasons for a shipping company to expand or not expand into other related sectors. This is also about a choice between "make" and "buy". From the viewpoint of specialisation and trade, more benefit can be obtained if production is more specialised as the average cost should be lower and the quality of the product higher. But there always remains a question of how far the specialisation should go or how to define the core activity in a sector. Usually, a core activity is the one that a firm is recognised for or identified with and it is also the one allowing the offerings to evolve and upgrade. Apart from the conventional criteria on out-sourcing, today some more important strategic considerations are increasingly relevant for the decision making regarding whether or not shipping companies, such as a shipping line, should expand the business in the area of logistics. In this regard, one key concept and two directions are of specific importance: the key concept is about "control" and the directions are about the business value chain and customer data.

- ***About the control of the business value chain***. Even undertaking more value-added activities and therefore creating more profit is not necessarily the main consideration, as shipping lines increasingly find that they have to offer a logistics service in order to safeguard their core shipping business. As discussed above, importers and exporters need integrated logistics solutions instead of isolated and separate transport arrangements. A shipping line can, in theory, take the cargo and "out-source" logistics services to other companies. But, by doing this, it does not have direct control of the whole logistics chain. The chain is from the origin to the destination including different modes of transport, port and storage services. That is why some leading shipping lines are very interested in having dedicated container terminals of their own, even if the total cost of operating an exclusive user terminal is not cheaper than that of a common user terminal. So shipping is no longer a complete service in itself, it is a part of a larger package. Today, whoever controls the whole logistics chain controls maritime transport.

- ***About the customer interface and data***. In the 21st century, data has become the most important asset and the most fundamental of economic resources. Among various data, that of customers is of very high value. This subject will be further elaborated on in Chapter 16. What we can say here is that a liner shipping company may lose direct contact with its customers if it does not control the logistics system. This is because the customer data is collected at the interface with them and most customers want to have only one single interface. For example, a freight forwarder that controls the logistics chain may be the one who has contact with the customers and therefore has the access to the data. The forwarder would then contract a shipping line to undertake the maritime transport but without necessarily providing the full information on the cargo and the customers. A shipping line in such a case may be a subcontractor responsible for a partial service for just one customer, i.e., the logistics service provider. So it is very important for a shipping line to expand into logistics activities in order not to be cut off from the link with the customers and access to the crucial data.

14.6 Summary

In this chapter we have examined the relationship between shipping and logistics from several aspects. First, we contrasted shipping with logistics in terms of the total sizes of business and the complexity of the two systems. The international shipping sector is a part of trade logistics. In 2018 the maritime transport market was about 7% of the global logistics market measured in US dollars. Due to the continuous improvement in productivity and the intensive competition, the maritime transport freight has been on the decline. On the other hand, logistics is a much bigger business. Its size varies from about 9% of GDP in industrialised countries to almost 20% in less-developed countries. While shipping focusses on the best transport outcomes, logistics is based on some broader concepts such as total cost and customer service.

The differences between international shipping and logistics are found thus at a geographical level in that the former is about transporting cargo from port to port while the latter is about the movement of cargo from the origin to the destination. At the level of cost, maritime transport generally contributes a much smaller portion in the total logistics cost, but at the level of time, the share of maritime transport in the total time spent on logistics is much larger. Within a shipping company, there are also logistics issues to tackle. These include fleet and ship management as well as container management in shipping lines. The introduction of containers in liner shipping has changed the maritime transport of general cargo completely by making the connections between shipping and other logistics activities seamless and by shifting the business emphasis from transport to logistics. The containerisation has greatly enhanced the efficiency of general cargo transport, storage and handling at both ends of each transport leg. It has enabled the development of the global supply chain.

The value of a traded cargo is higher at the destination than at the origin. The difference is created by logistics. Different Incoterms reflect the value changes from the seller's factory and the buyer's floor of a traded cargo at different logistics stages. Different companies specialising in various logistics activities provide services from transport to terminal and storage. While these companies are cooperating between themselves, there is also a competition for value added. The consequence is the tendency of logistics integration. The logistics integration follows some basic rules and principles, such as the optimal size of the operation, the sector's position in the logistics system, the technical/operational complexity condition and the financial capability/risk. As a result, some logistics sectors are in stronger and more leading positions than other sectors when logistics integration takes place. This effect can be expressed by the rate of domination and the rate of vulnerability of each logistics sector. For example, it is more likely that a shipping line will take over a port, rather than the other way round. Thus the shipping sector has a higher domination rate and a lower vulnerability rate than the port sector.

Whether or not a specialised company should expand its business to other logistics sectors is as much an economic and commercial decision as a strategic one. It is so because liner shipping is increasingly defined and deeply influenced by logistics because customers are looking for an integrated logistics package rather than individual transport solutions. Therefore, the responsibility vis-à-vis customers stays with the provider of the full-service package, not that of partial service. From an economic viewpoint, out of total trade logistics, the part of maritime transport is small and declining. Some leading shipping lines consider that transforming themselves into logistics service providers is vital for the future of the shipping business. From the strategic viewpoint, a shipping line may need to become a logistics service provider for the sake of the two controls: the control of the business value chain and the control of customer interface and data. In Chapter 16 this last point will be further discussed.

Notes

1 Lambert D., Stock J., and Ellram L. (1997).
2 Lambert D., Stock J., and Ellram L. (1998). The definition is given by the US Council of Supply Chain Management Professionals in *Supply Chain Management Terms and Glossary* and Lambert D., Stock J., and Ellram L. (1998).
3 Amstrong and Associates Inc (2019).
4 The IMF estimates suggest that maritime transport freight is about 5% of the total import value of merchandise trade. If about 70% of global trade is moved by maritime transport, the total freight would be in the region of US$650 billion in 2017 (WTO World Trade Statistics 2018, total import in 2017 was US$17,572 bn). When it comes to the total logistics cost as a percentage of the global GDP, there are different estimates ranging from 11% to 13%, with big gaps existing between countries.
5 The logistics performance of different countries is investigated by the World Bank and the result is published, every other year, in its "Logistics Performance Index" report.
6 World Bank (2018).
7 Ibid., note 4, p. 53.
8 Ibid., note 4, pp. 56–58.
9 Clarksons (2019). In 2018 the East–West trade (Transpacific, Transatlantic and Asia–Europe) was of 79 million teus, the total intra-regional trade was of 82.4 million teus and the intra-Asian trade was of 58.3 million teus.
10 UNCTAD (2018).
11 Bernhofen D., El-Sahli Z., and Kneller R. (2013).
12 Ibid., note 8, p. 7.
13 Levinson M. (2006).
14 Maersk Line has more than 80 container liner services calling at the Port of Singapore. That may mean more than 10 ships of the same company calling at the port per day, if most services are weekly. The situation for other leading shipping lines is similar, and it applies to many main ports in the world (retrieved 7 January 2019 at www.maersk.com/en/local-information/singapore/routes).
15 Milne R. (2018).

References

Amstrong and Associates Inc. (2019) "*Global Logistics Costs and Third-Party Logistics Revenues*", Retrieved 19 November 2019 from www.3plogistics.com/3pl-market-info-resources/3pl-market-information/global-3pl-market-size-estimates/.

Bernhofen D., El-Sahli Z., and Kneller R. (2013) "*Estimating the Effects of the Container Revolution on World Trade*", Lund University Working paper 2013:4 p. 11.

Clarksons (2019) "*Shipping Intelligence Network*", Clarkson, London.

Lambert D., Stock J., and Ellram L. (1997) "*Fundamentals of Logistics Management*", 1st Edition, Irwin/ McGraw-Hill, New York.

Levinson M. (2006), "*The Box – How the Shipping Container Made the World Smaller and the World Economy Bigger*", Princeton University Press, Princeton, NJ, pp. 64–65.

Milne R. (2018), "*World's Biggest Shipping Line Maersk Looks for Deals on Land*", Financial Times, 26 December 2018.

UNCTAD (2018) "*Review of Maritime Transport, 2018*", UNCTAD/RMT/2018, Geneva, p. 13.

World Bank. (2018) "*Connecting to Compete – Trade Logistics in the Global Economy, 2018*", The World Bank Publication.

Chapter 15

The economics of maritime safety and environmental regulations

For some people, maritime safety and marine environment protection are not economic issues because life is priceless and pollution should simply not be allowed. Such views are not wrong, but they are not entirely right either. One of the root causes of why the maritime transport industry still has too many casualties and generates too much pollution is precisely the ignorance of the economic dimension in the whole process of addressing the issues. Life is not priceless, but it might be priced too low, the problem of air emissions is not about elimination, but it is about optimisation. Economies should only grow if the growth is environmentally sustainable. By bringing the ship-related safety and environmental challenges into a specific economic framework, we will have a better chance of finding the right and effective solutions. In this chapter we will analyse the basic characteristics of ship-related safety and environmental issues and their special economic characteristics. We will then describe the concept of optimal levels of maritime safety and marine environment. This will lead us to a discussion of the risk-based regulation approaches and, finally, we will look at the market-based measures for the control of greenhouse gas emissions from ships.

15.1 The nature of maritime safety and environmental issues

In many ways, one can say that safety and environment-related negative consequences or costs are the by-products of economic activities. In the context of maritime transport, this is about the relationship between casualty or pollution on the one hand and the shipping production on the other.

Why are safety and environmental problems economic problems?

Economics is basically a study of the allocation of resources to alternative uses. In other words, it is about *choices* of using limited financial, human and natural resources for society's maximum benefits. Are maritime safety and environmental protection matters of choice? This has been a subject of debate,[1] and it is a fundamental question for understanding the economics of maritime safety and environment.

Occupational safety and most environmental problems are economic issues simply because economic activities are the origins of casualties and pollution. In any given technical and operational setting, the number of accidents threatening the safety of people or property is proportional to the scale of production. However, the environment or safety system and the economic system pursue different objectives, which cannot be optimised simultaneously. The environment system interacts with the economic system and the gain of the one is normally the loss of the other. The whole issue becomes a matter of choice: either more A at the expense of B or more B at the cost of A.[2] It is said, therefore, that safety and environmental questions fall within the sphere of economic analysis and the economics of safety and environment specialises in studying the relationship between the two systems. Such a study in general aims at achieving a balance or equilibrium between the objectives of the two systems. Although an economic issue, the problems associated with safety and environment cannot be completely tackled and resolved by using the traditional approaches of economics. In other words, a related but different branch of economics, the economics of safety and environment, should apply.

The core of neoclassical economic theories and approaches is the market mechanism. The market is believed to function in making economic choices by allocating resources with efficiency through a pricing mechanism. However, in practice, markets fail to deliver efficiency as far as safety and environment are concerned, because the property right of safety and environment goods is in most cases not identifiable. One of the cornerstones of the market economy is the clearly defined property rights, which are exclusive, transferable and protected. In the absence of such property rights, markets will fail. This is the case of maritime safety and environmental products. Safety and environment goods, i.e., safety and environment products and services, have the characteristics of public goods. For example, there is not a particular person who can be identified as the exclusive beneficiary of a cleaner sea or a polluted river. Contrary to exclusive property rights, which imply private and individual ownership, public goods are characterised as non-exclusive and non-rival in consumption. This means that the consumption of the goods by one does not reduce the amount available to others or that safety and environmental goods have zero marginal cost. Such weak or absent property rights results in an inefficient allocation of resources and a failure in achieving safety and environmental objectives, as there is a lack of any incentive for a rational person to make an investment since he cannot own and transfer the full benefits or cover an undefined and unclaimed environmental cost.

The public-goods nature of maritime safety and environment reveals another important feature, which is *externalities*. The market economic system is a "closed" system or a "linear" system in the sense that it does not take into account its relationship with and its impact outside the system, such as, for example, on the surrounding environment. A closed economic system considers only the production, consumption and exchange between economic agents within the system with a clearly defined property right. It ignores the flow of materials and energy that cross the boundaries. Un-priced activities and resources have no value in a closed economic system. This situation is illustrated in Figure 15.1. An externality is said to exist when an activity by one agent in the economic system causes a loss of welfare to another agent outside the system. For example, a ship disposes illegally of waste into the water incurring financial or recreational losses to other people who have no economic relationship with the polluter. One reason why externalities occur is the failure of the market to price the effects caused by one person on another person with such a failure leaving the affected person uncompensated. It is because of the lack of property rights, as mentioned above, which makes the sufferer unable to demand that the externality is reduced or to ask for compensation. The high transaction costs associated with the settlement of the externalities between the parties is another major cause of externalities.

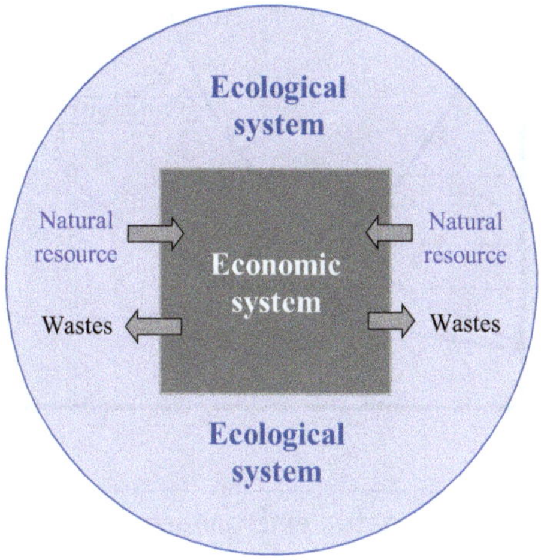

Figure 15.1 Economic activities and negative externalities.

Source: Shuo Ma.

Note: economic activities such as shipping generate wastes in the environment which are external costs of the economic system.

What is the purpose of maritime safety and environmental economics?

Externalities can be either positive or negative. When they are negative and not compensated for, they are said to have an external cost. If such an external cost is paid for, in the form of compensation, we then say that the externality is internalised. Maritime transport does cause negative externalities, mainly in relation to the pollution of the environment and the safety threat to the health or life of seafarers and dockworkers. Environment-related externalities include oil spills or greenhouse gas emissions from ships related to accidents, ship operations, terminal operations and dry-docking. Although oil is the most well-known source of marine pollution, other materials such as garbage and sewage from ships and many chemicals carried by sea may be as dangerous as, or even more dangerous than, oil to the marine environment. For example, externality caused by pollution in the atmosphere from emissions from ships is also becoming an increasing concern.

Occupational safety problems in maritime transport are also a primary source of externality. For analysing how externality occurs, the safety and health-related costs should be divided into economic costs and non-economic costs or private costs and social costs or direct costs and indirect costs. When the financial losses in the case of injury or illness happening to seafarers are covered, non-economic costs still exist in the form of pain, worry, fear, etc., suffered by the victims and their families. Such costs may persist for a long time and are difficult to evaluate and compensate.

The safety-related externality in the form of social costs is more complex. For example, let us say that for a shipping company the high accident rate with a particular item of equipment forces the company to pay an extra US$300,000 a year in medical, indemnity and replacement costs. Further, the consequent injuries and illnesses incur another US$200,000, which the company does not pay for, for the victims, families, insurance and social security system. Thus, a new safety device may solve the problem. However, if the company pursues only a financial interest, its decision to invest or not in

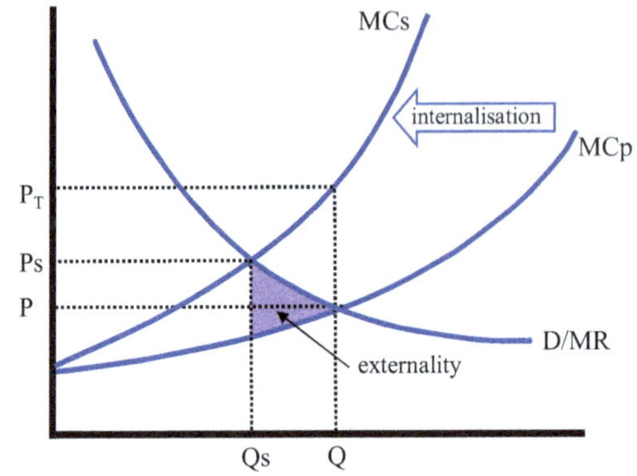

Figure 15.2 Internalisation of negative externalities.

Source: Shuo Ma.

Note: society's cost is higher than producer's cost due to a negative externality. When the negative externality is internalised by regulations, quantity is reduced to Qs and price is increased to Ps.

the new equipment will depend on whether it costs more or less than US$300,000 per annum. If the device costs US$400,000 each year, there might not be sufficient incentive for the company to make the investment. Spending US$400,000 to save a total of US$500,000 is a good deal for society, but not for the company. Such externality leads to an inefficient allocation of resources for society.

Using the above example as an illustration, as in Figure 15.2, we have the demand curve for the shipping service as represented by D, which is also the curve for marginal revenue in the case of a competitive market under the assumption that the marginal revenue for the producer equals that for society. MC_P is the marginal cost for the shipping company, and MC_S is the marginal cost for society. In this case, MC_S is always higher than MC_P since the externality is negative and society bears both the costs of production and the other environment-related costs resulting from the production. However, with unpriced environmental costs, the company considers only its direct marginal cost to maximise its surplus by keeping the production at Q. Such a production level will incur a direct production cost at P and a total social cost at P_T, creating a net externality unit cost, $P_T - P$. Such external costs are therefore paid by the direct victims of the pollution, the public and the society as a whole. Figure 15.2 indicates further that if such externality is internalised, i.e., the shipping company is made to cover the total cost P_T, then the producer cannot keep the production at Q because the demand will not pay the price at P_T. The shipping company will have to reduce the production to Q_S to arrive at a new demand–supply equilibrium with a higher price at P_S. At this reduced production level and increased price, the external cost or externality, which is represented by the shaded area, is internalised and covered by the transaction.

How do you internalise safety and environmental externalities?

How are externalities internalised? How do you make the producers, such as a shipping company, pay for the total cost, including external cost? There are three main approaches which have been used to deal with externality problems, namely through polluters' self-discipline, by governmental rules and regulations and by government-administrated market-based methods.

The first approach is to rely on self-discipline. Take maritime safety and the marine environment, for example. It has been suggested that up-grading safety and preventing pollution is a question of assuming corporate responsibility and good citizenship on the part of shipping corporations. In 2018, for example, a large shipping company, Maersk Supply Service, agreed to deploy its ships to support an effort to remove plastic debris from the sea.[3] Shipping companies as well as shippers should be honest and improve safety and the environment until it is no longer economically feasible for them to do so. This is certainly a noble approach with the major advantage being its simplicity and low cost. However, despite noticeable progress, some more effective, systematic, enforceable, sustainable and more forceful methods are needed. This is due to the fact that the self-discipline approach depends so much on the social and cultural environment, which, in a highly open and global sector such as shipping, is greatly diversified.

The second approach is using government intervention through rules and regulations to deal with the issues of externality. This is the most commonly used approach. The advantage of this approach is the applicability: it is a feasible and proven method. The main deficiencies of the approach are the lack of accuracy of the regulations because the process of rulemaking and enforcement depends on subjective judgement, bureaucratic procedures and political influence. One of the goals for the economics of safety and environment is, therefore, to study various aspects of government regulations to enhance accuracy and effectiveness.

As far as maritime safety and the environment are concerned, government regulation is nothing new. Although the first items of shipping-related regulation and law can be traced back to as early as the 15th century,[4] the real development and expansion of maritime regulation is something remarkably recent. In the area of maritime safety, for example, the first government regulation is believed to be the British Merchant Shipping Act of 1872, through which an office of Registrar General of Shipping was established with the main responsibilities of collecting official log-books, confirming that merchant ships obeyed applicable laws and recording deaths, accidents and casualties. Further, a series of marine safety provisions, such as the 1875 requirement for ships to be marked with load lines, were incorporated into Britain's Merchant Shipping Act of 1894.[5]

Compared with that on maritime safety, the first pieces of international regulation on the environmental problems related to maritime transport came much later. It was not until 1954 that the first International Convention for the Prevention of Oil Pollution from Merchant Ships was adopted at the Second International Conference on this subject. It was the first international agreement ever on environmental issues related to ships, though the convention was very limited as it covered only operational not accidental pollution. This last aspect will be discussed in a later section.

The third approach is called market-based methods. This is to create a system that allows free market systems to solve the problems based on the pricing mechanism through bargaining between the stakeholders of the safety and environmental products.[6] The advantage of the method is in its minimum requirement for direct government intervention, though the government often still has a role to play when the system is established. The major shortcomings are that the key assumptions, such as zero transaction cost, perfect competition and no income effects, are quasi-absent in the real world. The system does generate a cost. However, the shortcomings do not prevent the approach from being an effective way to internalise maritime externalities.

In this chapter we will focus on the last two methods, i.e., the regulations by the public authorities and the market-based approaches. We will analyse maritime risks and the appropriateness of the risk levels which are acceptable. We will then examine the issues regarding ship-related air emission control. Comparisons will be made between emission standards and market-based methods, not only for the sake of efficiency but also for the encouragement of using better and more advanced technologies.

Are maritime safety and environmental problems accidental or operational?

There are differences as well as similarities between maritime safety and marine environment protection regulations. This is because when an incident or accident occurs, it very often presents a threat to both the humans on board the ship and the surrounding environment. The most remarkable difference between maritime safety and environmental protection is that, while maritime safety-related regulations almost exclusively deal with accidental cases, environmental regulations deal with both accidental and operational circumstances. If maritime safety and environmental products can be measured by their occurrence and consequences, which means by the frequency of occurrence and severity of consequences of the safety and/or pollution events, then for all maritime safety and part of marine environmental products, the outcomes are uncertain. So these products are accidental such as, for example, a ship grounding, causing casualties and oil spills, happens accidentally not intentionally. On the other hand, for some environmental products, both occurrences and consequences are fairly predictable. For example, to legally discharge waste oil into the ocean or emit harmful exhausts from the operating engine into the atmosphere. Such discharges are allowed and are deliberately undertaken and are referred to as operational. Sometimes, operation-related safety issues do exist, for example working for a long time in a special environment with noise, vibration or odour might have an adverse impact on the health of seafarers. But most safety problems are linked to accidents.

Obviously, because of the differences in the nature of maritime safety and marine environmental products, the corresponding regulations should have different characteristics as well. For accidental cases, the statistical objective for the IMO regulations is normally what is called ALARP or *As Low As Reasonably Practicable*, which is defined as "a level of risk for which further investment of resources for risk reduction is not justified. When risk is reduced to ALARP, it is acceptable".[7] For operational cases, the objectives are to identify the optimal pollution conditions and levels and to make sure that these conditions and levels are met properly. Referring to the discussions of the earlier section, this means finding out the marginal environmental damage cost curve and the marginal pollution control cost curve. The type of measures to take for the implementation of the regulations is different too. For accidental cases, risk management principles should be followed and techniques should be employed. The IMO conventions such as OPRC and INTERVENTION or the double-hull requirements for tanker ships in MARPOL Annex I are examples of this type of measures. With regard to operational environmental cases, waste management principles and techniques should be utilised. This may include, for example, setting up the conditions and limits for the discharge of waste, such as oil or sewage into the sea or greenhouse gases into the atmosphere. Table 15.1 shows the main features and the distinction of maritime safety and environmental regulations between accidental and operational categories. This is important in understanding the objectives of the regulations and the appropriate measures to implement.

Table 15.1 Accidental and operational nature and characteristics of maritime safety and environmental issues

	Safety & Environmental Products			*Safety & Environmental Regulations*	
	Occurrence	*Consequence*	*Nature*	*Objectives*	*Measures*
Maritime Safety	Uncertain	Uncertain	Accidental	ALARP	Risk control
Marine Environment	Certain	Certain	Operational	Optimal level	Waste control

Source: Shuo Ma

Note: For accidental problems, regulations are based on risk management and control, while for operational problems, regulations are based on level management and control.

The decisions and regulations on maritime safety and environmental protection can be divided into three categories, namely prevention-related, preparedness-related and response-related. If an accident-based pollution event happens, it is often associated with a safety issue in the first place, though there may also be environmental accidents due to technical failure or human error. With a close look at the IMO regulations, one can easily observe that most maritime safety-related regulations are based on risk management and most environmental regulations are based on level control. In the next two sections we will discuss these two bases in more detail.

15.2 Risk-based safety and environmental regulations

One of the principles adopted by the maritime community is to establish safety rules and regulations on the basis of risk assessment. The assessment includes several stages of analysis on the risks and the mitigation methods and then making decisions accordingly.

What is the risk of maritime transport?

Safety risk comes from the uncertainty of the occurrence of various unexpected events with negative effects. It is defined as a function of the frequency and consequences of safety incidents. Risks are divided into individual and societal risks. The former refers to the risk of death, injury, illness, etc., experienced by an individual, while societal risks refer to the average risk of fatalities for a group of the population or the whole society. For societal risks, for example, a risk assessment estimates the probabilities of the frequency of such an occurrence and the severity of the consequences, using a risk matrix as shown in Figure 15.3. The low frequency of occurrence but high severity of consequence, such as a fatality, may be as risky as many frequently happening small incidents with less serious

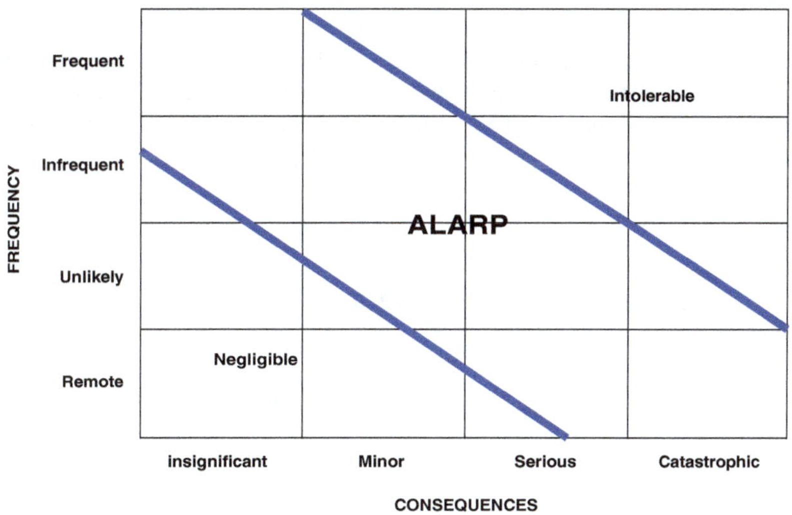

Figure 15.3 Matrix of maritime risk and actions required.

Source: Shuo Ma, based on data from IMO.

Note: a typical example in maritime safety is about frequency of fatalities. It can also be frequency and severity of oil spill accidents.

impacts. For the middle range, efforts should be made to reduce the risk to as low as reasonably practicable. If the risk falls above this range, the situation is intolerable and urgent and immediate actions have to be taken. If the risk falls below the middle range, it is considered to be negligible and, as such, no particular action is required. Experience and historical data are often used to make a risk estimation. In maritime transport, historical data such as casualty reports and pollution accident statistics are generally accessible, although they are perceived to be not in sufficient detail for more useful analysis. Such data normally give a certain kind of indication with regard to the frequency of accidents and their tendency. Based on such data, mathematical models can be used to calculate the probability of the occurrence of projected events.

Risk management aims to reduce the risk by either reducing the chances of the occurrence or mitigating the impact of the consequences, or both. In maritime transport, this is sometimes left to market mechanisms such as marine insurance, through which the risk is reduced by balancing the aggregated risks against the total premium income. However, as explained above, due to the externalities generated by maritime safety and environment incidents, the markets alone cannot achieve the efficient allocation of resources and therefore regulations are needed. Based on economic analysis, it is hoped that the risks can be kept at an appropriate level when the surplus for the whole society is maximised.

In 2014 the US Department of Transportation stopped a rule requiring truck drivers to file a report on vehicle condition before and after every trip, even when no faults were found. It was estimated that the change saved the industry US$1.7 billion.[8] A similar situation might also exist in maritime transport. In 2014 the IMO published a report based on a survey of over 3,300 respondents from the shipping industry and the national maritime administration, which revealed that almost 60% of respondents considered many instruments of the IMO's SOLAS Convention as an administrative burden, making it the most problematic of all IMO mandatory instruments.[9] This is quite an alarming signal given the importance and the impact of the convention. The 1974 version of the Convention is out of date, mainly due to the fact that it was developed with piles of amendments which have been added as prescriptions in response to often major maritime safety events. Instead of being based on a holistic and systematic risk assessment, such disaster-triggered regulations sometimes have been amended with urgency leaving little time and room for economic analysis in the process of regulation-making. As a result, it may, unfortunately, lead to under-, or more often over-dosing regulations or poor results of implementation. Such reactive or prescriptive regulations, even when fully implemented, have no built-in capabilities to prevent different accidents that may happen in the future, particularly in view of the technological progress in the shipping sector since 1974. A good maritime safety regulation system should be established based on risk assessment and a scientific, proactive, systematic, integrated approach.

What is the risk-based rule-making approach in maritime transport?

In 2002 the IMO adopted a risk-assessment-based method called *formal safety assessment* (FSA). The approach incorporates a risk assessment and a cost-benefit analysis in the rule-making process. Though not formally introduced until 2002 into the international maritime regulations, the idea of having an economic analysis component in safety and environment regulation-making was not new. In the USA, the Executive Order 12,291 of 1981 requires that benefit–cost analysis be performed for all major environment, safety and health regulations. FSA is "a rational and systematic process for assessing the risks associated with shipping activity and for evaluating the costs and benefits of IMO's options for reducing these risks".[10] The FSA approach comprises five steps:

1 ***Identification of hazards (or "what might go wrong?").*** This step consists of collecting all data about the accident under investigation, then identifying all hazards that might impair the functions of the

generic ship type used in FSA. Finally the hazards are screened and ranked using historical data and an expert system.

2 ***Assessment of risks associated with those hazards (or "how bad and how likely?").*** This is to evaluate the probability or frequency of each accident type and its severity or consequence. This step can be completed by examining, for example, using a Risk Contribution Tree, the risk contributors and quantifying the risks in terms of probability and consequence of outcome.
3 ***Consideration of alternative ways of managing those risks (or "can matters be improved?").*** This is to list all the possible measures of risk control with the attributes attached, which indicate the nature of each measure, for example whether the measure is preventive or mitigating, engineering or procedural.
4 ***Cost–benefit assessment of alternative risk management options (or "what would it cost and how much better would it be?").*** The standard CBA techniques are applied to each option to determine the economic costs and benefits in net present value terms.
5 ***Decision on which option to select (or "what actions should be taken?").*** Actually, FSA does not give a ready-to-use decision. Instead it provides a framework with more complete and systematically collected and presented information, which is necessary for the decision-making.

This approach tries to improve the quality of decisions based on cost-effectiveness for the maritime transport sector. It is expected that, by having a full picture and the knowledge of the entire scope of the risks encountered, as well as information on the possible ways of reducing the risks, this method will help create a safety culture. However, to accurately quantify the costs and benefits related to the implementation of safety and environment regulations has proved to be very difficult. The long-term, indirect and induced effects with costs and benefits make it harder still to have exact figures. So the real purpose of CBA is not to compare with a certain precision the cost and benefit of each regulatory item, but rather to have an overall feel for the rightfulness of the regulation concerned and for the trade-off between the alternative policy programmes

15.3 Optimisation of environmental standards

The environmental impact of shipping may be a consequence of a maritime accident; it may also be from the operations of transport production. This includes air emissions from ships. In this context, it is an optimisation process which is needed. The standards for the environmental performance of the shipping industry is, in the real world, a highly complex issue influenced by not only economic but also technical, social, cultural, political and other factors. The following discussions will be from a mainly economic perspective.

What are the aims of safety and environmental regulations?

Safety and environmental regulations are for the purpose of achieving a balance between the objectives of the economic system on the one hand, the social, safety and environmental system on the other hand, and also for achieving a balance between the needs of the current and future generations. If the word "society" is employed to embrace the entire beneficiary interests of such balances, the ultimate goal of the regulations should then be to maximise a society's total surplus. The basic economic principles tell us that when marginal cost equals marginal revenue, the surplus is maximised and the corresponding quantity produced is at its optimal level, as shown in Figure 15.4. In the context of maritime safety and marine environment regulations, marginal costs indicate the costs incurred by an individual or a company or a society at large to comply with the requirements of the regulations concerned. This means, in practice, the costs relating to safety control or pollution abatement. As far as marginal revenue is concerned, it signifies the benefits received by an individual, a company or the entire society resulting from enhanced safety standards or reduced pollution levels. In the real world, such benefits include the cost savings from reduced safety accidents or pollution and also the improvement in the quality of life.

The economics of safety and environment regulations and the introduction of external costs highlight the fact that the physical presence of pollution does not necessarily mean that economic pollution exists (no third-party interests affected). Discharging limited amounts of oil into the sea does create physical pollution, but it does not necessarily generate a cost to a third party if the level of discharge is well within nature's assimilation capacity. Hence, it is not seen as economic pollution, but more like the discharge of waste by the natural system. Another notable feature is that even if economic pollution or dangers to safety do exist, it may not mean that they should be eliminated. As illustrated in Figure 15.4, the level of pollution such as, for example, the amount of waste discharged, is represented by the horizontal axis, whereas the cost and benefit levels are represented on the vertical axis. The *MB* curve refers to the "marginal benefit" of the pollution-producing activity to society or the "marginal control cost" *MCC*, which reflects damage saved. *MC* refers to the "marginal costs" generated by the pollution to society or marginal damage cost, *MDC*. At a low production/pollution level, the marginal benefit is big and the marginal cost small. As the production/pollution increases, the marginal benefit falls and the marginal cost rises. The optimal production/pollution is at Q when the marginal benefit equals marginal costs at X. So "P" should be the objective for the optimal regulation.

The equilibrium of marginal cost and marginal benefit provides a foundation for optimal safety and environmental regulation. One of the ways to achieve this is to use rules in the form of compulsory emission standards, which are often referred to as the "command-and-control" method. This approach consists of the promulgation of laws, rules and regulations with the specification of objectives, standards, technologies and operational procedures that polluters must comply with. In the broad context of such laws and regulations, specific rules and standards are normally established aiming at agreed objectives. By using the "command-and-control" method, one could control the pollution at its optimal level through a "bargaining" process. This is because the optimal pollution level is achieved when marginal benefit and marginal cost are identical.

Through the process of bargain or competition, the equilibrium can be achieved. This means that under the pressure of public opinion, which can be represented by, for example, two opposing

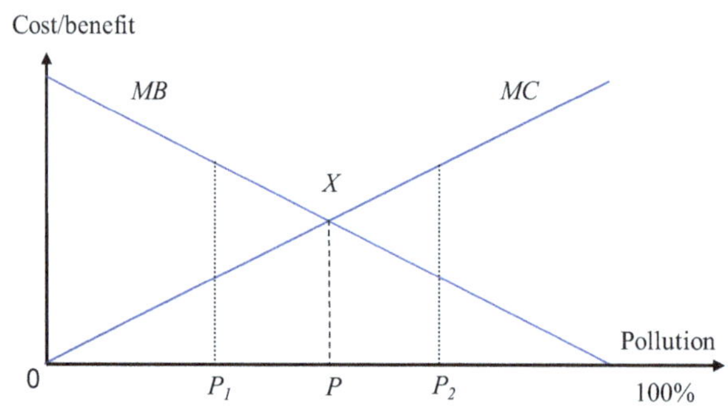

Figure 15.4 Optimal level of pollution control.

Source: Shuo Ma.

Note: when the environmental cost and benefit for society from pollution reduction regulation are equal, the optimal level of pollution control is achieved.

interest groups such as pro-business versus pro-environment groups, the emission standard would then be negotiated and moved, mostly by the government or similar public authorities influenced by the interest groups, towards the optimal level of pollution. This phenomenon can be seen in Figure 15.4. If the initial standard is set at P_1, which is stricter than the optimal level for society at P, such a policy will generate strong opposition from the producers who will request that the standard be revised. Then a re-evaluation of the pollution damage and pollution control costs will reveal that the initial standard set is too stringent and, as a consequence, an adjustment is likely to be undertaken in such a way that more pollution will be allowed. By the same token, if the emission standard set is too relaxed at P_2, which is below the optimal level of pollution, public opinion will lean towards the advocates of the environment, which will lead to a strengthening of the rules with the amount of pollution being permitted at a lower level. It is also more likely to be accepted because the marginal benefit is lower.

Such a pollution-standard-setting mechanism can also be seen in the establishment of maritime legislation at, for example, the IMO. At any given time and for a particular item of maritime regulation, optimal standards are sought through consultation, negotiation, debate and discussion, which collectively is a "competitive process" amongst various interest groups. As an outcome of such a policy-making or standard-setting process, the optimal pollution level, which is also the optimal regulation level, will be realised. An important implication of this analysis is that the bigger the differences between the interest groups, the harder the process will be and the longer time it will take to reach a consensus. It is also true that the bigger the divergence, the lower the average satisfaction level of all the stakeholders, due to the fact that the "optimal" standards please neither business-minded nor environment-minded people entirely.

How do you measure the cost and benefit of environmental regulations?

The externalities expressed in terms of the cost and benefit for society from pollution control and environmental regulations are difficult to measure. One of the commonly used ways is a state-preference method, which is to ask the individual to assign values to safety and environmental goods. Typically, for a specific scenario of a regulation, individuals are asked about the maximum amount of money they are *willing to pay* (WTP) for having, for example, a new environmental regulation. Alternatively, the question asked can concern the minimum amount of money they are *willing to accept* in compensation (WTA) to forgo a given safety or environmentally good service.

The level of WTP in relation to a given pollution changes from person to person, from community to community and from country to country, because it is affected by the conditions and environment people are in. The most important influential factors include the income level, the relevant education received and the awareness people have. Taking the income level as an example, the WTP for a person or a country is usually positively correlated with the income level, which means that, for a given pollution, the WTP amount is higher for persons who have a higher level of income and the WTP is lower for those with a lower income level. The WTP is never a static phenomenon because people's income level varies amongst individuals in a society. The education level and the awareness of the real cost and benefit of pollution have an impact on the level of WTP. This is why a major accident with the exposure of the consequences can change the WTP of a population quickly and completely. The economic structure of a region or a country may also have a direct impact on the marginal benefit and marginal cost of the pollution. The cost and benefit of marine pollution for a tourism- and fishery-dependent country must be different from that for an agricultural- or mining-dependent country. As a result, there is no uniform optimal pollution level. The difference in optimal pollution level for different persons, communities, regions or countries is illustrated in Figure 15.5. The marginal benefit, *MB*, of pollution can be expressed as marginal control cost, *MCC*, which is saved damage cost

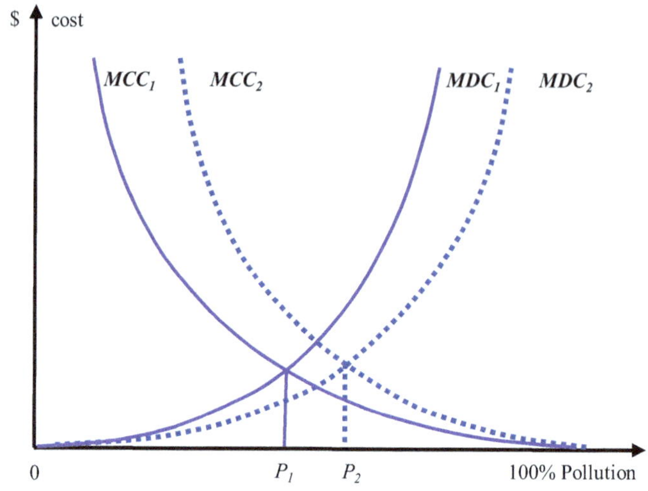

Figure 15.5 Divergence between optimal levels of pollution control.

Source: Shuo Ma.

Note: since marginal benefit (*MB*) or marginal control cost (*MCC*) and marginal damage cost (*MDC*) are measured based on WTP or WTA, which are in turn affected by factors varying from person to person or from one country to another, so there is not a unique optimal level.

thanks to the control. While marginal cost, *MC*, is the marginal social damage cost of pollution or *MDC*. Country A has its optimal level at P_1, country B's optimal level is at P_2, which means that country A benefits less from the polluting activity but has to pay a higher cost for corrective and preventive measures due to, say, a higher national income and a better-informed population.

The difference in optimal pollution level is the biggest difficulty for policy-makers in establishing and implementing uniform environmental regulations. While marine pollution is a global issue, the solution relies largely on national assessment and decisions. It is believed that the impact, both benefit and cost, of pollution should determine the application scope of relevant environmental regulations to see whether regulations should be better implemented at regional or national or international level. Once the scope is identified, ideally environment protection regulations should be made according to the optimal pollution level based on the average *MCC* and *MDC* so that the maximum net benefit is obtained for the society. The above economic analysis signifies that if an environmental regulation is targeted at the whole world, then the optimal pollution level, on which the regulations are supposed to be based, should be determined by the average benefit and external cost of the pollution in question for all countries in the world. Such "averaged" regulations are certainly the most appropriate regulations that will create the maximum value for the whole international community, although they will be probably disliked by many countries whose MCC and MDC are either much higher or lower than the average. To some extent, the large gap between optimal levels of countries generates great difficulties for environmental regulations at the international level. It is also the reason and justification for the introduction and implementation of some environmental regulations at regional or national levels. It is an acceptable approach as long as the major pollution impact is also national or regional.

The major international environmental regulations adopted at IMO are known as conventions. The conventions are developed to prevent or to respond to marine pollution and greenhouse gas emissions. Given the divergence of optimal regulations for different member countries of the organisation, ratifying an international convention by sufficient countries for the convention to enter into force is often a lengthy process. Political and other factors play an important role in it. Nevertheless, in many cases, it is economic considerations that are the end objectives and the decisive elements in the process. Criticism is often heard that the organisation is reactive rather proactive and new regulations are almost always introduced as responses to accidents or disasters. But there is an economic reason for this because it is the accidents and the much publicised negative consequences that are the key ingredients for the change of public WTP and consensus is necessary for moving the optimal pollution level P by adopting stricter and more costly measures.

The complexity in quantifying the cost and benefit comes from the fact that it is not based on direct and explicit gains and losses in an economic sense. As is the very nature of the WTP concept, the cost and benefit have social and political dimensions as well. Without the inclusion of social and political cost and benefit in the equation, some needed regulations will not pass the cost–benefit analysis test. Such cases are found in some key IMO mandatory instruments like SOLAS or MARPOL Conventions. For example, double-hull tankers are expected to reduce the probability of oil spills in the case of grounding or collision. But this type of ship is more expensive to build and to operate and there is also a loss of carrying capacity. It is estimated that double-hull implementation is expected to reduce oil spills in the event of an accident by 40% in small tankers and 70% in large tankers. Using the average annual total amount of accidental spill in the USA and the higher end of the clean-up/remediation cost per ton of spill, the total benefit of double-hull tankers in preventing oil pollution damage per annum would be US$370 million. The total cost of double-hulled tankers carrying the above cargo is estimated at US$1.6 billion. This leads to negative expected net benefits of the double-hull requirement with a benefit/cost ratio of 23%.[11] A similar conclusion is also drawn in another study where it is found that, based on a 20-year vessel life, a pure economic cost–benefit analysis suggests that the expected benefits of double-hull tankers are only 20% of the expected costs.[12] In the adoption process of the regulations on double-hull tankers, the decisive role played by the two major oil spill accidents, *Exxon Valdez* and *Erika* and their associated high political and social costs, is obvious.

The implementation of IMO regulations on the sulphur content of marine fuel in sulphur emission control areas (SECA) from 1.0% to 0.1% from 1 January 2015 showed a positive benefit to cost ratio of 1.9 to 3.5.[13] A similar positive result was recorded as the result of emission control of NOx from ships.[14] The cost of marine environmental regulations can be expressed in terms of two major economic impacts in the following two areas: on transport cost and subsequently transport mode choice; and on international trade and subsequently on national economies. It is estimated that these regulatory measures will increase transport costs and lead to some shippers considering alternative cheaper transport modes or routes. The cost impacts are relatively limited on transport choices, trade and national economies,[15] due to the facts that the price elasticity is generally low for the maritime transport of basic commodities and the low shipping cost to cargo value ratio for manufactured goods.

15.4 New environmental agenda and emission control methods

For the period of 2007 to 2012, about 846 million tons or 2.6% of global CO_2 and 866 million tons or 2.4% of global CO_2e for greenhouse gases combining CO_2, CH_4 and N_2O, are attributable to international shipping.[16] In the broad context of the 2015 Paris Agreement on Climate Change, the international maritime community agreed in 2018 on ambitious objectives regarding the reduction of CO_2 and GHG emissions from ships. It has taken a long time to reach this point. It remains a big challenge for the shipping sector to achieve the objectives.

What is the dilemma for the environmental agenda of international shipping?

It was in 1997 that the MARPOL Convention was amended by a protocol to include Annex VI on "Regulations for the prevention of air pollution from ships". The 1997 Kyoto Protocol indicated that countries should pursue limitation or reduction of emissions of GHGs from marine bunker fuel by working through the IMO. The main challenge facing the global maritime community with regard to the greenhouse gas emissions is that, on the one hand, ever stronger pressures are coming from many countries and organisations for the international shipping sector to have an emission cap and a timetable and, on the other hand, global trade continues to grow, which requires additional shipping capacities.

Figure 15.6 is about a challenging scenario. Between 2000 and 2018, seaborne trade in both tons and ton-miles continued to grow at a relatively fast pace. Seaborne trade almost doubled in size during this period. What is more important is that seaborne trade per capita has also steadily increased. With their economies developing, countries will always make more international trade. However, the productivity of ships has not had much improvement. As a consequence, the extra demand must be satisfied by additional shipping capacities. This situation is particularly challenging when, during recent decades, trade growth has come mostly from developing countries rather than traditional industrialised countries. Imposing an environmental target with an absolute amount of emissions allowed has been considered as a major hindrance to economic development, which remains the top national priority in most of these countries. Besides, since the mid-1990s, the fuel efficiency of ships has stagnated. In such a context, a relative target of carbon intensity should be considered as more acceptable.

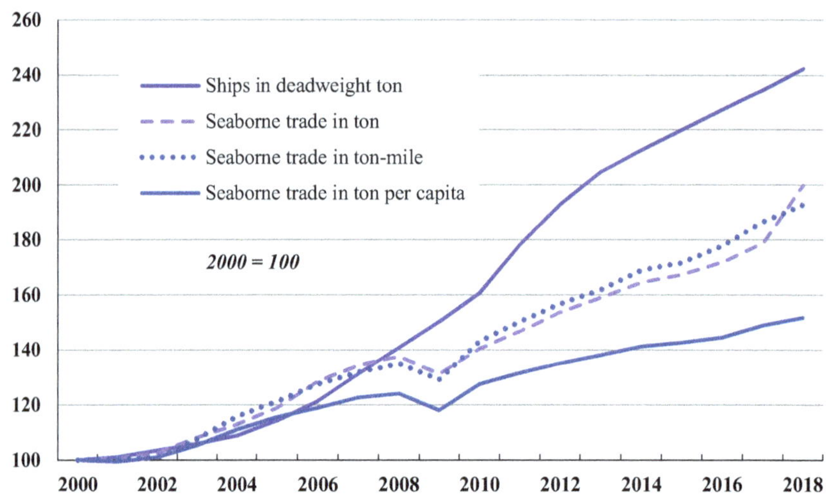

Figure 15.6 Growth Indices of world fleet, seaborne trade in ton, ton-mile and ton per capita 2000–2018, 2000=100.

Source: Shuo Ma, compiled based on data from UNCTAD and Clarksons.

Note: seaborne trade continues to grow in this period. Thanks to economic development and globalisation, seaborne trade per capita in 2018 is 50% more than that in 2000. The world ship tonnage in 2018 is 2.4 times as big as in 2000.

In the Kyoto Protocol, a differentiation scheme between the industrialised and developing countries was adopted. But, in international shipping, it is virtually impossible to make such distinctions. As a result, international shipping had been one of the last sectors without a carbon cap in absolute terms.

What is the new maritime environment agenda after Paris?

In 2015 the Paris Climate Agreement was concluded by the world leaders with an aim to strengthen the global effort to reduce carbon emissions so as to keep the increase of the temperature to well below 2 degrees Celsius and to pursue an effort to limit the temperature increase even further to 1.5 degrees Celsius. The IMO air emission control agenda established in 2018 is in three areas that can be summarised as follows:

> to continue to implement the energy efficiency design index (EEDI) for new ships; to reduce carbon dioxide emissions per transport work on average for international shipping by at least 40% by 2030 compared to 2008 and pursuing efforts towards 70% by 2050; to reach maximum greenhouse gas emissions from international shipping as soon as possible and to reduce the total greenhouse gas emissions by 50% at least by 2050 compared to 2008 and pursuing effort towards eliminating them.[17]

With this agenda, for the first time, a cap in absolute terms with a definite deadline for greenhouse gas emissions from international shipping was established. The total amount of greenhouse gas emissions from international shipping was estimated at 940 million CO_2 equivalent tons for 2008.[18] This means that, according to the ambitions laid out by IMO in 2018, the total amount of greenhouse gas emissions from international shipping should not be more than 470 million CO_2 equivalent tons by 2050. This objective is supposed to be achieved with a growing fleet, possibly at 3%–4% per annum. Continuous and more aggressive efforts ought to be made. It is almost certain that, by using only current technical methods, such as EEDI and operational approaches such as SEEMP, it is unlikely that the maritime transport industry will meet the intended emission goals. More innovative and radically different new technologies and energy are the only hopeful solutions. Based on the known technology and operational structure, it is expected that zero-emission shipping might lead to a 100% increase in freight costs.[19] As discussed previously, the maritime freight cost has been in decline in the long term. Measured in constant money terms, as shown in Figure 1.8, the liner shipping freight in 2018/2019, was merely about 10% of that in 1968. So the impact of such an increase in shipping could be acceptable as long as the whole shipping industry moves together to achieve the goal. It is also feasible to achieve emission-free shipping by going back to the origin of ships: sail. The effects of the future wind-powered cargo ships will mainly be the low speed and small size of shipments, which should also be acceptable.

How do you meet the GHG emission reduction requirements?

For achieving the greenhouse gas (GHG) emission reduction objective, the international maritime community works on a roadmap through the IMO. Possible measures were identified for short-term, mid-term and long-term implementations as a part of the IMO's initial strategy on reduction of greenhouse gas emissions from ships.[20] Among the short-term measures, the application of EEDI, SEEMP and the regulations on speed have a direct impact on the emission levels.

It is obvious that new technology has to be developed and applied to future and probably also existing ships. Between 2008 and 2012 the GHG emissions from international shipping declined by more than 10%, but, to a large extent, this reduction is attributable to slow-steaming, a practice which became popular among shipping companies in the wake of the 2008–2009 financial crisis. Reducing ship's speed is indeed the most effective way of curbing fuel consumption and subsequently cutting air emissions. But this was introduced and accepted thanks to several favourable conditions which happened at the same time. The first is the large and sudden decline of the freight market, which had double effects. On the one hand it forced the shipping companies to save cost by reducing ships' speed and, on the other hand, it made the shippers more willing to accept longer transit time because the additional inventory cost could be compensated for by the lower freight. The second is the high fuel cost which happened during the period and the bunker cost remained at a high level despite the economic crisis. The third factor was the very low interest rates of the major currencies, the US dollar, the Euro and the Yen. So the high bunker prices reinforced the need for slow steaming for the shipping companies and the low interest rates alleviated the pressure for the shippers of higher inventory cost due to slow-steaming. It is unrealistic to assume that such a situation will remain the same in the long run. Therefore, other methods, which are more innovative, sustainable, fundamental and radical than slow-steaming, need to be found.

Traditionally, when the target has been fixed, standards will be made in the form of regulations for industry-wide implementation and enforcement. For example, if "no more than 470 million CO_2 equivalent tonnes of greenhouse gas emissions by 2050" is the target, rules will be made so that the emissions are not exceeding the target. Often more specific technical methods and ways of ship operation are recommended or requested by the authorities. This is also called prescriptive standards. A different approach is known as "goal-based rules".[21] The biggest difference between them is that the former focusses on the means while the latter emphasises the objectives. A prescriptive standard specifies the exact technical method to be used. This method has many merits but limitations too. A goal-based standard sets up the final outcome to be met and the producers or shipping companies are free to use any solution in achieving the goal. It is believed that, by adopting goal-based standards and establishing a system that encourages shipping companies to innovate and find the most suitable and appropriate technical methods and solutions, the shipping industry will have a better chance to achieve the environmental ambitions.

15.5 Market-based measures for emission control

Once the right level of pollution or air emission levels have been identified, deciding on the appropriate course of action is the next critical factor for such levels to be achieved. The traditional method for achieving the objectives has been the so-called *Command-and-Control* approach. This includes the establishment of standards and the enforcement of compliance. So it is also referred to as a quantity instrument. However, command-and-control is not the only way to implement environmental regulations. Another approach is using *market-based methods*. This approach is to rely on a price or a tax, which is levied in proportion to the amount of pollution. So it is also referred to as a price instrument. As far as the authorities are concerned, either national or international, their support for the market-based measures does not contradict a "goal-based" philosophy because such options require the authority's decisions in the first place.

What are the "pros" and "cons" of command-and-control methods?

The "command-and-control" method has several advantages, which has made it appealing and is why it has become the principal method of pollution control of most governments and inter-government bodies such as the IMO. First, it is straightforward and with often an explicit target and clearly defined technical or numerical norms. Second, targeted actions can be quickly taken. When a substance is known to be extremely harmful, e.g., a particular type of paint used on ships, it can effectively limit or eliminate the substance from the market. Third, the producers may like this method partly because industry input is often called for when the standard is set and partly because it may be perceived as being a fair treatment to all producers. Fourth, this approach is quite attractive to both the environmentalists and the politicians because emission standards, which may well be in the form of strong statements, have a symbolic value to demonstrate the activity of a decision-maker in response to the expectations of specific interest groups or the general public.

The standards-based regulatory instruments or the "command-and-control" approach have a number of shortcomings too. A major shortcoming of this type of regulatory instrument is that the very principle of determining the emission standard level may become a disincentive factor for shipping companies to invest in new technology. An investment in new pollution control technology may lead to a reduced control cost, which means a higher optimal control level. We can use Figure 15.7 to illustrate this point. As explained above, the optimal pollution level at which an emission standard is established by the public authority is generally achieved through a competitive bargaining process and such a standard is stabilised and generally accepted when it is close to or at the intersection of the marginal control cost, *MCC*, and the marginal damage cost, *MDC*. Such a principle, however, implies that when costs change, either the *MCC* or *MEC* or both, the emission standard ought to be re-established against the point of the new equilibrium. This is, in fact, where the problem arises. Without regulation, a shipping company would not have taken any pollution-processing measures and would have emitted all waste at point P, whereas, with proper regulation, the initial emission standard was set at P_1. At this point, the ship's pollution control cost is A and B. By regulation, the ship cannot emit more than P_1, but it could improve its profitability by reducing the emission control cost if new technology is introduced. For the shipowner to invest in this technology, they have to be convinced that the cost savings from the use of the new technology will be big enough to recover the investment. Assuming the use of the new technology will enable the shipowner to shift the marginal control cost from *MCC* to MCC_1, and given that the emission standard is always at P_1, the new control cost will be B, the area below the MCC_1 curve, and the net cost saving will be area A. However, the shipowner knows well that such an investment would lead to a reduction of the marginal control cost to MCC_1 and consequently provides the regulatory authorities and environmental advocates with an argument

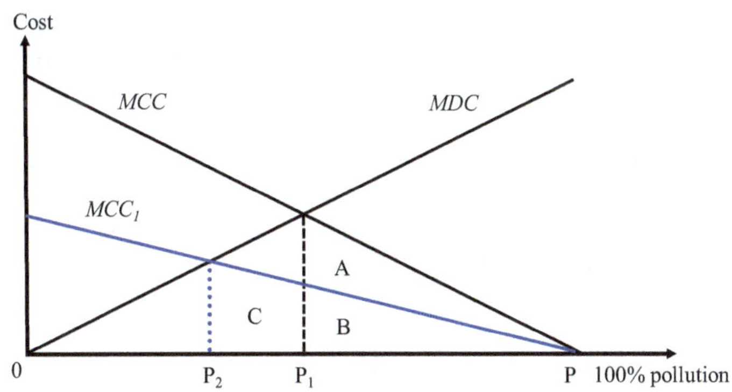

Figure 15.7 Disincentive effect on new technology investment.

Source: Shuo Ma.

Note: investing in new control technology may reduce control cost from *MCC* to MCC_1 allowing a surplus of area A. However, this effort may trigger the re-setting of optimal pollution from P_1 to P_2 and the surplus becomes A–C.

to revise the emission standard by making it more stringent. In such a case, to satisfy the principle of equilibrium of *MCC* and *MDC*, the emission standard will be set at P_2 and the cost savings for the shipowner from the use of the new technology will only be A–C, which may result in the shipping company not investing in the better control technology.

From the above discussion we can see an important implication that the bigger the technological innovation is, the more the reduction in the pollution control cost will be. On the other hand, given the increasing global concerns about the environment and decreasing tolerance level for greenhouse gas emissions, the societal marginal damage cost curve, *MDC*, is likely be higher in the future. So there will be a tendency of the optimal pollution level moving to the left, which means more stringent regulations. With regard to the use of new ship technology, there is an incentive for the shipping companies to advocate for not reducing the emission control cost, so as to maintain the optimal pollution level, and one of the best ways of doing this is by using existing control technologies continuously. This is not in the long-term interest of technological advancement in shipping.

Why are the "market-based methods" more efficient?

One of the most important weaknesses of the command-and-control method is when the technological level of different ships and shipping companies is not the same, which often is the reality. In such a case, a single uniform emission standard will prove to be inefficient. The cheaper and more effective technology should control more emissions than the less efficient technology does. If there are two ships and the marginal control cost is not the same between them, then a lower total control cost will be achieved by using a market-based method. If single emission standards are applied, there will be no distinction between the ships in terms of the type of technology they use. So, by the uniform emission standard, the most cost-effective pollution control can only be achieved if all the ships in question are using identical emission-processing technologies and have the same pollution control costs. The reality is that, in maritime transport as in most other sectors, such a condition does not exist.

Economic instruments for pollution control have several advantages over the "command-and-control" or regulatory approach. By properly employing a market solution, the public authority can effectively achieve the objectives of pollution control with minimum abatement costs and of encouraging the use of clean technology. The economic instruments are mainly in two forms: the first is *emission charges*, which is a kind of tax on emissions, and the second is *tradable emission permits*, which is allocating emission permits to shipping companies and allowing them to trade such permits on the market. By using either method, shipping companies receive an incentive for pollution abatement and greenhouse-gas-emission control on a sustainable basis. As a result, government intervention is minimal and, most important of all, producers are encouraged to adopt new and better technologies of emission control.

Let's begin our discussion on the emission charge approach and compare it with the command-and-control method to see the effect on total control cost and the investment in new technology. An emission charge is a kind of levy expressed in per unit money terms on pollutants or emissions, for example US$30/ton of CO_2 emitted. It is generally imposed by a public authority on producers for the effluent generated from the production. The charge actually represents a message that "pollution is not free". We are interested in how an emission charge would encourage a shipowner to invest in a better method of pollution control and the use of new technology and how much cost can be saved by using an emission charge system.

For example, a shipping company has two ships and, without control, each ship would emit 200 units of CO_2 in a given period. A new command-and-control regulation is introduced by the government to allow a maximum emission of 100 units per ship. To comply with this regulation, every ship ought to control 100 units of emissions. The two ships use different control technologies with different marginal control cost. Ship 1 has an old technology and ship 2 has a new technology which reduces the control cost. The question is about which method, uniform emission standard or emission tax, leads the lowest total control cost. In Figure 15.8 MCC_1 represents the marginal control cost of ship 1 with the old control technology. MCC_2 represents the marginal control cost of ship 2 equipped with the new technology. Under the command-and-control emission standard of 100 units, both ships have to control 100 units. The control cost of ship 1 is BDEFG, and the control cost of ship 2 is BD. The total control cost is BDEFG+BD. If an emission tax T is introduced, it is in the shipping company's interest to control the emission as long as the control cost is lower than the tax. So ship 1 will control 75 units and emits 125 units by paying the tax. As such, the control cost for ship 1 becomes DE. For ship 2, it will control 125 units and emit 75 units by paying the tax. The control cost for ship 2 becomes ABD. For both methods, the total emission and controlled units are the same, but the control costs are different. Compared with a single emission standard, using emission tax means the addition in control cost is A by ship 2 and the reduction in control cost is BFG by ship 1. As BFG is bigger than A, the difference is the gain of efficiency. For achieving the same objective of a total of 200 units of emissions, the market-based method is more cost-effective by allowing the ship with more efficient control technology to control more and the ship with less efficient technology to control less until the marginal control costs of both ships are the same.

This extra cost saving is the incentive for the shipowner to invest in new technology. To understand this point, we can assume that a ship is considering up-grading the control technology so it can move the marginal control cost from MCC_1 to MCC_2. Should such technology be employed, the total control cost would be the area ABD and the tax payment would be T×75. So the net cost savings would be EFGH with EFG as control cost savings and H as tax cost savings. Note that, in the same situation, the total cost savings would only be area EFG if the uniform emission standard is applied. Therefore, area H represents an extra incentive for the shipowner to invest in new technology.

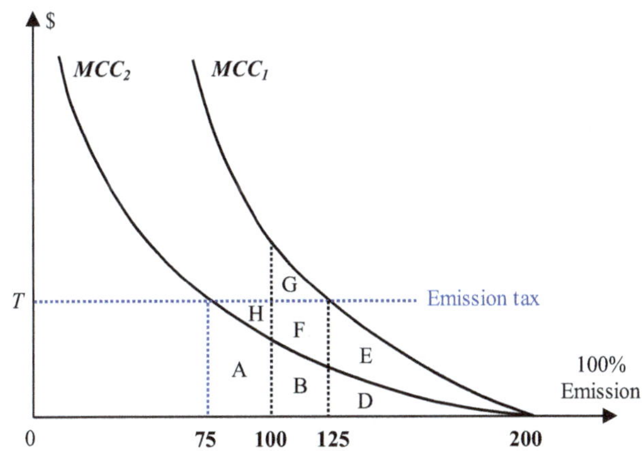

Figure 15.8 Effect of emission tax on control cost and technology.

Source: Shuo Ma.

Note: if two ships have different marginal control cost at MCC_1 and MCC_2, when the marginal control cost is the same for both ships, the total control cost will be the lowest. This can be achieved by pollution tax but not by uniform emission standards.

The positive aspects of emission tax include the following. It may be seen as a fairer system as it limits the chances for special interest groups to influence emission standards. It requires less government intervention than the regulatory approach. It rewards environmentally efficient ships and penalises the inefficient ones. It generates an income, which can be used to support environmental protection in general. However, the emission charge as a pollution control instrument is not perfect. Its major weaknesses include the following. It may be difficult to determine the right charge level, to monitor the pollution and to exercise policy enforcement. As a tax, it may represent a financial burden on producers. It may, therefore, create unfairness between shipping companies if the tax is not levied universally; with market fluctuation, in the short term, when the freight is high, shipping companies, short of sufficient control capability, may prefer to pollute more even if that means paying higher emission charges.

The idea of tradable emission permits finds its origin in the Coase theorem on property rights.[22] The principal idea is that instead of deciding on pollution standards, the public authority defines the total amount of allowable emission which corresponds to the total amount of tolerable pollution. It then lets the market decide on who can pollute or emit and how much. The tradable emission permit is, in essence, designed to create a market for emission rights. What is specific with the emission trading instrument is that periodically the public authority also allocates, either through sale or free distribution, the initial pollution rights or permits among polluters and allows them to trade such permits freely. In the same way as the emission charge system, an emission permit trading system can achieve the environmental objectives with cost efficiency and at the same time provide an incentive for the use of new technology. Let's see how it works.

Assume that two ships are independently operating in the market, which needs to be regulated, as shown in Figure 15.9. Without any environmental regulation, each ship will discharge 200 units of greenhouse gas emissions per year into the air from the operation. The public authority, after a consideration of all the relevant aspects and information, decides to cut the emission level by half and thus issues a total of 200 emission permits representing 200 units of emissions per year. The permits are

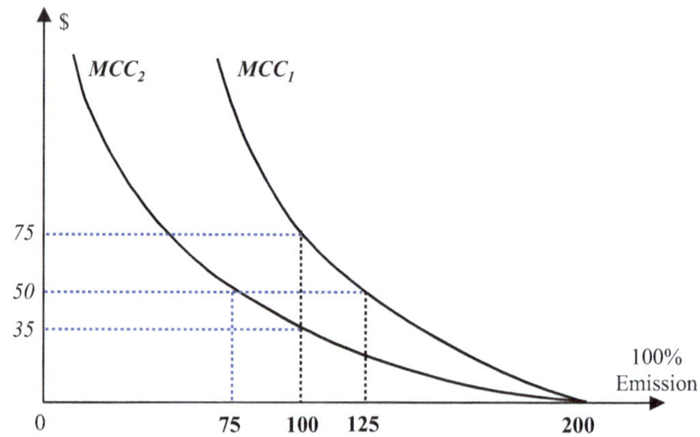

Figure 15.9 Effect of tradable permits on cost and technology.

Source: Shuo Ma.

Note: if two ships have different marginal control cost at MCC_1 and MCC_2, when the marginal control cost is the same for both ships, the total control cost will be the lowest. This can be achieved by pollution tax, but not by uniform emission standards.

equally distributed to the two ships, which means that each ship is allowed to emit 100 units per year into the atmosphere. Supposing that the two ships are using different technologies for emission control, ship 1, which is using less efficient technology, has a marginal control cost represented by curve MCC_1, while ship 2, which is using a new pollution control technology, has the marginal control cost represented by MCC_2. The marginal control cost at the 100th unit is \$75 for ship 1 and \$35 for ship 2. Since the emission permits are transferable, ship 1 would prefer controlling less than 100 units as long as it can buy a permit at a price cheaper than \$75. For the same reason, ship 2 would like to continue to control after 100 units so long as it can sell the permit at a price higher than \$35. The two ships will engage in a mutually beneficial trade of permits continuously until their marginal control costs are the same between them. In this example, this is when the price of the permit is at \$50/unit, the point of the most efficient emission control. Ship 1's benefit is the difference between the savings from controlling less and the cost of additional permits bought. Ship 2 makes a net benefit equivalent to the difference between the prices of permits sold and the additional control cost. From the above analysis we can conclude that, by using a tradable emission permit instrument, while the total emission level remains the same at 200 units, both ships are better off and so is society since the total pollution control cost is reduced. The positive impact of this tradable pollution permit on the use of new technology is similar to the emission tax shown in Figure 15.8.

Under the condition of freely tradable permits, the initial distribution of pollution permits, which is often considered to be a critical and difficult activity of the public authority, does not affect how the permits are finally allocated among emitters through the market mechanism. Obviously, a fair allocation of initial permits is an important issue. The example in Figure 15.9 is a simple case of only two ships. However, the tradable emission permit instrument works better in a big market with a larger number of parties involved in the transaction of the permits. By free trading, the best allocation of environmental resources is achieved, which means that efficient technology is rewarded by being utilised to the maximum while inefficient technology is discouraged through minimal use. Thanks to the free emission trading market, environmental products have a price, which, taking the above example, is \$50 per permit. The amount of transactions is positively correlated with the differences in marginal emission control cost, or the technology level, among the ships. The bigger the divergence of technological levels among ships, the more the trading will be and vice versa. There is no limit to newcomers, even when the maximum emission level has been attained in a market. Since such a cap-and-trade scheme is in a free market system, the price of permits is determined solely by market forces of supply and demand. So, during an economic recession, the price of emission permits may be very low, unless the authority scales down the total permits allocated.

From the analysis of emission tax and emission permit trading, we can see that the two approaches have the same effect regarding cost efficiency. By using either of these approaches, the total control costs can be minimised and the positive impact on incentives to use new technology is also similar. The ultimate choice by the authority between the two methods depends on the following aspects. First, the non-economic factors, such as political acceptability, are very important influential elements and effluent tax is often disliked because of the political sensitivity. The second aspect is concerned with implementation costs which include the transaction cost, for example, in the case of emission permit trading, or control cost.

15.6 Summary

In this chapter we began with an examination of the basic economic characteristics of maritime safety and environmental issues. We concluded that maritime safety and environment protection is an economic subject because it is about choices of, for example, an acceptable safety level or for an optimal emission level. However, traditional economics has failed to allow an efficient allocation of resources with regard to maritime safety and marine environmental products due to the lack of clearly defined property right. Consequently, there is an externality which is the cost external to the economic system generated by production and unpaid by the producer. The purpose of maritime safety and environmental economics is to measure such costs and the ways to internalise the external cost. There is a role for the public authorities to play to internalise externalities. But there are options concerning how and to what extent the government intervention should be.

We also discussed the major differences between safety and environmental problems which are the outcomes of either accidents or operations. Accident-related safety issues require the management of risks and operation-related environmental problems need proper management of wastes. Risk-based rulemaking, such as formal safety assessment, is a new way of establishing maritime safety-related regulations, in which an economic evaluation in the form of cost–benefit analysis is included. When it comes to operation-related waste management, the regulations are supposed to be established at the optimal level when the marginal benefit is equal to marginal cost of regulations. It is, however, difficult to accurately measure the true cost and benefit of environmental products and the reduction of them. The commonly used state-preference method is affected by the local environmental conditions. So, as a result, there is an absence of a common and universal optimal pollution level and regulation standard. Consequently, most regulations take a long time to enter into force and can easily be out of date.

International shipping is responsible for about 2.4% of global greenhouse gas emissions. Without control, this percentage will rise rapidly given the continuous growth of seaborne trade. However, the improvement of fuel efficiency based on the current technology of ship propulsion systems seems to be close to the limit. So, the size of tonnage supply will continue to increase in line with trade growth. It was not until 2018 that the shipping community agreed on an absolute amount of GHG emissions as a target for international shipping, which is to be no more than 50% compared with the 2008 level by 2050. In addition to the existing technical and operational methods, different sources of energy and innovative technologies, methods and practices are needed to meet the ambitious targets.

Market-based methods are demonstrably better and more cost-effective to internalise the external cost and achieve emission control objectives, rather than the traditional uniform standards scheme. What is even more important is that, unlike a command-and-control method with uniform standards that do not differentiate ships using different emission control technologies, market-based instruments provide incentives to those producers who invest in better technologies and favour those who can control emissions at lower costs. There are two main methods: emission charges or emission permit trading. The two different schemes lead to the same result efficiency, but the implementation, administration and operation aspects are different. Adopting market-based approaches does not suggest the absence of government. Actually, public authorities have a very important role to play in setting the appropriate level of emission charges or allocating the right amount of tradable permits.

Notes

1 Opinions were expressed to deny an economic treatment of safety and environment issues: McBurney S. (1990) and Sandel M. J. (1997). "It's Immoral to Buy the Right to Pollute", in Stavins R. N. (2000). Some others advocated that economy should be shaped by the principle of ecology rather than the market: Brown L. R. (2001).
2 Simpson R. D. (1998).
3 Maritime Executive (2018).
4 Farthing B. and Brownrigg M. (1997), pp. 6–21.
5 Drewry Shipping Consultant Ltd (1998), pp. 17–22, pp. 59–87, pp. 40–42, pp. 86–87.
6 Coase R. (1960). Coase developed the theoretical framework for environmental economics by introducing property right in the environmental products.

7 IMO (2013).
8 *The Economist* (2017).
9 IMO (2014a).
10 IMO (2018a).
11 Kite-Powell H. L., Jin D., and Farrow S. (1997).
12 Brown R. S. and Savage I. (1996).
13 Eelco den Beor et al. (2016).
14 Danish Ministry of the Environment (2012). *Economic Impact Assessment of a NOx Emission Control Area in the North Sea*, Environmental Project 1427, 2012. It was stated that "The total cost in 2030 of establishing a NECA is estimated to be €282 million. The environmental impact is assessed in the environmental impact assessment report by PBL at between €443 million and €1,928 million, depending on the applied assessment method and also reflecting the uncertainty of the assessment. The total net benefits to society will equal between €161 million and €1,928 million. This is equivalent to a benefit–cost ratio of 1.6–6.8. On the benefit side a range of benefits are not monetised, which implies an even better benefit–cost ratio."
15 Halin R., Smith T., and Englert D. (2019). It was found that "if a carbon tax of US$ 10–50/ton of carbon dioxide is applied, the maritime transport cost might increase by 0.4 percent to 16 percent and the import prices might increase by less than 1 percent".
16 IMO (2014b).
17 IMO (2018b).
18 Ibid., note 13, p. 72.
19 Bockmann M.W. (2019).
20 Ibid., note 14, pp. 6–8.
21 IMO (2011).
22 Ibid., note 6.

References

Bockmann M.W. (2019) "*Zero-carbon Shipping to Double Freight Costs*", Lloyd's List, 11 September 2019.

Brown L. R. (2001) "*Eco-Economy: Building an Economy for the Earth*", WW Norton, New York, pp. 26–72.

Brown R. S. and Savage I. (1996) "*The Economics of Double-hulled Tankers*", Maritime Policy and Management, Vol. 23, No. 2, pp. 167–175.

Coase R. (1960) "*The Problem of Social Cost*", *The Journal of Law and Economics*, Vol. 3, October 1960, pp. 1–44.

den Beor E. et al (2016) "*SECA Assessment: Impacts of 2015 SECA Marine Fuel Sulphur Limits – First Drawings from European Experiences*", Delft, CE Deltf, April 2016 Publication 16.7H83.43.

Denish Ministry of the Environment. (2012) "*Economic Impact Assessment of a NOx Emission Control Area in the North Sea*", Environmental Project 1427, 2012.

Drewry Shipping Consultant Ltd. (1998) "*Cost of Quality Shipping – The Financial Implications of the Current Regulatory Environment*", Drewry Shipping Consultant Report November 1998, pp. 17–22, 59–87, 40–42, 86–87.

Farthing B. and Brownrigg M. (1997) "*Farthing on International Shipping*", 3rd Edition, Lloyds of London Press, London, pp. 6–21.

Halin R., Smith T., and Englert D. (2019) "*Understanding the Economic Impacts of Greenhouse Gas Mitigation Policies on Shipping*", World Bank, Policy Research Working Paper 8695, January 2019.

IMO. (2011), "*Generic Guidelines for Developing IMO Goal-based Standards*", Annex 1, MSC89/WP.7.

IMO. (2013) "*Guidelines for the Approval of Alternatives and Equivalents as Proved for in Various IMO Instruments*", MSC.1/Circ.1455, 24 June 2013.

IMO. (2014a) "*Periodic Review of Administrative Requirements in Mandatory IMO* Instruments – *Final Report of the Ad Hoc Steering Group for Reducing Administrative Requirements*", C113/11, 20 October 2014.

IMO. (2014b) "*Reduction of GHG Emissions from Ships – Third IMO GHG Study, 2014 – Final Report*", MEPC 67/INF3.

IMO. (2018a) "*Formal Safety Assessment*", Retrieved 10 October 2018 from www.imo.org/en/OurWork/safety/safetytopics/pages/formalsafetyassessment.aspx

IMO. (2018b) "*Initial IMO Strategy on Reduction of GHG Emissions from Ships*", Resolution MEPC. 304 (72) adopted on 13 April 2018, MEPC 72/17/Add.1 Annex 11.

Kite-Powell H. L., Jin D., and Farrow S. (1997) "*Expected Safety Benefits of Electronic Charts and Integrated Navigation Systems*", *Journal of Transport Economics and Policy*, Vol. 31, No. 2, May 1997, pp. 147–162.

Maritime Executive. (2018) "*Maersk Deploys Plastic Clean-up Project in Pacific Garbage Patch*", 6 August 2018. Retrieved on 8 October 2018 from www.maritime-executive.com/article/maersk-to-deploy-plastic-cleanup-project-off-san-francisco.

McBurney S. (1990) "*Ecology into Economics Won't Go*", Green Books, Devon, UK pp. 47–73.

Sandel M. J. (1997) "*It's Immoral to Buy the Right to Pollute*", in Economics of the Environment 2000, edited by R. N. Stavins, W. W. Norton & Company Ltd, Liverpool, pp. 449–451.

Simpson R. D. (1998) "*Economic Analysis and Ecosystems: Some Concepts and Issues*", in Economics of the Environment 2000, edited by R. N. Stavins, W.W. Norton & Company Ltd, Liverpool, pp. 529–541.

The Economist. (2017) "*Grudges and Kludges*", Regulation, United States, The Economist, 4 March 2017, pp. 29–31.

Chapter 16

Digital disruption and the future of maritime transport

The maritime transport sector is about to undergo a technological transformation, probably the largest in history, which will change the entire industry completely. It is the digital transformation, a real process of disruption or the 3rd maritime technological revolution as described in Chapter 9. It is the application of advanced digital analytics methods and techniques, including machine learning, which can help interpret events so as to support and automate decision making and actions. The impact of the digitalisation is so significant that, within a foreseeable future, virtually every activity of the sector will be completely restructured. Many existing businesses will shrink and eventually disappear or will be integrated into others; some activities will grow and new ones will emerge. In any event, the way of doing business in the digital era will be very different from that of today. The reason for the digital disruption to have begun now is mainly because of the technological breakthroughs in three particular areas of digitalisation. The post-digitalisation maritime transport of the future will be more efficient thanks mainly to automation and more effective thanks mostly to the discovery of unknown business patterns. While the grand direction and the long-term perspectives are almost matters of certainty, the questions of when, where, how, by whom, etc., do not have precise answers. This is because, on the one hand, it is only the beginning of the great digital disruption and the technology is changing and progressing so rapidly that no one knows the exact processes. On the other hand, the answers to these questions depend partially on the barriers and resistance encountered in each specific circumstance as well as the abilities of the stakeholders to overcome them. In this chapter we will discuss the main reasons and the root causes of the changes. We will also examine the possible features of the maritime digital transformation.

16.1 An analysis of shipping and related activities

Maritime transport is about the physical and spatial movement of goods from one place to another by ships, and this is the ultimate purpose and the final product of the sector. For this to happen, a series of other related activities is also needed. We will first examine the digital nature of shipping and related tasks. What is the core activity? What are the inputs required? How are incomes made and expenses incurred? The discussion of these questions is vital for assessing the impact of digitalisation. In this section our analysis of the shipping-related activities will be from three angles: shipping-centric, outcome–input and cash-flow.

What are the shipping-centric maritime activities?

The transport of cargo by ship from one port to another is at the core of all maritime activities. All other activities are supportive activities. As the core activity is operated and managed by shipping companies, we will take a closer look at the activities and the systems supporting the core. Over the course of the last centuries, maritime transport has evolved to become an extensive and complex system, with the shipping of cargo at the centre supported by various other activities, as illustrated by Figure 16.1, and as in Chapter 13 we divide the shipping cost into three groups: the capital cost, the operation cost and the voyage cost. The supportive maritime activities can be divided in the same way into those regarding the ship, those regarding the operation and those regarding the voyage. We will discuss them briefly as follows.

- ***Ship-related activities.*** In this group there are activities such as shipbuilding, ship financial services provided by, for example, financial market or banks, the classification of ships, which begins from the stage of ship design until the end of the ship's economic life, and marine insurance.
- ***Ship-operation-related activities.*** In this group we have activities such as ship operation and management. The education and training of seafarers as well as technical, crewing and ship management companies should also be included in this group. Marine insurance, ship repair and maintenance are also provided. There are ship owners who outsource technical and manning management to specialised third-party companies. The national and international maritime administration also belongs to this group, which includes ship registration.
- ***Voyage-related activities.*** This is about cargo transport. In this group we have maritime legal services, which are needed sometimes for ship-related matters, such as chartering contracts, sometimes for shipping-related matters, such as freight payment or insurance claim on cargo damage.

Figure 16.1 Eleven core and supportive maritime transport activities.

Source: Shuo Ma.

Note: the above activities are the most important ones. Shipping companies doing ship operation and management is at the core which is supported by other maritime activities.

At ports, ship bunkering and supply services are provided to ships, in relation not only to the type of ship but also the type of transport it is engaged with. Other shipping services are also included such as shipbroking, and ship and port agency, which are activities concerning commercial aspects of shipping. Port and cargo handling are important activities in this category, which cover services to both ship/crew and cargo.

Figure 16.1 shows the complex shipping system which consists of 11 main maritime transport activities, with ship operation and management at the core and many supportive sectors. The diagram is representative rather than exhaustive, and there are more activities. Originally, all of them were all integrated and undertaken by the same trader/ship owner. But shipping developed, specialisation started and activities are divided into sectors.

What are the characteristics of maritime activities based on outcome and input?

Let's now look at the maritime activities summarised in Figure 16.1 but from the following two different angles, namely, the type of outcome expected and the type of input required. We will concentrate on the 11 types of activities, which cover the major aspects of what the shipping sector does. Regarding the expected outcome, our focus will be on the results to which the decision or action will lead. It is the purpose of an activity. Regarding the required input, our focus will be on the main elements needed for the decision or action to be taken. Such an analysis should allow us to understand the function and aim of each type of activity. Obviously, all activities are executed by people. So this can also be seen as a people-centric analysis. Reference is also made to Table 13.1 for our analysis.

Let's begin with the core activity of *ship operation and management*, which includes both shore- and ship-based operation of ships. The expected outcome is the carriage of goods from a loading port to a discharging port. The outcome is the physical movement of cargo. For this to happen, ships should be operated by seafarers. The seafarers need to take decisions and actions based on the information related to the ship and navigation. This includes information about the ship and navigational conditions and the instructions regarding the transport. The seafarers should use their knowledge and experience to evaluate the information and take decisions and actions accordingly. This process is illustrated in Figure 16.2, which reads from the right to the left: to produce the expected outcome of cargo transport, the activity of ship operation ought to be undertaken, which requires the input of information and instructions.

We can also make a similar analysis of input and outcome for the other ten main maritime activities in the same fashion, as shown in Table 16.1. We should keep in mind that most of these activities, though they look quite different from one another and are undertaken separately, were integrated

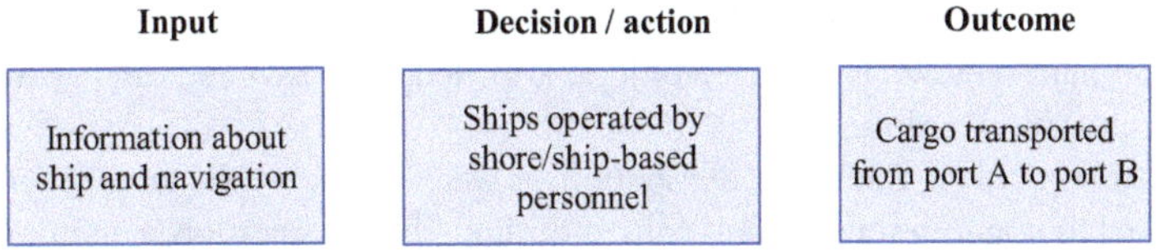

Figure 16.2 Input and outcome of ship operation and management activities.

Source: Shuo Ma.

Note: seafarers need the ship and navigation-related information as well as transport-related instructions to complete cargo transport.

at the early stage of international shipping before specialisation. Because of the differences between them, when the demand increased, and for the sake of productivity and efficiency, the activities were separated to become specialised operations. Here is a brief discussion of the nature of outcomes and inputs for the other ten activities. As far as the inputs are concerned, we use the data in Table 13.1.

- ***Shore-based ship operation and management.*** This is the kind of activity ship owners or shipping companies do. It was separated from on-board ship operation as maritime transport became more complex and ship–shore communication improved. The outcome is to take commercial decisions and subsequently to provide ships, crew and related people with directions and instructions for the transport of cargo. The activity is undertaken by people with the relevant knowledge and experience based on the input of information and data on the market.
- ***Shipbuilding and repair.*** Shipbuilding may or may not be considered as an integral part of the maritime transport system. It is more about the manufacturing industry than about transport services. This activity is to provide ships, the means of transport, to shipping companies. The outcome is obviously the ships built and sold. The activity is undertaken by shipyards based on the input of materials and information from the market.
- ***Ship financial services.*** These relate to the activities of financial institutions, including banks, which are involved in providing the funding for ships. Therefore, the outcome is the settlement of funding with agreed conditions. To do so, the financial institutions need mostly two sorts of information, as input, on the customer and the market.
- ***Classification of ships.*** The purpose of this activity is to set up, maintain, verify and certify technical standards of the ships from construction to operation. It is done by classification societies. The chief outcome is to provide ships with technical certifications. To do so, they need the input of technical and regulatory information.
- ***Marine insurance.*** This is to cover the loss or damage incurred to ships and cargo during maritime transport. The activity is undertaken by insurance companies. The outcome is in the form of coverage of the losses and damages, the input is the insurance terms and conditions and the activity is the information about the accident, etc.
- ***Shipbroking and agency.*** As the name suggests, the purpose of shipbroking and agency is to bring together sellers and buyers of ships or shipping services. The outcome of the activity is, therefore, an agreement reached and a contract concluded. The input required is the knowledge of the brokers and agents and the information about customers and the business concerned. Freight forwarders are not included here as they represent mainly importers and exporters.
- ***Port and cargo handling services.*** The outcome of port activities is safe berthing and the loading and unloading of cargo. Ports, which refers to the port community with different stakeholders, should, therefore, have the necessary facilities and equipment. They should also have the input of information and instruction from shippers and ship owners.
- ***Maritime court and legal services.*** The outcome of legal services is to prepare legal documents and to help customers settle legal cases. Legal workers or firms are employed to undertake the activity. The type of input required is the relevant legal knowledge on laws and cases as well as the information on customers' claims.
- ***Ship registration.*** This is about the registration of ships by the public authorities. The outcome includes establishing rules and regulations regarding ship registration, conditions on taxation, supervision of ship safety and marine environmental performances, flag state and port state control, etc. These activities require the input of policy as well as the information on the ships.
- ***Maritime education and crew management.*** Specialised schools and academies provide maritime education and training services. Crew management companies provide technical services to shipping companies. The outcome is educated people with specialised knowledge and crew management skills. Knowledge and information on maritime transport are the inputs needed for the activities.

To sum up the above discussion, as shown in Table 16.1, is that among the 11 main maritime transport activities there is a major difference between the outcomes and the inputs. Regarding the *outcomes*, there are more variations. Some activities have outcomes in the form of physical changes, such as ship management and operation, or shipbuilding, or cargo handling or bunkering service at ports. Other activities have outcomes of a rather intangible nature. They include, for example, the shore-based ship operation and management, or activities such as maritime administration, classification of ships, marine insurance, or shipbroking, or education and training. When it comes to the nature of the *input*, there are more similarities between activities. Data, information and instructions are the types of input needed for carrying out the activities.

Table 16.1 The types of input and outcome of major maritime activities

	Type of outcome	*Type of input*
1. Ship management and operation	Safe transport of cargo by ships	Navigation and ship knowledge and information
2. Shipbuilding and repair	Contract preparation and conclusion	Technical, commercial and operational knowledge and information
3. Ship financial services	Secured funding with conditions	Financial, commercial and market knowledge and information
4. Classification of ships	Class given on seaworthiness to ships	Technical, regulatory knowledge and information about ships
5. Marine insurance	Coverage of risks for ships	Technical, financial knowledge and information about ship and navigation
6. Ship broking and agency	Contract preparation and conclusion	Technical, commercial and operational knowledge and information
7. Port and cargo handling services	Safe berth of ships and loading/unloading of cargo	Information and instruction from ship owner and shippers
8. Ship bunkering and supply services	Ship bunker and provision supplied	Information and instruction from ship owner
9. Maritime court and legal services	Customer is assisted, its interest defended and legal case settled	Legal knowledge and information on cases
10. Ship registrition	Ship registery, regulation, survey, control	Policy, technical and organizational knowledge and information
11. Training and crew management	Education and management of crew	Knowledge and information about relevant maritime transport subjects

Source: Shuo Ma

Note: The input and outcome descriptions are indicative and representative rather than exact and complete.

What is a cash-flow-based analysis of maritime activities?

An important reason for the transport of cargo by ships as the unique core of all maritime activities is also the fundamental difference regarding the source of cash flow. As an activity delivering the final "product" to trade, the transport of cargo by ship is the only business that is paid for by the external source of the maritime transport system. And that is the inflow of cash from international trade in the form of maritime freight. All other maritime activities are selling services to the shipping companies, which use the cash received from trade to pay for the supportive services. Such differences are shown in Figure 16.3. The cash flow received in the form of maritime transport freight is shared within the sector. A very large part of this amount is passed on as out-going cash flow from shipping companies to other maritime activities against their services.

From cash-flow directions we can see the central position of ship operation and the supportive role of other activities. It is difficult to know the exact situation of cash flow of each activity or to tell how this total inflow of cash to ship operation is distributed among various businesses. However, there is a general difference in business size. Some are large, providing substantive value-added activities and absorbing large portions of cash flow, and others are rather small in business scope, often attached to the main sectors. Some activities employ many people, while others create fewer jobs. Based on the characteristics of cash flow, the 11 main maritime activities can be divided into four groups, namely, ship operation, ship acquisition, port operation and maritime services. A large portion of the cash flow received by shipping management and operation goes to each of the three groups, which are discussed as follows.

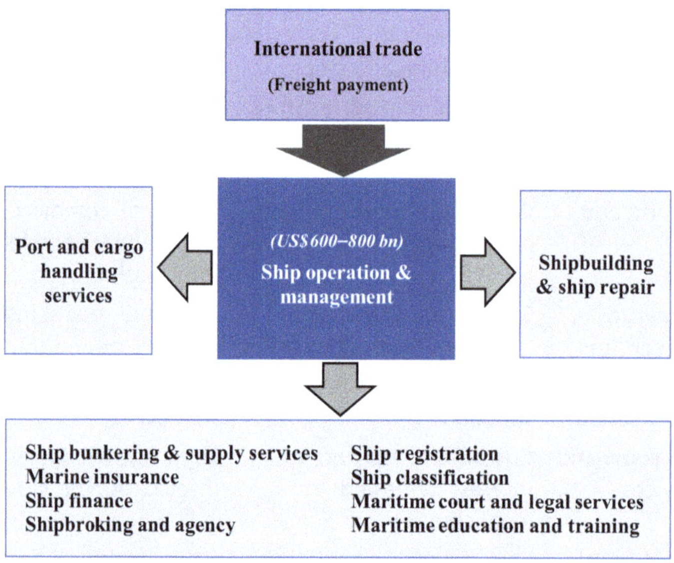

Figure 16.3 In-flows of cash for major maritime activities.

Source: Shuo Ma.

Note: as the activity delivers the final "product", the transport of cargo by ships operated by shipping companies is the only activity receiving in-flow cash from outside the maritime transport sector. All other activities receive cash from shipping companies by selling services to them.

- ***Ship operation***. Ship operation is placed before ship acquisition because this is the core business. This is the activity which is paid for directly by shippers and it is the in-coming cashflow from outside the shipping sector, while most other activities are paid for by shipping companies. As discussed in Chapter 14, the size of the international shipping market can be measured by the total freight received for the transport service. This amount is difficult to estimate due to the fact that the maritime freight market is highly competitive and volatile. But a gross calculation, based on the differences between the prices of trade on FOB and CIF terms, suggests that the total maritime freight is approximately 5% of the global import value. Taking the freight fluctuation into account, the total freight would be in the region of US$600 and 800 billion per year. The shipping companies receive freight against the provision of transport services. To do so they have to buy the necessary product and services by using part of freight received, as shown in Figure 16.3.
- ***Ship acquisition and ship finance***. The first asset a shipping company needs to have is a ship. Ships are expensive assets worth tens or even hundreds of millions of dollars apiece. The total capital cost of ships would be some 10% to 15% of the total freight received by the shipping companies.[1] If the cost of other equipment, such as containers, and the cost of ship repair and maintenance are included, the cash flow would be over US$100 billion per year.
- ***Port operation and cargo handling***. Port-related costs have two parts, service-based and time-based. Service-based costs include tax and dues, the cost of cargo handling, storage, etc. Cargo-handling cost can be very high at some ports. Time-based costs, on the other hand, refer mainly to the inventory cost of ship and cargo. Both ships and cargo spend a long time in ports. Many ships trading in short-haul markets may spend more time in ports than at sea. Depending on the value of vessels, the time cost varies and may be extremely high. As a result, shipping companies pay a substantial part of the cash received to cover port-related costs and services.
- ***Maritime services***. This is the third group of activities for which shipping companies buy inputs from other maritime sectors. An extensive range of activities is included here, from ship registration and classification to ship finance, insurance, shipbroking and maritime legal services. In this group the cost of seafarers and shore-based personnel is one of the most expensive inputs for shipping companies. Other costly items include bunkering and insurance costs. The cashflow needed for these services is not fixed because the services are subject to the changing markets.

In this section we have examined maritime transport activities from three distinctive aspects: from the relationship between them, from the nature of outcome and input of each activity and the features of cash flow of each activity. These discussions are necessary because they pave the way for the analysis of the rest of the chapter. The reviews help and enable us to appreciate how and to what extent each maritime activity is affected by digitalisation and automation as well as the possible consequences. They also help us understand the skills required for the activities and the impact of digitalisation on them. No maritime activity can escape from being disrupted by AI, digitalisation and automation. But the transport of cargo as the core activity will not disappear.

16.2 Digitisation and programmability of maritime activities

The bio-scientists say that at the deepest measurable microscopic level of matter is the information, or data, composed of bits or units of information expressed in binary notation as either zero or one.[2] Everything is digital or can be expressed digitally. Although it is a debated subject, for maritime transport we could say that most of the activities are about dealing with information and data, which can be converted, expressed and transferred digitally. If shipping is digital, it should possibly be done digitally. As all activity discussed in the above section refers to things done by a person or a group of persons, in this section we will concentrate on different maritime professions and the working procedure and method.

By *digitisation* we refer to the process of changes from analogue to digital form. This is different from *digitalisation*, which refers to the digital transformation or the restructuring process using digital technologies; by *programmability* we refer to the aspect of particular standardised ways of undertaking the activity in question. Based on the discussions in Chapter 13, particularly Table 13.1, and in the previous section, we will examine the digitisation level of information in shipping and the programmability degree of each maritime activity. We will concentrate on three groups of activities. First, we will look at the ship operation and management of both shore and ship-based activities, partly because this is the core activity of maritime transport and partly because it distributes cash flows to other businesses. Then we will analyse the port sector to see which part of the port operation is digital and programmable and which part is not. Finally, we will go through the major maritime services by examining the digitalisation and programmability nature of each of them.

To what extent are ship operations digitised and programmable?

Ships are operated by both shore-based managers and ship-based crew members. Ship managers make three kinds of decisions regarding financial, commercial and technical aspects concerning ship operation. Financial management includes the decisions related to purchasing and sale of ships, fund-raising and debt service, evaluation of investment options, etc. Commercial management involves the decisions related to ship-chartering, shipping route design, communication with shipmasters and agents, negotiation and conclusion of transport and service contracts with charterers, shippers, ports, agents, insurers, etc. Technical management involves the decisions mainly related to crew management, ship maintenance and repair, etc. Despite the differences between them, the three types of activities have many common features in terms of the skills and knowledge required. As we saw in Table 13.1, under Maritime Jobs – Category 3: Maritime Managers and Specialists, their activities consist mainly of planning, ship routeing, dispatching, tracking transport shipment, etc. The discussion below is about to what extent these activities are digitised and programmable.

- ***Financial management***. Can the inputs and outcomes of this category of activities be expressed digitally? A ship investment decision is usually highly complex. It requires the input of a wide range of knowledge and the analysis of a large number of variables covering multiple sectors. Most factors concerning technical specifications of ships and financial conditions can certainly be presented in a digital format. Other factors, such as market perspectives, economic sentiment, social and policy decisions and the situation of competition, etc., are more difficult to convert into digital formats. Regarding programmability, some financial-management-related decisions are standard and rule-based. They include, for example, the financial performance parameters and KPIs or credit rating of the borrowing companies, or loan conditions offered by the lending institutions. Many rules and principles can be developed and cause–effect relations can be established. There is, therefore, a possibility for some basic decisions to be structured and programmed. But, again, as financial decisions frequently involve competition, negotiation and personal relations, these may be too complex to be standardised and programmed for now.
- ***Commercial ship management***. The activities in this category include the negotiation and conclusion of the transport contract, but also marketing and customer service, etc. For doing so, the input, the outcome and the process could, in theory, be largely digitised, though some elements are highly complex, especially when they concern market forecasting, and are similar to the decisions of financial management. In many companies, particularly the liner shipping sector, a high level of digitisation is already a reality, in that most inputs and outcomes of management are all in digital format. With regard to the programmability of commercial management of ships, most of the decision making is still not totally standardised. In the liner shipping sector the work process is more structured with clearly defined rules and guidelines. The decision-making process is, to

a large extent, programmable because there is a definite number of variables to consider and the rules and the relations between the variables are known.

- ***Technical ship management***. Under this title the main activities include crew management and technical support for ships. It is possible to digitise the process though, when managing people, personal involvement is an important and inevitable part. Digitisation of the ship maintenance process is more feasible with technical records and scheduling of routine maintenance. However, when a major repair is to be undertaken, complex technical evaluation is required. The survey results can be in a digital format. With the need for personal contacts and given case-specific differences in the need for ship repair, the programmability level of the activities will not generally be very high.

As far as shipboard management is concerned, the seafarers' activities can be divided into two categories regarding navigation and engines. The digitisation of most of the operational input, outcome and processes has been going on for some time and the trend will continue and accelerate.[3] The shipboard activities belong to category 1 of maritime jobs according to Table 13.1 and they are much dependent on experience, which means a good memory of many cases and an ability to connect them with some rules.

- ***Navigation-related activities*** such as watchkeeping are undertaken by crew members and they involve making decisions and giving orders based on data collected, the rules, knowledge and experience of navigation and the observation of the environment. Part of the input has been digitised, for example electronic chart display and information systems (ECDIS) have replaced paper charts for navigation.[4] Some other parts are still analogue, such as printed rules and instructions in paper format. But they can be easily digitised. As far as programmability is concerned, the activities are theoretically programmable though, in practice, the activities can only be programmed after being digitised.
- Regarding ***engine-related activities***, the situation is less complex because modern merchant ships with unmanned engine rooms have been in service for a long time. Such autonomous systems rely on digital processes and operational programmes. So the input, outcome and process related to the operation of marine engines are digitised. The number and the characteristics of influential variables as well as the engine-related cause–effect relations are well known. As a result, activities related to marine engine and propulsion systems are highly programmable.

How digital and programmable are port operations?

As discussed in Chapter 10, port operations can be broadly divided into two main groups: ship related and cargo related. *Ship-related activities* include safe navigation, bunker and other supplies, repair and maintenance services. The provision of navigational aids and the maintenance of navigational channels can be digitised, though to digitise some navigational services, such as pilotage and towage, may be more challenging. The level of programmability varies. It is generally possible to programme a ship's navigational manoeuvring for auto-navigation-guidance in the port area. The supply of bunker, water and other provisions for ships and crew can be relatively digitised for a certain degree of automation, though the programmability relies on the integration of different systems. When it comes to ship repair and maintenance, the activities are complex and case-specific, so the input, outcome and process can be digitised, but, apart from some routine maintenance, they are hard to programme.

Regarding cargo-related port activities, there are four types of operations, namely, ship–shore operation, cargo-transfer operation, storage operation and delivery operation. One of the critical features of cargo-related port operations is that, given a high level of inter-dependence and interreaction between them, the four operations ought to be synchronised and closely coordinated as a whole. The efficiency of one operation cannot be improved unless that of other operations are also improved by a similar extent.

- ***Ship–shore cargo handling operation***. This is about the handling of cargo on and off ships. The information and data needed can be digitised and have generally been digitised. The work process is repetitive and standardised, so therefore is programmable. In an increasing number of ports the ship–shore cargo handling operation has been automated.
- ***Cargo transfer operation***. This is about moving cargo between the storage and the waterfront with specialised equipment. The information received and generated can undoubtedly be in a digital format. The working procedures are clearly defined and can be programmed. Again, some ports have automated this operation.
- ***Cargo storage operation***. This is about keeping the cargo temporally in a yard or a warehouse. Similar to the above situations, the information about this operation can also be digitised and the process is programmable.
- ***Cargo delivery and reception operation***. This is about what happens at the gate of a port. Information about the cargo and the transport concerned is collected. It can be presented in digital format. The process is programmable.

Based on the analysis in Chapter 13, people working in the port, such as stevedores, need a limited amount of education and preparation. The activities are of a repetitive and operational nature.

What is the situation of digitisation and programmability in maritime services?

Due to the similarities among maritime services and the fact that they are in support of shipping companies, we discuss the different services together. Based on the size of value-added, some services are significant, such as marine insurance or ship finance, others are less so, such as ship registry or legal services. We will see whether or not the information and data needed are in digital format and to what extent the processes are programmable. The analysis below is made based on Table 13.1 in which maritime services fall under category 2 of maritime jobs and some under category 3. Communication and coordination are the main skills required for undertaking the activities.

- ***Ship registry***. All information needed about the ship, the ship owner, as well as the conditions and the outcome of registration service is possible to hold in a digital format. There is a standard process to follow, though individual cases may require personal attention. The bulk of the work is programmable.
- ***Marine insurance***. This is one of the most specialised maritime activities requiring extensive experience. While most of the information and data used for marine insurance can be in digital format, the situation of claims is more diverse because each case is different and a specific investigation is needed, so, as a result, some of the processes are not programmable.
- ***Ship classification***. This is about the technical standards and conditions of ships. Both inputs and outcomes can generally be presented digitally. Although the physical surveys of vessels by classification societies will be needed much less in the future, it is not easy to do these digitally. Thus, not all the work processes can be programmed.
- ***Shipbroking***. The information used can be in a digital format. But the activity usually involves personal contact with the interpretation of the contract, explanation of the situation and negotiation of the conditions, so it is difficult to programme the process.
- ***Ship agency***. As a shipping intermediary, a shipping agent mainly collects and provides information on ship or cargo. They also provide services related to logistics. Such information can be put in a digital format. Some of the services can also be digitised. A good part of the process can be programmed.

- ***Ship finance.*** The financial institutions, such as banks, need the information to make decisions and this can be in a digital format. Decision making also requires market analysis and forecasting, which are usually difficult to programme, although this is about to change thanks to AI and algorithms.
- ***Maritime legal service.*** Lawyers work with information such as judicial rules, legal documents and cases. This can be in a digital format. A good part of their work process can be programmed. Although, when representing their customers in legal processes, personal involvement is necessary.

Which maritime activities are more digitisable and programmable?

Digitisation is the pre-condition for digitalisation. It means that, first of all, all information, data, knowledge, communications and activities of maritime businesses should be digitised. Then, by using digital technologies and analytics, the decision-making processes and activities are carried out automatically or digitalised. Not all decision-making processes and activities can be digitalised. Those that can be are called programmable processes, which are less dependent on subjective judgement. In the above discussion we selected some major maritime activities and made some estimates about the levels of digitisation and programmability of each activity. It was done mainly based on the earlier analysis in Chapter 13 of the skills and knowledge needed for undertaking the main maritime activities. It is difficult to measure the exact levels of digitisation and programmability because of the complex relations between different maritime activities and, even for the same activity, differences exist from one period to another and from one place to another. The purpose of such indicative estimates is to have an idea about the impact of digitalisation on various maritime activities.

The estimated levels of digitisation and programmability of the main maritime activities are shown in Figure 16.4, which is a matrix with four sections. The horizontal axis represents the digitisation level and the vertical axis represents the programmability level. The estimates are made based on the above analysis and Table 13.1. Cargo-handling activities are routine and repetitive with well-established operational rules and procedures. So it falls in the section of high digitisation and high

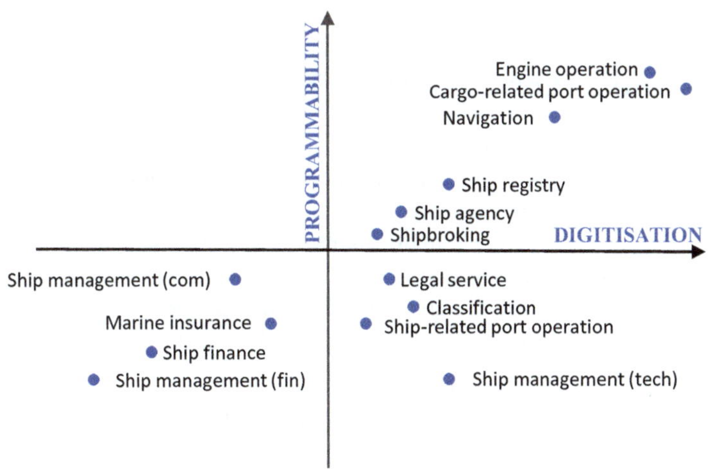

Figure 16.4 Digitisation and programmability of main maritime activities.

Source: Shuo Ma.

Note: the digitisation and programmability levels are estimates only and they vary over time and place. The two variables are correlated.

programmability. The same is true for shipboard operations and, to a lesser extent, ship registry, ship agency and legal service. Some other activities, such as ship-related port operations or ship-broking, have high digitisation levels but a low level of programmability because the decision making requires more analysis and subjective judgement. The activities like ship finance, marine insurance or shore-based ship operations are in the section of low digitisation and low programmability. These activities still require a lot of personal contact and the handling of specific cases with a complex and different background. For them the level of digitisation is low and there is a lack of standard decisions so far. There is no activity falling into the section with low digitisation but a high level of programmability. There are activities that are digitised but not as much programmable. It is important to notice that the two variables are positively correlated ($r^2=0.78$). It means that, generally, a sector with a high level of digitisation is more likely to also have a high level of digitalisation, and vice versa.

16.3 Breakthroughs in digital technology and the impact on shipping

Digitalisation is different from digitisation. Digitisation is about the change of form and digitalisation is about the change of action or the business itself. However, a pertinent question to answer is why many maritime activities have not been digitalised, even though many of them are already in digital form. In this section we will discuss why digitalisation of the maritime transport sector did not happen in the past and why it is happening now.

Part of the answer to the question is that digitalisation was not possible until recently because some key technological breakthroughs happened only recently. Such new digital technologies are of various kinds, which can be broadly divided into three groups tackling three critical areas of digitalisation: data acquisition, data processing and data mining. More specifically, the first area of technologies is about the collection, transfer and storage of all kinds of data. The second area of technologies is about the algorithms and analytics, which lead to the finding of answers to questions and the creation of customer value. The third area of technologies is related to the massive enhancement of processing and computing power for data mining. We will discuss them one by one.

Why is data acquisition a key factor?

Correct decisions can hardly be made without adequate information. However, people often have to make decisions with limited information due simply to the unavailability of sometimes even critical data. The causes of shipping accidents are very often linked to inadequate and incomplete information when making decisions. Of course, the information in this context should also include specialised knowledge and experience. So, information and data are the essential ingredients without which even the best analytical capabilities will not be able to produce the right decisions. So to collect, transfer and store necessary and as complete as possible data is the crucial first step. Let's discuss each of these steps.

- ***Technological breakthroughs in data collection***. In maritime transport a lot of information and communication is in digital form. Internally, the use of ERP systems in firms and organisations transformed the *data/information* from the analogue form on paper to the digital form in computers in an integrated manner. Externally, communication with customers, including all shipping documents, is increasingly made in a digital format and often integrated with the company's CRM system. There is still a lot of uncollected information regarding the work of seafarers, the conditions of equipment, the changes in the external environment and market conditions, etc. One of the main reasons for such data not being collected is the lack of technical means, not only for the collection but also for the process and use of the data. This situation has started to change. The *voice* *and image recognition and digitisation* technologies have made remarkable progress. The technology in the area of onboard *digital sensors* is quickly getting better and more affordable than before, which leads to the development of the *Internet of Things*, leading to an explosive increase in data collected.

- ***Technological breakthroughs in data transfer***. Most of the data/information is a kind of happening data that needs to be collected live in real-time. The difficulties are not only in the collection of such data but also how to transfer it to the database continuously and dynamically for data processing based on cloud computing or edge computing.[5] It ought to be moved back and forth between electronic devices and between computers. Optic fibre and wireless communication technologies have made the transfer of a large quantity of data possible. Ship–shore communications rely on satellite communication technologies. For land-based maritime activities, thanks to the development of new wireless communication technology such as 5G, autonomous vehicles are capable of operating at high speed. An example would be an automated container port, where the use of 5G wireless communication technology is critical for maintaining a high level of productivity and fast but safe cargo-handling operations.[6]
- ***Technological breakthroughs in data storage***. The storage of an enormous amount of data which increases at an explosive rate is always a challenge. Thanks to the technological advancements in the area of data memory as well as internet-based big cloud computing servers and distributed edge computing capability, data can generally be stored and processed either centrally or locally. With more progress made in the related technologies, the storage of an extremely large and ever-growing amount of data is highly likely to be more effective at an increasingly reduced cost in the future.[7] It is vital that data is adequately filtered and appropriately sorted and labelled before storage in a standard and structured way. For example, not all information during a charter party negotiation and conclusion needs to be kept. Irrelevant data are not the only elements to be filtered out as some sensitive information should also not be included. For retrieving and using the data stored, it should be labelled correctly in the first place. For instance, data reflecting the on-going process and data about results are to be identified with different labels.

Why is the algorithm a key to deriving value from data?

The significance and real meaning of *big data* are not about data or the size of it. It is about the findings from the data or the discovery of patterns, models and answers to questions from the analysis of a lot of data. Data is a resource, not a final product. To make sense of big data, one has to employ suitable methodologies for data processing. The outcomes are the solutions, decisions, tasks and actions.

In the same way as in any other business, to succeed in highly competitive maritime transport it is the quality of decisions that is paramount. So data adequacy and the ability to derive rules and solutions by linking relevant elements from the data are the determining factors. Or, in other words, all bad decisions are due to the lack of the right data and the ability to derive useful information from it. These are often expressed as uncertainties or risks. For example, a ship owner may buy a ship which does not have the expected market demand because he does not have the data. Or a maritime underwriter may accept a low premium for the ignorance of high risk because he does not know the key information. Thanks to the fast development of digitisation, data is becoming increasingly available. The crucial factor is, therefore, the ability to find the answers to questions by using the data. There are two basic methods for data processing which we will briefly discuss as follows.

- The first is ***to model the best practices***, so it is also called an expert system. The idea is to simulate the actions experts would take in similar situations. It relies on past experiences recorded in big data. Algorithms are used to identify the relationship between the variables and the expected action. Consequently, a course of action can be pre-programmed based on the known relationships and the inputs on the variables. For example, to assess a ship investment proposal, an expert system can be built based on the variable input and the cause–effect relations that an expert would use in dealing with similar cases. When a sufficient size of database is built with a big pool of cases, the algorithm should be capable of evaluating any new projects almost as well as the experts do. However, such a system can hardly solve a problem which has not been seen before or deal with unexpected circumstances. The system is meant to mimic human experts as closely as possible, but not to surpass them.

- Another method is about a "deep learning" approach. This comes from the relatively new development of artificial intelligence or AI. The system finds out the best solutions from the principles by using the algorithm called *machine learning*. With the input of the rules, principles and the expected goals, the algorithm can find the best solutions that were unknown previously. The calculation process is independent of the experience. Instead of relying on records of the past or the expertise of experts, the machine learning system generates its own data. It is validated by neuroscience. This is a very potent and revolutionary approach because it may reveal new and original ways to reach the best outcomes that people never know about. This development is so new that we have not seen its applications in shipping. However, it will not be long before some shipping decisions are made this way. The AI algorithms are capable of processing oceans of data, while human experts possibly can remember and process only a fraction of the data, so it is highly likely that the best practices and perfect solutions as known in shipping now are neither best nor perfect. Only AI can help discover the best and most appropriate ways of dealing with, e.g., transport service routeing, ship scheduling, avoidance of ship collision and many other critical issues.

Why is computing power the critical enabler for digitalisation?

To process millions of gigabytes of data within a short period requires enormous computing power. The computing hardware capability has been improving rapidly and continuously for many decades since the 1960s following the so-called "Moore's law". As of 2018, the fastest computer chip can perform 10 trillion calculations per second. The computing power of a smartphone in our pocket today is more than that of a supercomputer occupying an enormous room in the past. It is widely believed that such technological breakthroughs, like the parallel processing capabilities of GPUs, leading to a massive growth of computing power, have been one of the chief reasons for AI and digital transformation to take off.

However, as the world, including maritime transport, continues to be digitised, the increase of data generated will be exponential. In order to process such an astronomically significant amount of data even more computing power is needed. If data produced by driverless cars is used as a guide, crewless ships will generate several thousands of gigabytes per day. If cargoes, vessels, containers, ship equipment, etc., were all fitted with sensors as part of IoT application in shipping, the corresponding computing power needed for data processing would be tremendous. Fortunately, the progress of computing technology continues as well. Researchers and technology companies are working hard on the further improvement of the existing technologies and the promising new technologies such as the quantum computer, the 3-D computer chips, etc., to raise the computing power to new highs. In 2019 a milestone achievement on quantum computing was reported by Google to the effect that, for the first time, it was shown that quantum computers could outperform conventional computers by more than one thousand times.[8]

16.4 Digitalisation, automation and maritime transport

When talking about the forthcoming change, it is often referred to as the disruption of the existing business models caused by digital technologies. The technological breakthroughs are indeed the origins of the disruptive changes. But technology alone is not enough to cause the complete transformation of a sector. It is the new value, or a tremendous extra customer benefit created by the firm adopting the new technologies, that leads to the substitution of the old model for the new and causes the disruption. As far as maritime transport is concerned, the extra customer value enabled by digitalisation and AI takes mainly two forms: the automation of operations for better quality and efficiency and the identification of new models for making better decisions. In this section we will focus on the first form, automation.

For companies, giving up an old way of doing business for a new one is always costly and risky. So they often will not do it unless they have to, which usually means they are under the pressure of market competition. If adequate benefits can be generated by digitalisation, the companies that have taken the risk will be better placed to win in the competition. So the potential customer value created by the use of digital technologies could be a decisive factor. The technical development changes fast and there have not been standard ways of applying the technologies in maritime transport. So our discussions in this section will focus on the general trends in shipping as a result of digitalisation and automation rather than on specific predictions of what, where and when the disruption in maritime transport will be.

What are the new values created from digital disruption in shipping?

Many people think that the chief objective of digitalisation and automation in maritime transport is cost saving by replacing people with robots. But often this is not true. The most important benefits are the extra values created rather than more cost saved. Transport users always look for customer values with the best value for money. For most of them, quality and cost are inseparable. We will, again, discuss the maritime activities in three categories: ship operations, port operations and maritime services, by looking at the potential improvement in customer values through digitalisation and automation as well as by a general assessment, as shown in Table 16.2, of the conventional state versus the future state of the selected maritime activities.

Ship management onshore

In this aspect the level of digitalisation is not high. So far, most shipping companies manage their ships in a traditional way, with financial, commercial and technical managers making most decisions. Many of such management tasks are routine rather than original and repetitive rather than creative. It is likely that, when most tasks have been digitised, by using data mining methods and algorithms, superior business patterns can be discovered and better decisions can be made. It has already happened in other sectors, such as legal services or business consultancy, which share a lot of common characteristics with ship management.[9] The shore-based ship management will inevitably be affected by AI and some tasks will be automated. A very important benefit of AI application is related to risk management, which will be discussed in the next section.

Ship management at sea

News and reports on autonomous ships have been frequently in the headlines of the maritime press in recent years. Given the fact that shipboard operations are routine and rule-based, replacing ship crew with automation is not only technically feasible but, in time, inevitable. For this to happen more generally, much more data need to be collected through the digitisation of all shipboard activities. The electrification of ship propulsion is considered by many as a prerequisite for autonomous ships, in which case more time might be needed for new breakthroughs in battery technology. For other modes of transport, autonomous operations are making even more progress. We can see, with a Google search, that France, Japan and China will soon have autonomous high-speed trains in operation and it will not

Table 16.2 The future state of selected maritime activities as a result of digital transformation

	Conventional state	*Future state*
1. **Shore-based ship management and 00 operation**	Ship managers in office, many people especially for liner shipping companies	Wide use of AI and digitalisation to support and automate decisions
2. **Onboard ship operations**	A typical crew of 16-20 persons and similar number of standby seafarers	Unmanned autonomous ships with shore based monitoring and control
3. **Port cargo handling operations**	Many people working for cargo handling operations in port	Automated cargo handling operations with remote supervision and control
4. **Port ship-related services**	Pilots, tugboat crew, maintenance of safe navigation facilities	Automated services with remote monitoring
5. **Ship registration**	People handling ship registration work and carrying out flag State control	AI supported registry processes and Flag State control systems
6. **Ship broking and agnecy**	Ship brokers and agents providing information and advice	E-broker and e-agent system with AI supported optimisation
7. **Marine insurance**	Specialists evaluating applications and settling contracts and cases	Big-data and AI supported risk assessment and case handling
8. **Ship financial services**	Specialists evaluating cases with information on market, ship, shipowner	Big-data and AI supported application assessment and decisions
9. **Maritime legal services**	Lawyers preparing legal documents and settling cases	Big-data and AI supported case analysis and legal decisions
10. **Maritime education and training**	Instructors giving classroom and supervising practical training	More tailored education solutions by e-learning for continuous training

Source: Shuo Ma

Note: The future state refers to ultimate situation of shipping as the result of the current digital disruption and transformation.

Under 5. on "Ship registration", the maritime administration may delegate flag state control to recognised organisations, such as a classification society.

take long before driverless trucks are on the road. Their examples have shown that once the process has started, more data are collected and, through trial and error, the improvement pace will be fast and the transition from semi-automation to total automation will not take very long.[10] For shipping, in the same way as for all other modes of transport, the biggest gain from automation is improved safety and service quality by drastically reducing or eventually eliminating human error in ship operation.

Port operations

As far as container cargo handling is concerned, automated container terminals are already a reality. In those ports, the role of humans is limited to the supervision of cargo handling operations and the necessary intervention in case things go wrong. Some automated container terminals have outperformed the best conventional terminals in many areas, in particular the annual average crane productivity, the annual cost per teu and the annual energy consumption per teu.[11] Port cargo-handling operations have been the best test ground for maritime automation for two main reasons. First, the container terminal operations consist of repetitive, routine and rule-based tasks. Second, they are also carried out in a predictable environment and within a limited and closed space. On the ship-related port operations, replacing the current radio and radar information and communication by the IoT and AI technology to determine optimal times for ships to dock, load and unload based on the data about the ship, cargo, weather, water, traffic, berth conditions, etc., can improve port efficiency significantly.[12] Several leading ports have plans to introduce, within the short term, a remote-controlled pilot system and unmanned tug boat services.[13] The traditional concept of a cargo port located at the heart of the city with a lot of workers and busy traffic is quickly changing to that of a highly efficient, low-cost and entirely automated port situated far away from the city centre.

Maritime services

The situation of maritime services is more diverse. Take maritime administrative services such as ship registry for example – the procedures are routine and rule-based. Most steps from application to verification and approval can be automated to improve accuracy, efficiency and reduce cost. The maritime services that depend solely on providing information are in great danger of being replaced by internet-based virtual agents. Some maritime services are related to contract negotiations, such as brokers for sales and purchase or chartering of ships. This is very much like a two-party game based on basic principles and rules. An application of AI methodology such as machine learning would be a promising way to augment the quality and speed of decision making. In the traditional way of providing shipping services such as ship finance, legal services or marine insurance, personal interaction is an important element. However, such interaction involves mostly offering information and advice based on professional experience and analysis. Digitalisation can create additional value for such services. This is because much more information can be pooled from broader sources and covering wider areas and a more extended timeframe. As a result, the AI can not only emulate the best human performance, but it can also surpass humans by discovering solutions faster, with better precision than that of humans or find patterns unknown to people. Maritime education and training will remain most probably as one of the last sectors to be automated. But the AI and digitalisation can bring extra value to the customers, particularly through e-learning, with more tailored and individualised education solutions to help people not only acquire the necessary knowledge and skills but to also continuously reinvent themselves for the changing environment.

What are the challenges to maritime automation?

Automation and better decisions are the two linked but different outcomes of digitalisation. Both of them bring enormous extra customer value and, at the same time, challenges and long-term impacts. In this section we briefly discuss these factors of automation from various angles, such as economic, social, operational, technical, legal and regulatory.

Economic impact

It is not easy to carry out a cost–benefit analysis of automation for maritime transport because some costs and benefits are long term and indirect. The economic effects of automation in other sectors where robotics are widely used, such as the automobile industry, have been so positive that such production methods have become a standard feature in any modern car-making plant. As far as maritime transport is concerned, the economic justification is generally accepted by the industry. By 2019 virtually all major shipping companies, as well as many non-shipping organisations, have various kinds of autonomous ship projects. Some trial tests of autonomous ship systems have been undertaken;[14] the first commercial container ship, *Yara Birkeland*, a 120-teu autonomous, electric-powered container vessel, will be sailing in Norwegian coastal waters from 2020 for fertiliser company Yara. And the world's first autonomous shipping company, called Masterly, was established in August 2018.[15] Similar experiments have also been conducted in many other shipping nations in Europe, Asia and North America. Some recent research has confirmed the positive effect that owning and operating autonomous ships can result in significant cost savings.[16] While the construction cost of autonomous ships is higher, the direct benefits are from the savings in crew cost and fuel consumption due to the reduction of weight and air resistance when the accommodation structure is removed. The need for such a cost-saving is demonstrated in both the competition within the sector as well as that between modes of transport. Short sea shipping might see the cost advantage over road transport shrink should the cost of trucking decrease drastically due to full automation. In the port of Qingdao, China, investing in a fully automated container terminal is about 150% of the investment for a conventional terminal. After the first year of operation, the automated terminal is said to have achieved its main objectives. It reduced the workforce by 85%. Seven months after the opening, the automated terminal started to maintain the ship-to-shore crane productivity at 35 moves per hour per crane on average, which is an improvement of 30%[17] on the average of human driver alternative. And in a port where the typical crane driver's salary is about US$18,000 per year, it will take about 5–7 years to pay back the additional investment in automation. It is still too early to know the full cost and benefit of autonomous ships and the automation of other maritime activities, but it is very clear that the benefits will be more than cost-savings.

Social impact

This is probably the single most important concern regarding the current wave of maritime automation. This is partly because seafarers and dock workers are not the only ones affected. The threat of automation is for almost every activity and no job in maritime transport is totally safe. It is not the intention of this book to estimate the numbers, either in terms of employment positions to lose or a timeline for the people/automation substitution to happen. There are many reasons why such predictions are impossible to make. The most crucial ones are related to the ability to overcome the barriers, resistance and pains associated with the transformation. It is more meaningful to talk about the *automatability* of maritime jobs, based on a training dataset reflecting the knowledge, skills and abilities that different occupations need on the one hand, and what computers and AI can do on the other.[18] Based on such an approach, researchers at the University of Oxford calculated the likelihood of automation of some 702 occupations.[19] From these we selected 14, shown in Table 16.3, to represent some jobs in maritime transport. Certainly many of the occupations are not specific to maritime transport and they are based on the situation in the US only. But, taking the table as the indicative measures on the likelihood of automation, some interesting observations can be made. The people working in the maritime service sector are among the professions most threatened by automation. Insurance underwriters, agents and brokers are highly likely to be replaced by computers and AI. This is because the work consists of looking for data and offering information and standards as well as structured solutions. Port operations are more likely to be automated than ship operation. It is interesting to note that

Table 16.3 Maritime jobs, the likelihood of being automated.

Maritime jobs	*Likelihood of being automated (1–0)*
Insurance underwriters	99%
Cargo and freight agents	99%
Shipping, receiving and traffic clerks	98%
Brokerage clerks	98%
Transportation inspectors	90%
Crane operators	90%
Tank, truck and ship loaders	72%
Transport storage/distribution managers	59%
Financial specialists (all others)	33%
Captains, mates and pilots of water vessels	27%
Business operation specialists (all others)	23%
Financial manager	6.9%
Ship engineers	4.1%
Training and development specialists	1.4%

Source: Frey C. B. and Osborne M. (2013) "The Future of Employment".

Note: the above list is selected from a pool of 702 occupations to reflect maritime jobs or proxies from the most (1) to the least (0) computerisable.

ship engine officers are much less likely to be replaced by automation than ship bridge officers such as captains or mates. This echoes the general belief that so long as the ship propulsion system is not electrified, it is difficult to spare ship engineers. It is hard to make predictions about the automatability of the tasks which currently look to be not computerisable because of the fast technological progress as discussed in the previous section.

Operational impact

The most critical operational impact of automation is the vulnerability of the digital system related to technical breakdown or cyber-attacks. Because the digital world is like an interlocking network, a technical breakdown may have a more extended effect. However, such risks could be mitigated by different preventive and protective measures, which is what the big tech companies have been doing. Relevant cybersecurity principles have been developed. For example, the ISO/IEC 27001 standards which aim at the improvement and maintenance of an organisation's information security management system.

Technical impact

The future digitalised maritime industry would create a technological inequality. This is because, in the conventional system setting, a lot of shipping skills and know-how are acquired in various ways, including formal education and training but also through on-the-job training and learning-by-doing approaches. For most shipping organisations of the less-developed countries, operating modern and foreign-built equipment and facilities have not posed too much of a problem. But, in a digitalised environment, the establishment, control, maintenance and development of such new maritime transport systems would be a tremendous challenge. So it is essential that all organisations, big or small, should be open to and prepared to be part of the transformation processes, to adapt themselves and master the new technologies. Experience has shown that many AI applications can be implemented at large or small scales to tackle general or specific problems.

Legal and regulatory impact

The introduction of autonomous ships brings a series of legal and regulatory challenges. For example, under the current maritime regulatory systems, such as that of the IMO which governs international shipping, safe manning is always a central piece requirement. Ships being properly manned is also a basic requirement in virtually all current maritime legislation and contracts. An example is the specific duties and responsibilities designated to the Master of a ship, such as the IMO's International Convention for the Safety of Life at Sea (SOLAS) or the Convention on the International Regulations for Preventing Collisions at Sea (COLREG). The challenge is not limited only to the manning of ships but to a much broader scope of issues, from maritime jurisdiction, ship construction and safe navigation, to environment protection and marine insurance.[20] Having realised this, the world maritime community has begun to tackle the issue at national, regional and global levels. In 2018 a corresponding group on Maritime Autonomous Surface Ships (MASS) was established by the IMO. The group consists of 33 Member States, 1 Associate Member and 17 NGOs and IGOs. The aim of the group is to identify ways of improving the international regulatory instruments on maritime safety and security.[21] At the IMO's MSC-100 meeting, a report was submitted which contains the comments on the ten IMO maritime safety and security instruments for the use of MASS.

The various impacts or factors discussed above do not have the same kind of relationship with maritime automation. The economic factors are the leading cause of automation in the shipping sector, while the social and operational factors are the consequences of it and the technical and legal/regulatory factors are the conditions of it. Summarised in Figure 16.5, we may also say that, with regard

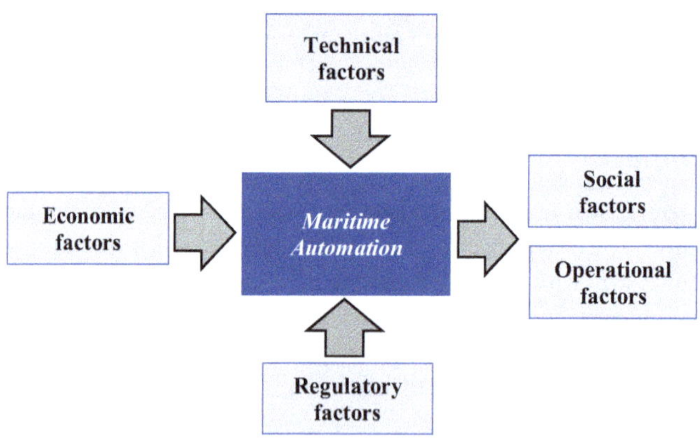

Figure 16.5 The nature of relations with maritime automation.

Source: Shuo Ma.

Note: as for maritime automation, the economic factors are the drivers to recognise, the technical and regulatory factors are the enablers to develop and the social and operational factors are the results to cope with.

to maritime automation, the economic factors are the drivers, the technical and regulatory factors are the enablers and the social and operational factors are the results.

16.5 The power of big data, AI and the future of maritime risks

To a large extent, success or failure in maritime business depends on the ability of a shipping organisation to handle risks. Of course, this is true for many businesses, but shipping is generally considered a high-risk sector. There are two main types of maritime risk, the market risk and the ship operation risk or, in other words, the commercial risk and the technical risk. The market risk includes all risks associated with the uncertainties of the shipping markets and high financial exposure of valuable ships. Operational risks are related to the safety threats affecting ships, crew and the third parties. Digitalisation and AI provide new tools for learning much more about maritime risks and subsequently enabling organisations to have more effective management of the risks. So direct cost saving is only part of the benefit brought by automation and AI; another part is the better management of risks. There will be an improvement of predictability and the discovery of better solutions. The consequent changes in maritime transport will be profound.

How can big data and AI help mitigate market-related maritime risks?

The market-related maritime risks are linked mainly to the uncertainties of the freight on the one hand and of the contractors on the other. The nature of maritime risks is uncertainty and the root cause of uncertainty is very often related to incomplete data and unknown relations between the data. When a commercial or operational decision ought to be made, the relevant information is required in order to make the right decision. But this can be extremely complex. For example, to order a new bulk carrier which can help to achieve the company's objectives, information would be needed on the demand, the supply, the competition, the investor itself and many other matters. The ideal list would be long, covering not only the current situation but also the historical data and future forecasts. Information on national policies, economic structure, demography, etc., is very important, so is information about the shipbuilding capacity, technology, financial conditions, etc., as well as information about the competition and information about every aspect of the organisation itself. The width and depth of the information needed is so great that few companies are really able to acquire everything they need. Those who have more ways, means and capabilities to obtain more data are likely to make better decisions. But, in most cases, decisions are made with incomplete information and data. This is the first source of risk. Similarly, credit risk comes from insufficient information about the contractors, suppliers, customers or partners.

To mitigate market-related maritime risks, adequate information and data not only should be available, but also should be well analysed and understood. It means that appropriate analytical methods should be employed to make sense of the data and reveal the relationships between the data for achieving the objectives. For this task, personal experience usually plays a decisive role and this can be acquired from both internal and external sources. Internally, experienced managers are called from different departments to provide expert inputs. Externally, the advice is often sought from consultants, brokers and agents. However, such personal experience is, by definition, subjective and variable according to the individual person's value judgements, analytical ability, professional background and knowledge profile, but also personal taste, preferences and bias. This is the reason why we see many companies change their major decisions, sometimes completely, after the CEO is changed. The quality of decisions depends on the experience and the ability of a ship owner to judge, derive and foresee the results based on available information. As a result, the market "secrets" are often not found and the experience-based approach produces no outcome. This is the second source of risk. Because of the above two deficiencies, there is always a high level of market-based maritime risk.

Thanks to big data and AI the above situation is changing. Today more market information is available in digital format and internal activities are increasingly digitised. At the same time, advanced analytical capabilities such as machine learning and other algorithms and significant computing power have enabled people to process the data in order to discover the unknown patterns and rules and the answers to the questions. In 2019 a Japanese shipping company started working with some partners on research and analysis of maritime logistics and shipping market conditions combining data and AI technology to develop market predictive models with high accuracy.[22] We will use some more examples to show how this can be done and to underline some related key issues.

- The first example is in the area of marine insurance. The purpose of marine insurance is to cover risks of loss or damages to ships, cargoes or third parties. To cover such risks, the marine insurance companies should have a lot of information on the ship, the shipping company, the freight it carries, the area the ship trades in, the historical records, and much more. But, in reality, only a fraction of such crucial data is available when an insurance decision needs to be made. It may typically include the static information about the ship such as the flag, class, records on deficiencies, detention and casualties, etc. Other critical data often do exist about businesses but they are usually not made available, even for some of the internal data in the insurance company. It might take a long time for the information from the claim department about an increase in claims concerning a port or a vessel to reach the underwriting department.[23] In addition to the above traditionally considered data for insurance companies, much more information and data are highly relevant for a good decision. For example, the Automatic Identification System (AIS) data, which is used mainly for navigational safety purposes, provides information such as a vessel's location, identification, course and speed not only currently but in the past. Such data can be highly valuable for marine insurance.

  Some non-traditional marine insurance companies began to consolidate a much more comprehensive database which is valuable for marine insurance and they used AI tools such as machine learning to analyse the data and to identify invisible patterns.[24] The dataset employs a full picture of the ship, its biodata, maintenance record and safety record, and it also includes the historical data showing how vessels navigated in, e.g., shallow waters, rough weather, narrow channels, port areas, the data about the total miles sailed during the defined period, the ports called, the days operated, etc. Then the data is processed using a machine-learning method to model all kinds of maritime risks by calculating the likelihood of ship accident, cargo damage, delay, port congestion, etc. Such services help maritime insurers to have a much better insight into the risks and thus to develop appropriate marketing and pricing strategies. The more data that can be used, the better the models will become. So, as more companies join the same "InsurTech" service, the database will become bigger and, subsequently, the accuracy of the predictions will be higher. If the insurance companies would agree to share the claim information/data from the past, more precise patterns can be built and more accurate solutions can be found. In conclusion, the use of AI and digitalisation can help marine insurance companies increase the efficiency of marine insurance activities and anticipate and reduce risks.
- One of the market-based maritime risks is related to credit concerning different kinds of transactions. At the same time, international trade and transport involve many parties. So a documentation system was created with sophisticated paper circulations. The use of such a system is usually complex, costly, time-consuming and open to fraud. A revolutionary record-keeping system based on cryptography and digital technology called *blockchain* provides a promising solution. A blockchain is a shared database of the secure and trusted ledger of transactions. All parties that share the database can enter and track transactions and see assets without any intermediaries or the possibility of changing a record. The assets can be any storage of value, such as a ship, a cargo, a contract, a bill of lading, a freight

payment, a certificate of origin or a ship's deficiency record. Compared with other transaction systems, blockchain technology provides many advantages. It increases efficiency significantly by eliminating intermediaries, transaction verification and document circulation; it drastically reduces the possibilities of fraud; it tightens security and it improves transparency and auditability. It is likely that by using blockchain technology trust will be ensured throughout transactional chains and, as a result, many existing market-related maritime risks together with huge associated costs will massively decrease.

A recent PwC survey of 600 executives from 15 territories shows that 84% of organisations have at least some involvement with blockchain technology.[25] Given the potential benefits and the wide application possibilities, many maritime companies, as well as existing or start-up tech firms, have begun to apply blockchain technology to shipping operations. There are many examples of using the technology in shipping and new cases emerge continuously from ship financing institutions and classification societies to shipping lines and ports. A critical issue regarding blockchains in shipping is about the nature and scope of blockchain with regard to who can write data onto the ledger and who can read the data. A distributed ledger system can either be public or private. Unlike the much publicised "bitcoin", which is open and permissionless, so far the blockchains established in shipping are private permissioned networks. They are usually set up by a starter or a consortium who administrates the blockchain by deciding on who is allowed to join the network. Public or private, the basic features of maintaining the replicas in sync of a shared ledger of digitally signed transactions remain the same. A private network provides more privacy and does not require as much computing power to operate and maintain as a public blockchain does.[26] The supply-chain-related blockchains embrace an extended network of stakeholders from trading companies, forwarders, customs, banks and insurance to shipping companies, land transport operators and ports, etc. However, for any such system to function correctly, solutions have to be found to overcome obstacles such as the lack of norms, standards, rules and jurisdictions, all of which are needed not only for interoperability but also for dispute settlement. The experience shows that a solution will ultimately be found, but it will take some time.

How can big data and AI help mitigate operational maritime risks?

Many of the maritime risks are linked to the operation of ships and navigational safety. Over the last 50 years we have seen tremendous progress in maritime safety and risk reduction. However, there are still thousands of casualties reported every year and too many accidents threatening people, ships, cargo and the environment. The magnitude of the maritime operational risks is reflected in the marine insurance premium, which is in the region of some US$30 billion each year.[27] The typical causes leading to maritime casualties are grounding, fire/explosion, flooding, collision, machinery failure, etc. The risks related to maritime operations can be examined under three headings, namely, navigational safety, system reliability and the issue of compliance. We will discuss them as follows.

- ***Navigational safety***. According to the statistics published by the marine insurance industry, more than 50% of total losses between 2003 and 2017 were related to foundered ships caused by heavy weather and grounding.[28] By permanently monitoring data on weather and sea conditions, vessel location, speed and ENC (electronic navigational chart) data and analysing them in real-time and comparing them against the benchmarks, one can detect abnormalities, anticipate dangers and alert the crew or the system in good time so appropriate preventive actions are taken. These may include the calculation of the best navigational routes and time windows. Also, for example, a minimum clearance between the keel and the sea bed ought to be kept and the COLREG requirements should be fully respected regarding passing-by ships. Such kinds of technological solutions exist already in the market.[29]

  A study published in 2018 regarding the analysis of 693 accident investigation reports of six major maritime countries from 2002 to 2016 revealed that collision and grounding were the most common types of accidents and human errors were the primary responsible factor in most cases.[30] Inadequate risk management, failure in communication, poor judgement, inadequate lookout, etc., are among the most frequently cited direct causes. The use of digitalisation technologies could reduce such risks in a sensible manner. If we take a vessel sailing on a particular shipping route as an example, by collecting and analysing the meteorological-ocean data, local regulations, AIS and GPS data, an optimal route, from both safety and economic aspects, can be calculated. This can be compared with the historical data on how ships navigated on the same route. Predictive ship-moving trajectories would then be calculated and optimal sailing instructions generated for ship officers and shore-based staff. If unusual manoeuvring or a deviation from the suggested route, or a potential collision or grounding is detected, seafarers as well as shore-based staff would automatically be alerted in good time and the corrective manoeuvring recommended[31] or appropriate actions would be taken in the case of an autonomous ship.

- ***System reliability***. Technical reasons such as ship structural defects or machine failure or equipment breakdown may no longer be the main source of operational risk. However, in the above-mentioned study of 693 accident investigation reports, technical failure is still responsible for 11.5% of all accidents. Advanced digital technologies, such as IoT, provide new solutions. The Internet of Things means the extension of internet connectivity to natural or man-made objects identifiable by IP addresses. Attached to the objects are web-enabled smart devices that use embedded electronics such as sensors, processors and communication hardware which collect and transfer data over a network to the cloud or locally at "edge" for process and analysis. Then solutions will be generated and actions are taken.

  Some organisations, such as marine engine manufacturers or classification societies, have already used AI and IoT technologies to bring predictive maintenance to shipping so as to increase the system reliability. When smart IoT devices are installed in the equipment, a continuous monitoring system is established by collecting data on the functioning and the technical conditions of the critical components. Then, using machine-learning algorithms, anomalies can be detected by analysing differences in data outputs such as, for example, identifying discrepancies from engine pressure sensor data. Based on the reports, human experts can assess the situation and come up with recommendations on, for example, repair or maintenance.[32] As possible machine and equipment breakdowns are prevented, downtime is minimised and operational risks reduced.

  With cameras and microphones installed on board ships, image and sound data can be collected and transmitted to the cloud. By using digital technologies such as sound and image recognition, ship classification societies can increase the efficiency, accuracy and effectiveness of ship survey activities. Because the AI algorithms can analyse the image data over time to discover corrosion and the trend of coating breakdown, the condition of a ship can be remotely assessed and coating and structure issues can be automatically detected at a very early stage for appropriate measures to be planned and undertaken in time.

- ***Compliance***. A national maritime administration is responsible for the enforcement of the international regulations that it has ratified regarding the ships under its registration. One of the major challenges in the aspects of maritime safety, security and marine environment protection is that some countries do not have the necessary expertise, experience and resources to implement an IMO convention that they have accepted to be part of their national law. The lack of experienced ship surveyors is believed to be one of the major causes. In this regard, using AI, blockchain and digital technologies can be a valuable solution to the problem, which could lead to more efficient, effective and accurate ship inspections. For example, using blockchain technology could prevent misdeclared cargoes which are believed to be responsible for about a quarter of incidents with container ships.[33] Most digital technologies used in transport contracts, documentation, marine insurance, predictive maintenance and ship classification, as discussed above, can equally be applied to the tasks of flag state implementation.

Table 16.4 Effects of digital technology on maritime risks

	Big data–AI	*IoT–AI*	*Blockchain*
Shipping market risks	major		
Credit risks	minor		major
Navigational safety risks	major	minor	
System reliability risks	minor	major	
Rule compliance risks	minor	major	minor

major *minor*

Source: Shuo Ma.

Note: digital technologies can mitigate maritime risks. The table shows the major and supplement effects on the common maritime risks between the 3 digital technologies.

In Table 16.4 we estimate which digital technologies could help mitigate major maritime risks as discussed above. Having the necessary data is the base and foundation for advanced analysis using AI and related analytics in the context of our discussion. So, broadly, there are two types of digital technologies which have direct impacts on maritime transport: blockchain and AI. AI needs big data that can usually be acquired through digitisation of business activities and IoT networks. The table indicates the digital technology that would have leading or supplementary disruptive effects on each of the five main types of maritime risk. Other digital technologies may also help to mitigate maritime risks indirectly.

16.6 Competition from trade integration for customer control

So far in this chapter we have discussed the disruptions triggered by digital technologies from within maritime transport. The disrupting force comes from outside of shipping too. In this section we will concentrate on the external disruptive influences on the shipping sector. It is hard to tell where, when and from whom the external challenges will come, but e-commerce is clearly a potential contender and its rapid development recently may affect the future of international shipping. We will discuss the perspectives of the integration of trade and transport, the critical factors regarding the development of the integration and the possible leaders of such integration.

Why was shipping separated from trade?

As mentioned in Chapter 7, traditionally shipping was offered as part of international trade. Traders were at the same time ship owners and a shipmaster used to be directly involved in trade negotiation with importers or exporters. Although industry-controlled shipping still exists now, transportation has been mainly separated from trade as an independent 3rd-party logistics service due to multiple factors. Payment is another aspect of trade which has been handled separately by banks rather than importers and exporters themselves. Today the factors that led to the separation of shipping from trade are changing due to the development of internet and digital technologies. We will look at these changes below.

- The first driving force for the separation of shipping from trade was the pursuit of scale economies. As trade grew and competition intensified, bigger ships and shipping companies were more competitive due to cheaper average transport cost. Most small traders had to give up their own ships and use large vessels operated by the common carriers. So shipping was separated from trade. For the same reason, activities such as bunkering or agency were also separated from shipping. With digital technologies, the concept of size and the level of scale economies are changing. For example, one of the most important benefits of a big vessel is from the savings in manning cost. This advantage would be much reduced or even disappear if ships were crewless.
- Another major reason for shipping to be separated from trade was specialisation. As the market developed, maritime transport became more sophisticated in terms of business modality, market mechanism, regulatory structure and operational techniques. The knowledge and expertise required grew beyond the ability of the trading companies. Today, as described above, the international shipping system is challenged and will be disrupted by digital technologies in all aspects. As a result, the organisation, process and operation of maritime transport will be simplified and automated. Internationally traded cargo will continue to be transported by ships in the future but, possibly, it will be done as an integral part of a trade.
- A shipmaster used to be the full representative of the trader because of the lack of the means of communication. It was later possible for the separation of shipping from trade when the importers and exporters were able to communicate remotely without relying on the ship crew. During the course of the last half century, one of the biggest technological changes has been in communication. It is now the age of the "internet of everything" and satellite communication allows people to access and receive full information anywhere in the world.

While the separation of shipping from trade has offered significant benefits to international trade in terms of low transport cost and high efficiency, it has also made trading much more complicated. A trader can no longer focus only on trade. Now they often have to be equally attentive to the transport because a poor deal for the latter can easily offset the gains from the former. In some cases the determining factor for a profitable trade is the transportation rather than the trading itself, particularly for the trade of commodities, where the shipping freight not only may be higher than the price of the cargo but also more volatile and unpredictable. In other words, for a trader, transport and trade are inseparable. Having to deal with the shipping market in addition to the trade market increases a risk that many traders would prefer not to have. Now digitalisation offers the solution.

Why are the customer interface and data the keys to supply chain dominance?

In the coming decade the biggest disruption of maritime transport may not come from inside the shipping sector, such as from automation or completely new models of operation that we have discussed so far in this chapter. The real challenge will more likely come from external factors that will eventually lead to a disconnection of maritime transporters from their traditional customers, the importers and exporters. There might be a transformation of maritime transport into a sort of affiliate or an add-on to trade. Possibly the shipping of the future will be an integral part of a trade, in the same way as the packing is a part of the trade.

Over recent years there has been a new development called the "platform economy", which has disrupted many consumer sectors such as retail, banking, music, taxis, hotels, etc.[34] These are the new tech companies using digital technologies to take over the most valuable and critical segment of the transaction: the supplier–consumer interface. They have done so with new platforms that greatly enhance the customer experience. This kind of competition was unexpected. It did not come with a full and better product or service, it just came with a better customer interface solution. The new customer value created by the platform economy has some common features in terms of incontestable superiority of speed, choice, convenience, mobility, seamlessness, transparency, integration, security, etc. Customers cannot resist the great value offered by the new services. As a result, the conventional business model is disrupted with two serious and interlinked consequences: (i) the customer interface is "hijacked" by platform companies; and (ii) the platform companies control the key data about transactions.

The consequences of the above mentioned "decoupling" of the customer interface from the rest of the businesses have disruptive effects on the future of the traditional suppliers. This is because today the most valuable asset is data, particularly the data on customers. Such data is indispensable for virtually all strategic decisions from the identification of development directions and the design of the product and service to the understanding of the market trends and competition. With digitalisation and AI, those who have the access to and control of the data will be able to get more insight into the customers and the market, which in turn allow them to keep improving the service, differentiating the offering, enhancing the customer stickiness, attracting more customers and strengthening their market positions. As far as the global supply chain is concerned, the customers are the manufacturers and consumers. So far, most shipping companies know who their customers are and, in many cases, they also have direct access to the customers, even in the liner shipping sector, in spite of the use of intermediaries. But as digitalisation further develops and expands, more challenges may come to maritime transport.

Who are the most likely disruptors for the shipping sector?

In maritime transport, how would a similar disruptive change happen? The most likely contenders are e-commerce companies, which have already used the advantages of the platform economy to disrupt the retail and wholesale business. There are numerous such e-commerce firms and, currently, two of them are considered as market leaders: Amazon of the US and Alibaba of China. These companies expanded quickly in the domestic market and are now extending their prowess to international trade. They all have the ambition to integrate maritime transport in their global trade eco-system.[35] They plan to create a "one-stop-shopping" service by integrating all trade-related activities and services from finance and import/export clearance, to full logistics such as packing, storage, shipping and port services. What a customer needs to do is just to have one-click on the app of a smartphone or a computer keyboard with one single payment to complete an international trade from the factory to the doorstep of the final consumer. Figure 16.6 illustrates the transition from a fragmented global trade system (A) to an integrated one (B).

The application of AI and other digital technologies have allowed a reintegration of all activities related to international trade. And this can be done without compromising the benefits of specialisation, as shown in diagram (B) of Figure 16.6. The building and organising of an integrative trade eco-system would be beyond the financial and technical ability of even the largest shipping companies. There are many cases of trading companies getting into the transport business, for example the shipping capacities of the oil majors. But we do not see a shipping company expanding into international trade. Amazon is more than thirty times as big as the largest liner shipping company in terms of market capitalisation.[36] Many leading shipping companies have made an effort to build their own "e-platforms". But, given the nature of their business scope, such e-platforms are about *transport ecosystems* focussing on amelioration of the current system.[37] When an integrated trade-ecosystem is available,

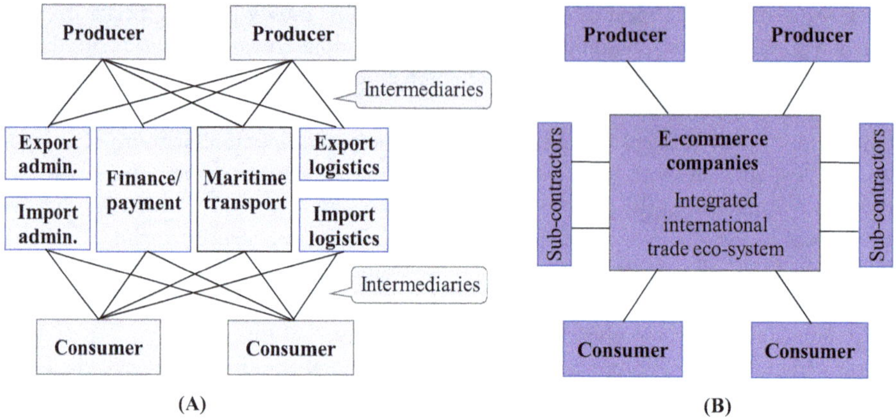

Figure 16.6 Fragmented vs. integrated international trade eco-systems and maritime transport.

Source: Shuo Ma.

Note: the figure to the left (A) refers to a fragmented international trade system whereby maritime transport and many other activities are undertaken separately from trade, whether or not this is via an intermediary. The figure to the right (B) represents an integrated and inclusive trade ecosystem offered by the e-commerce companies. All supportive activities, such as maritime transport, are inclusive parts of trade but sub-contracted to the traditional producers.

extra values are evident and the importers and exporters would most likely opt for trade-ecosystems rather than transport-ecosystems. Such developments may have very profound consequences for maritime transport and two of them are of particular importance.

- First, it might be possible that the e-commerce companies will control a significant part of international trade through their comprehensive e-platforms with an all-inclusive service package. As a result international shipping would be excluded from the import–export link to become a sub-contractor of the e-commerce companies for primarily the port-to-port transport. As long as the shipping market is competitive and the profit margin remains reasonably low, the e-commerce companies would most probably prefer outsourcing the maritime transport to the traditional shipping companies rather than in-sourcing the activity with involvement in shipping. But the shipping companies would lose direct contacts with the importers and exporters and, instead, they may have the e-commerce companies as the only clients. The importers and exporters would most probably like such an integrative modality due to efficiency and convenience.
- The second consequence is the reduction and eventual elimination of many shipping services. This may include brokers, agents and freight forwarders. When most activities have been digitised, the platform would offer the functionalities covering most of what intermediaries are offering now. Automation favours integration. When a good part of marine insurance, ship classification, etc., are automated, scale economies would become a decisive factor for gaining a business advantage. So many shipping services would be integral parts of the new international trade ecosystem.

16.7 The way forward for maritime transport: from digitisation to digitalisation and digital transformation

We have discussed so far all the digital technologies that could potentially disrupt the ways maritime transport has been done and transform the shipping sector entirely. However, many uncertainties remain still. Many people believe that the power of AI might have been overstated and exaggerated. In 2017 the AI-enabled software "AlphaZero", developed by Google's affiliated firm DeepMind, defeated the best players of the ancient Chinese chess game "Go". The AI software had the victory after playing games against itself for just three days and without using any data from human games. People may argue that chess playing is a particular case that is not comparable with shipping activities and particularly not with the operation of ships which are too complex to be fully digitalised and automated. In this section we will attempt to answer the following four questions. Will the shipping sector be digitalised and the current business model disrupted? If yes, when and to what extent will such a transformation happen? How will it happen? And what should one do about it?

Based on the earlier discussions of this chapter, we will try to address these questions in the context of two areas of challenges triggered by the disruptive digital technologies. The first is about the perspective of automation of most maritime transport activities. It is about revolutionary changes within the shipping sector. The second is about the integration of trade and transport. It is about disruptive changes outside the shipping sector. Foretelling the future is always risky, even when the digitalisation in the shipping industry has started and the trend is clearer by the day. So our analysis will be mainly based on the fundamental reasons rather than on forecasts of a specific timeline, business champions or development paths.

Why will most maritime transport activities be digitalised and automated?

Maritime transport, especially the operation of ships, is indeed complex and different from the operation of aeroplanes or trucks in the sense that deep-sea vessels are rarely identical.[38] But this should not be a barrier to prevent ships from being autonomous. Despite all the differences, there are sufficient technical and operational similarities between ships that an AI-enabled automation system could adapt itself and cope with the particularities. There are numerous reasons to believe that the shipping industry will be disrupted in favour of a large scale of digitisation and automation. Among these reasons, we will discuss the three that are the most fundamental for the superiority of the decision-making process in a digitised and automated system as compared with the conventional system.

- ***Completeness of data coverage.*** The quality of decisions, either on board ships or at the company level, is determined by the completeness of relevant data and information based on which decisions are made. In other words, poor decisions are often the result of insufficient or incomplete information. When actions and activities are digitised, the data, which would have been lost without digitisation, is collected. When such digitisation expands to cover all relevant internal and external activities, conditions and environment, the chances of discovering the critical information that reveals the secret rules of good decisions will be higher. This can be seen from the above example about the decisions on voyage optimisation. A much better decision can be made if it is based on the complete data regarding the past, the present and the future conditions about the sea route, weather, ship, engine, consumption, cargo and port, etc. A marine insurance company can improve its decisions if it uses the information on the vessel's behavioural-based information rather than the historical claims and static data. The system can weigh each of the behavioural-based data according to its correlation to the past claims. All data on the ship's management and operating patterns, as well as behavioural-based information such as vessel statistics, movements, machinery, cargo and port information, are very relevant for determining the potential claims.

- ***Capability and speed of data processing***. The digital technology has progressed very rapidly since the beginning of the 21st century. It is almost a reality that whatever people can sense, the technologies, such as radar, image and voice recognition and all sorts of sensors, can sense too. What is more important is that the improved speed and potential of the sensing abilities are clearly more promising for sensor technologies than for humans. So to collect a full set of data one has to rely on digital technologies. One other important aspect is about processing the data collected. The required capability and speed of processing the massive amount of data are simply beyond the ability of human beings. It has been proven that only the AI system built on powerful computing abilities and specific algorithms can achieve the desired outcomes.

  The situation is also the same for data storage. In this aspect, digital technologies outperform humans by a large margin. An experienced seafarer, for example, is someone who has been in the business for a long time and has the memory of lots of knowledge and information, and who can also make sense of this knowledge and information by linking the dots to come up with a good decision. The AI system can also learn and have such abilities too. So we may also say that an experienced seafarer is about, first, the ability to memorise or to store the data and, second, the ability to analyse or to make sense of the data. If so, AI will do better in both areas. Human-based accumulation of knowledge and information is limited to the physical ability and, usually, the life span of a human being,[39] while AI does not have such limitations. The AlphaZero example also shows that AI can beat humans in making sense of data.
- ***Accuracy and relevance of data use***. The AI system can process big data quickly and accurately thanks to a pre-sampling of the data collected so only the essential information is processed. Because of enhanced computing power and advanced algorithms, the modern AI system has the data-mining capabilities which can help discover relations, patterns and rules between the variables that have never been discovered by humans before. It is the significance of the AlphaZero case that has "devalued" the knowledge and experiences accumulated by humans and made the so-called expert system much less powerful, at least for this and many similar situations. This is because emulating experts would mean limiting the optimisation within the capability of the selected people, while it is clear that human beings can merely process a tiny part of data and thus discover only a fraction of all options. So the "ideal" voyage plan recommended by the most experienced shipmasters today may still not be the best plan. The most renowned marine insurance experts may still be ignorant of the most suitable underwriting solutions. A big-data-based AI system or the use of blockchain technology will provide a better chance for the financial institutions to catch a potential crook than experienced bankers before a ship loan decision is made.

The superiority of the AI system in the above areas, compared with human beings, suggests that there is a so-called "dark knowledge",[40] which is beyond the reach of humanity and in which the answers to many challenging questions reside. It is therefore not a surprise that the steps taken by AlphaZero were totally incomprehensible to the best Go players and were not in the chess books which record the masters' playing scripts over thousands of years. So, most probably, the best practices and the right solutions across the shipping industry have not been found. There is a sea of dark knowledge related to maritime transport that we do not understand and to which we have no access. But the answers to many of our problems will come from this dark knowledge so we have to rely on digitalisation and AI to find them.

It is important to note, however, that when it comes to much competition-oriented decision making, the use of AI and automation may not lead to advantage if everyone uses the same system.

Unlike the elimination of accidents, market-based decisions are more about a zero-sum game, where a decision can only win if it is comparatively better. So it may be possible that market-based and competition-dependent decision making will not be automated.

What is the timeline of digital shipping?

A disruptive change usually takes a long time to complete. But as the improvement of technology accelerates, global competition intensifies and the world is so closely connected, the time for the new technologies to replace the old ones keeps shortening. For example, it took almost a hundred years between the introduction of the first commercial steamship and the disappearance of the last merchant sail ship serving in foreign trade.[41] Maritime containers were first introduced in the mid-1950s and it took about 50 years for them to reach about a 75% share of the international seaborne trade of general cargo.[42] Although the implementation and generalisation of new technology are different in production, consumption and service, it is, nevertheless, interesting to note that, barely ten years after the iPhone was introduced in 2007, so many sectors have been disrupted, from cameras and wristwatches to music and newspapers. It is also expected that electric cars, and indeed autonomous cars as well, will become the mainstream, i.e., over 50% of new sales, within a shorter time than for transformations in the past.[43]

Many surveys and studies speculate on the time it will take for autonomous ships to become the mainstream of the ship supply.[44] It is very difficult to know. First, the ships built today are not autonomous and they have an economic life of about 25 years. Second, the development of digital technologies is not over yet. On the one hand, new technologies that could be applied to the shipping sector may still emerge and, on the other hand, there are still technical issues for digital transformation that remain to be tackled. Third, if the benefits of the digitalisation are not shared relatively evenly among all those concerned and the society in general, the short-term shocks from the destructive changes might cause so much political and social resistance that, in turn, this would slow the pace of changes.

In view of the above reasons, the transition, which has begun, will not be complete very soon, though it will most probably accelerate. Most maritime transport activities in advanced countries will most probably be digitised by around 2030. By then, the necessary technologies, including AI, blockchain and also electrification and communication, might have matured.

What are the main impacts of the digital transformation on maritime transport?

The experience of the past shows that the time and speed of the changes depend less on the technological capabilities of the suppliers but more on the political, social, cultural and organisational capability to accept and adapt to the changes. The impact of digital disruption will be profound and comprehensive. People's interest will be affected, their working conditions will have to be changed and many people may even lose jobs. So the success of the digital transformation is determined by the company's ability to deal with the resistance and manage change. The second challenge is related to data itself. Apart from technical aspects, there are also issues of ownership, privacy and use of data. The third challenge is about system reliability and security.

- ***Employment.*** The most significant barrier to digital transformation is related to the loss of jobs. The job losses in maritime transport will be a challenge to society. During the digital transformation process all three stakeholders: individuals, companies and governments, should work closely together to mitigate the risks and minimise the impact. As happened during previous disruptive changes, while old jobs may disappear, new positions will emerge. But the new posts will more likely be in the sectors such as health and education. It is highly probable that transport, including international shipping, will face a significant reduction in the labour force.

The effect of employment reduction will not be the same in terms of its geographical dimension for all maritime professions. Let's take seafarers and dockworkers as examples. In both cases, the development of digitalisation and automation will be at the expense of many jobs. But seafarer is an international job, supplied by a handful of countries, while dockworkers are locally recruited. According to the BIMCO/ISF, the total number of seafarers in 2015 available to international shipping was 1,647,500.[45] The number of people working in ports is much bigger. So autonomous shipping will affect only international seafarer supply countries such as the Philippines. For dockworkers, the effect of automation will be local.

One important aspect to minimise the impact is to ensure that the benefit of digitalisation and automation is shared fairly by all members of society. This may not happen automatically. It is particularly difficult to do because the bulk of the benefit is often only available in the long term, while the pain of the change would usually arrive as a short-term shock.[46] An even more important objective is to help those affected to re-integrate in the labour market with new skills. This can only be done by society as a whole rather than by the shipping industry alone because new posts will more likely be created elsewhere. By working together there will be a better chance for a smooth and successful digital transformation.

- ***Data issues***. Data is a resource and it is probably the most critical and valuable one in the 21st century. The biggest issues for maritime transport now are two-fold. One issue is that a lot of data has not been collected and the other is that, out of the data available, only a small portion has been translated into customer value and business opportunities. All activities and processes ought to be digitised and then they should be optimised and automated. The shipping sector is now at the early stage of digitalisation. However, it is time to discuss among all stakeholders across countries, such as customers, employees, companies and governments, the data-related issues. Many of these are at the policy level, for example the ownership of data, issues of data control, concentration, access, sharing and transfer. The privacy and commercial sensitivity of data is another aspect.
- ***System reliability and cyber security***. No system is totally free from breakdown or utterly immune to external hacking. System reliability and cyber security are relative terms and discussed within the concept of risk management. After changing from analogue to digital, the nature of risk and vulnerability differ. In risk management terms, the frequency of incidents would generally be lower while the consequences would be more severe. It is also one of the reasons why the underlying risks of digital systems tend to be overstated. Those proven as best practice in other sectors should undoubtedly be considered for use in maritime transport. They may include adequate laws and law enforcement measures, effective policy and training on system security, proper technical backup and necessary protections, etc.

Who will be the leaders of the digital transformation in maritime transport?

Virtually all companies involved in maritime transport have realised that their business will be affected by digitalisation and that there is a need to change. But not every organisation has begun taking concrete actions or has a clear idea about what actions to take or where to start. Some leading shipping companies have made more headway. But many others may still be at a loss, puzzled by the technical terms and concepts and wondering which technologies are the best and how to use them. Some people would prefer to adopt a "wait and see" attitude, pointing out that history shows that the pioneers of new technology often will not be the ultimate market leaders. The initial process through trial and error is indeed risky and costly, which might be avoided by those followers. But this time around things are different. The technology front runners could enjoy a unique advantage in the control of the critical mass of data on the operations and, especially, on the customers. Such advantage will enable them to be at the top for a long time and accumulate even more data, which will further strengthen their leading positions. So the price of being inactive for too long might be high when the full-scale competition based on digitalisation capabilities begins.

Containerisation is most probably the single most significant maritime innovation in contemporary liner shipping. It was not "invented" within the shipping industry; it was the boss of a trucking company who first introduced containers to shipping. Will the breakthroughs in the digital transformation of maritime transport come from the current shipping firms? Probably. It is interesting to note that in the marine insurance sector, which is one of the oldest maritime transport businesses, the leaders of the so-called "Insurtech" are new tech start-ups created after 2010 rather than those well-known names in dominating positions of the sector for hundreds of years.[47] When digital technologies disrupt other economic sectors, often the leaders of the disruptive changes are the names of new tech companies rather than the familiar established firms, for example Spotify for digital music, Tesla for electric and autonomous cars, Netflix for movies, Uber for urban transport, Airbnb for hotels and Amazon for retail.

Why are the champions of digitalisation often newcomers from outside the sector rather than the companies in the sector? There are two main reasons. The first is that the disruption is like pressing a "reset" button to put all players, old and new, at a new starting line. Many of the advantages enjoyed by the established companies, based on their size, cumulated knowledge, experience, market base, etc., will evaporate. This is why Tesla can beat many big car manufacturers – because the disruptive technology on electric cars reset everyone's button to zero. Past achievement is even a negative asset because it increases the opportunity cost for the established companies to have a completely new start. The second reason is that the success in the digital age depends less on sector-specific capabilities but more on the firm's digital technology capabilities, which many established companies are lacking. Since 2010 a new kind of start-up company has emerged which specialises in data analytics by using algorithms to convert raw data, e.g., from a machine's sensors at a customer's factory, into useful predictions.[48] So the leaders of digitalised and automated shipping of the future will most probably be those with the following common characteristics.

- ***They always identify and fulfil vital customer values that have not been provided for by the existing suppliers.*** The examples in the shipping sector may include the more accurate prediction of lenders' financial risk and credibility, the massive reduction of maritime frauds, the big decrease in navigation accidents and engine/equipment breakdown, the elimination of paperwork and speedy/guaranteed transactions and payment.
- ***They often decouple customer "interface" from the product or service, then sell it as a new offering and control the critical data.*** We have seen this happening in businesses like taxis, music or film sectors. The examples in the shipping sector may include the creation of Amazon's "Dragon Boat" project and its eventual development as a true "one-stop-shopping" trade service with international shipping included.
- ***They always master the digital technologies, explore the full potentials and create new business models fast.*** The examples in the shipping sector may include the InsurTech companies using AI-based data-mining technologies and algorithms to analyse risks, the use of blockchain technology to increase safety and efficiency and using IoT technology to improve ship and equipment reliability.

Because of the specialised expertise required and the scale economies needed and, at the same time, the extended periods of over-supply and fierce competition, the entry barriers to maritime transport, especially in the liner shipping sector, are high for outsiders. So today's liner shipping firms may be the leaders of the forthcoming maritime digital transformation. But it is also highly possible that the leaders will be new, unknown and coming from non-shipping-background companies. Among the reasons for this, two are more important: first, the most significant entry barrier to digitalised shipping is no longer the sectoral expertise but the capability to master digital technologies; second, outsiders are usually more open-minded, more inclined to take bold steps and make radical changes because they have lower opportunity costs, have little to lose and no legacy to maintain. Bold steps and drastic actions are the exact prerequisites for disruptive transformations. So far, shipping companies have not been fast and aggressive enough in investing in digital technologies.[49]

What are the principles for a successful maritime digital transformation?

The forthcoming digitalisation will transform our economies and societies alike in the same way as previous technological disruptions did in the past. The shipping industry will not be an exception and the sector will be restructured. To a great extent, the future of every shipping company depends on what they do today with digital challenges. There are many right and necessary things to do, such as investing in people and technology, making mid- and long-term strategies, or taking hard and drastic actions to restructure the organisation. But none of these is as critical as to have the direction right. There are a few fundamental principles with regards to the direction shipping companies ought to take. Based on the experience of other sectors and the nature of the digital disruption, we will discuss five core principles and key issues, which are also the typical areas in which many maritime organisations could easily get things wrong.

- ***The key is not about "choosing technologies", but about "solving problems".***
  "Blockchain, 5G network, big data, machine-learning, AI, IoT, data-mining, cloud-computing" – shipping executives and managers can be overwhelmed by the technology jargon and buzzwords as well as by countless stories about technology-triggered business successes and failures. They may be aware of the forthcoming digital disruption and the necessity to change. But when it comes to how to proceed, many of them tend to consider the selection of the right technology to be the most critical element in digitalisation. But this is to "put the cart before the horse". Although the looming changes in maritime transport are commonly described as technological disruptions, they actually are not. Because it is the customers, not the technology, that will dictate the changes by embracing the new business models and products with higher customer value, which are enabled by the new technology. It is the customer's choice that will disrupt the current businesses. Technology should not be the starting point because it is the tool, not the objective. The objective is to create new value for customers by solving their problems.

  In this particular context, the "problems" to solve are fundamental ones, the bottlenecks and the most critical issues, and they should be the problems for the customers or major unfulfilled demand or significant undelivered values. The "solutions" to the problems should be new and radical changes which solve the problem completely rather than by incremental improvements. We can come back to the example of the containerisation. McLean, the entrepreneur who invented sea containers, had one clear objective, which was to find a solution for the problem of slow cargo handling in port. Adding more cranes and extending working hours could help. But to solve the problem from the root, cargo handling has to be done entirely differently. Then containerisation was the solution and the maritime transport of general cargo was disrupted. Today, to solve a fundamental problem entirely or to create new values and a better experience for the customers, radically new approaches have to be used. And it is highly likely that digital technologies and AI will be deployed. The journey of digitalisation of any maritime organisation should not begin with the choice of technologies but with the search for the ultimate solutions to the critical problems and the creation of new customer values.

- ***The key is not about "cost-saving", but about "value-creation"***. Despite the tremendous pressure on most shipping companies to reduce cost, the aim of the digital transformation should not be to save money. Cost is important, but it is not the chief goal of the change. Instead, the objective of using AI and automation in shipping is to create new value for the customers. The competition in maritime transport is indeed focussing on price, but price cutting will not allow the company to go very far. AI and automation represent a far higher stake for the shipping industry and provide potentials with much more benefit than what cost-cutting can achieve. For example, when credit evaluation for ship finance or risk assessment for marine insurance are largely automated using AI and big-data-based solutions, it is not the savings of personnel cost that are the most important. What counts is the new value created in terms of the quality of credit evaluation and the accuracy of risk assessment, which were unachievable previously. Similarly, the real benefit from replacing crane drivers in ports or watch officers on board ships by AI and automation is not to save cost but to improve the quality of service, eliminate human errors and avoid accidents. The ultimate value for society would be the freedom of people from working under harsh and often dangerous conditions.
- ***The key is not about "improving operations", but about "building a business model"***.
Commonly, many shipping firms see AI and automation as the means for the improvement of their current operations. This is not the right way to go. Digital technologies can undoubtedly help improve existing operational processes, but it should not be the primary goal. The real end result of digitalisation should not be a better operation of the current system but a new business model which replaces the existing one. It is why the Amazon retail system is not an enhancement of the Walmart model. Similarly, in maritime transport, the purpose of TradeLens, the blockchain project jointly launched by the shipping line Maersk and the tech company IBM, is not to improve the documentation flows, but to create a new model of maritime trade by removing the documents altogether and making the transactions secure and transparent.[50]

  New business models can only be created by the companies that understand and see the power, possibilities and potentials of digital technologies in the disruption of old systems and the recreation of new ones. To solve the fundamental problems completely, such companies think out of the box, instead of inside it. By using digitalised and AI-empowered systems, the users of maritime transport will have a big benefit from new added value and improved customer experience. Whether or not the shipping industry will be digitised and automated is not determined by the shipping industry itself, but by the users. The extra added value from digitalised and automated maritime transport is so significant that those companies which fail to offer it will have little chance to survive.

  It is in this context that we can now discuss the relationship between automation on the one hand and AI/digitalisation on the other. Too often, automation is evaluated in isolation against a cost-saving effect or operation improvement or the two combined. But the phenomenon of automation in ship or port or maritime service operations is more complicated. It is because automation is inseparable from AI and digitalisation. It is one integrated process. The cargo-handling operation at a port cannot be automated unless it is first digitised. The latest examples show that to benefit fully from port automation, AI technology must be used. It is also true the other way round: when digitalisation and AI use are in place, automation will be a natural consequence or a must rather than a choice because people will be unable to process the huge amount of data and take actions quickly and accurately enough.
- ***The key is not about "to get cargo", but about "to get data"***. For many shipping companies, the primary objective of the operations is to have more business or cargo. But such a response is not necessarily correct anymore in the digital era. One of the essential aims of digitalisation and automation is actually about data. So if a discussion on whether a shipping organisation should

or shouldn't embrace digitisation and automation focusses on a cost-and-benefit analysis of cargo transport, the organisation is likely to be on the wrong track. In the 21st century, data is the most fundamental resource.

There are three aspects concerning the importance of data for shipping companies. First, we now know that, like any other businesses, even the best run shipping organisations have typically been managing their activities with the knowledge of a fraction of the data needed both internally and externally. So digitalisation is like opening the door to the precious data resources, without which a shipping company is highly unlikely to win in the competition of the future. Second, the data collected on shipping activities is not only crucial for managing the shipping sector, but it is also indispensable for value creation in other areas and the betterment of society as a whole. Therefore, it is unwise not to automate low-cost jobs based on economic considerations only. Shipping organisations ought to realise the huge stakes and make strategic decisions to ensure that their businesses are digitalised, even in the absence of a short-term economic incentive. Third, the customers of shipping companies are also the same customers of other organisations in logistics and international trade. There is a competition for customer data and who controls the customer data also controls the customers and controls the entire value chain.

- ***The key is not about "new technology", but about "new leadership, organisation and people".*** Digital technologies are very important, but they are not the most difficult part. If technology is the hardware, then it is the software in terms of leadership, organisation and people that is the key to the success in digital transformation. This is simply because a real digitalised shipping needs a different mindset and a digitalisation- and automation-compatible organisation. Such an organisation would mean that some people will lose their work and most others will have to change their usual ways of working and learn new skills. It is a difficult thing to do. It requires strong and totally committed leadership and adequate investment in people, in terms of communication and training. By leadership, it means whether or not the owner or the CEO of the shipping company has the full vision and understanding of the stakes. If the person does, a genuine and complete commitment could be made and, only then, will there be a chance to succeed. By investing in people, it is important that everyone in the organisation is fully aware of the stakes of the change and understands the consequences of no change or not enough change. Then appropriate training programmes ought to be implemented, along with the identification of the critical issues and the investment in suitable digital technologies.

It will take time before the value and benefits of digitalisation are delivered fully. It is because presently AI and digital technologies are still at the beginning of their development and most shipping organisations are at the very early stage in the process of digitisation. As digital technologies mature, we will see more transformative effects in maritime transport in the near future.

16.8 Summary

In this chapter we have discussed the economic basics of current disruptive challenges in maritime transport. Although the new digital technologies are the origins of change, the disruption of the existing businesses is driven by the customers who opt for digitalisation-based new services at the expense of the old models. To better understand the value of shipping activities to customers, we began with an analysis leading to the conclusion that shipping and the movement of cargo must be the core value that customers care about. Having transport-of-cargo-by-ships at the centre, we examined the supportive activities required, the input needed, and the cash-flow expected. These elements and features will determine the way the activities are affected by digitalisation. In the future, cargo will always be transported, but very differently.

Then we analysed the likelihood of each main maritime activity being digitised and automated. Some of those activities have already been digitised, with numerous cases of a high level of computerisation and automation, such as in engine operation or cargo handling. Some others are still in analogue formats such as marine insurance or ship finance. The aspect of programmability has also been examined to see if there are standardised and pre-determined ways of undertaking the activities. A process can be easier to automate if it is routine, repetitive and standardised, such as cargo handling at ports. Other less standardised activities such as legal services are harder to automate. Both standardisation and programmability are relative notions because, strictly speaking, there is always a standard for everything people do. Those activities labelled as not standardised merely have more options and variables.

In the past, it was always the technological breakthroughs that enabled the disruptive changes. In this chapter we reviewed the decisive role of the major breakthroughs in digital technologies and the subsequent digitalisation development. The technologies are all about data: its acquisition, its transmission, its processing and its use. Starting with computerisation and the internet, more lately with voice/image recognition, hard/software enhancement, sensors and the Internet of Things, the economic activities have been more digitised than ever. Then extraordinary improvement happened in data transfer and storage thanks to the new technologies. To make sense of the data collected, advanced algorithms and huge computing power are crucial. We have seen the technological breakthroughs in both areas. The development and evolution of these and other technologies are still at an early stage. New progress is made continuously.

We then evaluated the possible impact and perspectives of automation and AI in maritime transport. However, our emphasis is on the general trend rather than any specific forecasts. We began with an analysis of the new customer value from digitalisation in each of the main maritime transport services. In Table 16.2 we see the comparison for two such activities between the current situation and the new future production model. We took a particular look at the subject of maritime automation. Based on a research report by the University of Oxford, we examined the automatability levels of the main maritime transport activities, from the highest in marine insurance and cargo handling to the lowest in ship finance and training. Finally, we analysed the impact and challenges of automation on maritime transport from the economic, social, operational, technical, legal and regulatory aspects.

International shipping is a business of risk, either technically or commercially. In this section we examined the reasons why digitalisation and AI can help mitigate and massively reduce maritime risks. The origin of risks comes from uncertainty and uncertainty is often caused by the lack of adequate information and data and the relation between the variables. This is mainly because either the necessary information is not available or there is a lack of data processing capability and speed. The application of advanced digital technologies and automation are about to change this situation. With big data, AI, data-mining, blockchain, IoT, predictive analytics, etc., the situations of uncertainty can be radically changed. There have been an increasing number of good examples of using these technologies to manage maritime risks in the areas of ship finance, marine insurance and preventive ship maintenance.

One of the biggest challenges is that the new contenders of future shipping may come from outside maritime transport. The new leaders may be those technologically strong but non-traditional maritime firms. Usually the tech start-ups begin to penetrate in one specific shipping sector, for example shipping agency or marine insurance. They may also compete based on an established e-commerce background, such as Amazon or Alibaba, by annexing the entire maritime transport to their global trade ecosystems. Trade and transport, which were together in the past, are currently separate activities due to specialisation and the benefit of scale economies. In the digital age a reintegration is possible. One possible common feature of most newcomers to future shipping is that they will decouple the customer interface from the physical transport services. They will create extra value based on the customer interface while keeping total control of customer data. At the same time, they will rely on traditional maritime firms like sub-contractors for shipping services.

In the last section of the chapter we concentrated on the main environment and the ways in which maritime organisations will meet the disruptive challenges. By emphasising three data-related capabilities: data coverage, data processing and data use, we explained why there should be no doubt that most maritime activities will be digitalised and automated. It is because AI and automation out-perform humans in all three data-related capabilities. Regarding the timing of digitalised and automated maritime transport becoming the mainstream business model, we would rather be more cautious and not speculate about a timetable. When it comes to the impacts of disruptive changes, job losses come on top. Making sure that the costs and benefits are shared as fairly and evenly as possible among all stakeholders of society is one of the keys to a successful digital transformation. Other important impacts include data privacy, ownership, access, system reliability and cyber security. It looks likely that the leaders of the maritime digitalisation are those who can see the significant customer value in digital transformation, who can decouple the customer interface from other functions and effectively use the advanced digital technologies to deliver the value. We finally discussed some common misunderstandings about digital transformation. We explained why it is about "value creation" rather than "cost-saving", "business model building" rather than "improvement of operation", "solving problems" rather than "choosing technologies" and it is about "data" rather than "cargo" and it is about "people" rather than "technology".

Notes

1 KPMG (2012), pp. 13–14. It is estimated that the total value of the global fleet, including ships under construction, is worth a total of about US$1 trillion. If the average life span of a ship is 20–25 years, some US$40–50 billion per year would be needed for replacement. If the cost of financial service, the cost of other equipment and the cost of repair and maintenance is included the amount would be about US$150 billion per year.

2 Elvidge J. (2018).

3 Digital Ship (November, 2018), p. 20.

4 As a mandatory requirement of the IMO SOLAS regulation, by 2018 all cargo ships of 150 gross tonnage and above have to be equipped with ECDIS. See: IMO (2019).

5 The collected data is transferred to centralised *mobile cloud computing* (MCC) centres, such as Microsoft's Azure, Amazon's EC2, etc., or to localised *mobile edge computer* (MEC) installations for data processing and feedback.

6 It was reported at the Mobile World Congress 2019 in Barcelona that 5-G technology was introduced in the automated container terminal of the Port of Qingdao, China. The report says that "The 5G connection included data traffic from more than 30 high-definition cameras as well as control data for a programmable logic controller (PLC). These operations required millisecond-level latency control signals, as well as stable, remote and real-time control, requirements which only key 5G technologies can deliver." Source: *Ericsson and China Unicom announce 5G smart harbor at the Port of Qingdao*, 26 February 2019, retrieved 3 April 2019 at www.ericsson.com/en/press-releases/2019/2/ericsson-and-china-unicom-announce-5g-smart-harbor-at-the-port-of-qingdao.

7 A report revealed that

> the world currently produces many exabytes, i.e. billions of gigabytes, of data a day, and it could produce a great deal more in future … Storing a day's worth of the world's data using the most high density storage medium in current use would require enough very expensive magnetic tape to cover dozens of basketball courts.

However, with the technology on new molecules developed by synthetic biology, all those exabytes of data could potentially be stored in just 20 grams of DNA. One could put everything that happened in a century into a single warehouse and expect it to last fundamentally uncorrupted for thousands of years.See *The Economist* (April 2019).

8 Murgia M. and Waters R. (2019). In the report it says that the quantum process was able to perform a calculation in less than 3.5 minutes that would take today's most powerful computer, known as Summit, approximately 10,000 years. But this result was later challenged by IBM saying that 2.5 days would be enough. This is still more than 1,000 times longer than 3.5 minutes.

9 The leading consultancy companies such as McKinsey and BCG have developed the AI system, e.g., McKinsey Solutions, that can help produce standard reports automatically. It improves the quality, in terms of time and accuracy, and cuts cost. See Harvard Business Review (2017). The consultancy firm Deloitte uses its dynamic database and the AI-based automated report writing system, DeloitteSmartReports, to quickly produce three main types of reports for any client. See Deloitte (2018).

10 Waldmeir P. (2019) and *The Economist* (March 2019).

11 After one year of operation, on 11 May 2018, the Qingdao Port fully automated container terminal published the following performance record: annual average crane productivity was at 35 moves per hour, compared with a conventional terminal of Qingdao Port the average cost per teu was 48% lower and the average energy consumption per teu was 24% lower. (See: "Qingdao Port Fully Automated Container Terminal Handled More Than 790,000 teu in Its First Year", www.xinhuanet.com/fortune/2018-05/11/c_129870296.htm).

12 The Port of Rotterdam started to implement IBM's IoT and cloud computing technologies to collect and process real-time data on water, weather, traffics, berths, etc., from the sensors installed across the entire land and sea areas of the port. It is said that by using the new system "shipping companies and the port stand to save up to one hour in berthing time which can amount to about $80,000 US dollars in savings". (See: 20 April 2019, www.portofrotterdam.com/en/news-and-press-releases/port-of-rotterdam-teams-with-ibm-internet-of-things-to-digitize-operations).

13 Maritime Executive (2019) "Work starts on Singapore's autonomous tug", MAREX, 9 April. Singapore's MPA also announced a project on a remote piloting system (See: "MPA invests $7.2m in projects on autonomous shipping", *The Strait Times*, 10 April 2019).

14 The Finnish engineering company Wärtsilä completed successfully the test of its automated dock-to-dock solution on the ferry *Folgefonn* in Norway in 2018. It was reported that "the ship left the dock, manoeuvred out of the harbour, sailed to the next port of call, manoeuvred through the harbour entrance, and docked alongside the terminal – all without human intervention". (See: *The Digital Ship*, 29 November 2018).

15 World Maritime News (2019) and Willumsen T. (2018).

16 Kretschmann L., Burmeister H-C., and Jahn C. (2017), pp. 76–86. The research concluded that "the expected present value of cost of owning and operating the autonomous bulker over a 25-year period is mUSD 4.3 lower than for a conventionally manned ship".

17 On 15 May 2017 the first phase of a 2,088-metre full automated container terminal opened at Qingdao Port, China. The total investment is about US$1 billion. After one year of operation, it recorded 100% on schedule handling operation, an annual average crane productivity of 35 moves per hour, terminal productivity 30% higher, external truck terminal turn-around time less than 15 minutes. The workforce reduced from more than 60 to 9 persons supervising the terminal operation in a remote control room. (See: www.sofreight.com/news_31115.html.)

18 Frey C. B. and Osborne M. (2018).

19 Frey C. B. and Osborne M. (2013).

20 Ramboll and Core Advokatfirma (2017).

21 IMO (2018).

22 *The Digital Ship* (October, 2019).

23 Andrew Y. (2019).

24 Faulkner M. (2018). The leading "Insurtech" companies are relatively young tech companies rather than traditional large marine insurance corporations. By early 2019 one of them, Windward, has

the clients' underwrite of about 25% of the global merchant fleet and another, Concirrus, claims that using their service can improve marine loss ratio by 7%.

25 PwC (2019).

26 The Danish shipping line Maersk teamed up with IBM and launched a blockchain network called "TradeLens". It is a private system. Other leading shipping lines, such as COSCO Shipping, CMA-CGM, Evergreen and Yangming, also agreed to develop their own joint blockchain platform. See: Lloyd's List (January 2018).

27 In 2016 the total marine insurance premium was US$29.9 billion with 54% on cargo insurance and 25% on hull and machinery. The number of total losses per 1,000 vessels over 500 GT decreased from about 3.2 in 2001 to about 1.4 in 2017. About 50% of the losses were caused by weather. See: Seltmann A. (2018) "Global Marine Insurance Casualty Trends", IUMI based on data from Lloyd's List Intelligence.

28 Allianz *Safety and Shipping Review 2018*, AGCS, p. 14. Between 2008 and 2017 a total of 1,129 total losses were recorded. The three leading causes were ships foundered 52.5%, grounding 20% and fire/explosion 10%. According to IUMI, about 50% of total losses during 2008 and 2017 were caused by weather.

29 *The Digital Ship* (May 2019), Navigation, Autonomy and New Technologies, 2 May 2019. It was reported that two companies "GNS and StormGeo are combining their weather and navigation capabilities in a new partnership that will provide more than 20,000 vessels with fresh insight into voyage optimisation".

30 Acejo I., Sampson H., Turgo N., Ellis N., and Tang L. (2018).

31 Liang L. H. (2019). Similar solutions have also been available such as the "A-Suite" of the company Transas.

32 All major marine engine manufacturers, such as Man and Wärtsilä, are offering predictive maintenance services. The one by Man is called *Man Primeserv Online Service*, which sends key engine data, via satellite for example, from anywhere in the world for analysis. Wärtsilä, another marine engine maker, started the predictive maintenance system many years ago. Its AI-powered system is able to identify a fault four months before it occurs. (See: Lipsith G., "Smarter than human? How AI is revolutionising maintenance", *Maritime Digitalisation and Communication*, 22 January 2019).

33 Baker James (2019).

34 The Platform Economy examples include Amazon/EBay/Alibaba for retail, Airbnb for hotels, Uber/Didi for taxis, Apple Music/Spotify for music, etc. It is estimated that the global platform economy had a value of USD 7.18 trillion. For more details see: the KPMG 2018 Report on *Tech Giants – Race for the Platform*.

35 In 2013 Amazon started its ambitious global logistics arm called "Dragon Boat" to complete its enormous e-commerce system with a "one-click service for seamless international trade and shipping", from factories in Asia to customers' doorsteps in North America. See: *Forbes* (1 April 2016). Alibaba started in the same year a 4th party logistics platform called the "Cai Niao" programme, which consolidates the major 3rd party logistics service providers by a centralised information and data system, common distribution hubs and a shared final delivery network.

36 On 31 May 2019 the capitalisation of Amazon was USD 850 billion and that of A. P. Moller Maersk was USD 24 billion. Retrieved 3 June 2019 from https://ycharts.com/companies/AMZN/market_cap and https://ycharts.com/companies/AMKBF/market_cap.

37 Most leading shipping lines have built or are building their e-transport platforms in their effort of digitalisation, such as the reported ecosystem of CMACGM, a big French liner shipping company (source: "CMACGM unveils digital ecosystem", *The Digital Ship* (April 2019)).

38 "Liberty ships" built during World War Two is one of few examples of identical ships built in big numbers.

39 It is only a new scientific discovery that "parental responses can transmit heritable small RNAs that regulate gene expression transgenerationally", See: Posner R. et al. (2019).

40 Weijia W. (2019). The ancient Chinese game Go is considered to be one of the most challenging chesses. It has a total of 2^{361} possibilities to play. Over two thousand years a total of about 3,000 playing scripts have been recorded, which are studied by the professional players. But the scripts cover only a tiny fraction of the possibilities.

41 Stopford M. (2009).

42 ISL (2018).

43 In 2018 1,256,000 electric cars were sold in China, or about 4.5% of all new cars sold in 2018. This is an increase of 62% on 2017, while during the same period the total car sales in China dropped by 2.8%. Source: retrieved 29 June 2019 at: www.xinhuanet.com/fortune/2019-01/15/c_1123989803.htm.

44 Grace K., et al. (2017). In this article the findings of a survey of 352 of the world's leading experts on a forecast regarding when it will be that "'High-level machine intelligence' (HLMI) is achieved when unaided machines can accomplish every task better and more cheaply than human workers". With different probabilities for different sectors, the aggregate forecast is between 30 and 74 years.

45 BIMCO/ICS (2015).

46 Even at the automated container terminal of the Port of Qingdao, which opened in 2017 and which was built with the latest technology and benefitted from lessons learnt from earlier automated terminals, the gantry crane productivity was below that of driver-controlled cranes for the first six months. It took them a year to improve from 26 to 35 moves per hour per crane on average. Source: 3 July 2019, www.xinhuanet.com/fortune/2018-05/11/c_129870296.htm.

47 The two leading marine-focussed insurtech companies Windward and Concirrus were both created in 2010. Windward, e.g., started to offer their AI-based marine insurance services in 2017 and, within two years, they already had a client base covering about 25% of the global merchant fleet.

48 *The Economist* (September, 2019).

49 A market survey published by Informa Engage and Wärtsilä revealed that digital technology is still seen by many shipping executives as a cost rather than an investment and the shipping industry is interested in digitization but not yet interested enough to invest. See Clayton R. (2019).

50 Baker J. (August 2018).

References

Acejo I., et al. (2018) "*The Causes of Maritime Accidents in the Period 2002–2016*", Seafarer International Research Centre, Cardiff University, November 2018.

Allianz. "*Safety and Shipping Review 2018*", AGCS, p. 14.

Andrew Y. (2019) "*The Future Is Bright: The Future Is Digital*", IUMI Eye Newsletter, March 2019. p. 20. Retrieved 23 April 2019 from https://iumi.com/news/iumi-eye-newsletter-march-2019/the-future-is-bright-the-future-is-digital.

Baker J. (August, 2018), "*Maersk and IBM Launch Blockchain Product*", Lloyd's List, News, 9 August 2018.

Baker J. (2019), "*Pilot Project Seeks to Prevent Misdeclared Cargoes with Blockchain*", Lloyd's List, News, 25 June 2019.

BIMCO/ICS (2015), "*Manpower Report – The Global Supply and Demand for Seafares 2015*", BIMCO and ICS.

Clayton R. (2019) "*Why Is Shipping So Slow to Digitise?*" Lloyd's List, Analysis, 30 July 2019.

Deloitte. (2018) "*Leverages AI to Develop Strategic Market Reports and Benchmarks*" 15 January 2018. Retrieved from www.consultancy.uk/news/15463/deloitte-leverages-ai-to-develop-strategic-market-reports-and-benchmarks.

Elvidge J. (2018), "*Digital Consciousness: A Transformative Vision*", Iff Books, December 2018.

Faulkner M. (2018) "*Marine Insurers Sail to Forefront of Insurtech Revolution*", Lloyd's List, Analysis, 4 July 2018.

Forbes. (1 April, 2016), "*Amazon's Shipping Ambitions are Larger than It's Letting On*", Retrieved on 25 April 2019 from www.forbes.com/sites/robinlewis/2016/04/01/planes-trains-trucks-and-ships/.

Frey C. B. and Osborne M. (2013), "The Future of Employment: How Susceptible Are Jobs to Computerisation?", Working Paper, 17 September 2013, Oxford Martin School.

Frey C. B. and Osborne M. (2018) "*Automation and the Future of Work – Understanding the Numbers*", News Opinion, Oxford Martin School. 13 April 2018. Retrieved 20 April 2019 from www.oxfordmartin.ox.ac.uk/opinion/view/404.

Grace K., et al. (2017), "*When Will AI Exceed Human Performance? Evidence from AI Experts*", arXiv:1705.08807v2, 30 May 2017, Connel University.

Harvard Business Review. (2017) "*AI May Soon Replace Even the Most Elite Consultants*", 2 July 2017.

IMO. (2018) "*Regulatory Scoping Exercise for the Use of Maritime Autonomous Surface Ships (MASS)*", MSC 100/5, 28 September 2018.

IMO. (2019) "*IMO SOLAS Regulation*", V/19.2.10.

ISL. (2018), "*Shipping Statistics Yearbook 2018*", Port Surveys, Bremen, Germany, pp. 325–407.

KPMG. (2012) "*Ship Financing in Flux – Search for a New Course*", KPMG LLP, London, pp. 13–14.

KPMG. (2018) Report on "*Tech Giants – Race for the Platform*", KPMG LLP, London. Retrieved from kpmg.com/us/racefortheplatform.

Kretschmann L., Burmeister H-C., and Jahn C. (2017) "*Analyzing the Economic Benefit of Unmanned Autonomous Ships: An Exploratory Cost-comparison between an Autonomous and a Conventional Bulk Carrier*", Research in Transport Business and Management, Vol. 25, December 2017, pp. 76–86.

Liang L. H. (2019), "*Singapore Strait Benefits from Fujitsu's AI Ship Collision Prediction Technology*", Seatrade Maritime New, 4 April 2019.

Lipsith G. (January, 2019), "*Smarter than Human? How AI Is Revolutionising Maintenance*", Maritime Digitalisation and Communication, Tue 22 January 2019.

Lloyd's List. (January, 2018), "*Blockchain Comes of Age in Shipping*", Opinion, 16 January 2018.

Murgia M. and Waters R. (2019) "*Google Claims to Have Reached Quantum Supremacy*", Financial Times, 20 September 2019.

Posner R. et al. (2019) "*Neuronal Small RNAs Control Behavior Transgenerationally*", Cell, Vol. 177, No. 7, 13 June 2019, pp. 1814–1826.

PwC. (2019) "*Blockchain Is Here, What's Your Next Move?*", 23 April 2019. Retrieved from www.pwc.com/gx/en/issues/blockchain/blockchain-in-business.html.

Ramboll and Core Advokatfirma. (2017) "*Analysis of Regulatory Barriers to the Use of Autonomous Ships*", Danish Maritime Authority, December 2017.

Seltmann A. (2018) "*Global Marine Insurance Casualty Trends*", IUMI based on data from Lloyd's List Intelligence.

Stopford M. (2009) "*Maritime Economics*", 3rd Edition, Routledge, London, pp. 23–29.

The Digital Ship (November, 2018), "*Wärtsilä Completes New Tests of Autonomous Ship System*", *Digital Ship*, November 2018, p. 20.

The Digital Ship (April, 2019) "*CMACGM Unveils Digital Ecosystem*", Software, Big Data & IoT, 25 April 2019. Retrieved 3 May 2019 from https://thedigitalship.com/news/maritime-software/item/5999-cma-cgm-unveils-digital-ecosystem.

The Digital Ship (May, 2019) "*StormGeo and GNS in Voyage Optimisation Partnership*" Navigation, Autonomy and New Technologies, 2 May 2019.

The Digital Ship (October, 2019), "*K Line to Use AI for Greater Insight into Shipping Markets*", Software, BigData and IoT, 8 October 2019.

The Economist (March, 2019) "*Humans Struggles to Cope When Automation Fails, the Perils of the Human-machine Interfacer*", *The Economist,* Business, 14 March 2019.

The Economist (April, 2019) "*Synthetic Biology – The Engineering of Living Organisms Could Soon Start Changing Everything*", Technology Quarterly, 4 April 2019.

The Economist (September, 2019) "*Technology Firms Vie for Billions in Data-analytics Contracts*", Business, *The Economist*, 5 September 2019.

The Strait Times (2019) "*MPA Invests $7.2m in Projects on Autonomous Shipping*", 10 April 2019.

Waldmeir P. (2019), "*Driverless Cars Must Navigate Human Foibles*", Financial Times, 2 January 2019.

Weijia W. (2019) "Why Cannot Humans Understand the Magic of AlphaGo?", Presentation at Tencent Technology News, March 30 2019, China (Shenzhen) IT Leaders Summit. Retrieved 3 July 2019 from https://technology-info.net/index.php/2019/03/30/wang-weijia-why-cant-humans-understand-the-magic-of-alpgago/.

Willumsen T. (2018) "*A Commercial Reality Check for Autonomous Shipping in 2018*", Seatrade Maritime News.

World Maritime News. (2019). "*Workd's 1st Autonomous Shipping Company in the Making*", Retrieved 21 April 2019 from https://worldmaritimenews.com/archives/248731/worlds-1st-autonomous-shipping-company-in-the-making/.

Index

Page numbers in **bold** refer to content in **figures**; page numbers in *italics* refer to content in *tables*.

www.ingramcontent.com/pod-product-compliance
Lightning Source LLC
LaVergne TN
LVHW080803011026
849160LV00015B/1520
* 9 7 8 1 1 3 8 9 9 9 6 5 7 *